Literary Criticism: Plato to Dryden

LITERARY CRITICISM

Plato to Dryden

by

Allan H. Gilbert

Professor Emeritus of English Literature
Duke University

Detroit   Wayne State University Press

NOTE OF THANKS

o◯oo◯o

MR. EDWARD H. BLAKENEY has permitted the use of his translation of Horace's *Art of Poetry*. Various suggestions on his text of Aristotle's *Poetics* have been made by Professor Alfred Gudeman. The section on Sidney has been read by Professor Marcus S. Goldman. The Library of Cornell University has loaned essential volumes from the Dante Collection, and many books have been furnished by the Library of Duke University. The Research Council of Duke University has enabled me to expedite the work. Assistance, often involving the detection of serious errors and suggestions for improvement, has been rendered by Dr. Clara W. Crane, Dr. Raven I. McDavid, Jr., Dr. Olga Marx Perlzweig, Mrs. Freda Townsend, Miss Elizabeth Hopkins, Miss Dixie Swaren, Miss Lucetta Teagarden, and Miss Hessie Brawley Watts. To these and many others I wish to express my thanks.

ALLAN H. GILBERT

CONTENTS

∘◯∘∘◯∘

Introduction, 1

PLATO, 5

ARISTOTLE, 63

HORACE, 125

DIONYSIUS OR LONGINUS, 144

DANTE, 199

GIOVANNI BOCCACCIO, 207

GIANGIORGIO TRISSINO, 212

SIR THOMAS ELYOT, 233

GIRALDI CINTHIO, 242

CONTENTS

Literary Criticism: Plato to Dryden

INTRODUCTION

oᴑooᴑo

Tʜɪs ᴠᴏʟᴜᴍᴇ attempts to represent European theories of poetry from Plato's time to the year 1700. Sir Philip Sidney remarked that he deserved "to be pounded for straying from poetry to oratory," and I have endeavored to take warning from him by avoiding what is primarily rhetorical rather than concerned with the nature of poetry. This explains my rejection of Quintilian, Tacitus, and other such writers commonly treated in histories of literary criticism. I have also felt that details of versification, particularly when applicable to but one language, were better omitted. Similarly matters of language as such have fallen without the province I have defined; Dante's work *On the Vulgar Tongue,* and Du Bellay's well-known *Defense and Illustration of the French Language* are therefore not to be found here, though I do not underestimate their importance in the history of thought relating to poetry; without respect for the vernacular and preference for it over Latin there could have been no modern literature. In making necessary choices I have endeavored to select writers who in their own day spoke for the future rather than the past, and those whose conceptions are of value at present, either in developing our own critical thought or in interpreting the most important literature of their own ages. I have also tried to choose the great rather than the small man. For these reasons I tend to give but one side of a controversy, the vindications written by Tasso or Sidney, but not the attacks that provoked them; the nature of the objections is adequately revealed by the replies. Interest in the working of ideas rather than the history of an age—its perishing as well as its developing thought—has led to some omissions. For example, after a good many hours on the *Poetice* of Scaliger I was unable to feel that I could fit any extended selections into my plan; he so absolutely represents the ultra-classical spirit that the name of no vernacular writer appears in his pages. The Neo-Latin literature of the Renaissance was composed by men of ability and deserves from students of literary history more attention than it receives, but it is generally inaccessible, and hardly to be compared with literature in modern tongues from Dante's *Comedy* on. I have, however, quoted from Scaliger in the footnotes; all the passages can be found through the index. Vida is also omitted, though had I included him I could have justified my choice by such reasons as the obvious influence he exerted on Alexander Pope. A subsidiary reason for leaving Vida out is that the original and an

English translation of his *Art of Poetry* are accessible, while other critics of equal importance are not easily to be had in the original and not at all in English. Indeed, after including the works that must form the backbone of any knowledge of criticism, I have endeavored to make available what could not be easily obtained elsewhere. Certain defects in my selection can be attributed to the necessary restrictions on the size of the volume. Others—necessarily unknown to me—must be attributed to the limitations of my view of the subject. I trust that readers who do not find in the volume selections from various critics whose importance is better known to them than to me can find some consolation in what I do provide.

I offer a considerable amount of material that has never before been translated; the best apology for the present volume is to be found in its 250 pages from critics of the Italian Renaissance. An attempt has been made to give something new in other fields as well. For example, Aristotle's *Poetics* appears in a translation representing labors on the Greek text that differentiate it from the form on which any preceding English translation was based. Heywood's *Apology for Actors* has not been reprinted for nearly a century; I have been able to make corrections in the text of the selection I offer and to give some new material on its sources.

Believing that the history of criticism is essentially a matter of knowing the critics themselves, rather than what may be said about them, I have attempted to keep the accompanying matter as brief as possible. The introductions do not present biographical or historical facts except so far as they bear on the critical views expressed in the selections themselves. I have often attempted to interpret the selections as they appear to me, especially when I felt that I differed in some way from previous writers. A reader who does not like the introductions can easily pass over them; obviously he will be wise to do so if he is thereby enabled to devote additional time to thought on the words of the critics themselves. The notes vary according to the nature of the selection and the editor's understanding of it. There are some that merely explain allusions; others endeavor to interpret a passage; perhaps the most important are those that refer to similar or contrasting ideas of other critics, thus suggesting something of continuity in the process of criticism. The bibliographies of the various authors are intended to throw light on them only as critics; works appearing in the general bibliography are not repeated in the bibliographies of individuals. The index is designed to assist the reader in bringing together for comparison or contrast the chief conceptions of the various critics.

The behavior of the animal known as *homo sapiens* is usually interesting to those who have some desire to justify in themselves the application of the name. Such persons will find here examples, on a more generous scale than elsewhere, of what man has been able to do with the subject matter of the volume; it represents what he actually did achieve, for good or bad, in reflecting on the problem of poetry for some two thousand years, and includes two periods when human mental activity seems to have been especially important, Greece in the fourth century B.C. and Renaissance Europe.

But turning from such general considerations to the more specific, there are perhaps three main services such a book as this can render. At the outset one can neglect the person who desires merely to know about literary criticism—for he needs not the writings of the critics themselves but only a history telling about them—and turn to those who hope to know and understand criticism itself.

First, criticism is of some aid in enabling us to come more intimately into contact, on the intellectual side, with certain works of literary art, those on which the criticism is based, or those written under its influence. Obviously one should not be too casual in any assumption about this matter, for literature is precedent to criticism. Yet it seems that the productions of Milton and of Shakespeare, Jonson, Ford, and other dramatists would have been somewhat different—perhaps better—if the theorists had not spoken. While the critical doctrines of even a great poet must be observed with caution, yet no sensible judge will neglect what the artist says when he turns critic.

Second, the thinkers of the past said a great deal that is of permanent value and capable of application—now more, now less—by their successors, provided those successors grasp the principle of *mutatis mutandis*, and show power to translate into the thought of their own time the reflections of earlier and different ages. The usual assertion of the Renaissance that poetry has didactic value, for example, is not to be rejected as an outworn freak, but to be reflected on as involving a permanent truth likely to be bracing to thought in our day. Our problem is to find what parts of the doctrine we can now use, and how we must vary it in application. The true philosopher, represented by the professor at his best, as opposed to the sophist, the journalist at his worst, is not to be whirled away by surface currents in the thought of his day; he is fair to the contemporary, but knows there were brave men both before and after Agamemnon. His function is to keep the Aristotelian mean between a vicious worship of antiquity and a consuming zeal for the present.

But alas! even the best minds of any age are not perfect. The theories of the past furnish us far too many examples of how not to approach literature. In the present selection I have endeavored to keep the warning death's-heads as few as possible, and to present the works and parts of works that seemed to approach in method or content or both most nearly to what may be thought the truth, though I hasten to say I do not feel confident of my ability to recognize the form of a goddess who sometimes appears more shifting than the Renaissance Fortune. The history of criticism at its worst is the history of human error. Even so great a man as Aristotle is perhaps at times guilty of setting up standards of poetry that fit the idiosyncrasies of his own temperament rather than facts or eternal principles. The past may warn the modern critic against what he should not do, as well as aid him in further construction.

PLATO

o◯◦◦◯o

DIALOGUES

Between 400 and 348 B.C.

PLATO OWES HIS FAME not only to his power as a philosopher, but also to his literary gifts; he has been called a poet, as by Shelley, and a dramatist. In proportion as he deserves these names it is difficult to recover his matter-of-fact opinion on poetry. A dramatist must present ideas suitable to his characters, even though these ideas may be quite opposed to his own. Certainly the form of the dialogue has commonly been used since Plato's time for the presentation of matters that are to be debated rather than for the direct exposition of the beliefs of the author. Even up to the present, however, expositors of these dialogues have tended to accept as Plato's own opinion whatever is said by any of the principal speakers. Yet the only safe rule for the reader is to assume that though any opinion expressed is one Plato was sufficiently interested in to wish to present it, it need not be his; indeed it may even be the opposite of what he holds to be true. It should be remembered also that Plato does not set out even in a dialogue to discuss poetry in and for itself.

It is, however, inevitable that every reader of Plato will form for himself at least tentative opinions on the philosopher's own views. To the present writer they seem as follows: Poetry contains much truth, yet the poet may be quite wrong in some of the beliefs he expresses. He cannot be expert on all subjects of which he speaks but must of necessity know but little of some of them. He cannot, therefore, be taken as a reliable teacher of whatever subject he deals with. His presentations of the gods are not morally satisfactory; the divine must be true and unchanging, but the poet tells of many wicked deeds performed by the gods; if readers accept these stories they will be misled. Nor are all the human characters of poetry admirable; a young man should certainly not imitate all the actions of Achilles in the *Iliad*. Many of the ideas found in the poets are also not worthy of belief, such as that of the complete unhappiness of souls after death, as given in the *Odyssey;* proverbial sayings found in poetry do not always deserve full ethical approval. Hence poetry should not be used in education, as the Greeks of Plato's time used it, with the belief that it gives reliable ethical, theological, and factual instruction.

What, then, is poetry for Plato? He thinks it produced not by a rational process, but through inspiration. The poet is in the power of the Muses and utters what they put in his mouth. This may be taken to mean that the poet is not humdrum or matter-of-fact in his methods, that he often cannot well explain what he has written, and that much of his content expresses the thoughts and feelings of others than himself. He has creative power, as has the lawgiver, but on a lower plane, and is concerned with stories rather than with rational ideas. His productions because of their beauty are worthy to excite the admiration and love of the greatest men and can be charming even to the multitude. Pleasure rather than profit is the function of poetry. Yet because of its harmony and good taste it can have a salutary effect on the character of readers and hearers. The poet may, however, produce compositions not in good taste and fitted only to secure immediate applause from the ignorant. Such, perhaps, is Plato's position.

To some this theory will appear to make Plato too modern, too much in general agreement with enlightened criticism in the present era. The editor, however, is not disturbed by such an objection, being of the opinion that, with human nature and Greek art and thought before him, Plato's powers of mind were quite sufficient to enable him to take various positions that we associate with our own age. To one who insists on the theory of necessary historical progress and intellectual advance, such a position will evidently be untenable.

If, as the editor holds, Plato did succeed by his critical process in stripping poetry of the extraneous qualities and powers with which the current thought of his day endowed it, and putting it forth as poetry alone, in and for itself, he prepared the way for Aristotle, who was able to turn his scientist's eye on poetry as an autonomous activity of man, having its own particular function and giving its own peculiar pleasure.

Yet this purely aesthetic view of poetry is of importance to but a few, to those who apprehend its real nature as art and thereby have an antidote against any harm that may result from the poet's presentation of wicked characters or of matter that is half true or wholly untrue. They are the persons who can take poetry as fictitious or representative, rather than as matter of fact. But a large number are unable so to understand the art. Poetry to them is not a presentation by an artist, but an encouragement to the life of labor or licentious sloth that is presented. In an ordinary state, censorship can hardly be attempted. As Milton pointed out in his *Areopagitica*, it is not enough to censor poetry; all the activities of life must also be regulated if any real effect is to be gained even from the most enlightened regulation of the poet, and with any but the most enlightened government the censorship itself must be bad; there will be no one to censor the censors. But under Plato's ideal government there is competent supervision of all human activities to serve the ends of the perfect state. He does not, however, assume perfect human material on which the rulers may work. Therefore among the young citizens there will be many incapable of an aesthetic view of poetry and likely to receive injury from passages presenting aspects of life unfit for the imitation of citizens. To all such, poetry is interdicted, save as approved by lawgivers who have examined it and found suggestions of only such thought and conduct as they desire.

To the modern this may bring profit by indicating how to read poetry. As himself a lover of Homer, Plato tells us that we must read the *Iliad* aesthetically, as poetry and not as matter of fact or science. He warns us, however, that one part of us, equivalent to the unsophisticated in his state, is likely to forget the true nature of poetry and degrade it to the merely practical level. No small part of the history of criticism after Plato, as it appears in this volume, exhibits the tension between the practical and the aesthetic view, and warns us that for us too, if we forget ourselves, Plato may have spoken in vain.

The translation of the selections from Plato in this volume is by the editor.

BIBLIOGRAPHY

Gilbert, Allan H., "Did Plato Banish the Poets or the Critics?" in *Studies in Philology*, XXXVI (1939), 1–19.

Gilbert, Katharine, "The Relation of the Moral to the Aesthetic Standard in Plato," in *The Philosophical Review*, XLIII (1934), 279-94.

Grube, G. M. A., *Plato's Thought*. London, 1935.

Shorey, Paul, *What Plato Said*. Chicago, 1933.

Taylor, A. E., *Plato*. London, 1929.

Plato, *Dialogues*, translated by Benjamin Jowett. Oxford, 1892.

——, *Dialogues*, Loeb Classics Series. Cambridge, Mass., 1917–35.

——, *Œuvres complètes*, publiée sous la patronage de l'Association Guillaume Budé. Paris, 1920. (Unfinished.) Greek text and French translation.

——, *Laws*, translated by A. E. Taylor. London, 1934.

—— *Plato,* translated by Lane Cooper. New York, 1938. Contains the *Phaedrus,* the *Symposium,* the *Ion,* the *Gorgias,* and parts of the *Republic* and the *Laws.* The selections "should be of special interest to students of poetry and eloquence."

oᗌooᗌo

THE ION

Probably before 388 B.C.

The obvious thing about this dialogue is that it presents the theory of inspiration,[1] first that of the poet and then of those subject to his influence. In spite of the playful tone of the whole, Plato may have intended what he says on inspiration to be taken seriously. The theory is not without modern aspects if it be taken to mean that the state of mind of the poet himself, in some way unlike that of ordinary experience, is reproduced in anyone who receives from his work a truly poetical effect.

Still further, the dialogue may be taken as an attack on a confused practical criticism, which makes poetry consist in the knowledge of the poet and represents the critic as learning from the poet and therefore expert himself. The attack is here directed not on the poet, as in the *Republic,* but on the critic. Plato shows that the professional student of poetry is less able to judge the accuracy of passages involving any particular art than is a practitioner of the art. The critic is thus forced from the platform on which he explains the erudition and accuracy of Homer, except as by accident he may have had experience in war or agriculture, or some other activity. What then is left for the critic? The things everyone knows. Ion himself is allowed to suggest this when he says he understands what a woman or a slave would say. He does not develop, as he might, that his knowledge can apply to their actions and words as human beings, not as experts in anything. That was to be taken up by Aristotle,[2] and even by Wordsworth when he wrote that "the remotest discoveries of the chemist, the botanist, or minerologist" will be proper subjects for the poet whenever "the relations under which they are contemplated by the followers of these

[1] For some other Platonic references, see the appendix immediately following this dialogue. Girolamo Fracastoro refers to the *Ion* for the *furor poeticus* in his *Naugerius* 160D (Urbana, 1924), and Vincentius Madius knows it by the title *De furore poetica* (*In Aristotelis librum de poetica* [Venice, 1550], pp. 61, 187).   [2] *Poetics,* xv, first par., below.

respective sciences shall be manifestly and palpably material to us as enjoying and suffering beings."[3]

Plato does not represent Ion as of much ability, though he does not deny him feeling for poetry, in spite of mental confusion. Our conclusion may be that the first business of the critic is to concern himself with what is poetical in poetry. In that consists his highest function. To point out the poet's excellence or failure in knowledge is in itself of comparatively little value, no more so than for Aristotle's poet to understand the horns of the deer.[4] The poet must represent his themes artistically, and the critic must feel them and present them as did the artist himself. The critic is the ring suspended from the poet. This imaginative presentation of the ideal critic has its matter-of-fact parallel in the twenty-fifth chapter of Aristotle's *Poetics*.

THE ION (*complete*)

[The elocutionist. 530 A[1]]

Socrates. I am glad to see you, Ion. Where have you come from? from your home at Ephesus?

Ion. No Socrates, from the festival of Asclepius at Epidaurus.

Soc. Why, do the Epidaurians support elocutionary contests in honor of the god?

Ion. Yes indeed, and in music generally.

Soc. Did you compete? And what success did you have?

Ion. I won the first prize, Socrates.

Soc. Splendid; I hope you will win at the Panathenaic festival too.

Ion. Oh, I shall, *D.V.*

Soc. It is a fact that I have often envied the art of you elocutionists, Ion; for it requires you always to be well-groomed and to make a fine appearance, and you must all the time be in contact with a great many good poets and especially with Homer, the best and most divine of them, and to understand his thought and not his words alone is something to be envied. You could not be

---

[3] Preface to *Lyrical Ballads*. [4] *Poetics*, xxv, 60b23, below.

[1] The numbers and letters are those of Stephanus, commonly given in editions of Plato. I use the number proper to the first line of one of my sections to indicate the whole section.

an elocutionist if you did not have an intimate knowledge of the words of the poet. The elocutionist must be the interpreter of the thought of the poet to the audience, and it is impossible to do this well without understanding what the poet says. All these things make me envy you.

Ion. You are right, Socrates, this part of my craft requires a great deal of work, and I can talk about Homer better than anyone else. Neither Metrodorus of Lampsacus nor Stesimbrotus of Thasos nor Glaucon nor any other elocutionist that ever has lived has had so many beautiful things to say about Homer as I have.

Soc. I am glad to hear it, Ion. I assume that you will not object to explaining it to me.

Ion. Not at all, for it is worth your while, Socrates, to hear how splendid I make Homer appear. I know I deserve to be crowned with a golden crown by his descendants.

Soc. I'll make a point of getting an opportunity to hear you. But now explain this to me: Are you marvelous in presenting Homer alone, or are you just as good in Hesiod and Archilochus?

Ion. No, I concern myself only with Homer; that seems to me quite enough.

Soc. Do Homer and Hesiod ever say the same thing about something or other?

Ion. Yes, very often, I assure you.

Soc. Now when that happens can you present better what Homer or what Hesiod says?

Ion. It is just the same to me, Socrates, when they are alike.

[The poets' subjects. 531 B]

Soc. But how is it when they do not say the same things? Don't Homer and Hesiod both say something about divination?

Ion. Yes, they do.

Soc. Well, in these matters of soothsaying on which the two poets agree and disagree, would you give the better exposition or would a soothsayer, a good one, of course?

Ion. The soothsayer would.

Soc. Now supposing you were a soothsayer, if you could explain the passages in which they agree, would you not also understand how to set forth those in which they disagree?

Ion. Evidently I would.

Soc. How then can you be so wonderful in dealing with Homer, but not with Hesiod or the other poets? Does Homer deal with subjects not mentioned by all the other poets? Hasn't he said a great deal about war and about the relations with each other of good men and bad, ordinary men and craftsmen, and on the dealings of the gods with one another and with men, telling how they act, and on the phenomena of the heavens and Hades, and the beginnings of gods and men? Aren't these the things on which Homer has written his poetry?

Ion. That's right, Socrates, they are.

Soc. Well, then, didn't the other poets write about these things?

Ion. Yes, Socrates, but not in the same way Homer did.

Soc. What do you mean? That they haven't written so well?

Ion. Oh, not nearly.

Soc. Homer has done it better, then?

Ion. Infinitely better.

[Judges of accuracy. 531 D]

Soc. Well then, my dear Ion, when several persons speak of arithmetic and one of them speaks much better than the others, is there anyone who can select the one who speaks well?

Ion. Of course.

Soc. And will this be the same man who can recognize those who speak badly or some other?

Ion. The same one.

Soc. And will he be a man who understands arithmetic?

Ion. Certainly.

Soc. Now then, if several persons are telling what wholesome food is, and one of them speaks better than the others, will one man recognize the best speaker as the best, and another a pretty bad speaker as bad, or will the same man do both?

Ion. Without any doubt it will be the same man.

Soc. Who will he be? What would you call him?

Ion. A doctor.

Soc. In short, then, we have said that the same man will always be able to select, from among a number of speakers on the same subject, those who speak well and those who speak badly. And if he doesn't know who speaks badly, he evidently won't know who speaks well on the same subject.

Ion. So it is.

Soc. Then the same man is competent on both sides?

Ion. Yes.

[Judgment of Homer's accuracy. 532 A]

Soc. Didn't you say that Homer and the other poets, among whom are Hesiod and Archilochus, speak of the same things but not in the same way, since Homer speaks well and the others worse than he does?

Ion. Yes, and that is true.

Soc. Well then, if you recognize the one who speaks well, you should recognize also these who speak worse.

Ion. It seems that I should.

Soc. If that is so, we shall not be wrong in saying that Ion is equally competent for Homer and for the other poets, since he admits that the same critic is competent to judge all those who speak of the same things, and all the poets deal with the same subjects.

Ion. But Socrates, why is it that, when someone speaks of some other poet, I can't fix my attention and am unable to think of a thing worth saying, but am completely at a loss? When, however, someone mentions Homer, then I wake up, can direct my attention, and have plenty to say.

Soc. It is not hard to understand this, my friend; it is clear that you are not enabled to speak of Homer by skill and knowledge, for if you could do it through skill, you could discourse also on all the other poets; for there is a general art of poetry. Or don't you think so?

Ion. Yes.

[Judgment of the other arts. 532 D]

Soc. Then if I take any art in general, the method of investigation applied to it can be applied to all the other arts. Do you wish to hear how I explain this, Ion?

Ion. Indeed I do, Socrates; it is a great pleasure to me to listen to you wise men.

Soc. I wish what you say were true, Ion. But the wise men are you elocutionists and actors and those whose poems you recite;[2] I can do nothing but speak the truth, as a layman should. In this matter that I just now asked about, you can see how common and ordinary it is, and how every man knows what I said, namely that the method of inquiry would be the same if an art as a whole were examined. For example, is there a graphic art as a whole?

[2] Cf. the appendix to the *Ion*, sect. 2, below; *Republic*, x, 600 E.

Ion. Yes.

Soc. And are there not many painters, past and present, some good and some bad?

Ion. Quite right.

Soc. And have you ever seen anyone who was expert in showing when Polygnotus the son of Aglaophon painted well and when badly, but who had no power to judge other painters? When someone displays the works of the others, he goes to sleep and is at a loss and has nothing ready to say, yet when it is time for him to present his opinion on Polygnotus, or any other single painter you wish to name, he wakes up, collects his wits, and speaks fluently.

Ion. I never heard of such a case, never.

Soc. Then in sculpture did you ever know anyone who was thoroughly competent to expound the virtues of Daedalus the son of Metion, or Epeius the son of Panopeus, or Theodore of Samos, or any other single sculptor, but as to the other sculptors he was at a loss and without animation, having nothing to say?

Ion. No, I never saw anything like that.

Soc. And in addition, as I suppose, in flute-playing, lyre-playing, singing to the lyre, and elocution, you never knew a man who could comment excellently on Olympus or Thamyras or Orpheus or Phemius, the elocutionist of Ithaca, but who when he came to Ion of Ephesus was helpless and had no idea when he was reciting well and when badly.

Ion. I cannot contradict you there, Socrates, yet I am perfectly sure I talk on Homer better than anyone else and have plenty of ideas, and all the world says I speak well about him, but about the others I don't. That's the long and short of it.

[Inspiration. 533 C]

Soc. I understand, Ion, and I am going to explain to you how I think it is. As I said, it is not skill that enables you to speak well about Homer, but a divine power that moves you, just as it does the stone that Euripides calls the magnet but that most men call the stone of Heraclea. This stone not merely attracts iron rings but extends its power to the rings so they can attract others just as the stone does; thus there is sometimes a very long series of iron rings hanging one from another. The power of the stone reaches out to all of them. Thus the Muse inspires some and others are inspired by them until there is a whole series of the inspired. For all the epic poets, the good ones, utter all their beautiful poems

not through art but because they are divinely inspired and possessed, and the same is true of the good lyric poets. For just as the
Corybantes are not in their right minds, so the lyric poets are not
in their right minds when they compose their beautiful poems, but
when they enter into harmony and rhythm they revel as though
they were possessed, like the Bacchae who when they are possessed
draw honey and milk from the rivers but cannot do so when in
their right minds. The soul of the lyric poets, so it is said, experiences the same sort of thing. For the poets tell us, I think,
that they get their poems from the honey-flowing founts in the
gardens and vales of the Muses and bring them to us just as do the
bees, and that they too are winged. And they speak rightly, for
the craft of the poet is light and winged and holy, and he is not
capable of poetry until he is inspired by the gods and out of his
mind and there is no reason in him. Until he gets into this state,
any man is powerless to produce poetry and to prophesy. They
write poetry and say many beautiful things on various subjects, as
you do on Homer, not by art but by divine gift, each one being able
to compose beautifully only in accordance with what the Muse
grants to him, whether he produces dithyrambs or encomiums or
dancing songs or epics or iambics; but in other kinds of poetry each
one is without ability. For they do not utter the words they do
through art but by heavenly power, since if through art they knew
how to speak beautifully on one thing, they would be able to do
so on all the others.

Therefore the god, depriving these men of their reason, uses
them as helpers in prophecies and divinations, that we, when we
hear them, may know they are not the ones who utter the noble
words that issue from them, for their intellects do not produce
them, but the god himself is speaking, and through his human
mouthpieces he addresses us. Tynnichus the Chalcidian is an excellent example of this; he composed no poem that anyone thinks
worth remembering, except the paean everyone sings; this, perhaps the most beautiful of all lyric poems, he composed without
the aid of art, for, as he says, some muse invented it. Through this
example, above all, the god appears to me to remove our doubts
by showing that these beautiful poems are not human nor the
work of men but divine and produced by the gods; the poets are
nothing but the interpreters of the gods, each one under the influence of the divinity that lays hold of him. In order to make this
plain, the god uttered on purpose a lyric of the greatest beauty by

means of a worthless poet. Do I seem to you to speak the truth, Ion?

Ion. I am convinced you do. For you lay hold on my spirit with your words, Socrates, and good poets seem to me to interpret by divine aid what they derive from the gods.

[The elocutionist as interpreter. 535 A]

Soc. And do not you elocutionists in your turn interpret the works of the poets?

Ion. You are quite right; we do.

Soc. So you are interpreters of interpreters?

Ion. That is exactly it.

Soc. Well then tell me this, Ion, and don't withhold anything I ask. When you are speaking well and making the deepest impression on your hearers, whether you are telling how Odysseus leaped upon the threshold, revealed himself to the suitors, and poured out the arrows at his feet, or how Achilles attacked Hector, or of the sorrows of Andromache, or of Hecuba, or Priam, are you in your right mind or are you beside yourself, and does not your spirit seem to take part in the events you narrate, whether they are in Ithaca or Troy or any other place you tell of?

Ion. How vividly you present this proof to me, Socrates! I will answer you without reserve. When I speak of anything piteous, my eyes are filled with tears; when I mention anything fearful or terrible, my hair stands on end with fear and my heart throbs.

Soc. Is that the way of it? Shall we say, then, that a man is in his right mind who, when he is adorned with beautifully colored garments and golden crowns, weeps in the midst of sacrifices and public ceremonies, though he has lost none of his adornments, or who is afraid when he is surrounded by more than twenty thousand friendly persons, though not one of them is disposed to strip him or treat him unjustly?

Ion. You speak the truth, Socrates; he is not in his sober senses.

Soc. And do you not know that you produce the same effects on many of the spectators?

Ion. I know it right well, for when I look down from the platform I see them weeping and showing signs of terror and astonishment at my words. It is needful for me to give them the closest attention, for if I make them cry I shall laugh myself when I am paid, but if I make them laugh I shall weep because I get no pay.

[Inspiration in series. 535 E]

Soc. Don't you see that these spectators are the last of the rings I spoke of as obtaining their power one after another from the stone of Heraclea? You as an elocutionist and actor are in the middle, the poet comes first. The god through all of them moves the spirits of men as he will, by divine power suspending one from another. And like the rings that hang from that stone, there hangs down a whole chain of dancers and masters and sub-masters of choruses, suspended by the side of the other rings attached to the Muse. One of the poets is sustained by one muse, another by another—we call it possessed, for it is almost that, since he is held. Below the first rings, those of the poets, others are sustained; some are held by the power of Orpheus, some by that of Musaeus, but most are attached to Homer and possessed by him. You, Ion, are one of the rings in the chain attached to Homer, and when someone recites from another poet you fall asleep and have nothing to say, but when a verse from Homer is uttered, straightway you awake, your spirit dances, and your speech flows freely; for not by art or full understanding of Homer do you recite as you do, but by divine gift and inspiration, just as the Corybantes quickly recognize that strain only that proceeds from the god by which they are possessed, and for that song they have abundant dances and words, but to the others they give no heed. In this way, Ion, you abound in words when Homer is mentioned, but are mute at the names of the other poets. So in answer to the question why you are bountifully supplied for Homer but not for the others, I say your power to recite Homer is not derived from art but is a divine gift.

[Ion insists on his knowledge of Homer. 536 D]

Ion. You speak convincingly, Socrates. Yet I should be astonished if you could speak well enough to convince me that when I recite Homer I am inspired and out of my mind. I am sure I should not seem so to you if you heard me speaking of him.

Soc. I am eager to hear you, but not until you answer this question: Of what subject among those dealt with by Homer do you speak well? For surely you cannot deal with all of them.

Ion. Rest assured, Socrates, there is not one of them I cannot deal with.

Soc. Of course you do not include those discussed by Homer of which you happen to know nothing.

Ion. And what are the subjects that Homer speaks of, but that I don't understand?

[The arts in Homer. 537 A]

Soc. Does not Homer say a great deal and in many ways about the various arts? For example, chariot-driving; if you have forgotten the words I shall repeat them to you.

Ion. Oh, I'll repeat them; I know what they are.

Soc. Say over for me, then, the words of Nestor to his son Antilochus, when he advises him to be careful about the turning post in the chariot race at the funeral games of Patroclus:

> *Ion.* Lean thy body on the well-knit car slightly to their left, and call upon the off horse with voice and lash, and give him rein from thy hand. But let the near horse hug the post so that the nave of the well-wrought wheel seem to graze it—yet beware of touching the stone.[3]

Soc. That will do. Now Ion, would a physician or a charioteer know better whether Homer used these words correctly or not?

Ion. A charioteer, certainly.

Soc. Is it because he understands that art or not?

Ion. For no other reason than that he understands the art.

Soc. Does not the god grant to each of the arts to know something special? We cannot know through the art of the pilot what we know through medicine.

Ion. Certainly not.

Soc. Nor can we know from carpentry what pertains to medicine.

Ion. Certainly not.

Soc. Is it not the same for all the arts? for what we know through one we do not know through another. But first answer me this: Do you say that two arts differ from each other?

Ion. Yes.

Soc. Now in settling my ideas, when I encounter knowledge of certain things I assign them to one art, and the knowledge of other things I assign to another art; do you do the same?

Ion. Yes.

Soc. Now in respect to the knowledge of these matters, what can we assign to one art and what to another, when the same knowledge seems to pertain to both? I know that the fingers are five in

[3] *Iliad*, XXIII, 335 ff., trans. by Lang, Leaf, and Myers.

number, and you know the same thing, and if I should ask you whether you and I have the same knowledge through the same art of arithmetic or through some other art, you would say that we have our knowledge from the same art.

Ion. Yes.

Soc. To take up the question I was intending to ask, I want you to tell me whether it seems to you generally true of the arts that the same things are known by means of the same arts, and other things by means of other arts, and that if the arts are different they deal with different matter.

Ion. It seems that way to me, Socrates.

Soc. So if anyone has command of a certain art, will he not be the man who has an excellent knowledge of the words and deeds pertaining to this art?

Ion. You are right.

Soc. Then about the words you recited, will you or the chari-oteer know better whether Homer spoke properly or not?

Ion. The charioteer.

Soc. You are an elocutionist and not a charioteer.

Ion. Yes.

Soc. Is the art of the elocutionist different from that of the charioteer?

Ion. Yes.

Soc. If it is different, its knowledge is concerned with other matters.

Ion. Yes.

Soc. What of the time when Homer says that Hecamede, the concubine of Nestor, gave the wounded Machaon a posset to drink? He put it thus:

It was made of Pramnian wine, and she grated on it cheese of goat's milk with a grater of bronze; and beside it an onion as a relish to the drink.[4]

Does it pertain to the art of the physician or of the elocutionist to decide whether Homer speaks correctly of these things or not?

Ion. That of the physician.

Soc. And Homer writes also:

She sped to the bottom like a weight of lead that mounted on horn of a field-ox goeth down bearing death to ravenous fishes.[5]

[4] *Iliad*, XI, 638, 630.   [5] XXIV, 80–2.

Shall we say that it belongs to the art of the fisherman rather than of the elocutionist to judge whether this passage is well put or not?

Ion. Obviously, Socrates, to that of the fisherman.

Soc. Now consider this: suppose you are talking and you say to me: "Well, Socrates, since you have found in Homer passages that should be judged according to each of these different arts, go on and find some passages that belong to the soothsayer and the art of soothsaying, and which must be judged good or bad by one skilled in that art." See how easily I can give you a true answer. There are many passages of the sort in the *Odyssey*, such as the speech of Theoclymenus the prophet of the house of Melampus, who says:

> Ah, wretched men, what woe is this ye suffer? Shrouded in night are your heads and your faces and your knees, and kindled is the voice of wailing, and all cheeks are wet with tears, and the walls and the fair main-beams of the roof are sprinkled with blood. And the porch is full, and full is the court, of ghosts that hasten hell-wards beneath the gloom, and the sun has perished out of heaven, and an evil mist has overspread the world.[6]

And there are many such passages in the *Iliad*, as in the narrative of the battle at the stockade, where Homer says:

> As they were eager to pass over, a bird has appeared to them, an eagle of lofty flight, skirting the host on the left hand. In its talons it bore a blood-red monstrous snake, alive, and struggling still; yea, nor yet had it forgotten the joy of battle, but writhed backward and smote the bird that held it on the breast, beside the neck, and the bird cast it from him down to the earth, in sore pain, and dropped it in the midst of the throng; then with a cry sped away down the gusts of the wind.[7]

I say that such passages as these pertain to the soothsayer for examination and judgment.

Ion. And you are right, Socrates.

[What parts of Homer can the elocutionist judge? 539 D]

Soc. And so are you, Ion. And now just as I have selected for you from the *Odyssey* and the *Iliad* passages that pertain to the soothsayer and the physician and the fisherman, I wish you, Ion,

[6] *Odyssey*, xx, 351–7, trans. by Butcher and Lang.
[7] *Iliad*, xii, 200–7, trans. by Lang, Leaf, and Myers.

since you know Homer better than I do, would pick out for me the passages that pertain to the elocutionist and the art of elocution, and that are better judged by an elocutionist than by any other man.

Ion. In my opinion, the entire poems, Socrates.

Soc. Don't say the entire poems, Ion; are you so forgetful as that? An elocutionist should not be forgetful.

Ion. What have I forgotten?

Soc. Don't you remember you said the art of the elocutionist is different from that of the charioteer?

Ion. I do remember it.

Soc. Do you not admit then, that if it is different it deals with different things?

Ion. Yes.

Soc. According to what you have admitted, the art of elocution cannot be concerned with everything in Homer nor the elocutionist know everything.

Ion. Perhaps he won't know the sort of thing you have mentioned.

Soc. You mean most of the things with which the other arts are concerned. But what will he know, since he doesn't know everything?

Ion. He will know, I am sure, the language that befits every sort of person, a man, a woman, a slave, a free man, a subordinate, or a chief.

Soc. You mean, do you, that the sort of thing a sea captain will say when his ship is in danger will be better understood by the elocutionist than by the pilot?

Ion. No, the pilot will understand that.

Soc. But the language fitting one in charge of a sick man will be understood by the elocutionist better than by the physician?

Ion. Not that either.

Soc. But you mean the language suited to a slave, perhaps?

Ion. Yes.

Soc. You mean that the sort of thing a slave who keeps cattle will naturally say to quiet them when they are excited will be known to the elocutionist but not to the cowherd?

Ion. Oh, no.

Soc. The sort of thing, then, a spinner will say about the working of wool?

Ion. No.

[The elocutionist and generalship. 540 D]

Soc. Will he know the kind of thing a general will say in making a speech to his soldiers?

Ion. Yes, that is the kind of thing an elocutionist will know.

Soc. What's that? Is elocution the art of war?

Ion. I certainly should know what a general ought to say.

Soc. Perhaps you have had military experience, Ion. And if you have been trained in horsemanship you know when horses are well or badly handled, and the same for lyre-playing. So let me ask you: By which art, Ion, do you know whether horses are well managed? Is it because you are a horseman or because you are a performer on the lyre? What is your answer?

Ion. Because I am a horseman, certainly.

Soc. Hence if you understand who plays well on the lyre, you admit that you have this understanding because you are a lyre-player, not because you are a horseman.

Ion. Yes.

Soc. Since you understand military matters, do you understand them because you are an experienced general or because you are a good elocutionist?

Ion. I can't see any difference.

Soc. What? Do you mean there is no difference? Do you think the art of the elocutionist and that of the general to be the same or different?

Ion. I think they are the same.

Soc. So if a man is a good elocutionist he is also a good general?

Ion. Certainly he is, Socrates.

Soc. And he who is a good general is also a good elocutionist?

Ion. No, I don't think so.

Soc. But doesn't it seem to you that he who is a good elocutionist is also a good general?

Ion. Yes, indeed.

Soc. Are you the best elocutionist of all the Greeks?

Ion. There is no doubt of that.

Soc. And are you also the best general among the Greeks?

Ion. Be assured of that, Socrates; I have learned generalship from the teachings of Homer.

Soc. And why in Heaven's name, Ion, if you are the best man among the Greeks both as an elocutionist and as a general, do you travel around reciting to the Greeks, but never lead an army?

Does it seem to you that the Greeks are in great need of an elocutionist with a golden crown, but do not require a general?

Ion. My city, Socrates, is governed and provided with generals by yours and does not need a commander; neither you nor the Spartans would take me as a general, for you know both cities have enough of their own.

Soc. My good Ion, do you know Apollodorus of Cyzicus?

Ion. Who is he?

Soc. A man whom the Athenians have often chosen as their general, even though he is a foreigner. Then there are Phanosthenes of Andros and Heraclides of Clazomenae, who, being distinguished by their obvious fitness, were chosen by the city for high commands and other important functions, even though they were foreigners. And will not such a man as Ion of Ephesus be chosen as general and receive honors if he shows himself worthy? Why, were not the Ephesians originally Athenians, and is not Ephesus a city second to none?

[The elocutionist works by inspiration. 541 E]

But Ion, if you tell the truth about your capacity to praise Homer by means of art and knowledge, you don't do the right thing, for after forcing me to believe you know many fine things about Homer and saying you will point them out, you cheat me and don't come near pointing them out; you don't intend to show what it is in which you have such great skill, as I long ago asked you to do, but just like Proteus in all his shapes, you turn this way and that, until in the end you escape in the form of a general, in order that you may not show how skillful you are in explaining Homer. As I just said, then, if when you undertake to explain Homer through skill, you deceive me, you do not treat me fairly. And if you do not make use of skill, but through a divine gift receive inspiration from Homer, and without knowing what you do say many fine things about the poet, as I said you did, you do treat me fairly. Choose, then, whether you wish me to think you unfair or inspired by the god.

Ion. There is a great difference, Socrates, and it is much better to be thought inspired.

Soc. Well then, I'll choose the pleasant conclusion and consider that you are inspired and not making use of art when you praise Homer.

APPENDIX TO THE *Ion*

Three passages on inspiration

1. Thirdly, there is the madness of those possessed by the Muses. It seizes upon a sensitive and pure soul, which it rouses and fills with a strong desire for odes and other poetry, and thus by making splendid ten thousand deeds of the ancients instructs later generations. But if anyone approaches the poetic doors without this madness of the Muses, thinking that he will be a good-enough poet through art alone, he is ineffectual, and the poetry of the self-controlled man loses all its splendor when compared with that of the madmen (*Phaedrus*, 245).

2. On leaving the politicians, I [Socrates] went to the poets, the authors of tragedies and of dithyrambs and of other forms, thinking that they would catch me in the very act of being less wise than they were. So taking up the poems they had, as it seemed to me, elaborated most carefully, I asked then what they meant, expecting not merely that my ignorance would appear but that I would learn something from them. But I am ashamed, gentlemen, to tell you the truth; yet I must speak. I might say that almost all those who happened to be present could have spoken better than the poets did on the works they themselves had composed. So I understood at once that the poets do not compose their poems because of their wisdom but by genius and because they are inspired like prophets and givers of oracles, for these utter many fine speeches but know nothing of what they say. It seemed to me that the poets underwent much the same experience. And I saw also that because of their poetry they thought they were the wisest of men in matters of which they were ignorant (*Apology*, 22).

3. There is an ancient story that has always been repeated among ourselves and accepted by others to the effect that the poet, whenever he seats himself on the tripod of the Muse, is not in his right mind, but is a sort of fountain that allows its waters as they rise to flow freely, and since his art is imitative, he must often contradict himself in presenting contrasting characters, nor does he know which of two contradictory characters speaks truly (*Laws*, IV, 719).

THE REPUBLIC[1] (*selections*)

Book II

[Some literature is unfit for the young, 377 B]

[Socrates is speaking to Adeimantus.]
Shall we allow the children to hear any stories that chance to
be told by anyone without distinction and to take into their souls
teachings that are wholly opposite to those we wish them to be
possessed of when they are grown up?

If we are not to allow it, it appears our first duty is to regulate the
story-makers, and accept anything good they produce and reject
anything bad. We shall order the nurses and the mothers to tell
their children the stories we select, and to form their souls with
their stories even more than they form their bodies with their
hands. Most of the stories they now tell must be rejected.

We may see the less excellent stories in the better ones, for whatever their quality they are necessarily of the same type.

By the better stories I mean the work of Hesiod and Homer and
the other poets, for they composed false stories and told them to
men, and continue to do so.

First and above all, I condemn them because they tell lies, and
still further because their lies are not attractive.

I have in mind poems in which the author, writing on the nature
of gods and heroes, makes a bad likeness, as when a painter makes
a portrait that isn't at all like the person he was supposed to
portray.

[Lies about the gods. 377 E]

First there is that greatest of lies about the highest beings, which
is so wickedly and falsely related about the deeds of Uranus, as
Hesiod tells of them, and how Cronus revenged himself. These

---

[1] While the *Republic* is a dialogue and must be interpreted as one, the interlocutor in
the parts here presented seldom says much. It seemed that the omission of his words,
except in a few instances, would make the argument clearer; hence I have adopted
that plan. But that the reader may not wholly lose the effect of dialogue, each speech
by Socrates is begun at the left-hand margin. Plato does not present a dialogue between Socrates and others, but has Socrates report his conversation with them. I
have simplified it to a dialogue given directly by Plato. A few other slight modifications
have been made.

actions of Cronus and his sufferings at the hands of his son, even if they were true, should not lightly be related to the thoughtless and young, but should remain untold. If it is necessary to tell them, they should be heard in secret by as small an audience as possible, after the sacrifice not of a pig but of some great and unusual victim, so that as few as possible may be able to hear. These dangerous stories should not be permitted in our city, for a young man must not be allowed to hear that he does nothing strange when he commits the most shocking offenses, not even when he revenges himself in every way upon his father who has injured him, but that he is doing what the first and greatest of the gods have done.

And it is not fitting for a young man to hear that the gods fought with the gods and plotted against and injured each other (for that is not true) if we wish those who are to guard our city to think it a shameful thing to quarrel easily with each other. And we must not allow the stories of the wars of the giants and all the terrible deeds of many kinds committed by the gods and heroes against their relatives and neighbors to be told or worked in embroidery. But we should rather strive to persuade our youth that no citizen ever quarreled with another and that it would be impious to do so, and stories with such a purpose should be told to children by the old men and women, and the poets also must follow these principles in composing stories for those who are older. But the binding of Hera by her son, and the story that Zeus hurled Hephaestus out of heaven when he tried to protect his mother when she was being beaten, and the wars of the gods that Homer wrote of are not to be admitted to the city, whether they have a hidden meaning or not. A child is not able to judge which have hidden meanings and which do not, and because he is very young the stains he gets from the teachings of the poets cannot be washed out, but are firmly fixed.[2] For this reason, care of every sort must be taken about the first stories children listen to, in order that they may hear only what will have a virtuous influence.

Adeimantus answered: That is reasonable, but if anyone should ask what sort of poems you mean and what their stories are, what could we say?

---

[2] This implies that those who read the poets in maturity, when they are able to judge, will receive no stain; hence that private reading of poetry by the competent would be allowed. Cf. the reference to the antidote at the beginning of *Republic*, x, p. 42, below; also p. 52, below.

[Poetry should present God as he is. 378 E]

Socrates replied: You and I, Adeimantus, are not at present poets but organizers of a city. It is necessary for the organizers to understand the types according to which the poets must needs write and from which their poems must not be allowed to depart; but the lawgiver does not have to compose stories himself.

I shall explain the types of poetry countenanced by proper ideas about God. He must be presented as he really is, whether he appears in epic or lyric or tragic poetry.

Is not God really good and to be presented as such?

But nothing good is hurtful, or is it?

And does what is not hurtful do any injury?

And can what does no injury do anything bad?

And would what does no evil be the cause of evil?

Well then, is the good beneficial?

Is it the cause of good action?

The good is then not the cause of everything but merely of things that are beneficial; it is not the cause of evil things. So God, since he is good, may not be the cause of all things, as is usually said, but he is the cause of few things among men, and not the cause of many, for good is much less common than ill; good is caused by God alone, but we must seek out the cause of evil, for it cannot be God.

We are not, therefore, to believe Homer, or any of the other poets, when he foolishly charges the gods with something wrong, as when he says that

> Two jars are placed at the threshold of Zeus, full of lots, one of happy ones, the other of unhappy.[3]

and that the man to whom Zeus gives a mingling of the two

> experiences sometimes ill, sometimes good.

But the man to whom he gives the second unmingled

> terrible misery pursues over the sacred earth.

Nor does Zeus as a distributor

> provide for us something of good, something of ill.[4]

And as to the violation of the oaths and treaties, which was the doing of Pandarus,[5] if anybody attributes it to Athene and Zeus

---

[3] See *Iliad*, XXIV, 527–9.   [4] Author unknown.   [5] *Iliad*, IV, 69 ff.

we shall not approve, nor shall we when someone says that the strife and division of the gods was caused by Themis and Zeus, nor shall the young men be allowed to hear such words as those of Aeschylus:

> God implants in men the cause of wickedness when he wishes utterly to overthrow a house.

But if anyone should write a poem in which these iambics appeared, such as one on the sufferings of Niobe or on the woes of the family of Pelops or on the Trojan war or some such subject, either he will not be allowed to say that the ills he presents are the work of God, or if he is allowed to say so, a reason such as we are now seeking must be brought to light, and it must be said that God does things that are just and good, and that those who are afflicted are benefited by it. But the poet must not be permitted to say that those who are punished are miserable and that God is responsible for their misery. He shall, however, be permitted to say that the wicked are miserable and need punishment and that when they pay the penalty they receive benefit from God. But that God, though he is good, is still the cause of the ills of anyone must be denied in every way, nor must anyone say such things in the city if it is going to have good laws, nor must anyone, old or young, hear them, nor can they be told either in meter or without meter, and if anyone says such things he shall be considered impious, because his words are not useful to us nor consistent with each other.

This then would be one of the laws about the gods, and gives one of the criteria according to which those who speak must speak and those who write poetry must write, namely, that they are not to say that God is the cause of everything, but only of what is good.

[God is invariable. 380 D]

Now for the second law. Do you think God is a magician, who trickily appears sometimes in one form, sometimes in another, now as himself and again altering his appearance into many shapes, deceiving us and making such things seem true of him, or is God simple and wholly unlikely to depart from his proper form?

To continue, if anyone puts off his own form, does he not metamorphose himself either through his own power or that of another? But if things are as good as possible, are they not least likely to be changed by some alien power? Are not the healthiest and strongest bodies least altered by foods and drinks and labor, and the strongest plants by heat and wind and similar trials?

And external suffering will least affect and change the spirit that is most vigorous and wise?

And the same is true of every article that can be produced, dress and buildings and garments; those that are well made and in good condition are least altered by time and other destructive forces. Everything that because of art or nature or both is most nearly perfect can be least altered by something from without.

But God has in every way the best things that pertain to God. Hence God would be least likely to assume many forms.

If he should become different, would he not have to change and alter himself?

And could he change himself to a form better and more beautiful, or would it of necessity be one worse and less beautiful? for we can hardly say that God is lacking in beauty or excellence.

And under such a condition do you suppose any god or man would change himself for the worse?

It is impossible, then, for a god to wish to alter himself, but since, as it appears, each one is as beautiful and powerful as possible, he always remains simply in his own form.

So none of the poets must say to us that

> the gods in the likeness of strangers from distant lands, in all manner of disguises walk about the cities.

Nor must anyone speak falsely of Proteus and Thetis, nor in tragedies and other poems present Hera in disguise as a priestess asking alms from

> the life-giving sons of Inachus, the river of Argos;

and many other lies of this sort are not to be told to us. Under the influence of stories that make them timid, mothers tell these lies to their children, and present the myths badly, saying that the gods go about in the night in all sorts of strange disguises, but we must not permit this, for they at the same time blaspheme the gods and make their children cowards.

But is it possible that, even though the gods do not transform themselves, they make us think they appear in divers forms, by practising deception and witchcraft on us?

But would a god wish to deceive us either in word or deed by presenting a phantasm?

[After some discussion, it is concluded that God is altogether simple and true in word and deed, and is not metamorphosed nor does he deceive others, not by phantasms nor words nor by sending signs when men wake or when they dream.]

So this is the second method according to which it is necessary to speak and act about the gods, namely, to make clear that they are not wizards who transform themselves and that they do not deceive us with lies in word or in deed.

[Homer misrepresents the gods. 383 A]

If that is true, we can praise many things in Homer, but we cannot praise the dream that was sent by Zeus to Agamemnon,[6] nor can we praise Aeschylus for having Thetis say that, at her wedding, Apollo in his song

> told of her fair children, exempt from sickness and living in blessedness, and sang a paean saying that in every way my fortunes were dear to the gods, and put courage in my heart. And I trusted that the divine mouth of Phoebus was without falsehood, overflowing with prophetic wisdom. But he who sang the song, he who sat at the wedding-feast, he who spoke such words, he it is who has killed my son.

Whenever anyone says such things about the gods, let us blame him and refuse to give him a chorus and not allow teachers to use his works in the education of the youth, if we wish our guardians to fear the gods and be godlike themselves, so far as is humanly possible.

Book III

[Poetic accounts of Hades. 386 A]

[Socrates is speaking to Adeimantus.]

As to narratives about the gods it seems that some of them are fit to be heard and some not fit to be heard by children who are being so trained that they will honor the gods and their parents and put a high value on friendship for one another.

And if they are trained to be brave, should not stories be chosen that will lead them to fear death as little as may be? Or is it possible for anyone to be courageous who has that fear in his heart?

---

[6] *Iliad*, II, 1–34. The dream was false.

And if anyone believes the stories about Hades and its horrors, do you think he will be without fear of death and will choose to die in battle rather than suffer defeat and slavery?

It is necessary, it seems then, for us to devise positive instructions for those who undertake the telling of such tales and oblige them not simply to revile Hades, but rather to praise it, for otherwise they say nothing that is true or profitable for children who are going to be soldiers.

We shall get rid of everything of the sort then, beginning with this passage:

> I had rather live on the earth as the slave of some poor man than to rule over all the wasted dead.[7]

And these:

> Lest unto men and gods should appear those abodes, fearful to look on, dark and decaying, that the gods abhor.[8]

> Alas, in the abodes of Hades there remains to us a shade and image, but no intellect.[9]

> He alone had wisdom; the others were flitting shades.[10]

> Fluttering from the body, the soul went down to Hades, bewailing the doom that forced it to give up strength and youth.[11]

> The gibbering ghost went beneath the earth like smoke.[12]

> Just as bats in the depths of some mysterious grotto fly with squeak and gibber when one of the cluster falls from the rock where they cling together, so the gibbering ghosts flew about.[13]

We must ask Homer and the other poets not to be angry if we cancel all such passages, not as unpoetic and displeasing for the rabble to hear, but because the more poetic they are the less fit they are for the ears of boys and men trained to be free and to fear servitude more than death.

Then we must get rid of all the names that rouse terror and fear, like Cocytus, Styx, ghosts, and specters, and all those that by their very names make men shudder when they hear them pronounced. Perhaps there is some use in them, but we fear for our guardians lest they get feverish with horror and grow too soft.

So we must get rid of these names.

---

[7] *Odyssey*, XI, 489-91.   [8] *Iliad*, XX, 64-5.   [9] XXIII, 103-4.   [10] *Odyssey*, X, 495.
[11] *Iliad*, XVI, 856-7.   [12] XXIII, 100.   [13] *Odyssey*, XXIV, 6-9.

The opposite method must be chosen for them and used by the poets.

⌊Lamentations by famous men in poetry. 387 D]

And we must get rid of the complaints and lamentations the poets assign to famous men.

But consider whether we are right in getting rid of them or not. For we admit that a wise man will not think death terrible for a wise man who is his companion.

And he will not lament for him as for one who has suffered some terrible misfortune.

And we also admit that such a man is most self-controlled in making his life good, and that he differs from other men in having very little need for assistance.

It will not be very terrible to him to be deprived of a son or a brother or of his property or anything else of the sort.

He will not lament much, but will bear it meekly, if some of these things happen to him.

So it is right for us to get rid of the tears of famous men and turn them over to women (though not to women of high character) and to worthless men, so that those we agree we are educating for the protection of the country may scorn such actions.

Then we shall require Homer and the other poets not to say that Achilles, the child of a goddess,

> lay sometimes on his side, sometimes on his back, sometimes face down, and then he rose up and wandered distraught by the shore of the waste sea, and with both hands seized up the sooty ashes and poured them over his head,[14]

nor that he wept and wailed in all the ways Homer tells of. And we cannot allow Homer to say that Priam, a man of close kin to the gods,

> prayed and rolled in the dirt, and shrieked out the name of each man as he called on him.[15]

And still more insistently we shall ask Homer not to represent the gods as weeping and saying:

> Alas, wretched that I am, I have brought forth a child to sorrow.[16]

[14] *Iliad* xxiv, 10–12; xviii, 23–4, modified.   [15] xxii, 414–5.
[16] xviii, 54. The speaker is Thetis, goddess-mother of Achilles.

And if they do so represent the gods, they should not be so bold as to misrepresent the greatest of them by having him say:

> Woe is me, I behold a man dear to me pursued around the city, and my heart is torn with sorrow.[17]
> Oh! oh! no man was dearer to me than Sarpedon, and fate decrees that he shall fall at the hand of Patroclus, son of Menoetius.[18]

If, my dear Adeimantus, the young men take such things seriously when they hear them and do not laugh at them as foolish ideas, no one would think it unworthy for him as a man to act in the same way, nor would he rebuke himself if he should happen to say or do such things, and he would not be ashamed or try to restrain himself from uttering over small woes many a dirge and many a lament.

No, reason makes clear to us that it must not be allowed; we will hold to that until someone persuades us of something better.

[Unseemly laughter. 388 E]

Then our guardians must not be fond of laughter. For when anyone gives himself up to violent laughter, his condition calls for a strong reaction.

So if any poet represents men of sense as overcome by laughter, the verses must be deleted, and much more so if he says it of the gods.

So we shall have to cut out such a passage as this from Homer:

> Inextinguishable laughter burst forth among the blessed gods when they saw Hephaestus bearing the cup through the hall.[19]

It cannot be received according to our conclusions.

Adeimantus replied: Attribute the conclusions to me if you wish; at any rate such a passage is not acceptable.

[Truth, temperance, and respect for the gods in poetry. 389 B]

Socrates continued: Certainly we must set a high value on truth. If we were right in saying not long ago that falsehood is of no value to the gods but is valuable to men as a sort of medicine, evidently falsehood must be in the hands of a physician, and not permitted to laymen.

So the rulers of the city, if anyone, have the right to tell lies for

---

[17] *Iliad*, XXII, 168–9.   [18] XVI, 433–4.   [19] I, 599–600.

the good of the state in matters of war and politics, but none of the others must undertake to tell them. But we think that for a private citizen to lie to the rulers is a fault of the same sort, though greater, as if a sick man should not tell the truth to his physician or the athlete should deceive his trainer about the state of his body, or if in some matter he and his fellows have in charge, a sailor should misrepresent the ship and the crew to the pilot. Hence if the ruler should find someone besides himself in the city telling lies,

> any one of the workers, soothsayer, healer of ills, or joiner of timbers,[20]

he will punish him for bringing in a practice that will overthrow and destroy the city as though it were a ship.

Adeimantus replied: Yes, if the ruler acts according to reason.

Socrates continued: Do we wish the young men to be temperate?

And as to temperance, isn't the most important thing for the common people that they be subject to the rulers, and that the rulers themselves exercise temperance in drink, love, and feasting? And we shall approve the saying of Diomed in Homer:

> Friend, sit still and attend to my word.[21]

And what comes later:

> The Greeks moved on breathing courage, in silent awe of their leaders.[22]

And there are others of the same sort. Then there is this:

> Sodden with drink, having the eyes of a dog and the heart of a deer.[23]

Will you approve what follows that, and other passages in prose or verse in which privates speak insolently to their leaders? I think it does not make for temperance if the young men hear them. There is nothing strange about their being otherwise pleasing. But suppose a poet makes the wisest of men say that to him nothing seems fairer than when

> the tables are full of bread and flesh, and the cupbearer takes the wine from the mixing-bowl and carries it around and pours it into the cups.[24]

---

[20] *Odyssey*, XVII, 383-4. [21] *Iliad*, IV, 412. [22] III, 8, and IV, 431. [23] I, 225.
[24] Odysseus speaking in the *Odyssey*, IX, 8-10.

Does it seem to you that a young man will be influenced to temperance by hearing this? Then there is the passage:

> To meet one's death from hunger is the worst of fates.[25]

Then Homer writes that while other gods and mortals were asleep, Zeus alone was awake and making plans; yet he lightly forgot them all in his desire for sexual pleasures, and is so overcome with his emotions when he sees Hera that he does not wish even to go to their chamber but wants to lie with her there on the ground, and says that his desire is stronger than when they first came together, without the knowledge of their dear parents.[26] Then there is the story of the binding of Ares and Aphrodite by Hephaestus,[27] for the same sort of thing.

Do you think them fit for our young men to hear?

But the deeds and acts of great men that show extraordinary self-control should be seen and heard, such as this:

> Smiting his breast, he rebuked his heart in this wise: Stand fast, my heart; you have borne things worse than this.[28]

And we must not allow our men to accept bribes or love wealth.— So no one can be allowed to chant to them:

> Gifts persuade the gods, gifts move reverend kings.[29]

Nor is Phenix the attendant of Achilles to be praised for advising him in a song to come to the aid of the Greeks if they give him presents, but unless they do, not to lay aside his anger.[30] Nor shall we have so little esteem for Achilles as to admit he was so fond of money as to take gifts from Agamemnon,[31] and to give up the body of Hector if he received a ransom, but otherwise not.[32] I hesitate for Homer's sake to assert any impiety in saying these things about Achilles and in believing them when they are related by others, especially that he said to Apollo:

> You have hindered me, O Far-darter, you who do more harm than any other god; I swear I would take my revenge on you if I had the power.[33]

And it is also related that he was disobedient to the river-god, and was willing to fight with him,[34] and that he said he would cut

---

[25] *Odyssey*, XII, 342.   [26] *Iliad*, XIV, 294.   [27] *Odyssey*, VIII, 266 ff.   [28] XX, 17-18.
[29] Attributed to Hesiod.   [30] *Iliad*, IX, 515 ff.   [31] *Iliad*, XIX, 278 ff.
[32] *Iliad*, XXIV, 139, 502, 555, 560, 594. James Adam in *The Republic of Plato* (Cambridge, 1926) comments on this passage that Plato is "unfair" to Achilles. He does not cite line 139.   [33] *Iliad*, XXII, 15-6.   [34] XXI, 222 ff.

off the locks of his hair that were consecrated to another river, the Spercheius, and bestow them on the dead body of the hero Patroclus,[35] but we cannot believe that he did so. And it is said he repeatedly dragged Hector around the body of Patroclus and slew captives at the funeral pyre; but all these things we shall say are not truly reported; nor shall we allow our guardians to believe that Achilles, who was the son of a goddess and of Peleus—a most temperate man and third in descent from Zeus—and who was brought up by Cheiron, was so greatly disordered in spirit that he had in his breast two opposing maladies, slavish avarice and insolence to gods and men.

And moreover we shall not believe or allow it to be said that Theseus the son of Poseidon, and Peirithous the son of Zeus rushed on to the dreadful rapes reported of them, nor shall we think that any other son of a god or hero was so mad as to do the terrible and unholy deeds now falsely assigned to them. But let us oblige the poets either not to attribute these deeds to such men or not to say that they were the sons of gods; they must not combine the two, for by no means can we allow them to attempt to persuade the young men that the gods do evil deeds and that the heroes are no better than men. In the light of what we have said earlier, these stories are not holy or true, for we have explained that it is impossible for evil to come from the gods.

[Such harmful stories must be forbidden. 391 E]

And such stories are harmful to those who listen, for every wicked man will have his excuse, since he will believe such deeds are done and have been done by

the seed of the gods, near of kin to Zeus, who have high in the air on the summit of Ida an altar to Zeus their father, nor has the blood of the gods perished in them.[36]

For these reasons we must forbid such stories, that they may not produce in the young a strong inclination to evil.

Is there any other type of literature we should examine to see whether it is to be approved or not? We have said what is necessary about writings that deal with the gods and with spirits and heroes and things in Hades.

There remains the type that deals with men.

[35] *Iliad*, XXIII, 151.   [36] From the lost *Niobe* of Aeschylus.

But it is impossible, my friend, for us to consider this at present. I think we said the poets and orators speak badly on matters of the greatest importance to men, indicating that many unjust men are happy, and many just men miserable, and that injustice is profitable, if it is not found out, and that justice is good for others but damaging to ourselves. We should prohibit them from saying such things and command them to put the opposite sentiments in their chants and stories.

If you agree that I am right, I may say you agree with what we were searching for some time ago.

Then if it is necessary to speak of men as I have suggested, shall we bring that conclusion into harmony with what we have found justice is, and say that by nature justice is advantageous to those who possess it, whether it seems to be so or not?

[Narrative and dramatic diction. 392 C]

But this is enough on the ideas. We must next look at the diction, I think, and consider thoroughly what is to be said and how it is to be said.

Adeimantus answered: I do not understand what you mean.

Socrates replied: It is necessary you should. Perhaps this will be plainer. Does not everything narrated by myth-writers and poets deal with what has been or is or will be?
And do they not use either simple narrative or dramatic presentation or both?

Adeimantus answered: I need to know more about that.

Socrates continued: I seem to be a ridiculous and baffling teacher. Well then, like a poor speaker, I won't attempt to deal with the entire subject but will take a part and try to make clear to you what I mean about it. I know you remember the first part of the *Iliad*, where the poet says Chryses asked Agamemnon to release his daughter and the king treated him harshly and when the priest did not succeed he prayed to the god against the Greeks? Then you remember these words,

> He appealed to all the Greeks, but most of all to the two sons
> of Atreus, leaders of the people.

Now up to these words the poet speaks in his own person and does not in any way attempt to make us suppose that anyone else than himself is talking. But after this it is as though Chryses himself spoke, and the poet attempts to make it seem to us as though it were not Homer who is speaking but the priest, who is an old man. And he has used this same method in relating almost everything that happens at Troy and at Ithaca and in the whole *Odyssey*.

Now it is narrative when he tells what each one said and what happened between the speeches.

But whenever he speaks as though he were some other person, will he not adapt his language to make it as fitting as possible to the person who speaks?

Then when one makes himself resemble another in either voice or gesture, he imitates the one he makes himself resemble?

So this is the way, I think, in which Homer and the other poets carry on their narrative by imitation.

But if the poet does not at all conceal himself, the poem and the narrative will be carried on without any imitation. But that you may not say you do not understand, I shall tell you how this is. If Homer said that Chryses came with a ransom for his daughter, as a suppliant to the Greeks and especially to the kings, the poet in using that method would not speak as though he were Chryses but as Homer, and there would be no imitation but simple narrative. This is how he would have done it; I don't use meter because I am not a poet: The priest came and wished them success in the capture of Troy and safety for themselves, and asked them to reverence the god by taking the gifts and letting him have his daughter. The Greeks respected him and assented to what he proposed, except that Agamemnon was angry and commanded him to depart and not to return, threatening that the scepter and the insignia of the god should not protect him, and declaring he would not release his daughter but that she should grow old in Argos with him; he bade him depart and not show anger, if he hoped to return home in safety. The old man was afraid when he heard this and went away in silence, but when he was clear of the camp he prayed fervently to Apollo, calling upon the god by his various names, reminding him of the past, and asking for help if the god had ever taken any pleasure in the temples the priest had built or in the victims he had sacrificed on his altars. He asked the god as a sign of thanks to revenge his tears on the Greeks with the divine arrows. This, my friend, is a simple narrative without imitation.[37]

[37] See Aristotle, *Poetics*, III, first par., below.

Observe then that the condition is reversed when one omits what the poet says between the speeches and leaves only the dialogue.

Adeimantus answered: I see it's that way in tragedy.

Socrates replied: You understand perfectly and I think I can now make clear what was not plain before, that poetry and mythology sometimes appear as complete imitations, as you say tragedy and comedy are, and sometimes as narratives of the poet himself; the latter you find especially in dithyrambic poetry. The mixture of the two methods you find in the works of the epic poets and in many other places.

You remember that not long ago we said we had indicated what the poet was to narrate, and now we must see how he is to do it.

[Shall imitation be allowed in the city? 394 D]

This, then, was what I said, namely, that we must agree whether we shall allow the poets to give us their narratives by imitation, or by imitating some things and not others, or sometimes one and sometimes the other, or not to imitate at all.

Adeimantus said: I infer that you are going to consider whether we shall admit tragedy and comedy into the city or not.

Perhaps I am, replied Socrates, and perhaps I am going to consider some other things as well. I don't know just what, but wherever reason directs the spirit, there let it go.

Consider this then, Adeimantus: Ought our guardians to be imitators or not, or shall we follow our earlier decision that every man can carry on one occupation well, but not several; in fact, if he tries it, will he not fail in all he undertakes, and lose reputation? Is not the same thing true about imitation, that the same man cannot imitate many things so well as he can one?

The same man, then, will not be a good administrator of important affairs and also be a good imitator, nor will he be able to imitate many things, since the same persons are unable to do well in the two kinds of imitation that seem close to one another, that is, in the composition of comedy and tragedy.

The same persons are not elocutionists and actors either.

Even comic and tragic actors are not the same; and yet these are all imitations, aren't they?

[Are the guardians to be imitators? 395 B]

It seems to me, Adeimantus, that in these matters human nature is so specialized that it cannot produce good imitations of many

objects or do many of those things on which the imitations are
patterned.

So if we are going to hold to our first conclusion, our guardians
should differ from all other workers in being very skillful producers of the liberty of the city and should be concerned with
nothing that does not bear on this, and they should neither do
nor imitate anything else. And if they do imitate they should
from childhood imitate only what will aid them in their duties,
namely, the characters of the courageous, wise, holy, free, and the
like, but they should do nothing that is slavish nor be good at
imitating it, nor anything else that is evil, for fear that from the
imitation they may get some of the real thing. Have you not observed that imitations, when carried on steadily from childhood,
are established in the character and the nature and appear in
body, voice, and habit of thought?

Then since we are training men, we must not allow them, if we
hope they will be good men, to imitate a woman, either young
or old, quarreling with her husband or showing anger against the
gods or boasting loudly of what she believes is good fortune, nor is
she to be imitated when she is in affliction or distress or tears, and
much less when she is sick or in love or in the pangs of childbirth.
And we must have no imitations of slave women or slave men
carrying on their proper duties.

And we must not allow our youths to imitate bad men, cowardly
and opposite in character to those we mentioned a little back, who
revile and defame each other and use foul language, either when
they are drunk or when they are sober, or anything else bad that
such men do to themselves and to each other. And our pupils
must not be allowed to act like madmen in word or deed. They
must understand insane and wicked men and women, but must
not perform any of their acts or imitate them.

But then, what about the blacksmiths and other artisans, and
those who row triremes or beat time for the rowers? is anything of
this sort to be imitated?

Adeimantus agreed, saying: We cannot permit one of our pupils
to devote his mind to this sort of thing.

Then, said Socrates, can they imitate the whinnyings of horses,
the bellowings of bulls, the murmurings of streams, the roar of the
sea, and thunder, and all such things?

No, returned Adeimantus, they must neither be mad nor imitate the mad.

But, continued Socrates, if I understand what you say, there is a kind of diction and narrative in which a man really fair and good can tell a story, and another kind, quite different, which a man of opposite nature and education would use.

It seems to me that an upright person, when he comes in the narrative to some speech or act of a good man, will be glad to speak as though he were that man and will not be ashamed of the imitation, especially when he can imitate a good man acting firmly and intelligently, and he will be much less willing to imitate one who is overcome by sickness or love or wine or anything of the sort; and when he comes to someone unworthy of himself, he will not seriously wish to act like an inferior, except for a moment when the inferior man does something good, but will be ashamed of it, since he is not trained in the imitation of such characters, and is disgusted at having to mold and fit himself into their forms; he thoroughly despises it except in jest.

Hence he will use such a mode of narrative as we spoke of a little while ago with respect to the poems of Homer, and his language will without question be a mingling of both imitation and simple narrative, with a small amount of narration in a long work. But a man not of this sort, in proportion as he is worse, will the more gladly imitate all sorts of things and will think nothing unworthy of him, and will undertake to imitate everything seriously and before crowds; he will imitate the sort of thing we just spoke of: thunder and the noise of the wind and of hail and axles and pulleys, and the notes of trumpets and flutes and pipes and all sorts of instruments, yes and the barking of dogs, the baas of sheep, and the cries of birds. His diction will be composed of imitation with voice and gesture altogether or with very little narrative.

These are the two types of diction I was speaking of.

Now one of these is liable to small variations, for if we allow fitting harmony and rhythm to the diction, the one who speaks correctly is always on about the same note and employs one harmony, for the changes are but small, and likewise his rhythm is much the same throughout.

But doesn't the other type require just the opposite, and need every sort of harmony and rhythm, if it is going to speak appropriately, because it has variations of every sort?

And do not all the poets and orators make use of one or the other of these types of diction or mingle the two?

[The unmixed imitation of virtue to be allowed in the
state. 397 D]

What shall we do, then? Shall we receive into the city either of
the two forms or a mixture of them?

Adeimantus replied: If my opinion is of any worth, we shall
take the unmixed imitation of virtue.

But Adeimantus, continued Socrates, the mixed form is sweet,
and the one opposite to what you choose is the sweetest of any to
children and to the servants who care for them and to the crowd
generally.

But you may say it is not very fitting for our state, because we
don't have men of two occupations or of many, for each man does
one thing.

So in this city alone we shall find that the leather-worker is only
a leather-worker and not a pilot in addition, and the farmer is a
farmer and not a judge as well, and the soldier is only a soldier
and not a merchant too, and so for all the rest.

It seems, then, that if a man so clever that he can do a great many
things and can imitate all the occupations should come to our city
and ask to be received as a citizen, we should venerate him as holy
and wonderful and pleasing, but should say there is no man of the
sort in our city and according to law there cannot be, and should
send him away to some other city after having anointed his head
with perfume and crowned him with a garland; we need a more
austere and manly poet who will tell profitable stories, and will
imitate the speech of the virtuous man and will say what he has
to say according to the forms we fixed by law at the beginning,
when we set about the education of warriors. . . .

[The influence of beauty and virtue. 400 D]

Then superior style, harmony, grace, and rhythm follow good
character; I do not mean the stupidity called by the flattering
name of good character, but the intelligence that really makes the
character good and beautiful.

Are not these the things to be sought after by our young men, if
they are to do their duty in life?

And surely painting is full of these qualities and so are all the
similar arts, and weaving is full of them, and embroidery and
architecture and the manufacture of all the other needs of man,
and so is the nature of bodies and of all living things; all of them

either possess grace or lack it. And the lack of grace and the lack of rhythm and the lack of harmony are sisters to bad style and bad character, and likewise the opposite qualities are sisters and imitations of wisdom and good character. Shall we, then, consider the poets alone and require them to put the image of good character in their poems if they expect to write poetry in our city? Or must we consider the other artists and lay down the law that the immoral and unrestrained and false and ungraceful cannot be presented in the images of animals or in architecture or in any other art, and that a person of that sort of character shall not be allowed to work among us, in order that our guardians may not be brought up among ugly forms as though in a bad pasture, where every day they pluck and feed on all manner of things, a little at a time, until at last they have unwittingly gathered into their souls a great mass of ills? Are we not rather to seek for artists of a higher genius who are able to discover the nature of the beautiful and the graceful, in order that the young men, as though living in a healthful spot, may suck in virtue everywhere, and the influence of beautiful works may always be exercised on their sight and hearing, like breezes bringing health from happy climes, and may lead them unconsciously to resemble and love the beauty of reason with which they are in accord?

Book X

[Imitation is dangerous. 595 A]

[Socrates is speaking to Glaucon.]
Certainly there are many other reasons I think of why we were quite right in our organization of the state, and after considering the matter I think we did especially well about poetry.
We refused to admit it because it is imitative, for that it should not be admitted is the more apparent, I think, now that we have distinguished between the various parts of the soul. Between ourselves—for I hope you won't give me away to the tragic poets and the other imitators—all the imitative arts seem to me ruinous to the mental powers of all their hearers who do not have as an antidote the knowledge of what these arts really are.
The truth must be told, though I hesitate because from childhood I have felt a certain love and veneration for Homer. He seems to

me to be the chief teacher and leader of all the splendid tragic poets. Still a man should not be respected to the detriment of the truth, so I must explain what I mean.

But first answer a question.

[Imitation explained. 595 C]

Do you understand imitation well enough to tell me what it is? I don't myself understand very well what purpose there is in it.

It's likely that I should know, then, Glaucon answered.

Socrates replied: It wouldn't be strange that you should, since often those with dim vision make out objects more quickly than those with sharp eyes.

That's all very well, said Glaucon, but when you are present I hardly have the courage to tell what I do think; you give your opinion.

Shall we, then, said Socrates, begin our investigation in our usual manner? We are in the habit of putting in the same class all the various things to which we give the same name.

Now let us take any class of things you like. For example, there are a great many chairs and tables.

But only two ideas pertain to these objects, that of chair and that of table.

Well then, don't we say that the maker of either of these things, having the idea in mind, makes the chairs and tables we use and other things in the same way? For certainly none of the cabinet-makers devises the idea itself; how could he?

Now consider by what name you call this maker.

I mean the one who makes everything that each and every one of the handicrafts turns out.

Glaucon said: You are talking about some wonderfully clever man.

Wait a moment, replied Socrates, you must say something stronger than that. For this same being is the maker not merely of all implements, but he makes everything that grows out of the earth and produces all the animals, and himself too, and in addition the earth and the sky and the gods and everything in heaven and under the earth in Hades.

You are talking of a wonderful and wise being, said Glaucon.

Don't you believe it? replied Socrates. Now tell me, on the whole doesn't it seem to you that there is such a maker, or do you think that in one sense there is a maker of all these things and in

another sense there is none? Or don't you see that in a sense you
yourself can make all these things?

It is not hard; you can make things everywhere and without delay;
the quickest way is to take a mirror and move it about, for you
would quickly make the sun and anything that is in the sky and
the earth and yourself and the other animals and furniture and
plants and everything we have been talking about.

Yes, said Glaucon, reflections of them but not the real things.

[The artist's imitation. 596 E]

Good, Socrates answered, you have the notion I want. I think
the painter is one of these makers.

You may say that he doesn't really make what he makes, yet in a
sense the painter makes a bed, doesn't he, when he makes the
picture of a bed?

And what about the cabinet-maker? Yet he doesn't make the
idea, which is the real bed, but only one individual bed.

If he doesn't make the bed in its true essence, he doesn't make
the real bed, but something like it though not it; and if anyone says
that the product of the cabinet-maker gives us essence or being in
the full sense of the word, he is in danger of saying what is not true.
So we mustn't be astonished if the cabinet-maker's product turns
out to be only a shadow of the truth.

Shall we then, try to learn what this imitator really is?

Then there are altogether three beds, one in nature, which we
would admit, I think, to be the work of God, for it can hardly be
the work of some other being.

Then there is one made by the cabinet-maker.

And one is made by the painter, isn't it?

Then there are painter, cabinet-maker, and God; these three are
concerned with three different kinds of bed.

But God, whether because of his will or through some necessity
that not more than one bed should be produced in nature, made
just one bed, the real bed. But two or more of that sort were not
made by God and never will be made.

The reason is that if he had made two, there would be one behind
them whose appearance both of the others would have; that would
be the real bed, and not the other two.

Since God understood that and wished to be the real creator of the
real bed, but not a sort of cabinet-maker who makes an individual
bed, he produced in nature one bed.

Shall we then call him the natural creator of it, or by some such name?

But what of the cabinet-maker? Is he not the maker of the bed? And isn't the painter also the creator and maker of one?

Glaucon did not accept this, but answered: Not at all.

Socrates then asked him: But how do you say he is related to the bed?

It seems to me, answered Glaucon, most reasonable to say that he imitates what the others make.

So, said Socrates, you call him who is not in direct contact with nature an imitator.

The same thing is true of the writer of tragedy, for if he is an imitator he also is by nature out of direct touch with the king and the truth, and so are all the other imitators.

So we are in agreement about the imitator. But about the painter; does he attempt to imitate each object as it naturally is?

Shall we not rather say he imitates the works of the artisans?

[Appearance and reality. 598 A]

Does he imitate them as they are or as they appear to be?

If you look at a bed from one side or from the front or in any other way, isn't it different? Or doesn't it really differ, though it appears different?

And isn't it the same about other things?

Now consider this: to what is painting in each instance directed? Does it imitate the thing as it actually is, or the appearance that it presents? Is it not an imitation of phantasy rather than of truth? Then imitation is far removed from truth and, as it seems, produces things because it gets hold of a little of each object, namely, the image of each. The painter, for example, will paint us a shoemaker, a carpenter, and other workmen, though he does not understand the craft of any of them. And a good painter, if he is allowed to show at a distance his picture of a carpenter, will deceive children and simple men into thinking that it is really a carpenter.

But, my friend, this is the way we must look at such things: If someone tells us he has met a man who understands all the crafts and all sorts of other things, such as an expert in each craft knows, and that there is nothing he doesn't know more exactly than anyone else, we must think our informer a simple fellow who has been misled by encountering some enchanter and imitator. The

imitator seems to him to be all-wise because he himself is unable
to distinguish between knowledge and ignorance and imitation.

[The poet's knowledge. 598 D]

Then we must next examine tragedy and Homer who is at the
head of it, for we hear some say that the tragic writers know all the
crafts, and possess all human knowledge pertaining to virtue and
vice, and all divine knowledge; they argue that the good poet, if
he is to write on subjects he can treat properly, must deal with
what he understands; otherwise he cannot write at all. We should
find out whether men who argue thus have not encountered
imitators who have deceived them, for they do not realize that
something intervenes between the imitations they see and the
truth itself, and that imitations are easily produced by one who
does not know the truth; such productions are phantasms and not
realities. Or is there something in their belief, and do good poets
really have sound knowledge of the things on which they are
popularly supposed to speak well?
Do you think that, if a man were equally able to produce both the
thing imitated and the image of it, he would wish to give himself
to the production of images and make that activity prominent in
his life as the best thing he can do?
In my belief if he truly understood the things he imitates he would
much prefer to work in the things themselves rather than in
imitations, and would endeavor to leave behind him as monuments many beautiful works of his own; he would prefer to be
praised rather than to praise someone else.

[Is Homer a teacher? 599 B]

We need not, then, examine Homer or other poets by asking if
any one of them was a physician and not an imitator of the talk of
physicians, and if any poet is reported to have cured anyone in
antiquity or recently, as Asclepius did, or whether the poet left
successors instructed in medicine, as Asclepius did his descendants,
nor shall we ask anything about the other arts, but let them go.
We shall be satisfied with asking about the greatest and most
splendid things Homer undertakes to deal with, namely wars and
military affairs[38] and the government of cities and the. education
of a man, for it is proper to try to learn from him by asking: My
dear Homer, if in your knowledge of virtue you are not out of

[38] Cf. the emphasis on Homer's knowledge of generalship in the *Ion*, 540 D, above.

contact with truth, as a mere maker of images according to our definition of the imitator, and if you are in close touch with the truth, and in a position to know what activities make men better or worse individually or in groups, tell us in what city you made improvements in the government, as Lycurgus did in Sparta, and other men in many other cities great and small. What city recognizes that you have been a good lawgiver and have benefited it? Italy and Sicily have Charondas and we Athenians have Solon, but what city acknowledges you?

Can he point to any?

And what war is mentioned as having been skillfully conducted in the time of Homer with him as general or adviser?

But are the works of a wise man attributed to Homer, as many inventions and devices helpful in the crafts and in other activities are said to be the work of Thales of Miletus and Anacharsis of Scythia? But if it is not related that he did anything of a public sort, perhaps Homer when he was alive privately directed the education of various persons who loved to associate with him, and marked out for others a way of life called the Homeric, just as Pythagoras was greatly loved for this, and his followers to this day call their rule of life the Pythagorean and are distinguished from other men by it.

No, Glaucon answered, nothing of the kind is told of Homer. And, Socrates, perhaps Creophylos, the companion of Homer, would appear in matters of education more ridiculous than his name,[39] if the things reported of Homer are true. For when he was alive he was greatly neglected, it is said, by that friend of his.

Yes, so it is said, Socrates answered. But you know, Glaucon, that if Homer really was a person who could train men and make them better, and could speak on such matters not as an imitator but as one with real knowledge, he would certainly have acquired many companions and been loved and honored by them. Protagoras of Abdera and Prodicus of Ceos and many others would hardly have been able to produce such an effect on their associates as to make them suppose themselves unable to manage their houses and cities without using the principles of their teachers, if Protagoras and the others had not taken charge of their education. The pupils of these men love them so greatly for their wisdom that they almost carry them about as in a triumphal procession. But if the contemporaries of Homer and Hesiod had thought they were able to instruct men in virtue, would they have allowed those

[39] It means "of the beef-tribe."

poets to go about chanting verses? Would they not have clung to them regardless of expense, and forced them to stay with them? And if they could not persuade the poets to stay, would they not have accompanied them anywhere and everywhere, until they were sufficiently instructed?

[The poets are only imitators. 600 E]

Shall we decide, then, that all the poets beginning with Homer are imitators of images of virtue or of whatever they write about, and do not lay hold of the truth, but, as we just said, the painter, though he does not understand shoemaking, makes what seems to be a shoemaker to those who also do not understand and who judge from colors and gestures?

So, I take it, we shall say that the poet in his words and phrases uses the colors proper for each of the arts; and though he knows only how to imitate, yet to those who are as ignorant as himself he appears really to know. If he speaks of shoemaking, military affairs, or anything else, he seems to speak very well, for his ornaments of meter and rhythm and harmony naturally have great charm. But when the ideas of the poet are stripped of the colors of poetry, you know, I think, how they appear. You must have observed this.

Well then, do they seem to you like those faces that have freshness but not beauty, if you happen to see them when they have passed their bloom?

Let us go on to consider this: We said, didn't we, that the poet is an imitator of what he knows nothing about, of a mere appearance? Let us not leave this subject partly thought out, but treat it fully. The painter, we say, paints reins and a bit.

And the harness-maker and the smith make them.

Then does the painter know what reins and bits really are?

Or does the manufacturer, namely, the smith or the harness-maker, know, or does knowledge belong only to the man who understands a bridle?

In my opinion the horseman is the one who knows.

And this holds generally.

I mean that for all such things there are three crafts, those of the user, the maker, and the imitator.

Then the virtue and beauty and correctness of any implement of life and action is determined by nothing else than the need because of which each one is made or brought forth.

It must needs be that the user of each is well versed in it and can tell the maker which ones are good or bad for the use he makes of them; a flute-player can tell a flute-maker about the flutes he uses in playing, and will explain how they should be made, and the flute-maker will carry out his instructions.

Then the man who knows will explain about good and bad flutes, and the worker will follow his directions?

Then in this matter the maker will have a right belief about good and bad, since he is associated with the one who knows and is obliged to listen to him; but the one who uses the flute is the man who knows.

But does the imitator from using the thing he paints get to know what is good and what is bad?

Is his knowledge reliable because he is obliged to come in contact with somebody who knows and who gives him directions on what he should paint?

If not, the imitator will neither learn for himself nor be properly taught whether he imitates well or badly.

A fine imitator he will surely be in his knowledge of the things he works on!

So he will imitate without knowing how each thing is good or bad, but what seems excellent to the ignorant rabble—that, it appears, he will imitate.

It seems we agree on two points, then: that the imitator knows nothing worth mentioning of what he imitates, but his imitation is a sort of game and not serious, and all who undertake tragic poetry in iambic poems and in epics are imitators in the full sense of the word.

Can there be any doubt, I said, that this imitation is not in direct contact with truth?

[Protection against the imitator. 602 C]

Now on what part of the being of man does it exercise the power it has?

But I must explain. When you look at the same thing near at hand and from a distance, does it not appear different in size?

And a stick appears crooked when you see it in the water and straight when it is taken out, and objects appear hollowed or rounded because the vision is deceived by shading, and every sort of confusion is produced in our minds: painting that uses light and shade, in its effect on our easily deluded senses, doesn't fall at all short of witchcraft, nor do sleight-of-hand performances and similar tricks.

But measuring and counting appear to be excellent remedies against such deceptions, so that appearances of greater or smaller or more or less do not control us, but rather the faculty that has counted and measured and even weighed.

This work would be carried on by the part of the soul that can reckon.

And it often happens to this part of the soul that measures and counts that diverse things and equal things may appear larger or smaller than they are, and opposite things seem to agree. And did we not say that it is impossible for the same part of the mind to have diverse beliefs about the same thing?

Then the part of the soul that judges with respect to measure would not be the same as that which judges contrary to measure. But if the soul is to be healthy it must trust to measure and reckoning.

And anything opposed to this would of necessity be one of the worse parts within us.

Because I wished you to admit this, I said that painting and imitation generally carry out their work far from the truth and have to do with that part within us that is remote from the truth, and that the two arts are companions and friends of nothing wholesome or true.

So imitation is a wretched thing begetting wretched things on a wretched stock.

Is that true for what we see alone, or for what we hear and call poetry?

If it is true for poetry, we shouldn't trust merely to the likeness of poetry with painting, but should also consider that part of the reason with which the imitation of poetry is concerned, and see whether it is bad or excellent.

[Self-control. 603 C]

Let us proceed in this way: we may say that an imitative art imitates men who are performing either forced or voluntary acts, and thinking that as a result of their acts they are either happy or miserable, and in all these conditions they either lament or rejoice. And there seems to be nothing further. But in all these conditions does a man enjoy harmony of mind? Or, as he was confused in vision and had at one time opposite ideas about the same things, is he confused in his deeds and at war with himself? But I recollect that it is not now necessary for us to come to a decision about the matter, for in what we have already said we have sufficiently considered the whole subject, and decided that our spirits are full of ten thousand opposed things at the same time. And though that was correct, it now seems necessary to consider what we then omitted.

We think that a reasonable man, when he sees anything happen as a result of chance, such as the loss of a son or something else of greatest consequence, bears such an affliction more easily than others do.

But now let us consider whether he will display no sorrow at all or whether that is impossible and it is more likely that he will show moderate grief.

Now tell me this about him. Do you think he will be more likely to fight with his sorrow and restrain it when he is in the company of his equals or when he is completely alone?

When he is alone, I think he will dare to utter many things he would be ashamed of if anyone should hear him, and he will do many things that he would not like to have anyone see him doing. Are not, then, reason and law what require him to resist, but emotion what forces him to lament?

But since there is in man an opposite tendency in this matter, we say that there necessarily are two forces within him.

Is not one of these forces ready to obey the prescriptions of the law? The law says it is a splendid thing to bear the utmost affliction with a calm mind and not to cry out, because one cannot be sure what is good and what is bad in such things, and there is no future advantage in chafing under them, nor is anything human deserving of great eagerness, and grief hinders us from doing what should be done as quickly as possible in the circumstances. I refer to the need for showing reason about what has happened, just as in playing with dice one should adjust oneself to the outcome of chance, as good sense requires; we should not act like children when they have bumped themselves, for they put their hands on the part that has been struck and waste their time in crying out; but we should train the soul to seek a remedy as quickly as possible and to raise up what is fallen and sickly and dispel laments by remedies.

We agree, then, that the best part of the soul wishes to follow reason.

[Poetry imitates men who lack self-control. 604 D]

But what shall we say of that part of the soul that leads us to remember our sorrow and to complain and revive our lamentations? is it not irrational, lazy, and prone to cowardice? Yet the soul easily vexed is that which is imitated often and in various ways, but the thoughtful and calm man, always level-headed, is hard to imitate and an imitation of him is not easily understood, especially in a great assembly when all sorts of men are gathered together in a theater, for the imitation of such a man presents qualities outside their experience. It is clear that the mimetic poet is not naturally inclined to the rational part of the soul and his wisdom is not directed to its satisfaction, if he wishes to be acceptable to the many, but in order to be pleasing in his imitation he deals with the disturbed and unsettled character.

[Imitative poetry is corrupting. 605 A]

We can, then, properly consider him as parallel with the painter, whom he resembles in making things that are not in harmony with the truth; he is also like him in being occupied with another part of the spirit, and not the best part. Hence in justice we should not take him into the city that is to be well ruled, because he stirs up and nourishes and makes strong this bad part of the spirit, and destroys the rational part, just as anyone by making the wicked powerful would betray the city to them, and would destroy those of more insight. We shall say that the imitative poet sets up a badly governed state in the soul of each individual, rejoicing at the stupidity that cannot distinguish great from small but thinks the same things are sometimes large, sometimes small, for the poet makes images and is remote from the truth. But we have not said the worst of poetry. Its capacity for corrupting good citizens, with a very few exceptions,[40] is an exceedingly dangerous quality.

[Pity for the heroes of drama. 605 C]

Still further, when Homer or some other tragic writer imitates one of the heroes in distress, who gets off a long tirade of lamentation or pours forth verses and beats his breast, the strongest of us listen

---

[40] Perhaps the exceptions are the persons mentioned at the beginning of this tenth book of the *Republic* as having an antidote in the knowledge of the true nature of poetry.

with pleasure, you know; we surrender our spirits to the guidance of the poet and sympathize with the hero, and are eager to praise the author because he so powerfully stirs our feelings.

But when affliction comes into our own lives, you know we pride ourselves on conduct of the opposite sort and try to remain calm and self-controlled, as the behavior befitting a man, and think of what we have just praised as suitable only for women. But, when we see a man whose conduct appears to us unworthy and which we would be ashamed of in ourselves, is it proper for us not to censure him but to applaud and praise him? Yet there is one way in which it is not inconsistent.

If you consider that the part of our being we restrain by force in our own affliction is desirous of weeping and pouring out tears until it gets entirely rid of them, as nature urges it to do, you will see that part of us is the very same the poets satisfy and delight. If that portion of the soul best by nature is inadequately controlled by reason and habit, it abandons its watch over lamentation on seeing human sufferings that do not immediately afflict itself, as when a man who claims to be good suffers without cause; it then praises and pities the sufferer and feels that it gains something from the spectacle, namely pleasure, which it wouldn't get if it decided to reject the drama completely. I suppose there are not many who can understand that what applies to the sorrows of others applies to their own, for if they give free rein to pity for the characters of tragedy, they will not find it easy to practice restraint in their own sufferings.

[The comic. The emotions. 606 C]

And isn't the same thing true of the comic? You may be ashamed of a thing that causes laughter, but if you hear it in a comic imitation or in private you are much amused and do not hate it as a vile thing, just as was true of pity. Then you permit what formerly you had restrained in yourself by reason, when you wished to laugh at it, because you were afraid of appearing like a buffoon; as a result, having broken down your dignity at the theater, many times in your own affairs you let yourself go as though you were a comic actor.

And with regard to sexual emotions, anger, and all the passions and sorrows and pleasures of the spirit, which we think are always with us, does not the poetic imitation have the same effect on us? It feeds and waters these passions that ought to be dried up, and puts them in command of us when they should be so ruled that we may grow better and happier instead of worse and more vile.

[The poets must be banished. 606 E]

Well then, Glaucon, when you chance on those who praise Homer and say that poet has been the teacher of Hellas, and that he is of value to those who become familiar with him because they can learn to manage and understand human affairs, and that they can live their whole lives according to the instructions they receive from this poet, we should love and honor them as men of high character so far as their powers extend,[41] and should acknowledge that Homer is the greatest of poets and the first of the writers of tragedy, yet we must hold to the belief that hymns to the gods and praises of good men are the only poems that should be admitted to our state. If we do admit the muse who is so sweet with her lyrics and epics, pleasure and pain will rule in our city instead of law and what is generally accepted as right reason.

Now since we are back on the subject of poetry, let us defend ourselves by showing that we were quite right in banishing it from the city for being what it is, for reason compelled it. Let us say to poetry, that she may not impute to us harshness and rudeness, that there is an ancient quarrel between philosophy and poetry, shown by such sayings as that philosophy is a yelping cur howling at its master, and is strong in the silly talk of fools, and that the crowd of pretended wise men is too much for Zeus, and that the philosophers are carefully thinking out how poor they are; these and many others are signs of the ancient enmity of poetry and philosophy. But if poetry and imitation, the bringers of pleasure, have anything to say, let them speak and show that they have a place in a well-ordered state, for we shall listen with delight, being well aware that we are bewitched by them. But it is not right to give up what one looks on as true. Still, my friend, are you not captivated by poetry, especially when you see her as presented by Homer? Then is it not proper that she should come back to make her defense in a lyric or some other kind of poem?

---

[41] Of this sort was Protagoras, who said: "When the boy knows his letters and can get the meaning of what is written, as before of what was spoken, the teacher puts into his hands for reading, as he sits on a bench in the school-room, the works of good poets and compels him to commit them to memory; in these poems there are many wise sayings and many digressions that give the highest praise to the good men of the past, in order that the boy may be eager to imitate them and seek to be like them" (*Protagoras*, 325–6).

And we may also permit her defenders, even if they are not poets but merely lovers of poetry, to speak of her without meter, and assert that she is not merely delightful but that she is also profitable to states and human life; and we shall listen like friends. For we shall be the gainers if she not merely appears delightful but also brings us profit.

But if it cannot be done, my dear friend, we shall act like those who are in love but think their love is not to their advantage and force themselves away from it.

We have an inbred love of such poetry nourished in us by education in a splendid state, and shall be glad to look on her as altogether good and true; yet so long as she does not make good her case, we shall as we listen to her keep in mind the argument we have already accepted, as a charm to prevent us from falling again into the childish loves of the multitude. At any rate we know we are not to suppose this sort of poetry admirable because it has attained the truth and is of great worth, but when we listen we must be on guard, as though in fear for the city within our souls, and must observe the laws we have laid down for poetry.

It is a hard struggle, my dear Glaucon, greater than anyone realizes, between good and evil, and we must not allow honor or wealth or any kind of authority or even poetry to make us neglect justice and the other virtues.

o◯oo◯o

THE LAWS

About 335 B.C.

The Laws are thought to have been composed when Plato was more than seventy years of age; they may therefore be supposed to give his mature thought. Yet since the form of the dialogue is still employed and no speaker can be identified with the author, it is impossible to say that Plato's opinions are absolutely laid down. I find it impossible to think that the Athenian who takes the chief part, for Socrates no longer appears, is Plato himself, or at least represents more than aspects of Plato's mind. The comic picture of eminent generals and statesmen solemnly reciting bad verses is hardly to be explained as the serious opinion of a man who knew and loved Homer as Plato did. At the same time he may have believed that the ordinary literal-minded person should be deprived of all literature except that fitting to his comprehension. On, and apparently against, a purely utilitarian theory of poetry the Athenian speaks in much the tone of Socrates.

The idea of censorship is offensive to most persons who in this day think of themselves as intellectual, though practically there is (at least in America) little public concern about the indirect varieties of censorship. Moreover, no small number are under the influence of two curiously blended ideas, that of the irresponsibility of the poet and that of his marvelous wisdom. The second is shown at its worst in some of the nineteenth-century idolaters of Shakespeare; Shelley's *Defense of Poetry* is its best expression. In addition, the lover of poetry, such as Sir Philip Sidney, has usually tended to repel all attacks that seemed likely to interfere with his own enjoyment, using whatever weapons came to hand. But the attitude of unreasoning protest against all regulation is hardly that of a judicious critic. He at least should be able to inquire into the relation of the arts to society, to ask with calmness whether any particular examples are likely to be of benefit to the masses or not, and on what grounds judgments for and against general circulation of any piece of poetry or drama may judiciously be pronounced. Plato furnishes us an example of a lover of art who throughout his life did not shrink from such an inquiry.

THE LAWS (*selections*)

Book II

[Is tragedy devoted to pleasure? 2.658 E]

Athenian. I am on the side of the crowd in so far as I think that music[1] should be judged according to the pleasure it causes, but not the pleasure of chance comers, for I believe the most beautiful examples of the art are those which please the best men, those who are properly trained, and above all the man superior to the rest in ability and education. We say that the judges of music need ability, because they must possess wisdom, and courage too, for the true judge of a dramatic performance must not take his verdict from the rabble and allow himself to be overcome by their applause and his own incompetence, nor should he be so weak and timid that when he knows the truth he will utter a hasty and false

[1] The word *music*, as used by the Greeks, covered music in our sense, poetry, drama, and allied arts.

verdict with the very lips that pronounced his oath as a judge. For the judge is properly not the pupil but the teacher of the spectators, and should be opposed to those who give the audience pleasure in a way that is not fitting and right. Yet the custom of Sicily and Italy at present allows the audience to determine the victory by show of hands. This corrupts the poets, for they produce vulgar work to please the multitude, so that the spectators train the poets, and it corrupts the pleasures of the audience too.[2] For if the people always listened to characters better than themselves they would grow to enjoy pleasure of a higher type, but when, as at present, they make their own choice, just the opposite comes about. What conclusion can we reasonably draw from these considerations? Perhaps it is this.

Clinias. What?

[Poetry must be approved by law. 2.659 D]

Ath. It seems to me that for the third or fourth time our discussion has come back to this point, namely, that education is the drawing and leading of children toward right by the united experience of the best and oldest men, in order that the soul of the child may not get accustomed to pleasures and pains opposed to the law and to those who keep it, but will agree with them and be pleased and pained by the same things as the old man is. For these reasons we have what we call songs. They are really charms for the spirit, intended to bring about the agreement we spoke of, for since the spirits of the young cannot bear seriousness, we use the terms *plays* and *songs* and employ our charms as games, just as in treating those who are sick and weak, physicians attempt by using pleasant foods and drinks to give them proper nourishment, but to make unwholesome food unpleasant, so the sick will welcome healthful food and form a proper hatred for the unhealthful. In the same way the good lawgiver will persuade, or if he cannot persuade, will force the poet to work as he should, and present in his beauteous and well-wrought rhythms and harmonies the gestures and accents of men who are wise, strong, and altogether good.

Clin. But do you really suppose, stranger, that poetry is composed in this way in other cities? So far as I know, what you

---

[2] "And what of tragedy herself, that venerable and wonderful form of poetry? It seems to me [i.e., Socrates] that she devotes her effort and zeal merely to pleasing the spectators, and does not strive against evils that are sweet and charming and refuse to gratify the audience with them, nor will she speak and sing of anything unpleasant but beneficial whether her hearers like it or not" (*Gorgias*, 502 B).

describe is done only in my country and that of the Spartans, but elsewhere there is always something new in the dances and in all other music, not according to law but on the promptings of unrestricted pleasure, and music is far from being always uniform in matter and manner, like the Egyptian art you mentioned,[3] but is always undergoing change.

Ath. You are right, Clinias. But if I seemed to you to speak about what now is, I suppose I misled you and made a mistake by expressing my ideas badly. But I really did present just the opinion on music you assign to me. To find fault with things that are beyond remedy and far gone in error is not pleasant, though sometimes necessary. But since we agree on music, tell me this, please: is it better managed by your countrymen and the Spartans than by the other Greeks?

Clin. Of course.

Ath. But if the same measures should be adopted by the others, would we think their regulations better than they are at present?

Clin. There would be a great difference, if they followed my people and the Spartans, and adopted the plans you have just said are the best ones.

[The poets should say that the good are happy. 2.660 D]

Ath. All right, let us agree on this. In your country is the general practice in education and music such as I shall now describe? Do you compel the poets to say that the good man who is temperate and just is happy and blessed, whether he is great and powerful or little and weak, whether he is rich or poor; and that the unjust man, though richer than Cinyras or Midas, is wretched and lives in distress? Your own poet says, and truly I think, that he would not name or value an unjust man who did and acquired all the things commonly said to be good, even though he struck his enemy down at close quarters, nor would your poet represent an unjust man as daring to look on bloody death, or as swifter than Thracian Boreas, or as possessed of anything else to be called good. The things called good by the rabble are not really good. It is said that the first of good things is health, the second beauty, and the third riches, and then a thousand other things are called good: sharp sight and hearing and quickness in whatever the senses perceive, and to be a king and do just what one wants to,

---

[3] The Athenian has praised the art of Egypt as determined by law and unchanged for centuries (*Laws*, II, 656–7).

and the summit of all happiness is, after one has obtained all these things, straightway to become exempt from death. But what you and I say is that all these things are the best of possessions for just and holy men, but that, beginning with health, they are all as bad as possible for the unjust; we think that seeing and hearing and using the senses and life itself would be the greatest of evils to a man who, though not subject to death and possessing all these good things, was yet without justice and all virtue; the evil would be less if such a man lived but a short time. I suppose that in your country you will persuade and compel the poets to set forth these doctrines of mine, and by putting them into suitable harmonies and rhythms to give proper instruction to your young men. Isn't it so?

Book VII

[Poets must compose nothing contrary to law. 7.801 A]

Ath. The third law, I suppose, is this, that the poets, since they know that prayers are requests addressed to the gods, must be very careful lest by some error they ask for what is evil instead of what is good; it would be ridiculous to make such a prayer as that.

Clin. Of course.

Ath. Did we not a little while ago accept the argument that no Plutus of silver or gold should abide in a temple dedicated to him in our city?[4]

Clin. Yes indeed.

Ath. Now what shall we say this statement exemplifies? Does it not illustrate the truth that the race of the poets is not wholly capable of knowing exactly what is good and what is not? Hence a poet in composing either in words or in melody may make a mistake and in things of the highest importance cause the citizens to pray for the opposite of what they should; as we said, we shall not find many things more damaging than this. So shall we make another addition to our laws and patterns for music?

Clin. What do you mean? Tell me more clearly.

Ath. The poet shall compose nothing contrary to the laws and judgments of the city on what is fair and good, and shall not show anything he has composed to any private citizen before it has been put in the hands of the judges whose function it is to deal with such things and of the guardians of the law, and has been approved

---

[4] See the reference to this passage by Longinus, xxix, below.

by them. . . .[5] Well, shall we make this our third law, pattern, and example, or what is your opinion?

Clin. I think we should have it.

Ath. After these arrangements, then, hymns to the gods and praises mingled with prayers of just the right sort may be sung, and after the gods, the spirits and heroes may receive prayers and praises of the kind fitting to each one of them.

Clin. So they can.

Ath. Still further, we may without hesitation make this law: All citizens who have completed a life of splendid and difficult labors of both body and mind and have always been obedient to the laws may fittingly receive praises.

Clin. Surely they may.

[Regulations for poetry. 7.802 A]

Ath. But it is not safe to honor with praises and hymns those who are still living, before they have brought their lives to a noble conclusion. These praises should be awarded without distinction to both men and women who have been conspicuously good. This shall be the arrangement about the poems and dances. In the music of earlier times there are many ancient and beautiful poems and many dances for the body, which we can without scruple select as fit and proper for the state we are founding. To examine these and choose some of them we shall appoint men not less than fifty years of age, and whatever ancient poet appears worthy is to be taken, but whatever seems wholly unsuitable is to be entirely rejected, and whatever seems defective is to be carefully rewritten. For this service we shall enlist poets and musicians and make use of their poetical abilities, though we shall not rely on their pleasure or wishes except at rare intervals. In this way we shall carry out the plans of the lawgiver and arrange dancing and song and choric activity as much as possible according to his intentions. Every unregulated musical activity becomes a thousand times better when it attains proper order, even though not sweetened to the taste of the audience; delight is common to all kinds of music. If throughout the course of his life from childhood until the age of sobriety and discretion a man has been familiar only with sober and well-ordered music, when he hears the opposite he hates it and pronounces it unfit for free men, but those who have been nourished on the ordinary sugary music say its opposite is harsh

---

[5] Milton in his *Areopagitica* objects to such a law.

and unmusical. Hence, as I was saying, there is nothing to choose between the two kinds as to pleasure or displeasure, and, besides, one makes those brought up with it better and the other makes them worse.

Clin. You are quite right.

Ath. Now we must consider whether there is a type of music suitable for women and another suitable for men, and must provide each kind with its proper harmonies and rhythms. It would be terrible if the whole harmony and rhythm of a piece were wholly inappropriate, as it will be if these matters are not properly attended to for the various songs. It is also necessary to make laws giving general principles for them. We can lay down the rules for the harmony and rhythm of both kinds of song, and decide on those for the women after observing the natural differences between the sexes. We shall assume that according to law and reason the masculine temperament is majestic and inclined to courage, and the feminine is directed toward order and temperance.

[Poetry in education. 7.810 E]

We have a great many poets who write in hexameter and trimeter and all the other meters, some of whom aim at the serious and others at the amusing.[6] Thousands of persons keep saying young people who are well educated will be nourished with an abundant diet of these works, and will be expected to read until they have learned a great deal of poetry and committed whole authors to memory. Some educators collect summaries from all the poets and make anthologies and insist they be learned word for word, that the young may be good and wise as the result of the experience and wisdom brought before them. Do you now wish me to make perfectly clear to these believers in poetry wherein they are wrong and wherein they are right?

Clin. That is just it.

Ath. What single statement can I make about all of them that will be correct? Perhaps something like this, namely, that everyone would agree with me that each of the poets has said many things that are good and many that are quite the reverse. If this is true, I say that it is dangerous for the young to acquire this extensive knowledge of poetry.

[6] A little later he speaks of poems that give a "fortunate pleasure" (813 A). Cf. *Republic*, 606 E, above, and Horace, *Art of Poetry*, 333, below.

Book VIII

[Who shall write poetry? 8.829 C]

Ath. There shall be distribution of prizes and awards for merit, and the citizens shall compose encomiums and poems of censure upon one another, according as each one has conducted himself in the games and in all of life, praising the one who is believed to have done exceedingly well and blaming him who has not. Yet not every poet should compose these, but one who is, first, not less than fifty years of age, and not any of those who merely have in them a sufficiency of poetry and music but never have achieved any noble action. But the poems of those who are themselves noble and are honored in the city and are doers of splendid actions are to be chosen even if they have no poetical charm. The choice of them will lie with the superintendent of education and the other guardians of the law, who are to give them this privilege, namely that they are free to write as they please, but to the others no permission shall be given nor shall anyone dare to chant an unauthorized poem, unapproved by the guardians of the law, even though it be sweeter than the hymns of Thamyras and Orpheus, but only such poems as have been approved as holy and dedicated to the gods, and such as are written by good men and judged to be correct in the blame and praise they assign to various persons.

ARISTOTLE

oᴑ°°ᴑo

THE POETICS

About 334–330 B.C.

IN THE LAST FEW YEARS there have appeared two editions of the *Poetics*, that of Rostagni and that of Gudeman, which apparently represent a nearer approach to the original form than any of their predecessors. They owe their superiority chiefly to two sources. The first of these is an Arabic translation of a Syriac translation of a Greek manuscript of the fifth or sixth century. From this Arabic version of the *Poetics* can be inferred readings, believed to be authentic, unlike those otherwise accessible. The second source is a Greek manuscript of the thirteenth or fourteenth century, called Riccardianus 46. This contains a passage (15,1455a14) not found in other manuscripts of the *Poetics* but represented in the Arabic version, and in addition differs in other ways from the text hitherto accepted. That text, represented in its most recent form by the edition of Bywater, was based on the manuscript called Parisinus 1741. The belief that this manuscript is not superior to all others is chiefly the result of the publication in 1911 of the edition of Margoliouth, who studied the text in the light of the Arabic version and the Riccardianus 46. His first work on the subject was published in 1887.

In his edition published in 1927, Rostagni wrote: "The fact is this: He who publishes the *Poetics* of Aristotle today, even with an intention essentially exegetical such as mine, cannot walk in the path trod by the current editions of Vahlen, Christ, and Bywater. The text of the *Poetics* can be constituted today only by comparison of the authorities of the Parisinus 1741 and the Riccardianus 46 and with the aid, anything but untimely, of the Arabic version." He presents a text founded on this theory. In the year 1934 there appeared the edition of the *Poetics*, running to five hundred pages, by Alfred Gudeman, a lifelong student of the treatise. He was able to avail himself of various resources inaccessible to earlier students, such as two medieval Latin translations of the *Poetics* and a careful study of the Arabic version by Tkatsch.

Objections to Gudeman's text have been made, especially by Rostagni, partly because he believes it unduly dependent on the evidence of the Arabic version. To the translator the text of Gudeman appears generally acceptable. At any rate it is well to have an English translation representing the latest study of the *Poetics*, and better to take the risk of accepting a few readings that time will reject than to follow an antiquated text. Consequently, I have, with Professor Gudeman's kind permission, followed his text, except for a single conjecture (59b31, last sentence). In the instances in which his new readings appeared of importance to the general reader I have called attention to them in footnotes and frequently given the renderings of earlier translators. In interpretation I have been much influenced by the notes of Gudeman, Rostagni, and Albeggiani, but have had always at hand the other volumes listed in the bibliography.

On the content of the *Poetics* and its influence, there is little need for discussion here. The first can be gained from the work itself; the second is apparent in many of the succeeding selections in the present volume. Both are treated in books mentioned in the bibliography, yet perhaps a few suggestions may be ventured.

Though Aristotle possessed a philosophical view of the world and of the relation of poetry to society, the *Poetics* should not be made too abstruse. At least a simple meaning should be tried first, and the student should assume that he has some notion of what Aristotle means without seeking for the recondite. With respect to "imitation," for example, Aristotle first meant such copying of human activity as the resources of any art made possible. The imitation is refined by the skill of the artist; there is no slavish imitation of one man, for the copy must be convincing and credible rather than exact; the imitator makes his characters better or worse than they really were; there are many qualifications, yet the basis of a play or epic is a reproduction of what the artist sees when he looks at men around him.

While Aristotle's love for poetry is evident, there is another part of his nature still stronger, the passion for analysis and for reasoning from its results. The *Poetics* is prevailingly a work of analytical criticism rather than an exposition of the reader's pleasure. The second wars with the first at times, as when Aristotle, in spite of his delight in Homer, makes the epic inferior to tragedy because less concentrated. Did Aristotle really prefer tragedy to Homer because it was concentrated, or did his analytical theory indicate to him that he should? In somewhat the same way Dryden as a reader seems to have preferred Shakespeare, but as a critic gave the preference to Jonson. If Aristotle had been less inclined to analysis, to the working out of a system, he might have been inclined to see more aspects of even the art he looked at so closely, might have told us something of the artistic power of plays that achieve greatness without conformity to his system. Yet the system itself is one to which exception can hardly be made so far as it goes. It is founded on the observation of play and audience by a man who knew how to observe. Without it we should less clearly understand one of the important ways in which man looks at works of art, and in which human nature demands that he look at them, the obviously scientific method. Indeed some of Aristotle's observations, notably the analysis of recognitions, have not yet been assimilated by modern critics.

Whether the demand for unity in a work of art represents Aristotle's personal choice, or whether, as Tasso thought, it is a permanent principle, the *Poetics* is the great representative of the demand for artistic concentration. To it perhaps more than to the Greek tragedies themselves is to be traced the belief in classic as distinguished from romantic art. From Aristotle more than even from Sophocles came a body of belief expressed at its utmost in the theory of the unities, and still commonly thought of as peculiarly expressing the Greek spirit. Few Greek tragedies are wholly acceptable to Aristotle. If, in spite of his wisdom, he wrote somewhat as one who had settled his theory in favor of unity of structure, and judged tragedy as it conformed to his fixed beliefs, it is not strange that in the minds of smaller men his deductions became hardened into a system of rules according to which literature was to be judged. If the master himself felt that he could mold the artist's plastic mind, no wonder if his followers were still more inclined to set the critic above the artist. When the critic attempts to force the artist to conform to his system, the spirit of Aristotle at his worst is at work.

At his best the Aristotelian asks the causes of art in the nature of man, and points out how the natural demands of the audience can be satisfied. He keeps the author from supposing that his art is for himself alone and not for the hearers for whose sake it exists. For the confused impression of the rapt spectator, he substitutes a careful, clear analysis of what is before us and of its fitness for justifying its existence or performing its function. All who take pleasure in excellence of workmanship are disciples of Aristotle.

BIBLIOGRAPHY

Albeggiani, Ferdinando, *La poetica*, traduzione, introduzione, commento. Florence, La Nuova Italia, 1934. The translation is based on

Rostagni's text, with specified exceptions. It is not always in agreement with the interpretation in Rostagni's notes. The commentary is based on the Greek text. The same translation, with briefer introduction and notes designed for readers ignorant of Greek, was issued by the same publishers in 1933.

Anderson, Maxwell, *The Essence of Tragedy*. Washington, 1939. Discussion of the tragic hero and the recognition scene.

Butcher, S. H., *Aristotle's Theory of Poetry and Fine Art*, with a critical text and translation of the *Poetics*. Fourth edition. London, 1923. This volume, consisting of a translation and explanatory essays, has since the appearance of the first edition in 1895 been probably the most popular and generally influential of English works on the *Poetics*.

Bywater, Ingram, *Aristotle on the Art of Poetry*, a revised text with critical introduction, translation, and commentary. Oxford, 1909. An edition primarily for students who understand Greek, though the elaborate notes can be used to some extent by those who do not read that language. The text, based on the manuscript called Parisinus 1741, represents a very conservative position. The translation has been reprinted in *Aristotle's Poetics* [and] *Longinus on the Sublime*, ed. by Charles S. Baldwin. New York, 1930.

Cooper, Lane, *The Poetics of Aristotle;* its meaning and influence. Boston, 1923. An excellent summary of the *Poetics*, and a clear account of its influence up to the present.

——, *Aristotle on the Art of Poetry*, an amplified version with supplementary illustrations for students of English. The fruit of long experience in teaching the *Poetics* to American students. Illustrations from English literature and explanations are inserted in the text.

——, *An Aristotelian Theory of Comedy*, with an adaptation of the *Poetics* and a translation of the 'Tractatus Coislinianus.' New York, 1922. A reconstruction of Aristotle's lost discussion of comedy. The introduction includes suggestions on various ancient and modern writers on comedy.

Cooper, Lane, and Gudeman, Alfred, *A Bibliography of the Poetics of Aristotle*. New Haven, 1928. Indispensable. See also the supplement by Marvin T. Herrick in *The American Journal of Philology*, LII (1931), 168–74.

Fyfe, W. Hamilton, *Aristotle, The Poetics*, etc., with an English translation. London, 1927. The translation is based on Vahlen's edition of 1885, with some reference to later work, especially that of Bywater.

Gilbert, Allan H., "The Aristotelian Catharsis." *The Philosophical Review*, XXXV (1926), 301–14.

——, "Scenes of Discovery in *Othello*," in *The Philological Quarterly*, V (1926), 119–30.

Gilbert, Katharine E., "Aesthetic Imitation and Imitators in Aristotle." *The Philosophical Review*, XLV (1936), 558–73.

Gudeman, Alfred, *Aristotles über die Dichtkunst*, neu übersetzt und mit Einleitung und einem erklärenden Namen- und Sachverzeichnis versehen. Leipzig, 1921. This little volume, prepared for general readers, is based on studies in preparation for the edition listed below.

——, Aristoteles ΠΕΡΙ ΠΟΙΗΤΙΚΗΣ mit Einleitung, Text und Adnotatio critica, exegetischem Kommentar, kritischem Anhang und Indices Nominum, Rerum, Locorum. Berlin and Leipzig, 1934. An impressive volume intended for students proficient in Greek. The text is the most radical we have. The importance of the work, at least of the commentary, is admitted even by those who refuse to accept the text. See also the introduction preceding this bibliography.

Margoliouth, D. S., *The Poetics of Aristotle*, translated from Greek into English and from Arabic into Latin, with a revised text, introduction, commentary, glossary, and onomasticon. London, 1911. The first complete translation of the Arabic text to be published. Important also for its study of the other manuscripts, fuller than any other up to that time.

McKeon, Richard, "Literary Criticism and the Concept of Imitation in Antiquity." *Modern Philology*, XXXIV (1936), 1–35. Chiefly on Plato and Aristotle. Founded immediately on the works of the writers in question and presenting them as they are, without attempt to fit them into a system pleasing to the author.

Ross, W. D., *Aristotle*. London, 1930. An account of all of Aristotle's works, with a section on the *Poetics*.

Rostagni, Augusto, *La poetica di Aristotele*, introduzione, testo e commento. Torino, 1934 (preface dated 1927). The author does not present this as a true critical edition but as a reconstituted text, made necessary by the new estimate of the manuscripts that has rendered obsolete the text of Butcher and its predecessors; it has some of the qualities of a critical text. The introduction gives much space to Aristotle's relation to Plato and to the philosophical significance of the *Poetics*. The exegetical notes, in smaller type than the text, occupy perhaps three times as much space. I am much indebted to them.

Further bibliography will be found not only in the volume by Cooper and Gudeman, but in most of the volumes here listed.

The Contents of the *Poetics*

∘◯∘∘◯∘

THE POETICS

Chapter I

[Imitation. 47a8[1]]

Let us consider poetry itself and its species, dealing with the capacity of each one and showing how its matter must be arranged if a poem is to be good,[2] the number and kind of the parts of each type of poem,[3] and whatever else is properly considered in such an investigation; we shall follow the natural order and begin at the beginning. Epic poetry, tragedy, and also comedy, dithyrambic poetry, and most music on the flute and the lyre all fall into the general class of imitation. Yet they differ from each other in three things, for they imitate in different materials, or imitate different things, or do it in another way, not according to the same method. For just as color and form are used by some who, following a model, imitate many things, either working according to art or by rule of thumb, and others employ the voice, so all practitioners of the arts I have spoken of produce their imitation through rhythm and speech and harmony, either separately or combined. Music on the lyre or the flute and any other kinds of art there may be of a similar sort, such as music on the syrinx, make use of harmony and rhythm only. The art of dancers imitates by rhythm alone without harmony, and through the rhythmical movements of the dance imitates characters and feelings and deeds.

---

[1] An abbreviation for 1447a8, the page, column, and line in Bekker's edition of Aristotle's works; I use the number of the first line to indicate the entire paragraph.

[2] Chaps. VI–VIII.

[3] Chaps. VI–XII, and XVIII. See also the Appendix to the *Poetics*, note 4, pp. 118–121, below.

[Imitation by words only. 47a28]

But the art which imitates by means of words only, in prose or in meter that is either the same throughout or of several kinds, is up to the present without a name.[4] For we have no common name for the mimes of Sophron and Xenarchus and the Socratic dialogues,[5] nor would we have any if someone made an imitation in the meters of epics or elegies or anything else of the sort; yet by associating a composition with its meter people call some writers elegiac poets and others epic poets, giving them the name of poets not because of their imitation but in popular fashion according to the meter they use. Even if a writer presents medicine or natural philosophy in meter they still speak of him as a poet, yet there is nothing in common to Homer and Empedocles except their meter; the one is justly called a poet, but the other should be called a natural philosopher rather than a poet.[6] The same would be true if anyone should produce an imitation by mingling all the meters, as Chaeremon composed his *Centaur,* a rhapsody made up of all the meters; and Chaeremon is certainly to be called a poet. Enough on this matter.

[Imitation by various means. 47b24]

There are some arts that employ all the means I have mentioned, namely rhythm, melody, and metrical language, as the poetry of the dithyrambs and of the nomes and tragedy and comedy. These arts differ in that the first two use the three means throughout, the last two use them in various parts. These are the differences of the arts in the means through which they work out their imitation.

Chapter II

[Diversity of character. 48a1]

Since imitators imitate men who are doing something, these subjects of imitation are of necessity good or bad, for by these

[4] Croce comments: "There never can be such a name, because poetry and literature, though touching on one side, always remain two diverse things" (*La poesia* [Bari, 1936], p. 40).

[5] Mimes are comic, but not properly comedies. The chief Socratic dialogues are those of Plato.

[6] See also chap. IX, first par., below.

classes kinds of character are usually distinguished.[7] That is, men are better than we are, or worse, or like us, as the painters have made them.[8] For Polygnotus imitated them as better than we are, Pauson as worse, and Dionysius as we are.[9] It is clear that each of the imitative arts I have mentioned will have these differences and that one will differ from another as it represents different things in this fashion. In dancing, flute-playing, and lyre-playing these differences appear, and in prose and purely metrical imitation, for Homer represented men better than we are, Cleophon like ourselves, and Hegemon the Thasian, who first wrote parodies, and Nicochares, who wrote the *Deliad*,[10] represented them as worse. The same is true of dithyrambic and nomic poetry; one may imitate as Argas did[11] . . . or as Timotheus and Philoxenus did the Cyclopes. In this matter tragedy differs from comedy, for tragedy attempts to imitate men who are better and comedy men who are worse than those about us.[12]

Chapter III

[Difference in manner of imitation. 48a19]

There is a third difference in the method by which a poet imitates men of these three sorts. For in imitating the same things by the same means (i.e., harmony, rhythm, language) it is possible to tell a story either by speaking part of the time in character, as Homer does,[13] or by speaking in one's own person without any change, and it is possible to have the persons who are imitated act out and perform everything. These then, as we said at the beginning, are the three differences to be observed in imitation, namely those of means, object, and method. Sophocles, then, would be the same sort of imitator as Homer in that both imitate good men, and the same sort as Aristophanes in that both imitate by

[7] Gudeman rejects as a marginal comment a statement, immediately following, that men are distinguished from each other by the goodness and badness of their characters.

[8] Cf. chaps. xv, 54b8; and xxv, 61b9, below.

[9] Painters of the fifth century B.C. In the *Politics*, VIII, 5, Aristotle writes that "the young ought not to study the works of Pauson, but those of Polygnotus or any other painter or sculptor who expresses moral ideas."

[10] Nothing is known of this poem; perhaps it was a burlesque.

[11] Something, perhaps the title of Argas's work, is seemingly missing from the mss.

[12] Cf. chaps. v, first sentence; xv, 54b8; xxv, 60b32, 61b9.

[13] See also chap. xxiv, 60a5, below.

having their characters move and dramatize the deeds they are concerned with. Some say that dramas were so named because they imitate persons who are in action.[14]

[The origins of drama. 48a29]

Therefore the Dorians assert that they first produced tragedy and comedy.[15] Comedy is claimed both by the Megarians in Greece, who say it sprung up in their democracy, and by the Megarians in Sicily because Epicharmus the poet came from there before the time of Chionides and Magnes.[16] They point to the names as an indication of this, for they say that their word for the outlying hamlets is *comai*, while that of the Athenians is *demes*, and that the comedians are so called not from the word *comadzein* (i.e., *to revel*) but from their wandering around in the *comai* because they were looked down on in the city.[17] Concerning the differences in imitation, both in number and in kind, let what I have said suffice.

Chapter IV

[The origin of poetry. 48b4]

In general there seem to have been two causes for the origin of poetry, each of them natural. For imitation is natural to men from childhood and in this they differ from the other animals, because man is very imitative and obtains his first knowledge by means of imitation, and then everybody takes pleasure in imitation. An indication of this is found in experience. For we look with delight on pictures that accurately represent things that in themselves are painful for us to behold, such as forms of the most unpleasing animals and dead bodies. The cause of this is that to learn is very pleasant not only to philosophers but also in the same way to men generally, even though they partake of this pleasure but to a slight extent. For this reason they are pleased when they

---

[14] The Greek words for *drama* and *action* are etymologically related.

[15] Because they say that the word *drama*, used at Athens, is taken from their dialect. If the Athenians had invented drama, the name would have been Athenian and not Dorian. Gudeman indicates that the word *drama* is not exclusively Dorian, and Bywater thinks that "Aristotle does not accept this view" of the word.

[16] The traditional text, rightly according to Rostagni (*Gnomon*, 1935, p. 229), here says that the Peloponnesians claim the invention of tragedy.

[17] At this point most editors print a sentence substantially equivalent to the first two in the first note on this paragraph. Gudeman indicates that it should be omitted since it is not present in the Arabic version.

see images because they have the experience of learning by seeing and each man can reason about it, saying to himself that the picture is that of a certain person. But if it happens that a man has not seen the original, he will get pleasure not from the imitation but from the skillful execution or the color or some similar cause. Since imitation is natural to us, and harmony and rhythm too,[18] for the meters are evidently species of rhythm, those who from the beginning had a natural aptitude for them finally produced poetry from their improvisations by means of many small advances.

[Higher and lower types of poetry. 48b24]

Poetry, then, is divided into two kinds according to the natures of the poets, for those who were of a graver sort imitated splendid deeds and the actions of great men, but those of a lower type imitated the doings of meaner men, at first composing invectives, as the nobler writers composed hymns and encomiums. We cannot name such a poem by any of the authors before Homer, but it seems likely there were many; if we begin with Homer there are his *Margites*[19] and others of the sort. In these a fitting meter was used, now called the iambic because in that meter they iambicized or lampooned one another. So some of the old poets became heroic poets and others iambic poets. Just as Homer was in serious matters the poet of highest renown, for he did not merely write well but made his imitations dramatic, so he was the first to lay out the plan of comedy, presenting in dramatic form not invective but something ludicrous. For as the *Iliad* and the *Odyssey* have some analogy with tragedy, so the *Margites* has some with comedy. When tragedy and comedy arose, poets wrote one or the other of them according to their natural bent; some became comic poets instead of writers of invective, others became tragic authors instead of epic poets, because the new types of writing were grander and more esteemed than the older ones. The question whether tragedy is now sufficiently developed in its species or not, and the judgment of it in itself and in relation to the audience is another problem.

[18] Plato speaks of man's instinct for harmony in the *Laws*, II, 653–4. Cf. p. 40, above. Apparently Aristotle has in mind the design and order of metrical language, rather than harmony in the Greek technical meaning, partly equivalent to *scale*.

[19] A burlesque poem, no longer attributed to Homer, of which only small fragments have been preserved.

[The evolution of tragedy. 49a9]

Since tragedy was produced by the authors of the dithyramb, and comedy from the phallic songs that still remain as institutions in many cities, tragedy, as well as comedy, was from the beginning an improvisation. From its early form tragedy was developed little by little as the authors added what presented itself to them. After going through many alterations, tragedy ceased to change, having come to its full natural stature. As to the number of the actors, Aeschylus first increased it from one to two, diminished the activity of the chorus, and made the speeches of the actors the leading feature. Sophocles increased the number of actors to three and introduced the painting of scenery. Now as to the length of tragedy. It developed from short plots.[20] It abandoned comic diction, and in its development from the satyr drama it at last acquired dignity. The meter changed from tetrameter to iambic. For at first authors used the tetrameter because their poetry was satyric and related to the dance, but when dialogue became important, nature herself found a suitable meter, since the iambic is the meter most easily spoken. A proof of this is that we often utter iambics in conversation with each other, but hexameters seldom and only when we depart from the colloquial tone. Then there is the number of episodes. And as to the other things, let us proceed as though the traditions on the embellishment of each one had already been presented, for it obviously would be a long task to deal with them one by one.

Chapter V

[Comedy. 49a31]

As we said, comedy is an imitation of those who are worse than ourselves, yet not in every sort of evil but only in that baseness of which the ridiculous is a species.[21] For the laughable is a sort of fault and deformity that is painless and not deadly, as indeed the comic mask is an ugly sort of thing and deformed and yet does not suggest pain. The changes in tragedy and those responsible for them have not been forgotten, but comedy because it was not

---

[20] At this point there is an unintelligible passage in the Arabic version, indicating to Gudeman that the original Greek was longer than the versions we now possess.

[21] Cf. chaps. II, the last sentence; IV, 48b24, above.

taken seriously from the beginning has passed from our knowledge. And it was at a late date that the archon allowed a chorus to the comic writers, for in earlier times it was made up of volunteers. Comedy already had some definite forms when those called comic poets were first spoken of. It is unknown who introduced masks or the prologue or the employment of a number of actors and similar things.[22] As to the composition of the plots, it came in the beginning from Sicily, and Crates was the first of the Athenian poets to give up the invective manner and make speeches and plots of general application.

[The epic. 49b9]

The epic followed tragedy in that it was an imitation of serious actions by means of metrical language, but the two forms are unlike in that the epic has a single meter and is a narrative; as to length, tragedy attempts to keep within a single revolution of the sun or to exceed it but little,[23] but the epic is indefinite in time, and thus unlike tragedy; yet at first the time of both tragedies and epics was the same. Some of their parts are the same, some are peculiar to tragedy; therefore he who knows what is good and bad in tragedy knows what is good and bad in epic poetry, for whatever the epic has is found in tragedy, but not all parts of tragedy are found in the epic.[24]

Chapter VI

[Tragedy defined. 49b20]

We shall speak later of imitation in hexameters and of comedy.[25] Let us speak of tragedy by bringing together from what we have already said the definition of its nature. Tragedy, then, is an imi-

[22] For information on these matters in tragedy, see chap. VI.

[23] This is the only place in which Aristotle speaks of what later was established as unity of time. See the index under *unity of time.* Aristotle is here giving not a precept but a statement of the practice of his age, which he probably approved of as representing an advance in tragic construction. Something of the sort is implied in his remarks on the superiority of tragedy to epic in chap. XXVI.

On the length of tragedy see chaps. VII; XVIII, 56a10. On the length of the epic see chap. XXIII, 59a30.

[24] See also chap. XXVI, 62a14, below.

[25] Epic poetry is discussed in chaps. XXIII, XXIV, and XXVI. Comedy is not discussed, except incidentally, in the *Poetics* as we have it. See chap. II, the last sentence; IV, 48b24; V, the first sentence; XXVI, the last sentence.

tation of an action that is serious and complete and has sufficient size, in language that is made sweet, and with each of the kinds of sweet language separately in the various parts of the tragedy, presented by those who act and not by narrative, exciting pity and fear,[26] bringing about the catharsis of such emotions. By language made sweet I mean language having rhythm and harmony and melody; and by separately according to the species, I mean the setting forth of some things by the use of meters alone, and others again by means of melody.[27]

[The parts of tragedy. 49b31]

Since men who act produce the imitation, it follows of necessity that in the first place one part of tragedy is concerned with its appearance to the eye, and after that come melody and diction, for through these they produce the imitation. By diction I mean the putting together of the verses, and by melody that to which all the obvious meaning of the word can apply. Further, the action imitated is performed by agents who of necessity are of a certain sort in character and quality of thought, for because of these we say that actions are what they are;[28] now since the imitation is of an action, there naturally are two causes for dramatic actions, character and thought, because of which all the agents experience good or bad fortune. The plot is the imitation of the action. By plot I mean the synthesis of the individual acts, by character that according to which we say that those who act are of some certain sort, and by thought I mean those passages in which the speakers show something by argument or deliver an opinion.[29] Every tragedy, then, must have six parts, because of which the tragedy is of such a sort as it is. These are plot, character, diction, thought,

[26] Almost universally no comma is put at this point and the translation is substantially that of Butcher: "through pity and fear affecting the proper purgation of these emotions." The notion that pity and fear expel themselves seems to me unattractive (see "The Aristotelian Catharsis," in *The Philosophical Review*, xxxv [1926], 301–14), as it did to Vincentius Madius, *In Aristotelis librum de poetica*, Venice, 1550, p. 98. At any rate there is so little agreement about the meaning of the passage as to make the translation almost a matter of indifference. Fontanelle wrote: "I never have understood the purgation of the passions by means of the passions themselves" (*Reflexions sur la poétique*, sect. 45, in *Œuvres* [Paris, 1766], iii, 170–1). See *catharsis* in the index.

[27] Gudeman suggests that at this point there was originally an explanation of the catharsis, now lost.

[28] Cf. chap. xv, 54a33, below.

[29] The word used here is *gnomē*, which may mean a maxim, sententious saying, or sentence, of the sort commended in the Renaissance. They are discussed by Aristotle in the *Rhetoric*, ii, 21. See *sentence* in the index.

spectacle, and music. By means of these tragedians imitate. Two
are parts with which they imitate,[30] one involves the manner of
imitation,[31] and three cover what is imitated.[32] There are no
others. These parts, then, not a few writers of tragedy have used
as species, as it were.[33] Every tragedy has spectacle and character
and plot and diction and music and thought.

[Plot.[34]   50a15]

The most important of these is the putting together of the separate actions, for tragedy is an imitation not of men but of actions
and life. And happiness and unhappiness reside in action, and
the end is some sort of action,[35] not a quality, for according to
their characters men are what they are, but according to their
actions they are happy or the reverse. They do not, then, act in
order to represent character, but in the course of their actions they
show what their characters are; so in the actions and the plot is
found the end of tragedy, and the end is more important than
anything else.[36] Besides, without action there can be no tragedy,
but without characters there can be one. The tragedies of most
recent writers are deficient in character, and in general the same
thing is true of many poets. Among the painters Zeuxis gives the
same impression when compared with Polygnotus, for Polygnotus
was a good painter of character but the painting of Zeuxis does

[30] Diction and melody.   [31] Spectacle.   [32] Plot, character, thought.

[33] I have followed Gudeman's text, which contains one emendation wholly conjectural. Rostagni, though he thinks the passage very difficult, holds that it can be
explained without emendation. Part of his note I translate as follows: "Of these [six]
which are the forms or essential elements of tragedy not a few of the poets in general
have made use." Albeggiani, however, who usually follows Rostagni's text, accepts
the conjectural emendation and translates much as I have, explaining in a note, part
of which I render as follows: "In this passage he affirms that the single parts of a
tragedy have been used by many poets as forms of them, and hence there are many
tragedies founded on character, language, scenic spectacle, etc." The idea apparently meant something to Aristotle; at least it is repeated, with perhaps more vigor, at
the beginning of chap. XII. Cf. the remark on the four parts and species in chap.
XVIII, 55b32, and see the Appendix following the *Poetics*, note 4, and chap. XXIV,
first par.

[34] Plot is dealt with in chaps. VII-XIV and XVI-XVIII.

[35] Usually interpreted, as by Bywater, as "the end for which we live," but sometimes
as "the end of tragedy," as by Fyfe. The latter was the opinion of Castelvetro, who
wrote: "Characteristics cannot be the end of tragedy, since the end of a tragedy is
action, as has been said, and not quality" (p. 138; cf. Castelvetro 140,15, below).
Felicity for Aristotle involves activity; for example: "The good of man is activity of
the soul according to virtue" (*Nicomachean Ethics*, I, 6, 1098a16).

[36] The word *end* means *chief thing, ruling element.* Cf. the plot as the soul, in the next
section, and the beginning of chap. VII.

not show the minds of his subjects. Again if one should present in
the proper order ethical speeches, well handled both in diction
and thought, he would not produce the effect of tragedy, but that
tragedy in which those elements were inferior, yet which possessed plot and a suitable arrangement of actions, would produce
a much better effect.

[Reversal and recognition.[37] 50a33]

Besides this, the chief things by means of which tragedy moves
the feelings of the audience are parts of the plot, namely, reversals
and recognitions. A proof is that those attempting to compose
are able to work skillfully in diction and in character before they
show mastery in the arrangement of the incidents; this was generally true of the earlier poets. The first principle and as it were
the soul of tragedy is the plot; the characters are in the second
place. A comparison may be made with painting, for if anyone
makes a confused smear with the most beautiful colors, he will not
give so much pleasure as by drawing an image in white chalk.
The plot is an imitation of an action and presents characters primarily for the sake of what they do.

[Thought.[38] 50b4]

Thought comes third. This is to be able to say what is possible
and befits the conditions, namely, whatever in the speeches falls
under the arts of politics and rhetoric, for the older dramatists
made their speakers talk like statesmen and those of the present
like practiced rhetoricians.

[Character.[39] 50b8]

Character is that which reveals an agent's moral habit, showing
of what sort it is,[40] for there is no character in those speeches in
which the speaker does not clearly choose or avoid something,[41]

[37] For fuller discussion see chaps. xi, 52a29; xvi.

[38] See also chap. xix, first par.   [39] See also chap. xv.

[40] At this point the traditional text gives, with slight change, the words translated
"in which he does not clearly choose or avoid," which occur again just below. If they
were retained, as they are by most editors, they would mean: "in which the character
does not show by [his actions] whether he chooses or avoids something." Rostagni
comments: "It would be useless to reveal the moral intention of a person by means of
speeches showing character when it was already clear from the reality of his actions."
He also refers to chap. xv, third sentence. Gudeman omits the words in question,
which do not occur in the Arabic version.

[41] "Speeches in which moral intention is revealed possess character" (Aristotle,
Rhetoric, ii, 21).

but there is thought in those that show something as it is or as it is not or present a general idea.

[Diction.[42] 50b11]

The fourth of the literary parts is diction. I mean by diction, as I have already said, the expression of meaning by words; this has the same function in both metrical and non-metrical language.

[Melody and scenery.[43] 50b16]

Of the other elements which make tragedy pleasing, melody is the most important. Scenic display, though impressive, requires least technical skill and is least germane to poetry, for tragedy can produce its effect without performance and without actors,[44] and the art of the designer of scenery has more power to produce stage effects than that of the poets.

Chapter VII

[The construction of the plot. 50b21]

Having defined these things, let us discuss next what the arrangement of the incidents has to be, since this is the first and most important matter in tragedy. We have established that tragedy is an imitation of a finished and entire action having reasonable size, for a thing can be a whole and yet not have magnitude. A complete thing is what has a beginning, a middle, and an end. A beginning is what does not of necessity come after something else, but after which something else naturally is or happens; an end on the contrary is that which necessarily or for the most part is or happens after something else, but which has nothing after it; a middle is that which comes after something and has something after itself. Hence it is necessary for those who compose plots well neither to begin where they chance to nor to end where they chance to, but to conform to the ideas I have expressed.[45]

[42] See also chap. xix, 56b8.

[43] No independent treatment is given to these two elements. Spectacle is touched upon in chap. xiv, in chap. xviii (see the Appendix immediately following the *Poetics*, note 4), and spoken of as important in chap. xxvi, 62a14. For music see *ibid*.

[44] Cf. chap. xxvi, 62a5.

[45] Aristotle apparently does not intend to divide a tragedy into three parts—as though the first act were the beginning, the next three the middle, and the last the end—but merely to say that it must be a self-contained unit, intelligible and satisfactory to an auditor who has little or no knowledge of what went before and none of what follows.

[Beauty of plot. 50b34]

We shall now discuss beauty. A living creature or any subject that is made up of parts not merely must have these properly arranged but must have magnitude that is not a matter of chance. For beauty consists in magnitude and order; therefore an exceedingly small animal cannot be beautiful, because the vision is confused when it is applied to an object so small as to be almost invisible; nor can a very large animal—such as one a thousand miles long—be beautiful, for the eye does not take it in at once, but it presents no unity and completeness of view to those who look at it. Hence, as it is necessary for bodies and animals to have magnitude, but such as can properly be embraced in one view, so it is necessary for stories to have size, but such that they can be easily remembered.[46]

[Length of plot. 51a6]

The measure of length so far as it is determined by dramatic contests and the viewing of a work by spectators has nothing to do with the art of tragedy. If it were necessary to have a hundred tragedies in a contest, they would have to compete by the clock, as is required under other circumstances. But with respect to the length of a tragedy according to its nature, the larger it is, within the limits of clarity, the better it is. To speak simply and clearly, the space that permits a hero, according to probability or necessity and in regular order, to pass to good fortune from bad fortune or from good fortune to bad fortune gives a proper limit to size.

Chapter VIII

[Unity of plot. 51a16]

A plot is not unified, as some think, because it is concerned with one man, for a countless number of things happen to one man, some of which cannot be combined with others in a single unit; thus there are many acts by one man which cannot form parts of a unified action. Therefore all the poets who have written *Heracleids*, *Theseids*, and similar poems seem to have gone wrong, for they think that since Hercules was one man a plot dealing with him must also be a unit. But Homer, as he surpasses in other

---

[46] See chap. XXIV, 59b17; also chap. XXVI, 62a14.

things, seems also to understand this matter, whether because of art or nature,[47] for when he wrote the *Odyssey* he did not deal with everything that happened to Odysseus, such as his getting hurt on Parnassus,[48] or his pretending to be insane when the army was called together, for after one had happened there was no necessity or probability that the other should happen, but Homer wrote the *Odyssey* about one action, as we understand it, and likewise the *Iliad*.[49] It is necessary then, just as in other imitative arts there is one imitation of one thing, that the plot, being an imitation of an action, should be concerned with one thing and that a whole, and that the parts of the action should be so put together that if one part is shifted or taken away the whole is deranged and dis-joined, for what makes no perceptible difference by its presence or absence is no part of the whole.

Chapter IX

[Poetry and the universal. 51a36]

It is apparent from what has been said that it is not the business of the poet to tell what has happened, but what might happen and what is possible according to probability or necessity.[50] The his-torian and the poet do not differ by writing in verse or prose (for the history of Herodotus could be put in verse and yet it would be nonetheless history whether with meter or without meter), but they differ in that the historian writes of what has happened and the poet of what might happen.[51] Hence poetry is more philo-sophical and more serious than history, for poetry deals more with things in a universal way, but history with each thing for itself. To deal with them universally is to say that according to proba-bility or necessity it happens that a certain sort of man does or says certain things,[52] and poetry aims at this, when it gives names to the characters. But to deal with an individual for himself is to

---

[47] Cf. chap. XXIII, 59a30 , and note.

[48] This statement is not literally true, for Homer does tell of the injury of Odysseus in the hunt on Parnassus (*Odyssey*, XIX, 394–466). Editors point out that the story is incidental, and not part of the main narrative of the work. See the Appendix following the *Poetics*, note 9. Cf. chaps. V, 49b9; XVIII, 56a10, and XXIII.

[49] See chap. XXVI, 62a14.

[50] Aristotle speaks on this matter in chap. XXIV, 60a26, and chap. XXV, 60b32, and 61b9.

[51] See chap. I, 47a28; chap. XXIII, first par.

[52] Even inconsistent characters are provided for in chap. XV, first par.

tell what Alcibiades did or experienced. This universal quality of poetry has already been manifested in comedy, for having composed the plot according to probabilities, comic writers give the characters any names that occur to them and do not, like the iambic poets, write about specific persons. In tragedy they cling to the historic names. The reason is that the possible is credible; if a thing has not happened, we do not believe it is possible, but what has happened is clearly possible, for it would not happen if it were impossible.

[Original plots. 51b19]

But even among tragedies there are some plays that contain one or two familiar names though the others are fictitious, and in some tragedies there are no familiar names, as is true of the *Flower* of Agathon, for both its incidents and its names are devised by the poet, and yet it is nonetheless pleasing. Hence a poet need not strive to use exclusively the traditional myths on which the best tragedies are based. It would be ridiculous to strive for this, since even the stories that are known are known to but few, but please everybody. These things make clear that the poet must be the maker of plots rather than of meters, since he is a poet because of imitation and he imitates actions. Certainly if he happens to use in his poetry what has happened, he is not the worse poet, for nothing forbids some of the things that actually have happened to be such as are likely to happen; when they are so considered, he who writes of them is a poet.

[Episodic plots. 51b33]

Of imperfect[53] plots and actions the episodic are the worst. By an episodic plot I mean one in which the episodes do not have to each other the relation of either probability or necessity. Such plots are composed by bad poets on their own account and by good poets because of the judges,[54] for since the poets engage in contests and stretch out the plot beyond its capacity, they are often forced to depart from the proper order.

[53] From a conjectural reading; the usual word is *simple*. Cf. chap. x. Possibly *simple* may be retained on the ground that the involved plot, because it must be constructed with the peripety in view, will exhibit a necessary relation between widely separated parts. Hence it is unlikely to be episodic, or made up of a string of little-connected events.

[54] The more usual reading is "because of the actors." At any rate Aristotle did not wish the structure of a play to be determined by extra-artistic reasons. Cf. p. 87, below. For Plato on the judges, see pp. 56–7, above.

[Pity and fear. 52a1]

The imitation is not merely of a complete action but also of terrible and pitiable happenings, and these are most effective when they occur contrary to expectation and yet one depends on another; they then have more of the astonishing than if they happened of themselves or by chance.[55] Even chance incidents appear most astonishing when they seem to happen as the result of a cause, as when the statue of Mitys in Argos, by falling on the murderer as he was looking at it, killed the man who had caused the death of Mitys. It seems that such things cannot occur by chance. Hence it is necessary for the best plots to be such stories as I have spoken of.

Chapter X

[Simple and involved plots. 52a11]

Plots are either simple or involved,[56] for the actions of which the plots are imitations are of these kinds. If an action is knit together as a unit in the way already laid down,[57] I call it simple when the change of fortune takes place without peripety or recognition; but I call it involved when the change of fortune is accompanied by recognition or peripety or both. It is necessary for the recognition and peripety to result from the very construction of the plot, so that of necessity or according to probability they follow what has gone before. There is a great difference between *propter hoc* and *post hoc*.

Chapter XI

[Peripety. 52a22]

Peripety is a change to the opposite of actions performed according to probability or necessity, as we have said.[58] For example, in

[55] For further reference to the astonishing see chap. XVIII, 56a19; chap. XXIV, 60a11; chap. XXV, 60b23, below.

[56] *Explicit* and *intricate* (Milton, Preface to *Samson Agonistes*, below).   [57] Chap. VII.

[58] In chap. X. The peripety should not be confused with the change of fortune necessary, according to Aristotle, in all dramas. In chap. X he makes clear that this change can occur without any peripety. The example from the *Oedipus* has led to description of the peripety as a reversal of intention. Perhaps Aristotle did not demand that it always be quite so clear. Butcher (pp. 330–1) writes that the tragic peripety "suggests, if I mistake not, a series of incidents or a train of action . . . tending to bring about a certain end but resulting in something wholly different. The situation, as it were, turns upon the agent who is attempting to deal with it,—swings round and catches him in the recoil."

the *Oedipus*, a man who came to Oedipus with good intentions and
expected to remove his fear as to his mother by making plain who
he really was did the opposite of what was intended.[59] In the
Lynceus one man is led off to execution and the other follows to
put him to death, but it comes about from what happens that the
second is put to death and the first is preserved.

[Recognition.[60]   52a29]

Recognition, as the word indicates by its derivation, is a change
from ignorance to knowledge—resulting in love or hate—by
those marked out for good fortune or bad fortune. The best recognition is one combined with a peripety, as it is in the *Oedipus*.[61]
But there are other forms of recognition, for there is recognition
of inanimate objects and various other things, as has been said.[62]
It can also be learned whether someone has or has not done a
particular thing. But the recognition most closely connected with
the plot and the action is of the sort that has been mentioned.[63]
Such a recognition and peripety will produce pity and fear, and
tragedy is an imitation of actions producing these feelings, and
good fortune and bad fortune come about as a result of such recognitions and peripeties. When the recognition is a recognition of
persons it may be merely that of one man by another, when it is
clear who one of them is, or it may be necessary for both of them
to be recognized; Iphigenia is identified by Orestes because of
the sending of the letter, but a further recognition of Orestes by
Iphigenia is also needed.

[59]Aristotle apparently had forgotten the exact situation, for the messenger came to
summon Oedipus to Corinth as king, without any knowledge of the troubles in Thebes.
On talking with Oedipus and learning of his fears, he attempted to dispel them. This
well-meant effort served only to reveal to Oedipus the terrible truth that he was the
child of Laius and Jocasta.

[60]For further discussion of recognition see chap. XVI, and for references chap. XIV,
53b26, and chap. XXIV, first par., below.

[61]See the preceding section.

[62]The usual interpretation is that inanimate objects can be recognized. Castelvetro,
however, held that Aristotle thought that inanimate objects in some sense could be
said to recognize persons (248,39 ff.). The passage is difficult textually; Gudeman
writes that the words translated "as has been said" refer to nothing now in the *Poetics*
and that there is no good explanation. Bywater renders: "What we have said may
happen in a way in reference to inanimate things, even things of a very casual kind."
Rostagni seems to get about the same meaning from a different text.

[63]Gudeman suggests that this sort is that arising from the construction of the plot
and associated with the peripety, mentioned by Aristotle in chap. X. It would seem
to be that, or "the best recognition" of the present chapter, rather than "the recognition of persons" indicated by Butcher.

[Suffering. 52b9]

Two parts, then, of the plot are peripety and recognition; the third part is tragic incident.[64] A tragic incident is an action that is destructive or painful, such as deaths on the stage, tortures, wounds, and the like.[65]

Chapter XII

[The quantitative parts of tragedy. 52b14]

We have already spoken of the parts of tragedy that are to be used as species. According to its quantity and the parts into which it may be divided, it consists of the following.[66] . . .

Chapter XIII

[Plots to avoid in tragedy. 52b28]

In sequence to what has been said above, I shall now show what the poet must avoid and what he must seek after in putting together his plots and whence the effect of tragedy comes. Since, then, it is necessary for the structure of a tragedy of the most excellent sort to be not simple but involved, and for it to be imitative of things that are fearful and pitiable—for that is the peculiar quality of such an imitation—it is plain at the outset that it is not advisable to show good men falling from good fortune to bad fortune, for this is not fearful nor pitiable but abominable. And bad men should not pass from bad fortune to good fortune, for this is of all conditions the most unsuitable to tragedy, because it contains nothing that is necessary, since it does not touch our human feeling and is not pitiable or fearful.[67] Nor should very wicked men fall from good fortune to bad fortune; such a thing touches

[64] For further development of this topic, see chap. XIV.

[65] The violent death on the stage was condemned by Horace in the *Art of Poetry*, 185, and has been generally assumed to be contrary to Greek practice, in spite of the present passage. For Renaissance comment see the index under *death on the stage*.

[66] Most of this chapter is omitted not so much because the whole is sometimes thought an interpolation as because of its special application to Greek tragedy.

[67] The adjective *philanthropos*, here and just below rendered *touching our human feeling*, occurs also in chap. XVIII, 56a19. It seems important for Aristotle's theory but its meaning—if beyond the obvious—is disputed.

our human feeling but has nothing pitiable or fearful about it, for pity is felt for the undeserving man in his misfortune and fear for a man like ourselves, so that the fall of the exceedingly wicked man is neither pitiable nor fearful.

[The proper tragic hero. 53a7]

There remains then the man who occupies the mean between saintliness and depravity. He is not extraordinary in virtue and righteousness, and yet does not fall into bad fortune because of evil and wickedness, but because of some error of the kind found in men of high reputation and good fortune, such as Oedipus and Thyestes and famous men of similar families.[68]

[The most effective plot. 53a12]

The plot must also be single rather than double, as some think it should be, and the change it presents must not be to good fortune from bad fortune but the opposite one from good fortune to bad fortune, not because of wickedness but because of some great error either of such a man as has been indicated or of a better rather than a worse man. Proof of this is found in practice. For at first poets accepted plots as they chanced on them, but now the best tragedies are written about a few houses, as on Alcmaeon, Oedipus, Orestes, Meleager, Thyestes, Telephus, and others on whom it came to suffer or do terrible things.[69] According to the rules of art the best tragedy is of this structure. Therefore they are in error who complain of Euripides because he used such themes in his tragedies and many of them end unhappily. For, as I have said, this is right. The best proof of it is that in the contests and on the stage tragedies of this type appear the most tragic, provided they are skillfully handled; Euripides, even though he

---

[68] This error (*hamartia*) is also mentioned in the next paragraph. Bywater renders it "error of judgment." In chaps. xvi, 54b30, and xxv, 60b10, Aristotle uses it of errors or faults in artistic construction. In the *Ethics*, iii, 2, Aristotle writes: "Obviously every wicked man does not know what he should do and what he should abstain from, and through an error (*hamartia*) of that sort (i.e., dependent on ignorance) men become unjust and wholly bad." The word translated *wickedness* (*mochtheria*) in both instances in this chapter and the word translated *wicked* (*mochtheros*) in the *Ethics* are the same, except that one is a noun and the other an adjective. While Aristotle should not be held to a strict consistency, we can infer that the acts of the tragic hero, resulting from ignorance and error, seem like those of a wicked man, but are unlike them because not deliberately bad.

[69] See the end of chap. xiv, and the note there.

does not manage other things well, at any rate appears more tragic than the other poets.[70]

[A less effective plot. 53a30]

Second in quality is the kind of plot some put first; I mean the plot having a double arrangement, like that of the *Odyssey*, and concluding in opposite ways for the good and the bad. It seems to be first in rank because of the weakness of the spectators, for the poets in their compositions follow the wishes of the audience.[71] But this type does not furnish the pleasure properly derived from tragedy but rather that suitable to comedy, for those who are the bitterest enemies in the story, as Orestes and Aegisthus,[72] go off together as friends at the end and no one is killed by anyone.

Chapter XIV

[The sources of pity and fear. 53b1]

Pity and fear, then, may be aroused by the spectacle, and also by the arrangement of the events; the latter is preferable and the mark of a better poet, because it is necessary for the plot to be so put together that, without seeing, one who hears what has been done is horrified and feels pity at the incidents;[73] one might experience this on hearing the story of Oedipus. To bring about this effect through the spectacle is less artistic and dependent on the attention given to staging. Those who by means of the spectacle seek to produce not the fearful but merely the monstrous have nothing in common with tragedy, for one should not seek every pleasure from tragedy but only that proper to it. Since it is necessary for the poet to provide this pleasure by means of pity and fear through imitation, it is clear that this effect must be worked

[70] Gudeman suggests that Euripides is not here compared with Aeschylus and Sophocles, but with dramatists whose plays were appearing on the stage when Aristotle was living. The traditional text requires the translation: "Euripides . . . appears the most tragic of the poets." Rostagni emphasizes the word *appears*, as having reference to the spectacle. In *Gnomon*, XI, 229, he vigorously asserts the validity of the traditional text.

[71] Cf. Plato, *Laws*, II, 659: "The ancient and common custom of Hellas . . . did certainly leave the judgment [of tragedy] to the body of spectators, who determined the victor by show of hands. But this custom has been the destruction of the poets; for they are now in the habit of composing with a view to please the bad taste of their judges" (trans. by Jowett).

[72] Aegisthus was the paramour of Clytemnestra, who murdered her husband Agamemnon, father of Orestes. Orestes then slew Aegisthus. See, for example, the *Electra* of Sophocles.   [73] Cf. chap. XXVI, 62a5, 14.

into the incidents. Let us find out then what sorts of event are terrible and what sorts are pitiable. It is necessary for such deeds to be those of men who feel affection for one another, or of enemies, or of those who are neither. But if an enemy acts against an enemy, there is nothing pitiable either in the deed or in the anticipation of it except the actual suffering that takes place, nor is there if they are neither friends nor enemies. But when the sufferings are those of persons who feel affection for each other, as when a brother kills a brother, or a son his father, or a mother her son, or a son his mother, or is about to do so, or anyone does something of the kind, these are the deeds to look for. The traditional myths are not, therefore, to be abandoned—I mean such as that Clytemnestra was killed by Orestes or Eriphyle by Alcmaeon —but it is necessary for the poet to find suitable matter in them and to use skillfully what is handed down to him.

[Tragic situations. 53b26]

As to what we mean by *skillfully,* let us explain more clearly. It is possible for the deed to be done, according to the practice of the ancient poets, by those who know and understand, as Euripides had Medea kill her sons.[74] It is possible for the deed not to be done by those who know.[75] It is possible to act without knowing that one is doing something terrible and then later to discover one's relationship with the persons concerned, as did the Oedipus of Sophocles. In this instance the terrible deed is outside the play,[76] but it can be within the tragedy, as in the instances of Alcmaeon in the play by Astydamas or Telegonus in the *Wounded Odysseus.* Finally one who is about to inflict some deadly injury may recognize the person he is about to injure in ignorance before he acts.[77] Besides these there is no other, for it is necessary to act or not to act, knowingly or not knowingly. Of these, for the person who knows to be on the point of acting and not to act is the worst; it is horrible and not tragic because there is no suffering. Therefore, no one has a character act in this way except a few poets now and then, as in the *Antigone* where Haemon acts thus to

---

[74] Euripides, *Medea,* 1236 ff.

[75] This sentence is inserted by Gudeman on the basis of the Arabic and medieval versions. Rostagni (*Gnomon,* p. 229) objects to the insertion as implied by the sense.

[76] Oedipus ignorantly killed his father and married his mother before the opening of the play. The tragedy itself deals with the revelation of what he has done.

[77] For explanation of this and the following references to recognition in this chapter, see chap. XI, 52a29, and chap. XVI.

Creon.[78] Next comes the carrying out of the action by one who knows. But it is still better for one who is ignorant to act, and after acting to recognize the other character, for there is nothing abominable in it and the recognition astounds us. Best of all is the last, I mean such an instance as that in the *Cresphontes* when Merope is about to kill her son yet does not kill him but recognizes him;[79] similarly in the *Iphigenia* the sister recognizes the brother;[80] in the *Helle* the son recognizes his mother when he is on the point of giving her up. Because the last type is the most tragic, the best tragedies have for a long time dealt with not many families, as has been said.[81] The reason is that the poets, who did not look for material systematically but in a haphazard fashion, discovered that what they wanted was to be found in the myths; so they needs must rely on those houses in which such tragic events have occurred. But I have said enough on the composition of tragedies and the nature of the plots that ought to be used in them.

Chapter XV

[Character. 54a16]

With respect to the characters there are four things it is necessary to aim at. The first is that they be good. There will be character, as has been said,[82] if speech or act clearly shows a moral choice indicating what sort of person an agent is; his character will be good if his choice is good. There is goodness in every type of person, for a woman is good and so is a slave, though one of these is perhaps inferior, the other paltry.[83] The second necessity

[78] Sophocles, *Antigone*, 1231 ff.

[79] According to the story as told by Hyginus (*Fables*, 137), Merope had an axe in her hand to kill a sleeping boy whom she thought the murderer of her son; just in time she recognized him as her son himself.

[80] Euripides, *Iphigenia among the Taurians*. For further discussion of the recognitions in this play see chap. XVI, throughout.

[81] In chap. XIII, 53a12, above. If the poets had been more scientific in their search would they have found material elsewhere than in the few myths that, as they learned by experience, were suitable for tragedy?   [82] Cf. chap. VI, 50b8.

[83] Fontanelle wrote: "The vices also have their perfection. A half-tyrant would not be worth considering; but ambition, cruelty, and perfidiousness when raised to their highest point become grand. Tragedy demands that the author make them, so far as is possible, splendid objects. There is an art of embellishing vices and giving them an air of nobility and elevation. Ambition is noble when satisfied with no lower object than a throne; cruelty is of the same sort when supported by an unyielding spirit; even perfidiousness when accompanied by extraordinary ability . . . The theatre is not opposed to what is vicious but to what is low and trivial " (*Reflexions sur la poetique*, sect. 17).

is that character be appropriate, for there is a manly character, but it is not fitting for a woman to have a masculine character or to be powerful. The third necessity is that character have resemblance.[84] For this is something else than to make characters good and appropriate, as has been said above.[85] The fourth necessity is that character be consistent. For if a character is not consistent because the man who is imitated was such a character, nevertheless it is necessary that he be consistently inconsistent. An example of unnecessary baseness of character is furnished by Menelaus in the *Orestes*,[86] and instances of unfitting and inappropriate character appear in the lament of Odysseus in the *Scylla*,[87] and in the speech of Melanippe.[88] An example of inconsistent character is found in the *Iphigenia at Aulis*, for Iphigenia as a suppliant is unlike the later Iphigenia.

[Probability and necessity in character.[89]   54a33]

In the characters as in the arrangement of the actions one must ever seek for the necessary and the probable, so that a certain sort of person does or says certain sorts of things according to necessity or probability, and one thing happens after another according to necessity or probability. It is clear therefore that the solutions of the plots ought to come from character itself,[90] and not as in the *Medea* from a stage mechanism and in the *Iliad* in the events relating to the sailing away of the Greeks.[91]

[84] Aristotle does not explain what the characters are to resemble. Some students understand him to mean that they must be true to life. Cf. the remark on the portrait painters (p. 91). It is also suggested that he means they should resemble their mythical prototypes. This opinion is perhaps supported by Horace's prescription that Medea should be fierce and unyielding, etc. (*Art of Poetry*, 123–4, below).

[85] There seems to be nothing above. Bywater translates "appropriate, in our sense of the term." Suggestions for emendation and omission have been made.

[86] Mentioned also in chap. xxv, 61b15.

[87] See Plato's remarks on lamentation in *Republic*, III, 387D, immediately above.

[88] Gudeman accepts an earlier suggestion that an example of character differing too much from its historical prototype has fallen out of the text at this point.

[89] For probability and necessity in plot, see chaps. IX, X, XI.

[90] This reading, important for Aristotle's view of the relation of plot and character, is adopted by Gudeman and Rostagni; its only manuscript support is that of the Arabic version. Most other students accept a reading which makes the solution of the plot come from the plot itself. For character as the cause of action, see chap. VI, 49b31.

[91] Euripides, *Medea*, 1317 ff. She escaped in a magic chariot. In the second book of the *Iliad*, the goddess Athene keeps the Greeks from abandoning the war against Troy. Aristotle obviously has in mind the machinery used in bringing a god on the stage. Some translators use the words *deus ex machina*. Though Aristotle does not elsewhere mention the *deus ex machina*, objection to it is obviously implied in his belief that a tragedy should be self-contained, as expressed, for example, in chap. VII, first par.

[Stage mechanism. 54b2]

One should use stage mechanism only for things outside the drama or for what has happened before it, or for what man cannot know, or for later things that need to be foretold or announced, for we admit that the gods see these things.

[The irrational. 54b6]

There should be nothing irrational in the incidents themselves, and if there is an irrationality, it should be outside the tragedy, as in the *Oedipus* of Sophocles.[92]

[Tragedy imitates better men. 54b8]

Since tragedy is an imitation of better men than our contemporaries,[93] the dramatists should imitate good portrait painters who, though presenting the right form and making their portraits like the originals, make them more beautiful.[94] Thus the poet in his imitations of wrathful men and cowardly men and others of comparable traits must still represent them as good, as Homer makes Achilles an example of hardness and yet good.[95]

[Further warnings to the poet. 54b15]

The author must be careful about these things and also about the rules governing the visual matters necessarily connected with poetry, for errors are often made in them. But enough has been said on this in my published writings.[96]

Chapter XVI

[The kinds of recognition: (1) Token. 54b19]

What recognition is has already been explained.[97] As to the five kinds of recognition, the first and least artistic kind, used by many writers through incapacity, is recognition through signs.

[92] It is irrational to represent Oedipus as remaining ignorant of the manner of the death of Laius (*Oedipus Tyrannus*, 103 ff.). Cf. chap. xxiv, 60a26.

[93] Some editors prefer a reading that means "than we are."

[94] See also chap. ii; chap. xxv, 60b32, 61b9.

[95] A difficult passage. Some editors find a reference to the poet Agathon.

[96] Perhaps in a lost dialogue *On the Poets*. The *Poetics* itself was not designed for publication.

[97] In chap. xi, 52a29. There are references to recognition also in chaps. xiv, 53b26; and xxiv, first par.

Some of them are congenital, such as "the spear the Earthborn have on their bodies,"[98] or stars like those Carcinus uses in the *Thyestes;*[99] or they may be acquired, and of these some are on the body, as scars, and some are apart from it, like necklaces and such things as were found in the little boat in the *Tyro.*[100] There is a better and a worse in using these, as is shown when Odysseus is recognized through the scar in one way by the nurse and in another by the swineherd, for scars and everything of the sort used for the sake of proof are rather inartistic, but when they cause shock, as in the Bath Scene, they are better.[101]

[(2) Recognition by the poet's arrangement. 54b30]

Second are recognitions added to the traditional plot by the poet, and therefore inartistic.[102] For example, in the *Iphigenia* the heroine recognizes that the man before her is Orestes; she has been recognized by means of the letter,[103] but Orestes says what the poet wishes, not what the plot demands; therefore this method comes close to the error just mentioned, for Orestes might have been provided with tokens.[104] And there is the voice of the shuttle in the *Tereus* of Sophocles.[105]

[98] A birthmark on the descendants of those sprung from the dragon's teeth sowed by Cadmus at Thebes.

[99] A mark on the shoulders of the Pelopids derived from Pelops's ivory shoulder.

[100] In this lost play by Sophocles two children seem to have been exposed in a little boat; perhaps garments and ornaments found in it served to identify them. Margoliouth translates as follows: "and the disclosure in the *Tyro* by means of the Ark"; Rostagni gives the same interpretation; some other translations are still more paraphrastic than the present one.

[101] In the *Odyssey*, XXI, 207 ff. Odysseus announces himself to the swineherd and the neatherd and proves it by drawing aside his clothing to display as proof the scar received in the hunt of the wild boar on Mount Parnassus. In the Bath Scene (*Odyssey*, XIX, 386 ff.) the same scar is seen by the nurse by accident and against the wish of Odysseus; in her astonishment she would have cried out had he not seized her by the throat. This latter recognition differs from "the best recognition" (p. 93) in that the scar is employed only for the sake of the recognition and is of no other use in the plot.

Butcher (p. 331) looks with some favor on the translation "accidentally" for the words I render "cause shock"; certainly they contrast with "for the sake of proof."

[102] Literally this clause runs: "made by the poet," etc. Aristotle's intention, as the context shows, is to indicate something brought into the story purely for the sake of the recognition, as a variation on the display of a scar or jewel not otherwise necessary.

[103] Aristotle implies that she is recognized in an artistic fashion.

[104] Euripides, *Iphigenia among the Taurians*, 747 ff. Orestes describes certain objects in the house of the family at Argos. This is not much better than to show a scar, as in the *Electra*, 573. In Shakespeare's *Twelfth Night*, v, i, Viola, in proof of her identity, says that her father died on the thirteenth anniversary of her birth and also that he had a mole upon his brow. She might almost as well have shown one on her own brow.

[105] Philomela used her shuttle to disclose through the web she wove her rape by Tereus, who had cut out her tongue to keep her from telling of his deed.

[(3) Recognition through memory. 54b36]

The third method is that by means of memory, when a man's mind is aroused as he sees or hears something, as in the instance in the *Cyprians* of Dicaeogenes, for on seeing a picture, a character burst into tears; there is another instance in the story of Alcinous, for on hearing the minstrel and remembering, Odysseus shed tears;[106] so the two were recognized.

[(4) Recognition by means of reasoning. 55a4]

The fourth type is recognition by means of a train of reasoning, as in the following from the *Choephoroe:* someone like me has come; no one is like me except Orestes; hence Orestes has come.[107] There is also that of Polyidus the Sophist about *Iphigenia*, for it is probable that Orestes would have reasoned that his sister had been sacrificed and that he was to be sacrificed. Then there is one in the *Tydeus* of Theodectes when the father reasons that he came to find his son and met his own fate. And there is one in the *Phinidae* in which on seeing the spot the women infer their fate, namely that there they are fated to die, for there they were exposed.[108]

[(5) Incorrect recognition through false reasoning. 55a12]

There is also a conclusion drawn from false reasoning on the part of an observer, as in *Odysseus the False Messenger*. That no one except Odysseus can string the bow is a fact devised by the poet; if then the false messenger says he will recognize the bow he has not seen, his words are a further step in the argument; the poet gives an example of bad reasoning when he has the observer recognize the false messenger as Odysseus because of what has been said.[109]

[The best recognition. 55a16]

The best recognition of all is the one arising from the events themselves in such a way that the shock of the discovery is

---

[106] *Odyssey*, VIII, 521 ff.; IX, beginning. On hearing the minstrel sing of the siege of Troy, Odysseus is reminded of the friends with whom he was associated there. Similarly King Claudius, when reminded of the murder of his brother by Hamlet's "mouse trap," shows emotion that suggests his guilt.

[107] Aeschylus, *Cheophoroe*, 168 ff. Electra reasons that the unknown visitor is her brother, even before she sees him. The other examples are from works now lost and cannot be explained with certainty.

[108] The *Tydeus* and the *Phinidae* are lost. We can only guess at the nature of the recognitions alluded to.

[109] See the Appendix to the *Poetics*, note 1, below.

produced according to probability, as in the *Oedipus* of Sophocles[110] and in the *Iphigenia*,[111] for it was probable that the heroine of the latter play would wish to send a letter. Recognitions of this sort are the only kinds without signs such as necklaces devised by the poet.[112] The next best is that coming from a syllogism.

Chapter XVII

[Practical advice to the author. 55a22]

It is necessary that the author when putting together his plots and laboring on their diction should bring the play before his own eyes, for thus seeing everything in the clearest light as though he were actually present when the events happened, he will find what is suitable, and incongruities will be very unlikely to escape him. A proof of this is what was censured in Carcinus. Amphiaraus came out from the temple, but his act escaped the notice of the poet, who did not see it as a spectator; yet on the stage the play failed because the audience were displeased by this defect.[113] As far as possible the author should act out his piece with gestures, for the most persuasive poets are those who have the same natures as their characters and enter into their sufferings; he who feels distress represents distress and he who feels anger represents anger most genuinely.[114] Therefore poetic art is the affair of the gifted man rather than of the madman,[115] for men of the first kind can adapt themselves well but those of the second are beside themselves.

[The outline. 55a34]

It is necessary for the poet as he composes tragedies to make a general scheme of his narratives, even of those he has constructed

[110] There is no formal scene of recognition, but the truth is borne home to Oedipus, as earlier to Jocasta, by what is said by characters bent on something else than the discovery that is made (ll. 1002 ff.).

[111] As has been said earlier in the chapter, it is only the recognition of Orestes by Iphigenia that is unskillful. That of Iphigenia by Orestes comes from her attempt to communicate with home; the discovery comes as a shock, with no presentation of material that is useless except for the securing of the recognition.

[112] See the Appendix to the *Poetics*, note 2, below.

[113] This play is now unknown.

[114] Cf. Horace, *Art of Poetry*, 102–3, below.

[115] See the Appendix to the *Poetics*, note 3.

for himself,[116] and after that to fill in the episodes and give the works their full length. By making a general scheme I mean what I shall illustrate from the *Iphigenia:* A certain maiden, about to be sacrificed to a god, was snatched away in a manner not clear to those sacrificing her, taken to another country where the custom was to sacrifice strangers to the god, and made priestess; at a later time her brother happened to come to the temple (the fact that the god commanded him for some reason to go there is outside the general plan, and the purpose for which he went is outside the plot); on his coming, after he had been seized and was on the point of being sacrificed, he recognized his sister; then whether it was Euripides or Polyidus who so arranged it, as probability required, he said it was necessary not merely for his sister but for himself to be sacrificed, and in that way rescue came. After a general scheme has been made and the names given to the characters, the episodes may be composed, with a view to making them fitting, as the attack of madness because of which Orestes was taken prisoner and his rescue through his purification. In dramas the episodes are short, but an epic poem is lengthened out by them. The story of the *Odyssey* is not long: A certain man has been away from home many years, has been always under the eye of the god, and is alone; matters at home have come to such a pass that his property is being wasted and his son is being plotted against by the suitors to his wife; he arrives at home after great sufferings; making himself known to a few friends, he falls on his enemies; he is saved but destroys his foes. This, then, is indispensable, all the rest is episodic.[117]

Chapter XVIII

[The two parts of the plot. 55b24]

For every tragedy there is a tying of the knot, or complication, and an untying of it, or solution. The tying is composed of what

[116] The normal translation is represented by that of Butcher: "As for the story, whether the poet takes it ready made or constructs it for himself, he should first sketch its general outline." In his note on the words equivalent to *even of those he has constructed for himself*, Rostagni translates "*anche quelli inventati*," and explains that the words imply "beside the traditional." Both Gudeman and he refer to chap. IX, where traditional and made-up plots are discussed. Margoliouth translates the Arabic into Latin: "*Debet ipse etiam dum facit ponere ea universe.*"

[117] See chap. XXVI, 62a14, and note.

is without the plot and many times of some things within it; the rest is the untying. By the tying I mean what extends from the beginning to that part nearest the point from which the hero changes to good fortune or to bad fortune, by the untying the part from the beginning of the change until the end. So in the *Lynceus* of Theodectes the tying includes the actions that took place before the beginning of the play and the kidnaping of the boy and then the explanation of these events.[118] The untying is from the accusation of murder to the conclusion.

[Species of tragedy. 55b32]

The species of tragedy are four, for the same number of parts has been mentioned; the involved, which is all peripety and recognition, the pathetic, such as the *Ajaxes* and *Ixions,* the tragedy of character, such as the *Phthiotides* and the *Peleus,* and the fourth, which is simple, such as the *Phorcides* and the plays on Prometheus and all that have scenes in Hades.[119]

[Poet and critic. 56a3]

It is necessary for the poet as far as possible to make use of all the types, or if he cannot attain that to employ the most important ones and as many as possible, especially because of the way in which they now censure the poets, for since there have been poets who were good in each part of tragedy, the critics think that any one poet of the present should surpass his predecessors when each is at his best.

[What tragedies are alike. 56a7]

It is proper to say that tragedies are alike or not in respect to their plot only, and plots are alike that have the same tying of the knot and untying. Many who have skillfully twisted the threads together disentangle them badly.

[Tragedy must be limited. 56a10]

It is necessary, as has been said, for the poet to keep reminding himself that he should not make an epic scheme for a tragedy; by epic I mean that which has many stories in it, as though someone should make a tragedy of the whole *Iliad.*[120] For because of the length of the epic its parts take their proper size, but in dramas

---

[118] The play to which Aristotle refers is lost and the text is bad; consequently the passage is unintelligible.   [119] See the Appendix to the *Poetics,* note 4, below.
[120] Cf. chap. v, last sect.; chap. VIII; and chap. XXIII, 59a30.

the result is strikingly contrary to expectation. There is proof of this, for the poets who take the whole story of the fall of Troy, and not a part of it as Euripides did, or take the whole tale of Thebes and not a part as Aeschylus did, either fail completely or do not come out well in the dramatic contests, since even Agathon failed for that reason alone.

[Effective plots. 56a19]

Yet both in plots involving peripeties and in simple actions these poets succeed in attaining the tragic effect they aim at by means of the astonishing, for this quality is tragic and arouses human sympathy.[121] It requires a plot in which a shrewd but wicked man, such as Sisyphus, is deceived, and a brave but unjust man is worsted; these are probable according to the saying of Agathon, for it is probable many things will happen contrary to probability.[122]

[The chorus. 56a25]

The chorus should be treated as one of the actors, should be an integral part of the whole, and should participate in the action, not as in the plays of Euripides but as in those of Sophocles. In other poets the songs are not more closely connected with the plot in which they appear than with some other tragedy. Therefore they are now singing interpolated songs, a practice that Agathon first introduced. Yet what difference is there between singing interpolated songs and transferring a speech from one play to another?

Chapter XIX

[Thought.[123] 56a33]

Since the other species of tragedy have been discussed, it remains for me to speak of diction and thought. A discussion of thought may be found in our treatment of rhetoric,[124] for the sub-

---

[121] My translation of this sentence is derived from Rostagni and Albeggiani. Bywater translates: "Yet . . . the poets I mean show wonderful skill in aiming at the kind of effect they desire." Cf. xiii, 52b28, note, above. For the astonishing see chap. ix, last sect.

[122] This section is apparently a defense against the critics mentioned in the section of the present chapter headed "Poet and critic" and is perhaps misplaced here.

The saying of Agathon is repeated in chap. xxv, 61b9. See the note there.

[123] For references to thought see also chap. vi, especially the secs. headed Plot, Thought, Character. [124] The first two books of Aristotle's *Rhetoric*.

ject properly belongs to that department. Thought is shown in everything that the characters must bring about by means of speech; the subdivisions are proof, refutation, arousing of emotion —pity, fear, anger, and the like—and the feeling that things are important and trivial. It is clear also that it is necessary to make use of the same principles in actions as well, whenever it is needful to present pitiable or fearful or great or probable things, except that there is this difference, that it is necessary for actions to produce their effects without explanation, but the effects of spoken things must be prepared by the speaker himself and result from what he says. For of what use would the speaker be if the idea appeared in some other way than through his words?

[Diction. 56b8]

As to diction, one part of the investigation deals with the various kinds of expression, which are the concern of those who are skilled in elocution and professionally occupied with that art, to wit, the nature of command, prayer, narrative, threat, question, answer, and everything else of the sort. Whether the poet knows these things or not, no censure worthy of respect is cast upon his art.[125] For who would think there is anything worthy of blame in the passage in which Homer said, "Sing, goddess, of wrath"?[126] Yet Protagoras censured it, asserting that the poet gave a command when he supposed he was uttering a prayer, for, says Protagoras, to bid someone to do something or not is a command. Therefore we may pass over this inquiry as belonging to something else than the art of poetry.

Chapter XX

[Grammar. 56b20]

[This chapter is omitted.]

Chapter XXI

[Classes of words. 57a31]

Words are divided into two classes, simple and double. By simple I mean those that are not put together from significant

---

[125] For further remarks of this sort, see chap. xxv, 60b23.　　　[126] *Iliad*, I, I.

parts, such as *earth*. The double may be made up of a significant and a nonsignificant part, except in certain cases,[127] or from significant parts. There are also threefold, fourfold, and manifold words, like so many Massilian words,[128] for example, *Hermocaïcoxanthus*.

[Types of words. 57b1]

Every word is either an ordinary word or an imported word or a metaphor or an ornamental word or a coined word or a lengthened word or a curtailed word or a modified word.

[The ordinary and the imported word. 57b3]

By *ordinary* I mean a word that ordinary men use, and by *imported* a word that foreigners use. Hence it is clear that the same word can be both imported and common, but not for the same users. The word *sigunon*, "spear," is an ordinary word for the Cyprians but an imported word for us; but *doru*, "spear," is an ordinary word for us but an imported word for the Cyprians.

[Metaphors. 57b6a]

A metaphor is the transfer of a name that belongs to something else either from the genus to the species, or from the species to the genus, or from one species to another, or according to analogy. "Here stands my ship"[129] illustrates transfer from genus to species, for lying at anchor is one kind of standing. "In truth Odysseus has done ten thousand noble deeds"[130] exhibits transfer from species to genus, for it uses *ten thousand* instead of many. "Drawing forth the life with bronze" and "cutting off the stream with the sharp bronze" illustrate transfer from species to species, for here *draw forth* means *cut off* and *cut off* means *draw forth;*[131] both signify to take something away. I mean by analogy the condition when a second thing is related to a first as is a fourth to a third; then one may put the fourth instead of the second and the second instead of the fourth. And sometimes poets add the thing with which the supplanted word is connected. I mean that as the cup is related to Dionysus the shield is related to Ares; so one may

---

[127] The text of this exception is uncertain; I do not attempt to give an exact rendering.

[128] Marseilles was founded by Greeks from Phocis.

[129] *Odyssey*, I, 185; XXIV, 308.   [130] *Iliad*, II, 272.

[131] Both are from Empedocles (Fragments 138, 143). The meaning is disputed, but Aristotle's purpose seems clear.

call the cup the shield of Dionysus and the shield the cup of Ares.[132] Or old age is to life as evening to day. Hence one can call evening the old age of day, or old age the evening of life or the sunset of life.[133] Sometimes there is no word analogous to those employed, but nonetheless the poet will speak according to proportion. For example, to scatter seed is to sow, but we have no verb for scattering light, when said of the sun, yet this nameless process has the same relation to sunlight as sowing to the seed; hence it is written: "sowing a god-created flame." It is also possible to use this kind of metaphor in another way, for after the metaphorical term has been applied something normally connected with it can be denied, as when the shield is said to be not the cup of Ares but the wineless cup.

[The ornamental word.[134]]

[The coined word. 57b33]

The coined word is one that never having been used by anyone is brought forward by the poet himself, for it seems there are such words, such as *ernuges*, "sprouters," for horns and *areter*, "supplicator," for priest.[135]

[The lengthened word and the curtailed word. 57b35]

As to the lengthened word and the curtailed word, the first is one that has adopted a longer vowel than belongs to it or an added syllable; the second is one of which some part has been removed.[136]

[The altered word. 58a5]

The altered word is one in which part of the usual form is untouched and part is changed.[137] [Some ten lines at the end of the chapter contain a discussion of the gender of nouns and the endings of those of each gender. Since they relate only to matters of grammar of the Greek language, they are omitted.]

---

[132] Timotheus, Fragment 22 Wilam.   [133] Probably from Empedocles.

[134] This section is lacking from our texts.

[135] *Iliad*, I, 11, 94; v, 78.

[136] The examples that follow require a knowledge of Greek, and the text is corrupt. Analogous are the Elizabethan use of *girl* as a dissyllable, and the shortening of *Diana* to *Dian*.

[137] The examples here also are not significant in English. An analogy is furnished by *pacifist* and *pacificist*.

Chapter XXII

[Good and bad style. 58a18]

The virtue of style must be that it is clear and not pedestrian; the clearest is that made up of common words, but it is pedestrian. An example of this is given by the poetry of Cleophon and Sthenelus. But diction that employs unusual words is elevated and goes beyond ordinary speech. By unusual words I mean borrowed words, and metaphors, and lengthening, and all that goes beyond the ordinary. But if one composed altogether in this sort of language, a riddle or barbarism would result; a riddle if he composed in metaphors, barbarism if in borrowed words, for the nature of a riddle lies in joining together absurdities to express things that exist; this cannot be done by joining together non-metaphorical words, but with a metaphor it is possible, as in the expression: "I saw a man fastening bronze on another with fire,"[138] and the like. Barbarism comes from the use of borrowed words.

[How to use ornaments of style. 58a31]

It is necessary to make use of these elements in some way, for the borrowed word and the metaphor and the ornamental word and the other kinds of elaborated diction I have mentioned will cause a composition not to seem common and abject; ordinary language will produce clarity. But lengthening and contraction and alteration of words contribute no small part to making diction clear but yet not common, for the departure from the normal method of using the ordinary language keeps the diction from appearing common, and yet the relation to the norm secures clarity for it. So they do not rightly censure who blame such a habit of speech and make game of the poet, as did Euclid the elder, saying it was easy to write poetry if one were permitted to lengthen and shorten words as one wished, and satirizing the practice by writing lines to illustrate it.[139] . . . To be at all conspicuous in

---

[138] The medical operation of cupping with a bronze cup.

[139] I omit the examples. A parallel is the statement that it would be easy to write regular verse in English if one were permitted to accent words as one pleased. There are English lines the accent of which is debated by editors. For example in Milton's *Samson Agonistes*, 134, regular accent would require Adámantéan proóf. Can it be read Adamántean proóf, making the line consist of two anapaests? Is a better reading Ádamantéan proóf? Did Milton observe the normal accent or did he indulge in the poetic modification permitted by Aristotle?

using this device is laughable, and moderation should be practiced in all the parts of poetical composition, for he who uses metaphors, borrowed words, and the other kinds of ornament improperly and he who uses them deliberately and for the purpose of
exciting laughter will produce the same effect.

[Examples of ornament. 58b15]

Let us see how different the proper use of them is by inserting
the words in their usual forms in the verses of an heroic poem; and
when the common words are substituted for borrowed words,
metaphors, and other kinds of ornament, it will appear that we
are speaking the truth. For example, Euripides and Aeschylus
write the same lines, except that by the change of a single word a
borrowed term is substituted for a common and ordinary one, and
the work of the first seems splendid but that of the second paltry;
for Aeschylus in the *Philoctetes* wrote:

> A cancer eats the flesh of my foot.

But Euripides substituted for *eats* the word *feasts on*.[140] Or take

> A man low of stature and of slight esteem and unseemly,[141]

and read it after substituting the common words:

> A man short and weak and shabby.

And again:

> He set out an unseemly stool and a pygmaean table.
> He set out a mean stool and a little table.[142]

Further, "the shores are yelling," and "the shores are clamoring
loud."[143]

[Unnatural changes. 58b30]

Then Ariphrades ridiculed the tragedians because they put
their speeches in forms no one would use in conversation. . . .[144]
But because things of this sort are not used in ordinary speech they
make the diction appear other than commonplace; the critic did
not understand that.

---

[140] The plays are both lost.　　　　[141] *Odyssey*, IX, 515.　　　　[142] *Ibid*, XX, 259.

[143] *Iliad*, XVII, 265. The examples are apparently more effective in Greek than in
English.

[144] Some translators, including the present one, do not attempt to render the examples given at this point. Professor Cooper finds an excellent equivalent in Wordsworth's
"That glides the dark hills under" (*Yarrow Unvisited*, 26). Less exact as an equivalent
is Milton's "in field great battles win" (*Paradise Regained*, III, 73).

[The significance of the devices mentioned. 59a4]

It is a great thing to use properly each of the devices I have spoken of, both compound words and borrowed words, but much the most important is the metaphor; this alone cannot be learned from others and its use is a sign of genius, for to use metaphors well is to see resemblance.

[Their use in various types of poetry. 59a8]

Of the various words I have mentioned, the compound ones are most suitable in dithyrambs, the borrowed words in heroic poetry, and the metaphors in the iambics. In heroic poetry all the means I have mentioned are useful, but in the iambic, since it especially imitates speech, those words are most suitable that are used in conversation, such as the common word, and the metaphor, and the ornamental word. What has been said may suffice for tragedy and imitation in action.

Chapter XXIII

[Narrative poetry. 59a17]

Concerning narrative that imitates in one meter, it is obviously necessary that, as in tragedies, the plots be dramatically put together, and deal with one action that is whole and complete and has a beginning, a middle, and an end, so that as a complete living creature it may give the proper pleasure. And such works are not put together like histories, in which it is necessary for the composition to deal not with one deed but with one time, and to tell whatever happened in that time to one or more men, no matter what relation one event has to another. For example, the naval battle that took place at Salamis and the battle with the Carthaginians in Sicily at the same time had no relation to the same end, as often one thing comes after another in time but the two do not have the same guiding principle. Yet nearly all the poets use such historical material.

[Homer's skill. 59a30]

Therefore just as Homer appears admirable in comparison with the others in the things already mentioned, so he does in this too: though the Trojan war has a beginning and an end, he did not attempt to treat the entire war in his poem, because the plot would have been too long and could not have been comprehended in one view, or if he could have moderated the length of the plot, it would still have been too complicated in its variety of incident.[145] But he selected one part and used many of the other incidents as episodes, such as the catalogue of the ships[146] and other episodes with which he diversifies his poem. But the others treat one man and one time and one action of many parts, as did the author of the *Cypria* and the *Little Iliad*. As a result, from either the *Iliad* or the *Odyssey* there can be made one tragedy, or only two, but from the *Cypria* many can be made, and from the *Little Iliad* eight,[147] namely, *The Award of Arms*, the *Neoptolemus*, the *Philoctetes*, *The Beggar's Song*, *The Fall of Ilium*, *The Embarcation*, *Sinon*, and *The Trojan Women*.

Chapter XXIV

[Epic resembles tragedy. 59b7]

In addition epic poetry of necessity has the same species as tragedy, for an epic is either simple or involved or concerned with character or pathetic.[148] The parts of the epic are also the same as those of tragedy, except that the epic does not have melody and spectacle; for the epic requires peripeties, and recognitions, and scenes of suffering, and the thought and the diction must be well handled.[149] Homer was the first to use all these species and did it well. Of his poems each is composed in a different way: the *Iliad* is simple and presents scenes of suffering; the *Odyssey* is involved, for there are frequent recognitions,[150] and is concerned with character. In addition, they surpass all the other poems in diction and thought.

[145] For other remarks on the length and unity of the epic, see chaps. v, 49b9; xviii, 56a10; xxvi, 62a14, and the Appendix to the *Poetics*, note 9.

[146] *Iliad*, ii, 484–779.

[147] I follow Butcher and Gudeman in reading *eight*; other editors give *more than eight*. The substance of Aristotle's thought is not affected by one or two more or less in the list.

[148] See chap. xviii, 55b32, and the Appendix to the *Poetics*, note 4.

[149] See the Appendix to the *Poetics*, note 5.

[150] For some of the recognitions in the *Odyssey* see chap. xvi, above. There are various others, such as the discovery by the suitors that Telemachus has eluded them ("whether someone has done something or not," *Poetics*, xi, 52a29) in Bk. iv, 624 ff., and the recognition of Odysseus by the suitors at the beginning of Bk. xxii. See Plato's reference to the latter, *Ion*, 535, above.

[How epic differs from tragedy. 59b17]

Epic differs from tragedy in the length of the composition and in the meter. A good limit of length is that which has been given, for it is necessary to take in the beginning and the end in one view.[151] This is possible if the compositions are shorter than the old epics and equal the length of the tragedies presented in one program.[152] With respect to extending its length, the epic has a capacity wholly peculiar to itself, because the nature of tragedy does not admit of the imitation of many parts of an action that occur at the same time, but only of the one part imitated on the stage by the actors.[153] In the epic, however, because of its narrative form, many parts that happen at the same time can be included; by these, if they are closely connected with the rest, the majesty of the poem is increased. Hence the epic has this advantage tending to magnificence of effect, variety for the hearer, and the weaving of dissimilar episodes into the action, for uniformity quickly satiates an audience and makes tragedies fail on the stage.

[Epic verse. 59b31]

As to meter, the heroic has stood the test of experience.[154] If anyone should compose a narrative poem in any other meter or in several, it would seem unfitting, for the heroic is the most stately and weighty of the meters and therefore most easily receives borrowed words and metaphors and ornaments of all sorts; in this respect imitation in narrative has an advantage over other kinds. The iambic and the tetrameter are meters of activity, the first being suitable for action, the second for the dance. It would be still more absurd if one should mix them all together, as Chaere-

---

[151] See chap. VII, 51a6; chap. XXVI, 62a14.

[152] Three tragedies, altogether about 4000 lines long, or about one fourth the length of the *Iliad* and one third that of the *Odyssey*.

[153] This is sometimes said to have given rise to the notion of unity of place (see the index under *unity of place*). Castelvetro (57, 1 and notes, below), however, establishes unity of time in his commentary long before he comes to this passage, and without reference to it; his basis is rational, not that of the authority of Aristotle. This statement, then, he takes as a matter of course, writing: "As has been said, tragedy can present only an action that has happened in one place and in the course of twelve hours" (535, 41–3; cf. *Poetics*, V, 49b9, above, and the note). The meaning of Aristotle here, he indicates, is that the writer of tragedy should confine himself to his proper business. For the entire passage see Castelvetro, in the section on tragedy and epic compared, 535, 32, below.

[154] The Greek epics are in hexameter.

mon did. Hence no one should produce a long composition in any other meter than the heroic, but as we said, nature herself teaches us to choose the proper measure.[155]

[Homer's dramatic method. 60a5]

Homer, worthy of praise in all other respects, deserves it also in that he alone of all the poets is not ignorant of the part he himself should take. It is necessary for the poet to speak in his own person as little as possible because he is not an imitator in what he says then.[156] Yet the other poets appear in their own persons throughout the poem and their imitations are few and far between. But Homer, having said a few words in introduction, straightway brings forward a man or a woman or some other agent, and not someone without character but someone having it.

[The astonishing. 60a11]

It is also necessary for the poet to put into his tragedies something astonishing,[157] but the improbable, which is the most usual basis for the astonishing, is better employed in the epic than in tragedy because the actor is not seen; the circumstances of the pursuit of Hector would appear laughable on the stage, the Greeks standing still and not pursuing and Achilles shaking his head as a signal to them,[158] but in the epic the laughable qualities escape notice. The astonishing is pleasing; a proof of this is that all men in telling stories add to them in the belief they will please their audience.

[How to tell lies. 60a18]

Homer has been very influential in teaching the other poets how lies should be told. It is done by using a paralogism.[159] For if when one thing exists a second thing exists or happens, men think it is also true that if the second exists the first must also exist or happen; but this is false. Now it is necessary for the poet, when the first is false and yet if it were true the second would of

---

[155] With the first sentence of the paragraph in mind, Gudeman emends this sentence to mean "experience itself teaches us," etc. Cf. the remark on nature in chap. IV, 49a9, above.

[156] See also chap. III, first par., and Plato's discussion of imitation in the *Republic*, III, 393 ff., above.

[157] See chap. IX, last sec.; chap. XVIII, 56a19; chap. XXV, 61b9.

[158] *Iliad*, XXII, 205.

[159] A piece of false reasoning or pseudo-syllogism. Cf. chap. XVI, 55a12.

necessity exist or happen, to present the second. Then the minds of men, knowing that the second is true, accept the false conclusion that the first is also true. There is an example of this in the bath scene in the *Odyssey*.[160]

[The improbable. 60a26]

The poet should choose probable impossibilities rather than incredible possibilities.[161] The plots should not be made up of improbable parts; indeed they should above all contain nothing improbable, but if the unreasonable cannot be avoided, it should be outside the plot, as that Oedipus did not know how Laius came to his death; it should not be in the play itself, as in the *Electra* the persons telling of the Pythian games,[162] or in the *Mysians* that a man came from Tegea to Mysia without speaking. Hence to say that the plot would be ruined without such events is ridiculous; one should not devise such plots from the beginning. But if a poet does take such a plot and appears to have handled it with some appearance of probability, the absurdity may be pardoned.[163] Even the improbabilities about putting Odysseus on shore in the *Odyssey* would clearly not be tolerable if treated by an inferior poet.[164] As it is, the skill of Homer conceals the absurdity and makes it pleasing.

[Diction relative to other elements. 60b2]

The results of labor on the diction should appear in the parts where there is no action and no presentation of character or thought, for diction that is too splendid conceals both character and thought.

---

[160]*Odyssey*, XIX, 164–260. Penelope concludes from the truth of the description in ll. 220–48 that the narrative in ll. 164–200 is also true. In l. 203 Odysseus is said to have "told many a false tale in the likeness of truth."

[161] See also the discussion of the impossible in chap. XXV, 61b9, and the beginning of chap. IX.

[162] See the Appendix to the *Poetics*, note 6.

[163] The text of this sentence is corrupt; I have followed Gudeman. He quotes from the work on poetry by Philodemus of Parium a passage that may be translated as follows: "It is possible for a poet who has selected a plot and foundation for his work that is improbable to work it out poetically, and there have been poets who have done so. He is a finished and excellent poet who takes thought in the choice of such things" (*Philodemos über die Gedichte*, ed. by Jensen [Berlin, 1923], p. 21).

[164] Odysseus is put on shore by the Phaeacians without their rousing him from slumber, though they run the vessel ashore for half her length, lift the hero, all wrapped in his bedding, out of the ship, and pile on the ground the goods he had brought with him. (*Odyssey*, XIII, 114 ff.)

Chapter XXV

[The fundamentals of criticism. 6ob6]

Problems and their solutions and the number and nature of their kinds will be clear to those who look at them as follows. Since the poet, like a painter of animals or any other maker of likenesses, is an imitator, he must always imitate some one of the three aspects of things: either as they were or are, or as men say they are and they seem to be, or as they ought to be.[165] He presents these in language which employs borrowed words and metaphors. And there are many modifications of diction, for we allow these to the poets. In addition, there is not the same sort of correctness in politics as in poetics, nor in any other art as in poetics. There are two kinds of error in the art of poetry, one coming from the essence of the art, the other accidental. If the poet chooses to imitate something and fails because of lack of imitative ability, the error is in the poetic art itself. But if he makes a mistake about what he chooses to imitate or writes of impossible things—for example, a horse that moves both its right legs forward at the same time,[166] or the faults that can occur in dealing with every one of the arts, as a mistake about medicine, or something in any other art whatever—then the error is not germane to poetry.[167] It is necessary to dispose of the objections brought up in the problems by considering them with these things in mind.

[Errors that touch the poetic art. 6ob23]

First, as to matters that concern the art of poetry itself. If he has represented impossible things, he has committed a fault, but he is right if he attains the end of poetry, and he does attain the end, as has been said, if he thus makes one part or another more

[165] Cf. chaps. II; XV, 54b8.

[166] Aristotle obviously did not know of the pacing horse, which has the gait he speaks of as impossible. See his *De incessu*, XIV, 712a.

[167] The passage is corrupt, but its purport seems to be clear, namely that the poet is to be judged for his skill in imitation and not for his scientific accuracy. Philodemus objected to the demand for great learning on the part of the poet: "It is too much to expect the excellent poet . . . to study all manners and customs, and to have a knowledge of natural science. The idea should not be taken too seriously that the poet should associate with all sorts of characters. Moreover, he is dreaming who says that the poet should know all about geometry and geography and astrology and law and seamanship. For if geography is a necessity to the poet, why not also the handicrafts?" (*op. cit.*, p. 11). Cf. Plato's discussion of the poet's knowledge, *Ion*, 538, *Republic*, x, 598, above, and see the index under *poet, his knowledge*.

astounding.[168] The pursuit of Hector is an example of this.[169] If, however, he could have managed to attain the end better or not worse and at the same time conformed with the art from which he has taken his subject, his fault is not justified; for it is necessary, if it is possible, to be at fault in nothing whatever. Then we may ask whether the fault is one of those essential to the art or is only incidentally connected with it; it is less serious for a painter not to know that a female deer has no horns than to represent one inartistically.[170]

[Poetry does not always present truth. 60b32]

Further, if a poet is blamed for not presenting things truly, the objection can be removed by saying, perhaps, that they are as they should be, as Sophocles said he presented men as they ought to be but Euripides as they were.[171] If a poet presents men neither as they are nor as they should be, he can be defended by saying that his characters are as men say they are, as in accounts of the gods. Perhaps one cannot hold that the poet when dealing with them presents something better than the reality or tells truths,[172] but must suppose Xenophanes was right in asserting that "no man now lives or ever shall live with knowledge of the truth about the gods";[173] yet at any rate men do say that the gods are as the poets represent them. In other instances one cannot defend the poet as presenting something better than the reality, but can say he is in accord with historical facts, as in the matter of the weapons: "The spears were driven into the ground erect on the spikes of the butts";[174] for so they were in the habit of doing then, as the Illyrians do now. As to the question whether something is said or done by someone rightly or not, not merely should one examine the thing itself that has been done or said to see if it is good or bad, but one should examine also the one who acts or speaks, and to whom and when and how and on account

---

[168] Cf. chap. XXIV, 60a11, and chap. IX, 52a1.
[169] See chap. XXIV, 60a11, above.
[170] This error was made by Pindar, *Olympian Ode*, III, 52.
[171] See the present chapter, 61b9, below.
[172] "Better than the reality" is equivalent to *as it should be*; cf. the preceding sentences. This is a controverted passage. I give what seems to me the meaning to be derived from the text as accepted by Rostagni and Gudeman; the latter printed the form I follow only among his variants, but has written to me that he now prefers it.
[173]*Fragments*, 34, Diehls. Aristotle does not quote Xenophanes; I have inserted the words he is supposed to have had in mind.
[174]*Iliad*, x, 152.

of what, as for the sake of attaining a greater good, or avoiding a greater ill.[175]

[Defense through explanation of language. 61a9]

Some objections may be disposed of by recourse to the language. There may be a borrowed word in the passage, "First did he assail the mules,"[176] for perhaps he means not the mules but the sentinels. And in what is said about Dolon, "Verily he was badly shaped to look upon, but swift of foot,"[177] the meaning is not that his body was deformed but that his face was ugly, for the Cretans used the word *well-shaped* to mean handsome of face. And again, "Mix the wine stronger,"[178] may not refer to undiluted wine for drunkards but may mean "Mix it faster." Words may be used metaphorically, as when Homer says: "All the gods and chariot-driving men slept throughout the night";[179] yet at the same time he says: "As often as Agamemnon turned his gaze to the Trojan plain, he marveled at the sound of flutes and pipes."[180] Here *all* is used instead of *many* in a metaphor, for all of anything would include a large number. And again "alone unsharing"[181] is metaphorical, for the best known is thought of as the only one. There may be a change in the way of reading; Hippias of Thasos in that way explained: "We grant he will obtain the thing prayed for" as "Allow him to obtain the thing prayed for."[182] Similarly he

[175] There is some discussion whether the right and wrong of this sentence is moral or artistic. There are suggestions in the *Poetics* of the moral view of poetry (chap. xv) as possibly held by Aristotle himself. At the same time he rejects the perfect hero (chap. xiii). Is it not likely that on the whole, like Plato (see the introduction to the selections from Plato, above), he had rejected the merely moral view? The present passage may, then, either be wholly artistic in reference; or it may be an answer to those who insist on perfect characters, showing how artistic reasons may justify an imperfect character. See also a further reference in this chapter, 61b15, below.

[176] *Iliad*, I, 50.   [177] *Ibid.*, x, 316.   [178] *Ibid.*, IX, 202.

[179] Apparently Aristotle confused, perhaps by a lapse of memory, *Iliad*, II, 1 and *Iliad*, x, 1. In neither passage does the word for *all* now occur in texts of the *Iliad*. I have followed Gudeman's reading.

[180] The passage in full is as follows: "As often as he turned his gaze on the Trojan plain, he wondered at the many fires that burned before Troy and at the sound of flutes and pipes and at the noisy crowd of men" (*Iliad*, x, 11-13). Aristotle seems to have quoted only enough to bring the idea before his pupils, or the text is corrupt.

[181] *Iliad*, xviii, 489; *Odyssey*, v, 275: "The Bear . . . that alone hath no part in the baths of Ocean." It was known in antiquity that what is true of the Bear is true of northern constellations generally.

[182] An older reading of *Iliad*, II, 15. Aristotle gives only one form of the sentence, apparently supposing that the other would be understood. The change is merely in the accent of a single word, changing it from a statement by Zeus to a command to the God of Sleep. A parallel is found in the sign *Umbrellas recovered*; according to the accent of *recovered* they are found when lost or provided with new coverings.

explained "It is not rotted by the rain" as "Part of it is rotted by the rain."[183] Or the difficulty may be explained by a change in punctuation, as in the lines of Empedocles: "Suddenly things become mortal that before had learnt to be immortal and they are unmixed that were mixed before," which may be read: "Suddenly things become mortal that before had learnt to be immortal and they that before were unmixed are mixed."[184] In the words, "The greater part of the night had gone by,"[185] the explanation is that of ambiguity, for *the greater part* is ambiguous. Another explanation is that of the habit of language, as in calling a mixed drink wine. For the same reason Ganymede is said to pour out wine for Zeus, though the gods do not drink wine.[186] According to the same principle Homer writes of "greaves of newly-wrought tin,"[187] and we call those who work in iron bronzesmiths. Perhaps these can also be explained as metaphors. It is also necessary when a word seems to suggest some self-contradiction, to examine how many meanings it can have in the passage in question. For example, when the poet writes, "In this the bronze spear stuck fast,"[188] in how many ways can *stuck fast* there be understood?

[Bad critics. 61a34]

By taking it in this way or that, one acts in a way opposed to the conduct described by Glaucon when he says that some critics take up an irrational opinion and, having decreed its truth for themselves, proceed to draw conclusions from it, and assuming the poet has said what their fancy requires, blame him if he writes something inconsistent with it.[189] This appears in the circum-

[183]*Iliad*, XXIII, 328. Aristotle gives but one form of the statement.

[184]*Fragments*, 35, 14f., Diehls. Aristotle gives but one form of the sentence. The explanation seems to be that the Greek word for *before* can by punctuation be related to either preceding or following words.

[185]*Iliad*, X, 251: "More than two parts of the night have gone by, and a third part is still left." How could a third part be left when more than two thirds had passed? The word meaning *more than* perhaps means also *fully*.

[186]*Iliad*, XX, 234.

[187]*Iliad*, XXI, 592. "Of tin" is a standing epithet for greaves, though they probably were of some other metal.

[188]*Iliad*, XX, 272. When Aeneas flung his spear at Achilles, it pierced two layers of Achilles's shield only, for the layer of gold wrought by Hephaestos stopped it. But presumably the layer of gold was the outermost. How then could the spear pass through two layers and yet be stopped by the gold? Attempts at explanation seem somewhat absurd; apparently either the passage was corrupted or the key to its interpretation lost at an early date.

[189] Still a habit of critics in matters of more consequence than Aristotle here deals with. A large proportion of the adverse criticism of great authors is of this type.

stances relating to Icarius. The critics think he was a Laconian, and if he was, it is strange that Telemachus, when he went to Lacedaemon, did not see him. But perhaps it is as the Cephallenians say, for they declare that Odysseus married among them and that the name is Icadius and not Icarius.[190] Hence it is likely that the problem came into existence because of the mistake of the critics.

[The impossible. 61b9]

It is in general necessary to account for the impossible in poetry by saying that it makes a work better than the reality[191] or that it is in harmony with opinion,[192] for in poetry a credible impossibility is to be chosen before an incredible possibility.[193] Perhaps it is impossible that men should be such as Zeuxis painted them,[194] but it is better for them to be superior to the reality, because the artist ought to improve on his model. As to the irrational, it can be defended because it presents what is commonly said and also because sometimes it is not wholly irrational, for there is a probability things will happen contrary to probability.[195]

[Contradictions in language. 61b15]

Contradictions in language are to be examined like proofs in a debate, to see whether they indicate the same thing in the same relation and are used in the same way, that we may explain the

[190] *Odyssey*, IV. If Icadius, father of Penelope and therefore grandfather of Telemachus, lived at Sparta, Telemachus when in that city would hardly have failed to visit him.

[191] Tragedy represents men as better than those we know; see chaps. II and XV, 54b8. Cf. "as they ought to be" at the beginning of this chapter; it is another way of saying that men may be represented as better than the common run, as is shown by the remarks on Sophocles, Euripides, and Xenophanes earlier in the present chapter. Note "improve on his model" just below.

[192] Discussed just below as "what men say." The words translated thus and the verb corresponding to the word *opinion* (*dokeo, doxa*) are used near the beginning of the present chapter in setting forth the second aspect to be imitated, "as men say they are and they seem to be." Somewhat farther on the tales about the gods are justified for the artist because "men say so."

[193] Cf. chap. XXIV, 60a11, 60a26.

[194] See the Appendix to the *Poetics*, note 7, below.

[195] This saying is attributed to Agathon in chap. XVIII, 56a19, above. It is not wholly in harmony with Aristotle's saying that "the poet should choose probable impossibilities rather than incredible possibilities" (chap. XXIV, 60a26, above, and the beginning of chap. IX). From the present context one may infer some conflict between what seems rational to a cultivated reader and to a credulous one. Evidently, too, the author would be obliged to give some appearance of rationality to the event contrary to probability.

poet's work according to what he himself says or what a man of sense would assume. It is right to blame irrationality and wickedness when a poet uses irrationality without any necessity, as Euripides does in the instance of Aegeus,[196] or wickedness such as that of Menelaus in the *Orestes*.[197]

[What the critics object to. 61b22]

The matters objected to by critics, then, are of five species, the impossible, the irrational, the immoral, the contradictory, and that which violates correctness in poetic art. As may be seen from the twelve heads already given, the justifications are twelve in number.[198]

Chapter XXVI

[Epic and tragedy compared.[199] 61b26]

One may debate whether the epic imitation is better than the tragic. If the less vulgar is the better, and that is the one addressed to the better spectators, it is clear that the vulgar form of imitation is that addressed to everyone, for the performers, as though they were appearing before a stupid lot of hearers, indulge in a great deal of action; bad flute-players, for instance, twist about when they have to represent discus-throwing and tug at the leader of the chorus when they are playing the music relating to Scylla. Tragedy is said to do the same sort of thing, as the earlier actors thought the later ones did, for Mynniscus called Callippides the ape because he carried action to excess, and the same opinion was held of Pindar.[200] The whole art of tragedy is said to have the same relation to the epic as the later to the earlier actors. They say epic poetry addresses itself to cultivated spectators who do not need gestures, but tragedy to the vulgar. It is clear, then, that tragedy as a vulgar art is the lower one.

[Tragedy defended. 62a5]

In answer it may be said that this objection applies not to the poet but to the actor, since it is possible to overdo gesture in recit-

---

[196] Euripides, *Medea*, 663 ff. Aegeus appears without any reason to assure the safety of Medea.

[197] Already mentioned in chap. xv, first par.

[198] See the Appendix to the *Poetics*, note 8, below.

[199] Aristotle also compares epic and tragedy in chap. v, 49b9, chap. xviii, 56a10, and chap. xxiv, first two pars.   [200] An actor otherwise unknown.

ing an epic, as Sosistratus did, and in a lyrical contest, as Mnasitheus of Opus did. Then not all action is to be rejected, unless the dance is to be abolished, but only vulgar action, such as Callippides was blamed for and as at present is laid to the charge of others because they do not imitate free women. Tragedy may produce its effect without movement and action just as the epic does, for through reading we can find of what sort a play is.[201] Hence if tragedy is superior in other respects, the defect of vulgar action does not necessarily pertain to it.

[Tragedy superior. 62a14]

And it is superior, because it has everything the epic has, for it can even use the same meter, and in addition it has, as no trifling component, music and spectacle, in which the pleasure of tragedy to a great extent consists.[202] Then it has power both when read and when acted, and the end of the imitation is attained in less space, and the more concentrated is more pleasing than what is made thin by occupying a long time, as if one should put the *Oedipus* of Sophocles into as many words as the *Iliad* contains. Besides, the imitation of the epic poet is less compact; a proof of this is that from any epic poem several tragedies can be formed.[203] Hence if they compose a single plot, either it appears too short if concisely told, or watery if it conforms to the normal demands for length. I have in mind a poem made up of several actions, for the *Iliad*, and the *Odyssey* too, have many parts of this sort, and each part has a size of its own; yet these poems cohere perfectly, so to speak, and are as much as possible imitations of one action.[204] If then tragedy is superior in all these ways and in fulfilling the func-

[201] For the effect of tragedy without the performance of the play compare chap. VI, end; and chap. XIV, beginning.

[202] On the pleasure of tragedy see chaps. VI, 50a33 and IX, 51b19. The traditional text, defended by Rostagni, makes the last clause refer to music only. A conjectural emendation, to include spectacle also, made by Vahlen, is supported by the Arabic translation.

[203] See the Appendix to the *Poetics*, note 9, below.

[204] Even the admired Homer seems to have carried his use of the episode too far, for the old epics are too long to be taken in at one view (chap. XXIV, 59b17); they have, however, the advantage of variety (*ibid.*). Did Aristotle know an epic that is too short in contrast to the "watery" plot of even the Homeric poems? It is suggested that he had in mind the work of Chaeremon, mentioned in chaps. I, 47a28, and XXIV, 59b31.

Milton referred to "the two poems of Homer, and those other two of Vergil and Tasso" as "diffuse" models of the epic form and called "the book of Job a brief model" of the same form (*The Reason of Church Government*, Introduction to Bk. II), perhaps echoing Aristotle's "watery" and "short," though it seems without suggestion of censure.

tion of the art—for it is necessary that poems produce not any
pleasure they happen to but such as I have spoken of—it is clear
that tragedy is superior to the epic because it attains its end better.

[Comedy. 62b16]

About tragedy and epic in themselves and about their species
and parts, with their number and differences, and the causes of
good and bad quality, and critical objections and their solutions I
have said enough. On iambic poetry and comedy. . . .[205]

APPENDIX TO THE *Poetics*

Note 1

Recognition through false reasoning, chapter XVI, 55a12.

One Greek manuscript, Riccardianus 46, supported by the Arabic
translation, gives a number of words not found in the traditional text.
These, with one correction, are admitted into the text by Margoliouth
and Rostagni. Gudeman holds that with the longer form as a basis the
Austrian scholar Tkatsch has with probability restored the genuine
text, yet does not admit the longer form into his own text. I have,
however, incorporated a translation of Tkatsch's reading. Margoliouth
translates as follows: "That Odysseus and no one else could string the
bow is assumed in the fiction by Homer, though Penelope *thinks*
'Odysseus will know the bow which this beggar has not seen'; to produce the disclosure by the *knowing*, when it was to have been by the
stringing, is a case of misleading." The Riccardianus has the false
messenger say he would string it. If this be accepted, the false reasoning
might consist in believing the messenger when he says he can string the
bow instead of demanding that he do it. But the word translated *string*
is probably an error for *recognize*.

I render Rostagni's translation and explanation as follows: "*That he
[Odysseus?] and no one else should be able to string the bow is a thing imagined
[or given as a fact] by the poet, and constitutes the presupposition.* To understand this I turn to the definition of paralogism in chap. XXIV, 60a21,
where I read that a truth, B, follows from a false presupposition, A, laid
down as true; then through paralogism the hearers are led to hold that

---

[205] One ms. shows letters interpreted to mean something like the words in the last
incomplete sentence. They apparently indicate a second book of the *Poetics* in which
Aristotle kept the promise to discuss comedy made in chap. VI.

the presupposition A is also true. Then, in our case, it was an incredible thing that Odysseus alone and no other man was able to string the bow; it was a false presupposition given as true by the poet; but since through that means Odysseus really makes himself known, men are induced to admit that what was presupposed was also true."

He then continues to translate and comment: "*If also [Odysseus?] said that he was able to recognize the bow which he was unable to have seen.* Here Aristotle perhaps refers to some expression of the drama which made still greater the incredible quality of the presupposition."

And further: "*Even though by means of it he caused himself to be recognized, there is a paralogism in thinking it true for that reason. . . .* Then the paralogism consists in laying down as true the false or incredible presupposition, because by means of this Odysseus (or whoever it may be) is truly caused to be recognized."

Part of Albeggiani's note may be translated: "The most probable explanation seems to me the following. Aristotle says there exists among others a form of recognition resulting from a paralogism in which the public has a part. The paralogism contained in the tragedy of *Ulysses the False Messenger* would consist in the fact that Ulysses is recognized through his own recognition of his bow, instead of through stringing it, which would be a justifiable recognition. The recognition of Ulysses by means of the fact that he recognizes his bow implies a paralogism, because even if the owner of an object is in a position to recognize it, not everyone who recognizes it is therefore the owner. This interpretation, though not confirmed by any knowledge of the tragedy mentioned, seems to me acceptable because the most probable, when compared with the others. The interpretation indeed (Rostagni's, as given above) which makes the recognition by paralogism depend on the stringing of the bow, in which Ulysses succeeds, does not indicate how it is a paralogism, because the recognition by the stringing that Ulysses performs on a bow he alone is able to string is not a paralogism. Valgimigli also deals with a recognition by paralogism, in that the public is inclined to believe Ulysses is identified through his recognition of the bow, but, not to mention other difficulties, this interpretation takes away the character of a paralogism from the recognition, and therefore is inacceptable."

The passage is obviously difficult, and the more so because in our ignorance of the drama referred to we are likely to be too much or too little influenced by the apparently related passages in the *Odyssey*, that of the return of Odysseus in disguise (*Odyssey*, XIX, 164-260) alluded to by Aristotle in chap. XXIV, 60a18, and that in which Penelope promises to marry the man who can string the bow of Odysseus and make a certain skillful shot with it; all fail to string the bow except Odysseus himself (*Odyssey*, xxi). For false reasoning see also chap. xxiv, 60a18.

Note 2

Recognition, chapter xvi, 55a16.

The poet must always prepare for his scene of recognition, and the more for one of the best class. But the other classes require the poet to have something done or to provide something for the sake of the recognition. Even the recognition by a syllogism is not free from this. In the *Choephoroe*, used by Aristotle as an example, the hair of Orestes and his footprints serve as the basis of the syllogism, which is reinforced by bringing proof according to the first and least artistic method. In some of Aristotle's other examples of the syllogism probably no material objects are used; still the character says something "devised by the poet" to serve as the basis of the reasoning. Aristotle's principle evidently is that as little effort as possible should be obvious in the recognition; the poet should not have devised some addition to the story for the sake of the recognition, but, as in the *Oedipus Tyrannus* and the recognition by Orestes in the *Iphigenia*, it should be incidental to what is done for other purposes of the action rather than an end in itself.

For him the matter was clearer than for critics of modern literature. The traditional plot is the same for plays by several Greek authors. That plot involves a recognition, as of Orestes by Electra, but the tradition does not specify its method. The most skillful author is he who is obliged to "devise" for himself and add to the traditional story the smallest amount, not demanded by the plot, for the sake of the necessary recognition. Euripides, for example, was obliged to make and put on the brow of Orestes a scar through which Electra could recognize him (*Electra*, 573). Cf. chap. xvi, 54b30, and notes, above.

Note 3

Poetic madness, chapter xvii, 55a22

The traditional text presents an alternative: "either the gifted man or the madman." Gudeman, whose text I follow, justifies his reading from the Arabic translation of the *Poetics* and from the manuscript called Riccardianus 46. Castelvetro suggests the same reading, though

it is not in his Greek text (on *Poetics*, XVII, pp. 352–3, below). Margoliouth translates the Arabic as follows: "Quare est ars poetica ingeniosi
magis quam dementium." Bywater does not accept the Arabic text,
but his translation is somewhat softened, being "one with a touch of
madness in him." Something of the sort was suggested by Tyrwhitt in
1806. On this "furor poeticus" see the index under *inspiration*.

   There is difference of opinion about Aristotle's meaning in the word
madman. Does it refer to the mentally deranged person or to the
inspired poet? Is it an attack on Plato, who sometimes uses the word
madness (*mania*, from the same root as Aristotle's word) in speaking of
the inspiration of the poet (*Phaedrus*, 245)? In the *Ion* words from a
different root are generally used, that meaning *inspired by some god*
being frequent. Aristotle uses the latter word when he says that
"poetry is a thing inspired by the god" (*Rhetoric*, III, 7, 1408b19).
Though less vigorous than that, the present passage does not suggest
that the poet can succeed by art alone, as might be inferred from
Poetics, VIII, and as Aristotle's analytic habits might influence us to
suppose he would have thought; natural endowment at least is needed.
Socrates in Plato's *Phaedrus* says that madness is indispensable to the
poet (the appendix to the *Ion*, above).

   Dryden writes: "They who would justify the madness of poetry from
the authority of Aristotle have mistaken the text, and consequently the
interpretation; I imagine it to be false read, where he says of poetry that
it is εὐφυοῦς ἢ μανικοῦ that it had always somewhat in it either of a
genius or of a madman. 'Tis more probable that the original ran thus,
that poetry was εὐφυοῦς οὐ μανικοῦ, that it belongs to a witty man,
but not to a madman" (Preface to *Troilus and Cressida*, Ker's *Essays of
Dryden*, I, 221–2). Dryden is believed to have derived his idea from
Rapin, who attributes it to Castelvetro.

Note 4

The species and parts of tragedy, chapter XVIII, 55b32

   This is a difficult passage. Gudeman would make it a reference to
the six parts of tragedy (plot, character, thought, diction, melody,
spectacle) with the exception of the last two; these parts are used as
species (see chap. VI, 49b31). This opinion is supported by the opening of chap. XXIV, where the parts are mentioned with the exception of
the last two, and the species are given as the simple, the complex, that
dealing with character, and that dealing with suffering.

Rostagni objects to any connection with chap. VI or chap. XXIV, writing in part as follows: "The four species of tragedy, graduated from the best to the worst, are the involved, the pathetic, that emphasizing character, and a fourth, a little apart from these, founded on spectacle. Referring to chap. XXIV, where Aristotle says that the species of epic are the same as those of tragedy and enumerates them as simple, complex, emphasizing character, and pathetic, the critics usually hold that there is a lacuna or error in the classification here and that the simple species should in some way be restored to it. I believe they are wrong, for various reasons: (1) We have here a sliding scale, based on a special conception of tragedy, and there an enumeration. (2) The difference between one classification and the other is not so great that, when the point of view is changed, Aristotle could not in the end have thought them identical, especially since the tragic species labeled as spectacular was essentially simple. (3) With the present classification it is possible to decide the corresponding parts of tragedy, the determination of which is one of the cruxes most troublesome to commentators." Continuing, he comments on the words *the same number of parts has been mentioned:* "This clearly refers to the parts or elements of tragedy as they respectively correspond with the four species of tragedy. They cannot be the quantitative parts discussed in chap. XII, nor the qualitative parts of chap. VI, because the latter are six and not four; strictly they cannot (in spite of all the efforts of the commentators) be four of the six, because if, in order to get four of them, we exclude diction and thought, which indeed Aristotle has not yet treated (see chap. XIX), we should for the same reason exclude melody; there would remain three, plot, character, and spectacle, which would not correspond, as such, to the species taken one by one. Consequently, Aristotle has employed the word *parts* with complete freedom, as he often does, referring not to the letter and not to a specific paragraph, but to the marrow of his own treatise. Certainly according to that, the parts or elements that appear essential to the specifically tragic aspect, in relation, I assert, to the function of tragedy are (1) peripety and recognition, closely connected (see chap. XI) and constituting at bottom a single thing, or the elements contrary to expectation [chap. IX, last paragraph]; (2) suffering, which Aristotle has treated at length and clearly in chap. XIII; (3) character, treated in chap. XV; (4) the fourth (with Greek *de,* as an element a little lower in rank) the spectacle, of which it has been said in chap. XIV that even from this it is possible to obtain the effect proper to tragedy, though to avail himself of it is a sign of a poet of the lower rank.

"It is to be understood that in substance the preceding is equivalent to the group of three—plot, character, and spectacle—of the first and general classification (since the plot includes peripety and recognition and suffering as its three parts—chap. xi), and if for that we merely substitute this new terminology and grouping into four (which is confirmed in chap. xxiv, first sentence) we obtain the number and the exact correspondence with the four species."

If Aristotle's meaning can be worked out—I am not sure it can be—Rostagni's explanation is an ingenious one. I find it difficult, however, to accept the spectacular as the fourth class, for the following reasons: (1) chap. xxiv does give four classes, of which the simple is one; (2) the *Prometheus*, used as an example in chap. xviii, being without peripety and recognitions, has a simple plot; (3) I am not sure that the simple and the spectacular can be identified; (4) while Aristotle does speak of the effect of the spectacle,[1] he yet so stigmatizes it as inartistic (chap. vi, at the end; chap. xiv, first par.) that I hestitate to believe he would have allowed it even a subordinate position among his four classes. In his discussion of the marrow of tragedy (chaps. vi–xviii) it seems to me he is concerned chiefly with plot and character, leaving thought and diction for later treatment and giving no sign that he intends independent consideration of melody and spectacle. The passages on spectacle (chap. vi, end; chap. xiv, beginning) I take as incidental to the discussion of plot. The latter reference seems to be more favorable than the first, in admitting that pity and fear can come from what meets the eye, yet still indicates that the good artist does not rely on the extraneous aid of the staging but on the plot. If Aristotle is dealing with the marrow of tragedy, he can dismiss spectacle.

I should, then, modify Rostagni's exposition by finding the four parts, corresponding to the four species, in plot and character alone, and follow the editors who consider as a species the simple tragedy mentioned in chap. xxiv instead of the spectacular. The word *simple* applied to a plot is not wholly negative, since such a plot imitates an action of a simple type, must be composed according to the principles of art, and has a change of fortune (chap. x, beginning). This change of fortune might without much straining be considered one of the parts of the plot; it occurs in all plots, while the peripety is a part found only in some of them; there are two sorts of change, one without peripety, the other with it. In the present chapter (xviii) as in chap. x, the word meaning *involved* is applied to both involved plot and involved tragedy. It seems

[1] Chaps. xiv, 53b1; xxvi, 62a14 and note. In the last Rostagni's note seems to work against the importance he gives spectacle in the paragraphs just quoted.

that the same thing might be true of the word for *simple*, and the simple tragedy be that with the simple plot, as the involved tragedy has an involved plot. If in chap. xiii we are told that the structure of the most excellent tragedy is involved, we yet see in chap. x clear recognition that there are tragedies of simple structure.

Chap. xxiv indicates that the classes of epic are not always mutually exclusive, for the *Iliad* is simple and pathetic, and the *Odyssey* is involved and emphasizes character. Unless it is impossible for an involved tragedy to depend on the art of the designer of stage effects, the spectacular tragedy can hardly be identified with the simple, for an involved tragedy might also be spectacular, but a simple tragedy cannot ever be involved. Need it be spectacular?

In my discussion I have disregarded what editors say on the evidence of the manuscripts. Bywater and Rostagni hold that three unintelligible letters are an error for part of the word for *spectacle*. Butcher accepts the reference to spectacle, but thinks there is an omission such that Aristotle gave the fourth class as the simple. Gudeman holds that the three letters cannot signify *spectacle*. Albeggiani, who usually follows Rostagni, prefers the reading meaning *simple*.

Note 5

The parts of tragedy, chapter xxiv, 59b7

Various commentators remark on the absence from this sentence of character, the second of the elements of tragedy in importance (chap. vi, 50a33), which has just been said to determine one of the species of tragedy and epic, as recognition and discovery determine the involved tragedy, and suffering the pathetic tragedy. An emendation, with no manuscript authority, has even been suggested to supply the omission. While there seems to be no support for the emendation, the reasons against expecting a reference to character given by Rostagni and Bywater seem to me unconvincing. Perhaps this is one of the instances where the quality of the *Poetics* as a collection of notes rather than a logical treatise appears. The second sentence of the chapter, "The parts of the epic . . . be well handled," is thrust into the current of the thought, for the "all these" (third sentence) that Homer used are the species of epic that immediately appear in classifying the *Iliad* and the *Odyssey*. Obviously in using these species, he used the elements of plot, and also thought and diction—which are specified—and character, which is not.

I do not understand that the number of the species and parts is here said to be the same (see chap. vi, 49b31, and note, chap. xviii, 55b32, and the note immediately preceding the present one).

Note 6

The improbable, chapter xxiv, 60a26

In the *Electra* of Sophocles, Orestes himself, Pylades, and an old servant come to Argos pretending that they have in an urn the ashes of Orestes, killed in a chariot race at the Pythian games. An early suggestion, still approved by commentators, is that the improbability referred to by Aristotle is the anachronism of employing the games in an action that took place before they existed. But, as Castelvetro says (567, 10, below), Aristotle is not speaking of historical improbability, but of one in the structure of the plot, as in the *Oedipus*. Bywater is willing to consider the opinion of Robortello that it is absurd for Clytemnestra to learn the news first from the old servant, for Argives must have been returning from the games with news of them. Castelvetro presents the same opinion at length (568, 1). News of the games might have reached Argos before the false messengers if they had really seen the contests, but since they did not see them they could arrive when they pleased. According to their tale, however, they waited long enough for the funeral rites of Orestes, yet an early arrival is accounted for when Sophocles has the old servant say that the body was "straightway" burned on the pyre. Are we to suppose that Clytemnestra, Electra, and Aegisthus knew the program of the games and the time at which the first news might arrive, so they were well prepared to suspect either a too-early arrival of news or an addition to the first reports? A further improbability is that Aegisthus has heard how Orestes met his death, but not that ashes rather than a body have been brought (ll. 1441 ff.).

Note 7

Men as represented by Zeuxis, chapter xxv, 61b9

Zeuxis appears as an artist who represented men as better than they are; Polygnotus is used for the same purpose in chap. ii. The two are contrasted in chap. vi. Aristotle's opinion is confirmed by the well-known story of the artist's choice of the five most beautiful virgins in Croton, that their qualities might be combined in his painting of Helen, who would thus appear physically superior to women as they are (Cicero, *De inventione*, II, 1). Quintilian (XII, 10) said of him that "he gave greater size to the parts of the body, because he thought it made his work more splendid and impressive, and is said to have followed Homer, who admired women with the most vigorous bodies."

I translate the text with an addition from the Arabic version accepted by Butcher and Rostagni; Gudeman thinks the addition should be printed as a variant. Butcher translates: "It may be impossible that there should be men such as Zeuxis painted. Yes! we say, but the impossible is the higher thing." "Superior to the reality" refers to the second point in the first sentence of the present paragraph.

Note 8

The twelve critical justifications, chapter XXV, 61b22

Gudeman's list of the twelve is as follows:

I The impossible is justified thus:
   1 It "serves the end of poetry" (60b23).
   2 It is incidentally connected "with the poem" (*ibid.*).
II The irrational is justified thus:
   3 It is as men "were or are" (60b32).
   4 "They are as they should be" (*ibid.*).
   5 It is "as men say" it is (*ibid.*).
III The immoral is justified thus:
   6 We should consider "the one who acts or speaks, and to whom and when and how and because of what" (*ibid.*).
IV The contradictory is justified thus:
   7 Poetical speeches "are to be examined like proofs in a debate" (61b15).
V Violations of correctness in poetic art are justified thus:
   8 Through explanation of a "borrowed word" or a metaphor (61a9).
   9 Because of "change in the way of reading" (*ibid.*).
  10 By "a change in punctuation" (*ibid.*).
  11 By "ambiguity" (*ibid.*).
  12 By "the habit of language" (*ibid.*).

Rostagni gives the same list, except that he breaks no. 8 into two and compensates by omitting no. 7; the contradictory, thus omitted, for him includes—if I may infer from a note on the contradictions discussed in the preceding paragraph—the matter listed under headings 8–12.

Note 9

Epic unity, chapter XXVI, 62a14

In this and the following sentences, Aristotle shows that even the work of Homer, which he so greatly admired, is structurally inferior to the best tragedy; tragedy can imitate one action, while the epic can only do so to a limited extent, in Homer "as much as possible." The remark on the unity of the Homeric poems in chap. VIII, is, then, to be taken with implied qualification, though Homer's works appear absolutely unified in comparison with those of other epic poets. The central story of the best epics, as appears in the summary of the *Odyssey* in chap. XVII, 55a34 has this unified character. The added parts are episodes and do not pertain to the plot proper. Chap. XXIII is devoted to the same matter; the central plot of a Homeric epic can provide one or two tragedies, while other epics may furnish as many as eight. That Odysseus was wounded on Parnassus is for Homer an episode to explain the scar; for an inferior poet it would have been part of the plot (chap. VIII, above). Homer can, however, elaborate it to more than a hundred lines (*Odyssey*, XIX, 392 ff.); a tragedy cannot properly make use of a similar episode (see chap. XXIV, 59b17, above); for example Euripides, to explain a scar on the forehead of Orestes (*Electra*, 573–4), crowds in a line and a half. Cf. chap. XVI, 54b30 and notes.

HORACE

o◯oo◯o

THE ART OF POETRY

Perhaps composed in 14 or 13 B.C.[1]

THE MODERN READER who comes to this poem of Horace for the first time is likely to feel some disappointment on observing its quality as an "unmethodical miscellany," as Coleridge called it.[2] Parts are even to be called perfunctory, as though Horace on being asked to say something on poetry turned to the most convenient treatise on the subject and borrowed freely; it is established that he followed a Greek book on poetry by Neoptolemus of Parium. Why did an author so experienced as Horace prefer to repeat conventional matter rather than rely on his own observations? Why did he write chiefly on the drama rather than on the sort of verse he is famous for? A satisfactory answer would involve an understanding of the mind of Horace and his relation, especially on the intellectual rather than the emotional side, to his art; it would furnish suggestion for thought on the nature of poetic genius and the extent to which any poet is likely to be capable of rational or logical observation of his own processes and those of his fellow artists. It is at least important for the student of criticism to observe such a production as the first in a long series of utterances of poets on their own art.

But though parts of the work seem lifeless and the arrangement haphazard, even the modern reader who is not repelled by his first view will find that many passages bear the impress of an observing mind and are illuminated by the genius of the poet. Reasons will be discovered why the *Art of Poetry* has been the guidebook of so many artists, such as Dante, Ben Jonson, and Byron. In the history of criticism only Aristotle's *Poetics* surpasses it in influence.

Recent study indicates that the *Art of Poetry* is less formless than has been supposed, that even though it obviously has the qualities of an

---

[1] This is the date preferred by Rostagni (see the bibliography). Immisch prefers a date some years earlier.

[2] Scaliger says that Horace in his *Art of Poetry* teaches without any art (*Poetice* [1561], Epistola, sig. a. IV).

epistle and is the work of a poet, it is also a formal discussion of the poetic art. The construction is that of the treatises on poetry—especially the drama—developed on an Aristotelian basis and known to the contemporaries of Horace. Their basis is a threefold division into what may be called *poetry* (concerned with poetic content), *poetics* (technique, language, verse), and *the poet*. The first two concern the art, the last the artist. The same topics are properly considered in different aspects under different heads; this gives, however, a superficial appearance of disorder. In fact the tripartite system is not one that commends itself to the judgment of the present. With this method in mind, Rostagni divides the *Art of Poetry* as follows:

1–41 The content of poetry.

   1–37 Simplicity and unity.

   38–41 Adaptation to the powers of the writer.

42–294 The technique of poetry.

   42–45 Arrangement.

   46–72 The choice of words.

   73–85 Composition.

   86–92 The style should be appropriate to the subject or the literary type.

   93–113 But there are exceptions; style must be appropriate to the passions represented.

   114–118 It must be appropriate to the characters.

   119–127 Traditional and consistent characters.

   128–130 Originality.

   131–152 Originality in respect to well-known themes.

   153–294 Concrete applications.

     153–219 Tragedy (with principles applicable to comedy).

       153–155 Introduction.

       156–178 Characters in tragedy.

       179–188 Tragic action.

       189–190 Length.

       191–192 *Deus ex machina*.

       193–201 The chorus.

       202–219 Music.

     220–250 Satyric drama.

     251–274 Verse.

     275–294 History of the drama.

295–476 The poet.

   295–308 Introduction.

   309–332 Philosophical preparation of the poet.

Immisch gives a somewhat different division, making the three main sections 1–152, 153–294, 295–476. The first deals with the art of poetry in general, without special treatment of its historical species; the second with poetry as divided into its species; the last with the poet.

To Klingner preceding outlines seem too exclusively concerned with one aspect of the epistle, such as its relation to Greek sources, too little regardful of the concrete situation in which Horace found himself, and prone to neglect the satirical character of the poem; it should be looked on as an expression of the mind and situation of Horace rather than as a formal treatise. Such divisions as he makes, however, often coincide with those of Rostagni; for example, the second main division begins with line 295.

The translation by Edward Henry Blakeney, M.A., slightly modified according to his directions, has been used with his kind permission. The editor is responsible for the notes.

BIBLIOGRAPHY

Blakeney, Edward H., *Horace on the Art of Poetry*. London, 1928. This volume contains the Latin text, English prose translation, the verse translation of Ben Jonson, introduction, and notes.

Cook, Albert S., *The Art of Poetry*. New York, 1926. This volume contains translations of the poetical treatises of Horace, Vida, and Boileau, edited with introduction and notes.

D'Alton, J. F., *Horace and His Age*. London, 1917.

Fairclough, H. Rushton, *Horace, Satires, Epistles, and Ars Poetica*. Latin text with an English translation. Loeb Classics, 1926.

Fiske, George C., *Lucilius and Horace, a Study in the Classical Theory of Imitation*. Madison, 1920.

Fiske, George C., *Cicero's "De Oratore" and Horace's "Ars Poetica."* Madison, 1929.

Immisch, Otto, *Horazens Epistel über die Dichtkunst* (*Philologus*, Supplementband, xxiv, Heft 3). Leipzig, 1932.

Klingner, Friedrich, *Horazens Brief an die Pisonen*, in Berichte über die Verhandlungen der Sächsischen Akademie der Wissenschaften, Phil.-hist. Klasse. Leipzig, 1937.

Rostagni, Augusto, *Arte poetica di Orazio*. Torino, 1930. Latin text with introduction and notes. I am much indebted to this edition.

Sellar, William Young, *The Roman Poets of the Augustan Age: Horace and the Elegiac Poets*. Oxford, 1892.

Showerman, Grant, *Horace and His Influence*. Boston, 1922.

THE ART OF POETRY

SUPPOSE a painter chose to couple a horse's neck with a human head, and to lay feathers of every hue on limbs gathered here and there,[1] so that a woman, lovely above, foully ended in an ugly fish below; would you restrain your laughter, my friends, if admitted to a private view? Believe me, dear Pisos,[2] a book will appear uncommonly like that picture, if impossible figures are wrought into it—like a sick man's dreams—with the result that neither head nor foot is ascribed to a single shape, and unity is lost.[3]

"But poets and painters have always had an equal right to indulge their whims."[4] Quite so: and this excuse we claim for ourselves and grant to others: but not so that harsh may mate with gentle, serpents be paired with birds, lambs with tigers.

Frequently grave openings, that promise much, have one or two purple patches tagged on, to catch the eye and enhance the colour. Thus, for example, we get descriptions of "Diana's grove and altar,"[5] "the moving waters hurrying through fair fields," or get a picture of the Rhine, or of a rainbow; but all the time there is no place for these scenes. Perhaps you know how to limn a cypress;[6] but what avails this if you have to represent a sailor, who has paid to have his portrait painted, as struggling hopelessly to shore from a wreck? A wine-jar was designed: why, when the wheel goes round, does it come out a pitcher?[7] In short, be your subject what you will, only let it be simple and consistent.

[1] That is from animals of various species.

[2] The *Art of Poetry* is an epistle addressed to a father and two sons bearing the family name of Piso.   [3] Cf. Aristotle, VIII, 51a16, above.

[4] Poetic license. Lucian (*Pro imaginibus*, 18) refers to an old saying to the effect that poets and painters are not to be held accountable.

[5] Perhaps a reference to the sanctuary called Numus Dianae, near the town of Aricia, in the forest on the slopes of Mt. Albanus and on the shore of what is now called the lake of Nemi.

[6] The painter's skill is the more unsuitable because the cypress is the tree of funerals.

[7] Instead of a large and elegant vessel the unskillful potter produces a small and undistinguished one.

Most of us poets—O father, and sons worthy of your father,—are misled by our idea of what is correct. I try to be terse, and end by being obscure; another strives after smoothness, to the sacrifice of vigour and spirit; a third aims at grandeur, and drops into bombast; a fourth, through excess of caution and a fear of squalls, goes creeping along the ground. He who is bent on lending variety to a theme that is by nature uniform, so as to produce an unnatural effect, is like a man who paints a dolphin in a forest or a wild boar in the waves. If artistic feeling is not there, mere avoidance of a fault leads to some worse defect.

The humblest bronze-smith who lives near the Aemilian training school will depict you nails, and imitate waving hair in metal, yet fail in his work because he cannot represent the figure as a whole.[8] Now, if I wanted to compose a work, I should no more wish to be like that smith than to live admired for my dark eyes and dark hair while I had a crooked nose.

You writers, choose a subject that is within your powers, and ponder long what your shoulders can and cannot bear.[9] He who makes every effort to select his theme aright will be at no loss for choice words or lucid arrangement.

[42] Unless I am mistaken, the force and charm of arrangement will be found in this: to say at once what ought at once to be said, deferring many points, and waiving them for the moment.

Careful and nice, too, in his choice of words, the author of the promised poem must reject one word and welcome another; you will have expressed yourself admirably if a clever setting gives a spice of novelty to a familiar word.[10]

[47] If by chance some abstruse subject needs new terms to make the meaning clear, it will be right to frame words never heard of by old-fashioned folk like the Cethegi, and the licence will be allowed if not abused; new and lately-minted words will be accepted if drawn from a Greek source, provided this be done sparingly. Why should a Roman grant to Caecilius and Plautus a

[8] Workers in bronze had their shops at the Aemilian school for the training of gladiators, near the Forum. For the idea cf. Catullus, *Epigram* 87, as translated by Lovelace:

> Quintia is handsome, fair, tall, straight; all these
> Very particulars I grant with ease.
> But she all o'er's not handsome; here's her fault:
> In all that bulk, there's not one corn of salt.
> While Lesbia fair and handsome too all o'er
> All graces and all wit from all hath bore.

[9] Referred to by Dante in his work *On the Vulgar Tongue*, II, 4.

[10] Cf. Aristotle, *Poetics*, XXI, 57b1, above.

privilege denied to Virgil and Varius? Why am I myself, if I can capture a phrase or two, grudged this freedom, seeing that the works of Cato and Ennius[11] have enriched the mother-tongue and broadcasted new names for things? It has always been and always will be permissible to circulate a word stamped with the hall-mark of the day.

As forests suffer change of leaves with each declining year, so the earliest-invented words are the first to fall: an elder generation passes away and new-born words, like youth, flourish and grow. Death claims both us and our works. What matter if the sea, let into the heart of the land, shelters our ships from the north winds— a right royal work; or the marsh, long barren and fit for boats alone, feeds neighbouring cities and groans under the ploughshare; or the river, taught a better channel, has changed its course once ruinous to crops? The works of men's hands must perish, much less can the glory and charm of words endure undecaying. Many a word long disused will revive, and many now high in esteem will fade, if Custom wills it, in whose power lie the arbitrament, the rule, and the standard of language.[12]

[73] Homer has shown in what metre the deeds of kings and captains and the sorrows of war may be written. First came the voice of lament, in couplets unequally paired; then the joy of the successful lover: but who the author was that first published the dainty measures, critics dispute, and the matter is still unjudged.

It was fury that armed Archilochus with his own device, the iamb; this metre comedy and stately tragedy adopted, as fitted for dialogue, drowning the din of the audience, and born for action.[13]

The Muse has assigned to the lyre the work of celebrating gods and heroes, the champion boxer, the victorious steed, the fond desire of lovers, and the cup that banishes care.

---

[11] Ennius was called the father of Roman poetry. Only fragments of his works (tragedies, comedies, epic poetry, and other writings in verse and prose) are now extant. He is thought to have been somewhat younger than Plautus. Horace speaks disparagingly of him in lines 259–62.

[12] Horace was well aware that works of art grow old-fashioned and lose their power. Cf. Giraldi, *Romances*, sect. 28, below, and Phillips, *Theatrum Poetarum*, sect. 2, below. Pope renders the idea:

> Our sons their fathers' failing language see,
> And such as Chaucer is shall Dryden be.
>
> *Essay on Criticism*, 482–3.

[13] Aristotle makes Homer the first iambic poet known by name (*Poetics*, IV, 48b24, above). Horace follows Alexandrian scholars.

[86] In works of genius are clearly marked differences of subject and shades of style. If, through ignorance, I fail to maintain these, why hail me Poet? Why, from a false shame, do I prefer ignorance to knowledge? A subject for comedy refuses to be handled in tragic verse; the banquet of Thyestes disdains to be rehearsed in lines suited to daily life[14] and right enough for comedy. At times, however, even Comedy exalts her voice, and an angry Chremes rants and raves;[15] often, too, in a tragedy Telephus or Peleus utters his sorrow in the language of prose, when, poor and in exile, he flings aside his paint-pots and his words a yard long, in eagerness to touch the spectator's heart with his lamentable tale.[16]

[99] It is not enough for poems to be fine; they must charm, and draw the mind of the listener at will. As the human face answers a smile with a smile, so does it wait upon tears; if you would have me weep, you must first of all feel grief yourself;[17] then and not till then will your misfortunes, Telephus or Peleus, touch me. If the part assigned you is not in character, I shall fall asleep or laugh.

Sad words suit a gloomy countenance, menacing words an angry; sportive words a merry look, stern words a grim one. For Nature shapes first our inner thoughts to take the bent of circumstance; she moves to gladness or drives to anger, bows the heart to earth and tortures it with bitter grief. After, with the tongue her aid, does she express emotion.

[112] If a speaker's words are out of gear with his fortunes, all Rome, horse and foot, will guffaw. It will make a world of difference whether god or demigod be talking; an old man well on in years or a stripling in the first flush of youth; a wealthy dame or some bustling nurse; a roving trader or a son of the soil; a Colchian or an Assyrian; one reared in Argos or in Thebes.[18]

[119] Either stick to tradition or see that your inventions be consistent.[19] If when writing a play you introduce yet again the "far-famed Achilles," make him impatient, hot-tempered, ruthless, fierce; he must disown all laws: they were not made for *him;* his appeal will be to the sword. In like manner let Medea be high-

---

[14] Or *to private affairs.* Theophrastus's definition of comedy ("a harmless bringing together of private affairs") seems to have been in the mind of Horace. For Heywood's use of it see *Apology for Actors,* Bk. III, sect. 3, below. For the general acceptance of this notion, see *comedy* in the index.

[15] Perhaps a reference to Terence, *Heautontimorumenos,* Act V.

[16] Cf. Giraldi, *Orbecche,* 108, below.

[17] A well-known line. Cf. Aristotle, *Poetics,* XVII, first par., immediately above.

[18] See also ll. 153 ff., below.

[19] Cf. Aristotle, *Poetics,* IX, 51b19, immediately above.

hearted and unconquerable, Ino tearful, Ixion a traitor, Io a wanderer, Orestes forlorn.

[125] If you bring on to the stage a subject unattempted yet, and are bold enough to create a fresh character, let him remain to the end such as he was when he first appeared—consistent throughout.[20] It is hard to treat a hackneyed theme with originality,[21] and you act more rightly by dramatizing the *Iliad* than by introducing a subject unknown and hitherto unsung. [240–3] I shall aim at a poem so deftly fashioned out of familiar matter that anybody might hope to emulate the feat, yet for all his efforts sweat and labour in vain. Such is the power of order and arrangement; such the charm that waits upon common things.[22] [131] The common quarry will become your own by right, if you do not dally in the cheap and easy round; if you do not, an all too faithful translator, essay to render your author word for word; if you do not—a mere copyist—take a plunge into some narrow pit from which diffidence or the conditions of the work itself forbid you to escape.

Nor should your exordium be like that of the cyclic poet of old: "I'll sing the fate of Priam, and the famous war of Troy." What will this writer produce worthy of such mouthing? it will be a case of "mountains in labour and—a mouse comes out!" Much better he who makes no ill-judged effort: "Sing me, O Muse, the tale of that hero who, after the capture of Troy, surveyed the manners and cities of mankind."

[143] His aim is to fetch not smoke from a flash but light from smoke, that afterwards he may bring you marvels of the picturesque—Antiphates and the Cyclops, Scylla and Charybdis. He does not date "the Return of Diomed" from Meleager's death,[23] nor the Trojan war from the twin eggs:[24] he ever hurries to the crisis and carries the listener into the midst of the story as though

---

[20] Cf. Aristotle, *Poetics*, xv, first par., immediately above.

[21] The Latin word *communia* (hackneyed theme) has caused much debate. Rostagni holds that it means subjects not appropriated by tradition and history, quoting from a scholiast: *communia . . . idest intacta*. Such an explanation fits with the rest of the sentence.

[22] The four lines preceding seem to Mr. Blakeney to belong here rather than in their usual position.

[23] Diomedes took part in the second expedition against Thebes, conducted by the Epigoni. Meleager was an older son of Diomedes's grandfather, Oeneus. On the death of Meleager, his mother Althaea committed suicide. Oeneus then married Periboea, who bore Tydeus, the father of Diomedes.

[24] Leda was loved by Zeus, who visited her in the form of a swan. She produced two eggs, from one of which issued Castor and Pollux, and from the other Helen of Troy.

it were already known;[25] what he despairs of illuminating with his touch he omits; and so employs fiction, so blends false with true, that beginning, middle, and end all strike the same note.[26]

[153] Now hear what I, and the world at large, expect. If you want an appreciative audience that will sit quiet till the curtain drops and the call for "cheers" begins, you must observe the characteristics of each age and assign a fitting grace[27] to natures that shift with the years. The child who can just talk and feel his feet with confidence longs to play with his peers; is quick to anger, as quick to cool; his moods change hourly. The beardless boy, his tutor out of the way, finds delight in horses and dogs and the turf of the sunny plain. Pliant as wax to vice, he is gruff with his counsellors, slow to provide for his own best interests, lavish with his money; high-spirited, passionate, ready to discard his fancies. With manhood comes a change of tastes: his aim now is money and friendship; he will be the slave of ambition, and will shun doing what, later on, he might wish to undo.

Many are the discomforts of age, partly because the old man, ever amassing, shrinks from his gains and dares not enjoy them; partly because he handles everything in chill and listless fashion,— irresolute, a laggard in hope, lazy, greedy of long life, cross-grained, querulous, one who extols the past as it was "when I was a boy"; a censor and critic of the rising generation. The years as they come bring many blessings: many do they take as they go. Lest an old man's part be given to a youth, or a man's part to a boy, we shall do wisely to dwell on the attributes proper to each period of life.[28]

[178] An action either takes place on the stage, or is announced as having taken place off it. What finds entrance through the ear strikes the mind less vividly than what is brought before the trusty eyes of the spectator himself. And yet you will not present incidents which ought to be enacted behind the scenes, and will remove from sight a good deal for the actor to relate on the stage by

[25] The Latin words here, *in medias res*, were obviously in the mind of Milton when he wrote in the argument of the first book of *Paradise Lost:* "The poem hastes into the midst of things."

[26] Cf. Aristotle, *Poetics*, VII, first par., above.

[27] "Fitting grace" translates *decor*. The following paragraph may be said to deal with *decorum*, an important subject in later criticism (see the index under *decorum*).

[28] Lines 153–77 perhaps rest on Aristotle's *Rhetoric*, II, 12–4. So stereotyped a rendering of the qualities of the various ages was the easier for Horace because of the use of conventional masks by the actors on the Roman stage; the type of old man or young man is determined from the beginning of the play by the mask adopted.

and by—so that, for example, Medea may not butcher her boys or savage Atreus cook human flesh in front of the audience, Procne turn into a bird or Cadmus into a snake. Anything you thrust under my nose in this fashion moves my disgust—and incredulity.[29]

[189] A play which is to be in demand and, after production, to be revived, should consist of five acts—no more, no less.[30] A god must not be introduced unless a difficulty occurs worthy of such a deliverer; nor should a fourth actor be forward to speak.[31] The Chorus should discharge the part and duty of an actor with vigour, and chant nothing between the acts that does not forward the action and fit into the plot naturally. The Chorus must back the good and give sage counsel; must control the passionate and cherish those that fear to do evil; it must praise the thrifty meal, the blessings of justice, the laws, and Peace with her unbarred gates. It will respect confidences and implore heaven that prosperity may revisit the miserable and quit the proud.

[201] In days gone by the pipe, not as now bound with brass and rival of the trumpet, but soft and simple with its few stops, was useful to accompany a Chorus and give it its note. It could fill with sound the not yet overcrowded benches, to which of course the people would gather, readily counted (for they were few)—a thrifty folk, chaste and honest. When victorious nations began to extend their boundaries, and an ever-widening wall to compass their cities, and people were free to enjoy themselves uncensored on feast-days with early revels, a greater licence was granted to rhythms and tunes. What taste could you expect in some unlettered rustic, out for a holiday, when in company with a townsman—clown and gentleman together? So the piper added movement and wanton gestures to his art of old, and would trail his robes as he strutted about the stage; so were new notes added to the sober lyre; bold eloquence brought with it a language unknown before; and wise saws, prophetic of the future, would match the oracles of Delphi.

[220] The poet who competed in tragic verse for a paltry goat soon made the rustic satyrs doff their garments and ventured on

---

[29] The effect of verisimilitude necessary to the drama is not produced.

[30] This piece of advice was taken seriously by Renaissance writers, as is exemplified by many Elizabethan plays. In the preface to his *Samson Agonistes* (below) Milton speaks of a drama that is "not produced beyond the fifth act."

[31] Cf. Aristotle, *Poetics*, IV, 49a9, above. The passage illustrates Horace's preference for an arbitrary rule from Greek practice rather than for Roman usage in earlier times; Plautus did not limit himself to three actors.

coarse jests without loss of dignity, sure that a spectator, fresh from the sacrifice, drunk and subject to no law, must needs be held by the charms and enticements of novelty.

[225] It will be well so to commend to your audience the quips and laughter of Satyrs, so to pass from grave to gay, that no god or hero who is to be staged—so conspicuous of late in royal gold and purple—should in his discourse sink to the level of tavern-talk; or again, while shunning the ground, catch at clouds and emptiness. It is beneath the dignity of Tragedy to blurt out trivial verse: like a matron bidden to dance on holy days, the Muse, if she has to move among saucy Satyrs, will show a due reserve.

[234] If I write satyric plays, I shall not choose only bald and everyday terms; nor so try to vary from tragic diction that none can guess whether Davus is the speaker, or bold Pythias[32] who won a talent by wiping her master's eye, or Silenus—guide, philosopher, and friend of a god.[33]

[244] In my judgement, when woodland Fauns are brought on to the stage they should be careful not to languish in love-verses, like city exquisites, nor rap out filthy and shameful jests. For those who possess horse, father, or estate take offence; nor do they receive with favour or award a crown to everything the purchaser of fried peas and chestnuts may approve.[34]

[251] A long syllable following a short is termed an "iambus" —a lively foot; hence the word "trimeter" was given to iambic lines, although, uniform from first to last, they yielded six beats.

---

[32] Davus and Pythias represent the male and female slaves of comedy; the latter deceived her master. Perhaps they appeared in a comedy by Caecilius, mentioned by Horace in line 54, above.

[33] Silenus is here mentioned not in his character as a drunkard but as the wise teacher of Bacchus. Socrates was compared to him, as possessing wisdom underneath an uncouth appearance (Plato, *Symposium*, 215 A, 216 D, 221–222). The last passage is as follows: "Silenus and the satyrs . . . represent in a figure not only himself, but his words. For . . . his words are like the images of Silenus which open: they are ridiculous when you first hear them; he clothes himself in language that is like the skin of the wanton satyr—for his talk is of pack-asses and smiths and cobblers and curriers, and he is always repeating the same things in the same words, so that any ignorant or inexperienced person might feel disposed to laugh at him; but he who opens the bust and sees what is within will find that they are the only words which have a meaning in them, and also the most divine, abounding in fair images of virtue, and of the widest comprehension, or rather extending to the whole duty of a good and honorable man."
At this point most texts give four lines (240–3) that Mr. Blakeney transfers to follow line 130. The conventional numbering of the lines is, however, preserved.

[34] Horace prefers the taste of the rich to that of the poor. The latter apparently were in their habits like those who purchase popcorn at the circus, or like the "nut-cracking Elizabethans."

Not so long ago, to permit of a slower and more sedate movement, the iambus granted the staid spondee a share in its native rights, with the proviso that it kept its place in the second and fourth feet, in friendly fashion. The iambic foot is rarely found in the much-vaunted trimeters of Accius,[35] and brands those ponderous lines which Ennius launched on to the stage with the dishonouring charge of over-hurry and carelessness in workmanship or, worse, of ignorance of the poetic art.

[263] It is not every critic that notices false rhythms; and it is true that needless indulgence is given to Roman poets.[36] Am I, therefore, to run riot and break the rules? or shall I assume that the public will mark my slips? If so, then, wary and safe within the hope of forgiveness, I have indeed escaped censure, praise I have deserved not.

Do you, my friends, study the Greek masterpieces: thumb them day and night.[37]

"But," someone answers, "your forebears praised the measures and pleasantries of Plautus."[38] True: they admired both far too tolerantly, not to say foolishly, if only you and I know how to distinguish vulgarity from wit, and are quick with fingers and ears alike to catch the right cadences.

[275] Thespis is said to have discovered Tragedy—a form of poetry hitherto unknown—and to have carried his plays about in tumbrils, to be chanted and performed by actors with faces smeared with lees. After him Aeschylus, inventor of the mask and comely robe, laid his stage on short planks, teaching his company how to talk grandiloquently and strut with buskined feet. Next came the Old Comedy, praised by all; but freedom degenerated into licence and violence, to be checked by law; to law it yielded,

[35]Accius was a Roman writer of tragedies admired by Cicero. Only fragments of his works remain. His "oderint dum metuant" was echoed in the Renaissance; Richard Edwards has his tyrant, King Dionysius, say:

Let them hate me, so they fear me (*Damon and Pythias*, 729).

Horace did not admire archaic work such as that of Accius, Ennius, and Plautus (mentioned some lines below). He expresses himself in *Epistles*, II, I, in which occur the well-known words: "Captive Greece captured the savage victor and brought the arts into rustic Latium." The whole epistle is a plea for recent literature based on Aristotelian principles.

[36]Rostagni would interpret: "Indulgence unworthy of poets is given to the Romans."

[37]Rostagni thinks this addressed to the Romans in general, not merely to the Pisos, as is shown by the word *your* in the next paragraph.

[38]Quintilian (*Institutes of Oratory*, x, 1, 99) admired Plautus, and Cicero speaks of his jests as "refined, polite, clever, witty" (*De officiis*, I, 104).

and the Chorus, robbed of its power to hurt, fell silent—to its shame.

Our own poets have left no style untried; not the least of their merits was when they boldly forsook the footsteps of Greece and celebrated, in comedy and tragedy alike, our national deeds. Latium would not be mightier in valour or feats of arms than in letters, if only her poets, one and all, did not scorn the long labour of the file.[39] Do you, O Pisos, sprung from Numa, censure the poem that has not been pruned by time and many a cancellation—corrected ten times over and finished to the finger-nail.[40]

[295] Because Democritus believes that genius is happier than miserable art, and shuts the gates of Helicon on all sane poets,[41] a good few will not cut their nails or beard, but court solitude and shun the baths. The fact is, a poet may win a poet's name and reward if only he has never entrusted to Licinus, the barber, a pate that not three Anticyras could cure![42]

What a fool I am to get rid of the bile when spring comes on! but for that, no poet would write better. But nothing is worth that! I'll serve as a whetstone which, though it cannot cut of itself, can sharpen iron. Though I write nothing, I'll teach the business and duty of a writer; show where his materials may be found; what it is that trains and moulds a poet; what becomes him, what does not; whither knowledge tends, and whither error.

[39] The file would be used in giving a smooth and perfect finish to the work of a carver. Some modern wood carvers object to its use as giving a result so smooth as to lack strength and individuality, for example: "Glass-paper [sandpaper] must on no account be used on the carving. The student should . . . never have recourse to glass-paper or a file. . . . Glass-paper not only spoils the texture of the wood, but it destroys the delicate details of the carving, by which the carver expresses his feeling in the work" (Eleanor Rowe, *Practical Wood-Carving* [London, 1930], part I, p. 8). Acceptance or rejection of the file perhaps marks the difference between the taste of the age of Horace and the present. It is also expressed when critics of the present say a painting is good in that it preserves the qualities of the sketch, which may be lost in careful finishing. Would the age of Horace have admired, as we do, the sketches of Michaelangelo or Leonardo?

[40] *To the fingernail: ad unguem.* The figure is taken from the method used by sculptors in testing the polish of the surface of their work.

[41] According to Cicero (*De divinatione*, I, 80; *De oratore*, II, 46), Democritus, the philosopher of Abdera, denied that any man could be a great poet without madness (Democritus, fragment 17, Diehls). See *furor poeticus* in the index. In *Satires*, I, 4, 43 Horace himself approaches the theory, saying he only can be called a poet who has a soul possessing much of divinity.

[42] There were two or three places named Anticyras; they produced hellebore, used in the treatment of madness. Blakeney quotes from Burton's *Anatomy of Melancholy*, II, 4: "*Naviget Anticyram:* a common proverb to bid a dizzard or madman go take hellebore."

[309] The secret[43] of all good writing is sound judgement.[44] The works of the Socratics will supply you with the facts: get these in clear perspective and the words will follow naturally.[45] Once a man has learned his duty to friend and fatherland, the just claims of parent, brother, or guest on his love, the obligations of senator or judge, or the duty of a general sent on active service, he will infallibly know how to assign to each character its fitting part. I shall bid the clever imitator look to life and morals for his real model, and draw thence language true to life. Sometimes a play, tricked out with commonplaces and with characters well drawn, even though it be void of charm, force, or artistic skill, delights the populace and holds their interest far better than "lines without sense, and tuneful trifles."

It was the Greeks, aye, the Greeks covetous of praise alone,[46] that the Muse endowed with quick wit and rounded utterance. Our Roman youths by long calculations learn how to divide the shilling into a hundred parts. "Come, young Albinus, tell me this: take a penny from sixpence, and what is over? You ought to know." "Fivepence." "Good! you'll hold your own some day. Now add a penny: what's the result?" "Sevenpence." Ah, once this canker of avarice, this money-grubbing, has tainted the soul,

---

[43] *The secret:* more literally, *the source and fount.* Ben Jonson puts it *the root and spring.* Cicero said that wisdom was the foundation of eloquence (*Orator*, 70).

[44] Perhaps directed against the theory of the poet's madness, certainly an assertion of the intellectual quality of poetry, chiefly, as the following lines show, in the understanding of practical duties. If, as is supposed, Horace included Plato among the Socratics, he could hardly have recalled as he wrote that Plato spoke of the poet as possessed by divine madness.

[45] Milton wrote: "True eloquence I find to be none but the serious and hearty love of truth, and that whose mind so ever is fully possessed with a fervent desire to know good things and with the dearest charity to infuse the knowledge of them into others, when such a man would speak, his words (by what I can express) like so many nimble and airy servitors trip about him at command, and in well ordered files, as he would wish, fall aptly into their own places" (*An Apology for Smectymnuus*, sect. 12).

[46] Contrasted with the Romans, who desired money. On avarice as an enemy of poetry Boccaccio wrote: "They say poets can hardly be called wise to have spent their whole time following a profession that, after years of labor, yields never a cent. This explains, they add, why poets are always stark poor; they never make brilliant showing with dress, money, nor servants; from this they argue that, because poets are not rich, their profession is good for nothing. Such reasoning along with its unexpressed conclusion, finds easy access to the ears and minds of others, since we are all somewhat given to love of money, and foolishly take wealth to be the greatest thing in the world. If they come to examine my work, I daresay they will be enough smitten of this disease to say: 'Oh yes, a very pretty work, but of no use whatever!' " (*Genealogy of the Gods*, trans. by Osgood [Princeton, 1930], p. 22). In other parts of the same work Boccaccio speaks of the neglect of poetry because it does not bring in money.

can we hope that poems will be written worthy of cedar oil and to be treasured in polished cases?[47]

[333] The poet's aim is either to profit or to please,[48] or to blend in one the delightful and the useful. Whatever the lesson you would convey, be brief, that your hearers may catch quickly what is said and faithfully retain it. Every superfluous word is spilled from the too-full memory. Fictions made to please should keep close to the truth of things; your play should not demand an unlimited credence; it will not do to describe how a living boy is ripped from Lamia's belly after she has just eaten him. Elder folk rail at what contains no serviceable lesson; our young aristocrats cannot away with grave verses: the man who mingles the useful with the sweet carries the day by charming his reader and at the same time instructing him.[49] That's the book to en-rich the publisher, to be posted overseas, and to prolong its author's fame.

[347] Yet some faults there are that we can gladly overlook. The string does not invariably give the note intended by mind and hand; we listen for a flat, and often get a sharp; nor does the arrow always hit the target. But whenever beauties in a poem form a majority, I shall not stumble at a few blemishes that are due to carelessness or that the weakness of human nature has failed to guard against.

[353] How, then, do we stand? A copyist who continually makes the same blunder, spite of constant warning, gets no quarter; a harpist who is for ever fumbling with the same string is laughed at; so, too, I rank the slovenly poet with Choerilus,[50] whose occasional fine lines, though surprising, move one to mirth. Am I, then, to be indignant whenever good Homer nods?[51]

[360] "Yes, but it is natural for slumber to steal over a long work. Poetry is like painting: one piece takes your fancy if you stand close to it, another if you keep at some distance. One courts a dim light, another, challenging keen criticism, will fain be seen

[47] Worthy of preservation.

[48] Thomas Heywood used this as a motto on the title pages of plays and other writings.

[49] Perhaps the most influential paragraph in the entire work.

[50] A poet who accompanied Alexander the Great. Rostagni thinks Horace took his name from tradition, without reading his work.

[51] Aristotle thought Homer often could be defended (*Poetics*, XXIV, immediately above). The notion that a great author might nod (fall asleep, take a nap) was tradi-tional; according to Plutarch, Cicero said it of Demosthenes (*Life of Cicero*, 24). For the right attitude to the defects of a great poet, see Longinus, XXXIII, immediately below.

in the glare;[52] this charms but once, that will please if ten times repeated."

[366] Hope of the Pisos! although you have your father to guide your judgement aright and are yourself wise to boot, cherish this lesson and take it home: that only in limited fields is mediocrity tolerable or pardonable. A counsel or second-rate pleader at the bar may not rival Messalla in eloquence, nor possess the knowledge of Cascellius; yet he has his value; but mediocrity in poets has never been tolerated by gods, men, or—booksellers. Just as, at some pleasant banquet, ugly music, coarse perfume, and poppy seed mixed with Sardinian honey offend the taste, because the meal could have passed without such things: so a poem, created to give delight, if it fails but a little of the highest sinks to the lowest. One who is ignorant of games will abstain from the weapons of the Campus; and if he knows nothing of ball, or quoit, or hoop, will hold aloof, lest the thronging onlookers laugh with none to check them; yet he who is no poet, presumes to write verses! "And why not? Is he not free, of gentle birth, rated at a knight's income, with nothing against him?" *You*, I know, will say and do nothing "against the grain"—such is your resolve, such your good sense. If, however, you should one day produce something, pray submit it first to Maecius the critic, to your father, to me; and then put back the manuscript in your desk and let it stand over for a decade. The unpublished may be cancelled; but a word once uttered can never be recalled.

[390] Orpheus, seer and bard in one, weaned savage forest-tribes from murder and foul living; whence the legend that he tamed tigers and fierce lions.[53] It was said, too, that Amphion, founder of Thebes, moved stones by the sound of his lyre and drew them where he would by the magic of his entreaty. This was the poets' wisdom of old—to draw a line between the Man and the State, the sacred and the common; to build cities, to check pro-

[52] Editors suggest, rightly I fear, that the work which when seen in bright light still defies critics is in the opinion of Horace the better one. Possibly, however, he is saying that there are various kinds of poetry and that it is the duty of the critic to get the right light on each; if so, he is anticipating the insistence of Manzoni that the critic must ask: "What is the intention of the poet?" (Preface to *Il Conte di Carmagnola*). Only after a reader has done so has he a right to judge.

[53] An example of the allegorical interpretation of poetry, such as had a great vogue in the middle ages. Sidney uses the reference to Orpheus and the following one to Amphion in his *Defense*, sect. 2, below. Dante, referring to Ovid's story of Orpheus, gives much the same explanation in *Convivio*, II, I, 25–34. Cf. also Dante's letter to Can Grande, sect. 7, below.

miscuous lust, to assign rights to the married, to engrave laws on
wood. Thus did praise and honour come to divine poets and their
lays. Following upon them, noble Homer with impressive art
depicted the character of heroes and their wrath, while Tyrtaeus
with his songs kindled men's hearts to warrior deeds[54]; in verse
were oracles delivered, and the path of life shown forth, while the
favour of monarchs was courted by Pierian strains,[55] and festivals
were devised to sweeten human toil. This I say lest perchance you
should be ashamed of the lyric Muse, and of Apollo lord of song.

[408] Whether a good poem be the work of nature or of art is a
moot point. For my part I fail to see the use of study without wit,
or of wit without training: so true is it that each requires the
other's aid in helpful union.[56]

The athlete who is eager to reach the longed-for goal has endured and done much in boyhood, has borne heat and cold, has
abstained from women and wine; the flute-player who plays at
the Pythian games has first learned his lesson and trembled before
a teacher. Nowadays people think it enough to say: "I make wonderful poems; devil take the hindmost! it's a shame for me to be
outdone and to own I really do not know what I have never
learned."

[419] As a crier collects a crowd to buy his wares, so a poet, rich
in land and rich in investments, bids flatterers flock to him for
their profit. If there is one who can provide a costly feast, who will
go bail for a poor man and rescue him from the law's grim toils, I
shall be surprised if, for all his wealth, he is clever enough to distinguish the false friend from the true. Whether you have given
another a present, or mean to do so, never call him, when filled
with joy, to listen to your verses; for he will be sure to cry, "Splendid! bravo!" He will change colour over them, drop tears of
pleasure, leap, beat upon the floor.

Hired mourners outstrip in word and action those whose sorrow
is real: so is the sham admirer moved far more than the honest one.
Wealthy folk, when keen to mark whether a man be worthy of

---

[54] The martial elegies of Tyrtaeus were greatly esteemed in ancient Sparta.

[55] Pieria was a district to the north of Mt. Olympus, the birthplace of the Muses.

[56] "An inward prompting ... now grew daily upon me that by labor and intent
study (which I take to be my portion in this life) joined with the strong propensity of
nature, I might perhaps leave something so written to aftertimes, as they should not
willingly let it die" (Milton, *Reason of Church Government*, introduction to the second
book). In the context Milton mentions inspiration also, though Horace does not. See
the selections from Milton below.

friendship, are said to ply him with many a bumper and put him to the ordeal of wine; so, if you write poems, you will never fail to detect the spirit that lurks beneath the fox's skin.[57]

In days gone by, whenever you read a piece to Quintilius[58] he would exclaim, "Correct this, I pray, or that." If you replied that you could do no better, that you had tried twice or thrice in vain, he would bid you cut out the ill-turned lines and bring them to the anvil again. If you chose rather to defend than to mend the faulty line, not a word more would he say, or waste his efforts. Henceforth you might hug yourself and your works, alone, without a rival.

[445] A kind and sensible critic will censure verses when they are weak, condemn them when they are rough; ugly lines he will score in black, will lop off pretentious ornaments, force you to clear up your obscurities, criticize a doubtful phrase, and mark what needs a change[59]—in fact prove another Aristarchus.[60] He will not say, "Why should I take my friend to task for mere trifles?" —it is such trifles that will bring into sad scrapes the poet who has been fooled and flattered unfairly.

[453] As men shun the patient troubled with itch, jaundice, insanity, or moonstruck frenzy, so wise men dread to touch a mad poet, and avoid him: boys jostle him and fools pursue. If, spouting his lines and roaming, head in air (like a fowler watching thrushes), your bard falls into a pit or ditch, he may bawl, "Help, neighbours, help!" but there's no one to pull him out. Should somebody minded to assist throw a rope, I shall say, "Who knows whether he has not thrown himself there on purpose, and does not want to be saved?" And then I shall relate the Sicilian poet's end: "Empedocles, wishing to be thought a god, in cold blood leapt

---

[57] Cf. Plutarch's essay on *How to Discern a Flatterer from a Friend*. The friend must censure, though with tact, when it is necessary.

[58] For his "incorruptible faith and naked truth," see Horace, *Odes*, I, xxiv, 7.

[59] Perhaps derived from Horace is the following: "The poet with diffidence approaches his faithful friends, asking that they be willing to adopt an unfriendly spirit and to assume the stern brows of severe judgment. May they have no pity on error! He renews this request again and again. When he has been admonished for a hidden defect, he is glad to give thanks for it, and of his own will admits his faults, even when he is condemned with unjust judgment and is able to refute the accusation as untrue. . . . Now this, now that he rejects, for he is suspicious even of what is well done; he adds improvements, plucks off and shears away foliage and redundant branches, and bit by bit trims off ineffectual profusion; he is an exacting master" (Vida, *Art of Poetry*, III, 466–85).

[60] Aristarchus was an Alexandrian critic of the second century B.C., famous for his edition of Homer, in which he marked as spurious the lines that did not seem to him excellent.

into blazing Etna."[61] Suffer poets to destroy themselves if they choose; he who saves a man against his will as good as murders him. No first attempt, this; if pulled back straightway, he'll never become like other folk nor lay down his desire for a theatrical ending. Nobody quite knows why he fashions verses: possibly he has fouled his father's grave or violated some sacred boundary, and so lost caste. Well, he's mad: that's clear; and like a bear that has managed to break its prison bars this pitiless reciter stampedes scholar and dunce alike. Once he has captured his victim, he sticks till he slays him with reading—like a leech that will never let go till gorged with blood.

[61] According to Aristotle (*Poetics*, I, 47a28, immediately above) Empedocles was a physicist rather than a poet, even though writing in meter. Horace follows a different tradition, which completely neglects the greatness of Empedocles and makes him a bad poet. Horace's word *frigidus* (in cold blood) alludes to the importance of fire or heat in the system of Empedocles and at the same time means *insipid* or *stupid*. Milton follows Horace in his lines

> He who to be deemed
> A god, leaped fondly into Aetna flames
> Empedocles.
>
> *Paradise Lost*, III, 469–71.

DIONYSIUS OR LONGINUS

ο◯οο◯ο

ON LITERARY EXCELLENCE

Perhaps about 80 A.D.

THIS AUTHOR is commonly known as Longinus and his work as *On the Sublime*. Traditionally he has been thought of as the secretary of Zenobia, queen of Palmyra, who lived in the third century, but that view is now generally abandoned, though without giving us any historical Longinus in his place. It is comforting to feel that there is at least one literary man whose biography cannot be studied; we must consider his work itself or nothing.

Undergoing for ages, it appears, neglect more complete than fell to the *Poetics* of Aristotle, the work was first published in the Renaissance in 1554 by Robortello, one of the early modern students of Aristotle. Other editions and translations, first into Latin and then into other languages, followed. The first English translation was that of 1652. The most famous and probably most widely circulated was that by Boileau into French in 1674, which has been many times reissued. Longinus has been rendered into at least twelve modern languages. Isaac Casaubon, who died in 1614, called it a "golden book," and Dryden, near the end of the century, said that Longinus "was undoubtedly, after Aristotle, the greatest critic amongst the Greeks."[1] As my notes indicate, Dryden several times quoted from him. His age of greatest direct influence was perhaps the eighteenth century, though in the present century there have been at least three new English translations.

And the greater influence in the eighteenth century may be more apparent than real, for the method of the book has entered into all our judicial criticism of the details of literature. If Aristotle may be said to have determined our view of the structure of a literary work, Longinus has shown us how to approach an individual passage. If his method is less analytic than that of Aristotle, it is more aesthetic. If it seems to leave more to the possibly erring taste of the individual, it deals with what is more immediately and apparently poetical. Though it de-

[1] *Apology for Heroic Poetry*, near the beginning.

mands taste from the critic, it also requires his whole capacity, intellectual and emotional, even physical. There is still value in the opinion of Gibbon: "Till now, I was acquainted only with two ways of criticizing a beautiful passage: the one, to show, by an exact anatomy of it, the distinct beauties of it, and from whence they sprung; the other, an idle exclamation, or a general encomium, which leaves nothing behind it. Longinus has shown me that there is a third. He tells me his own feelings upon reading it; and tells them with such energy that he communicates them. I almost doubt which is most sublime, Homer's battle of the gods, or Longinus's apostrophe to Terentianus upon it." [2]

Longinus attained what he did partly by bursting his bonds. His first purpose was to write something of value to public speakers; not poetry but rhetoric is his concern. But by a process that Sidney was later to reverse, he has strayed from oratory to poetry, thus emphasizing the resemblances between them, and showing that there are fundamental similarities in all types of literary composition. He has become one of the critics of poetry by virtue of his love for it and understanding of its qualities. There are few who will not profit by attempting to criticize poetry according to his explicit suggestions; they will do still better if they succeed in criticizing in his spirit.

It has long been recognized that the word *sublime*, as employed in modern English, is not a proper translation of the title. Wordsworth wrote that "Longinus treats of animated, empassioned, energetic, or, if you will, elevated writing. . . . His ὕψος when translated 'sublimity' deceives the English reader by substituting an etymology for a translation." [3] But in spite of that, translators have continued to make more or less use of the word until recently, when Professor Tucker issued a translation entitled *On Elevation of Style;* in his introduction he suggests *excellence of expression* as another rendering for what has been called sublimity. In the present translation, made by the editor of this volume, the word *sublime* has also been avoided. The change at least makes it easier for the reader in this day to apply the treatise to modern poetry.

BIBLIOGRAPHY

Henn, T. R., *Longinus and English Criticism.* Cambridge, 1934. Additional examples, from English literature, are given.

[2] *Journal*, Oct. 3, 1762.
[3] Letter to J. Fletcher, in Knight, *Letters of the Wordsworth Family*, II, 250.
  R. Rapin wrote: "I make this sublime consist in the highest summit of perfection, which is the supreme stage of excellence in each condition" (*Du grand ou du sublime dans les mœurs et dans les differentes conditions des hommes*, in *Œuvres* [Amsterdam, 1709], III, 446). Generally, however, Rapin's notions seem to have been more conventional.

Monk, Samuel H., *The Sublime: A Study of Critical Theories in Eighteenth-Century England*. New York, 1935.

Longinus, *On the Sublime*. A new translation chiefly according to the improved edition of Weiske, designed for the use of English readers in general, by a Master of Arts of the University of Oxford. London, 1830. Many further illustrations, especially from the Bible.

——, *Libellus de sublimitate*, recognovit . . . Arturus Octavius Prickard. Oxford, 1906.

—— ——, translated by H. L. Havell, in *Theories of Style in Literature*, arranged . . . by Lane Cooper. New York, 1907.

—— —— The Greek text, edited after the Paris manuscript, with introduction, translation, facsimiles, and appendices, by W. Rhys Roberts. Cambridge, 1907. The most elaborate English edition.

——, *De sublimitate libellus*, in usum scholarum edidit Otto Iahn; quartum edidit Ioannes Vahlen. Leipzig, 1910.

——, *On Elevation of Style*, translated by T. G. Tucker. Melbourne and London, 1935. Worthy of a place with the earlier translations. Not quite complete.

——, *On the Sublime*. The Greek text with an English translation by W. Hamilton Fyfe. New York, 1927 (Loeb Classical Library, in the volume with Aristotle's *Poetics*). The text "is based on Vahlen's fourth edition (1910) of Otto Jahn's text." I have generally followed this text, though with reference to the others mentioned.

ON LITERARY EXCELLENCE

[Part I, Introductory: Faults and Virtues]

Chapter I

[The treatise of Caecilius]

[1[1]] My dear Postumius Terentianus, you know that when we considered together the work on excellence of style by Caecilius we found that it did not rise to the height of the whole subject, and especially that it was not very helpful on the main points which the writer must make clear if he will benefit his readers. Two requirements may be made of every treatise on an art; first, the author must make clear what he is about to deal with; then, as second in order though first in importance, he must show us the

---

[1] The numbers of the paragraphs apply to the present translation only.

methods of attaining the goal he sets before us. But Caecilius, while in a thousand ways he endeavors to show the nature of excellence as though to readers ignorant of it, still has strangely omitted as unnecessary all instruction on how we can develop our natures up to the necessary power over excellence. But perhaps we should not blame the man for what he has omitted but rather give him thanks for having attempted the subject and done something with it.

[The power of excellence]

[2] Since you have asked me without fail to put together, for your own use, my observations on excellence of style, I shall consider whether my conclusions are likely to be useful to men active in public life. You, my friend, will assist me by acting as a frank critic of my work, to the utmost of your abilities, for he who was asked what we possess in common with the gods answered well when he said "good will and truth." Writing to a man so well-trained as yourself, I feel there is no use in a long preface showing that excellent style consists in striking distinction of language. Nothing else than this has given the greatest poets and historians their high place and secured them fame and immortality. Genius does not merely persuade an audience but lifts it to ecstasy. The astonishing is always of greater force than the persuasive or the pleasing; it is within our own powers whether to be persuaded or not, but that is truly effective which comes with such mighty and irresistible force as to overpower the hearer. Skillful assemblage of matter and arrangement of parts according to a good plan[2] do not appear in one or two sentences; they must gradually become apparent as the order of the whole work is unfolded. But a well-timed example of genuine power over language strikes the hearer like a flash of lightning that rends everything before it, revealing the full might of the orator. But you know all about that, my dear Terentianus, for you have often observed it in your experience.

Chapter II

[An art of achieving excellence]

[3] First, one must consider whether there is any art for reaching the heights or plumbing the depths, for some think it a delu-

[2] The word here is *economy*, often used by later critics; see the index.

sion to suppose that a body of precepts can be applied to such
matters. The great man, they hold, is born and not taught, and
the genius is what he is only by the gift of nature. The productions
of native ability are thought to be ruined when subjected to the
dry-as-dust technologist. But I believe this popular notion can be
proved false, if only we consider that while in the strongest emotions Nature is a law unto herself, yet even she does not like to
work rashly and entirely without method. Though she supplies
the germ and primary element for everything, yet method must
determine how much and when each one is to be employed and
must assist in training the natural powers. Moreover great qualities are in danger when not controlled by the intelligence but left
without ballast or stabilizer, and abandoned to the sway of ignorant audacity. Many times the spur must be used on them, but
the curb is also needed. Demosthenes, speaking of the course of
human life, says that good fortune is the greatest of human blessings, but that the second, and not less important, is good judgment, since if it is lacking the first is useless. The same may be
said of language, for nature corresponds to fortune and art to good
judgment. Above all, we must learn from art that there are some
things in language that depend on nature alone. If those who
object to scientific study would consider what I have said, they
would, I think, no longer look on methodical analysis as a useless
waste of energy. [At this point there is a gap in the manuscript
amounting to about a twenty-fifth of the whole.]

Chapter III

[Bombast]

[4] What though they check the towering blaze of the furnace!
If I see but one man at the hearth, I'll whirl upon him a wreath of
flame like a torrent, and consume the house to a heap of ashes.
Not yet have I raised my noble strain.[3]

These words are not tragic but pseudotragic: the wreaths, and the
"vomiting to the sky,"[4] and making Boreas a flute-player, and the
rest. The language is like muddy water and the images are confused rather than impressive; if you examine them carefully in a

[3] From the lost *Oreithyia* of Aeschylus.
[4] Some of the quotation seems to be missing, if these words were part of it.

good light, they shrink little by little until they are absurd instead of terrible. If even in tragedy, where a stately and high-flown style is natural, tasteless bombast is unpardonable, surely it cannot be suitable to practical oratory. Hence it is right to laugh at Gorgias of Leontini for writing that "Xerxes is the Zeus of the Persians," and that "vultures are living tombs," and at some of the expressions of Callisthenes as not admirable but merely high-flown, and still more at some phrases by Cleitarchus, for the man is a frivolous creature of whom Sophocles says that "he blows on puny flutes, without regulating his breath." The same sort of language is found in Amphicrates and Hegesias and Matris, for often when they think they are inspired they act not like bacchanals but like children. Bombast seems to be one of the faults most difficult to avoid. All those who strive after what is great, somehow fall into bombast when they are attempting to avoid censure for seeming feeble and dry, thinking that "greatly to fail is a noble error." Swellings and tumors are dangerous for both bodies and words, because they may produce an effect opposite to what is expected; no one is more parched than a hydroptic.

[Puerility]

[5] The inflated style comes from attempting to outdo what is excellent, but puerility is the opposite of greatness; it is completely paltry and mean-spirited and indeed a most contemptible fault. What is this puerility then? Is it not a painstaking habit of thought which overconcern develops into rigidity? Writers stumble into this fault through trying too hard for something unusual and original and especially for something attractive.

[Ill-timed pathos]

[6] A third species of mistake comes in the use of the pathetic, what Theodorus called "recourse to the thyrsus." This is pathos empty and ill-timed, used without reason, or excessive when it should be restrained. For it often happens that speakers as though they were drunk give way to bursts of emotion that have nothing to do with the matter in hand and are simply the results of their own efforts. Hence to their hearers, who have no strong feeling, they seem absurd, as excited men usually do to those not under excitement.[5] But we intend to treat of the emotions elsewhere.

---

[5] Apparently the passage Dryden had in mind when he wrote: "Longinus, whom I have hitherto followed, continues thus: 'If the passions be artfully employed, the dis-

Chapter IV

[Frigidity]

[7] Of the second fault of which we spoke, I mean frigidity, there are many examples in Timaeus; he is in other matters an able writer, for sometimes he shows great excellence of language and he is well-informed and ingenious, though very critical of the faults of other writers while blind to his own. Yet because he is always subject to the urge for novelty he often falls into the most childish excesses. I shall instance only one or two, since Caecilius has already pointed out a number of them. In lauding Alexander the Great, Timaeus says that "he conquered all Asia in fewer years than Isocrates needed for the composition of his panegyric oration on the Persian war." An extraordinary comparison of the Macedonian conqueror with the sophist! It makes clear, Timaeus, that the Spartans are far inferior in vigor to Isocrates, for they captured Messene after thirty years of effort, while he composed his oration in less than ten. Then how Timaeus plays with sounds in speaking of the Athenians who were captured in Sicily! He says: "After they had acted impiously against Hermes by mutilating the statues of that god, they suffered punishment chiefly at the hands of one man, Hermocrates the son of Hermon, who was descended from the god they had outraged." I wonder, dear Terentianus, that he did not write of King Dionysius: "Since he showed impiety toward Jove and Heracles, he was deprived of his throne by Jovius and Heraclides."[6]

[Frigidity in Plato and Xenophon]

[8] But why should I speak of Timaeus when great men like Xenophon and Plato, though educated by Socrates, sometimes forget themselves for the sake of such cheap ornaments? Xeno-

course becomes vehement and lofty; if otherwise, there is nothing more ridiculous than a great passion out of season' " (Preface to *Troilus and Cressida*, in W. P. Ker, *Essays of Dryden*, I, 221).

[6] In the original the first words in the pairs are *Dia* (the accusative of Zeus) and *Dion*; I have changed them in order to preserve the "turn" (see entry under *turn* in the index).

Is it possible that from this passage might have been derived the objection to the pun (so much enjoyed by the Elizabethans) held by Dryden (*An Essay of Dramatic Poesy*, p. 637, below) and Addison? Addison censured them in Milton (*Spectator*, no. 297 [February 9, 1712]); he also objects to Milton's use of "a kind of jingle in his words" (*ibid*).

phon writes in the *Polity of the Lacedaemonians:* "You would get an
answer from a marble statue sooner than from them; you would
more quickly attract the gaze of a bronze figure; you would suppose they were more modest than the maidens in their eyes." [7] To
call the pupils of the eyes modest maidens is to be expected from
Amphicrates but not from Xenophon. And what a devil of a
notion it is to assume that the pupils of the eyes of every man in the
company were modest, when it is said that immodesty is shown
nowhere so quickly as in the eye; "boozer, with the eyes of a dog,"
says Homer. Yet Timaeus has not left this piece of frigidity to
Xenophon, but has seized on it as though recovering stolen property, for telling how Agathocles carried off from the wedding ceremony his cousin who had been betrothed to another man, our author says: "Would he have done this if he had had virgins in his
eyes instead of harlots?" And what of Plato, generally divine in
his diction, when he says that "after they had written they put in
the archives memorials made of cypress-wood?" And again he
says: "As to walls, Megillus, I should agree with Sparta to let them
lie sleeping on the ground, never to rise up."

[Frigidity in Herodotus]

[9] Herodotus is not far behind when he calls beautiful women
"irritations to the eyes." [8] Yet he has some excuse, for his speakers
are barbarians and half-drunk, but it is not wise to make a poor
figure to posterity by being trivial even in speeches put in the
mouths of such characters.

Chapter V

[The craze for novelty]

[10] All these gaudy weeds spring up in literary style from a
single root, namely the craze for novelty, over which the literary
men of the present are running wild. Our virtues and our vices
are nourished in the same soil. So while beauties of expression and
well-written passages, and pleasing ones too, conduce toward success in composition, yet these same things are at the bottom not
merely of a happy result but of its opposite as well. What I have

---

[7] A "turn" which assumed that the word *parthenōn,* in the text, would remind the
reader of the word *korā,* which means both *maiden* and *pupil of the eye.*
[8] The opposite of the modern phrase "easy on the eyes."

in mind are shifts in construction, hyperboles, and changes in number; further on I am going to show the danger that seems to accompany their use. At present it is necessary to investigate the matter and find out how we can escape the faults that accompany attempts at distinction in style.

Chapter VI

[Literary judgment]

[11] It is, my friend, possible to do this if we first obtain a clear and accurate conception of stylistic excellence. This is no easy matter. An accurate judgment in literature results only from long experience. But if I must say something by way of precept, perhaps what I am about to present will not be wholly useless to anyone who wishes to become an intelligent critic.

Chapter VII

[True value]

[12] It is necessary for us to realize, my dear friend, that nothing which the high-minded man despises is of great import in human life. Thus no wise man would think that wealth, honors, fame, high position, and whatever else makes a great show in the world are the things of surpassing value, for he knows that contempt for them is to be commended not a little. Certainly we give more honor to those who could have these things and magnanimously reject them than to those who have them. The same principle applies to the criticism of poetry and prose. We must look closely to see whether a passage has merely a counterfeit appearance of greatness that enables it to seem very impressive, though when a test is made it is found to be worthless—something to be despised rather than admired.

[What is a classic?]

[13] But our spirits are naturally mastered by the truly excellent and, acquiring a sort of vigorous exaltation, are filled with a sense of happy attainment, as though they had themselves produced what they hear.[9] If then a passage after being heard several times does not impress with a sense of its greatness a man of

---

[9] This sentence suggests some recent aesthetic theories.

good judgment and much experience in literature, and does not make him feel that "more is meant than meets the ear," but the more he considers it the less admirable it appears, it cannot be genuinely excellent, because it does not outlast the moment in which it is heard.[10] But what is rightly great will bear close examination,[11] attracts us with an irresistible fascination, and imprints itself deeply in our memories. Consider a passage fully and genuinely excellent only when it pleases all men in all ages. When men of different occupations, habits, ideals, and ages all agree that a verse is excellent, such unanimity of opinion on the part of diverse critics secures strong and unshakable confidence in the object they admire.

Chapter VIII

[Five sources of excellence]

[14] Excellence in style rises from five fountains, as one may call them, though common and essential to all the five classes is ability in the use of language, for without this nothing can be done. The first and most important, as I have said in my work on Xenophon, is a firm grasp of ideas.[12] The second is vigorous and inspired emotion.[13] These two constituents of poetic excellence are for the most part in-born. The other three come from art. The third is the formation of figures,[14] of which there are two kinds, those of idea and those of word. Next is notable language,[15] which has as its parts the choice of words and figurative and individual diction. The fifth, which serves to hold all the others in union, is fitting and dignified arrangement.[16] Let us consider the elements that enter into each of these classes.

[Emotion not essential to excellence]

[15] But first by way of introduction let me say that Caecilius omitted part of our five elements; for example, he does not deal with strong feeling. If he means that excellence and what moves the feelings are the same and are co-existent and connatural, he is wrong. There are some feelings that are mean and remote from

---

[10] May this be applied to the "book of the moment" of which the Rev. Hugh Black said he thought he could let that moment pass?

[11] See Horace, *Art of Poetry*, 361–5, above, note.   [12] Discussed in chaps. IX–XV.

[13] Not specially discussed in this treatise because the author intended to deal with it elsewhere; see the ends of chaps. III and XLIV.

[14] See chaps. XVI–XXIX.   [15] See chaps. XXX–XXXVIII.   [16] Chaps. XXXIX–XLIII.

excellent expression, as pity, worry, and fear. On the other hand, many passages of high quality have nothing to do with emotion, as among hundreds of others Homer's bold lines on the sons of Aloeus:

> In their rage they strove to pile Ossa on Olympus, and Pelion with its trees on Ossa, that they might have a ramp reaching to heaven.[17]

And more boldly he adds:

> Yea, and they would have wrought their purpose.

Oratory, panegyrics, and elaborate ceremonial speeches contain plenty of examples of the dignified and the excellent, but for the most part they are without strong feeling. Hence emotional orators do not succeed in eulogy and makers of set speeches lack emotion.

[Emotion and excellence]

[16] If on the other hand Caecilius thought emotion had nothing to do with excellence and therefore supposed he could pass over it, he is quite wrong. For I make bold to say that nothing is so effective as feeling of a high order when it is called out by the occasion; it seems to issue from a sort of divine rapture and enthusiasm and fills the words with inspiration.

[PART II, GREAT IDEAS, THE FIRST SOURCE OF LITERARY EXCELLENCE]

Chapter IX[18]

[The great soul]

[17] Of the five sources of excellence the first, namely great genius, is the most important. Hence, though it is true that such genius is a gift rather than an acquirement, yet we should try to

---

[17] *Odyssey*, XI, 315.

"Longinus has observed that there may be a loftiness in sentiments where there is no passion. The pathetic, as that great critic observes, may animate and inflame the sublime, but is not essential to it. Accordingly, as he further remarks, we very often find that those who excel most in stirring up the passions very often want the talent of writing in the great and sublime manner, and so on the contrary" (Addison, *Spectator*, no. 339 [March 29, 1712]).

[18] This chapter was called by Gibbon "one of the finest monuments of antiquity" (*Journal*, October 3, 1762).

discipline our spirits into greatness that they may be always ready to bring forth noble thoughts. How can this be done? you ask. Elsewhere I have written to this effect. Excellence of style is the concomitant of a great soul. Sometimes also, without a word being uttered, a bare conception amazes us because of the nobility of soul it expresses; the great silence of Ajax in the Book of the Dead is more impressive than any utterance. First of all, then, we must make every effort to determine the source of this quality, for the true orator must have no paltry and ignoble spirit. It is impossible that those who think and act in a mean and slavish fashion all their lives long should utter anything admirable and worthy of an eternity of fame. Surely great words are spoken only by those who think great thoughts. For this reason impressive speech comes only from noble spirits. When Parmenio said: "I would accept the terms of the enemy if I were Alexander," the Macedonian answered: "And I, were I Parmenio." [Almost one-eighth of the manuscript is missing at this point.]

[Illustrations from Homer]

[18] Homer says of Strife:

> At first her crest is but humble, but afterwards she raises her head
> to the heavens while her feet are planted on the earth.[19]

Only a noble spirit would have conceived the space between earth and the heavens. This does not give the measure of Strife more truly than it does that of Homer.[20] Quite different Hesiod's description of Sorrow (if the *Shield of Hercules* is really his):

> From her nostrils streams of snot were running.

He has made a picture that is not terrible but disgusting. But what greatness Homer gives to the affairs of the gods:

> As far as the eyes of a watchman on a hilltop can pierce the haze
> of the distance, as he looks out over the wine-colored sea, so far
> stride the shrill-neighing horses of the gods.[21]

---

[19]*Iliad*, IV, 442–3. Here, as in the anecdote of Alexander, I have added what is generally agreed upon as written by Longinus.

[20]Addison quotes:

> Satan alarmed
> Collecting all his might dilated stood
> Like Teneriff or Atlas unremoved;
> His stature reached the sky, and on his crest
> Sat horror plumed.
> *Paradise Lost*, IV, 985–9.

He comments that this "is at least equal to Homer's description of Discord, celebrated by Longinus" (*Spectator*, no. 321 [March 8, 1712]).   [21]*Iliad*, V, 770.

He measures their stride by the extent of the earth. Could not anyone properly say of such an extravagant distance that if the horses of the gods should stride a second time they would not find room enough in the world?[22] Magnificent too are Homer's imaginations of the battle of the gods:

> Round about rang like a trumpet the vast heaven and Olympus. Hades, the king of the dead, trembled in the depths of the earth; he leaped from his throne and cried aloud, in fear lest Poseidon the Land-Shaker should cleave asunder the earth, and his dreadful and decaying mansions that even the immortals shudder at should be seen by men and gods.[23]

Note, my friend, how when the earth is torn up to its depths and Tartarus is laid bare, and the whole cosmos is turned upside down and rent apart, everything at once, heaven and hell, mortal and immortal, is made to share in the combat and undergo its dangers.

[The true nature of the gods]

[19] These things are surely terrible, but otherwise, unless one takes them allegorically, they are wholly ungodlike, with no regard for the fitness of things.[24] For it seems to me that in telling of the wounds of the gods, their feuds, punishments, tears, bonds, and all their distressful experiences, Homer has done all he could to make the men of the *Iliad* into gods and the gods into men. Yet to us men death is appointed as a haven of refuge from misery, but Homer has given eternity not to the being of the gods but to their misfortunes. Much better than the account of the war of the gods are those passages in which he presents the divine nature as it is, undefiled, great, and in its unmixed being, as it appears in the familiar lines on Poseidon:

> Then the ridges of the hills and the forests and the peaks and the city of the Trojans and the ships of the Achaeans trembled beneath the immortal feet of Poseidon as he passed. He went riding

[22] On this passage Gibbon remarks: "I am sorry to criticize such a chapter, but what would Longinus have said had another made his observation upon that passage of Homer where the celestial horses leap at one bound the extent of the visible horizon? One would think, says he, the world could not have afforded space [for] another leap. To what faculty does the visible horizon appear above half the world? To the eyes it appears the whole; to the understanding, and even to the imagination, a very small part" (*Journal*, October 3, 1762).

[23] A mingling of *Iliad*, v, 750; xx, 61–5; xxi, 388.

[24] The word is *prepon*, the equivalent of *decorum*; see the index.

over the waters and the sea-monsters rose from the depths and gamboled about him, acknowledging their king. The waves parted in delight and on flew the horses of the god.[25]

So also the Jewish lawgiver, no common man, expressed the power of his god according to the worthy conception he had formed, when among the first words of his laws he wrote: "What did God say? Let there be light, and there was light. Let there be earth, and there was earth."[26]

[Heroic greatness]

[20] I hope, my friend, you will not think I am a bore if I quote one more passage from Homer—this one dealing with men—to show how he is wont to attain superhuman greatness. Fog and impenetrable darkness suddenly descend on the battle array of the Greeks. Then Ajax, wholly at a loss, prays:

O Father Zeus, deliver from the darkness the sons of the Achaeans, make it bright day, permit us to use our eyes; at least destroy us in the sunlight.[27]

How truly this represents the feeling of Ajax! He does not ask for life—such a petition would be too mean for a hero—but since in the thick darkness he can make no worthy use of his valor, and is chagrined that he is of no avail in the battle, he begs for instant light, for if that is granted he will secure a winding sheet befitting his courage, even though Zeus has ranged himself against him. In this passage Homer is carried along with the rush of the action and has himself the feelings of the lion that

rages like Ares the spearman or like a devouring fire among the hills in the thickets of the great forest; foam hangs about his mouth.[28]

[The *Odyssey* written by an old man]

[21] Homer shows throughout the *Odyssey*—and there are many reasons for attention to what I say—that a love of stories is a peculiarity of old age, when even a great genius is beyond its acme. It is also clear from other reasons that he composed this as his second work, and especially because all through the *Odyssey* he brings in as episodes remnants of the sad tales of Troy; he even

[25] *Iliad*, xiii, 18, 19, 27–9; xx, 60.   [26] Genesis 1, 3 ff. Not exactly given.
[27] *Iliad*, xvii, 645.   [28] *Iliad*, xv, 605.

pays the heroes their dues of lamentation and tears as though his reader knew all about their fates. The *Odyssey* is nothing else than the sequel to the *Iliad:*

> There lies Ajax, fierce as Mars, there Achilles, there Patroclus, an adviser prudent as the gods, there my own dear son.[29]

For the same reason I think the *Iliad,* written when Homer was at the height of his powers, is essentially dramatic and full of activity, but the *Odyssey* is mostly narrative, as befits old age. Hence one can compare the Homer of the *Odyssey* to the setting sun, which retains its size but not its dazzling brightness. He is no longer capable of a tone such as the verses of the *Iliad* possess, nor of the consistent excellence that never flags; there is not the same abundance of strong emotions, one after another; the style is not marked by rapid transitions and the feeling for public affairs, and the poem does not abound with imaginative pictures drawn from life. Homer like the ocean seems to be withdrawing into himself and lying quiet within his own bounds, so that henceforth his verses appear at the ebb tide of their greatness, as though he were wandering among myths and incredible legends. I do not say this in forgetfulness of the storms in the *Odyssey,* or of the tale of the Cyclops and similar matters, for if I am speaking of old age, it is the old age of Homer; yet in everyone of these parts of the poem the spirit of narrative dominates that of action.

[Old age and story-telling]

[22] As I said, I have spoken of him to show that great natures in their decline are sometimes easily turned toward trumpery, as is apparent in Homer's stories of the bag of winds and Circe's transformation of the men into swine, whom Zoilus called weeping porkers; then there is the feeding of Zeus by doves as though he were a young bird, and the ten days' fast of Odysseus when he was shipwrecked, and the incredible events at the slaying of the suitors. What else can we call these but actually dreams of Zeus?

[Declining emotion makes way for character]

[23] Then let us consider the qualities of the *Odyssey* for a second reason. I wish you to realize that the decline of emotion in great literary men and poets causes them to put emphasis on character. Hence the presentation of the traits of men about their

---

[29] *Odyssey,* III, 109–11. The aged Nestor is giving his reminiscences.

daily tasks in the house of Odysseus is suitable for a comedy in which character is the chief subject.

Chapter X

[Selection and arrangement of matter by Sappho]

[24] But now let us see whether we can find something else that can give distinction to language. Since there are in all things by nature certain parts that are of necessity involved with their primary matter, it must follow that one cause of excellence is the power to choose the most suitable of the constitutive elements and to arrange them so that they form a single living body. One part of the process pleases the reader by its selection of matter; the other by its putting together of what has been chosen. Sappho always presents the emotions that characterize passionate love by selecting the manifestations that in very truth accompany it. How does she show her ability? In selecting the chiefest and most impressive of them and binding them one with another:

> That man seems to me equal to one of the gods who sits face to face with you, and is close to you as he hears your sweet speech and your love-enforcing laughter; it makes my heart flutter in my breast. When I but look on you I lose all control of my voice and my tongue has no power; my skin tingles as with fire; my eyes cannot see, and my ears are filled with sound; I drip with sweat; shivers run over me; I am paler than grass; I seem on the point of death.[30]

Are you not amazed at the way in which she summons the spirit, the body, the ears, the tongue, the eyes, the color, as though all

---

[30] Ben Jonson imitated part of this ode as follows:

> Thou dost not know my sufferings, what I feel,
> My fires and fears are met; I burn and freeze,
> My liver's one great coal, my heart shrunk up
> With all the fibres, and the mass of blood
> Within me is a standing lake of fire,
> Curled with the cold wind of my gelid sighs,
> That drive a drift of sleet through all my body,
> And shoot a February through my veins.
> Until I see him, I am drunk with thirst,
> And surfeited with hunger of his presence.
> I know not whêr I am, or no, or speak,
> Or whether thou dost hear me.
> *The New Inn*, v, ii, 45–56.

This perhaps illustrates Longinus's own view of imitation (chap. xiii, below), as well as that of Jonson. See the introduction to the section on Jonson, below.

were apart from her, and at how in the most contradictory way she at once shivers and burns, is irrational and sane, and fears she is at the point of death;[31] she intends to show not merely one of the effects of love, but all its passions together. These feelings are all experienced by lovers, but as I said, Sappho achieves distinction by laying hold on the most impressive and uniting them.

[Homer's selection in describing a storm]

[25] It likewise appears that in the description of a storm Homer selects the most alarming of its accompaniments. The composer of the *Arimaspeia*, however, thought these verses terrifying:

> And here is another thing that fills my soul with wonder. There are men who live far from the land in the midst of the waters of the sea; they are wretched beings and live a life of toil, with their eyes fixed on the stars and their souls among the waters; oftentimes they pray with their eager hands uplifted to the gods and their hearts sick within them.

It is, I think, evident that this is flowery rather than impressive. But how does Homer express it? He writes (to quote one example from many):

> He fell upon them as when a wave nourished by the winds rises up under the clouds and smites a swift ship; the vessel is buried in foam, the fearful blast of the storm bellows in the sail, and the hearts of the sailors tremble with fear; narrow is their escape from underneath destruction.[32]

Aratus attempted to modify and imitate this passage:

> A little piece of wood is all that keeps death away.[33]

Yet he has made the idea small and well finished instead of awe-inspiring. He limits the peril when he says that "a piece of wood keeps death away." It is enough to keep it away. But Homer does not limit the danger to one time; he gives a picture of the sailors as continually in peril of destruction by one wave after another. Moreover, by forcing together prepositions that do not naturally unite, in the words "from underneath destruction,"[34]

---

[31] The original of the last clause is apparently faulty; I have not attempted to follow it.

[32] *Iliad*, xv, 624 ff.   [33] *Phaenomena*, 299.

[34] The nearest equivalent to the Greek preposition seems to be "out from under," not quite dignified enough for Longinus's letter.

he has tortured his phrase into resemblance with the woe that hangs over the sailors and thus by the tension of the words has admirably suggested the suffering they indicate, and has almost made the language itself express the peculiar quality of the danger, "hupek thanatoio ferontai."

[Selection and arrangement by Archilochus and Demosthenes]

[26] Of the same quality is the passage in Archilochus on the shipwreck,[35] and that on the arrival of the news by Demosthenes.[36] "It was evening," he begins. One might say they have chosen the striking features on their merits and united them, witnout any intermixture of cheap, trivial, or labored verses, which are enough to ruin the whole work by making holes and weak spots, for things are great because of their connection with others so ordered with them as to make a firm structure.

Chapter XI

[Amplification]

[27] Associated with the virtues we have named is what is called amplification; this may be used when narratives or arguments are so divided into sections that they permit of many fresh beginnings and pauses, and one great effect is reinforced by another still greater and they come upon us with continually augmented power. This may be done by developing a theme, or by emphasis for the strengthening of facts or arguments, or by skillful control of actions and feelings. In fact, there are a thousand means of amplification. But the orator must realize that none of these will bring him to the end he seeks unless they are of high quality. I admit one can make an exception of complaints and undignified sections, but if you take away excellence of style from other amplified passages you remove the soul from the body, for if they do not receive support from the qualities of the style their vigor declines and vanishes. What I have just spoken of differs from what I mentioned a little earlier, for I then had in mind the limitation of the main themes and their unified arrangement. Clearness demands that I show accurately the general difference between excellence and amplification.

---

[35] Only fragments of this lyric poet survive. See p. 185, below, and Horace, *Art of Poetry*, 79, above.   [36] *On the Crown*, 169.

Chapter XII

[Amplification defined]

[28] The definition given in technical treatises does not satisfy me; they say that amplification is language that confers an appearance of magnitude to the subject. That description could just as well be applied to style that is elevated or emotional or figurative, since all of these give a composition something of greatness. But to me these seem distinct from each other, for excellence consists in high quality, but amplification depends on abundance. The first often resides in a single thought, but the second is impossible without a certain plenty and copiousness. To speak generally, amplification is the amassing of all the different elements and sources of description that can be associated with the matters in question, and that enable the author to strengthen his presentation by lingering over it. In this it differs from demonstration, which makes clear what is sought for. [At this point about a twenty-fifth of the work is lost.]

[Cicero and Demosthenes compared]

[29] Plato pours forth his treasures in abundance, like a sea that spreads out in a great expanse.[37] So I should say that while Demosthenes as more emotional has a more fiery and flaming spirit, yet Plato, standing firm in weighty and majestic dignity, is by no means frigid, though he does not give forth flashes. If it is possible for a Greek to express his opinion, my dear Terentianus, it seems to me the greatness of Cicero differs from that of Demosthenes in just the same way. Demosthenes is superior in absolute excellence, Cicero in scope. Our countryman may be likened to a tornado or a thunderbolt because of the way he burns and scatters everything with his vehemence, speed, power, and energy. But Cicero, I feel, like a far-reaching conflagration seizes upon and sweeps up everything; he has always within him a great and inexhaustible fire, turned now in one direction, now in another, and fed with a steady supply of fuel.[38] But you as a Roman can judge this better than I can.

---

[37] It is supposed that Plato was mentioned in the part that is lacking. He is superior in magnificence, but Demosthenes is more concentrated.

[38] Dryden alludes to this passage and sums it up by saying: "One persuades, the other commands" (Preface to the *Fables*, in Ker, *Essays of Dryden*, II, 254).

[Profusion]

[30] The fitting moments for the excellence and nervous energy of a Demosthenes are those of intense and violent feeling when the audience must reel under a staggering blow. The time for profusion comes when they are to be overwhelmed. It should, then, be used mostly in the treatment of well-known themes, and in epilogues, digressions, and descriptions of all sorts, in historical and scientific speeches, and in not a few other types of composition.

Chapter XIII

[The greatness of Plato]

[31] To return to Plato, though he flows with a noiseless current, he nevertheless attains greatness; you have read the *Republic* and are not ignorant of his style:

> Those who have no experience of wisdom and virtue but are ever devoted to feasts and such things are borne downward, as it seems, and so they wander uncertainly through life, and in truth never have looked upward nor been carried upward nor tasted lasting and pure pleasure, but like cattle that always look down and feed from the earth, they feast at the tables, stuffing themselves and copulating, and in their greed for these delights they kick and butt each other with horns and hoofs of iron and slay each other in their lust.[39]

[Imitation of great predecessors]

[32] Plato also points out, if we will but not neglect his counsel, that another road, in addition to those we have mentioned, leads to excellence. And what road is that? It is imitation and emulation of the great prose writers and poets of antiquity.[40] Let us apply ourselves to this, my dear friend, with all our might. Many are in this way inspired by the spirit of another, just as report says

[39] *Republic*, ix, 586 AB, slightly abridged.

[40] For the Renaissance view, see the index, under *imitation*. Addison writes: "Longinus, among the rules which he lays down for succeeding in the sublime way of writing, proposes to his reader that he should imitate the most celebrated authors who have gone before him and been engaged in works of the same nature. . . . By this means one great genius often catches the flame from another, and writes in his spirit without copying servilely after him. . . . Milton, though his own natural strength of genius was capable of furnishing out a perfect work, has doubtless very much raised and ennobled his conception by such an imitation as that which Longinus has recommended" (*Spectator*, no. 339 [March 29, 1712]).

that the Pythian priestess, on drawing near to the tripod where there is a chasm in the earth breathing forth a divine exhalation, is so filled with the heavenly power that she utters oracles under its influence. So from the great spirits of the ancients an influence as though from the holy cave of the oracle passes into the spirits of the emulators; inspired by this, even those not susceptible share enthusiastically in the greatness of others. Was it only Herodotus who was thoroughly Homeric? No, Stesichorus and Archilochus were before him; and above all there was Plato, who diverted into his own stream a thousand little rills from the Homeric spring. We should need to indicate some of these if Ammonius and his pupils had not sought them out and made a classified list of them.

[Imitation is not plagiarism[41]]

[33] Such a proceeding is not theft; it is like obtaining a pattern from beautiful forms or images or other works of art. Plato would not have reared so many flowers among the precepts of philosophy or so often employed poetic material and language if he had not, I tell you, striven with all his heart against Homer for the pre-eminence, a young antagonist against one who had attained high honors, perhaps fighting with too great eagerness and pride, but still deriving great benefit from the contest. For, as Hesiod said, "Good is this strife for mortals."[42] Of a certainty the crown of victory is fair and the strife for fame is most honorable when even to be worsted by one's forefathers is not inglorious.

Chapter XIV

[What would Homer, Plato, or Demosthenes have said?]

[34] We then, when we are toiling on something that requires excellence of expression and greatness of thought, would do well to ask in our hearts how Homer would have said it or how Plato or Demosthenes or Thucydides, in his history, would have given it distinction. For these great characters appearing to us as objects of emulation and standing prominently before us will raise our souls to the pitch we have imagined.[43] Still more if we try in

---

[41] This paragraph is quoted by Dryden in his Preface to *Troilus and Cressida* (Ker, *Essays of Dryden*, I, 206).   [42] *Works and Days*, 24.

[43] Rendered by Dryden (*loc. cit.*): "Those great men whom we propose to ourselves as patterns of our imitation serve us as a torch which is lifted up before us to enlighten our passage, and often elevate our thoughts as high as the conception we have of our author's genius."

addition to formulate in our minds an answer to the question: If Homer or Demosthenes were present how would he react to this thing I am saying? How would he be affected by this other passage? Certainly our efforts will be great if we set before ourselves such a group of critics and such an audience for our utterances and imagine we are presenting our writings for examination to such superhuman judges and witnesses.

[How will posterity regard a composition?]

[35] We shall be still more stimulated if we go on to ask: How will all the ages to come respond to what I am writing? For if at the outset a man is afraid he will utter something too good to be appreciated in his own city and in his own day, his conceptions cannot be other than imperfect and blind abortions, brought forth before they have completed the time of development required for a life of fame.

Chapter XV

[Imagination and images]

[36] Imaginative pictures (the name by which some people call poetic images) are highly effective in producing massiveness, grandeur, and energy. The name imagination is commonly applied to any idea that enters the mind and produces speech, but the meaning that prevails is the one I employ, namely, that in your enthusiasm and strong feeling you seem to see what you speak of and put it before the eyes of your audience.[44] It will not escape you that imagination is defined in one way by the orator and in another by the poet, nor that in poetry it strives to strike the hearer with a sudden shock, but in oratory it seeks vividness. Both, however, aim at the latter and at excitement.

[Images in Euripides]

[37] O mother, I beg you, do not excite against me the bloody-footed and snaky maidens. They are here; they are close enough to leap upon me.

And

Oh, she'll kill me! Whither shall I flee?[45]

---

[44] "Imaging is, in itself, the very height and life of poetry. It is, as Longinus describes it, a discourse, which by a kind of enthusiasm or extraordinary emotion of the soul makes it seem that we behold those things which the poet paints, so as to be pleased with them and to admire them" (Dryden, *Apology for Heroic Poetry*, in Ker, *Essays of Dryden*, I, 186). [45] Euripides, *Iphigenia among the Taurians*, 291; *Orestes*, 255.

When the poet wrote these lines he saw the Furies, and all but forced his hearers to see what he imagined. Euripides especially uses all his powers in giving tragic expression to the two passions of madness and love, and I believe is more successful in these than in any of the others, though he has no hesitation in attempting various other imaginative forms. Having little elevation of spirit, yet in many passages he forced his nature to become tragic, and always in his great verses is like the lion of whom Homer wrote:

> With his tail he scourges his ribs and loins on either side, and ever lashes himself on to the combat.[46]

Of Helios giving over the reins to Phaethon he writes:

> Take care not to drive into the Libyan air, for since it is not tempered with moisture, it will dry up and split the wheels of thy chariot. . . . But ever direct thy course by the seven Pleiades. On hearing this the boy caught up the reins, and bringing down his whip on the flanks of his winged horses, he was off; the horses spread their wings in flight over the cloud-bands of the air. Behind him his father rode on the back of the Dog Star, cautioning his son. "Drive there," he said, "turn thy chariot this way, now turn it that way."[47]

Would you not say that in spirit the poet stepped into the chariot with Phaethon and shared his danger as the winged horses flew on? He could never have imagined such things if he had not been in the chariot and borne a part in those celestial deeds. The same imagination appears in his lines on Cassandra beginning: "Now, ye horse-loving men of Troy."[48]

[Images in Aeschylus]

[38] Aeschylus ventures on the most heroic imaginations, as when in the *Seven against Thebes* he writes:

> Seven strong men, ardent captains, have slain a bull over a black-rimmed shield, and dipping their fingers in the blood of the bull, have sworn by Mars, and the god of Destruction, and Panic-Rout the lover of blood.[49]

---

[46] *Iliad*, xx, 170.   [47] From a lost play, the *Phaethon*.
[48] Nothing is known of the context.
[49] Lines 42–6. The last expression is perhaps based on the fact, observed by so late a general as Robert E. Lee, that the slaughter of the flight is greater than that of the well-ordered array of battle.

Each man swears to the others that he will die with them without any sound of lamentation. Sometimes, though, Aeschylus brings in ideas that are not fully worked out, as though he had left wool unscoured or leather untanned. Yet in his desire for fame Euripides thrusts himself into similar perils. According to a startling phrase in Aeschylus the palace of Lycurgus is seized with divine frenzy on the apparition of Dionysus:

The house is in a frenzy, the roof reels like a Bacchic reveler.[50]

Euripides expressed the same idea in a different way, making it more pleasing:

The whole mountain joined with them in Bacchic revelry.[51]

[The imagination of Sophocles]

[39] Sophocles shows splendid imagination when he describes the dying Oedipus going to his own sepulcher accompanied by strange portents in the heavens;[52] and Achilles at the embarcation appearing above his tomb to the Greeks as they leave the shore; perhaps no one has made a more vivid image of this scene than has Simonides. But I cannot give all the examples.

[Imagination in poetry and oratory]

[40] As I said, the instances found in the poets are of a very mythical quality greatly in excess of the fact, but the imagination of the orator is at its best when it gives an effect of truth and reality. Exceptions to this rule, when the substance of the speech is poetical and mythical and runs over into the impossible, seem repellent and alien. Yes, by heaven, the wonderful orators of our day are like tragic poets; the noble fellows see Furies before them, and cannot understand that Orestes was beholding the phantasms of a madman when he said:

Loose me. You are one of my Furies; you grip my body fast to hurl me into Tartarus.[53]

[Imagination in the orator]

[41] What then can the orator's imagination do? It surely can introduce into his speeches many instances of vigor and true feeling, and when combined with practical arguments it does not

---

[50] From a lost play by Aeschylus.   [51]*Bacchae*, 726.
[52] *Oedipus at Colonus*, 1586–1666.   [53] Euripides, *Orestes*, 264.

merely convince the hearer but subjects him to its force. Demosthenes says:

> If at this instant we should hear a tumult in front of the courthouse and someone should say that the prison had been opened and the criminals were escaping, I am certain there is no man, either old or young, so careless that he would not come to the rescue to the limit of his ability. But if someone were to come and say that the very man before us is he who let them loose, the culprit would be slain before he had a chance to utter a word.[54]

Then there is the instance of Hyperides, when he was on trial because after the defeat he offered a resolution that the slaves should be set free. "This resolution was not proposed by the orator," he said, "but by the battle of Chaeronea." The orator has used his imagination along with a practical argument; hence he raises his conception far above the limits of persuasion. In all such speeches we naturally always hear the strongest part; hence we are snatched from the expository to the striking imaginative effect, and the practical basis is concealed in dazzling light. This is not an abnormal experience, for whenever two forces are united in their effort, the stronger invariably diverts to itself the power of the weaker.

[42] I believe I have said enough on the excellences of thought that are derived from greatness of soul, imitation, and imaginative power.

[PART III, FIGURES, THE THIRD SOURCE OF LITERARY EXCELLENCE]

Chapter XVI

[43] The topic of figures comes next in order. As I have said,[55] these, if rightly employed, make no slight contribution to greatness. But since it would require too much effort, indeed would be a boundless task, to treat them all in detail at present, we shall merely run through a few of those that contribute to a strong effect, in order to establish our assertion.

[The oath as used by Demosthenes]

[44] There is a passage in which Demosthenes is attempting to explain something about his political measures. What was the natural treatment of the subject?

[54] *Timocrates*, 208.   [55] In chap. VIII.

You were not wrong, O men of Athens, in undertaking the struggle for the liberties of Greece. You have proofs of this close at
hand: for they were not wrong who fought at Marathon nor at
Salamis nor at Plataea.

But instead, as though suddenly inspired by heaven and seized
upon by the might of Phoebus, the orator utters his oath by the
bravest men of Greece:

It is impossible you are wrong, no, by those who faced the dangers of Marathon, you are not.[56]

By employing the figure of adjuration, which here I call apostrophe, he seems to have put his forefathers among the gods, for
he implies that men who died as they did should be sworn by as
though they were gods; he has filled the judges with the spirit of
those who faced the dangers of the battle. Changing the nature
of his argument, he has given it the highest distinction and pathos
and all the reasons for belief demanded by strange and preter-
natural oaths. At the same time, he has made his speech a sort of
remedy and antidote for the spirits of his hearers, for comforted by
his eulogies they were made to feel that the battle with Philip was
as creditable as the victories at Marathon and Salamis. Thus by
the use of the figure he carries his audience along with him. It is
true he is said to have found the germ of his oath in Eupolis:

By my fight at Marathon not one of them shall vex my soul
unpunished.[57]

But it is not enough to swear some great oath; the place and the
manner and the time and the reason are what count. In Eupolis
there is nothing but the oath, in a speech directed to the Athenians
when they were prosperous and needed no encouragement.
Moreover the poet does not swear by men he ranks with the immortals that the listeners may have a just notion of their virtue, but
from soldiers in danger wanders off to something lifeless, the fight.
Demosthenes, on the other hand, adapts the oath to men who have
been conquered in battle, that Chaeronea may no longer appear a
disaster to the Athenians, and at the same time it is a demonstration that no error has been made, an example, a solemn assurance,
a eulogy, an encouragement. The orator foresaw that someone
would object: you are speaking of a defeat caused by your admin-
istration, and still you swear by victories. For this reason he meas-

<hr>

[56] *On the Crown*, 208.   [57] From a lost work by the comedian Eupolis.

ures his words one after another and acts cautiously, teaching us that even in a Bacchic dance we must keep sober,[58] for he says:

> Those who faced the dangers of Marathon, and those who fought in the naval battle at Salamis and at Artemisium, and those who stood in battle array at Plataea.

He does not use the word *conquered* but cleverly keeps from naming any result, since in the others it was fortunate and the opposite of what happened at Chaeronea. For the same reason he anticipates his hearer by adding immediately:

> The city gave a public funeral to all its dead, Aeschines, not to the victors alone.

Chapter XVII

[Figures and excellence of style]

[45] At this point, my dear friend, I must not omit one conclusion from my experience, though I shall state it briefly: Figures naturally work in harmony with excellence of style and in turn receive marvelous reinforcement from it. Where and how? I will explain.

[Figures liable to suspicion]

[46] The clever use of figures is peculiarly subject to suspicion; it excites men to infer treachery, craft, and fallacy, above all when employed in addressing judges who have absolute power, especially tyrants, kings, and administrators of high rank. Such a man is indignant if like a simple child he is overreached by the figures of speech of a clever orator. Taking the fallacy as an insult to himself, he becomes thoroughly enraged and, even though he keeps his temper, is made completely hostile to the argument of the speech.[59] Hence the figure seems to be best when the hearer does not notice that it is a figure.

[Emotion justifies the figure]

[47] Literary excellence and strong feeling are wonderful guards and protectors against the suspicion aroused by figurative

---

[58] Adapted from Euripides, *Bacchae*, 317.

[59] Cf. Cicero, *De oratore*, II, 37: "I think . . . all suspicion of artifice is prejudicial to the orator with those who have the decision of affairs; for it diminishes the authority of the speaker and the credit of his speech."

language. When the craft with which it has been elaborated is concealed by its beauty and grandeur, the figure is no longer obvious and escapes all suspicion.[60] An excellent instance is the one mentioned above, "I swear by those who fought at Marathon." How did the orator conceal that figure? Clearly by its own brilliance. For as lesser lights vanish when their brilliance is swallowed up by that of the sun, so the devices of the orator are wholly concealed by the glory that surrounds them. There is something in painting not very different from this, for the shadow and the lights are side by side in colors on the same plane, yet the lights are what strike the eyes, and seem not merely conspicuous but actually much nearer. So in a speech the passages characterized by strong feeling and elevation of style, lying closer to our hearts because of some inborn quality and because of their splendor, are much more quickly seen than the figures; they seem to throw a shadow over their own art and keep it concealed.

Chapter XVIII

[Question and answer]

[48] What are we to think of oratorical questions and answers?[61] Is not what is said made more vigorous and impressive by the imaginative power of such figures? Demosthenes asks:

> Tell me, do you wish to go around asking each other: Is there any news? What news could be more striking than that the Macedonian is conquering Greece? Is Philip dead? Not dead, by Zeus, though he is sick. But what difference does it make to you? Whatever happens to him, you will quickly make yourselves another Philip.[62]

And again Demosthenes says:

> Let us sail to Macedonia. Someone asks: "Where shall we land?" The war itself will find out the weak points in Philip's strategy.[63]

Stated simply this idea would have been altogether lacking in force, but when the figure is used, the inspired effect and quick

---

[60] Cf. the similar remark on the hyperbole, chap. xxxviii, below.

[61] The Greek text gives a second word for *question* instead of one for *answer*. An emendation has been suggested.

[62] *Philippics*, I, 10, slightly altered.   [63] *Ibid.*, I, 44, slightly altered.

play of question and answer and his reply to himself as to someone else not only give the speech higher oratorical quality but also make it more convincing. An emotional passage is always more effective when it seems not to have been planned by the speaker but to have sprung from the occasion. The question put to himself and its answer simulate spontaneous emotion. Those who are subjected to questioning by others get excited and without hesitation answer questions vigorously and with truth. Thus the device of question and answer seems to lead the hearer into the false assumption that each of the carefully prepared figures was thought of and spoken on the spur of the moment. We may further quote that passage from Herodotus which has always been thought one of his most excellent: "If thus. . . ." [About a twenty-fifth of the manuscript is missing at this point.]

Chapter XIX

[Asyndeton]

[49] In the figure of asyndeton,[64] the phrases fall unconnected as though in a torrent, almost getting ahead of the speaker himself. Xenophon writes:

> With their shields striking together, they pushed, they fought, they killed, they were killed.[65]

Take also the words of Eurylochus:

> We came, as you ordered, through the wood, glorious Odysseus. We saw in the glade a beautiful palace standing.[66]

Since the phrases are disconnected and yet rapid, they make emphatic the excitement which both hampers the man's speech and makes it more rapid. This the poet achieves by leaving out the connectives.

Chapter XX

[The combination of figures]

[50] The combination of figures seems to be especially effective when two or three are joined together for one purpose and each contributes its share of force, conviction, beauty. This appears in

---

[64] Omission of conjunctions.   [65] *Hellenica*, IV, 3, 19.   [66] *Odyssey*, X, 251.

a passage in the speech against Meidias, where asyndeton is combined with anaphora [67] and diatyposis: [68]

> The assailant may do many things which the victim sometimes cannot describe to anyone else—by gesture, by expression, by voice. [69]

Then, that this speech may not continue in the same way (for in monotony there is quiet; but emotion, since it is a violent disturbance of the soul, is expressed by disorder) straightway he rushes on to further employment of asyndeton and anaphora:

> With his gestures, with his expression, with his voice, when he insults you, when he acts like an enemy, when he uses his knuckles, when he treats you like a slave.

Here the orator does nothing other than the assailant does; he smites the mind of the jury with blow upon blow. Then he retires to make another onset, as do gusts of wind, saying:

> When it's with the fist, when it's on the face, this excites, this stirs up men not accustomed to being insulted. No one by telling of this can make it seem as terrible as it is.

Thus he fully maintains the quality proper to his anaphoras and asyndeta with continual variation, so that his order is disordered and his disorder takes on a certain order.

Chapter XXI

[To supply the conjunctions ruins the effect]

[51] Now then, if you please, put in the connectives, as Isocrates and his followers do:

> And one must not overlook this too, that the assailant may do many things, first with his gestures, and then with his expression, and further with his mere voice.

If you rewrite the rest in the same way, you will see that when you level it to smoothness with conjunctions the effect of breathless haste and roughness wholly collapses and the passage has no fire left in it. For just as one who ties together the bodies of runners deprives them of their speed, emotion hampered with

---

[67] Repetition of sounds.   [68] Vivid presentation.   [69] *Meidias*, 72.

conjunctions and other inactive words is kept from displaying its force; they take away its freedom for the race and its impetus as though hurled from a catapult.

Chapter XXII

[Hyperbaton]

[52] In the same class is the figure of hyperbaton. This consists in a violent disruption of the natural order of words and ideas, and seems to show the most unmistakable signs of violent feeling,[70] because those who really are angry or afraid or violently irritated or in the grip of jealousy or some other passion (for there are so many emotions that no one can hope to number them) come forward with one idea and then rush off to some other, after having thrown in something quite irrational; then they circle back to the first, and in their excitement, as though driven by an uncertain wind, shift their words and ideas now in one direction, then to the very opposite, and change their arrangement from the natural into a thousand shifting forms. The best prose writers, using hyperbaton to imitate nature, get the same effect. For art is perfect when it seems to be nature, and nature succeeds when it has art concealed within.[71] Take the speech of Dionysius the Phocaean in Herodotus:

> On a knife edge our cause is poised, men of Ionia; shall we be free? shall we be slaves, runaway slaves? Now then if you have a mind to endure afflictions, you will suffer hardships for the present, but you will overthrow your enemies.

In normal order this would be:

> Men of Ionia, now is the time for you to endure afflictions, for our cause is poised on a knife edge.

But he has displaced the words "men of Ionia," then he sets out with fear, anticipating his beginning as though dire need did not

---

[70] Dryden, apparently with Longinus in mind, writes: "A man in such an occasion of passion is not cool enough either to reason rightly or to talk calmly. Aggravations are then in their proper places; interrogations, exclamations, hyperbata, or a disordered connection of discourse, are graceful there because they are natural" (*Apology for Heroic Poetry*, in Ker, *Essays of Dryden*, I, 186). Dryden is obviously drawing on sections of Longinus from XVII onward.

[71] Cf. chaps. XVII, above, and XXXVIII, below, and Dryden, *An Essay of Dramatic Poesy*, sect. 65, below.

allow him time to address his hearers. Then he has reversed the order of the ideas; instead of saying that it is necessary for them to suffer (for to that he would exhort them) he first gives the reason for which they must suffer; "On a knife edge," he says, "our cause is poised." His words seem not carefully thought out but forced from him.

[Hyperbaton in Demosthenes and Thucydides]

[53] Thucydides shows yet greater skill in using hyperbaton to break apart what is by nature one and inseparable. Demosthenes, though not so rash as Thucydides, is the most excessive of them all in the employment of this figure; he frequently applies inversion to give the effect of tremendous violence and actually seems to be speaking extempore; he even drags his hearers along with him into a perilous maze of inverted phrases. For many times throwing aside the thought he was rushing on to express, and introducing some strange and unlikely arrangement, he takes disconnected ideas and piles them up in the middle until his audience is afraid he will scatter his thought to the winds and gets so excited that it is obliged to accompany the speaker in his perilous path. Then unexpectedly after a great interval he produces the long-awaited phrase at the end in just the nick of time, so that he astonishes his hearers the more by the very daring and hazard of his hyperbata. Examples are so common I shall not trouble to quote any.

Chapter XXIII

[Polyptotes]

[54] Then there are the figures included under polyptotes[72]— accumulations, startling turns, and climaxes—which, as you know, are very powerful aids in securing beauty and every kind of excellence and emotional effect. Then the variations of case, of tense, of person, of number, of gender, how they give diversity and vigor to a presentation![73]

[72] Literally *the figure of many cases*; it seems to include all changes of case, number, tense, etc., for the sake of rhetorical effect.

[73] English, with its relative lack of inflection, can do little of this sort, though it does occur, as in Milton's lines:

Knowing both good and evil as they know (*Paradise Lost*, IX, 709).

Mean I to try, what rash untried I sought (*ibid*, 860).

[The plural for the singular]

As to number, those instances are beautiful where a singular form when carefully considered is found to have the force of a plural, for example:

> Straightway a measureless crowd far and near along the strand was roaring "the tunny." [74]

But still more worthy of note are the instances in which the plural impresses us with its more mouth-filling sounds and gives a splendid effect by the very sense of multitude that it conveys. This is illustrated by the lines of Sophocles on *Oedipus:*

> O marriages, marriages, you gave us birth and when you had given us birth, you sowed the same seed again and produced fathers, brothers, sons—all of one blood—brides, wives, mothers, and whatever deeds most shameful have been wrought among men.[75]

The first three can be summed up in one name, that of Oedipus, and the others in that of Jocasta, but when the counting is spread out into plurals it multiplies the misfortunes as well. There is the same multiplication in this:

> Forth came Hectors and Sarpedons as well.[76]

And there is the passage in Plato about the Athenians, which we have quoted elsewhere:

> For no Pelopses, nor Cadmuses, nor Aegyptuses, nor Danauses, nor others of barbarous race too many to name dwell with us, but we are Hellenes, not half-caste barbarians,[77] etc.

Naturally the facts seem more imposing when the names are thus brought together in shoals. But this should not be done save in passages where the subject calls for augmentation or fullness or loftiness or strong feeling—one or more of these, since wearing anklets as well as bracelets is trying too hard to be splendid.

---

[74] By an unknown author. The fishermen in great numbers are to go out after a school of fish just reported by a lookout.

[75] *Oedipus Tyrannus*, 1403–8.   [76] From an unknown work.

[77] *Menexenus*, 245 D. Cf. Milton's Gorgons and Hydras, and Chimeras dire (*Paradise Lost*, II, 628).

Chapter XXIV

[The singular for the plural]

[55] Then on the contrary sometimes it gives a most excellent effect to descend from the plural to the singular. Demosthenes says:

> The whole Peloponnese was then at variance.[78]

and Herodotus:

> When Phrynichus presented his tragedy of *The Capture of Miletus,* the theater burst into tears.[79]

To include many separate individuals within a singular number enhances our impression that they behave as a unit. The cause of the splendid effect is, I think, the same in either instance. When the words are singular, to make them plural contrary to expectation is the act of a man in a state of strong feeling. When they are plural and you combine them all into one euphonious singular, the effect lies in the unexpected change of things in the opposite direction.

Chapter XXV

[The present for the past]

[56] When you bring in events that happened some time since as taking place at the moment when you speak, you make your speech not a narrative but a drama. Xenophon writes:

> Someone has fallen under Cyrus's horse and when he is trodden on plunges his sword into the belly of the horse; the horse rears and unseats Cyrus, who falls to the ground.[80]

Thucydides makes frequent use of this figure.

Chapter XXVI

[Direct appeal to the reader]

[57] Change of persons also produces a powerful effect, many times making the hearer feel as though he were moving in the midst of the dangers the poet sets forth.

---

[78] *On the Crown,* 18.   [79] *Histories,* VI, 21.   [80] *Cyropaedia,* VII, 1, 37.

You would say that unworn and untiring they met in battle, so fiercely they fought.[81]

And Aratus writes:

In that month see to it thou art not in the midst of the wash of the sea.[82]

Herodotus does much the same thing:

You will sail up the river from the city of Elephantine until you come to a smooth plain. Passing this place, you will again take ship and sail two days, until you come to a great city called Meroë.[83]

Do you see, my comrade, how he lays hold on your spirit and leads you through the places and turns hearing into sight? Such direct personal application puts the hearer immediately in contact with events. When you speak as to one man alone rather than to all who may care to listen (as Homer does when he says:

You could not tell to which side Tydides belonged),[84]

you will move him more deeply and make him more attentive and fill him with interest in the battle, for he will be aroused by these direct appeals to himself.

Chapter XXVII

[Changes to the first person]

[58] In other instances the writer, when speaking of one of his characters, suddenly turns and is changed into the very character himself; this figure is a sort of outburst of feeling:

Hector with a great shout called to the Trojans to rush upon the ships and let the bloody spoils alone. "Whatever man I see of his own will far away from the ships, for him will I seek instant death."[85]

Here the poet has chosen the narrative method as suitable, yet suddenly and without any explanation he puts the threat in the mouth of the angry leader. It would have seemed frigid if he had prefixed: Hector said thus and so. But as it is, the method of the poem changes even more quickly than the speaker does. Hence

---

[81] *Iliad*, xv, 697.   [82] *Phaenomena*, 287.   [83]*Histories*, II, 29, somewhat altered.
[84] *Iliad*, v, 85.   [85] *Iliad*, xv, 346.

the best place to use this figure is where the rapid movement of the action does not allow the author time for a transition, but without delay he must shift from one character to another, as was done by Hecataeus:

> Troubled by these things, Ceyx straightway commanded the children of Hercules to depart. "I am not able to aid you. Hence, that you may not ruin yourselves and hurt me; be off to some other people."

[Change to direct address]

[59] In the *Aristogeiton*, Demosthenes has used a different method for making his change of persons passionate and sudden:

> Will not one of you be found who is disturbed and indignant at the violent deeds of this disgusting and shameless fellow, who—oh you, most wicked of all men! when you were deprived of the right to speak not by gratings or doors, which someone might open.

While his sense is still incomplete he makes a sudden change and almost divides a single phrase between two persons: "who—oh you, most wicked." He turns aside to speak to Aristogeiton and appears to abandon the jury he is addressing, that so much the more he may come back to it with strong feeling. Penelope does the same thing:

> Henchman, wherefore have the noble wooers sent thee forth? Was it to tell the handmaids of divine Odysseus to cease from their work, and prepare a banquet for them? Nay, after thus much wooing, never again may they come together, but here this day sup for their last and latest time; all ye who assemble so often, and waste much livelihood. . . . Long ago when ye were children, ye marked not your fathers' telling, what manner of man was Odysseus.[86]

Chapter XXVIII

[Periphrasis]

[60] Then there is periphrasis, which, as I suppose no one will deny, produces excellent effects. For as in music the main theme is made sweeter by the so-called accompaniments, so periphrasis many times fits in with normal language and adds greatly to its

---

[86] *Odyssey*, IV, 681–9, trans. by Butcher and Lang.

beauty, especially if it is not puffed up and unmusical but tempered with sweetness. A sufficient witness for this is Plato at the beginning of his funeral oration:

> In truth we have given them their due reward, and having obtained it, they may now go on their appointed journey, receiving their last farewells as a group from the whole city, and as individuals each one from his kinsmen.[87]

In this passage he calls death an appointed journey and the receiving of due rites a sort of public escort to the grave by their fatherland. Has he not by these things considerably dignified the thought? for he has taken the literal expression and made it musical by wrapping it in the sweet harmonies of his periphrasis. Xenophon too makes use of periphrasis, writing:

> You look on labor as the guide to a happy life, and you have stored up in your souls the fairest and most soldierly of treasures, for before all else you desire to be praised.[88]

Instead of saying "You wish to labor," he says, "You look on labor as the guide to a happy life," and by developing the rest in the same way he has been able to include in his eulogy a great idea. Consider also that inimitable phrase in Herodotus:

> On the Scythians who sacked her temple the goddess sent a female disease.[89]

Chapter XXIX

[Periphrasis misused by Plato]

[61] Periphrasis, wrongly used, is more likely than any other figure to produce an effect the reverse of desirable, for when it is dull and savors of verbiage it soon sinks down in weakness. Hence some ridicule even Plato (a man who will have his figure, even out of season) because he says in the *Laws* that

> we should not allow either silver or golden Plutus to get a footing in the city and remain there.[90]

---

[87] *Menexenus*, 236D.   [88] *Cyropaedia*, I, 5, 12.   [89] *Histories*, I, 105.

[90] *Laws*, VII, 801B, above. The Greek word *plouton* is ambiguous here; it might be either a common or a proper noun. Herodotus uses the same words, in a different case, to mean "treasure in silver" (II, 121, I). It has been suggested that Plato is here quoting from a poet unknown to Longinus.

Would Longinus have approved Milton's "tame villatic fowl" (*Samson Agonistes*, 1695)?

They say that if he had wished to forbid the possession of animals he would have called them ovine and bovine Plutus.

[The value of figures]

[62] But, my dear Terentianus, this is enough by way of digression on the use of figures in securing literary excellence. They all enable speeches to be more passionate and expressive of feeling, and emotion plays the same part in the most excellent compositions as character does in those that are merely pleasing.

[PART IV, NOTABLE LANGUAGE, THE FOURTH SOURCE OF LITERARY EXCELLENCE]

Chapter XXX

[63] Now since the thought and the diction of a literary composition are mutually dependent, let us see if there is something still to be said on diction. It would be superfluous to explain to those who already know it that the choice of noble and grandly appropriate words is wonderfully effective in moving and influencing the reader, and that all orators and historians set the attainment of this as their chief object. For this in itself gives at one time grandeur, beauty, antique richness, weight, energy, strength, and a sort of polish like that on the most beautiful statues; it endows the facts with a speaking soul, as it were. Truly beautiful words are the very light of thought. Yet majesty in diction is not always to be desired: to array petty affairs in noble and stately words would be as though one put a great tragic mask on a puny child. Yet in poetry and history . . . [More than one twelfth of the entire manuscript is lacking here.]

Chapter XXXI

[Ordinary words]

[64] . . . full of thought and suggestive. And the words of Anacreon:

My mind is no more fixed on the Thracian filly.[91]

---

[91] The word meaning *filly* is supplied by a modern editor; hence the meaning may be *Thracian woman* or *girl*. The word *filly* has often been used in English to mean a young woman, as in Sedley's "Hyde-Park filly" (*The Mulberry Garden*, I, 1, 45).

In the same way the phrase of Theopompus, though less praise-worthy,[92] seems to me to be full of expression because of the analogy; I do not understand why Caecilius finds fault with it. He says:

> Philip was a great fellow for swallowing what political necessity told him he must.[93]

Sometimes the homely word is much more illuminating than the ornate one. Because it comes from ordinary life, it is immediately understood, for the familiar is more convincing than the unusual. The word "swallow" is very expressive when applied to a man eager and glad to put up with the disgraceful and sordid because of an ambition that enables him to endure anything. Much the same thing is true of the following phrases from Herodotus:

> Cleomenes in his madness cut his own body to pieces with a short sword until he chopped himself into mincemeat and died.[94]

> Pythes kept on fighting in the ship until he was cut up like a meat-carcass.[95]

These approach vulgarity but are not vulgar because they are full of meaning.

Chapter XXXII

[Metaphors]

[65] With respect to the number of metaphors Caecilius seems to take his stand with those who think two or at most three should be applied to the same matter. We may get our rule from the example of Demosthenes. The right time for their use is when the feelings roll on like a spring torrent and sweep along the whole mass of them as though they were inevitable. Demosthenes says:

> Detestable men and parasites, each one of whom has horribly mangled his own native land, pledging away their liberty by drinking first to Philip, then to Alexander, measuring their happiness by their bellies and their lowest appetites, and utterly subverting that liberty and determination never to submit to a despot which to the earlier Greeks were the standards and canons of felicity.[96]

---

[92] The text is here in dispute; some editors prefer a reading that would mean "the novel coinage" or "original expression of Theopompus."

[93] The reference is to the diet prescribed for athletes by their trainers.

[94] *Histories*, VI, 75.   [95] *Histories*, VII, 181.   [96] *On the Crown*, 296.

Here the orator's feeling against the traitors keeps us from realizing the number of the metaphors.

[The qualification of metaphors]

[66] For the same reason Aristotle and Theophrastus say that there can be some softening of bold metaphors by inserting *as if*, and *as it were*, and *if I may use the figure*, and *if I may be so bold as to say*.[97] The qualification, they say, atones for the boldness. I admit this, but yet, as I said in speaking of figures, the right antidotes for number and violence of metaphors are well timed and vigorous emotion and noble excellence of style. By the vigor of their current these naturally sweep along and push forward the rest, or rather they demand highly figurative language as a necessity and do not allow the hearer to object to their number, because he is fired with the enthusiasm of the speaker.

[Metaphorical description]

[67] Moreover, in the treatment of a generally accepted idea and in descriptions there is nothing so expressive as connected and interdependent figures. By means of these Xenophon gives a splendid description of the construction of the house of the body,[98] and Plato still more divinely. The head he calls the citadel of the body, the neck is an isthmus between it and the chest. The vertebrae, he says, are placed beneath like pivots. Pleasure is evil's bait for man, and the tongue the tester of taste. The heart, the meeting place of the veins and the fountain of the rapid-flowing blood, is in the guard house. The various tubes extending through the body he calls alleys. And he says:

> Since the leaping-up of the heart on the approach of danger or in the violence of passion is the result of fire, the gods, to counteract it, prepared and put in the body the lungs as a sort of cushion, soft, bloodless, and cellular in make-up, so that when the passions boiled up in the heart it might have its impact on a yielding surface and take no damage.

The seat of the sexual desires he compares to the apartments of the women, and that of anger to those of the men. The spleen is the towel of the entrails, for being soaked with their discharges it becomes swollen and fetid. After this the gods covered all the

---

[97] Milton apologizes for an elaborate comparison by saying: "If great things to small may be compared" (*Paradise Lost*, x, 306). [98] *Memorabilia*, I, 4, 5.

inner parts with flesh, making it a protection on the outside like a mat of felt. He calls the blood the pasturage of the flesh, and continues:

> For the sake of nourishment they provided the body with canals for the blood, cutting channels as though in gardens, so that, the body being like a canal with many outlets and inlets, the streams of the blood might run as from a flowing fountain.

He adds that when the end comes, the cables of the spirit are loosed like those of a ship and she is allowed to go free.[99] These and a thousand others like them occur throughout. Those we have pointed out show how grand figurative passages naturally are, and how metaphors conduce to literary effectiveness, and that emotional and descriptive writing most readily employs them.

[The misuse of metaphor]

[68] That the use of metaphor, like that of the other beauties of diction, is likely to be carried to excess is evident without my mentioning it. For these passages Plato is much censured, for again and again he is carried away as in some frenzy of diction into violent and intemperate metaphors and allegorical bombast. He writes:

> It is not easy to see that a community ought to be blended like wine in a mixing-bowl, where the wine seethes in madness when it is poured out, but being chastened by the other sober god and entering into a pleasant harmony with it, it makes a good and well-blended drink.[100]

They say that to call water a "sober god" and mixing a "chastisement" is the act of a poet who is not himself sober. Caecilius, discussing such defects in his writings on Lysias, has the courage to say that in every way Lysias is better than Plato, but in so saying he has yielded to two uncritical feelings: he loves Lysias more than he does himself, yet his hatred for Plato is actually more than his love for Lysias. He is moved by prejudice, and even the principles he lays down are not, as he thinks, generally admitted. He presents the orator as without defect or blemish, and holds that Plato is oftentimes faulty, but this is certainly not the truth—far from it.

---

[99] *Timaeus*, 65C-85E. This type of description was much admired in the Renaissance; see especially Spenser's *Faerie Queene*, II, 9.   [100] *Laws*, VI, 773.

Chapter XXXIII

[The faultily faultless][101]

[69] But suppose we take some writer who is really faultless and irreproachable. Cannot we still ask the general question: Which is preferable in poetry and prose, greatness with some flaws, or only moderate success but with everything sound and impeccable? Yes, I say, do virtues of composition get the first prize because of their greatness or because of their number? These are proper questions in a treatise on excellence of style and in every way demand an answer. For my part, I realize that the greatest geniuses are far from faultless. Precision risks triviality, and in great writings, as in the management of a great fortune, something must needs be overlooked. Perhaps it is inevitable that lowly and mediocre natures, because they never run into danger and never attempt to attain any heights, should for the most part be faultless and all but perfectly safe; but in the very nature of things, great dangers accompany greatness. I am certainly aware that human nature leads us to look at all earthly things from their worst side, and the memory of faults can hardly be erased, though that of beauties quickly disappears. I have myself observed not a few blemishes in Homer and others of the first rank, and I do not at all admire their faults. Yet I prefer to call them not willful errors but careless and accidental oversights casually permitted by the heedlessness of a great mind.

[The great preferred to the perfect]

[70] Even if the greatest abilities do not keep a uniform level in everything, I believe they should nonetheless always get the first prize, if only because of their capacity for grand conception. Apollonius Rhodius in the *Argonautica* appears as a faultless poet, and, except for a few externals, Theocritus in his *Pastorals* is most fortunate, yet had you not rather be Homer than Apollonius? And does Eratosthenes in his *Erigone* (a little poem faultless in every respect) surpass Archilochus with all his faults of workmanship? Is not the latter a greater poet because of the bursting forth of that inspired spirit which it is so hard to bring under law? In lyric poetry would you prefer to be Bacchylides rather than Pindar, and in tragedy Ion of Chios rather than Sophocles him-

[101] Taken over by Dryden, *Apology for Heroic Poetry* (Ker, *Essays of Dryden*, I, 180).

self? Yet the first are beyond blame and have wrought an excellent finish for all their work, while Pindar and Sophocles, though they seem sometimes to set the world aflame with their energy, often unaccountably lose their fire and fall most unhappily. Yet would any sensible man think all the works of Ion arranged in order equal to the single drama of the *Oedipus?*

Chapter XXXIV

[Hyperides more nearly perfect than Demosthenes]

[71] If excellence were decided on number of merits and not on their greatness, Hyperides would altogether surpass Demosthenes, for he has a greater variety of notes and more virtues, and like a champion in the pentathlon can make a good showing in any contest; in each event he is beaten by the best men, yet he overcomes every ordinary contestant. But Hyperides, in addition to imitating all the merits of Demosthenes except his excellent arrangement, has moreover laid hold on all the virtues and graces of Lysias. He speaks plainly where it is proper and not in one series and monotonously as Demosthenes does, and he has presented character pleasantly and with simple charm. He shows also innumerable signs of wit, plenty of urbane ridicule, good breeding, skillful irony, jests neither tasteless nor ill-bred as in the well-known Attic orators, pointed ridicule, and much comic stimulus with plenty of keen humor, and what may be called inimitable fascination in all these. He is naturally gifted with the power to inspire pity, can tell a story fluently and go through it with fresh spirits, as he does in his poetical narrative of Leto; and his funeral oration is an example of declamatory oratory hardly to be surpassed. Demosthenes, on the other hand, has little gift for characterization, does not possess a flowing style, is not facile or declamatory, and generally has little share in the merits I have mentioned; when he attempts to jest or cause laughter, he is laughed at rather than with, and when he wishes to approach the charming he is farthest from it. If he had attempted to write the little speech on Phryne or that on Athenogenes, he would have recommended Hyperides still more strongly.

[Demosthenes greater]

[72] Even so the high qualities of the other, though many, in my opinion are lacking in greatness; born of sober sense, they

lack vigor and do not move the hearer, for no one feels terror when he reads Hyperides. But when Demosthenes speaks, he reveals the virtues of a great spirit directed to the highest ends, a tone of high distinction, soul-stirring emotion, fullness of matter, readiness of mind, rapidity at the right moment, vigor and power wholly unrivaled. Then he gathers to himself these abundant and marvelous gifts of the gods (for I dare not call them human), and with the excellences he has, surpasses all those of his rival, and to make up for those he is without strikes down as with a thunder-bolt the orators of all the ages. You had better with open eyes face the lightning as it descends than gaze upon his repeated expressions of strong feeling.

Chapter XXXV

[Plato and Lysias]

[73] With respect to Plato the matter is different, as I have said. Lysias is far inferior to him in both the magnitude and the num-ber of his virtues, and exceeds Plato in his faults more than he falls short of him in his merits.

[The measure of man's mind]

[74] What then did those demigods have before their eyes when they strove to attain the greatest things in literature and despised minute accuracy? Among other things this, that nature did not create man to live a lowly or ignoble life, but as to some great public assembly, she has brought us into life and into the midst of the universe, to behold it in its entirety and contest whole-heartedly for its honors, and has endowed our souls with an irresistible desire for what is great and more divine than our-selves. Thus in our sight and imagination not merely does the whole creation lie open to human enterprise, but many times our thoughts even surpass the bounds of the universe.

[The unusual is admired]

[75] Anyone who will examine life in all its aspects, and see how completely what is great and beautiful has the primacy in every-thing, will quickly understand for what we are created. Thence as though led by a natural impulse we do not admire the little streams, clear and useful though they are, but the Nile, the

Danube, and the Rhine, and still more the Ocean. Nor because it keeps its light clear are we amazed by the little flame that we kindle ourselves more than by the heavens, even though they are often darkened, nor do we think it more to be wondered at than the craters of Aetna, from the abyss of which the eruptions hurl forth rocks and whole hills and sometimes pour out rivers of that pure fire generated within the earth. On all these things I shall merely remark that men hold cheapest what is useful and necessary; the exceptional gains our wonder.

Chapter XXXVI

[The great may be faulty]

[76] In dealing then with writers of genius, whose greatness falls within the bounds of the use and profit of man, we first conclude that though far removed from perfection, all such men yet have more than human capacity. Other qualities show those who possess them are men, but artistic excellence raises them close to the mental power of a god. Lack of errors prohibits censure but greatness demands our awe.[102]

[True greatness redeems its errors]

[77] Is it necessary to say that each of these great men again and again redeems all his errors by a single instance of excellence and successful composition? This is thoroughly proved for us if we pick out the mistakes of Homer, Demosthenes, Plato, and others of the first rank and put them all together, for we shall find that they are but a tiny part, indeed a microscopic fraction, of the excellences to be found everywhere in the works of those heroes. For this reason all ages of the world—and such a decision even jealousy cannot condemn for folly—have conferred the rewards of victory on the great men I have named; moreover to this day the ages have guarded their reputations against all attack, and bid fair to continue the watch,

So long as the waters run and the trees grow tall.[103]

[102] Addison writes: "I must also observe with Longinus that the productions of a great genius with many lapses and inadvertencies are infinitely preferable to the works of an inferior kind of author which are scrupulously exact and conformable to all the rules of correct writing" (*Spectator*, no. 291 [February 2, 1712]).

[103] Quoted by Plato in *Phaedrus*, 264C.

[Greatness in art and nature]

[78] To one who says that the Colossus with its faults is no better than the Doryphorus of Polycleitus,[104] various answers can be made. It may correctly be said that in art we admire the most accurate work but in the works of nature we seek for grandeur, and by nature man has the power of speech. Also in a statue we expect similarity to man, but in speech, as I said, something more than human. However (and this doctrine goes back to the beginning of my treatise) since infallible correctness for the most part depends on art, but striking elevation, even though not consistent, is dependent on greatness of soul, it is proper that art should give assistance to nature. When the two work in harmony, they should produce perfection. What I have said was necessary to decide the matters before us, but let each man enjoy what pleases him.

Chapter XXXVII

[Similes]

[79] But to resume. Comparisons and images are closely related to metaphors, differing only . . . [A twenty-fifth of the manuscript is lacking; the following section begins in the middle of a word.]

Chapter XXXVIII

[Excess in hyperbole]

[80] . . . such hyperboles as this:

If you do not wear your brains in your heels and trample on them.

Therefore a writer must know where to set the limit in each case, for he may ruin his hyperbole by going too far; such things give way when they are overstrained, and then their effect is the opposite of what is desired. Isocrates fell into strange childishness because of his ambition to speak of things as bigger than they are. The theme of his *Panegyric* is that the city of Athens surpasses Sparta in the benefits it has conferred on Greece. But this is what he says at the outset:

Since orations have such power that they can even make great things humble, give magnitude to the small, speak of the old as

[104] This statue was looked upon as a standard of perfection and called the "canon."

though it were new, and deal with what has just happened as though it were ancient.[105]

But Isocrates, says someone, is this the way you intend to reverse the actions of the Spartans and the Athenians? For by his praise of the power of words he makes the introduction of his speech almost a warning to his hearers that they are not to trust him.

[It is art to conceal art[106]]

[81] Certainly then the best hyperboles, as we said above of figures, are those that do not appear to be hyperboles. They are such as are uttered with deep feeling in the midst of some great emergency, as when Thucydides spoke of those who perished in Sicily, of whom he wrote:

> The Syracusans descending began to slay especially those in the river, so that the water was immediately polluted, yet nonetheless they drank it mingled as it was with blood and mud, and to many of them it was even worth fighting for.

Strength of feeling and extraordinary conditions win our belief that a drink made up of blood and mud was worth fighting for. Of the same type is what Herodotus said of those who fought at Thermopylae:

> Here the Persians buried them with missiles as they fought with knives—those who still had them—and with their fists and teeth.

You may ask how it is possible to fight with the teeth against men fully armed and how soldiers can be buried with missiles, yet Herodotus still convinces us, for he does not seem to have mentioned the fact for the sake of the hyperbole, but the hyperbole seems to be a normal result of the fact. For I reiterate that all daring phrases find complete justification in deeds and feelings that are akin to ecstasy.[107] So statements in comedy that are extreme enough to be incredible are accepted when they are laughed at:

> His field is no bigger than a letter from Sparta.[108]

---

[105] Cf. Milton's words: "If the Athenians, as some say, made their small deeds great and renowned by their eloquent writers, England hath had her noble achievements made small by the unskilful handling of monks and mechanics" (*Reason of Church Government*, Preface to Bk. II).   [106] Cf. chaps. XVII and XXII, above.

[107] The quotation from Herodotus, with the comment of Longinus, appears in Dryden's *Apology for Heroic Poetry* (Ker, *Essays of Dryden*, I, 185).

[108] Better than our phrase, "no bigger than a postage stamp." Letters from Sparta, in Laconia, were "laconic."

Laughter is emotion in a pleasant form. Hyperboles may reduce as well as magnify size, for stretching of the truth is common to both, and belittling is an increase in insignificance.

[PART V, ARRANGEMENT, THE FIFTH SOURCE OF
LITERARY EXCELLENCE]

Chapter XXXIX

[The emotional effect of order]

[82] Now my good friend, there remains for discussion the fifth of the factors contributing to excellence we specified at the beginning, namely, the orderly arrangement of the words themselves. Of this I have already given a sufficient account in two treatises, so far as I understand it, and need add only what my present purpose requires, namely, that harmony is not merely an instrument of persuasion and pleasure to men but also has wonderful power for expressing great and strong feeling. Does not the flute cause certain emotions in those who listen to it, does it not carry them out of themselves and inspire them with a sort of corybantic frenzy? Establishing a certain interval of time, it forces the hearer to move with its rhythm and to harmonize himself with its melody, even though he may be quite unmusical. Yes, and the tones of the harp, though in themselves meaningless, yet by the changes in their sounds, their harmony with each other, and their musical combination often, as you know, exert over us a powerful charm, yet these are but the images and spurious imitations of persuasion and not genuine activities of our human nature.

[Variety and unity]

[83] We know that literary composition, as a harmony of words natural to man and laying hold not of his ears alone but of his very spirit, sets in motion manifold ideas of words, thoughts, actions, beauty, and melody, all of them produced and nourished within us. At the same time, through the various forms of their mingled words, the emotion of the speaker is introduced into the spirits of those who listen and they share his feelings as he brings together great conceptions in the verbal structure he erects. Through these means does he not at once charm us and dispose us for the

majestic, the worthy, the excellent and all that it includes, and wholly master our minds? But it appears madness to raise a question on matters thus agreed on, for experience seems a sufficient test.

[The ordering of words by Demosthenes]

[84] That conception which Demosthenes attached to his decree is excellent and truly amazing: τοῦτο τὸ ψήφισμα τὸν τότε τῇ πόλει περιστάντα κίνδυνον παρελθεῖν ἐποίησεν ὥσπερ νέφος.[109] But it is effective not less because of its harmony of expression than because of its idea. Its rhythm depends entirely upon the dactyls, for they have a noble and elevating quality, and therefore the heroic, most beautiful of measures, consists of them. If you transfer words from their proper place, and write: τοῦτο τὸ ψήφισμα ὥσπερ νέφος ἐποίησε τὸν τότε κίνδυνον παρελθεῖν, or even if you cut off a single syllable and say: ἐποίησε παρελθεῖν ὡς νέφος, you will realize how the melody of the passage is united with its excellence. The words ὥσπερ νέφος depend on the length of the first foot, which consists of four beats. If one syllable is removed, as in ὡς νέφος, the shortening reduces the grandeur of the passage; on the other hand if you lengthen it, thus producing παρελθεῖν ἐποίησεν ὡσπερεὶ νέφος, the meaning is the same but it does not have the same effect, because the lengthening of the last syllables destroys the energy and power of its absolute excellence.[110]

Chapter XL

[United we stand]

[85] Composition is of the greatest importance in giving weight to noble passages, in the same way as the synthesis of the parts gives beauty to the body, for any one member cut from the

[109] *On the Crown*, 188: "By this decree the danger that hung low over the city was made to pass away like a cloud."

[110] Because of our imperfect knowledge of Greek rhythms, translation of the preceding passage is useful only in suggesting that an English sentence might be analyzed in some such way, but with the differences required by the different language. The experiment might be tried with such a sentence as one near the end of Burke's speech *On the Nabob of Arcot's Debts:*

> Baffled, discountenanced, subdued, discredited, as the cause of justice and humanity is, it will be only the dearer to me.

Will be may be abbreviated to *is*, or *to me* lengthened to *in my sight*. Or by a transfer we may read:

> As the cause of justice and humanity is baffled, discountenanced, subdued, discredited, it will be only the dearer to me.

others and taken by itself is of no great account, but when they are all together they make up a perfect harmony. Likewise when great things are scattered about, some here and others there, excellence is scattered with them, but when they are united in one body and secured to one another by the bonds of harmony, by their union they acquire power. In such well-rounded sentences greatness depends almost entirely on the union of a multitude.

[Ability in organization overcomes other faults]

[86] Many prose writers and poets, not having a natural gift for excellence of expression, even distinctly lacking it, and employing only common and current words which for the most part suggest nothing of moment, yet merely by uniting and harmonizing them have been able to attain dignity and distinction, and no longer appear ordinary. Among many others I may rightly name Philistus, Aristophanes at times, and Euripides usually. After slaying his children, Hercules says:

> I am full of evils and have no room for more.[111]

The phrase is certainly ordinary but becomes excellent because skillfully molded. If you give the words another order, it will appear to you that Euripides is a poet of arrangement rather than of thought. Of Dirce when she is dragged along by the bull, he says:

> Wherever he chanced to make a turn, he seized and dragged along woman or rock or oak, as it might be.[112]

The idea is a noble one, but gains force because the harmony is not as though it ran along on rollers, for the words furnish support to each other and, sustained by the pauses, have arrived at grand stability.

Chapter XLI

[Excessive rhythm]

[87] Nothing has so weakening an effect on an excellent passage as a weak and wavering rhythm, such as pyrrhics, trochees, and dichorees,[113] which become pure dance music. All excessively rhythmical passages seem overdecorated and tawdry and

---

[111] *Hercules Furens*, 1245.

[112] From the lost *Antiope*. Uncertainty of text adds to our slight knowledge of Greek rhythms in making the example ineffective.

[113] The pyrrhic of two short syllables, the trochee of a long and a short, the dichoree of four syllables, namely a long, a short, a long, and a short.

in their prevailing monotony wholly lack strong feeling.[114] And the worst of it is that just as lyrics used on the stage divert attention from the plot and fix it on themselves, so over-rhythmical words do not bring home to the hearers the emotion of a passage but only its rhythm, for sometimes inferring the rhythm that is to come they listen for it, and getting ahead of the speaker set the step for him as though they were a chorus. Also without grandeur are passages that are too concisely expressed and broken up into small fragments and short sections roughly fastened together as though with nails and fitting badly.

Chapter XLII

[Excessive brevity]

[88] Too much curtailment of phrase also lowers excellence, for a great passage is mutilated when it is made too short. You must apply this not to proper compression[115] but to what is downright tiny and divided into small parts. Too much compression cripples the sense, but brevity brings it to the goal. On the other hand, it is clear that long-drawn-out passages are spiritless, since their joints are loosened by their undue length.

Chapter XLIII

[Undignified words]

[89] Triviality in words also depresses a great passage. In Herodotus the storm is divinely described so far as the ideas are concerned, but he certainly brings in some words unworthy of his subject. In the phrase *sizzling sea*,[116] the word *sizzling* detracts greatly from excellence because it is cacophonous. But he also says:

> The wind let up, and an unpleasant end awaited those who were hanging to the wreck.[117]

Let up is too colloquial to be dignified and *unpleasant* is not suited to terrible suffering.

---

[114] Milton wrote: "True musical delight . . . consists . . . not in the jingling sound of like endings, a fault avoided by the learned ancients both in poetry and all good oratory" (the Verse, prefixed to *Paradise Lost*). Longinus seems to be speaking not of verse but of oratory in prose.

[115] The original means *improper compression*, but various editors omit the negative.

[116] *Histories*, VII, 188.   [117] *Histories*, VII, 191; VIII, 13.

[An example of undignified language]

[90] Likewise Theopompus, after having magnificently described the descent of the Persian king into Egypt, uses some trivial words that destroy his whole effect:

> What city or what nation in all Asia did not send envoys to the king? What is there of beauty or honor, whether produced by nature or the work of art, that was not brought to him as a gift? Were there not many costly coverlets and mantles, some purple, some in many colors, some white, many golden tents provided with all their furnishings, many robes and costly? Then too you might see plate of silver and gold of fine workmanship, and goblets and mixing bowls, some of them studded with precious stones, and others wonderfully and richly wrought. In addition to these things there were countless thousands of weapons both Greek and barbarian, baggage animals beyond number and beasts fit for slaughter, and many bushel baskets of spices, and many bags and sacks and jars of onions and of all other sorts of supplies; such stores of salted meat were piled up that the heaps grew so great that anyone approaching from a distance would think there were mounds and hills before him.

From the excellent he descends to the humble, when he needed rather to ascend in the scale. By mingling bags and spices and sacks with all the other wonders provided, he makes us imagine we are in a wholesale grocery establishment. If in the midst of this elaborate show, someone had come in laden with bags and sacks and set them down among the golden bowls set with precious stones and the silver plate and the tents all of gold and the drinking cups, it would have been an act not befitting the scene. Similarly such words are a disgrace to his presentation, and appear like brands of infamy when they are brought in at the wrong time. It would have been better to have dealt generally with the things he says were heaped together in hills, and altering his method of describing the other preparations, to have mentioned camels and a multitude of beasts of burden laden with everything that can be provided for the luxury and enjoyment of the table, or he might have called them heaps of every sort of grain and of whatever pertains to cookery and high living, or if he were determined to be more explicit about these things, he could have spoken of all the fine things known to caterers and cooks.[118]

[118] Cf. Milton's "all fish from sea or shore" (*Paradise Regained*, II, 344).

[Dignified words for dignified matter]

[91] In lofty passages we should not descend to the sordid and mean unless forced by some strong necessity, but should take care that our words fit the dignity of our subjects, and imitate nature in the creation of man, for she did not place our secret parts and the refuse of the whole body in full view, but concealed them as well as she could, and as Xenophon said, turned their channels as far backward as possible, to avoid doing any shame to the beauty of the whole animal.

[Mean effects]

[92] But I do not need to give a systematic discussion of the causes of a mean effect, for since I have dealt above with all the causes of noble and excellent diction, it is clear that the opposite of these will generally make it low and unseemly.

[PART VI, LITERARY EXCELLENCE AND THE SOCIAL ORDER]

Chapter XLIV

[Democracy and literature]

[93] One matter is left for examination, my dear Terentianus, and knowing your love of sound learning I shall not hesitate to put it before you. One of the philosophers recently inquired of me about it, saying: "It seems strange to me, as doubtless to many others, that in our age we find men gifted with powers of persuasion, well versed in politics, keen and versatile, strikingly rich in literary charm, but nevertheless natures capable of true excellence and genuine greatness are never or but seldom produced. In our times there is a world-wide dearth of great literature. Must we," he asked, "accept the trite belief that democracy is a good nurse of noble minds and that great men of letters reached their acme with democracy and perished with it? Liberty, it is said, is able to nourish the intellectual powers of able men and to fill them with high hopes, and in an age of self-government there prevails a spirit of competition with others and of desire for the highest place. Moreover, because of the prizes offered by republics, the intellectual powers of the orators are always kept sharp by practice, are as it were rubbed bright, and in their freedom are

likely to shine when applied to affairs of government. But in this age," he continued, "we seem to be schooled from our earliest days in strict servitude, and not merely are we wrapped in the swaddling clothes of its manners and actions when our minds are still tender, but we never drink of the most beautiful and freely flowing fountain of literature, namely freedom. Therefore," he asserted, "I say that we produce no great capacity except that for flattery."

[The incapacity of the slave]

[94] For that reason he maintained that all the other capacities fall to the lot of menials, but no slave can ever become an orator, for straightway there rises to the surface the cautious speech and guarded manner of one who has always been accustomed to punishment. As Homer says, "The day of enslavement takes away half of our virtue." "If what I hear is true," continued the philosopher, "the cages in which pygmies or dwarfs are kept not merely prohibit the growth of those kept within them, but actually make them smaller by means of the bonds that press on their bodies; in the same way all slavery, even the most just, might be called a cage for the spirit and a common prison."

[Avarice and luxury destroy literary power]

[95] But I took him up and answered: "My good friend, it is easy and a common trait to find fault with the age in which one lives. But consider that perhaps it is not universal peace that ruins great natures, but rather this war without a truce that has possession of our spirits, yes and still more the passions that keep watch over life in these days and utterly lay it waste. For the love of money, from which all are now sick beyond cure, and the love of pleasure hold us in slavery, or rather, as it might be put, submerge us under their waves, body and soul. For love of gold is a plague that shrivels up the spirit, and love of pleasure is wholly ignoble. After considering the matter I fail to see how, if we give such honor to boundless wealth, indeed, to tell the truth, make a god of it, we can fail to receive the evils that are akin to it when they seek to enter our souls. For on the very heels of measureless and insolent Wealth, Extravagance comes following, they say, and as soon as Wealth has opened the gates of cities and the doors of houses, Extravagance enters and dwells there. And after some time, according to the sayings of the wise, they build nests in our

lives, and quickly set about reproduction; as offspring they engender Swaggering, Folly, and Softness, not bastards but their own true issue. And if one allows these children of Wealth to come to maturity, they quickly bring forth in our souls implacable tyrants, Insolence, Lawbreaking, and Shamelessness. Of necessity this is the process. Then men no longer look upward or take any thought for their fame, but in the circle of these vices the ruin of their lives is little by little completed, the great qualities of their souls shrink and wither and grow parched because they set value only on the mortal and perishable parts of them, and neglect to develop what is immortal.

[Dishonest criticism]

[96] "A judge who has once been bribed cannot pronounce a free and sound judgment on the just and the fair, for to him who takes bribes his own advantage seems fair and just. But bribes and hunting for the deaths of others and schemes for legacies determine the whole courses of our lives; we are bargaining for gain everywhere at the price of our souls, since each one of us is enslaved by profit. In such a plague-stricken ruin of life can we expect to find remaining any free judge of great things and those that endure to eternity,—a man who is unbribed and does not seek office because of his desire for gain?

[No hope for the age]

[97] "But perhaps it is better for such as we are to be in bondage than to be free. If we were completely set free, like criminals from prison, our appetites for the goods of our neighbors would overwhelm the world with evils." I said also that the talents of the present are wholly wasted by the sluggishness in which all but a few pass their whole lives, not laboring or undertaking any task except to secure praise and pleasure and never to obtain the benefits of true blessedness and honor.

[The emotions]

[98] "It is best to let these things go at random," [119] and continue with what is next in order. This is the subject of the emotions on which I previously undertook to write in a separate treatise, for since they have a share in discourse generally and especially in excellence . . . . [The manuscript breaks off here.]

[119] Euripides, *Electra*, 379 (part of the line).

DANTE

oᴏᴏᴏᴏ

LETTER TO CAN GRANDE DELLA SCALA

1319

Of all medieval poets Dante would be universally thought best fitted
to give an account of poetic activity. Perhaps unsurpassed in artistic
power and rationally gifted as few poets have been, he had at his command both his own experience as poet and philosophical equipment
for its analysis. Yet he tells us nothing especially significant. In fact,
one who set out to prove that the theories of the poets but echo the
thoughts of their age could do no better than take Dante as an example,
for though one of the most original of poets, he is far from an original
theorist. For that very reason he may be chosen to represent medieval
critical theory.

In dedicating the *Paradise* to his friend and patron, Can Grande della
Scala, Dante gives some explanation of the work. The poem is properly
arranged; it belongs to the part of philosophy called ethics and is practical in intention; it has literal and allegorical meanings such as St.
Thomas had described and every student knew. Moreover, Dante's
letter—and the parts omitted more than those printed here—is presented in the manner and with the ideas of those who followed Aristotle according to the scholastic method. Whether one can go so
far as to say that many others in the early fourteenth century could
have written it is possibly doubtful; any other man would have been
less personally interested and perhaps would have seen less clearly the
purpose of the whole. Something at least is suggested by the debate,
now apparently settled, on the genuineness of the letter; there have
been men who held that it was not Dante's own, partly, it would seem,
because it is so much in the spirit of the age.

To be sure the epistle is illuminating and the poem should be read in
the light of it, for Dante had too clear a mind to describe something he
had not done. But from the dedication one would have but the slightest
notion that the work being analyzed was a great poem, or indeed a
poem at all. Of its artistic qualities or those that might be supposed to

relate especially to beauty, nothing is said. The thought and moral teaching, explained in the manner fashionable in Dante's time and seeming very strange in ours, take all the expositor's attention. The reader cannot but wonder if Dante's originality is wholly that of artist, not at all that of critic.

Perhaps the most astonishing thing about the letter is that it really does describe the poem. One is tempted to say that one reason for Dante's greatness lies in his capacity to use the thought of his time; he had so well absorbed it that he followed its prescriptions with no sense of bondage, but with complete artistic freedom. It is almost as though the age had been created for Dante, that it and his temperament might unite for the utmost excellence in his poem. Or are we to say that Dante's mind adapted itself to the age to such an extent that no unified explanation of the poem is possible save in its terms? In any other time Dante would have been a different poet as well as a different critic. We seem to have here, so far as the explanation goes, poet and critic at one. Our objection must be not that the criticism is untrue, but that it covers so very little of what we see in the poem. If Dante had written in any other age, would he have given very different reasons for a poem not essentially different? In his instance I suspect the poem would have fitted the age in lesser matters, but in the essentials that depend on the spirit of the poet it would have been little different. Yet the matters of the spirit are those of which Dante the critic tells us little or nothing.

No one, at any rate, can be so foolish as to suppose that Dante did not realize the artistic qualities of poetry. Before he even undertook the *Comedy* he had, partly through imitation of Vergil, attained what he calls "the beautiful style that has done me honor." [1] In his work *On the Vulgar Tongue*, in which he discusses the language of Italy and its fitness for poetry, he analyzes various styles as suited for various types of writing. [2] In the *Convivio* he states incidentally what may be called his principle for the make-up of poetry:

> I composed it [the *tornata*, a part of the canzone] when it was needful to say something in adornment of the canzone that was not part of the main idea . . . Therefore I say at present that the goodness and the beauty of every composition are distinct and separate from each other. Its goodness is in its idea and its beauty in the adornment of its words; both of them are delightful, though the goodness of the canzone should be especially pleasing. Therefore, because the goodness of the canzone was hard to see

[1] *Inferno*, I, 87.   [2] Bk. II, chap. IV.

because of the diverse persons that come forward to speak in it
and the many distinctions sought for, and its beauty was easy to
see, it seemed to me inevitable that people generally would give
more attention to the beauty than to the goodness of this canzone
(II, 11).[3]

This dualism is apparently the basis of Dante's theory of poetry,
thought on the one hand, beautified language on the other. Such unity
as appears is found in the proper fitting of the style to the nature of the
poem, and perhaps in the theory of inspiration, rather cautiously suggested in the letter to Can Grande, and variously exemplified in the
Comedy. At least such emphasis on the thought of his poetry and its
moral effect shows that Dante was far from any theory of mere beauty
in art. He belongs clearly to the group who insist on the intellectual
demands upon the artist. His opinions may serve as gadflies to rouse
us up when we are uncritically comfortable in the belief that thought
and expression form a necessary unit, or when we are inclined to dis-
count the importance of the poet's convictions.

The translation is by the editor.

BIBLIOGRAPHY

Dante, *A Translation of Dante's Eleven Letters*, with explanatory notes
    and historical comments, by Charles Sterrett Latham. Boston and
    New York, 1891.
——, *Epistolae*, ed. with translation by Paget Toynbee. Oxford, 1920.
——, *A Translation of the Latin Works of Dante Alighieri*. London, 1904.
——, *De vulgari eloquentia*. Ridotto a miglior lezione e commentato da
    Aristide Marigo. Florence, 1938.
——, *Convivio*, translated by William Walrond Jackson. Oxford, 1909.
Dinsmore, Charles Allen, *Aids to the Study of Dante*. Boston and New
    York, 1903. Chapter VI contains a translation of the letter to Can
    Grande.
Grandgent, Charles H., *Dante*. New York, 1921. See especially Chap.
    XI.
Bartsch, Karl Friedrich, "Dantes Poetik," in *Jahrbuch der deutschen
    Dante-Gesellschaft*, III (1871), pp. 503–67 [separately printed, Leip-
    zig, 1871].

[3] Somewhat similarly in the work *On the Vulgar Tongue* poetry is referred to as "rhetorical fiction and feigned music" (II, 4). For the word translated *feigned*, I follow
Aristide Marigo, "Il testo critico del *De vulgari eloquentia*," in *Giornale storico*, LXXXVI
(1925), 289 ff.; but whatever the adjective may be, there seems to be a dualism of subject and diction.

LETTER TO CAN GRANDE DELLA SCALA (*in part*)

[The subject of inquiry]

[6¹] Wishing to say something by way of introduction to the part [i.e. the *Paradise*] of the entire *Comedy* already mentioned, I have decided first to say something on the work as a whole, that the approach to the part may be easier and more adequate. There are six things to be inquired about at the beginning of any work of instruction, to wit the subject, the author, the form, the end, the title of the work, and the genus of its philosophy. There are three of these in which the part I have determined to address to you varies from the whole, to wit the subject, the form, and the title. In the others it does not vary, as appears to him who looks at it; hence, in respect to the consideration of the whole the three are to be separately inquired into. When this has been done, the way to the introduction of the part will lie open. Then we shall examine the other three not merely with respect to the whole, but also with respect to the part in question.

[Many meanings]

[7] For the clarity of what is to be said, one must realize that the meaning of this work is not simple, but is rather to be called polysemous, that is, having many meanings. The first meaning is the one obtained through the letter; the second is the one obtained through the things signified by the letter. The first is called literal, the second allegorical or moral or anagogical. In order that this manner of treatment may appear more clearly, it may be applied to the following verses: "When Israel went out of Egypt, the house of Jacob from a people of strange language, Judah was his sanctuary and Israel his dominion."[2] For if we look to the letter alone, the departure of the children of Israel from Egypt in the time of Moses is indicated to us; if to the allegory, our redemption accomplished by Christ is indicated to us; if to the moral sense, the conversion of the soul from the woe and misery of sin to a state of grace is indicated to us; if to the anagogical sense, the departure of the consecrated soul from the slavery of this corruption to the liberty of eternal glory is indicated. And though these mystic senses may be called by various names, they can all generally be

---

[1] The numbers of paragraphs are from the standard editions. [2] Psalms 114, 1-2.

spoken of as allegorical, since they are diverse from the literal or historical. For allegory is derived from *alleon* in Greek, which in Latin appears as *alienum*, or diverse.[3]

[The subject double]

[8] When these things have been observed, it is evident that the subject with which the alternative senses are concerned ought to be double. So one must look at the subject of this work as it is accepted according to the letter; then at the subject as it is understood allegorically. The subject of the whole work, then, taken merely in its literal sense, is simply the state of the souls after death, for from that subject comes the course of the whole work and with that it is occupied. But if the whole work is taken allegorically, the subject is man as by reason of meriting and demeriting through the freedom of the will he is liable to the rewarding and the punishing of justice.

[The form double]

[9] The form is double: the form of the treatise, and the form of treatment. The form of the treatise is triple, according to a triple division. The first division is that by which the whole work is divided into three *cantiche*. The second is that by which each *cantica* is divided into cantos. The third that by which each canto is divided into verses. The form or mode of treating is poetic, fictitious, descriptive, digressive, transumptive, and withal definitive, divisive, probative, improbative, and with the positing of examples.

[Comedy]

[10] The title of the book is: "Here begins the *Comedy* of Dante Alighieri, a Florentine by nation but not by habits." For the explanation of this it must be known that comedy gets its name from *comos*, a village, and *oda*, a song; therefore comedy is as it were a villagers' song. And comedy is a certain genus of poetic imitation differing from all others. It differs from tragedy in its matter in this respect, that tragedy in the beginning is good to look upon and quiet, in its end or exit is fetid and horrible; for this reason it gets its name from *tragos*, which is goat, and *oda*, as though to say *goatish song*, that is, fetid in the manner of a goat; this

---

[3] *Allegory* is now said to be derived from the Greek *allegoria*, from *allos* and *agoreuo*. Dante did not know Greek. The Latin *alius*, from which comes *alienum*, "alien," is related to *allos*.

is made plain by the example of Seneca in his tragedies.[4] Comedy, however, at the beginning deals with the harsh aspect of some affair, but its matter terminates prosperously, as is shown by the example of Terence in his comedies.[5] Hence certain authors in their salutations are in the habit of saying, instead of the usual greeting, "a tragic beginning and a comic end." Likewise the two differ in their mode of speaking: tragedy speaks in an elevated and sublime fashion, but comedy in a lowly and humble way, according to the prescription of Horace in his *Art of Poetry* where he grants that sometimes comic actors may speak like tragedians, and conversely:

> At times, however, even Comedy exalts her voice, and an angry Chremes rants and raves; often, too, in a tragedy Telephus or Peleus utters his sorrow in the language of prose (93–6).

From this it is clear why the present work is called *Comedy*. For if we consider the material, at the beginning it is horrible and fetid, since it begins with Hell, but at the end it is attractive and pleasing, since it ends with Heaven. As to mode of expression, its mode is lowly and humble, since it is the speech of the masses in which even womenfolk converse. . . .

[Literal and allegorical subjects]

[11] In what I am going to say I can make plain in what way the subject of the part now in question is to be assigned. For if the subject of the whole work taken literally is the state of the souls after death, with no restrictions but taken simply, manifestly the subject of this part is the same, but with a restriction, namely it is the state of sainted souls after death. And if the subject of the whole work taken allegorically is man as by reason of meriting and demeriting through the freedom of the will he is liable to the rewarding and punishing of justice, it is manifest that the subject of this part is limited to man as by reason of meriting he is subject to the rewarding of justice. . . .

[The end of the poem]

[15] The end of the whole and the part can be multiplex, that is, near at hand and remote; but omitting all subtle investigation,

---

[4] There has been an attempt to prove by parallel passages that Dante had read Seneca's dramas. It still seems possible, however, that, if he had seen them at all, he had seen only excerpts.

[5] There is no proof that Dante had read any of the works of Terence.

one may say briefly that the end of the whole and the part is to remove those living in this life from a state of misery and to lead them to a state of happiness.

[Ethics dominates the work]

[16] The genus of philosophy under which the work proceeds in the whole and in part is moral activity or ethics, for the whole and the part are devised not for the sake of speculation but of possible action. For if in any place or passage the method of discussion is that of speculative thought, it is not for the sake of speculative thought but for the sake of practical activity, since, as the Philosopher says in the second of the *Metaphysics*, "practical men now and then speculate on something or other."

[17] Having said these things by way of premise, we draw near to the exposition of the letter as a sort of offering of the first fruits; as to this it should be understood beforehand that the exposition of the letter is nothing other than the manifestation of the form of the work. This part or third *cantica* which is called *Paradise* is then divided chiefly into two parts, to wit a prologue and a part giving the main development. . . .

[18] Concerning the first part it should be known that though in ordinary speech it can be called the exordium, in accurate speech it should be called nothing other than the prologue, as the Philosopher seems to hint in the third book of the *Rhetoric*, where he says that the "proemium is the beginning in rhetorical speech as is the prologue in poetry and the prelude in music on the pipes." It is also to be observed beforehand that this prefatory matter, which commonly is called the exordium, is handled in one way by the poets and otherwise by the orators. For the orators have agreed to prefix some words to prepare the spirit of the auditor; but the poets not merely do this, but after it they utter a certain invocation. And this is proper for them, since they have great need of an invocation, because something contrary to the way of life common among men is to be sought from the superior beings, as a sort of divine gift. Hence the present prologue is divided into two parts, since in the first what is to be said is introduced, and in the second Apollo is to be invoked. . . .

[33] On the part giving the main development, which in the division was set over against the prologue, nothing will be said at present either by way of dividing or explaining, except this, that everywhere the procedure will be that of ascending from heaven

to heaven, and something will be said on the blessed souls found in each orb, and that true beatitude consists in perceiving the beginning of truth, as is made clear by John when he says: "This is life eternal, that they might know thee, the true God, etc."; likewise by Boethius in the third of the *Consolation:* "To see thee is the end." Thence it is that, to show the glory of blessedness in those souls, from them, as from those who see all the truth, many things are asked that have great utility and delight.[6] And when the beginning or the first thing, to wit God, has been found, there is nothing beyond that can be sought for, since he is Alpha and Omega, that is, the beginning and the end, as the Vision of John relates; hence the treatment is ended in God himself, who is blessed world without end.[7]

[6] For example, in *Paradise*, XIII, Dante learns from St. Thomas Aquinas the relation of the wisdom of Adam, Solomon, and Christ. This and other theological passages have often been objected to by critics of the *Comedy* as over learned; the question has even been raised whether they are genuinely poetry. Benedetto Croce finds some poetical justification for them (*The Poetry of Dante* [New York, 1922], pp. 224-30). Dante obviously felt that they were of the essence of poetry, fulfilling the demand of Horace for profit and delight (*Art of Poetry*, 333, p. 139, above), to which Dante alludes in the sentence now under consideration. Horace's work was known to Dante (*On the Vulgar Tongue*, II, IV, 4).

[7] *Paradise*, XXXIII, 49-145.

GIOVANNI BOCCACCIO

o◯ooo◯o

THE LIFE OF DANTE

1363-4

BOCCACCIO'S FIRST QUALIFICATION as a critic is his own experience in various sorts of literary composition. His most famous work is the *Decameron*, a collection of prose stories; he also composed a prose romance, the *Filocolo*, long poems, the *Teseide* and the *Filostrato*, and various other Italian works. In Latin he wrote *De claris mulieribus*, on famous women, and *De casibus virorum illustrium*, on the fall of famous men, as well as other works in verse and prose. Among the latter is a geographical dictionary. The Latin work most immediately interesting to critics of literature is the *Genealogy of the Gods*, "the first attempt on a large scale to assemble, arrange, incorporate, and explain the vast accumulation of legend, and reduce it, after the manner of his times, to convenient encyclopedic form." But in his character as one of the first scholars of his time, he was not satisfied merely to present a book of reference on mythology; he wished also to establish the propriety of the use of such material by Christian poets. This purpose appears chiefly in the preface and the fourteenth and fifteenth books, which have been translated by Professor Osgood (see bibliog.), and should be read entire. Some of the ideas developed at length in the *Genealogy* are more briefly given in a digression in the *Life of Dante*, which is here presented.

BIBLIOGRAPHY

Boccaccio, Giovanni, *Vita di Dante*, in *Il comento alla Divina Commedia e gli altri scritti intorno a Dante*, a cura di Domenico Guerri. Bari, 1918.

Osgood, Charles G., *Boccaccio on Poetry, being the Preface and the Fourteenth and Fifteenth Books of Boccaccio's* "Genealogia Deorum Gentilium" *in an English Version with Introductory Essay and Commentary*. Princeton, 1930.

Smith, James Robison, *The Earliest Lives of Dante*. New Haven, 1901.

THE LIFE OF DANTE (*selections*)

Chapter XXI (*in part*)

[Poetry is theology]

[1] Since many who do not understand such matters think that poetry is nothing else than a mere fabulous narrative, I have decided to exceed my promise and show that it is theology. . . .

Chapter XXII (*in part*)

[Poetry for wise and simple]

[2] If we wish to lay aside the passions and look reasonably at the matter, I believe that we shall easily enough be able to see that the ancient poets, so far as it is possible to human capacity, followed in the footsteps of the Holy Spirit, which, as we read in the sacred Scriptures, revealed its lofty secrets to future times through the mouths of many writers, making them beneath a veil speak what it intended at the proper time to show in deeds, without any veil. Therefore, if we look well at their writings, we shall see that these men, wishing the imitator to be not unlike the thing imitated, under the cover of fictions described what had been, or what was in their time, or what they desired or presumed would come about in the future. Hence, without assuming that all kinds of writing have the same end, but considering only their method, with which I am now most concerned, the same praise can be given to both Scripture and profane writings, in the words of Gregory. He says of the sacred Scriptures what can also be said of poetry, namely, that in relating anything it explains the text and the mystery subordinated to it in the same words. Thus at the same time it occupies the wise and gives comfort to the simple; in the obvious sense there is something to sustain babes, and in the hidden sense it keeps that with which it holds in admiring awe the minds of the wisest hearers. Thus it appears to be a river, if I may use the figure, both shallow and deep, in which the tiny lamb can go on its feet and the great elephant has ample room to swim. But I must go on to prove what I have stated.

[Allegorical interpretation]

[3] The sacred Scripture, which we call theology, in the guise of a story, now with the seeing of some vision, again by hearing

some lament and in many other ways, sets out to show us the high mystery of the incarnation of the divine Word, his life, the events of his death, his victorious resurrection, his miraculous ascension, and all his other acts. If we are instructed by these, we can come to that glory which he, by dying and rising, opened to us after it had long been shut to us through the sin of the first man. Likewise the poets in their works, which we call poetry, with fictions about various gods, with transmutations of men into varied forms, and with pleasant persuasions show us the causes of things, the effects of virtues and vices, and what we should avoid and what we should follow, in order that by working righteousness we may attain that end which they who did not fully know the true God thought was complete blessedness. In the green bush in which Moses saw God like a burning flame, the Holy Spirit wished to show us the virginity of Her who was purer than any other creature, and that she was to be the dwelling and shelter of the Lord of nature and that she would not be defiled by the conception or the birth of the Word of the Father. By Nebuchadnezzar's vision of the statue made of several metals struck down by a rock that was changed into a mountain, the Spirit wished to show all succeeding ages that they ought to submit to the doctrine of Christ, who was and is the living rock, and that the Christian religion born of this rock would become a thing immovable and eternal, as we see that the mountains are. In the lamentations of Jeremiah the Spirit intends to set forth the future destruction of Jerusalem.

[Poetry teaches allegorically]

[4] Similarly our poets, when they feigned that Saturn had many children and devoured all but four of them, wished to have understood from this fiction nothing else than that Saturn is time, in which everything is produced, and as everything is produced in time, it likewise is the destroyer of all and reduces all to nothing. Of the four children that he did not devour, the first is Jove, that is the element of fire; the second is Juno, the wife and sister of Jove, that is the air, by the means of which fire works its effects below; the third is Neptune, god of the sea, that is the element of water; the fourth and last is Pluto, god of the inferno, that is the earth, lower than any other element. Likewise our poets feigned that Hercules was changed from a man into a god, and Lycaon into a wolf. By this they wished to show that by acting virtuously, as Hercules did, man becomes a god by participation

in heaven, and that by acting wickedly, as Lycaon did, though he appears a man, he is truly to be called by the name of that beast which is known by everyone to have the quality most like his vice. So because of his rapacity and avarice, qualities like those of a wolf, it is feigned that Lycaon was changed into a wolf. Likewise our poets feign the beauty of the Elysian Fields, by which I understand the sweetness of paradise. From the darkness of Dis I learn the pain of the inferno. Hence I infer that attracted by the pleasures of one and frightened by the woe of the other we should follow the virtues that will lead us to the Elysian Fields and avoid the vices that will cause us to be hurled into Dis. I omit more particular expositions of these things, though they would be pleasing and would make my argument stronger, because I fear they would take me further than my chief subject demands and than I wish to go. And surely if no more were said than has been said, it ought to be well enough understood that theology and poetry are in agreement as to their form of working, but in subject I say that they are not merely wholly diverse, but in some parts contradictory. The subject of sacred theology is divine virtue; the ancient poets treat the gods of the Gentiles and men. They are contradictory in so far as theology brings forward from the beginning nothing unless it is true; poetry brings forward things as true that are wholly false and erroneous and against the Christian religion. But because some foolish men rise up against the poets, saying that they have composed disgusting and wicked fables that have no harmony with truth, and that in some other way than by fables they should show their ability and give their teaching to men, I wish to go somewhat farther with the present discussion.

[Poetry like Scripture]

[5] Let men of this sort, then, consider the visions of Daniel, those of Isaiah, those of Ezekiel, and the others in the Old Testament that were written by the divine pen and presented by Him to whom there has been no beginning and will be no end. Let them consider also the visions of the evangelists in the New Testament, full of marvelous truth to the understanding, and, if any poetic story is found so far from truth and from the verisimilar as these in many places appear on the surface, it may be conceded that the poets alone have written fables because they were unable to give delight or benefit. Without saying anything on the charges they bring against the poets, in so far as they have presented their

teaching in fables or under a fabulous veil, I could properly pass on, since I know that when they foolishly blame the poets for this, they rashly stumble into blaming that Spirit that is none other than the way, the truth, and the life. Still I intend to give them some satisfaction.

[Advantages of allegory]

[6] It is obvious that anything that is gained with fatigue seems sweeter than what is acquired without any effort. The plain truth, since it is quickly understood with little difficulty, delights us and passes from the mind. But, in order that it may be more pleasing, because acquired with labor, and therefore be better retained, the poets hide the truth beneath things apparently quite contrary to it. For that reason they produce fables, rather than some other covering, because their beauty attracts those whom neither philosophical demonstrations nor persuasions would have been able to allure. What then shall we say about the poets? Shall we hold that they are madmen, as their senseless adversaries, saying they know not what, have thought them? Certainly not; on the contrary they employ in their productions the most profound thought, which is equivalent to everything hidden in the fruit, and admirable and splendid language, which corresponds to the rind and the leaves. But let us resume the thread of our discourse.

[Poetry is theology]

[7] I say that theology and poetry can be called almost the same thing, when they have the same subject; I even say that theology is none other than the poetry of God. What else is it than a poetic fiction when the Scripture in one place calls Christ a lion, in another a lamb, and in another a worm,[1] here a dragon and here a rock, and many others that I omit for the sake of brevity? What else do the words of Our Savior in the Gospels come to if not a sermon that does not signify what it appears to? It is what we call—to use a well-known term—allegory. Then it plainly appears that not merely is poetry theology but that theology is poetry. And surely if in so important a matter my words deserve little reliance, I am not disturbed by it; for I put my trust in Aristotle, an excellent authority in any important matter, who affirms he found that the poets were the first to write theology.[2]

---

[1] Perhaps a reference to Job 25, 6: "the son of man, which is a worm."
[2] See Osgood, p. 163. A reference to *Metaphysics*, III, 4, 1000a9.

GIANGIORGIO TRISSINO

o◯oo◯o

POETICA

1529[1]

I:ECEIVED INTO THE FAVOR of a pope and an emperor in his lifetime, Trissino's career and accomplishment is not such as to give him a high reputation in the present. His epic poem and his dramas are not of the sort our age tolerates easily, being written to demonstrate a theory and revealing the habits of a literary man and humanist rather than a poet of original power. It can, however, be maintained that they are of higher quality than historians of literature commonly indicate. In the circumstances of his critical work Trissino was also unfortunate. The last two divisions of his *Poetica,* those in which general ideas appear, were printed only after his death; their chief conceptions had been formulated and even put into writing early in his career; they waited some twenty years for their author's final revision. It is true that they consist in large part of an expanded paraphrase of the *Poetics* of Aristotle; Trissino intended they should. Had he completed and issued them at the time of their formulation, he would have been the first to introduce the *Poetics* to Europe in the vernacular; they would have appeared as something new and strange to a world that knew Aristotle only vaguely. To us, expecting an original treatise, they are more disappointing than if they presented themselves as merely a translation. But when they are looked at further, they appear as of no mean quality. They present Aristotle clearly and intelligently, with no substitution of the critic's own theories for those of the Philosopher. Trissino knew Greek literature and understood the references of his author. Nor was he confined to the *Poetics* for his theory, for he apparently had read all that was available from both Greek and Latin criticism. His use of both critics and poets in comment, illustration, and even dissent is admirable.

---

[1] This is the date of publication of the first four divisions. The fifth and sixth parts seem to have existed in a rough draft at that time. They were not completed for some twenty years, and not published until 1563. The literary position they indicate was obviously arrived at before 1515, when Trissino presented his tragedy of *Sofonisba.*

He adds sections, such as that on comedy, where Aristotle's work is defective. Moreover, he also employs examples from modern literature. For the early sixteenth century, and even when finally printed in 1563, the last two divisions of the *Poetica* can be presented as a most attractive and helpful presentation of Aristotle to the Italian reader, more helpful than a simple translation and more succinct and of more pleasing literary quality than a commentary.

BIBLIOGRAPHY

Trissino, Giangiorgio, *Tutte le opere*. Verona, 1729.

Morsolin, Bernardo, *Giangiorgio Trissino*. Florence, 1894.

POETICA (*selections*)

Division I

[The value of poetry. 1[1]]

It is a splendid thing to benefit humanity, and is thought the more noble not merely as the benefit extends to a larger number of persons, but also as the pleasure of those benefited is greater, as in the instance of the physician who is thought more skillful when he not merely restores many to health but also does it without pain and with pleasant medicines. Now the greatest benefit that can be rendered to human beings is to teach them to live well, because this gives them while they are alive a tranquil and pleasant existence without any perturbation, and after death secures them eternal felicity in that other very long existence. Since the greater part of men are of such nature that they unwillingly lend their ears to instruction and listen with delight to stories and pleasant things, I judge those ancient poets should be greatly praised who considering delight and general usefulness have mingled with fables and stories of battle the most excellent instructions on human life, and in that way have made them pleasing to the people, whereas if these teachings had been unadorned they would perhaps have pleased little. Since then the poets are those who mingle with delight precepts designed to make the lives of men perfect, poetry should of right be thought by everyone a most excellent thing. Now without this most just cause can it be believed that it would have been in such high repute as it has

---

[1] The numbers of the sections are also those of the pages in the edition of 1729.

been in all ages and perhaps among all the nations of the world? Since it has been so fully treated by Greek and Latin authors in their tongues, I have formed the wish to deal with it also in our Italian language. . . .

Division V

[Rhyme. 91]

Since we have spoken of all the modes of making rhymed verses and of all the species of poems that are made with them, it will be well to lay them aside, because verses without rhyme, that is without agreement of the termination of the last words, are more fitted to all sorts of poetry than those with rhyme.[2] It is true that in the choruses of tragedies and comedies and in poems whose matter is love or praise, where sweetness and attractiveness are especially desirable, rhymes with their rules are not to be given up, but ought to be received and adopted as principal causes of this attractiveness and sweetness; and perhaps for this reason alone that period of antiquity, in which as though through some heavenly influence not merely literature but all the fine arts were brought down to the lowest point, adopted rhyme with great eagerness, so that in the time of the decay of the Latin language men of unpolished abilities pursued it with great zeal, as the hymns of the church clearly show.[3] And although rhyme was invented by the Greeks, though not much used by them because of its defects, that age of which I have spoken, finding it in the Latin which was growing corrupt and disappearing, embraced it with so much ardor that it not only was established in the vulgar tongue of Sicily and Italy, but also passed into France and Spain, and even returned into Greece itself; one can say, perhaps without falsity, that it was received by most of the nations of the world, but by the languages of *si*, of *oc*, and of *oi*, as Dante calls them, rhyme was arranged and classified with abundant rules. Hence, since I wish to write the Art of Poetry in the language of *si*, that is in Italian, it appears necessary to treat of rhyme, in which almost

---

[2] Trissino's epic of *Italy Liberated from the Goths* is unrhymed, as is his tragedy of *Sofonisba*, except for irregular use of rhyme in the choruses and related passages, somewhat as in Milton's *Samson Agonistes*, though more generally.

[3] For example the hymn by Thomas a Celano beginning

Dies irae, dies illa
Solvet saeclum in favilla,
Teste David cum Sybilla.

all the poems of that language are composed, and it appears the more necessary to treat of it because after the age of Dante and Petrarch, poets of the highest order, rhyme has always been much used, but its rules, as it were, abandoned. Though our age has well begun to throw light on rhyme, the explanation of the craft has not gone so far that it needs no aid. Hence some men of noble and quick parts such as Sannazaro, Bembo, and others, composing in rhyme, have not dared to step aside from mere imitation of Petrarch, and if they did abandon this imitation and wander off by themselves, they made great mistakes, for some of them could not distinguish the madrigal from the ballata, nor the latter from the canzone, nor could they discern the *serventesi*[4] from other kinds of poetry, as can be easily seen in their writings. Hence for the sake of the Italian language I have set myself to explain rhyme at length, and in doing it I have not spared labor, for besides Dante's work *On the Vulgar Tongue* and the rules of Antonio da Tempo, I have read also almost all the ancient Sicilian and Italian poets, as well as the Provençals and Spaniards I have been able to find, among whom I have observed all who use the rules I have set forth in my third and fourth books. My labors will be less irksome in proportion as I shall learn that I have satisfied many excellent minds who have an eager desire to know of such things. So after a long voyage I have come to poetry, which if it abounds in beautiful and learned ideas, yet forces me to treat with all possible brevity every part of it, in order that I may keep the promise I made at the beginning. I will not part from the rule and the precepts of the ancients, and especially of Aristotle, who wrote divinely of this art. . . .

[Character in tragedy. 104]

In the following division, where we shall discuss heroic poetry and comedy, in which moral qualities are equally useful and necessary, we shall treat them more particularly and fully than Aristotle has done in the *Poetics*. Hence in this part we shall follow the division of moral traits made by Dionysius of Halicarnassus,[5] which in my opinion is copious and excellent. Since tragedy is an imitation of the most important and greatest people, the composer of tragedy ought to act like the best painters, who in their

---

[4] These forms are explained by Trissino in division IV.

[5] Author of *On the Arrangement of Words* and other works. He taught oratory at Rome in the first century B.C.

pictures, although they give the true likeness of those whom they draw, nevertheless represent them as more beautiful;[6] so the poet, when imitating the wrathful, the timid, the lazy, and the like ought to make their moral traits better, that is, more gentle and more benign—not prouder and more malignant—as did Homer, who represented Achilles as wrathful, but loving and good; and Terence in the *Hecuba* made the mother-in-law pleasant to the nurse, and the harlot to the wife. Therefore the poet should observe what we have said, and afterwards take care of those things which of necessity come to the senses from poetry, that is, to the sight and the hearing. I say he should consider that the tragedy he is writing is to be recited, and the gestures seen, and the speeches and the melody heard. Hence he should treat the fable with words pleasing and fit, and in putting it together he should put everything before his eyes, and act as though he himself had a share in those actions, because if he does so he will see plainly all the moral traits, and will easily find what is suitable to each one, and things contrary and repugnant will not be concealed, and if he places as far as possible before his eyes the gestures and movements of those under the influence of the passions, he will as it were put himself under the influence of those passions, because those who are under the influence of the passions show through nature itself exactly how the tormented man is tormented and the troubled man is troubled. Therefore Aristotle says that those of the highest ability are suited to poetry, and those who are moved by violent feeling,[7] because the first know well how to investigate and the others how to form the passions.

[Plot. 105a]

It is necessary then that the poet, in order to do this, first lay out the speeches generally and then insert the episodes; to lay out the speeches generally is nothing other than to note the whole action that he wishes to imitate; this is exemplified in the *Sofonisba,* the action of which is that in a war between two republics one of them made a league with a king; the other republic, in order to detach the king from that league, gave him as wife the daughter of its general and thus did detach him. Then when the two republics fought together the one that had gained the king was

[6] Cf. Aristotle, *Poetics,* xv, 54b8, above.

[7] The word is *furore.* He has in mind the *furor poeticus,* though the actual allusion is to more general passions. See Aristotle, *Poetics,* xvii, first par., above.

routed in battle by the other, and the king was taken prisoner. Another king, an ally of the victorious republic, entering the city of the captive king, was besought by the wife of the prisoner not to give her into the hands of the conquering republic; he promised to do what she wished and, in order to do it better, took her for his own wife. After the wedding there arrived a messenger from the captain general of the victorious republic, who demanded the queen; the king who had espoused her did not wish to give her up and went to the captain general, who wished to send the queen as a prisoner to his republic. Therefore the king who had wedded her, not being able to keep his promise, sent her poison, saying that by taking it she could prevent herself from falling into the hands of her enemies; she accepted it, drank, and died. This then is the action, and the rest of the play is made up of the episodes; therefore the poet ought first to outline the simple action, and then insert the names and weave in the episodes; these episodes should be few and short, and suited to the action, as are in the *Sofonisba* the coming of Cato, the speech of Scipio with Syphax, and the sacrifice of Sofonisba, for these are few and brief and most suitable, and are in no respect like the episodes of heroic poetry, which are many and long, like those of the *Odyssey* of Homer and the *Aeneid* of Vergil.

[Thought. 105b]

The discourse or expression of thought in the play, the conceptions that Aristotle classes under *dianoia*,[8] ought to be taken from rhetoric, for it is proper to that art; to discourse pertain all those things which are necessary in preparing a speech the parts of which are to prove, to make clear, and to move the passions, such as pity and wrath, though such passions, and likewise greatness and littleness, are equally employed in preparing a play, which takes them from the same models as does an oration; but in this they are different: for a tragedy they are prepared from the nature of things without artifice, but in an oration they are made by the ability and the artifice of the speaker. Dionysius of Halicarnassus holds that the said discourses or speeches should be neither superfluous nor defective nor paradoxical; of the superfluous an example is furnished by Homer, who has Thersites utter much superfluous nonsense at which the Greeks laugh; so superfluous talk runs into chattering, defective into weakness, and paradoxical into

---

[8] *Poetics*, xix, first par., above.

peril. From this is manifest that eloquence does not consist in abundance but in proper and skillful arrangement; speeches should not be too brief, that they may not be weak, but should be enough to suffice, and this demands measure; which ought always to be preserved with security; security is gained by not saying contrary things and by proceeding always with propositions that are known and which all believe and admit, as that God is good and just, and that virtue is an honorable thing, and that one should revere his father and his mother; Plato and Xenophon say that Socrates always did this.

[Pity and fear.[9] 106a]

But because pity and fear are things with which tragedy is especially concerned, I wish to say something of their nature and origin, following the *Rhetoric* of Aristotle.

[Fear.[10] 106b]

Fear then is a sorrow or perturbation through the imagination of some deadly or painful evil which is likely to come, for not all evils are feared, because no one is in fear of becoming unjust or slothful, though these are evils, but merely those evils are feared which can bring about death or the greatest pains and sorrows; and these are not always feared but merely when they appear near us and are likely to come on us, for when evils are uncertain or very distant they are not feared, such as death, which everyone

---

[9] Aristotle, *Poetics*, VI, first par., above.

[10] This section is borrowed from Aristotle's *Rhetoric*, II, 5, yet to anyone who has read Italian political writers of the fifteenth and sixteenth centuries, above all Machiavelli, it is apparent that it is in their spirit. See, for example, Machiavelli, *The Prince*, chap. VII, last par.; chap. XXI, next to last par.; chap. XXIV, end; *Florentine History*, III, 19; and Gilbert, *Machiavelli's "Prince" and Its Forerunners* (Durham, 1938), pp. 48, 98–117. But however true, vivid, and familiar to his contemporaries Trissino's discussion may be, is it still a political rather than a literary discussion? Has the author forgotten he is writing about the drama? The answer is to be found in the repeated assertion of the critics that tragedy is concerned with kings and men of high rank (see the index, *tragedy, its subjects and characters*). Nor did the Renaissance author stop with such a choice; not only would he deal with a king, but a king in his public capacity; the function of tragedy is to make kings fear to be tyrants, as Sidney put it (sect. 32, below). Consequently any study of political fear is also a study of fear as the tragic writer is to use it. *Macbeth*, for example, may be considered in this light. Macbeth fears Banquo because the latter knows something of the reasons for his conduct. Macduff is to be feared because he has been injured. Malcolm and Donalbain fear Macbeth because he is evil and has power to hurt them. Banquo should have feared and the audience fear for him because he has put himself at the discretion of another, and a wicked man. In a similar way many Renaissance tragedies exemplify the theories of Trissino.

Fear is discussed in much the same way by Minturno, *De poeta*, pp. 209–12.

knows he must undergo, but because it is not near we do not think about it. If this is what fear is, it is necessary that all things are fearful that seem to have great power to kill us or to do us the most painful injuries; therefore the apparent approach of them causes us fear, because the formidable appears to be near at hand; so the near approach of the formidable is properly called peril. Therefore, the enmity and wrath of those who are able to injure us is formidable, because, since they are enemies or angry at us, it is obvious that they are able and wish to injure us and therefore are on the point of doing it. Injustice also excites fear when it is strong because the unjust man is unjust through choice, which indicates he will do what he wishes so far as he can. Likewise a capable man injured is worthy of fear when he has power, because manifestly he always can do what he wishes when he is injured and has power; therefore, because of both will and power, evil is at hand. Fear on the part of those who are able to do evil is also an indication of danger because such as these are of necessity always prepared and because, moreover, most men are ill-disposed and allow themselves to be overcome by gain and are timid in perils; for this reason it is almost always a fear-inspiring thing to stand at the discretion of others; hence, those who are conscious of some serious misdeed committed by someone seem formidable to him because he fears they will reveal it or will abandon him; and those who can do injury are formidable to those who are likely to receive it because men are for the most part inclined to do injury when they can. And those who have been injured or think they are going to be injured are dangerous because they are ever watching their opportunity. And equally those who have done injury are to be feared if they have power because they fear vengeance from someone else and such vengeance is put among objects of apprehension. And those also are formidable who contend about things which they cannot possess together because such as these ever war one with another. Those also who are afraid of those more powerful than themselves are equally dangerous to the more powerful because they can easily injure those stronger than themselves. For the same reason they are to be dreaded who are feared by those stronger than themselves; and also those are to be dreaded who have killed men stronger than themselves, and those who have attacked men less powerful than themselves are dangerous at that time or when they are made great. Of those who have been injured, and enemies, and adversaries, the choleric and free are less to be feared than are the mild, and two-faced, and malignant, because it cannot be known when such as these are about to act and when they are far from it. Of all formidable things those are most to be dreaded which, though they cannot be carried out, yet cannot be changed either because change is impossible or because it is not in the power of the doers but in that of their adversaries. Formidable also are those things that cannot be helped, or against which aid, though possible, is not easy to obtain.

To put it very briefly, I say those things are worthy to cause fear that excite pity, when they are put into action or are about to be put into action. These then are all the things disposed toward terror, and to be feared, or at least the chief ones.

[Who are those who fear? 107a]

Let us see then who those are who fear them. It is manifest that, since fear is the expectation of undergoing some deadly or painful sufferings, those who think they are not going to suffer any evil do not fear, because they cannot fear either things they suppose they cannot undergo or men who cannot cause them suffering or at a time when no suffering can come to them. It is necessary, then, that those should fear who think that they can suffer evil, and that they should fear those who can make them suffer it, and such evil as can actually happen to them, and at the time when it can happen. The persons, then, who do not fear they will undergo any evil are those who are or who think themselves to be in great prosperity, and these are the rich, the strong, the powerful, those abounding in friends, and the like, and for that reason they are almost always proud, disdainful, and audacious. But those who have suffered the greatest ills do not fear they are going to suffer them, nor do those who are cold and as it were dead to the future, such as those under torture and near death, for he who fears must have some hope that he can deliver himself from what afflicts him; the indication of this is that fear makes a man take counsel because no one ever takes counsel about a thing that is beyond hope. Hence in giving counsel to another and in comforting his fear one usually says that men commonly suffer similar ills and that they have suffered others greater than these, and one usually points out that many like to them suffer and have suffered ills they have not foreseen, and at the hands of unexpected persons and at unexpected times. So what we have said will be sufficient in order to understand what fear is and what things are feared and who those are that fear.

[Pity.[11] 107b]

Let us come then to pity, which is sorrow because of some evil, or what appears an evil, which may be deadly or painful, and comes to someone who does not deserve to suffer it, and the observer thinks this evil can come to himself or to some of his relatives; this is especially true when the evil seems near at hand. Whence it is manifest that he who would have pity must be such a person that either he or some of his can suffer such evils or similar or equal ones. For those who are totally ruined do not have pity because they think they can suffer no more, having already suffered so much; nor are the compassionate those who think themselves very prosperous, for such persons are rather contemptuous of the afflicted, because, believing they have everything that is good, they think they cannot suffer evil, for not to be able to suffer evil is surely to be placed among the good things of life. They feel pity, then, who think they themselves can suffer, having at other times suffered and been freed; also the old feel pity because of their prudence and experience. And so the weak and the timid and the practiced are liable to pity because they are governed by reason. They are also quick to show compassion who have fathers, wives, brothers, and children, because these appear to them able to suffer the things mentioned above. On the contrary they are not likely to feel pity who are subject to the passions of the strong, as wrath and audacity, because they do not think of what can come; nor do those feel commiseration who are by nature malicious and unjust, because such men do not consider that they are able to suffer. But they are subject to pity who stand in a middle place, that is, who are neither irascible nor audacious, nor malicious, nor unjust. The very timid also do not feel compassion, for when in terror they do not pity others because they are occupied with their own feelings, which arise from their belief that some of those who suffer are good and kind, since he who did not think anyone good would judge all men worthy of affliction. But generally those will be compassionate who remember that to themselves or to some of their relatives similar accidents can come, or who fear that they will come to themselves or some of theirs.

[11] From Aristotle's *Rhetoric*, II, 8.

[What is pitiable? 108a]

The things for which there can be commiseration are matters of suffering and sorrows that are death-bringing and excessive, and all those great ills of which Fortune is the cause. The things grievous and excessive are deaths, wounds, and afflictions of the body, such as old age, diseases, and need of necessary food. An evil of which Fortune is the cause is to have no friend or to have very few; therefore violent separation from friends and companions is full of misery. Pity is also caused by ugliness, weakness, the lack of some member of the body, and the receiving of evil from a person from whom good should be received—something that often happens. It also moves pity when to a man who has suffered greatly some good comes after he is dead. It is also pitiable never to have had anything good, or to have had it without ever being able to use or enjoy it. These are the things that excite pity.

[Who are pitiable? 108b]

Pity is excited by those whom we know but are not closely connected with, for when our intimates suffer or are about to suffer we feel sorrow as for ourselves. Hence Aristotle says that Amasis did not weep for his son who had been condemned to death and did weep when he saw one of his friends begging, because to see his friend beg was pitiable and the fate of his son was atrocious; for atrocity is a thing diverse from pity and expulsive of it, and often is useful to bring about the contrary; yet there is pity when the horror of the evil is near at hand. We have pity for those who are like us in age or characteristics or disposition or dignity or race, because in such as these it clearly appears what things can happen to us. So it can be generally said that all those things which we fear as able to happen to ourselves move compassion in us when we see them happen to someone else. And when such sufferings appear near at hand, then are they most piteous, because things done ten thousand years ago or which will be done ten thousand years later, since we neither expect them nor remember them, do not move pity at all or very little. Hence it is needful for those who wish to excite commiseration with ancient stories that they should be made pitiable with masks, language, and clothing, and in a word with the stage presentation, for the evil which is done or about to be done, being placed before our eyes by the means just mentioned, comes to appear near us, and what is near at hand, being done at the moment or going to be done, is the more piteous. For that reason such things as the outer garments and shirts of those who have suffered, and the words of those who are under the influence of the passions, especially when it appears that at the same time they are deserving of love and are virtuous, move us greatly. All the things that show that sufferings are near us, and that those who suffer are suffering unjustly, produce the greatest pity. This will suffice us on pity.

[Sentences.[12] 109]

The sentences or wise sayings in which not merely tragedy but also heroic poetry, comedy, and the other poems ought to abound are speeches short, moral, conclusive, and full of meaning, which the Greeks call *gnomai*, and they exhort either to do or not to do something; some are affirmative, some simple, some compound, some credible, some true, some hyperbolical. The exhortations to act are like this of Dante:

> Aye to that truth which has the face of falsehood,
> A man should close his lips as far as may be,
> Because without his fault it causes shame.

The exhortations not to do something are like this from my *Italy Liberated from the Goths:*

> He should never sleep the entire night
> Who stands at the helm of a nation.

The affirmatives are such as this from Petrarch:

> It is less shameful to err in youth.

The simple are as is this line from him:

> Ever sighing relieves naught.

The compound are like this one from the same author:

> The end crowns a life and the evening a day.

The credible are like this from Dante:

> Love, that exempts no one beloved from loving.

The true are like the following from the *Sofonisba:*

> This mortal life cannot run its course without sorrow.

The hyperbolic are like this line from Petrarch:

> Infinite in number is the troop of the fools.

[12] See the index under *sentences.*

It should be noted that nothing forbids the same sentence to have
two, three, or four of the qualities mentioned, that is, it can be
at the same time an exhortation to a deed, and simple, and true,
and affirmative, and so it is with the other qualities, provided
they are not opposites and contraries, for the same sentence cannot be at the same time an exhortation to act and not to act, both
simple and compound, and both hyperbolic and true. . . .

Division VI

[Comedy. 120a]

It remains, then, to treat the imitation of actions and traits less
dignified and of a worse sort, which may be done by deriding and
censuring them, and in that way teach men virtue, something
usually done by comedies, in which the poet does not speak for
himself but, in the same way as in tragedy, always brings in persons to speak and act. So it is also in pastoral eclogues, though in
these there is sometimes utterance by the poet, as is apparent in
Theocritus and Vergil. Comedy, then, imitates worse actions
with speech, rhythm, and harmony, as does tragedy; and it imitates an action single, complete, and large, which has a beginning, a middle, and an end. But in this it differs from tragedy,
that as tragedy carries on its teaching by means of pity and fear,
comedy teaches by deriding and censuring things ugly and
vile. . . . It suffices to know that comedy is an imitation of the
wicked and the vicious, yet not in every extremity of the vices,
but merely of that which is ugly, whence springs the ridiculous,
which is an ugly defect without pain and without deaths; of the
ridiculous we shall treat at length in its place.

[The comic plot. 120b]

Comedy, then, has the same substantial parts as tragedy, that
is, the fable, the human traits, the thought, the words, the stage
presentation, and the melody, because to make a comedy that
would be perfect it is necessary to represent it on the stage, where
it needs the chorus and melody. The comic fable, then, is made
up of actions diverse from those of tragedy, and as it were contrary to them, because tragedy produces the effect of its teaching
with pity, with tears, and with fear, which are sad things, while
comedy does it with jokes and with laughter, which are pleasant
things; hence as for tragedy are sought out piteous acts of great

and illustrious men, so in comedy it is necessary to use jocose acts of persons of low rank and unknown, and as in tragedy there come about sorrows and deaths and it almost always ends in unhappiness, so in comedy, though there are some disturbances, they do not involve wounds and deaths, and all terminate in good, as weddings, peaceful agreements, and tranquillity, through which characters issue in peace from the scene. . . .

[Comedy resembles tragedy. 121a]

The moral type is that in which morals are most prominent, as the *Hecyra* of Terence, and the ridiculous is that in which jokes and ridiculous things prevail, as the *Menechmi* of Plautus, from which we have adapted the *Simillimi*. And nothing forbids that the same comedy should be simple and moral, as is the *Adelphi*, and double and moral, as is the *Hecyra*, simple and ridiculous, as is the *Aulularia*, and double and ridiculous, as the *Simillimi*. But it cannot at the same time be simple and double, for they are contraries. So he who wishes to compose a comedy well should first arrange the fable, that is, find the action and write a summary of it, and put it before his eyes, and consider well the moral traits, and see what is fitting and what is contrary or repugnant, and then put in the names, and insert the episodes, and treat it with excellent sententious sayings, and with words familiar, ornate, and suitable, as we have said about tragedy.

[Comedy differs from tragedy. 121b]

But comedy will differ from tragedy in that while in tragedy the actions and names are true, either all or the greater part, in comedy the actions and names are all invented by the poet, though Plautus in his *Amphitryo* did not do it, whence it is called a tragicomedy. Yet such a thing was not afterward imitated either by himself or by any other, but rather they have all abandoned true names, especially since in Athens, to restrain the license of comedy, which unjustly blamed and derided worthy men, it was established by law that in comedies no one should be permitted to call anyone by name; thence was derived the custom of the new comedies, in which no real names are introduced, but all are invented by the poet. Such names are formed either from countries, as in *Mysis* from *Mysia*, *Syrus* from *Syria*, or from cities, as *Messenius* from *Messina*, or from mountains or rivers, as *Pachinus* and *Alesa*, or from qualities, as is *Phaedria* meaning *joyous*, *Sophrona* meaning *prudent*, *Chremes* meaning *avaricious*, and the like. The formation of such names from traits or qualities of men is the best way and the most suitable to comedies of all, and the plan of forming them from the Greek language is good, because they are formed more appropriately, although they are also appropriately derived from the Latin, *Mizio* from *mitis*,[13] and from the vulgar tongue, as *Scovoletto* from *scovolo*,[14] and the like.

[The ridiculous. 127a]

In this place we shall especially treat of the ridiculous, which, as Aristotle says, pertains to comedy. Of the ridiculous Aristotle says in his *Rhetoric* that he has dealt with it in his *Poetics;* perhaps it was in the part dealing with comedy, which has been lost through the ravages of time, and with it the treatment of the ridiculous which was included in it. So it is necessary to investigate it, which we shall do according to a method other than that used by Marcus Tullius and Fabius Quintilianus, because their method was rather oratorical than philosophical. The ridiculous then, as Aristotle says, is a mild form of the ugly, and is a defect and an ugliness that is neither deadly nor painful. Tully then and Quintilian, who perhaps took their idea from Aristotle, say, not badly, that the place and seat of the ridiculous is in ugliness and deformity, but from what cause this ugliness moves laughter they do not say, and the part of Aristotle which perhaps gave it is lost. Hence we shall investigate it in the following manner.

[Laughter. 127b]

It is evident that laughter comes from the delight and pleasure of him who laughs, and this pleasure cannot come to him except through the senses, that is from seeing, hearing, touching, tasting, and smelling, or from the memory of the pleasures they have had from something, or from the hope that they are going to have them. Such pleasure does not come from every object that delights and pleases the senses but merely from those objects that have some share of ugliness, for if a man sees a beautiful lady or a beautiful jewel or something similar that pleases him,[15] he does not laugh, nor does he laugh on hearing music in praise of him, nor on touching, tasting, and smelling things that to the touch, the taste, and the smell are pleasant and grateful; rather these together with pleasure bring admiration and not laughter. But if the

[13] Gentle. [14] Sponge. [15] Cf. Sidney, *Defense*, sect. 50, below.

object that is presented to the senses has some mixture of ugliness, it moves laughter, as an ugly and distorted face, an inept movement, a silly word, a mispronunciation, a rough hand, a wine of unpleasant taste, or a rose of unpleasant odor moves laughter at once, and those things especially cause laughter from which better qualities were hoped, because then not merely our senses but also our hopes are slightly offended, and such pleasure as this comes to us because man is by nature envious and malicious,[16] as is clearly seen in little children, for almost all of them are envious, and always delight to do evil, if they are able. It can be observed also that man never naturally delights in the good of others, except through accident, that is, through some good which he hopes from it for himself, as Plautus says:

> There is no one who would not envy the obtaining of something pleasant.

Hence if anyone sees that someone finds some money, he does not laugh or take pleasure, but rather is envious, but if he sees that someone falls into the mud and soils himself, he laughs, because that evil which does not come on ourselves, as Lucretius says, is always pleasant to observe in others. But if we have like sufferings, the sight of them in others does not move us to laughter, for no hunchback laughs at another hunchback nor a lame man at another lame man, unless he thinks that these ills are in him less ugly than in the other. If the evils, then, that we see in others are deadly and painful, as are wounds, fevers, and injuries, they do not move laughter, but rather pity through fear that similar ills may come to ourselves or to some of our circle, for we think those who belong to us parts of ourselves. The small ill, then, not painful or deadly, that we see or hear in others, as ugliness of body, and folly of mind, when it is not or we believe it is not in ourselves, is what pleases us or makes us laugh.

[Laughter and deformity. 127c]

As man is composed of mind and body, so ugliness in him is double, of the mind and the body, and the special deformities of the mind are ignorance, imprudence, credulity, and the like, which often depend one on the other, and therefore in jokes we laugh at the ignorance, imprudence, and credulity of someone else, and especially when we see them in persons who are thought

---

[16] Cf. Dryden, *Of Dramatic Poesy*, sect. 59, below.

substantial and of good intelligence, for in such as these many
times opinion and hope are deceived. To such instances of ugliness may be reduced all the jokes and jibes written by Boccaccio
and the Courtier, and likewise all the ridiculous stories and jokes
and clever sayings gathered up by Tully, Quintilian, Boccaccio,
Poggio, and the Courtier.[17] It is well to know that if the ugliness
and deformity of mind we have spoken of are great, such as be-
trayals and perjuries, they do not move laughter, but disdain,
and are condemned and rebuked, as are lies, exhibitions of ignorance, and similar awkward things of mind or body. But if they
are slight, they move laughter and are mocked at and delight is
taken in them. All these ridiculous deformities are either pointed
out, or narrated, or observed with some urbanity. Those which
are pointed out are of the sort that Tully assigns to Crassus, who,
when speaking against Helvius Mancia, said: "Now I shall show
you who you are." Mancia urgently answered: "Who will you
show that I am?" Then Crassus, turning, pointed with his finger
to a Cimbrian shield of Marius on a shop, on which was carved
the face of a Frank, brutal and distorted, which certainly resembled the face of Mancia, at which everyone began to laugh.[18]

[Comic stories. 128]

Deformities can also be shown in narrative only, as was that of
Strepsiades in Aristophanes,[19] who was narrating the disagree-
ments between himself and his wife; since he was a countryman
and avaricious, and she a citizen and proud, they disagreed in
many things, and especially in the name they were going to give
the son who was born to them; Strepsiades wished to give him the
name of Pennysaver, and the proud mother the name of Horse-
master; in the end they agreed to give each half a name, to wit
Savehorse or Phidippides. Such a story as this excites laughter
everywhere, because it throughout makes plain the ignorance and
avarice of the countryman, and the pride and imprudence of the
lady, which are all of them deformities of mind. Such deformities
either of body or mind can be pointed out with some word, an
action called urbanity;[20] an example appeared when someone
indicated the deformity of body of Testio Pinario, who twisted

---

[17] Castiglione in the *Courtier*, Bk. II, secs. 42–89, discusses comedy, with illustrative
examples. His discussion, like that of Trissino, owes much to Cicero's remarks in
De oratore II, 54–71.
[18] The story is told by Cicero, *De oratore*, II, 66, but assigned to Crassus by Pliny,
Natural History, XXXV, 8.   [19] In the *Clouds*.   [20] In the Latin sense of cleverness.

his chin in speaking as if he had a nut in his mouth, and his adversary said to him: "Say what you wish, when you have cracked the nut you have in your mouth." Similarly a buffoon pointed out a deformity in the face of the Emperor Vespasian of such a sort that it appeared to strain to get away from the body; the emperor asking him if he were going to say something, the buffoon replied: "I will speak when you have got away from your body." Also M. Bartolomeo Pagello noted the deformity of mind in M. Lionardo da Porto, who said it was easy to provide so that the hail would not injure Vicentio by placing some cannon in certain mountains above which the hail-bringing clouds were accustomed to come, and when those clouds were seen coming to discharge the cannon into them so that they would burst and let out their water and the hail would not fall on the lower ground. Pagello then put his hand into his purse and took out two *marcelli* and gave them to M. Lionardo, saying: "Please take these, and say that it was I who have spoken of so fine a remedy." At this everyone laughed, and so with urbanity he made plain the folly of such a remedy, without answering at all. This urbanity is a thing brief, sharp, swift, and excellently fitted to keen and ridiculous sayings, and it appears in speaking and answering, and it is a good source for anything involving ridicule, such as ambiguity, deceiving the expectation, scoffing at the nature of another, comparison with something still more deformed, dissimulation, inept sayings, and rebuking the silly; and all of the aforesaid things have many parts that excite ridicule, either in denying or refuting or defending or diminishing; and these all move laughter because they point out some deformity either in oneself or in some other.

[Ambiguity. 129a]

An example of ambiguity is that sonnet of Antonio Alemani on Alemano Salviati. This Alemano was with other citizens on a committee which did not wish to please the said Antonio in something he wished; so Alemano to excuse himself said to Antonio: "It is not I, that is, I am not the one who did not wish to please you." Antonio, feigning to think that he said that he was not Alemano Salviati, wrote as follows:

Alemano says to me, I am not I,
And this is not true, because he is he.
But when he denies that he is himself
He wonders whether he will speak the truth of my action.

Here the ridiculous rises from the ambiguity of *I am not I,* with which he feigns ignorance in himself and a lie in Alemano, both of which are deformities of the mind. Much like this was that circumstance of Scipio Nasica and Ennius the poet that Tully tells. Nasica, going to the house of Ennius and asking if he were at home, heard Ennius answer the servant that he was not. A few days later, Ennius, going to the house of Nasica, asked if he were there, and Nasica answered in a loud voice that he was not, and Ennius said: "What, do I not know your voice?" Then Nasica said: "You are not very courteous, for the other day when your servant told me you were not at home I believed him, and now you are not willing to believe me when I tell you myself." Here are two defects of mind that produce the ridiculous, one the ignorance that Nasica feigns in himself in wishing that Ennius should believe he was not at home when he heard he was there; the other is the lie which is revealed in Ennius who when he was at home had his servant say he was not there. Similar humor was that in a reply of Pievano Arlotto, who, finding himself on a street in Florence and passing a beautiful and bold girl, said to his companion: "This is a beautiful lady." The bold girl turned toward him and said: "I cannot say as much for you." Pievano instantly answered: "Yes indeed, since you wish to tell a lie of me, as I have of you." Thus Pievano, by feigning in himself deformity of mind that led him to lie, discovered the deformity of an ungrateful spirit in the lady who censured a man who praised her, and at the same time he made game of deformity of body in her. These two comic conditions are not very different from that above of Alemani, except that these do not come from ambiguity as does that.

[The pun. 129b]

Of this ambiguity there are many kinds, such as the changing of letters which by some is called a pun, as Garifilo to Garofolo, Luca Michiele to Licamelculo,[21] and the like; it is also done by means of some addition, as *moral* and *mortal,* as in that sonnet of Aretino as follows:

> Though you are, I confess it,
> Both poet and mortal philosopher
> Without a *sesino* and without natural.[22]

---

[21] *Garofolo* means *clove;* the English equivalent would be to call Mr. Clive, **Mr. Clove.**

[22] The pun on *natural* is obscene in both English and Italian.

Here the ridiculous is produced not merely with the ambiguity, by saying *mortal* in place of *moral*, but also with irony, when he says, *Though you are, I confess it,* and with synecdoche, by saying *sesino,* which is a kind of money, in place of money, which is the genus, and then he turns again to ambiguity, saying *without natural,* in place of *without natural philosophy,* for ambiguity, as though always feigning ignorance in itself, reveals deformity in others, as equally irony does, with which Aretino and Bernia produced many ridiculous passages, and not merely with these but also with sarcasm, allegory, hyperbole, and the other things we have mentioned. . . .

[What is contrary to expectation. 129c]

That which deceives expectation is the mode most appropriate to the ridiculous, because it reveals the imprudence of the one who waits, as in the jest of Giovanni Cannaccio with Prior Pandolfini, who believed for a certainty that Frate Girolamo Savonarola was a saint and that though then dead he should rise up; therefore he said one day to Cannaccio, who was one of those who sentenced the Frate to death: "What will you say, Giovanni, when you see Frate Girolamo raised from the dead?" Cannaccio responded, contrary to the expectation of Pandolfini: "I shall say that next time we ought to have him hanged." But here since the expectation is deceived in so grave a matter, it does not move so much laughter as if the thing were less serious, because every slight thing in which a man deceives himself moves laughter not only in others but also in the man himself, when he understands it, that is, when he sees he has uttered one word instead of another or has taken up one thing for another. Therefore the *Amphitryo* of Plautus and *I Simillimi* are very gay comedies because the persons in them many times deceive themselves, and because of resemblance take one person for another, and speak to one when they think they speak to another; thus they reveal that they themselves and the others are in some slight way ignorant, and frequent ridiculous situations arise. . . .

[The acute response. 130a]

A laugh is also roused by an acute response to some proverb that is uttered, such as was made by Maestro Gerardo Bolderico, a Veronese physician, to that lady of the Malaspini who asked from him a remedy for her only son. The physician answered nothing was wrong with the boy and she should not wish to have medicine given to him, but the lady still insisted that he should use some remedy, and wishing to excuse herself for such insistence, did it with a proverb, saying to him: "O sir, he who has but one eye often wipes it." The physician added: "And wipes it so much that he digs it out." The comedy sprang from the revelation of the imprudence of that lady, who believed that medicine would help one who was not sick.

[Literary comedy. 130b]

And finally all the comic passages in Aristophanes, Plautus, Terence, Apuleius, and others, and in some Italian authors, as Boccaccio, Burchiello, Poggio, Pulci, Ariosto, Aretino, Bernia, and Mauro, all show and point out little or ordinary deformities of body or of mind of some person, and with pointing out or otherwise revealing in different ways those deformities, produce ridicule, and pointed sayings, and jests. And what we have said will suffice for the ridiculous, so far as it pertains to comedy. It is manifest, then, that words in comedy should not attempt to be lofty and sounding and lordly, as do those of tragedy, but should aim to be low, clear, and urbane, and that the metaphors and other figures should be easy and such as are common in ordinary speech, which comedy especially imitates. Comedy therefore should not have diversity of foreign expressions or things that may make it appear foreign, nor should it show too much pains or too much ornament, because, as we have said, words very splendid and labored hide ideas and human traits; moreover expressions not in common use produce elevation, a thing not fitting to comedy.

SIR THOMAS ELYOT

o◉ooo◉o

THE GOVERNOR

1530

In the reign of Henry VIII, Sir Thomas Elyot, an experienced public official, wrote a work "on the education of them that hereafter may be deemed worthy to be governors of the public weal under your highness." Poetry occupies a small part of the volume. Though primarily concerned with education, Elyot does not lose sight of the general principles of poetry nor of its relation to society. His work gives a view of English and indeed European theory just before the *Poetics* of Aristotle became generally known. The popularity of the work, of which eight editions appeared by 1580, was such that Sir Philip Sidney probably had seen it. Possibly the coincidences between Elyot's "defense" (see sect. 6) and Sidney's are the result of Sir Philip's knowledge of *The Governor*.

BIBLIOGRAPHY

Elyot, Sir Thomas, *The Book Named the Governour*, edited from the first edition by H. H. S. Croft. London, 1880. A fully annotated edition necessary to careful study.

————. London, 1907 (Everyman's Library).

THE GOVERNOR (*selections*)

Book I, Chapter X

[Homer]

[1] I could rehearse divers other poets which for matter and eloquence be very necessary, but I fear me to be too long from noble Homer, from whom as from a fountain proceeded all eloquence and learning. For in his books be contained and most perfectly expressed not only the documents martial and disci-

pline of arms, but also incomparable wisdoms and instructions for politic governance of people,[1] with the worthy commendation and laud of noble princes, wherewith the readers shall be so all inflamed that they most fervently shall desire and covet, by the imitation of their virtues, to acquire semblable glory. For the which occasion, Aristotle, most sharpest witted and excellent learned philosopher, as soon as he had received Alexander from King Philip his father, he before any other thing taught him the most noble works of Homer, wherein Alexander found such sweetness and fruit that ever after he had Homer not only with him in all his journeys, but also laid him under his pillow when he went to rest, and oftentimes would purposely wake some hours of the night, to take as it were his pastime with that most noble poet. For by the reading of his work called *Iliados*, where the assembly of the most noble Greeks against Troy is recited with their affairs, he gathered courage and strength against his enemies, wisdom and eloquence for consultations and persuasions to his people and army. And by the other work called *Odyssea*, which recounteth the sundry adventures of the wise Ulysses, he, by the example of Ulysses, apprehended many noble virtues and also learned to escape the fraud and deceitful imaginations of sundry and subtile crafty wits.[2] Also there shall he learn to ensearch and perceive the manners and conditions of them that be his familiars, sifting out, as I might say, the best from the worst, whereby he may surely commit his affairs and trust to every person after his virtues. Therefore I now conclude that there is no lesson for a young gentleman to be compared with Homer,[3] if he be plainly and substantially expounded and declared by the master.

[Vergil]

[2] Notwithstanding, for as much as the said works be very long, and do require therefore a great time to be all learned and kanned, some Latin author would be therewith mixed, and specially Vergil; which, in his work called *Aeneidos* is most like to Homer, and almost the same Homer in Latin. Also by the joining together of those authors the one shall be the better under-

---

[1] The theory refuted by Plato (*Republic*, x, above), but accepted by many in later times. See Sidney, *Defense*, sect. 24, below.

[2] "Homer gives us a useful example of what virtue and wisdom can do" (Horace, *Epistles*, I, 2, 17–18).

[3] Cf. with Spenser's letter to Raleigh; he writes for a gentleman in the manner of Homer and Vergil.

stood by the other. And verily, as I before said, no one author serveth to so divers wits as doth Vergil. For there is not that affect or desire whereto any child's fantasy is disposed but in some of Vergil's works may be found matter thereto apt and proper. For what thing can be more familiar than his *Bucolics?* nor no work so nigh approacheth to the common dalliance and manners of children, and the pretty controversies of the simple shepherds therein contained wonderfully rejoiceth the child that heareth it well declared, as I know by my own experience. In his *Georgics,* Lord, what pleasant variety there is, the divers grains, herbs, and flowers that be there described![4] that, reading therein, it seemeth to a man to be in a delectable garden or paradise. What plough-man knoweth so much of husbandry as there is expressed? who, delighting in good horses, shall not be thereto more enflamed, reading of the breeding, choosing, and keeping of them? In the declaration whereof Vergil leaveth far behind him all breeders, hackney-men and skorsers.[5] Is there any astronomer that more exactly setteth out the order and course of the celestial bodies or that more truly doth divine in his prognostications of the times of the year in their qualities, with the future estate of all things pro-vided by husbandry, than Vergil doth recite in that work? If the child have a delight in hunting, what pleasure shall he take of the fable of Aristeus![6] semblably in the hunting of Dido and Aeneas, which is described most elegantly in his book of *Aeneidos.* If he have pleasure in wrestling, running, or other like exercise, where shall he see any more pleasant esbatements[7] than that which was done by Euryalus and other Trojans, which accompanied Aeneas? If he take solace in hearing minstrels, what minstrel may be com-pared to Iopas, which sang before Dido and Aeneas? or to blind Demodocus, that played and sang most sweetly at the dinner that the king Alcinous made to Ulysses? whose ditties and melody excelled as far the songs of our minstrels as Homer and Vergil excel all other poets. If he be more desirous, as the most part of children be, to hear things marvelous and exquisite, which hath in it a visage of some things incredible, whereat shall he more wonder than when he shall behold Aeneas follow Sibyl into hell?

---

[4] Milton wrote:

> For earth hath this variety from heaven
> Of pleasure situate in hill and dale.
> *Paradise Lost*, VI, 640-1.

See *variety* in the index.

[5] Horse traders.   [6] Vergil, *Georgics*, IV, 317-558.   [7] Pastimes, sports.

What shall he more dread than the terrible visages of Cerberus, Gorgon, Megaera, and other furies and monsters? How shall he abhor tyranny, fraud, and avarice, when he doth see the pains of Duke Theseus, Prometheus, Sisyphus, and such others tormented for their dissolute and vicious living! How glad soon after shall he be, when he shall behold in the pleasant fields of Elysium the souls of noble princes and captains which, for their virtue and labors in advancing the public weals of their countries, do live eternally in pleasure inexplicable! And in the last books of *Aeneidos* shall he find matter to minister to him audacity, valiant courage, and policy to take and sustain noble enterprises,[8] if any shall be needful for the assailing of his enemies. Finally, as I have said, this noble Vergil, like to a good nurse,[9] giveth to a child, if he will take it, everything apt for his wit and capacity; wherefore he is in the order of learning to be preferred before any other author Latin.

[Ovid and Horace]

[3] I would set next unto him two books of Ovid, the one called *Metamorphoses*, which is as much to say as changing of men into other figure or form; the other is entitled *De fastis*, where the ceremonies of the Gentiles, and specially the Romans, be expressed; both right necessary for the understanding of other poets. But because there is little other learning in them concerning either virtuous manners or policy, I suppose it were better that, as fables and ceremonies happen to come in a lesson, it were declared abundantly by the master, than that in the said two books a long time should be spent and almost lost, which might be better employed on such authors that do minister both eloquence, civil policy, and exhortation to virtue. Wherefore in his place let us bring in Horace, in whom is contained much variety of learning and quickness of sentence. This poet may be interlaced with the lesson of *Odyssea* of Homer, wherein is declared the wonderful prudence and fortitude of Ulysses in his passage from Troy. And if the child were induced to make verses by the imitation of Vergil and Homer, it should minister to him much delectation and courage[10] to study; nor the making of verses is not discommended in a

---

[8] Cf. Sidney, *Defense*, sect. 24, below, and note. A stratagem for the purpose of surprising the enemy is devised by Turnus (*Aeneid*, XI, 511ff.).

[9] For poetry as a nurse see Sidney, *Defense*, sect. 2, below.

[10] Inclination and desire.

noble man, since the noble Augustus and almost all the old emperors made books in verses. . . .

[The effect of poetry]

[4] Leonidas, the noble king of Spartans, being once demanded of what estimation in poetry Tyrtaeus,[11] as he supposed, was, it is written that he answering said that for stirring the minds of young men he was excellent, for as much as they being moved with his verses do run into the battle, regarding no peril, as men all inflamed in martial courage. And when a man is come to mature years, and that reason in him is confirmed with serious learning and long experience, then shall he, in reading tragedies, execrate and abhor the intolerable life of tyrants,[12] and shall contemn the folly and dotage expressed by poets lascivious.

Book I, Chapter XIII

[The wisdom of poets]

[5] They that make verses, expressing thereby none other learning but the craft of versifying, be not of ancient writers named poets, but only called versifiers.[13] For the name of a poet, whereat now, specially in this realm, men have such indignation that they use only poets and poetry in the contempt of eloquence, was in ancient time in high estimation, in so much that all wisdom was supposed to be therein included and poetry was the first philosophy that ever was known, whereby men from their childhood were brought to the reason how to live well,[14] learning thereby not only manners and natural affections but also the wonderful works of nature, mixing serious matter with things that were pleasant, as it shall be manifest to them that shall be so fortunate to read the noble works of Plato and Aristotle, wherein he shall find the authority of poets frequently alleged. Yea, and that more is, in poets was supposed to be science mystical and inspired, and therefore in Latin they were called *vates*, which word signifyeth as much as prophets.[15] And therefore Tully in his *Tusculan Questions* supposeth that a poet cannot abundantly express verses sufficient

[11] Horace, *Art of Poetry*, 402, above.
[12] Cf. Sidney on tragedy, *Defense*, sect. 32, below.
[13] Aeneas Silvius is quoted as saying that in comparison with Vergil, Ovid, Lucan, and Statius "the others who write heroic verse are far inferior and are to be called versifiers rather than poets" (*Tractatus de liberorum educatione*). Cf. Sidney, *Defense*, secs. 16, 37, below. [14] Cf. Sidney, sect. 3, below. [15] Cf. Sidney, sect. 6, below.

and complete, or that his eloquence may flow without labor words well sounding and plenteous, without celestial instinction, which is also by Plato ratified.[16]

[The defense of poets]

[6] But since we be now occupied in the defense of poets, it shall not be incongruent to our matter to show what profit may be taken by the diligent reading of ancient poets, contrary to the false opinion, that now reigneth, of them that suppose that in the works of poets is contained nothing but bawdry (such is their foul word of reproach) and unprofitable leasings.[17] But first I will interpret some verses of Horace wherein he expresseth the office of poets, and after will I resort to a more plain demonstration of some wisdoms and councils contained in some verses of poets. Horace, in his second book of *Epistles*, saith in this wise or much like:

> The poet fashioneth by some pleasant mean
> The speech of children tender and unsure,
> Pulling their ears from words unclean,
> Giving to them precepts that are pure,
> Rebuking envy and wrath if it dure.
> Things well done he can by example commend;
> The needy and sick he doth also his cure
> To recomfort, if aught he can amend.[18]

But they which be ignorant in poets will perchance object, as is their manner, against these verses, saying that in Terence and others that were writers of comedies, also Ovid, Catullus, Martialis, and all that route of lascivious poets that wrote epistles and ditties of love, some called in Latin *Elegiae* and some *Epigrammata,* is nothing contained but incitation to lechery.

[Comedy]

[7] First, comedies, which they suppose to be a doctrinal of ribaldry, they be undoubtedly a picture or as it were a mirror of man's life, wherein evil is not taught but discovered; to the intent that men beholding the promptness of youth unto vice, the snares of harlots and bawds laid for young minds, the deceit of servants,

---

[16] See Plato's *Ion* above, and *inspiration* in the index.
[17] See Sidney, sect. 38, below. Boccaccio deals with the same objections (Osgood, *Boccaccio on Poetry*, xiv, xiii, and the selection from the *Life of Dante*, above).
[18] *Epistles*, ii, 1, 126–31.

the chances of fortune contrary to man's expectation, they being thereof warned may prepare themselves to resist or prevent occasion.[19] Semblably remembering the wisdoms, advertisements, counsels, dissuasion from vice, and other profitable sentences most eloquently and familiarly showed in those comedies, undoubtedly there shall be no little fruit out of them gathered. And if the vices in them expressed should be cause that minds of the readers should be corrupted, then by the same argument not only interludes in English, but also sermons wherein some vice is declared should be to the beholders and hearers like occasion to increase sinners. And that by comedies good counsel is ministered it appeareth by the sentence of Parmeno, in the second comedy of Terence:

> In this thing I triumph in my own conceit
> That I have found for all young men the way
> How they of harlots shall know the deceit,
> Their wits, their manners, that thereby they may
> Them perpetually hate; for so much as they
> Out of their own houses be fresh and delicate,
> Feeding curiously; at home all the day
> Living beggarly in most wretched estate.[20]

There be many more words spoken which I purposely omit to translate; notwithstanding the substance of the whole sentence is herein comprised. But now to come to other poets, what may be better said than is written by Plautus in his first comedy?

> Verily Virtue doth all things excel.
> For if liberty, health, living and substance,
> Our country, our parents and children do well,
> It hapneth by virtue; she doth all advance.
> Virtue hath all thing under governance,
> And in whom of virtue is found great plenty,
> Anything that is good may never be dainty.[21]

[Sentences in Ovid and Martial]

[8] Also Ovid, that seemeth to be most of all poets lascivious, in his most wanton books hath right commendable and noble sentences; as for proof thereof I will recite some that I have taken at adventure:

[19] Cf. Sidney, *Defense*, sect. 31, below, and Heywood, *Apology*, sect. 10, below.
[20] *Eunuch*, v, 4, 8–18.   Cf. Heywood, *Apology*, sect. 10, below.   [21] *Amphitryo*, 648–52.

Time is in medicine if it shall profit;
Wine given out of time may be annoyance.
A man shall irritate vice if he prohibit
When time is not met unto his utterance.
Therefore, if thou yet by council art recuperable,
Flee thou from idleness and alway be stable.[22]

Martialis, which for his dissolute writing is most seldom read of men of much gravity, hath notwithstanding many commendable sentences[23] and right wise counsels, as among divers I will rehearse one which is first come to my remembrance:

If thou wilt eschew bitter adventure
And avoid the gnawing of a pensifull[24] heart,
Set in no one person all wholly thy pleasure,
The less joy shalt thou have but the less shalt thou smart.[25]

I could recite a great number of semblable good sentences out of these and other wanton poets, who in the Latin do express them incomparably with more grace and delectation to the reader than our English tongue may yet comprehend.

[Reading is not to be censored]

[9] Wherefore since good and wise matter may be picked out of these poets, it were no reason, for some little matter that is in their verses, to abandon therefore all their works, no more than it were to forbear or prohibit a man to come into a fair garden lest the redolent savors of sweet herbs and flowers shall move him to wanton courage, or lest in gathering good and wholesome herbs he may happen to be stung with a nettle. No wise man entereth into a garden but he soon espieth good herbs from nettles and treadeth the nettles under his feet while he gathereth good herbs. Whereby he taketh no damage, or if he be stung he maketh little of it and shortly forgetteth it. Semblably if he do read wanton matter mixed with wisdom, he putteth the worst under foot and sorteth out the best, or, if his courage be stirred or provoked, he remembereth the little pleasure and great detriment that should ensue of it, and withdrawing his mind to some other study or exercise shortly forgetteth it.[26] And therefore among the Jews,

---

[22] *The Remedy of Love*, 131–6.   [23] See *sentences* in the index.
[24] Sorrowful, brooding.   [25] *Epigrams*, XII, 34.
[26] This section on the reading of poetry has much affinity with parts of Milton's *Areopagitica*, for example: "Good and evil we know in the field of this world grow up together almost inseparably; and the knowledge of good is so involved and interwoven

though it were prohibited to children until they came to ripe years to read the books of Genesis, of the Judges, *Cantica Canticorum*, and some part of the book of Ezekiel the prophet, for that in them was contained some matter which might happen to incense the young mind wherein were sparks of carnal concupiscence, yet after certain years of men's ages it was leefull for every man to read and diligently study those works. So although I do not approve the lesson[27] of wanton poets to be taught unto all children, yet think I convenient and necessary that when the mind is become constant and courage is assuaged, or that children of their natural disposition be shamefast and continent,[28] no ancient poet would be excluded from the lesson of such a one as desireth to come to the perfection of wisdom.

---

with the knowledge of evil, and in so many cunning resemblances hardly to be discerned, that those confused seeds which were imposed on Psyche as an incessant labor to cull out and sort asunder were not more intermixed. . . . To all men such books are not temptations nor vanities, but useful drugs and materials wherewith to temper and compose effective and strong medicines which man's life cannot want."

[27] *Lesson:* reading.

[28] Cf. Plato's suggestion that readers might be provided with an antidote against injury by poetry (p. 42. above). Milton also wrote of the education of boys: "With wariness and good antidote, it would be wholesome enough to let them taste some choice comedies, Greek, Latin, or Italian" (*Of Education*, Columbia University Press, IV, 285).

GIRALDI CINTHIO

o◯oo◯o

DISCORSI AND OTHER WRITINGS

AMONG THEORETICAL STUDENTS of literature, as distinguished from untheoretical readers, the problem of literature in Italy, as in less measure throughout Europe, was that of the new methods versus the old ones. This was summed up in the debate on the *Orlando Furioso*. To what extent is the new form to be accepted; is it to be entirely rejected for the classical epics and their modern imitations? For the drama there was also the same problem, less acute in Italy in proportion as full-length Italian tragedy and comedy resembled Seneca and Plautus more closely than the *Orlando Furioso* its classical analogues. As a scholar, the theorist tended to look with veneration to the past and to consider the present as less authoritative. A voice in favor of the poets of modern times was needed. The opportunity lay open to Giraldi as one practiced in various forms of composition both prose and poetry, not primarily a scholar, yet not unversed in classical theory and practice. His great assertion is that the classical method of construction is not the only one; there are principles of literature other than those followed by the ancients and formulated by Aristotle and Horace. Nor need the recent author feel apologetic, for Italians writing on their plan have equalled, yes, surpassed, the greatest works handed down from antiquity. No effort need be wasted in apologizing for modern literature by showing that in some way not immediately apparent it does carry out the principles of Aristotle; it stands on principles of its own.

The translations are those of the editor.

BIBLIOGRAPHY

Crocetti, Camillo Guerrieri, *G. B. Giraldi ed il pensiero critico del secolo XVI.* Genoa, 1932.

Giraldi Cinthio, Giovambattista, *Discorsi intorno al comporre de i romanzi, delle commedie, e delle tragedie, etc.* Venice, 1554.

——, *Le tragedie.* Venice, 1583.

——, *Scritti estetici.* Milan, 1864.

AN ADDRESS TO THE READER BY THE TRAGEDY OF *ORBECCHE*

1541

[Tragedy in disrepute]

[1¹] Now, dear reader, my sad conclusion has come about, and if I could have disposed of myself according to my wish, I would have remained in concealment and not have annoyed anyone with my plaints and lamentations. For though I know that the wisest set the royal gravity of tragedy ahead of every sort of poetry because they well understand that nothing exists in the world better fitted to enable the human race to live a more excellent life, yet I see wantonness so increased (thanks to the decline of the world) that not only is tragedy not in esteem but its regal name is odious to many. Yet since the wishes of others have conquered my will and I am constrained to issue out into the light in my own despite, if there is any pity in you I pray that you may be willing to be rather a kind and benignant censor than harsh and rude, in order that you may not add to my sorrow, which is of itself hard because of the affliction that lacerates me. And if perhaps it seems that I do not appear in the proud habit that befits me, let the force of my sufferings excuse me, for they have so deprived me of the desire to ornament myself that I have sometimes envied the rudest pastorals; in their humble garments there is repose, while the grave and royal are full of care.

[Not in accord with ancient practice]

[31] And though I have sprung from a recent event and not from ancient history, I do not deserve the less praise, for he who with a just eye looks on the truth will see that without censure a new tragedy may be permitted to rise from new matter and new names. Nor should I be blamed because my prologue is separated from the acts themselves, for the times in which I am born and my novelty and some other special reason make me carry the prologue with me. Indeed he would be insane who in his effort to use nothing except what was customary among the ancients should abandon what without dishonor the place and the time require. And if I am not in everything like the ancients, it is be-

---

¹ The numbers are those of the lines of the original.

cause I was born just now of a young father and can appear only as young; perhaps my green youth will remove the displeasure you feel at my deep sadness. Nor should it be held a fault that I am divided into acts and scenes, but it should make me appear much more pleasing, for as a man would make a strange figure in the world who did not have limbs distinct from each other, so I think it would be disagreeable to see me confused in one large whole. And indeed Seneca and the ancient Romans realized how wrong the Greeks appear in this. And that I should be large and have my parts great beyond what is proper is not natural. Yet, on the other hand, greater beauty reigns in bodies that are larger than others of their species.

[The characters]

[64] And if there is anyone for whom it is hard to hear reasons able to move to pity a soul disposed to revenge, perhaps Malecche may seem tedious;[2] such a one may shorten that part as he wishes, for I shall not contend with him about it. Nor should it appear strange to you that the ladies I have in my company are wiser than some think is suitable for them, for in addition to the light that a woman like a man has from reason, the great wisdom possessed by that lady whose high and royal name in its splendor I hold hidden within me, with the greatest reverence and the greatest honor, has the power to make evident to every fair judgment not merely how much worth a gentle lady can have in herself, but that in prudence and in discretion (when the envy of others is banished) she can be the equal of the wisest man in the world. In addition let it not appear strange to you that I do not have Cyruses, Dariuses, and Statiras,[3] although I confess that I am from Persia. From such blame my birth can excuse me, if one looks closely, nor to a man who knows what desperation and deep sorrow can accomplish in the heart of a woman should it appear hard that a daughter plunged into sorrow without hope should have inflicted violent death on her cruel father. And though the savage tyrant comes to his death, no one will ever accuse me of wickedness who with a sane eye sees how much pity is roused in human hearts by the fate of those from whom I have my origin.

---

[2] His part is that of a prudent adviser, a frequent, almost conventional, character in Renaissance tragedies presenting kings; his function is to utter "wise saws and modern instances."

[3] First ed. *Satipne.*

[Death on the stage]

[99] And if the Stagirite,[4] who saw and knew and wrote so much, and initiated the art of composing tragedies, has taught me to cause the queen from whom I take my name to die by her own hands on the stage to end her evil condition, there is nothing very strange in my departing from the laws of the Venusine at this point and wishing that in the sight of the people she should violently slay herself with a dagger on the stage.[5]

[Diction]

[108] There are those who, intent on the matter of elocution, ever anxiously seek for swelling words and strong epithets and if they write a lament fill their pages with blind horrors and bloody dead men from Acheron, and with black and horrid nights, and if they write of gladness nothing other is heard than flowers, herbs, shadows, caves, waves, soft breezes, rubies, pearls, sapphires, topazes, and gold. I should say that to such selection the force of sorrow that oppresses me makes me unfitted, and I have wished rather to have for a guide nature with fit ornament than feigned art with pompous words. There are many today who write in the vulgar tongue and abandon the custom of approved authors, trusting in themselves, since they were born in a place where, as it seems to them, the vulgar speech is perfect, though in fact it is without value if ancient authors do not give it honor. To them you can easily respond, if perchance they wish to speak against me because in part I have followed the great Tuscan who for the sake of Laura exchanged the Arno for the Sorgue, and the good Certaldese, those two eternal and shining lights of the sweet vulgar speech,[6] that such was the Roman and such the Greek tongue as the vulgar is now, and both gained their renown not from common speech but from writers who showed themselves excellent in them. And they were esteemed in proportion as one or the other was like those three or four or six who have made the choice of the best from the speech of the illiterate vulgar, and whoever sought fame for his use of words followed those good authors and did not rely on having been born in Greece or in Rome. It is certainly true that since this pleasing common speech is alive, it is permitted to anyone who writes in this language to

[4] Aristotle, *Poetics*, XI, end, above.
[5] Horace (the Venusine), *Art of Poetry*, 185-7, above.   [6] Petrarch and Boccaccio.

use some words (selected, however, with excellent judgment) that are not found in the aforesaid Tuscans. Therefore to those who have limited our language to the words used by the two famous Tuscans (and there are many today who hold such an opinion), I prefer that the divine Bembo should make response, if there is a word in me that is not found in them, the divine Bembo, who has freed the vulgar tongue from its dark prison and from the obscure kingdom of Dis with a plectrum of happier sound than Orpheus used for his beloved wife. And may there also be an answer from the gentle Trissino, who with his song was the first to bring tragedy from the Tiber and the Ilissus to the waves of the Arno. And from the great Molza, whose honored name flies everywhere with sounds of fame. And the good Tolomei, who with a new method has already adapted verses in the vulgar tongue to Latin numbers and the Roman form. And that one who from Thebes beyond the frozen Alps has put into Tuscan dress the piteous sister of Polynices; I mean Alamanni, who because of my rare good fortune saw me come on the stage. The happy and exquisite abilities of these men, with the others who have followed in their steps, as well as those two celebrated authors, should be esteemed as they deserve. Seeking to enrich this language, with firm choice and sound judgment they have preferred to obtain by effort, in praiseworthy liberty, words that would set forth their thoughts rather than with fetters on their feet to remain silent in prison. Leaving then to you and to them such a burden, I shall wait under the secure protection of that nobleman through whose favor I have come out, hoping that some other, aroused by my words, may show tragedies in a more noble dress, more worthy of honor, and of rarer beauty; (if only it be not out of harmony with my sorrow) I shall seek with all my power to imitate their virtue, gifts, and rare and wondrous beauty.

THE APOLOGY FOR *DIDO* (*in part*)

1543

[Objections. 131[1]]

I shall now deal with the objections that have been made to my work. The first is that it would be better if I had composed this tragedy in prose rather than in verse. The second is that Aristotle

---

[1] The numbers are those of pages in the edition of 1583.

objects to the introduction of gods into tragedy. The third is that it is blameworthy to divide plays suited to the tragic stage into acts and scenes, because it was never done by the Greeks, from whom should be taken the laws and the true rules for composing plays creditably as Aristotle worked them out. The fourth is that the objector does not praise the use of a great number of interlocutors. The fifth is that the speeches people make about themselves are not according to decorum. The sixth is that I do not give in my *Dido* that image of the *Oedipus Tyrannus* from which Aristotle has taken his precepts, as from the true idea of the perfection of tragedy. The seventh is that it is too long in the presentation. All of these I see are the result of the slight understanding of the objector.

[Prose or verse for tragedy. 132]

Coming then to the objections, I say to the first that I do not know why this great censor should wish tragedies to be composed in prose, since not merely Aristotle in his *Poetics* says they should be composed in verse, and shows of what sort the verses should be, but we read the same thing in Horace, and besides this it can be seen that the tragic writers have all composed their works in verse. . . . But Ariosto revealed his ideas about material for the stage in his comedies, for though they were first issued in prose, on seeing their unfitness in that guise, he turned them into verse, for it appeared to him that prose was not at all suitable for such plays. It likewise appeared to Signor Trissino that prose was not at all adapted to tragedy. Therefore, he composed his *Sofonisba* in that sort of verses which he before anyone else most suitably gave to the stage in place of the iambic which the Greeks and Latins used. For it appeared to him that these verses loosed from the obligation of rhyme carried with them the same reason for being as the senarii, composed of iambics, in the Greek and the Latin tongues, namely, that they are similar to the familiar speech of our times, and fall, like the iambics, from the mouths of speakers (though they do not know it) in common speech. To the opinion of this excellent tragic writer Ruscellai conformed in his *Rosmonda*, which appeared with great acclaim soon after the *Sofonisba*, and I believe that in the future all those who give themselves to such compositions and seek honor from them will conform. And this is enough to answer anyone who ill says that our language does not have verses suitable to the stage.

[The god must not bring about the solution. 138]

Aristotle blames the introduction on the stage of gods who through their sole power and authority bring about the solution of the plot. This solution should come from the nature of the subject and the resourcefulness of the poet, and when both of these are lacking and the machine that carries the god is introduced to end the plot, as in the *Iphigenia among the Taurians* and in the *Andromache* and the other similar plays, and in the *Philoctetes* of Sophocles, it merits no praise at all. And that this was the opinion of Aristotle is perfectly clear from the passage in which he accuses Euripides, for though he says that dramatist can be called supremely tragic and praises him for most ingeniously tying the knot of a plot, he says that nonetheless some of his solutions are inept, and Aristotle says this because Euripides in a solution resorts to the machine. Thence it appears that he does not condemn the introduction of the gods in the beginning and in the other parts of a tragedy, but only in the solution, if it is brought about merely by the intervention of the god. . . . But, returning to Aristotle, if he had so blamed the introduction of the gods in the beginning (as is seen in Sophocles and Euripides), he would not have said that Euripides tied the knot ingeniously and would not (as I have said) have blamed merely the solution but the beginning also and the other parts, since in the tying of the knot gods appear in many dramas. Besides that, it seems to me it can reasonably be said that when the solution necessarily requires a god, it is not merely not unfitting to introduce him but it would be an error to leave him out. In the *Io,* for example, Minerva was suitably brought in to make known that Io was a child of Apollo; in this way the knot is easily untied, as Mercury had suggested at the beginning.

[Acts and scenes. 141]

Now passing from this objection to that on the division of tragedies into acts and scenes, I confess that the Greeks did not use this device; among them the stage never remained empty, because the chorus was always there, as is made clear not merely by the authority of Aristotle, but by the Greek plots that have survived the injuries of time. But I hold it certain that in this matter the Romans were much wiser than the Greeks, because it is not probable that great and lordly persons would wish to consider matters of great importance, such as appear in tragedy, in the midst of a multitude of people, even though these were their servants, but in matters which deal with honor or shame or the life or death of great persons, they have with them merely their secretaries, counselors, and other prudent and wise persons in whom they confide and who have been chosen by them for such matters, and surely they often speak with them alone of important affairs; nor is it probable that in the course of their activities and in their considerations pertaining to an important act they would speak of them to others about the court in the midst of a multitude. If the Greeks did not understand this matter of decorum, the Romans did, and knew how to give to the majesty of royal actions the persons who would manage them in such a way as would be fitting to so great majesty. . . . Homer sometimes did not consider what fitted the majesty of the actions he had in hand.

[The number of actors. 148]

In regard to the fourth objection, that on the number of the speakers, it is manifest that in ancient tragedies their number is not certain and defined, for some of them have six, some seven, and sometimes eight and nine are seen, and sometimes ten and eleven, nor are those lacking which have twelve and thirteen; this has led me to think that the interlocutors can be as many as suffice to develop the parts of the plot to an end magnificently and without confusion. And I am the more confirmed in this opinion when I see that the ancients who have given their judgment on the Greek tragedies praise highly those that carry with them the largest number of persons; the reason for this number, as it seems to me, is that regal actions are on a grand scale and individuals of various conditions appear in them on the side of him who suffers as much as of him who is the cause of the action; such actions cannot be carried to an end without a great deal of speaking by the characters. Therefore it seems to me that the number of persons introduced represents in large measure the majesty of the action, if only that number of persons is judiciously brought in. This is especially true when the kings of divers nations with their courts appear on the stage, for I know that Your Excellency[2] saw in the time of your illustrious father how unhappily that comedy turned out that was represented with but five actors, and with what great difficulty (though the argument was pleasing) it was car-

[2] This apology is a letter to Ercole II, duke of Ferrara.

ried to its conclusion, for the spectators were bored by having the same persons in their eyes and ears all the time. And if this monotony appears strange in comedy, where actions of the common people only and of not much importance are seen, how clearly should it be rejected in the presentation of regal affairs, and especially in our times, when the courts of great princes are crowded with a multitude of the most noble persons. Therefore, so long as unnecessary actors are not introduced and they do not make confusion but take the parts and produce the effects suitable to them, plenty rather than poverty of persons will make the conduct of the stage appear always more magnificent and more pleasing. The argument from the *Oedipus Tyrannus* is of no avail, for Aristotle does not adduce that story because of the number of the persons but solely because of the quality of the knot and the solution of the argument and because if that tragedy could properly prescribe the number to all the others there would not be seen in some ancient tragedies a greater number and in others a smaller number. And this greater number is so much the more fitting to the *Dido* because it contains the suites of two royal persons of diverse nations who have courts befitting the rank they hold. . . .

[Soliloquies. 152]

And the objection of my critic that it is not according to verisimilitude that kings should discourse in public on their affairs and that they should walk alone reasoning within themselves is so foolish that I blush to respond to him truly; if his objection should hold, it would not be proper to introduce on the stage the discussions of kings and queens with their secretaries and councilors and their servants, for none of the said discussions are carried on in public and yet they are introduced on the stage. But poor fellow that he is, does he not understand that though the stage represents a city, such speeches are not thought of otherwise than if they were carried on in the most secret and concealed rooms of the rulers? Hence they are shown on the stage in the same way as if they spoke in their chambers, for so stage presentation requires. And this speech in soliloquy appears to me to bring so much of regal gravity to the action that the omission would be rather a fault than the reverse. And this was so thoroughly approved by Roman practice that in it soliloquies were very frequent, both in comedies and in tragedies. And they were able to do it properly, gradually bringing the actors on the stage according to the requirements of the play. Wherefore only those were found there (as it would be in our times) who were speaking either alone or accompanied, with the chorus completely off the stage except when it was introduced as a speaker or when it divided one act from another. And I do not know why, in confirmation of his opinion, he brings up the argument that the spectators hear them speak. For he should know that the spectators are not to be regarded by the actors, who speak as though they were in their own houses and in their private rooms where they would naturally speak of their affairs.

[Imitation of the *Oedipus Tyrannus*. 153]

And because this is so manifest of itself that to set it forth completely is superfluous, I will turn to respond to the sixth objection that he has made against me, that is that the *Dido* is not like the *Oedipus Tyrannus*. And this I concede to him without question, with respect to the material, since the subject of the *Oedipus Tyrannus* is such that one like it has never existed before, does not now, and probably never will again. And if Aristotle selected this play as a sort of Idea for the composition of tragedy, he did it with the judgment he has used in all his other compositions, for this material is truly unique among the others. And he who was the author of the drama shows without any doubt a marvelous acuteness of ability, because the plot is excellently knit and loosed. And Sophocles found the material so disposed and had little trouble in making it into a tragedy, and needed only to ornament it with words fitting the subject. But if we wish to respect the judgment of this slanderer we shall be obliged to say that all the tragedies that have been composed before and after the *Oedipus Tyrannus* are of no value, for there is none that is like it in subject. And if all the other Greek and Latin plays must for this reason be of no value, I do not intend to feel shame if also this of mine and the others which I have composed on the commission of Your Excellency or because of the desire I have to be of avail to the men of this age and of our language, to the best of my knowledge and ability, suffer the same fate. But if the desire my critic has to oppose me does not blind the eyes of his intellect, he will be able plainly to see what is evident to all the judicious, namely that however much Aristotle esteemed the *Oedipus*, nonetheless he did not have so little esteem for the others that he did not avail himself also of them in giving ordinances and laws for the praiseworthy

composition of tragic matter. I confess then without any concealment that the *Dido* in its matter is diverse from the *Oedipus Tyrannus*. But I do not wish to concede that in the parts which are
proper to tragedy and in workmanship it is not of the same sort
as the *Oedipus* so far as was permitted by the subject taken from
Vergil that I had before me. And if perhaps I have sometimes
departed from the rules given by Aristotle in order to conform to
the customs of our times, I have done so after the example of the
ancients, for it may be seen that Euripides did not begin his stories
as did Sophocles and that, as I just said, the Romans arranged
their plots in yet another way than did the Greeks, and besides
this Aristotle himself has conceded it to me. For he does not forbid at all, when it is demanded either by place or time or the quality of the matters dealt with, to depart somewhat from those arts
which he reduced to the precepts that he gave us.

ON THE COMPOSITION OF COMEDIES
AND TRAGEDIES *(selections)*

1543

[The moral end of tragedy and comedy. 206[1]]

Tragedy and comedy have their end in common because both
endeavor to introduce good morals, but in this agreement there is
the difference that comedy is without terror and without commiseration (because in it there are no deaths or other terrible chances,
but instead it seeks to bring about its end with pleasure and with
some pleasing saying), and tragedy, whether it has a happy conclusion or an unhappy one, by means of the pitiable and the terrible, purges the minds of the hearers from their vices and influences them to adopt good morals. . . .

[Where can tragic and comic plots be obtained? 208]

Though the plot is common to both comedy and tragedy, still
some think that the plot of a tragedy should be taken from history
and that of a comedy should be feigned by the poet. It appears
that an adequate reason can be given for such a difference: Comedy deals with actions that occur in the ordinary life of citizens
while tragedy deals with famous and regal deeds, for comedy presents private men and tragedy is concerned with kings and great

[1] The numbers designating the sections are those of pages in the edition of 1554.

persons; hence it would not be true to life, since great men are in the eyes of the world, that any strange deed could be done by them which would not, as soon as it is performed, come to the ears of everyone. Therefore, since tragedy deals with illustrious acts, by treating of persons who perform them, it does not appear that such acts can be brought on the stage without their having been known before. But private actions can properly be feigned because for the most part they do not get beyond private houses and in a short time are forgotten. Hence the poet has a large field for feigning what he wishes in order to bring new comic plots on the stage. But though this reasoning carries with it much appearance of truth, I hold nonetheless that the tragic plot can be feigned by the poet as well as the comic. Aristotle, judicious here as everywhere, conceded it in more than one passage of his *Poetics*, and Cornutus[2] after him among the Latins, though saying that comedy feigns its fables and tragedy usually takes them from history, shows that it is not always necessary to take them from history. It appears to me also that reason is able to present the same truth to us with sufficient probability, because the power of moving tragic feelings depends only on imitation which does not depart from probability, and facts do not move the feelings without words fitly and poetically joined together. Therefore it seems to me that it is in the power of the poet to move at his wish the tragic feelings by means of a tragedy of which he feigns the plot, if that plot is in conformity with natural habits and not remote from what can happen and often does happen. And perhaps the feelings are moved to the adoption of good morals the more in proportion as by coming anew into the minds of the listeners the feigned plot gains for itself the greater attention. For since the spectator knows that he cannot learn of the action which is presented on the stage except through that presentation, as soon as he gets some knowledge of the plot and it seems to him that it probably is ingeniously composed, he arouses his attention and seeks not to miss a word of it. . . . That a feigned plot can have this power, experience has shown in the case of my *Orbecche* (such as it is) every time that it has been played, for not merely new spectators (permit me, M. Giulio, to speak of the truth, not to praise myself but to confirm with a very recent example what I am now saying) but those who had seen it every time it was acted were unable to restrain their sighs and sobs. . . .

[2]A literary man and critic of the time of Nero.

[The double plot. 214]

And here it should be understood that though double tragedies are little praised by Aristotle (though some think otherwise) double structure is nonetheless to be much praised in comedy and has made the plays of Terence succeed wonderfully. I call that plot double which has in its action diverse kinds of persons of the same station in life, as two lovers of different character, two old men of varied nature, two servants of opposite morals, and other such things, as they may be seen in the *Andria* and in the other plots of the same poet, where it is clear that these like persons of unlike habits make the knot and the solution of the plot very pleasing. And I believe that if this should be well imitated in tragedy by a good poet, and the knot so arranged that its solution will not bring confusion, double structure in tragedy will not be less pleasing (always remembering the reverence due to Aristotle) than it is in comedy. If there have been those who have favored this method and held an opinion unlike that of Aristotle, they are not, I think, to be blamed, especially if the tragedy has a happy end, for this kind of end is much like that of comedy, and therefore such a tragedy can be like comedy in its imitation of the action. . . .[3]

[Characters. 217]

Persons then who are in part good and in part evil (being half way between the good and the bad) awaken wonderful compassion if something horrible comes upon them. The cause of this is that it appears to the spectator that the person who suffers the evil is in every way deserving of some penalty, but not of one so heavy. And this justice, combined with the weight of the penalty, induces that horror and that compassion which is necessary to tragedy. Among all the stories that have ever been brought on the stage, none was ever more fitting or more likely to produce compassion than that of Oedipus as presented by Sophocles, for Oedipus was searching to punish one who had killed his father, and feared he would be united in marriage with his mother, and being as a result very eager in his desire to inflict just punishment on the criminal and to find a mode for avoiding the other error, early in the unraveling of the plot he recognized that he was the one who had imprudently run into such grave errors. Hence, whatever evil came to him he endured in such a way as to

[3] For a related discussion see Guarini, *Tragicomedy*, sect. 21b, and *passim*, below.

excite the greatest compassion, for he appeared as one who, holding such sins abominable, found himself immersed in them while he was preparing punishment for the malefactor. From this can be seen that ignorance of the sin committed, when the evil doer incurs punishment for the evil he has done, causes the greatest horror and the greatest compassion. And this wonderfully purges the mind from such errors, because the spectator drawing a silent conclusion says to himself: If the tragic character has suffered as severely as he does because of an involuntary error, what would happen to me if I should voluntarily commit such a sin? The illustrious actions of tragedy are so called not because they are praiseworthy or virtuous but because they are enacted by men of the highest rank. They must be chosen and arranged, if the work is well done, in accord with the demands of the times in which the poet writes, as regards the thoughts expressed, the characteristics of the person presented, his fitness in general, and other circumstances. Those who have their minds and natures turned toward low things will not be capable of making this choice because they will be inclined toward things that are base and of little honor, as Aristophanes was among the Greeks. . . .

[Happy and unhappy conclusion. 219]

Of the two sorts of tragedy there is one that ends in sorrow. The other has a happy end, but in bringing the action towards its conclusion does not therefore desert the terrible and the compassionable, for without these there cannot be a good tragedy. This type of tragedy, to which Aristotle gives the name of mixed, is shown to us by Plautus in the prologue of the *Amphitryo* when he says that in this play less noble persons are mingled with the great and royal. This he took from the *Poetics* of Aristotle where there is a passage on this sort of tragedy. It is in its nature more pleasing to the spectators because it ends in happiness. In this kind of tragedy the recognition or, as we prefer to call it, the identification of persons is especially in place; through this identification those for whom we feel horror and compassion are taken from perils and from death. Among all the identifications of which Aristotle teaches us (for it does not appear to me pertinent to speak of all of them) that one is praiseworthy more than the others by means of which there is a change of fortune from miserable to happy, as in its place we shall explain. But this noble kind of recognition is not so closely connected with the tragedy of a happy ending that it is not also very suitable to that of an unhappy ending, in which it produces an opposite effect to that just mentioned; that is, it makes the happy become miserable and turns friends to enemies.

[Concession to the audience. 220]

Among the Latins, Seneca never undertook tragedies with a happy ending, but devoted himself to the sad conclusion with such excellence that in nearly all his tragedies (as it seems to me) he surpasses in prudence, gravity, decorum, majesty, and skill in the use of sentences all the Greeks who ever wrote, though in language he might be chaster and more painstaking than he is.[4] Yet in spite of that I have composed some with happy conclusions, the *Altile*, the *Selene*, the *Antivalomeni*, and others, merely as a concession to the spectators and to make the plays appear more pleasing on the stage, and that I may be in conformity with the custom of our times. For though Aristotle says this is to cater to the ignorance of the spectators and the other method has its defenders, I have still thought it better to satisfy him who has to listen with some lesser excellence (if the opinion of Aristotle is to be accepted as the better) than with a little more grandeur to displease those for whose pleasure the play is put on the stage, because it would be of slight use to compose a play a little more praiseworthy that would be odious when acted.[5] Plots that are terrible because they end unhappily (if it appears the spirits of the spectators abhor them) can serve for closet dramas; those that end happily for the stage.

[Technique of the happy conclusion. 221]

Nonetheless the happenings in these less terrible tragedies should come about in such a way that the spectators are suspended between horror and compassion until the end, which, with a happy outcome, should leave everyone consoled. And this holding of the

[4] Giraldi writes further on Seneca: "Though these characters [Hecuba and Polyxena] are well presented by Euripides, they are still better presented by Seneca, as can be seen in the *Troades*, in which, though they appear to be taken from Euripides, they are nonetheless so treated by Seneca that good judges would set him above Euripides if only his Latin were as pure as the Greek of Euripides, for there is no one who can judge accurately who would not set Seneca higher in majesty, in power to move the feelings, in the observation of character, and in the vigor of his sentences" (p. 262). This unhesitating preference for Seneca gives an example of the rise and decline of literary reputations in various ages. Giraldi was not alone in his belief. Seneca seems to have been more in accord with the taste of the Elizabethans than were the Greeks. For Sidney's use of Seneca as a standard of good tragedy, see sect. 48, below.

[5] Cf. the opinion of Lope de Vega, *New Art of Making Comedies*, sect. 1, below.

spectator in suspense ought to be so managed by the poet that it is not always hidden in clouds, but the action goes on unrolling the plot in such a way that the spectator sees himself conducted to the end but is uncertain how the play is coming out. And in this sort of play often for the greater satisfaction and better instruction of those who listen, they who were the cause of disturbing events, by which the persons of ordinary goodness in the drama have been afflicted, are made to die or suffer great ills. Euripides does this in the *Children of Hercules* and Sophocles in the *Electra*, the first having Eurystheus killed and the second Aegisthus. I also, following their example, in the *Altile* had Astano die and Gripo in the *Selene*, at the very time when either one through his wickedness thought he would be more happy than anyone else. For it gives extraordinary pleasure to the spectator when he sees the astute trapped and deceived at the end of the drama, and the unjust and the wicked finally overthrown.

[Death behind the scene. 222]

These deaths, however, come about behind the scenes, because they are not introduced for commiseration but for the sake of justice. The action is so planned that the spectators hear the voices of the dying from behind the scenes, or their deaths are narrated either by a messenger or by some other person whom the author selects as suitable to do it. And this method of using narration by a messenger is found not only in tragedies that end happily but in those that end unhappily, when the action of the play demands it. And such deaths should be without cruelty, which in the best plays must not come near those persons from whose sufferings the terrible and the pitiable arise. I believe this is what Horace wished to indicate when he commanded us not to introduce Medea killing her children on the stage,[6] and that he did not (as many think he did) intend to forbid the use of a suitable death on the stage when the nature of affairs demanded it. I have always thought it very strange that Seneca departed from the advice of Horace in his *Medea*, and so much the more because Aristotle did not praise Euripides for having made the heroine in his *Medea* kill her children on the stage not in error but voluntarily. . . . Since Aristotle had condemned Euripides for having Medea kill her children with full knowledge of the conditions,[7] though the deaths happened off the stage, I cannot imagine how Seneca thought to gain renown

[6] *Art of Poetry*, 185, above.   [7] *Poetics*, xiv, 53b26, above.

by having her do it on the stage. But leaving to better judges the loosing of this knot, I return to say that Horace with his precept did not mean to forbid that appropriate deaths should be openly enacted but that those accompanied with cruelty should be avoided. This is especially true because Aristotle says that the deaths, torments, and wounds that come about through error among relatives, if they are done openly, are well suited to tragic compassion, though I know there are those who interpret Aristotle's words *en to fanero* otherwise than we do or than Valla and Paccio have done before us.[8] But in truth (as Horace himself says) our spirits are less quickly moved by things that are heard than by those that are seen.[9] Therefore the action that is narrated is less terrible and less compassionable than when it is seen. If, then, events are not incredible (as that Procne should be made into a bird or Cadmus transformed into a serpent) or do not come on the stage with cruelty, as when children are deliberately killed by their father or mother (which in addition to cruelty carries also with it incredibility), happenings that are terrible and compassionable can be presented on the stage in order that they may be more effective on the minds of the spectators than when merely related. And if some say there is no example of this in Greek tragedies, I say that we do not have all those that were read in the time of Aristotle, because if we had the examples he adduces, when he speaks of presenting deaths before the audience, we should see that they were not removed from the stage but rather were accepted in those times and by those poets. If our lack of examples were a decisive argument, we ought to say, because we do not now find among the tragedies we read any with feigned plots, that there never were any and that we should not now compose them, though Aristotle does not blame them but rather allows them. . . .

[Various endings for tragedy. 224]

You ought to know that tragedies that end happily are better adapted for intricate knots and are more praiseworthy when dou-

---

[8] The words *en to fanero*, "on the stage," are not, as Giraldi seems to suggest, connected with Aristotle's discussion of terrible deeds involving relatives (*Poetics* xiv). Among those who give another interpretation is Castelvetro, who, in his desire to reconcile Horace and Aristotle, suggests that these words do not mean "on the stage" or "before the audience," but "famous deaths, and not those of common ordinary persons, but such as those of Clytemnestra, Ajax, and Hercules, which, because of the person to whom they happened and the causes whence they came about and their manner, have come to the knowledge of the world through either history or fame" (*On Poetics*, XI, p. 255).   [9] *Art of Poetry*, 180–2, above.

ble than those that end unhappily, for the latter are rather better simple than double. By the simple I do not understand those that are opposite to the intricate, but those whose action rests on a single quality of person and is not managed on the stage with actions of diverse nature; to wit, there should be but one wise man, one foolish man, one who is cruel, one mild, one avaricious, one liberal, one simple, one astute. Hence plays ending unhappily are more like the *Iliad*, those ending happily like the *Odyssey*, both in the argument and the mingling of persons, so that it appears that in these two compositions Homer wished to give us the example of one and the other type of tragedy, as in the *Margites* he gave us an example of comedy, which was less to be blamed in his times (though Plutarch condemns those who believe the *Margites* is by Homer); from this can be seen how greatly they are deceived who have said that the *Iliad* gives us the form of tragedy and the *Odyssey* that of comedy, since both furnish an example of tragedy, the first of a tragedy ending unhappily, and the second of one ending happily. Critics fell into this error because they were of the opinion that there cannot be a tragedy which ends happily. And though we have said that for wicked persons no compassion is felt, and their fate is not terrible, I do not wish you therefore to believe that such persons cannot give a tragedy its name, for there are successful instances among the ancients, as we see from the *Medea* and the *Thyestes* of Seneca, and others of the kind. It often comes about that the name is given to tragedy by those persons from whom the events of the play have their origin, though these persons are fitted neither for horror nor for compassion, because they are not introduced there for that type of effect, which does not come from wicked persons but from those of a middle sort, as we have said. . . .

[Realistic language in the drama. 228]

Those verses which are called *sdruccioli* [ending with an accent on the antepenult] because of their hasty cadence at the conclusion have been accepted by our Ariosto and his followers for comedies, though this is not satisfactory to me because these verses are not in harmony with the speech of every day, for comic speech should be assimilated more nearly to that than to any other, but they carry with them a suggestion of literary labor such as should not appear on the stage. The speeches of comic characters should be so like familiar conversation that they seem like the talk of

friends and intimates when they have occasion to speak of such
things as are dealt with in the play; yet persons of this kind do not
utter a *sdrucciolo* once a day. There is, however, in familiar
speech a great number of verses of eleven syllables. Therefore, it
seems to me that this is the type of verse in which both tragedy and
comedy should be composed, though the verses used in comedy
should be like the speech of the common people, and those of
tragedy like the language of the great and noble.

[Rhyme in comedy. 229]

In comedy, however, these verses should be wholly without
rhyme, for verses with rhyme are farther from the speech of every
day than any others, carrying with them more suggestion of the
study than those without rhyme. On the contrary, rhyme is in
place in some parts of tragedy in dialogue and chiefly in speeches
by the chorus, and for greater harmony there should be a mingling
of irregular with regular rhymes; I refer, though, to the choruses
that divide one act from another, and not to those speeches by
the chorus that are mingled with those of the other actors, for in
the latter instance but one person of the chorus speaks and not the
whole body as one. . . .

[Rhyme in tragedy. 234]

Rhyme is also suitable for tragedy, in the moral parts and in
affecting scenes, such as are brought in for the sake of producing
compassion or showing unexpected gladness, for pleasant feelings
and sentences composed for persuasion can sometimes be set forth
in similar verses, that they may the more easily be received into
the mind of him who listens, but this is not so necessary that it cannot be omitted without blame. The other parts of a tragedy
should be of full-length verses without rhyme, for full-length verses
with rhyme are not more suitable for tragedy among us than are
heroic verses among the Greeks and Latins. . . .

[Five acts. 255]

The Latins have held that a plot should be divided into five
acts.[10] In the first the argument should be contained. In the
second the things contained in the argument begin to move toward their end. In the third come impediments and perturbations. In the fourth begins to appear a way to remedy what is

[10] Horace, *Art of Poetry*, 189, above.

causing trouble. In the fifth is given the expected end with a fitting solution for all the argument. These reasons serve only for comedy, but with the proper changes can serve also for tragedy, and this division has been common to both tragedy and comedy.

[The language of tragedy. 264]

The speech of tragedy should be grand, royal, magnificent, and figurative; that of comedy should be simple, pure, familiar, and suited to men of the people.

Hence only occasionally is it fitting to use in comedy those ornaments of speech, those lofty modes of speaking, those similitudes, those comparisons, those figures, those oppositions of words that the Greeks call antitheses, and those other ornaments that are suitable to tragedy, since this is foreign to the persons of comedy, and he who thinks by their means to give splendor to his composition brings to it darkness and unsuitability. Tragedy on the contrary loves all these things, for there is not a form of speech so figurative, so long as it is according to decorum and fitting, that is not properly used in tragedy, so much is tragedy superior in gravity to every other sort of composition. . . .

It was said that the language of tragedy should be according to decorum and suitable, for these figurative and lofty modes of speech are little suited to persons who are weighted down with great sorrow, for it appears hardly true to life that a person crushed by grief could turn his mind to this manner of language. . . .[11] Yet these figures of speech are fitting to that person who under the name of the messenger comes to reveal what has been done behind the scenes, on which depends the suffering and the horror of the play, and because of the station of the persons who suffer or of those to whom the unhappy chance is narrated, these figures of speech are suited, as is shown by examples in Greek and Latin tragedy. And we also have followed their steps in our *Orbecche*, in the messenger who brings tidings of the death of Orontes and

---

[11] Elizabethan practice is often at variance with this belief. For example, Othello, having discovered too late his horrible mistake in thinking Desdemona unfaithful, says:

> . . . Must you speak . . . of one whose hand
> Like the base Indian, threw a pearl away
> Richer than all his tribe; of one whose subdued eyes
> Albeit unused to the melting mood,
> Drop tears as fast as the Arabian trees
> Their med'cinable gum
>
> *Othello*, v, ii, 342ff.

of the children. And I believe that this is conceded to such a person because from him comes all the horror and the compassion that is the sinew of the play, and which should be made strong with every manner of speech that is fitted to it. Besides, the horror of what has come about induces awe and a certain shuddering, which he who has seen it with his own eyes can produce; therefore the messenger, as though touched with fury, can utter only grand words, full of the horror he has in his mind, and he should use all his powers in narrating the pitiable and horrible chance, to show the actions, the plaints, the words, the cruelty, the desperation, the manner in which the sufferer fell, and other such things, all of which are comprehended in saying that he was very cruelly killed; those few words would say it all, but less effectively than by giving it in detail.

ON THE COMPOSITION OF ROMANCES (*selections*)

1549

[The non-Aristotelian epic. 19[1]]

If a good poet should set himself to treat the deeds of Hercules or of Theseus . . . and should wish in a single poem to describe the whole life and all the illustrious actions of either one in order to put before the eyes of the reader the honored and praiseworthy life of a brave man, as Xenophon did for Cyrus in his *Cyropaedia* and as perhaps Statius wished to do in his *Achilleid* and as Silius did for Hannibal, I do not believe it would be unfitting to commence from the beginning of their lives and go through them to the end, for such a poem would not be written without splendor in the composition and without the pleasure and profit of the reader. For if we are glad to read in prose the lives of Themistocles, Coriolanus, Romulus, and other excellent men, why should it be less pleasing and less profitable to read them when arranged in verses by a noble and wise poet who knows how the lives of heroes should be written in verse in the guise of history as an example to mankind? I believe also that Suidas had such a poem in mind when he said the epic, which is not other than heroic composition in verse, was history, for he does not hold it improper to set forth in verse, in the manner of history, the life of a man who fully deserves the name of hero. And as the composition of history

---

[1] The numbers indicating the sections are those of pages in the edition of 1554.

begins with the beginning of things,[2] so works dealing with the whole life of a man open with the first of his illustrious deeds. And if in the cradle he gave sign of his greatness, with the cradle should begin the actions of his life. And if you say to me that Vergil did not do so for Aeneas nor Homer for Achilles in the *Iliad* and for Ulysses in the *Odyssey*, it seems to me proper to answer that both were attempting poems of a single action and not the poem that follows the style and manner of history. And though it appeared to Aristotle that if a man set out to produce such a composition it would be infinite, and therefore he did not praise it,[3] yet I am of the opinion (and I wish to speak with all the reverence I feel for so great a writer as Aristotle) this is not a sufficient cause to deter a judicious poet from undertaking such a work. There are a thousand means of shortening a work without giving up the description of the whole life of the man on whom the poet has set out to write, such as to have some things predicted by a diviner, to have others painted, and still others narrated. In this way can be treated all events not so splendid as to deserve such description as the others. By these means the poet will keep the work from surpassing its proper limits; for he should not wish to write of every thing so fully as to leave no place where the reader would not need to linger somewhat and exert a little effort to understand the passage. And that this can easily be done by an ingenious poet Ovid has shown in his *Metamorphoses*, for delivering himself with admirable skill from Aristotle's laws of art, he began the work with the beginning of the world and with astonishingly good sequence treated a great variety of things, and nonetheless covered them in a smaller number of books than Homer used in the *Iliad* and in the *Odyssey*, though each of these contained but a single action. Nor was Pisander among the Greeks unlike Ovid in treating a diversity of things, for he too began his work with the wedding of Juno and Jove and wrote in sequence all that happened up to his own times.[4] This is enough to show that the laws given by Aristotle have reference only to poems of a single action, and that all the poetical compositions that contain the deeds of heroes are included within the limits Aristotle gave the poets who write poems of single actions. . . .

---

[2] Apparently a common theory. Sir Walter Raleigh began his *History of the World* with the creation.

[3] This section is directed against the view expressed in *Poetics* VIII, above, and accepted by many Renaissance critics. [4] Pisander's work is now lost.

[Variety of subject. 23]

If the subject of the work includes many and various actions of many and various men according to the make-up of the romances in our tongue, as we have indicated above, the work will take its origin from the matter that is of greatest importance and on which all the rest appears to depend; this appears in the practice of Ariosto and Boiardo. In this matter it should be considered that Ariosto, though he began his composition with Orlando and finished with Ruggiero, does not deserve on that account the censure that some give him, for he follows the order of the events that he has set before him. And just as Ruggiero was the last in the presentation, so his victory (if the intention of the writer is to be respected) concludes the whole work laudably. . . . It appears to me that if a poet is to deal with ancient material in the form of a romance it is better to apply himself to many actions of a man than to one only. For I think this method better suited to composition in the form of romances than is the use of a single action. Diversity of actions carries with it variety, which is the spice of delight, and gives the author wide scope for introducing episodes, or pleasant digressions, and for bringing in events which in poems dealing with a single action cannot come about save with some hint of blame. . . . And these digressions the poet should be very careful to treat in such a manner that one may depend on another and be well joined with a continuous thread and a continuous chain to the parts of the subject he has undertaken to treat, and that they may carry with them the probability that pertains to poetic fictions, as we shall show below in its place. For if these digressions were otherwise handled, the poem would become faulty and wearisome, just as it delights and pleases when they appear to arise in such a way as though born at the same birth with the main topic. . . . The writer should use great diligence that the parts of his work fit together like the parts of the body, as we said above. And in putting together the bony frame he will seek to fill in the spaces and make the members equal in size, and this can be done by inserting at suitable and requisite places loves, hates, lamentations, laughter, sports, serious things, beauties, descriptions of places, temples, and persons, fables both invented by the author himself and taken from the ancients, voyages, wanderings, monsters, unforeseen events, deaths, funerals, mournings, recognitions, things terrible and pitiable, weddings, births, victories, triumphs, single combats, jousts, tournaments, catalogues, laws, and other like matters, which perhaps are so many that no little effort must be made by him who would wish to recount them one by one. For there is nothing above the heavens or below,[5] nor in the very gulf of the abyss, which is not ready to the hand and choice of the judicious poet, and which cannot with varied ornaments adorn the whole body of his composition and bring it not merely to a beautiful but to a lovely figure, for such things give to all the parts their due measure and fit ornament in such proportion that there emerges a body well regulated and composed. . . .

[Imitation. 28]

And because I have said that the light of judgment should be one's guide in literary composition, I will make known that this judgment is acquired in two ways. One is conversation and discussion with men who are learned and accustomed to compose. . . . The other way in which judgment is acquired is to read and observe diligently what has been written by authors who have attained excellence in the narrative kind of poetry, and to select their virtues and seek with all diligence to follow them, because so doing will not only develop the judgment but also will stimulate the young poet to practice composition. For often there will work in him the spirit that caused the activity of the poet whose work he reads, and it will awaken in him a flame that little by little will set his mind on fire and fill him with the fury that the Greeks call enthusiasm; roused by this, as though stung by a gadfly, he will be as it were forced to put on paper those things that are born in his mind because of his reading of that author. It has many times happened to me . . . that when I had no thought of composing anything, by the reading of some poet I have been forced in spite of myself to seize my pen and write out the things that have come into my mind. I believe this results from the sympathy of our souls with that of the poet, for since they are full of the seeds of things fit for harmony and the spirit of poetry, as soon as they are excited and aided they produce their fruit. Or it may be that this comes about because, as Aristotle says, poetry is natural to man, and our minds easily turn to that to which nature calls them. Therefore, the judicious reader should take the utmost care to flee from the vices of those he reads and to attend to their virtues only, for even in good authors are found things that should rather be avoided

[5] Cf. Sidney's phrase, *Defense*, sect. 24, below.

than followed. These, being mingled with other things that are full of good, enter unobserved, unless they are foreseen, into the minds of others, and at times because of the imperfection of our nature, which easily turns to the imperfect, have more power over readers than virtues have. Faults of this sort arise for the most part from the place where the good poets we read were born, or from the age in which they wrote, or from the nature of the poet. Vergil, by being too modest, has in matters of love often missed that graceful lasciviousness which went to excess in Ovid because he was of another nature than Vergil. . . . We see in the *Odyssey* of Homer many similar things, and specially where he has Nausicaä, the daughter of Alcinoüs, go to the river with other young women to wash clothes, which in our time would be impossible, I will not say to the daughter of a noble or a gentleman, but even of a simple artisan. This came about then because the poets of those early times followed a certain rough simplicity far remote from that majesty, with face royal and full of reverence, that appeared together with the excellence of the Roman empire; majesty which (though the greatness of the empire is past) has endured in a high degree even to our day. It would be a great error now to follow Homer in those things which, though suitable to his time, were unsuitable to the majesty of Rome and similarly are unsuitable in our times. . . . Though the age of Homer and the customs of his times and the singular virtue of that divine poet made such things tolerable in him, to do the same thing now would not be other than deliberately to select from the gold of his composition the dung (which came there not through the fault of the poet but through that of his age and time), and yet to suppose that one had selected the purest gold, as can be seen in the *Italia* of Trissino. . . . He who wishes to take literary material from Homer should therefore be careful to apply himself merely to those things which fit the age in which he writes and not to those which, though indeed they can be allowed in Homer for the reasons I have mentioned, appear very faulty today in those writers who need to have authority given to them that they may bestow it on things that are themselves lacking in it. . . . Though the compositions of Homer might offer material for composition to all the poets (as in fact they do give it to them), not all that Homer wrote was suitable in every time, in every age, in every condition of person. And what is taken from him needs to be better digested and brought to such perfection that it may fit in all its parts the time in which it is written, in such a way that what is taken from him may become better. This Marcus Tullius Cicero teaches us when he says that the Romans have taken many things from the Greeks, but that they then have made them better.[6]

[The arrangement of a romance. 39]

Taking up again our discussion of arrangement . . . I say that when it is judiciously used it carries with it the chain with which one part is joined and combined with another just as the parts of the human body are bound together by the muscles and other ligatures. Hence it should be considered that the poetic romances have another sort of connection than the heroic poetry of the Greeks and the Latins, who composed poems of a single action, as did Homer and Vergil. . . . For these have joined one book with another merely in a continued narration with a certain relation which they have had with each other with respect to the matter. But the writers of romances of highest reputation have not been content merely with relation but have striven to do something further, namely to put in one canto after another, before they come to the continuation of the matter, something to prepare the way for what they intend to say. In this Ariosto has succeeded admirably. And because there are those who blame in him what to me appears worthy of the greatest praise, that is, the beginnings of his cantos,[7] it seems to me not out of place to give a reason for this and to show how much more praiseworthy it is to do this than to follow in this matter the order of Vergil and of Homer. And to make this plan better known, it will not be too much for me to run back to what I first said, namely that the romances are divided into cantos. For our poets either sing or pretend that they sing before great princes, according to the custom of the ancient Greeks and Latins. And so, because they promise at the ends of their cantos that they must at some other time sing what they have left unfinished and similarly at the beginnings of their cantos feign that they have come back to sing what they left unfinished, before they come to the matter that they wish to continue they need to dispose the minds of their hearers to attention. Therefore, they act like a good player on the lyre or the lute or any other similar instrument who, before he begins to play the tune for which he has taken up

---

[6] Milton thought there was no plagiary if what was taken was "bettered by the borrower" (*Eikonoclastes*, chap. xxiii).

[7] Cf. *Paradise Lost*, beginnings of iii, vii, ix and beginnings of books in *Tom Jones*.

his instrument, seeks to catch the ears of those before whom he plays. So our poets, seeking to catch the attention anew from canto to canto, with some striking introduction rouse the minds of their hearers, and then come to the continuation of their matter, thus binding one canto to another with admirable workmanship. ... There is also another difference to be found between the connections made by these poets of ours and by the ancient heroic poets. For as the writers of the romances set out to deal with the actions of many, they have not been able to continue one matter, fully connected, from one canto to another. But they have been obliged, in order to bring their work to any end, to speak first of one of their characters, then of another, and breaking off their first subject to enter upon the deeds of another character, and in this way to continue their materials to the end of the work, a thing they have done with remarkable skill. For, when they break off their narrative, they lead the reader to such a point before they make the break that they leave in the mind an ardent desire to return to take up the narrative again; this secures reading for the whole of their poem, since the principal matters always remain imperfect until the completion of the work. . . .

[Variety.[8] 42]

Perhaps the method of composition with a single hero deserves more praise than the other, for that beauty which the writers of romances seek to secure by means of variety in the actions of many men can in various ways properly be introduced into a poem which contains many actions by a single man, and so relieve the reader from the satiety of reading continually on the same subject. . . . Yet actions with a continuous thread can be arranged by an ingenious poet with admirable variety . . . but if this can be done by Homer and Vergil in the course of describing a single action in many books, how much better can it be done by him who describes many actions. . . . In the compositions of Homer and Vergil can be found loves, unexpected events, examples of courtesy and justice, injuries, liberality, vices, virtues, attacks, defenses, stratagems, faith, loyalty, fortitude, instances of worthlessness, hopes, fears, useful things, harmful things, and other episodes or digressions in great numbers, which in combination with the knitting together and disposition of the work can bring about so much variety and delight that the poem will become very at-

[8] See the index.

tractive and pleasing, without those breaks in the action that have been used by our writers. Yet I do not blame the romancers, but rather praise them, since under the compulsion of the causes I have mentioned they cannot do otherwise if they wish to bring their works to an end. . . .

[Literary freedom. 43]

And now to speak generally, I say that authors who are judicious and skillful in composition should not so restrain their liberty within the bounds set by their predecessors that they dare not set foot outside the old paths. In addition to being a bad use of the gifts that mother nature has given them, such restraint would also prevent poetry from ever going beyond the bounds that one writer has given it, nor would it ever move its foot from the path in which the early fathers made it walk. Hence, knowing that it is permitted to architecture, to the military art, to rhetoric, to geometry, to music, and to the other arts that deserve the attention of a liberal spirit, to add, increase, diminish, and change, the great Vergil judged that such a procedure was still more appropriate to the poet in so far as to him is given the same power that the world has agreed to give to the excellent painter, of varying likenesses according to his own judgment as appears to him most to his purpose. Hence he shows in a great number of places how good writers, treading the same path in which the ancients have walked, can turn aside somewhat from the course already laid down, and leaving the beaten track, make their own ways to Helicon. Nor is this seen merely in the Latins but even in the Greeks, and among them in Homer, and much more in our Tuscan poets, whose compositions are of no less value in this language than were those of Greek and Latin poets in theirs, although the Tuscans did not follow in the ways of their predecessors, for, to speak truly, our tongue also has its forms of poetry, which are proper to it and do not belong to any other tongue or nation. Therefore no one should wish to confine the Tuscan poet within the limits to which the Greeks and the Latins are restricted . . . but he ought to walk in those paths which the best poets in our language have indicated with authority equal to that of the Greeks and Latins in their tongues.

[Classical principles do not apply to romances. 44]

And this is the reason why I have often laughed at those who have wished to bring the writers of romances under the laws of the art given by Aristotle and Horace, without considering that neither of them knew our language nor our manner of composing. Hence romances should not be subjected to classical laws and rules, but left within the limits set by those among us who have given authority and reputation to this species of poetry. As the Greeks and the Latins have derived the art of which they have written from their poets, so we should also take our art from our poets and hold to that form which the best writers of romances have given them. . . .

[The marvelous. 56]

There is nothing marvelous in that which happens often or naturally, but there is in what appears impossible and yet is assumed to have happened if not in truth at least in fiction, such as the changes of men into trees, of ships into nymphs, of branches into ships, the union of the gods with men, and other such things which, though they are false and impossible, are still so accepted by custom that a composition cannot be pleasing in which these fables do not appear. And perhaps the poet is called poet for this more than for any other reason, for this name of poet signifies nothing other than maker.[9] And not because of his verses but chiefly through his subjects he is called a poet, in so far as these subjects are made and feigned by him in such a way that they are fit and suitable for poetry.[10] If he should merely take the things already made and not feign new ones, he would lose the name of poet, for he would not make but merely would recite what is made. . . .

[Anachronism. 57]

While the historian is obliged to write only of deeds and actions that are true and as they really happened, the poet presents things not as they are but as they should be, that they may serve to instruct his readers about life.[11] And this is why, though the poets write of ancient affairs, they nonetheless seek to harmonize them with their own customs and their own age, introducing things unlike those of ancient times and suitable to their own.[12] This is seen

[9] Cf. Sidney, *Defense*, secs. 8 and 9, below, and the index under *maker*.

[10] Cf. Sidney: "not rhyming and versing that maketh a poet. . . . But it is that feigning" (*Defense*, sect. 16, below).

[11] "As they should be" is from Aristotle, *Poetics*, xxv, 60b32, above. The last clause, giving the moral purpose, is the conclusion of the Renaissance.

[12] It has often been supposed that the anachronisms of Shakespeare and his contemporaries are the result of ignorance. This passage suggests that they may often be deliberate. To Renaissance dramatists history was subordinate to the higher purposes of poetry; the present age gives history relatively a higher position.

in Vergil's account of Aeneas, for though he came from Troy, and the methods of sacrificing, conducting funeral ceremonies, and arming in Asia were not like those in Italy, yet Vergil has the Trojans sacrifice, bury, and fight according to Italian habits and not even according to the habits of the time before Rome was founded but those of the age of Octavian. And good poets have not merely taken this license, but have named things that did not exist in the time of the men of whom they write, not otherwise than as if in early times customs had been in use that appeared much later, as can be seen in Homer and Vergil. The writers of romances have also made some use of this method, for the reason that the poet (as I have said) does not write of things as they were or are, but as they should be, in order to give at once profit and delight by satisfying the men of that age in which they write,[13] a thing that is not permitted to those who write histories. . . .

[Poetry and history. 58]

I hold the belief of Aristotle, who says that the poet is far ahead of the historian in his power to benefit. And perhaps this is true because the historian, unable to part from the truth, is obliged to write of the vices no less than the virtues of men; hence he injures them as much as he benefits them. But the poet in his fictions imitates illustrious actions, presenting them not as they are but as they ought to be, and suitably accompanying things that have vice in them with the horrible and miserable (for the heroic poet does this as much as the tragic one when the material demands it), purges our minds from like passions and arouses them to virtue, as is seen in the definition that Aristotle gives of tragedy. . . .[14]

[The moral function of the poet. 59]

The function then of our poet, with respect to affecting morals, is to praise virtuous actions and to blame vices and by means of the terrible and the piteous to make them odious to the reader. In these two things the writers of the romances in our language are much more copious than were the Greek and Latin heroic poets, for, as they merely indicate blame and praise in such matters, our poets do it at length, especially in praising and blaming things of

---

[13] A good example of the Renaissance combination of Aristotle (see the beginning of this paragraph and the note) and Horace (*Art of Poetry*, 333) and a conclusion from it.

[14] *Poetics*, VI. Giraldi assumes that Aristotle's catharsis (see the index) implies the moral effect of tragedy.

our times. This habit (so far as I can understand) was first introduced by Dante and passed on to the times that came after him.[15]
It was then most happily taken up by our judicious Petrarch, not
merely in his canzoni and his sonnets, as in the canzone on Italy
and the sonnets on Rome, but in his *Triumphs,* in which he frequently passes into digressions of the type mentioned and then
easily returns to the theme he has left.[16] And in the same thing
Ariosto is great and wonderful, as he has also been very successful
in treating in his poem subjects and events not included in his first
intention but which add extraordinary beauty to his accomplished
work. And the same things add beauty to the compositions of
others who make use of them with judgment and grace. And here
it is to be observed that in digressions that contain jousts, tournaments, loves, beauties, passions of the soul, fields of battle, buildings, and similar other things, the author of romances is much
more copious than Vergil and Homer have been. . . .[17]

[Decorum. 63]

The poet should ever have his eye on decorum, which is nothing
else than what fits places, times, and persons. And therefore it
comes about that the ancient observers of the nature of things say
that decorum was that beauty, that grace, which springs from the
forms of speech that are joined together with judgment and with
measure and carry with them some exposition of characters,
which should shine out in words just as the beauty of color shines
out in a beautiful body. In short, decorum is nothing other than
the grace and fitness of things and should be considered not merely
in actions but also in the speeches and answers of men among
themselves. For we speak with a king in a way unlike that in
which we speak with a gentleman. And a king replies to another
king not as he does to his vassal or to another lesser prince. And

---

[15] Cf. Mazzoni, *Of the Defense of the "Comedy,"* Bk. IV, chap. XXXVI ff., below. He
apparently has in mind such passages as Dante's invectives against Florence, e.g.,
Purgatorio, XXIII, 94–108.

[16] Canzone 16, *Italia mia;* Sonnets 105 (*Fiamma dal ciel*), 106 (*L'avara Babilonia*), 107
(*Fontana di dolore*); *The Triumph of Fame,* part II, ll. 142–4, furnishes an instance of a
digression. Dante himself recognized his method as digressive (Letter to Can Grande,
sect. 9, above).

[17] Was it classical feeling that led Milton to say that he would not tell of

> tilting furniture, emblazoned shields,
> Impresses quaint, caparisons and steeds
>
> *Paradise Lost,* IX, 34–5.

as the romancers had done?

he speaks in one way to his soldiers, to arouse them to battle, and in another to his people to quiet them when they have risen in armed rebellion. . . .[18] And this principle of decorum should be applied not merely to actions, persons, places, and circumstances, as we have said, but also to words. For words are without force when they do not serve as the covering for things, nor can things be made manifest without words. Nor should this decorum be considered merely in the work as a whole but in each part of it, as in expository passages, invocations, narrations, and other parts as they come, so that each part may have what is individually suitable to it. Therefore he who would acquire fame as an author must give much attention to decorum in things and in words, in the whole and in the parts, for the composition and arrangement of the parts will avail little if the parts are ineptly placed and show some lack of decorum, and they cannot help lacking decorum whenever the writer does not take prudence as his guide in things and in words. [He then deals with decorum in persons, developing Horace, *Art of Poetry*, 153 ff.[19]]

[18] The king in *Hamlet* (iv, v, 119 ff.) addresses Laertes on his rebellion.

[19] Decorum is also discussed in Giraldi's work on the drama, where it is made "what befits the disposition of the doer and the speaker" (p. 259). Cf. Milton's description of decorum as "the choice of such persons as he ought to introduce, and what is moral and decent for each one" (*Reason of Church Government*, sect. 3, below)

ANTONIO MINTURNO

oᴗooᴗo

L'ARTE POETICA

1564

IN 1564 ANTONIO MINTURNO, bishop of Ugento, published the work usually called *L'arte poetica* but to which he refers in the dedication as *Della toscana poesia* (*Of Tuscan Poetry*). Some years before, he had issued a Latin work on the poet in six books, of which he writes: "On it I used almost twenty years and the best part of my life, in order to make plain those precepts for writing poetically which the fathers of the Greek and Roman Muses abide by; and they show how these rules should be kept."[1] The work on Tuscan poetry is, then, a mature performance, represented as giving his reader a chance to hear in Tuscan what had already been presented in Latin. Its concern is with Italian literature, thrown against a background of classical theory and practice. His claim is that he was the "first to give perfectly instructions on poetry to those speaking Tuscan as well as those speaking Latin, according to the way that Aristotle and Horace pointed out and that was taken by Homer, Vergil, Petrarch, Dante, and all the other ancients who were in esteem." He is perhaps to be thought a follower of Giraldi Cinthio (selections just above), though more conservative in position than his leader. The work is in the form of a dialogue between Minturno and various friends. It has been suggested that the bishop's Latin work, referred to above, was carefully studied by Sir Philip Sidney.

The translation, by the editor, is based on the edition published at Naples in 1725.

BIBLIOGRAPHY

Minturno, Antonio, *De poeta libri sex*. Venice, 1559.
——, *L'arte poetica*. Venice, 1564; Naples, 1725.
——, Myrick, Kenneth Orne, *Sir Philip Sidney as a Literary Craftsman*. Cambridge, 1935.

[1] For references to this work see the index.

L'ARTE POETICA (*selections*)

Book I

[Romantic[1] and classical; epic structure. 24[2]]

Minturno. He will compose correctly the plot of an epic poem who imitates and describes excellently a subject that is entire and perfect, made up of actions that are illustrious and serious, and having suitable size, because, as has been said, the plot is the imitation of an action which is one and complete and of proper length; but by means of episodes a poem is increased in length, and an epic poem especially, because it has taken as its characteristics great size and length,[3] for it is a narration. But because every narrative is able to include many things at one time, the epic feigns that many of them happened at the same time in different places. . . . Hence by reason of this prerogative the heroic poem has in itself great magnificence, and because of the variety of matter taken from outside often refreshes the mind of the hearer with wondrous delight, and renews his attention, not to mention driving away the boredom that the length of the work might generate. . . .[4] But though the epic has this prerogative of being carried to a great length, the plot should not be made up of more than one unit of material nor composed of actions that came about in a longer time than a single year,[5] for the epic narrative is not a history; the latter narrates not merely all the things that happen in the same time and all the things that happen to one or more persons, and which have come together by chance and without reason, but also things that have happened during many years and which come in order one after another. . . . But in a space of many years, as in the wars of the Romans with the Carthaginians, many things follow one after another of which it cannot be said that they terminate in a single manner. But the poet, as we have shown (since in one poem he comprehends those things which tend to one end), does not treat everything that happened to one

---

[1] On the romances see Giraldi, *Discourse on the Romances*, above.
[2] The numbers given to the sections are those of the pages in the edition of 1725.
[3] Joachim du Bellay called the epic "the long poem" (*Defense and Illustration of the French Language*, Bk. II, chap. v).
[4] See *variety* in the index.
[5] This corresponds to the single day allowed to the drama. See *unity of time*, in the index.

man at the same time and in the same group of events, if they are varied and not of one sort. . . . Vergil did not set out to describe all that happened in ancient Latium as a result of the coming of the Trojans. . . . If he had described so many and so various things, the work would have become immense in size and not easy to understand, and even if it had not increased more than was fitting, it would have been in the utmost confusion because of its great variety. And if, according to the habit of the historians, the facts had been briefly narrated and the poem ornamented with no episode, the poetry would have been despoiled of its beauty.[6] As the most skillful of poets, they undertook to write about what among so many things was clearest and most suitable to be written about, and what would make up a unified and perfect action. And in order to enrich their works they interposed many and dissimilar things, but such as, even though they were introduced from without or were merely attached to the plot, were not so remote from it that they did not direct themselves to the same end. Hence those plots are thought the worst in which we see many things mingled neither according to versimilitude nor necessity. Authors who fill up their pages with dreams commonly make this mistake.

[The romances popular. 25]

Vespasiano. You are referring to the loves and the famous deeds of the Paladins, which indeed deserved to have their memory kept alive for eternal ages by the most noble writers.

Min. But do you not find in such books many episodes much removed from the principal action and the matter in hand and introduced there for no suitable reason, and are not their poems truly the idle tales of the romances?

Vesp. But for all that, people repeat or read some song of the loves and deeds of Rinaldo or Orlando more gladly than any of the more graceful *canzoni* or the better sonnets of Petrarch.

Min. True. But by whom is it done or with what judgment? Certainly by the common herd who do not know what poetry is nor understand in what the excellence of the poet consists. For my part I value a sonnet by Petrarch higher than all the romances; this indicates that the rabble is mistaken in its wishes.

Vesp. Is it not possible of that same material to compose a poetic plot and produce an excellent poem?

---

[6] The primary purpose of the episode is adornment (see the index). It falls among things that the poet uses for delight rather than for profit.

Min. Why not? But with another order and another method and another style. Anyone who carefully considers our argument will easily understand this.

[The origin of the romance. 26a]

Vesp. Since we have gone on so far in our reasoning, just what is the romance?

Min. I shall not deny that it is an imitation of great and illustrious actions that are worthy of epic poetry. But certainly the word is strange, and in the Spanish as well as in the Provençal I believe it refers to the vulgar tongue. In Spain and in Provence because of the Roman colonies Latin was generally diffused to such an extent that men spoke there in a Romanized fashion (for the Romans occupied both regions, and barbarous nations dwelt there). Since the Roman language persisting in those lands, though for the most part contaminated and destroyed, was nevertheless more regular and more graceful than the Gothic and the Alanic, their native tongues, they applied themselves to learning and retaining it, and called it Romance and wrote in it. Therefore, because they dealt in that language with the actions and the loves of the knights more than with any other subject, the compositions made on that theme were called romances. The same word passed into Italy, because our writers began to imitate the romantic and classical compositions of the barbarians. And since our authors, as Cicero teaches us, always improve what they find in others, they make also the poetry of the romances more graceful and beautiful, if in truth it is to be called poetry.

[The greatness of Ariosto. 26b]

Vesp. Why is it not worthy of this name? Is not M. Ludovico Ariosto a most excellent poet, as he is a most noble writer of romances?

Min. Yes, indeed, nor do I judge that a lower estimate should be made of him. But I cannot affirm that his romances and those of the others contain the kind of poetry that Aristotle and Horace taught us.

Vesp. Of what consequence is it that the romance is not such poetry but another kind taken over from the Ultramontanes and made more splendid and more beautiful by the Italians, if the world is pleased with it and accepts and receives it with delight?

Min. I do not wonder about the common crowd, which often-times accepts things it does not understand; and when once it has adopted a thing with great pleasure, it always retains it and favors it; nor if anything better than that should present itself does it receive it willingly; such is the power of opinion firmly impressed on the human mind. But I cannot but be greatly astonished that there are some learned men, well versed in good literature and of excellent abilities, who (as I understand) acknowledge that there is not in the romances the form and the rule that Homer and Vergil follow, and that Aristotle and Horace command as appropriate, and who nevertheless labor to defend this error.[7] Nay more, since that sort of composition gives the deeds of errant knights, they obstinately affirm not merely that it is not fitting to write poetry in the manner of Vergil and Homer, but even that it is desirable that poetry also should be errant, passing from one manner to another, and binding together various things in one bundle.

[How the romance differs from the heroic poem. 27a]

Vesp. Will you teach us in what the romance differs from the heroic poem?

Min. The heroic poem, as I have said, sets out to imitate a memorable action carried to its conclusion by one illustrious person. The romance, they say, has as its object a crowd of knights and ladies and of affairs of war and peace, though in this group one knight is especially taken whom the author is to make glorious above all the others; he is to treat as many deeds by him and by the others as he thinks sufficient for the glory of those he is disposed to praise (though he may select the more memorable ones), and he takes for description diverse and contrasted lands and the various things that happened in them during all the time occupied by the fabulous story of the matter he sets out to sing.

Vesp. Does not the father of poetry do the same, since he deals with many very striking deeds of Ulysses, Diomed, the two Ajaxes, Menelaus, King Agamemnon, Nestor, and the other demigods, though he intends to praise Achilles above all the others?

[The method of Homer. 27b]

Min. Yes, that is true; but he makes all spring from one beginning, and directs all to one end. This is not done in the romance.

[7] Perhaps Giraldi, *On the Romances*, immediately above.

Homer takes as his subject the wrath of Achilles, and how injurious it was to the Greeks and how much damage it caused them, because while that demigod was fighting, none of the Trojans had the courage to issue out of the city. But when he turned against King Agamemnon because of the injury received from him and for that reason decided to fight no more against the enemy in aid of his own people, the Trojans took courage, summoned their energies, and many times came to combat to the disadvantage of the Greeks. Thus, treating with superhuman genius all that followed the wrath of Achilles, within that one action Homer included many things fitly joined to each other, such as the combat of Menelaus with Paris, of Hector with Ajax, and of Patroclus with Hector, and the plan Ulysses made with Diomed to kill Rhesus and take away his horses, the burning of the ships, and other actions not a few, until the wrath of Achilles was changed by the death of Patroclus and turned against the Trojans, with the result that Hector was miserably killed.

[The method of Ariosto. 28a]

In the *Orlando Furioso* the author could have followed the same order and method, if he had wished, and could have directed his poem to a similar end, for he could have undertaken to sing the amorous fury of Orlando and all that followed that madness, showing that the Moors did not have courage to undertake war against King Charles of France while Orlando was sane, but when he grew mad for love they passed into France and did very great damage to the Christians. In this he would have been able to treat the things done at that time because of love or any other cause, by the knights on one side or the other, who took part in that war. And after Orlando regained his first sanity, he was able to give the victory to the Christians through his valor.

Vesp. This was not the design of that poet, but he wished to show clearly that Ruggiero was worthy of praise above all the others, since from him the illustrious house of his patron, whom he intended to praise, had taken its origin.

Min. If he was not content to treat the deeds of Ruggiero, as of the most excellent of all the knights present in the war caused by the madness of Orlando, he could have composed another narrative about him, as Homer composed the *Iliad* in praise of Achilles and the *Odyssey* in praise of Ulysses, though Ulysses in the *Iliad* did many things greatly deserving praise. And so he would not have indicated by the title of the work that he was writing about Orlando and then written about another, as a principal character, nor would he have put forward a great number of persons and things, some of which are such that one of them alone would furnish a subject for an entire poem.

[How poems are named. 28b]

Vesp. Has not the *Iliad* its name from the place where the war was fought, and yet the subject of the work is the wrath of Achilles? And the tragedy entitled *Medea* and the other which is called *Tereus*, do they not have for their objects compassion directed to neither the one nor the other person named?

Min. The wrath of Achilles is not the subject of the divine *Iliad* in the sense of causing the action of the poem to show how great was the valor of the hero. While he appeared in the field the Greeks were victors, but after his wrath had so much power over him that he gave up bearing arms in their behalf, the victory went to the Trojans. And in the tragedies you speak of, what else is dealt with except the infelicity of the person from whom they have their names? I do not intend by what I have said to blame so great and noble a poem by so rare and excellent a poet, whose powers I marvel at; rather I exhort all to read the work, since it has power to give great delight and no little profit to those who understand it well. And I excuse the author, who, not because he did not know what was better but rather to give pleasure to the many, chose to follow the bad method he found in the romances. And if he put in the title of his poem the name of Orlando and not of Ruggiero, whom he set out to praise, he did it, as his defenders say, in order that the work should be more acceptable and more gladly read, because he thought the name of Orlando, as a more famous knight, would make it more pleasing than would that of Ruggiero or some other hero less known and less important in the romances. Ruggiero was so famous and well known from the romances of Boiardo that if Ariosto had written a book named after Ruggiero he would have been able to make it acceptable because of the beauty of his language, though the making of two separate poems, one on Orlando, the other on Ruggiero, would have been a heavy task and would have required a long time; nor, though he was not very old, did he have any certainty of so long a life that he would be able to finish both of them. Yet nonetheless he chose to base on the romances a single work in which these two heroes should be indicated as the chief and most glorious of all, the one to give his name to the poem, the other as providing the goal to which all might be directed.

[Ariosto knew the classical methods. 29]

Nor can it be believed that Ariosto was of the opinion that in the romances the form of Homeric poetry could not be kept, for the reason that in the *Odyssey*, to which the romance is more similar than to the *Iliad*, the only travelers introduced are Ulysses and Telemachus, the latter of whom pretends he is traveling in order to get news of his father, but in the romances many of the characters go on travels. Nor can it be believed for the reason that in the romances there are so many wandering knights they cannot be represented in any banquet or in any picture or in any guise whatever, as they are in the *Odyssey* in the case of Alcinous, Nestor, and Menelaus, and in the *Aeneid* in the case of Dido, Anchises, and Evander, and in the description of the shield, for the things the knights do can be narrated, as are in the *Iliad* the deeds of Ulysses and of Diomed and many other demigods. Nor can it be credited that Ariosto believed he could not follow the epic form on the ground that the epic founds its imitation on things that have truth in them or at least are accepted as true, because there can be no doubt that Aeneas came to Italy and acquired the kingdom of the Latins and the Rutulians, nor that the things described in the *Iliad* were the most memorable that happened in that war, nor that Patroclus was killed by Hector and Hector by Achilles, nor that after long wanderings Ulysses returned to his native land and his house and at last revenged himself on the suitors. On the contrary the writers of romances without any regard to the truth feign what never was, since neither written history nor fame gives any testimony to the love or the madness of Orlando, yet Boiardo feigned that he was in love and Ariosto that he was mad. Yet tragedy, which follows the truth or at least that which is held true, sometimes makes use of a novel event that has never really happened.[8] Nor, even though it always has been and always will be permitted to the poet to leave the path followed by the others, is it to be believed that the right to pass the bounds prescribed to poetry should be given him. Vergil rejected subjects to the narra-

---

[8]Aristotle, *Poetics*, IX, first par., above. Cf. Jonson's "truth of argument" (*Sejanus*, below).

tion of which idle spirits would have listened intently, as already
written on by others and generally known, and set himself to follow that road by which he would be able

> To raise himself from earth, and, famous and victorious
> Through the praise of others, wheel in flight.

Yet he did not go so far as to abandon the bounds set down for
the poet and preserved by the most worthy authors.

[The Italian language. 30a]

I do not believe that it ever came into the mind of Ariosto to think
of the Italian language as so rustic and barbarous that it could
not receive Homeric and Vergilian poetry, merely because the
rabble had its ears prepared for the follies of the romances and because the verses of Italian are of other measure and other harmony than those of Greek and Latin, and the Christians have
another religion, other laws, and other customs than the Gentiles
did. God grant that a poet so judicious and of such excellence
should not fall into such a thought! since it cannot be denied that
Italian is so serious and graceful and fit to set forth in language
every subject that can be expressed in words, that it can treat
gracefully and seriously any sort of poetry.[9]

[Romantic possibilities. 30b]

If modern melic poetry follows the footsteps of ancient poetry,
though with a different harmony of words, and dramatic poetry
in our time begins to appear beautiful for no other reason than
that it endeavors to assimilate itself to that of the ancients, cannot
the epic, represented by the romances, take its example from the
idea expressed in the books of Vergil and Homer? It cannot be
denied that the *Teseid* of Boccaccio, which narrates deeds and
loves not of knights but of heroes (although in it very little or no
semblance of Homeric poetry can be seen), is no more pleasing
to judicious and learned men than the *Ancroja*, or the *Spagna*, or
the *Altobello*, or even the *Morgante*[10] or any other romance which
in years past has gladly been read by the unlearned. This result
would not have come about if the romances in themselves possessed such excellence as today some attribute to them in order to

[9] Cf. Sidney's praise of English, sect. 55, below.
[10] The *Morgante maggiore* of Pulci is the best known of the romances in this list; a
translation of the first canto may be found in the works of Byron.

praise Ariosto. But they would assuredly praise him more if they would show that all their praise comes not from themselves but from the great powers of the noble genius of that author, who by his style made appear so beautiful and pleasing to all a thing in its nature barbarous and naked of all grace. Petrarch surely would not have called them dreams of sick men and follies of romance if in his times the opinion had been held that in them some vestige of poetry appeared. And it is not credible Dante would have said he could not find that any Italian up to his time had sung of arms, for the reason that no such composition was to be found in the hands of the common people, but rather because no person worthy of praise and esteemed for his pursuit of the muses had written of them, for it is held that the first writer of romances in whom some light of poetry shone was Boccaccio. Moreover Bembo would not have attempted,[11] as it is understood he did, to divert Ariosto from giving his efforts to romances and direct him to epic poetry if he had not thought the romances were ignoble. What shall we say of the verse? If it is worthy to have heroic matter sung in it, can we not infer that it also is such that he who writes in it can observe that law according to which, as poets of the first rank show us, an epic subject should be treated?

[Poetic themes of past and present. 31a]

What shall we say of the diverse religion and of the different customs if not that, though the poet should properly harmonize himself with his times, he should not depart from the law of poetry? Antiquity had the celestial gods as well as those infernal and earthly; modern times have the angels and the saints in heaven and one God only, and on earth the monks and the hermits. Antiquity had oracles and sibyls; modern times have necromancers and magicians. Antiquity had enchanters, such as Circe and Calypso; recent times have the fates. In ancient days the messengers of Jove were Mercury and Iris; but now some of the angels are sent by God.[12] But all this does not make it impossible that the subject matter of recent poetry should not and cannot be made up of one single entire and perfect action, as it was in ancient poetry. Though in Athens the judges conducted themselves in another manner than in Rome, the speech of those who accused or de-

---

[11] An Italian cardinal and literary dictator, as it were, in the early sixteenth century.
[12] This passage may be said to foretell what was to be done by Tasso in *Jerusalem Delivered* and by Milton in *Paradise Lost*.

fended did not change its form and method. Marcus Tullius, wishing to teach the Romans the perfect manner of speaking, would not have translated what Aeschines and Demosthenes said to the judges, the one accusing and the other defending Ctesiphon, if, even though the form of managing a case in Greece was different from that which prevailed in Rome and some diversity is to be found in the words, he had thought he could not use their speeches as good examples.

[Romantic heroes. 31b]

Just because no other names in Italian poetry are so well known as those of Orlando and Rinaldo, it is not, I think, impossible that a poem in the language now commonly written in Italy can be acceptable, even though it does not deal with one of those heroes, because I think that not the fame of the person celebrated in the verses but rather the ability of the poet gives a work authority and reputation. The name of Aeneas was known to but few (since no poem especially on him was read when Vergil commenced to write of him), but nonetheless the excellence of that divine poet made him famous and known to everyone, and gave the work composed on him so much favor that no other in the Latin tongue is so gladly read. Moreover the fame of Achilles and of Ulysses was not widespread until Homer, the prince of poets, wrote of them; and yet the *Iliad* and the *Odyssey* from the first day they were heard until the present have been most acceptable to all the world and ever will be. Even though it was not known in Italy what a paladin was and no one had heard such a name before men began to write of them, common readers did not at all hesitate to accept first a romance composed about some knight of the court of King Arthur of England, and then one on King Charles of France.[13]

[Barbarism and education. 32]

Even if the giant is more beautiful than the pigmy, and he is better who is defective in being too big rather than too small in stature, still the animal which is great beyond measure and whose members are not proportionate with each other will not appear in the least beautiful. And though Ariosto and Boiardo, to whom either their own virtue or fortune (if it is indeed true that every

[13] Charlemagne, who is important in the *Orlando Innamorato* of Boiardo and the *Orlando Furioso* of Ariosto.

poem like every other work has its fate) or both together have given a very great reputation, have chosen to follow the way discovered by crude and barbarous writers, their authority ought not to render it improper to walk on the road trodden by the best of the ancients, for I do not believe it is possible to deny that things invented take from their inventors authority, force, and vigor. . . . Now we see what sort of men are the inventors of epic poetry, of which we are speaking, and what sort invent romances. Certain it is that the most noble poets of the Greeks and Latins gave us the idea of epic poetry expressed in their works and the most excellent writers of either tongue composed the poetic art from it. The inventors of the romances were barbarians, men who never had any reputation for learning, but were as if guided by the light of nature. But all affirm that natural endowment without art is not able to make a perfect work.[14] And it appears to me that those who endeavor to find in these dreams a new type of art are seeking for leafy trees and green herbs in the sands of Ethiopia. Certainly this is nothing other than to seek for law in people who are naturally at enmity with reason, for the truth in vanity, and for certainty in error. And though to show that they are strong in ability and learning they make an effort to introduce a new poetic art into the world, they are not therefore of so great authority that we should believe them rather than Aristotle and Horace.

[The principles of art are immutable. 33]

But if these two, using Homer's poetry as their example, have taught a true art of poetry, I do not see how another diverse from that can be set up, for the truth is one, and that which is once true must of necessity be true always and in every age; nor can the differences between various ages change what is true, though they may be able to change customs and life, yet in all their mutations the truth still remains stable.[15] Hence the variety that comes from different times cannot bring about the possibility of treating in poetry more than one action that is entire and of suitable size, with which all the rest may truly and reasonably harmonize and join. Besides, this Art gives all her effort to the imitation of Nature, and does well in proportion as she approaches her. But in everything of every sort Art holds to a law with which she

[14] See *genius* in the index.
[15] On the permanence of artistic principles see Tasso, *The Heroic Poem*, secs. 28 ff., below.

is regulated in her work and by which she directs everything. One also is the idea in which Nature is mirrored when she works, and one is the form on which Art looks in carrying out her function. Architecture always has one law to which she ought to hold fast even though the building is often varied. Equally in its imitation painting makes an effort to keep one law, and so does sculpture and every other imitative art. And though now this art and now that one has been subject to variety, there has been no change in its inner being but only in some accidental quality, or in the mode of imitating and the ornaments. Though painting commenced by drawing outlines and then added color, and after that the art, distinguishing itself, found light and shade and that splendid quality which, because it is between the other two, is called tone by the Greeks, and found the law for adapting one color to another, yet in this art the imitation does not change so much that it is not, as it always has been, of one complete action. Nor because kinds of poetry are diverse (for we see that epic is one thing, dramatic poetry another and lyric another, and each holds to its own method, its own instrument, its own style, its own form, and its own way) do they therefore fail to guard in the same way the unity of the matter taken for imitation. And the epic, though it is much more extensive and takes in more things, never thought that it was permitted to depart from the same law. Colossi surely do not differ from pygmies in this. And what art, what science, what discipline can be found (not architecture, not music, not painting, not sculpture, not military affairs, not medicine) in which anyone works without endeavoring to follow the steps of the ancients, and in which he will not be most praised who follows them most closely? Only poetry presumes in our times to do what has always been blamed by wise men, and those are not lacking who hold it more beautiful and better than ever.[16] But it is according to reason that in every poem there should be treated one sole and single action which should be perfect and of suitable length, since on searching through all the arts and all the sciences you will not find a written work which has more than one subject under which may be put all that is treated in it, and to which everything may be directed as to the unique object of that work.

---

[16] As did Giraldi in the works given immediately above. In his epigram beginning "Three poets," Dryden asserted the superiority of Milton to Homer and Vergil. The claims of the ancients and the moderns were much discussed in the eighteenth century. See Swift's *Battle of the Books*.

[Un-Aristotelian poetry in antiquity. 34a]

Vesp. Not to contradict your opinion, the reasons for which seem to me conclusive, but to make the truth clearer, I shall ask you about this thing. How is it that the rule Aristotle gave us and Horace confirmed can be true if he who wrote the *Heracleid*,[17] and he who composed the *Theseid*, and Papinius, who wrote the *Achilleid*, and Ovid, who narrated the metamorphoses of the gods, of men, and of things, are by all looked on as poets? . . .

Min. . . . I surely will concede to you that those authors, who, you say, are put in the number of the poets, wrote stories in verse, and Ovid in the *Metamorphoses* made a fabulous story, since he brought together all the fables, knitting one after the other into the narration with wonderful power for arrangement, and much more appropriately than it had been done by those Greeks who wrote it in prose and left it for us to read. Yet as those Greeks are not for that reason reputed to be poets, so Ovid does not merit the name of poet because of it, just as he does not deserve it because he wrote the *Fasti*.

[Verse does not make a poet. 34b]

I shall never affirm that there is epic poetry in these works; why then are their authors to be called poets? I will explain to you. It is both because the common people attribute the name to all those who write in verse, whether they treat of agriculture, as Vergil and Hesiod, or of astrology, as Aratus, Manilius, and Pontanus, or of medicine, as Nicander, or of things done in war, as Quintus Calaber, . . . Silius Italicus, and Lucan, and because they adorn them with poetic splendors and add to them things feigned, as Vergil did in the *Georgics*[18] when he narrated the fable of Aristaeus. And all of this sort they call epic, as I said in my Latin treatise on the poet.

Vesp. Cannot the romancers stand among these, since they write fabulous stories?

[Romantic structure. 34c]

Min. You say what those content themselves with who presumptuously set Ariosto in many things before Homer and Vergil. And in truth it seems to me that the romancers can reasonably be

---

[17] For this and the *Theseid* see Aristotle's *Poetics*, chap. viii, first par.
[18] *Ibid.*, iv, 315 ff.

called neither by one nor the other name, since they set out to
follow now these, now those, and now go by the way followed by
neither one nor the other, for, like the pure epic poets, they narrate things of many persons and many years; like the true epic
writers, who are called heroic,[19] they use recognitions and peripeties and depict customs and passions, and make choice of someone
whom they present for praise before all the others, and increase
the size of the poem with many episodes, and following their own
peculiar custom often break the course of the narrative, and in-
terrupt what they are dealing with, leaping from one part to
another, and then take it up again, returning to the place whence
they departed. This they do both when time allows and when it
forbids. Time allows that when one action has been narrated,
what has happened elsewhere at the same time should next be
told, and that then returning to the narrative that was broken off
the author should proceed with it; as was said above, the epic does
this not without the pleasure of the auditor in the variety of
things narrated, which naturally pleases. But time does not allow
that when a battle has been joined or a tempest or some other
thing commenced, it should be interrupted in the middle, and
when the end of it is awaited, it should be left off for the sake of
treating some other matter which happened to other persons in
other places at the same time, as is the peculiar custom of the
romancers without regard to what time demands or the desire of
the reader, for they leave in the minds of their readers rather pain
than delight, for it should reasonably please no one that a thing
should be interrupted when it is most delightful. And I do not find
it true that the attention is stimulated but rather that it is less-
ened, because it is fired with desire of knowing the end not when
the narrative that has been begun is abandoned for another, but
when the outcome is delayed by many accidents that pertain to
the same subject. If that is a virtue the epic poet is not without it,
because he is intent on a single principal action of a single man.
For though he is not episodic, as are the romancers, yet he inserts
so many episodes in his poem that if episodic structure were not a
vice he would sometimes be able to use it. Vergil, for example,
could have left Turnus shut up in the Trojan fort and passed to
the council and to the assembly of the gods, and then returned to
liberate Turnus, not without injury to his enemies, if he had
thought that this leaving off of his narrative could reasonably

19 Cf. the distinction made by Edward Phillips, *Theatrum Poetarum*, sect. 8, below.

delight; he could also have found occasion in other places for use of the same method.

Book II

[Fortune and purgation in tragedy. 76]

Min. You will understand the end of tragic poetry when you have learned the function of the tragic poet, which is nothing other than to speak in verse in such a way that he may so teach, delight, and move[20] that he purges the passions from the minds of the spectators. Like every other dramatic poet, he is said to teach when he presents his poem in the theater, and in addition he brings especially before our eyes the example of the life and the manners of those who surpass others in greatness and in dignity and the favors of Fortune, and yet are through human error thrown into extreme unhappiness, so we may understand that in prosperity we are not to put our trust in worldly things, and that there is no one down here so long lived or so stable that he is not frail and mortal, no one so happy that he cannot become miserable, no one so great that he cannot become humble and low. And seeing in another so great a change of fortune, we should know how to guard ourselves that no unexpected evil may come upon us.[21] And if any evil does come upon us (since our nature is so subject to evil that it often molests us) we may know how with a patient spirit to sustain it. The same poet also, in addition to the pleasing quality of his verse, and the ornaments of speech, also delights us greatly with song, with the dance, and with spectacle, nor does he represent to us anything that does not please us, nor does he move us without delight;[22] but with the power of his words and with the weight of his thought he arouses passion in the mind and induces astonishment in it, both filling it with horror and moving it to pity. What is so tragic as to move another? And what moves so much as a terrible and miserable and unexpected happening, such as the cruel death of Hippolytus, the

[20] For the addition of *moving* to the Horatian *teach and delight* (*Art of Poetry*, 333, above) cf. Sidney, *Defense*, sect. 26, below, and the appendix to the *Defense*.

[21] The concept of Fortune is highly important in Renaissance tragedy, as is apparent on reading Jonson's *Sejanus.* Cf. Sidney's presentation of the tragic uncertainty of life and the overthrow of the great (*Defense*, sect. 32, below). Perhaps there was some influence of the line from Horace: "Then the fortune of kings, with their hands bound behind them, is dragged on the stage" (*Epistles*, II, 1, 191). See *fortune* in the index.

[22] See Aristotle, *Poetics*, VI, 49b20, above, and *purgation* in the index.

fierce and compassion-moving madness of Hercules, the unhappy exile of Oedipus? Yet this horror and this pity by delighting us purge us from like passions, because more than anything else they restrain the untamed fury of the human soul, for no one is so overcome by unrestrained appetites that if he is moved by fear and pity for the unhappiness of another, his soul is not purged of the passions which have been the cause of that unhappy state.[23] And the recollection of the grave misfortunes of others not merely makes us quicker and better prepared to support our own, but wiser and more skillful in escaping similar evils. A physician will not have greater capacity to expel with poisonous medicine the fiery poison of an illness which afflicts the body, than the tragic poet will to purge the mind of mighty perturbations with the force of the passions charmingly expressed in verses. And if music with the singing of words in the sacrifices purged the human soul, will not the harmony of the poet as well be able to do it?

[Experience brings about purgation. 77]

Let us consider then how much assistance experience in adversity gives in bearing lightly the chances of human life, and how easily is sustained that fatigue to which one is accustomed. Now will not being accustomed to the passions make more easy the bearing of them? Neither is it true that in proportion as we listen to trage-dies our passions are increased because the tragic stories move our spirits and perturb us.[24] On the contrary if it happens that we must be perturbed very seriously, we may bear our sufferings very lightly, for when we receive a wound we have foreseen, it must needs give us less pain, since no unexpected evil comes to him who is accustomed to be moved by the many and strange things that happen to others. Besides, if exercising ourselves with labors makes our bodies more apt to endure them without distress, and to this end the ancient laws and customs of Crete and Sparta are directed, will it be beyond reason that if we often hear and see in the theaters that which greatly disturbs us and horrifies us, our spirits may learn to bear easily the blows of fortune? Therefore, it may be held that no teaching is to be found which so much abates the passions of the mind as does tragic poetry, since she does not present before our eyes a single thing that cannot come

---

[23] Horace, *Art of Poetry*, 344, note, above.

[24] A marginal note indicates that this passage is a refutation of the opinion of Plato that tragic perturbations augment the passions (*Republic*, III, above).

about, and clearly presents to us the condition of man as though she were a brightly shining mirror;[25] and he who in this mirror sees the nature of things and the variety of life and the weakness of man does not grieve over it, when he thinks carefully on it, but wishing to act like a wise man, he will be able when fortune is adverse to console himself in three ways. First, because for a long time he will have considered that adversity might come upon him, and such a thought is excellent above every other remedy in its power to free the soul from every affliction. Next, because he understands that men must bear the accidents that happen to them. Lastly, because he knows nothing is evil except sin, and there should not be attributed to sin what does not proceed from a man's own will.

Angelo. From this discourse of yours I understand you have wished to show not merely that it is true that tragedy by means of pleasure purges the passions from the soul, as Aristotle thinks, but that one ought to hold the opinion of Plato false, for he blamed poetry because it fills the mind with perturbations.

Min. You have completely understood everything.

[Subjects and characters of tragedy. 78]

Ang. Since you have made the end of the tragic poet open and plain to us, tell us what his matter is.

Min. It cannot be doubted that it should be magnificent and serious, dealing with great and famous persons and marvelous and notable actions, since it represents to us what in ancient times chanced to the demigods and describes to us the things they did and suffered, yet not all of them, but only those that had a terrifying and miserable end. But because you will find that some men of this excellent type are good and some are evil and some partake of both qualities, being neither superior to the others in virtue nor so vicious that the responsibility for the unhappiness with which they are wounded by Fortune should be wholly attributed to them, it is not reasonable that the good, or even the evil, should be represented in the theater in whatever adversity they have fallen into; it is not merely unsuitable but is esteemed an unworthy and abominable thing to bring into the view of

---

[25] Cf. the prologue to Marlowe's *Tamburlaine:*
    View but his picture in this tragic glass,
    And then applaud his fortune as you please.
    See *mirror* in the index.

others those who, being of the best morals and ornamented with the greatest virtue, find themselves crushed by the blows of some wicked and horrible chance. . . . We may feel indignant, then, and have great displeasure at the adverse fortune of men famous for their virtue and perfect, but the ills of wicked and vile men do not appear to us worthy of pity. . . . Whence among those who are on a high level of glory and fortune, that man will be represented in the theater by the tragic poet who is not best and most excellent in virtue, nor altogether void of it; in fact, he will be rather more good than bad, and unhappy rather more through human error than through his own deliberate wickedness, as were Oedipus, Thyestes, and Creon. For this same reason the fortune of tragedy does not make a miserable and sorrowful man glad and happy, since there is nothing in such a change that is shocking or excites pity. This is confirmed by the fact that the business of the tragic poet is to put his reader into a condition of astonishment. And we consider those accidents astonishing that move us to compassion or horror, and yet the more when they come about with probability against our hopes and opinions, since events brought about by fortune, though of themselves they do not appear very worthy to cause astonishment, yet greatly excite us to wonder when we think they come about through the divine will or as the result of a plan.[26]

[Tragic subjects not approved by Aristotle. 81]

Min. That especially belongs to the tragic poet which fills the hearer with astonishment by horrifying him or moving him to compassion, and what we receive from an enemy is not so horrifying nor so pitiable that we ought to marvel at it, for it is not a very strange thing that one enemy should fiercely kill another, and evil that happens to the good excites in us anger and vexation rather than horror or compassion, as we have shown. You cannot deny, then, that if we are intent on what pure tragedy demands as suitable to it, we are forced to include its truly appropriate material within such narrow limits. Yet since tragedies are found of which the plots are double, as we shall explain, and many things happen which cause great astonishment not because of the person to whom they happen or by whom they are done, but in themselves, either through their novelty, as in the death of

[26] This whole section may be compared with Aristotle, *Poetics* XIII, above, as an example of Renaissance modification of Greek theory.

Macaria,[27] or because the action is full of inhumanity, as was the case of the miserable Trojan women,[28] we may widen the range of subjects suitable to tragedy and define it in such a way that whoever suffers a marvelous thing, if it is horrifying or causes compassion, will not be outside the scope of tragedy, whether he be good or whether he be evil.[29] As to Aristotle's saying that the finest tragedies are few for no other reason except that it comes to few to suffer or do things serious and terrible, you see clearly that in such cases one must consider him who suffers the ill and him who causes it. And with regard to him who causes it there is no doubt that the precept is true that he should be a friend or relative to him who receives death or wounds or similar afflictions. But considering him who suffers, even though he be an enemy and deserves pain, his case is not therefore wholly unworthy of compassion.

Book IV

[Sentences.[30] 282a]

Ferrante. Since to complete this discussion of Tuscan poetry there remains only to speak of ideas, which are also called sentences, and of words, what do we need to know to explain this part which is concerned entirely with speech?

Min. That which the rhetoricians and the masters of poetry teach, that the language should be Tuscan, that it should be clear, that it should be ornamented, and that it should be decorously suited and well-fitted to what is treated and narrated.

Fer. But since all that we include under the word *speech* means what is perceived by the mind and is conceived within before it is expressed outwardly, one should ask about sentences before words. What is a sentence?

[27] In *De poeta*, p. 184, Minturno writes: "In the *Children of Hercules* by Euripides, the Pythia answered that the brothers of Macaria would not be safe and victorious unless some virgin should be slain as a victim to Ceres. Therefore, that they might gain the victory, Macaria of her free will presented herself to be sacrificed."

[28] Euripides, *The Trojan Women*.

[29] In *De poeta*, Minturno argues for the death of Christ as a tragic subject: "Events are not lacking that can strike terror to our spirits" (p. 184).

[30] See the definition on p. 294, *sentence* in the index, and Webster's *New Int. Dict.*, 2d ed., under *sentence*, nos. 1, 3, 11.

Scaliger says that sentences are "columns or pillars that support the whole fabric of tragedy" (*Poetice*, III, 97, p. 145D1).

Min. I do not wish you to think that anything contained in the mind and then unfolded in words is included under the name of the sentence, because Aristotle (than whom no one ever taught better about it and its components and where it is properly uttered and by whom) defines it as a saying by means of which at a fit time a grave person, not ignorant of the things he speaks of, gives judgment not on any chance topic but on the course one should follow as excellent and good or flee as bad and wicked, generally and not particularly.[31] Or anything may be said particularly and yet illustrate the general idea of the sentence. The sentence does nothing else than argue and prove what the judgment says, or oppose it or bring forward something against it or entirely refute it. It serves also to awaken in the mind fear, pity, wrath, envy, and other passions, to amplify and increase what of itself does not appear marvelous, and to diminish what is too much so; for the chief glory of the poet is held to consist in his power to augment things that are by nature great or miserable or hateful; and to what is not of that sort he gives the reputation of being so.

[Examples of sentences. 282b]

Hence sentences are sometimes the beginnings of arguments, as

Gluttony and sleep and mattresses that encourage repose have driven all virtue from the world.

The conclusion is that he who is eager to acquire virtue flees a lazy and soft life. Sentences also form the conclusions of arguments, as

Therefore, alas, it must needs be that lamentation crowds close on laughter.

The cause is added, that Fortune is envious,

And a glad season endures but a little while.

The argument can easily be completed. There are also to be found sentences which, though they are not parts of an argument, yet have some likeness to one, since they include within themselves the cause; and these are much praised, as

But it does not please you to look so low with your proud spirit.

And

What do you do? What do you think? for you only look back to the time to which you can never return.

[31] This definition is apparently derived from Aristotle's *Rhetoric*, II, 21.

Because she has a proud spirit, it does not please her to look so low. And, since the time that is past cannot return, in vain he looks upon it. There are other sentences that do not need to be confirmed by reason; they may be commonly accepted, as

> Oh, how easy he is to deceive who is sure of himself!

And

> What the heavens forbid cannot well be done by a man.

Or they may be plain and clear, such as these:

> Truly we are dust and shadow; truly our desire is blind and greedy; truly hope is not to be trusted.

Sentences that like these are simple and require no reason (since they contain nothing to cause astonishment) are very pleasing. From this can clearly be seen that sentences on things doubtful and uncertain and beyond the knowledge of anyone properly have a reason added. This can be done in two ways; the reason can go before, as in

> Whence I, because eager ever to keep together what an hour dissipates, wish to embrace what is true, abandoning shadows.

Or the reason may follow, as

> O blind men, what does it avail to be so busy?
> You all return to your great ancient mother
> And your name is scarcely heard again.

And in things which are not beyond all doubt, brief and cautious sayings go well, provided you have shown why they are uttered, as

> You find me in action much more slow and weak than a little branch, bent by a great weight. And I have said he is likely to fall who climbs too high.

Also obscure sayings, as

> What are you doing? What are you thinking of? Why do you always look backward, disconsolate spirit? Why do you keep on adding wood to the flame with which you burn?

And countrymen, who often utter praiseworthy sentences on matters of which they have experience, teach us that sententious sayings are appropriate to the aged, as well as to those who do not lack authority and are not ignorant of the affairs of which they speak sententiously. Therefore aged men are brought on the stage in order that with sayings full of reason they may commend, reprehend, admonish, comfort, and terrify. Nor should there be any doubt that it is proper for one who understands them to speak universally of particular things, in order to secure belief and confidence, either when something is decided or there is an intention to decide what was taken up for demonstration; that is especially appropriate which comprises some general idea, if everyone or almost everyone accepts it. It is reasonable for the poets to use generally known and familiar sayings as common property, such as are the following:

> That which so pleases the world is a brief dream.
> Human resistance does not avail against the heavens.
> A beautiful death sheds honor on a whole life.
> He makes a good end who dies loving well.

Proverbs are also of this sort:

> It is possible in fine quarters to be unhappy, and there is good lodging in every city.

And obscure sayings:

> An evil tribute is a heavy load to carry.
> The fig is a bitter sight.
> He spreads his nets to catch nothing.

To sentences commonly accepted, human feeling and bad morals are sometimes opposed. There is no one who does not praise virtue above everything else and set the pursuit of it above everything else; yet against this there is a common sentence:

> What beauty has the laurel, what the myrtle? Philosophy goes poor and naked, says the throng intent on vile gain.

In conformity with the common opinion is the following complaint:

> This has made me love God less than I should, and care less for myself.

Contrary to it is this reply:

> Who is in favor then, who realizes it, with God and with the people?

This has its place in a few instances. That class of sentences in which some have dealt with things does not displease me, as

> Wrath is a brief madness.

Others in this group deal with persons, as

> Infinite is the troop of the fools.

Nor do I reject the group of sentences in which some pertain to intellectual habits, of whatever sort, through which we get the knowledge of things; there are not a few examples in the *Rime* of Dante, and in the *Triumph of Time* and the *Triumph of Divinity*.[32] Others in this group deal with morals, and their purpose is to make life better and encourage good works; the *Canzoniere* of Petrarch are full of such sentences. An intellectual sentence is the following:

> Just as eternal life is to behold God, and nothing more is to be desired nor is it possible to desire more; so, Lady, to see you makes me happy in this short and frail life of mine.

This one is moral:

> Miserable is he who puts his hope in a mortal thing (but who does not put it there?); and if he finds himself deceived at the end, there is a good reason for it.

Since the functions of the poet are that he should teach well, that he should delight, and that he should move, another excellent classification of sentences is that they should be of these various kinds. Those that teach are acute, as the following:

> The end praises life, the evening the day.

Those that delight are witty, as

> Blessed are thy eyes that see her alive.

And

> If he was blessed who saw her on earth what will he then be who sees her again in heaven?

Those that move are serious:

> So in the world each man has his chance from the day he is born.

And

> Truly we are dust and shadow.

[32] Semi-epical and allegorical poems by Petrarch.

Commonly sentences are given in the direct order of the words, as

> The miserable man is he who puts hope in mortal things.

Yet when the order of the words is changed they acquire greater force, as

> Miserable world, unstable and shameless, he is wholly blind who puts his hope in you.

And with how much more spirit was that saying that Death is ready in a moment to take from us the fruit of many and long labors uttered by Petrarch, crying out with the accent of sorrow and turning his speech to Death!

> Ah, wicked Death, how ready you are to pluck off the fruit of many years in a few hours!

And that other:

> One hour scatters what was hardly gathered together in many years.

And does not a sentence affect us more forcibly when there is an outcry and demand for hearing in this manner?

> Oh, our life, which is so beautiful to look on, how in a morning man easily loses what in many years he earned with great pain!

And

> What does it avail to subjugate so many cities and make strange peoples tributaries, with their minds ever fired by their woes?

This has more vigor than if it were put in a statement:

> It does not avail to subjugate so many cities.

The vigor of a sentence is augmented when its application is transferred from the general to the particular, as in

> If I love with such wondrous faith a little fading mortal earth, what noble thing ought I to do for you?

The general and direct statement would be that one should love with greater faith the celestial and holy things than the earthly and fading, but what pertains to the universal is attributed to a special person. Nor are they expressed merely with an outcry and violent sighs, as in this:

> O time, O rolling heavens, how in your flight you deceive blind and miserable mortals!

It may be put with gravity to confirm what is spoken:

Everything flies toward its end, so great is the power of a custom that is laid down.

Not seldom are sentences based on unlike things, as

Death cannot make the sweet sight bitter, but the sweet sight can make Death sweet.

They are also based on contraries:[33]

I see the better and apply myself to the worse.

Not a few sentences deal with things similar and things unexpected and things repeated and there are many other classes which the masters of rhetoric treat.

[How to use sentences. 286]

Sentences give vigor and light to speech if they are used rarely and when need requires them, for the silent auditor agrees with them, understanding that something which is uttered as appertaining universally to life and morals is in conformity with his particular opinion. The sentence will conform to the judgment of the hearer if, as the dramatic poet writes, he attains in his conjecture what the reader commends and accepts. These sentences enable the poem to present characters and habits, because through them the disposition and tendency of the mind, and the qualities and appetite of the man who speaks are revealed. Therefore, since the sentiments of the mind are thought to be the same as the affection and the desire and the choice and habit of conduct of each man, good speeches signify goodness, and wicked ones signify wickedness on the part of him who utters them. And an author must take care not merely that his sentences shall not be false, or inappropriate, but that they shall not be obscure or intricate or too abundant. Who ever agrees to what he does not understand? How can that be luminous which is hidden? And how can the multitude of these illuminate the work if it is less splendid because of their number? The stars do not show themselves to us as more shining or more beautiful when they are crowded than when they are scattered. Nor does gold ornament purple into which it is woven if the masses of gold have no in-

---

[33] This and the unlike or diverse things mentioned just above are from Renaissance logic. See the translation of Milton's *Art of Logic*, I, 14–15, in his *Works*, Columbia University Press, XI.

tervals between them. The fruits also on the trees in proportion as they are fewer become larger and more beautiful and finer. It results from too great profusion that the language of a verse that is short and cramped will be made up rather of pieces than of members, and it will lack that round and full and graceful composition that brings majesty and beauty to the work, nor can such verses escape appearing cold, weightless, sapless, and badly planned, since selection is lacking where number is great. And when you insert sentences in your poem, remember you are not a teacher of manners nor of learning, but one who is narrating; you should introduce them in the action and the words of someone else.

[Where sentences are most used. 287]

Fer. What poet most often uses the sentence?

Min. The tragic poet more often than all the others, since he treats the matter to which the sentence is most suited, and he introduces characters whom it is fitting to commend, to blame, to admonish, and to comfort sententiously. After him comes the comic poet and especially the poet of Old Comedy, who brings the chorus into the theater to say things useful to the city, since they wish that comedy shall be found to bring about reform in men's lives. After the comic comes the satiric poet, as one who reprehends vices and indecent things. Then follows the lyric poet, who, whether he praises or dispraises, treats many things pertaining to morals. Finally comes the heroic, who, though in the gravity and abundance of high sentiments he surpasses the others, yet scatters but sparingly in his poem things usually thought of as sententious, since it is not his function to reprehend or to blame,[34] and his speakers do not enter into contests of words, but he undertakes to narrate, sometimes simply and sometimes imitatively, illustrious acts and those worthy of eternal memory; in certain places he brings in sentences as though they were lamps, especially when there appears something new and unexpected which can be illustrated with the sentence, as

But grace divine was never slow.

And

What more than a single day is human life, cloudy, short, cold, and full of sorrow? It may seem beautiful but has no worth.

[34] This was a matter of debate. See Mazzoni's opinion, *Of the Defense of the* "*Comedy,*" Bk. IV, chap. XXXVI, below.

Book IV

[Imitation; whom to imitate. 445 a]

It is of no little importance what sort of poet you set before yourself for imitation,[35] since imitation is not strong enough to equal the thing chosen for imitation and to represent it as it is; moreover copying may encounter the difficulty that nature herself cannot bring it to pass that copies cannot be distinguished from the things that are represented and imitated. Hence if we take as our examples poets of little merit, we shall fall to such a depth that we shall deserve no praise. If we use as our models those of greater merit, when we fall we shall nevertheless remain among the number of those who are much praised. It is true that we shall not have much difficulty in making choice of those whom it is wise to imitate, since among us Petrarch alone is found to whom we ought to make ourselves similar with all our industry and all our zeal. I do not wish what I say to be understood as meaning that I think there is nothing in the others that should be imitated. But things worthy of imitation are not easily recognized, especially by one who, being far from perfection, hopes by imitation to attain it. Nor does that imitation please me that takes over some passage in similar words, or rather in the same words, unless it is from a writer of foreign speech, since the taking of word for word from strange authors, as the Latins did from the Greeks, and as ours have from the one and the other of them, always has been and always will be praised.

[How to imitate. 445 b]

But who will ever praise imitating the moderns, if you do not make what is taken yours to such an extent that it will not any more appear to belong to others? In such borrowing your activity is properly to be praised not merely in that it is like that of the bees, who sometimes change the softness of the flowers into the sweetness of honey, in such a way that in the honey nothing of the flowers can be recognized, but also because it knows so well how to make another's work its own that what is borrowed seems to

[35] On imitation see Horace, *Art of Poetry*, 268–9, 318, above; Longinus, xiii, above; and the index. The precept of imitation is carried to the utmost in Vida's *Art of Poetry*, especially Bk. iii, 185–95, 210–32, 257–63. Vida's work, with an English translation, appears in Albert S. Cook's *The Art of Poetry* (Boston, 1892), and later editions. Erasmus says something on imitation in his *Dialogus Ciceronianus*, *Opera* (1703) I, 985 B-E.

have sprung up in your own garden and not to have been transplanted from that of another. Wherefore I think it is permitted to everyone to use the manner of speech of the author he has selected for imitation, the words being either his own or changed, and he may also be so bold as to change his speech according to the example of the one imitated, for since the very model has taken many things from others, and yet has changed many words, our author permits himself to do only what the one imitated thought was permitted. Among the other things the imitator finds in his model, I rank that poetic style itself which he ought to follow as suitable to him. He will follow this way who does not take the facts and the words of which his poem is composed, but who uses the same method of obtaining and arranging matter and the same form of speech.[36] And since it has been demonstrated from what logical places[37] are taken those ornaments which make speech splendid, our imitative author will take changes in words and ornaments of speech to be used in describing the same thing or a similar thing from no other place than that whence the one set up for imitation took them.

[Examples of imitation. 446 a]

For example, Petrarch drew on the place of consequences when, wishing to signify where he was born, he said:

> Is not this the land that I first touched?

Taking your thought from the same place you will easily write:

> Is not this that heaven in the light of which I first opened my weak eyes?

Or

> Is not this that clime where were heard the first cries I uttered?

And Vergil having said:

> If they arrive at the lights of life,

---

[36] This topic is developed with examples in the *Della imitatione poetica* (Vinega, 1560) of Bernardino Parthenio.

[37] The classes of things from which the logicians and rhetoricians drew the arguments were called places or, by a name derived from the Greek, topics. Cicero wrote a work called *Topica*, to which Minturno refers in a discussion of places in Bk. IV, p. 417. Some of the places are genus, species, similarity, difference, equality, and cause. Ramus presents these in his rhetorical logic. See the translation of Milton's Ramist *Logic* in his *Works*, Columbia University Press, XI.

cannot it likewise be said:

> If ever they come to perceive the cold down here.

For before they issue from the wombs of their mothers they perceive nothing other than heat. And as Vergil changing place and taking from the antecedents said:

> From the high heaven now a new race is coming,

so not dissimilarly you may say:

> When the gentle soul descended from the sky.

Taking from one and the other place, Petrarch said:

> Which had descended to suffer heat and cold.

LODOVICO CASTELVETRO

o◯ooo◯o

THE POETICS OF ARISTOTLE TRANSLATED AND ANNOTATED

1571

IT IS NOT AN ACCIDENT that in recent times Lodovico Castelvetro has attracted perhaps more attention than any other Italian critic of the Renaissance, certainly more than any other who is not both poet and critic. His commentary on Aristotle is full, explicit, and painstaking, and yet often acute; he is, moreover, not afraid to take what in his day were unpopular positions, as in his assertions that pleasure is the end of poetry and that the poet need not be a learned man. Yet his abilities were recognized to such an extent that the references of sixteenth-century writers to critics and commentators are likely to include him or to refer to him alone. It is not strange that in the next century Milton thought of him as one of the chief expositors of Aristotle's *Poetics*. Notwithstanding his well-deserved reputation, he is not without faults, usually those of the scholar. He is unnecessarily prolix, and though willing to revolt against the thought of his own age, he is under the authority of Aristotle. Though familiar with Italian literature, he yet regards it through the eyes of former critics rather than seeing it as something not quite amenable to Greek principles. Thoroughgoing in his rationalism, he has the unenviable distinction of having formulated the so-called unities of place and time. Yet within his limits he is admirable; he sees how Aristotle can be applied, and few important ideas in the literary thought of his age escape his analysis, as will appear on looking in the index for any of the topics he treats.

The translation is by the editor.

BIBLIOGRAPHY

Castelvetro, Lodovico, *Poetica d'Aristotele vulgarizzata et sposta*. Basel, 1576.

Charlton, H. B., *Castelvetro's Theory of Poetry*. Manchester, 1913.

Fusco, Antonio, *La poetica di Lodovico Castelvetro*. Naples, 1904.

ON THE POETICS (*selections*)

Chapter I

[Poetry and matter-of-fact. 28, 13¹]

Aristotle writes that the sciences and the arts and history are not subjects for poetry. And I, who in this matter hold an opinion not at all different from that of Aristotle and think it wholly true, believe that I can bring forward the reasons that have induced me to hold such beliefs, which, if they are not the very same as Aristotle presented, are perhaps not very different; I have already incidentally mentioned some of them and taken them for granted; they are these. Poetry is the similitude or likeness of history. Just as history is divided into matter and words, so poetry is divided into two principal parts, which are likewise matter and words, but in these two parts history and poetry differ from each other, because history does not have matter that is given to it by the abilities of the historian, but its matter is furnished by the course of worldly events, or by the will, either manifest or hidden, of God. It has, in truth, words given to it by the historian, but they are such as are used in reasoning. The matter of poetry is found and imagined by the ability of the poet, and its words are not such as are used in reasoning, since men do not generally reason in verse, but the words of poetry are composed in measured verse by the exercise of the poet's powers.

[The poet's effort. 28, 30]

Now the matter of poetry should be like the matter of history and resemble it, but it ought not to be the same, for, if it were the same, it would not be like it or resemble it, and if it were not like it or did not resemble it, the poet in dealing with such material would not have labored at all, and would not have showed keenness of intellect in finding it; therefore he would not merit praise and especially he would not merit that through which he is reputed to be more divine than human, for he knows how to deal with a story, imagined by himself about things that have not happened, and yet to make it not less delightful nor less like the truth than

---

¹ The figures indicate the page and first line of the section in the edition of 1576; they are used to indicate the whole section. The division into sections is the work of the present editor, who is also the translator. Chapters are those of Aristotle's *Poetics*.

is the history produced by the course of mundane events or by the infinite providence of God, whether manifest or hidden. In taking his matter from history, that is, from things that have already happened, the poet does not endure any fatigue, nor does it thence appear whether he is a good poet or a bad one, that is, whether he knows or does not know how skillfully to find things like the truth, and he cannot be praised for producing a resemblance of them; rather he is to be blamed and is thought of as endowed with but a weak judgment because he has not recognized this. Moreover he is thought to have a wicked and deceptive nature, because with the force and color of poetic language he has wished to dupe his readers or hearers, making them believe that beneath his words there was some poetic matter, and acquiring false commendation for it. Therefore Lucan, Silius Italicus, and Girolamo Fracastoro in his *Joseph*[2] are to be removed from the ranks of the poets and deprived of the glorious title of poetry,[3] because they have in their writings dealt with matter already treated by historians; and even though it had not first been treated by the historians, it is enough that it had happened before and was not imagined by the authors mentioned.

[Science in poetry. 29, 10]

From this it can also be comprehended that science and art cannot be matter for poetry and cannot well be included in a poem, since, so far as the poet is concerned, the science and the art which have already been considered and understood through reasons necessary and having the appearance of truth, and through long experience by philosophers and artists, take the same position as history and things that have already happened. The poet merely covers with poetical words a subject from science or from art that has been found and written about by others, and on which it can be said that history has already been composed; the

---

[2] This passage raises the question of the suitability of the life of a Biblical hero for poetry. In England poems by Sylvester, Quarles, and Cowley (*Davideis*) are of this type. Milton must have been interested in the problem as well, for *Paradise Lost* is to some extent a poem on the life of Adam, though it also has affinities with the cosmological Biblical poem, such as that of Du Bartas.

[3] Dante considered Lucan one of the five great poets of antiquity into whose company he represented himself as admitted in *Inferno* iv, 90. Dante's theory of poetry obviously did not deny the poet a well-known subject. His belief in allegory probably influenced him. See the selection from Dante, above. Ben Jonson said of Du Bartas "that he thought not Bartas a Poet but a Verser, because he wrote not Fiction" (*Conversations with Drummond*).

poet has no part in it by reason of which he can boast himself a poet. Therefore one should not marvel if those versifiers,[4] Empedocles,[5] Lucretius, Nicander, Serenus, Girolamo Fracastoro in his *Siphylis*, Aratus, Manilius, Giovanni Pontano in his *Urania*, Hesiod, and Vergil in the *Georgics* are not received into the number of the poets, for even though they have been the first to think out some science or art and have not taken it from any philosopher, they should not therefore be called poets, because if they have thought out the truth of some science or art, and have discovered something that was and will be perpetually in the nature of things, and with which that science is concerned and by which that art is constituted, they have still performed the function of a good philosopher and of a good scientist but not that of a good poet.

[Poetry is delightful. 29, 32]

The poet's function is after consideration to give a semblance of truth to the happenings that come upon men through fortune,[6] and by means of this semblance to give delight to his readers; he should leave the discovery of the truth hidden in natural or accidental things to the philosopher and the scientist, who have their own way of pleasing or giving profit which is very remote from that of the poet. Besides, there is another reason more manifest to sense why the matter of the sciences and the arts cannot be the subject of poetry; poetry has been discovered solely to delight and to recreate,[7] I say to delight and to recreate the minds of the crude multitude and of the common people,[8] who do not understand the reasons and the divisions and the arguments, subtle and far from the practice of ordinary men, which the philosophers use in investigating the truth of things,[9] and professional men in their labors. It is not proper that a listener, when anyone addresses him, should feel irritation and displeasure, for it naturally annoys us excessively when anyone speaks to us in such a way that we are

[4] See *versifiers*, in the index.
[5] See Aristotle, *Poetics*, I, above. The authors mentioned all wrote on scientific subjects, such as astronomy, medicine, and agriculture.
[6] Fortune would have no power over nature.
[7] For Tasso's opposite opinion see *Of the Heroic Poem*, sect. 7, below. Castelvetro repeats this idea (122, 13; 275, 30; 279, 24; 295, 6; 505, 40; 552, 42; 592, 14; 696, 26; and elsewhere).
[8] This belief is reiterated near the end of the work (679, 35). Cf. Mazzoni, *On the Defense of the "Comedy,"* Bk. v, chap. IV, below.
[9] Cf. Sidney's remark on the "quiddity of *ens* and *prima materia*" (*Defense*, sect. 42, below).

unable to understand him. Therefore if we concede that the matter of the sciences and of the arts can be the subject of poetry, we should concede also either that poetry was not discovered for delight or that it was not intended for the plain people, but in order that it might teach and for the benefit of persons well skilled in letters and in disputations. This will be recognized as false through what we shall prove as we go further.[10]

[Poetry is for the common people.   30, 7]

Now because poetry has been discovered, as I say, to delight and recreate the common people, it should have as its subject those things that can be understood by the common people and when understood can make them happy.[11] These are the things that happen every day and that are spoken of among the people, and that resemble historical accounts and the latest reports about the world. For this reason we affirm, with respect to matter, that poetry is the similitude or resemblance of history; this matter, because it only resembles the truth, not merely renders its inventor glorious, and makes and constitutes him a poet, but delights more than does the history of things that have happened. . . . Because, then, the matter of the sciences and the arts is not understood by the people, not merely should it be avoided and shunned as the subject of a poem, but care must also be taken that no part of these arts and sciences is used in any part of the poem. In this matter Lucan and Dante in his *Comedy* have especially sinned without any necessity, for these poets by means of astrology show the seasons of the year and the hours of the day and the night.[12] Homer and Vergil in his *Aeneid* never fell into this error. I cannot do other than wonder somewhat at Quintilian, who thinks that no one can understand the poets well who is not versed in the art of astronomy and instructed in philosophy.[13]

[10] On the erudition of the poet see 591, 30, below.
[11] Milton invoked his muse thus: "Fit audience find, though few" (*Paradise Lost*, VII, 31). But he probably had in mind moral rather than intellectual fitness. When he addressed the learned, as in his *Christian Doctrine*, he wrote in Latin. For suggestions that he held a popular theory of poetry, see the *Reason of Church Government*, sect. 2, below.
[12] Against the charge of too abstruse reference to astrology Dante is defended by Mazzoni (*Dalla difesa di Dante*, v, 12). A passage he especially vindicates is *Paradise*, I, 37–42: "The lantern of the world rises to mortals through divers openings, but from that which joins four circles with three crosses it issues with a more propitious course and joined with a more favorable star."
[13] *Institutes*, I, 4.

Chapter III

[Drama and narrative. 56, 28]

The dramatic manner, which, as we said, employs things where the original had things, and words in direct discourse where the original had words, is different from the narrative, first, in that it uses words and things instead of the original words and things, while narrative uses words alone in the place of things and indirect discourse in the place of direct discourse. It is further different in that the dramatic is less ample, in respect to places, than the narrative, for the dramatic method cannot represent places very far apart, while the narrative method joins together places that are widely separated. It is also different in that the dramatic method is less ample with respect to time, for the narrative method joins together diverse times, something the dramatic method cannot do. In addition there is between them the difference that the narrative method tells things that are visible and invisible, audible and not audible, and the dramatic represents only things that are visible and audible. Still further they seem different in that the narrative does not so much move the hearers in those things that are connected with the feelings as does the dramatic. They are also much different in that the narrative relates many things, even though they are connected with the feelings, much better and more fully than the dramatic method presents them.

[Dramatic verisimilitude. 57, 1]

Because of the difficulty of representing actions and making them verisimilar, dramas do not present on the stage murders and other things that it is difficult to represent with dignity, and it is proper that they should be done off stage and then narrated by a messenger.[14] Still they are different because the narrative is able

[14] Castelvetro says also: "Reason shows that we are more moved by the sense of sight than by the sense of hearing; that is, we are more moved when we see something with our eyes than when we hear it narrated and take it in with our ears [from Horace, *Art of Poetry*, 180 ff.]. Therefore the poets should have murders and horrible things represented on the stage and make the people see them, exerting their powers to the utmost to produce terror and compassion in the audience. Yet they do not represent these horrible things, and if they do they are blamed for it, but they introduce a messenger or some other person who by the method of narrative makes the audience hear only, for experience has shown that such cruelty and horror cannot with verisimilitude be shown in action and that when shown they make the audience rather laugh than weep and that they produce the effect not of tragedy but of comedy" (289, 29–40). Cf. 296, 38; 550, 18–22. Is this illustrated by O'Neill's *Mourning Becomes Electra?*

to relate in a few hours many things that happened in many hours, and to relate in many hours a few things that happened in a few hours. But the dramatic method, which spends as many hours in representing things as was taken by the actions themselves, is able to do none of these things; thence it comes about that tragedy and comedy, which are members of the dramatic class, cannot last longer than the time allowed by the convenience of the audience, nor represent more things than those which come about in the space of time that the comedies and the tragedies themselves require.[15] And as I say, there must always be regard to the ease of the people, for after some hours the people have to leave the theater because of the human necessities for eating, drinking, sleeping, and other things.[16]

Chapter IV

[Poetic inspiration. 65, 11]

Aristotle was not of the opinion that poetry was a special gift of God bestowed on one man rather than on another, as is the gift of prophecy and other similar privileges that are not natural and common to all. Without doubt he intends, though he does not say it openly, to refute the opinion that some attribute to Plato, that poetry is infused into men through divine madness. This opinion had its origin and source in the ignorance of the common people and has been increased and favored by the vainglory of the poets for the following reasons and in the following manner. Anything done by someone else is highly regarded and seems marvelous to those who have not the power to do it themselves, and because men commonly measure the forces of the body and of the ability of other men by comparison with their own, they reckon as a miracle and a special gift of God that which they do not know how to attain by their own natural powers, and see that others have attained. Hence the first poets were thought by the ignorant people to be full of the spirit of God and to be

[15] "The epic, narrating by means of words only, can relate an action that occupied many years and happened in various places without any difficulty, for the words present to our intellect things remote in place and time. But tragedy cannot do the same, for it must needs have as a subject an action that happened in a short space of time, that is in the extent of place and time just such as the actors actually use in the performance, and not otherwise as to place and time. . . . It is not possible to make the audience suppose that several days and nights have passed when they have the evidence of their senses that only a few hours have gone by" (Castelvetro, 109, 13-29).

[15] Similarly 109, 21-7; 534, 3.

aided by God. For the people admired beyond measure the invention of the story in poetic compositions and likewise the long
series of verses with which the story was set forth, and especially
so when they saw that the divine responses of Apollo were given
in such verses, for they thought that through these the gods spoke.
. . . This belief of the people, though false, was pleasing to the
poets, since through it great reputation came to them and they
were looked on as dear to the gods. Hence they nourished it with
their approval, and making it appear that the condition was as
the people thought, they began at the beginnings of their works
to call on the aid of the Muses and Apollo, the god set over poetry,
and to make it seem that they uttered their poems as though with
the mouths of the aforesaid gods. . . . It is wrong then to attribute
to Plato this opinion of the *furor* infused into the poets[17] because,
as I said, it originated with the people and the poets agreed to it
for the sake of their own interests. Plato, when he mentions it in
his books, surely is jesting, as in similar instances he often does;
for example, in the *Phaedrus* he says that the lover is possessed by
a *furor*. But since Plato wishes to prove that this does not mean
that the poet is therefore in the power of something evil, he adds
that it is a good madness which overcomes the priestesses in Delphi and the priests in Dodona, and the Sibyl and other diviners,
and the poets. Yet by this he does not prove that the poets are
possessed by a divine *furor*, but merely brings forward as examples
some similar things, in harmony with the popular belief. . . . He
writes in jest in the *Apology* of Socrates, when he says the poets do
not understand what they write in their poems when moved by
the divine *furor*.[18] This is clear enough, for if he were telling the
truth and believed that their poems proceeded from divine inspiration, why did he forbid them in his republic? . . .[19]

[Imitation. 68, 25]

The imitation that is natural to men is one thing and that
which is demanded of the poet is another.[20] For the imitation of

---

[17] See especially Plato's *Ion*, above, and for further references to the *furor poeticus*, or
inspiration of the poet, see the index.

[18] *Apology*, 22, quoted in the appendix to Plato's *Ion*, above.

[19] See Castelvetro's comment on *Poetics*, XVII, 374, 6, below.

[20] The Italian word here translated *imitation* is *rassomiglianza*, the equivalent of the
English *resemblance*. I regret that the English word has lost the flexibility and breadth
of meaning it once possessed, for it perhaps is less likely to mislead than the word
imitation. *Imitation*, however, is now generally used to render the Greek *mimesis* in the
passage Castelvetro is here considering (*Poetics*, IV, first par.).

others that is natural to men, that is in them from childhood and
by means of which they first learn, and to which all men are more
disposed than are the other animals, and which consequently
they are much pleased to engage in, is nothing else than a following of the examples of others and a doing of the things the others
do without knowing any cause why they should do so. But the
imitation the poet is expected to use not merely does not
follow the example laid down by another, or do the same thing
that has already been done without knowing the cause for doing
it, but does something completely separate from what has been
done and sets before itself, so to speak, another example to follow.
In following it, the poet must needs have an excellent knowledge
of the causes why he does what he does and must spend time in
reflection and careful reasoning, to such an extent that it can
securely be affirmed that the imitation demanded from the poet
is not and ought not to be called directly or properly imitation,
but should be or can be called the strife of the poet and the disposition of fortune, or of the course of mundane things, in finding
an incident of human conduct delightful to listen to and marvelous.

Chapter V

[Comic deception. 93, 4]

The second[21] class of pleasing things able to raise laughter in
us consists of deceptions; I mean those deceptions by reason of
which someone says or does or suffers things which he would
neither do nor say nor suffer if he were not deceived. The deception of someone pleases us excessively, then, and delights us and
constrains us to laugh for pleasure. The cause of this is our nature,
corrupted through the sin of our first parents, which rejoices at
the coming of evil upon someone else as at some benefit to ourselves, and especially rejoices at evil which proceeds from that
part which is peculiar to man, that is from the natural intellect,
for it appears to those who are not deceived, when they see others
deceived, that they are themselves better and that they surpass
them in that quality,[22] namely reason, in which men are nearest
to God and greatly superior to all the other animals. This is known

---

[21] He has been discussing laughter that is not comic, such as that of a mother on
seeing her children.

[22] This suggests the feeling of superiority in the theory of comedy associated with the
name of Hobbes.

to be true because men do not laugh or take pleasure, or at least not so much, if a neighbor is constrained by force or chance to say or do or suffer things against his will, provided that in him is seen no diminution of reason or of intellect, though he may receive a great deal of injury or dishonor. Now the deceptions that are material for laughter can be divided in four ways. The first is of the deceptions that come about through ignorance of those things which are in ordinary use and in the common understanding of men, as through drunkenness or sleep or delirium. The next class contains the deceptions that come about through ignorance of the arts and the sciences and of the powers of the body or the mind, when someone, before he has correctly estimated his capacity, boasts of something he cannot do. The third class contains those deceptions that result from an unexpected movement of things in another direction or through a turning of the point of a jest against the person who is the author of it. The last class contains those deceptions that proceed from tricks or from chance. [Castelvetro then gives a number of illustrations from the *Decameron* of Boccaccio.]

[Comic wickedness and defect. 97, 4]

The third type of amusing things that can move us to laughter comes from wickedness of the spirit and from defects of the body, with their results. Sometimes they are presented to us covertly, in such a way that we are able to appear to laugh at something else than such wickedness and defects and actions, for, as we have said, our nature, corrupted by the original sin handed down to us from our first parents, enjoys recognizing a defect in others, either because it appears less defective if it has many companions, or because the appearance of being much superior fills it with pleasure and pride, since it seems to itself to be without these defects. But it is true that such defects would not make us laugh if they were not revealed under some covering in such a way that anyone is able, by excusing himself and feigning, to give the appearance of laughing at something else. For no one would wish to have it appear that wickedness or the defect of someone pleased him, however much it might really please him, for so much of the light of God is given us that we would judge such pleasure to be evil. So when Master Ermino Grimaldi asked Guielmo Borsiere to tell him of something that had never been seen before to paint in his house, Guielmo said to him, indicating something that

Ermino had never seen: "Have courtesy painted there."[23] It was possible to understand this saying literally, that Master Ermino had never seen courtesy, since it is not a thing that can be seen or subjected to the bodily eyes, and yet it can be otherwise understood, namely, that he had always been avaricious and never had exercised courtesy. . . .

[Comic indecency. 97, 38]

The fourth and last kind of pleasing things that move us to laughter are all the things that pertain to carnal delight, as the secret parts of the body, lascivious connections, memories of them, and things that are like them. But it is to be noted that the aforesaid things do not make us laugh when they are set openly before the eyes of the body or of the mind in the presence of others; rather they overcome us with shame and make us blush, and especially if we are or can be such persons of whom under the circumstances there can be a suspicion that we enjoy such things and desire to do them or to experience them. For if we do not laugh or make some sign or say some word by which we give obvious testimony that this does not please us, it will be presumed that we would consent to similar indecencies and desire them because nature inclines us without restraint in their direction. . . . Then the aforesaid pleasing things make us laugh when they are presented in the presence of someone else under a veil by means of which we are able to give the appearance of laughing not at the indecency but at something else. This without any example is much more than obvious to everyone. They also make us laugh when they are presented without a veil, in fact or in word, in such a place that we are seen by no one.

Chapter VI

[The purging power of tragedy. 116, 34]

Since it appeared to Plato that tragedy through the example of the tragic persons might injure the citizens and lower their moral tone, making them vile, cowardly, and full of pity, he did not wish tragedy to be presented in his republic, for he thought, if the people heard and saw men of high reputation do and say the things they do on the stage, that the too compassionate, the

---

[23] *Decameron*, I, 8.

timorous, and the vile would console themselves, and pardon in themselves their softness of mind and fear and pusillanimity, for they would see that they have companions among the great, such as kings, and would learn to allow themselves to be carried farther than is fitting by such passions.[24] But Aristotle, in order that men should not believe on the authority of Plato that he himself, when writing on tragedy, had set out to present an art injurious to the citizens and likely to contaminate their morals, in a few words rejects what Plato says, affirming that tragedy has just the opposite effect, that is, that with its example and its frequent representation it changes the spectators from vile to magnanimous, from fearful to firm, and from over-pitying to strict,[25] for it is the opinion of Aristotle that continual experience with things worthy of pity, fear, and baseness does not make men too pitying, nor fearful, nor vile, because tragedy by means of the aforesaid passions, terror and pity, purges and drives out of the heart of men the passions that have been mentioned. Now I wish to make clearly understood what Aristotle perhaps has wished to say, and says rather obscurely and scarcely indicates, either because, as has been often said, the things put in this book are brief notes to be used for a larger work,[26] or because he did not wish openly to blame the opinion of his master Plato, being restrained by a certain reverence. It must be understood, then, that as pure wine of a certain quantity, with which not a drop of water has been mixed, has more vigor and spirit than has the same amount of wine of the same quality with which a large proportion of water has been mingled, for though it exceeds the other in quantity, yet through the addition of so much water it becomes watery and loses all its original vigor and spirit, so the love of fathers for their children is much greater and more fervent and they take better care of them when they have a few of them, that is, three or two or one, than if they have a large number, as a hundred or a thousand or more. In the same way the compassion and the fear of men, when exercised on a few pitiable and terrible cases, are more vigorous and more moving than when they are scattered over a large number of events deserving of pity and fear. Then tragedy, which represents

---

[24] See *Republic*, III, above.

[25] This astonishing overstatement represents a common interpretation of the catharsis; see the index.

[26] "We may, then, be certain of what we have many times said, namely, that this little book is a collection of confused matters and of memories of material from which a well-ordered art of poetry could be compiled" (Castelvetro, p. 280).

to us similar actions, and makes us see them and hear them much more frequently than we would see them or hear them without tragedy, causes fear and compassion to diminish in us, since we have to divide the effect of this passion among so many diverse actions. The clearest proof of this comes before our eyes in a time of pestilence, for at the beginning, when three or four persons die, we are moved with pity and terror, but when we see hundreds and thousands die, the emotion of pity and horror ceases in us. We know this also by experience in perilous skirmishes, for in these, new soldiers are at first terrified by the thunder of the guns and the arquebuses and have the greatest pity for those who are wounded and killed, but after they have been in several fights they stand firm and without being much affected by pity see before their eyes their companions wounded and die. These reasons, perhaps, though they are very strong, are not of so much importance that because of them the law forbidding tragedy should be annulled, for they are directed elsewhere, namely, toward what Plato had in mind in making his prohibition. And in order to see clearly how the matter stands, one must realize that there are persons who undergo experiences that are terrible and able to excite pity, such as those mentioned. These persons are of two sorts, that is the strong and the timid, and the actions in question are also of two sorts, namely the frequent and the infrequent, and the one and the other according to diversity of manners bring about diversity of effect. Hence if the persons who suffer are strong and enduring, with the example of their fortitude and endurance they affect the spirits of others and drive pity and fear away from them. But if the persons are timid and weak, with their example they increase the terror and the compassion of the beholders and confirm them in their fear and weakness of spirit. ... Likewise, if terrible and pitiable actions are uncommon they move men the more to terror and to compassion, but if they are frequent they move them the less, and because of their frequency are able to purge the terror and the compassion of mortal hearts. This comes about through two causes, of which one is that when we see many misadventures come about, and none of them touch ourselves, little by little we grow secure and make ourselves believe that God, as he has guarded us many times in the past, will also guard us in the future. The other is that those mishaps which come about often and to many do not appear so terrible and consequently do not appear to us so deserving of compassion, though we may be certain that they will touch us when we see that they do not spare so many others.

[Poetry not primarily moral. 140, 15]

If the plot is the end of tragedy,[27] and consequently of every sort of poem, for the plot holds the same place in every sort of poem as in tragedy,—if the plot is final and not a thing accessory to the morals of the agents, but on the contrary the morals do not hold the final place and are accessory to the plot, it follows that many authors of high reputation for letters among the ancients and the moderns, among whom is even Julius Caesar Scaliger,[28] have greatly erred, for they think the intention of good poets, like Homer and Vergil in their most famous works, the *Iliad*, the *Odyssey*, and the *Aeneid*, has been to depict and show to the world, let us say, a general portrayed in the most excellent manner that is possible, or a valorous leader, or a wise man, and their nature, and like absurdities.[29] For if this is true the moral habits of characters would not have been chosen by poets to second the action, as Aristotle says, but the action would have been chosen to second the characteristics. In addition, it would happen that if such material were principal and not accessory, it could not be poetic material, since it is naturally philosophical and taken from many philosophers, especially Aristotle and Theophrastus.[30]

[27] *End*, a logical word, indicates here determining component. Castelvetro is repeating Aristotle's statement (*Poetics*, VI, 50a15, above).

[28] Scaliger entitles chap. III of his seventh book "Whether the poet should teach morals or actions." He agrees with Aristotle that "beatitude is nothing else than perfect action," and that a poem leads men toward that beatitude. He cannot, however, admit that there can be a poem without character, as Aristotle suggests (50a15, above), and decides that the poet teaches moral habits through actions. "Action is therefore a mode of teaching; and the moral habit is what we are taught to apply. Hence the action will be a sort of example of instrument in the narrative; the moral habit will be its end."

[29] With his opinion that "the end of poetry is to teach pleasantly," Scaliger was forced into such a belief as Castelvetro assigns to him. He devotes several pages to showing that Aeneas is the perfect character in all functions (*Poetice*, III, 12, pp. 91 ff.) of both public and private life. Vergil showed extraordinary skill "when he set out to unite in Aeneas alone the fortitude of Achilles and the prudence of Ulysses, and added to them piety. He eliminated the rashness of the one and removed the craft of the second, and transferred rashness to Turnus and craft to Sinon" (*ibid*, III, 20, p. 107 BC1). Cf. Spenser's letter to Raleigh, given below.

[30] The *Ethics* of Aristotle and the *Characters* of his pupil Theophrastus deal with typical characters and their traits. Their works and those of imitators apparently furnished suggestions to Renaissance dramatists. There are many points of contact between English works of the sort, such as Earle's *Microcosmography*, and the playwrights of the early seventeenth century.

Chapter VIII

[Unity of plot. 178, 39]

Aristotle . . . firmly requires that the action making up the plot should be one and relate to one person only, and if there are more actions than one, that one should depend on the other. He brings forward no reason or proof for this except the example of the tragic poets and Homer, who in composing their plots have used a single action by one person. But it can easily be understood that in tragedy and in comedy the plot contains one action or two which because of their interdependence can be reputed one, and more often of one person than of one family, not because the plot is not fitted to contain more actions but because the space of time of twelve hours at most in which the action is presented and the limitation of the space in which it is acted do not permit a multitude of actions or even the actions of one family, nor indeed the complete presentation of one action, if it is somewhat long. This is the principal and necessary reason why the plot of tragedy and comedy ought to be one, that is, ought to contain one action of a single person or of two that through their dependence may be thought of as one. This reason of limited time and place could not cause Homer to take a single action of a single person in the epic, which can recount not merely one action but several very long ones that happened in diverse countries.

[Unity demands constructive skill. 179, 14]

It is to be said that in the singleness of the action there is something else in view, namely, that he judges the plot will be more beautiful and the author more admired if he takes only a single action of a single person.[31] For it is not to be wondered at if a number of actions by one person, or one action of one people, or a number of actions by several persons delight us and render us eager to hear them, for because of the number of actions, variety, novel happenings, and multitude of persons and peoples, the plot carries with it pleasure and greatness and magnificence. Yet in that narration, though in itself it brings about the end of poetry, the ability of the poet does not show to much advantage. But in the narration of a single action of a single person, which at first sight does not appear to have power to cause an audience to listen

---

[31] Cf. Tasso, *Heroic Poetry*, sect. 32, below.

with pleasure, there is revealed the judgment and the industry of the poet, since he does with one action of one person what others scarcely are able to bring about with many actions by many persons.[32] Therefore Homer is much to be commended, for with but one action by Achilles, and that of lesser importance, namely an instance of anger, he knew how to plan the fabric of so excellent a plot. Similarly from one action by Ulysses, that is, his return from Calypso to his native land, he planned a second web not less wonderful. From this it is to be concluded that the plot of a tragedy or of a comedy should of necessity contain one action of one person, or two that are mutually dependent, and the plot of an epic should contain one action by one person, not of necessity but to show the excellence of the poet.

Chapter IX

[Tragedy and epic deal with kings. 188, 12]

In the plot of tragedy and of the epic there are necessarily to be found occurrences that happen to have taken place in the life of a particular man, and are known in outline, as for example, Orestes accompanied by Pylades his friend, and aided by him and by Electra his sister, kills Clytemnestra his mother, but no one knows in detail and exactly the ways he took and the methods he used in accomplishing this murder. Now the reason is manifest, and so clearly manifest that it can be spoken of as proved, because it is fitting that the plot of a tragedy and of an epic should accept such actual events as are common to it and to the truth of history. For the plot of the two kinds of poem mentioned should contain action not human alone but also magnificent and royal. And if it ought to contain action by a prince, the conclusion follows that it contains action that has happened and is certain, and that concerns a ruler who has been and who is known to have been, since we cannot imagine a king who has not been nor attribute to him any act, and so far as he has been and is known to have been, we cannot attribute to him an act that has not really happened. . . . For kings are known through fame or through history and equally their notable acts are known, and to introduce new names of kings and to attribute to them new actions is to contradict history and fame, and to sin against the manifest truth, a much greater sin in the composition of the plot than to sin in veri-

[32] Cf. Giraldi, *Romances*, sect. 42, above.

similitude. Therefore the plots of all tragedies and all epics are and should be composed of happenings that can be called historical, though Aristotle had a different opinion. . . .[33] But these incidents should not be set forth by history or fame except briefly and generally, in order that the poet may be able to perform his function and show his ability in finding the ways and particular methods through which the aforesaid incidents were accomplished. For if the ways and special methods through which these incidents were brought to completion were also known, there would be no matter fitted for the plot and it would not pertain to the poet but to the historian. Nor withal should we allow anyone to form the opinion that it is easier to compose the plot of a tragedy or of an epic than of a comedy, because in the plots of the first two the poet does not find out everything for himself as he does in comedy. . . .

[Comedy is the poet's invention. 189, 13]

Now to compose the plot of a comedy the poet searches out with his own powers a happening in its universal and particular aspects, and because everything is invented by him and no part is given to actual events or to history, he gives names to the persons as it pleases him and is able to do it with no inconvenience and in a reasonable way. He is able to shape a happening he has invented in all its parts, and therefore it should concern a private person of whom and of the things that have happened to him no one has any recollection, nor will they be given to the memory of the future through history or fame. Hence he who forms a complete and new experience of private persons and gives them names as he pleases cannot be rebuked by history or fame as a falsifier. And, if he wishes to be thought a poet in the true meaning of the word, that is an inventor, he ought to invent everything, because, since the private material makes it easy for him, he is able to do it. But no one should think that he who composes the plot of the comedy has license to make up for himself new cities that he has imagined, or rivers or mountains or kingdoms or customs or laws, or to change the course of the things of nature, making it snow in summer and putting harvest in the winter, and the like, for it befits him to follow history and truth, if in forming his plot it happens that he needs such things, just as it equally befits him who forms the fable of a tragedy or of an epic.

[33] *Poetics*, IX, first par., above.

[The historical plot truly poetic. 213, 38]

It appears that if things that have happened cannot constitute a poem[34] and do not tend toward the constitution of a poem, they should tend toward the destruction and diminution of a poem, when they are mingled with things that can possibly happen and things devised by the poet, if with the mixture made up of the things that have come about and those that can come about we compare those that can come about by themselves alone. That is, it appears that the plot of a tragedy or of an epic, when it is formed from an action that has really happened and retains the real names, as we have shown that it ought to be formed, ought to render its maker less deserving of the name of poet than is he who, in forming the plot of a comedy or of a tragedy, devises for himself the entire action and all the names, as did Agathon for his tragedy named the *Flower*. For if the plot made up wholly of things that have happened does not permit the author to be a poet at all, the plot made up partly of things that have happened would in its proportion take from him his poetic being; consequently he would be less a poet than the man who is considered a complete poet because he uses plots entirely of his own devising and events that might happen. Nevertheless I judge that the man who forms the plot of a tragedy or an epic taken from history with real and true names is not the less to be esteemed a poet than the maker of a plot containing only imaginary things; on the contrary he should perhaps be thought greater. For things that have happened, which the aforesaid composer considers in forming the plot of the epic and of the tragedy, are not so many nor set out in such a way that they deliver him from the effort of invention, since everyone can imagine for himself such things without much cleverness of intellect. We may suggest something that any man can easily imagine, such as the outline that a son has killed his mother who has murdered her husband and driven her son from the realm that she may enjoy herself with her paramour. But the difficulty is to find the ways in which the son may come to this killing in a marvelous fashion such as has not happened before. This difficulty is greater than that of devising the action in general and the particular ways and means through which it came to a conclusion, since the outline devised by the poet is not so fixed and determined

---

[34] Here and in two succeeding instances I have substituted the reading *poema* for the *poeta* of the text.

that it cannot be altered and changed, if it seems good to him, and that he is unable to make his characters clever or stupid or possessed of other qualities, as he judges these changes in harmony with the methods for constructing a good plot that earlier presented themselves to him. But he who takes his plot from things that have already happened cannot do that, because he is kept within certain bounds from which he cannot issue.

[An example from sculpture. 214, 32]

To show by an example what this difference is, I say that not many years ago, when excavations were going on in Rome, there was found a marble statue of a large and beautiful river god, with the beard broken and lacking, and yet, judged by the part that still remained on the chin, the beard if entire would, if properly proportioned, reach to the navel, though the point of the beard still remained high up on the breast without reaching any further; at this everyone marveled and could not imagine how that beard was arranged when it was complete. Michelangelo Buonarroti alone, a sculptor of great ability who was present, having stood solitary for a while, understood the state of things, and said: "Give me some clay." When he had it, he formed the part of the beard that was lacking of such a size as to be properly proportioned to the remainder, and joining it on drew it down as far as the navel. Then knotting it with one turn he showed clearly that the point of the beard formed by him touched high up on the breast in the very same place as the point of the broken beard. So to the wonder of all who were present he showed how the beard that was lacking was made and how it was knotted. And there was no one there who did not think that Michelangelo, for his quickness of wit in restoring so marvelously the lacking beard, was to be preferred to any other artificer who might have made a complete beard acceptable to his mind without regard to the pieces of the beard remaining.

[Another difficulty in the historical plot. 215, 10]

There is another difficulty much greater than that mentioned in actions taken from history, which is not found in imaginary actions, namely, that it is true of the ways and means of bringing to completion the actions taken from history that they are of necessity few, and have often been employed by earlier poets, and the most fitting and marvelous and workable devices have been discovered by others to such an extent that one must needs be a very skillful inventor and almost transcend the state of man if he wishes to deserve the name of a worthy poet in an action taken from history. Truly then there is need of superhuman ingenuity on the part of one who wishes, for example, to use in his plot the killing of his mother by Orestes, since it has been handled so many times and so well by so many poets in the past, and to bring about this murder there have been found so many ways and methods and such verisimilar and extraordinary ones, none of which the new poet can employ without incurring the infamy attaching to theft. From this restriction the inventor of the action that has not happened is free. Hence he who forms the plot of a comedy or a tragedy from an action wholly imaginary is not more a poet or more to be esteemed than he who forms the plot of an epic or a tragedy from an action that has actually happened.

[Plagiarism. 215, 27]

"And if he should happen to write of what has happened, he is not for that less a poet" [*Poetics*, IX]. These words are to be understood sensibly, that is, if it happens that the poet, not knowing that things have happened, and having imagined them for himself, puts them in his poem, he will be a poet just as much as though those things had never happened, since he has undergone the labor by which others gain the title of poet. But if he had before known that it had come about, he would have undergone no labor in finding it out and would not be a poet, as for the same reason no one is a poet for turning into verse what has been written by Herodotus. Now this reason which forbids the poet to take things that have happened also forbids him from taking things that have been written and invented by another poet, even though they have not happened. In that instance he would undergo as little labor in taking over the things written by others, as he does in taking things that have happened, and it appears that it is a more blameworthy theft to steal what another man has found and which is his own product, than it is to steal what has been produced by the course of the world under the control of Fortune and therefore seems in some sense common and not the special property of anyone. Now not merely in poetry is it reputed a theft to steal something that has been found by another poet, but also in any other subject, when one publishes the discovery of his neighbor as his own. The lawyers say that a doctor of laws who, in lecturing or counseling, gives as his own an opinion on the laws acutely found out by another doctor is liable to the penalty pronounced against those who do injury and commit theft. And such thefts as these of the inventions of another are pointed out with the finger and jeered at by the world, in the same way as is the crow who adorns himself with the feathers of the other birds in order to appear worth looking at and beautiful beyond all the others, and then, when each one takes away from him its feathers, he remains without feathers and fit to be mocked at and base. But if any thief of the inventions of others ought to be mocked at and punished, the poet who is a thief should be, for the essence of a poet consists in his invention, since without invention he is not a poet.

[Examples of plagiarism. 216, 12]

Nonetheless there are many poets greatly acclaimed who have borrowed from histories or other poets part or all of the inventions of their poems, and they find some men so stupid and so ignorant as to admire and commend them when they ought to blame and despise them. For example, Giovanni Boccaccio puts in the tale of the Count of Anguersa the love of Giacchetto for Gianetta,[35] taken from the story of the love of Antiochus for his mother-in-law. And Ludovico Ariosto, taking now one part from Ovid and now another from Statius and then another from Marullo and other from others, fills out his *Orlando Furioso*, especially stealing without changing anything the story of Zerbino from Heinrich the storyteller of the Emperor Henry the Fourth.[36] Nor does Petrarch guard himself from taking the invention of many of his sonnets from Latin and Italian poets, and that of the sonnet *O little chamber, that you were a port* from Pliny the Younger.[37] What more will you have? Vergil himself, if we believe Macrobius,

---

[35] *Decameron*, II, 8.   [36] *Orlando Furioso*, xx-xxiv.

[37] The sonnet runs as follows: "O little chamber, once a port of refuge against the severe tempests of every day, now you are a nightly fountain of tears, which in the day I conceal for shame." In his comment Castelvetro writes: "This sonnet is taken from an epistle of Pliny, Bk. vii [no. 5], to Calpurnia: 'I lie awake a great part of the night with your image in my mind, and by day, as it is commonly but truly put, my feet of their own accord take me to your room, but knowing it is vacant I turn back from it in sorrow and disappointment like an excluded lover. I escape these torments only when I am in the forum engaged in the lawsuits of my friends.' And consider how much better advised than the words of Petrarch are those of Pliny, for the latter had been in the habit of visiting his lady in that room" (*Le rime del Petrarca*, esposte per Lodovico Castelvetro [Venice, 1756], Sonnet 198).

stole various and not a few parts from Homer, which the critic gathers and tells about, and believing to exalt the poet by it, makes him out clearly a thief to no great credit of his. Entire comedies have been stolen from the Greek poets by Plautus and Terence, and entire tragedies by Seneca too from the Greek poets. And likewise entire tales of Boccaccio, such as the one on the Gascon lady, from ancient stories,[38] and that one about Guido Cavalcanti from Petrarch,[39] and those of Peronella and of Hercolano from Apuleius.[40] And Apuleius did not find it for himself but took from someone else the invention of his *Golden Ass*. But no more, for this is not the place to reveal all the blameworthy thefts of these and the other authors.

[Plagiarism justified. 216, 36]

I shall merely add that some of these thieves, who wish to be thought poets, are found to be so shameless that they dare to affirm it is permissible to steal things found by other poets, because the theft is committed without any damage to those from whom something is taken, and mockingly they say: If you do not believe it, go to see if in their books anything is lacking because of our theft. Or at least they say: The theft is not made against the will of the master. And still mocking they say that those who do not guard their property cannot reasonably complain when they are robbed, and that of this sort are the authors who leave their poems unwatched and publish them too without sending with them any guardian who will defend them from theft. They have even greater presumption and affirm that they do not commit theft nor take anything from anyone whenever they write what others have already written in earlier poems, since the others do not find or are unable to find anything that has not been said before.

[The inventor is entitled to his fame. 217, 6]

To this it is possible to say in a brief response that when the invention which was the property of the inventor becomes, through the theft of someone, common to him also, and it is believed that the thief is as much its inventor as the one who found it, the glory that ought to be entirely that of the first finder and limited to him

---

[38] *Decameron*, I, 9.   [39] *Decameron*, VI, 9.
[40] *Decameron*, VII, 2, from Apuleius, *The Golden Ass*, IX, 5–7, and *Decameron*, V, 10, from Apuleius, IX, 22–29. The second story is much more modified by Boccaccio than the first.

is diminished when it is shared with another. But when because of a theft the invention is attributed to him who stole it, the first finder wrongfully and completely is deprived of his deserved glory. Of this glory everyone who takes delight in the graceful labor of the inventor ought to be the eager and faithful guardian and conservator, holding in abomination the thieves of invention as ingrates and men without understanding who deserve heavy punishment. Now it is true that nothing is said which has not been said before, if we consider the fundamental parts of which each thing is composed and consists. But if we consider it as a whole, it is not true that everything has already been said. If so, we should have to say that all poems which from time to time have been made in succession are one, and that the *Odyssey* of Homer, which was made after the *Iliad*, is the *Iliad* or some poem composed before it, because the *Odyssey* has been first given either in the *Iliad* or in another poem composed before it.

[Episodes. 218, 27]

The episodes and digressions here blamed by Aristotle are those particular things that ought to fill up the action as a whole and show how it has been brought to its end. These digressions are blamable when they do not depend one from the other like rings joined in a chain, or are not joined to things pertaining to the plot as a whole. . . .

[Digressions. 219, 8]

Plots that have inartistic digressions of this kind are made by bad poets and by good ones, but for diverse reasons, for they are made by the bad ones through ignorance in the belief that they are good, but by the good because they turn aside from the right path not through ignorance but knowingly, and realizing that they are doing what is bad, to please others. As Aristotle explains, the poet should not, to please others, insert some inartistic digression into his poem. If Vergil had paid attention to Aristotle's advice he would not, in order to flatter and please the Roman people, have inserted into his poem the digression of the unregulated love of Dido for Aeneas. This digression is defective because it is a regal action that is false and rejected by history in manner and in time. It is rejected in manner because Dido for the preservation of her honor killed herself, since she wished to keep her faith to her husband who was already dead. It is rejected as to time because Aeneas could not have arrived in Africa when Dido was alive. Not to mention that it does not appear that he understands that the infamy with which he attempts to soil the glory of the founder of Carthage, by speaking to the liking of the Romans, is common to Aeneas their founder, for the affair is not conducted much to his honor but shows his great ingratitude. And perhaps it can be said that the digression made by him with this same purpose of flattering the people of Rome or Augustus, that of the journey of Aeneas to the lower world inserted into the *Aeneid,* is not artistic, since in neither history nor fame did anything appear earlier of his going into the underworld, though fame does mention the journeys of Hercules, Theseus, Pirithous, and Orpheus.[41] Thence also it can be seen how much less daring Homer was, who causes Ulysses to see the spirits of the dead by way of incantation,[42] while Aeneas, through the unrestrained daring of Vergil, goes in person to the lower world through a way permitted to few who are alive, and sees the souls not merely of the dead but also of those not yet born and learns the name of each one and their special actions and hears details about Anchises his father, as he would learn them from a historian; in this Vergil sins against the proprieties of prophecy, which usually does not condescend to proper names nor to things so plain and particular, but, keeping silent as to names, is in the habit of revealing persons and their actions with figures of speech somewhat obscure, as may be observed in the prophecies of sacred scripture and in the *Alexandra* of Lycophron.[43] Against this propriety Catullus errs similarly in making the Fates, at the marriage of Peleus and Thetis, prophesy of the birth and glorious deeds of Achilles under his own name and with every particularity.[44] But Ovid, when he has Proteus prophesy of the same thing to Thetis, does not name Achilles by his own name, but, including his actions under generalities, says, as is fitting to prophecy:

> Listen, you will be mother of a son who in feats of arms will surpass the acts of his father and will be called greater than he.[45]

But let him who wishes to see an example of unfitting digressions

---

[41] All of these descended to Hades.

[42] Apparently an error, for Ulysses does go to the "dank house of Hades" (*Odyssey,* x, 512).

[43] A poet of Alexandria. The *Alexandra* or *Cassandra* is a poem proverbial for its obscurity.

[44] Catullus, LXIV, 323–71.   [45] *Metamorphoses,* XI, 225; XV, 856, etc.

brought in to please others read those in the *Orlando Furioso* of Ariosto, introduced now by way of prophecy, now by other methods, yet none of these paths is legitimately trod by him.[46] Now according to Aristotle good poets are led to produce the digressive plots of tragedies to please the actors of their tragedies,[47] who are engaged in a contest with other actors presenting the tragedies of other poets, so that the tragedies with digressions, that otherwise would be too brief to take up the time prescribed by the judges, could fill up the whole time and the actors would not lose their contest because of the brevity of their tragedy. And perhaps these digressions written to please the actors are more concerned with what the actors know how to perform than with the material naturally suited to the plot, that they may show what they can do in that in which they are best trained and therefore may most easily obtain the victory.

[The marvelous. 221, 11]

There is presented here the sixth thing required of the plot that it may be beautiful, namely that it should be marvelous, since it is said in the definition of tragedy that it should be not merely an imitation of an action that is magnificent, perfect, etc., but also an imitation of things terrible and worthy of compassion. And because these things are terrible and excite compassion chiefly by means of the marvelous, it is not well to omit speaking of the marvelous, which generates and increases terror and compassion, in order that there may be full knowledge of terror and compassion as principal parts of the action or of the fable of the tragedy. But before we undertake the exposition of the words of the text of Aristotle, it appears that three things must be discussed. The first is, what is the true end of tragedy or of the plot of a tragedy? and at the same time, what is the true end of comedy or of the plot of a comedy? Then of what sort is the person peculiarly suited to tragedy and to the plot of tragedy and what are his characteristics? And finally, what sort of astonishing event can make the action more terrible and more fitted to arouse compassion? If we can make these things clear, the words of Aristotle will be clearly and plainly explained to us.

---

[46] In canto III Ariosto gives by way of a vision an account of the Estensi. In canto XXVIII is the story of Fiametta, told by the host of an inn at which one of the characters stops. The story of Doctor Anselmo is told in canto XLIII.

[47] *Poetics*, IX, 51b33, note, above.

[The end of tragedy. 221, 28]

So, commencing with the first thing laid down, I say that the end of tragedy or of the plot of tragedy is gladness or sadness but not every gladness or sadness, in order that the gladness and the sadness connected with the end of tragedy may not be confounded with the gladness or the sadness that are the ends of comedy or of the plot of comedy, as will be said. The gladness of the end of tragedy, then, consists in and is restricted to the escape by oneself or by persons dear to one from death or from sad life or from the loss of royal station. On the other hand, its sadness consists in and is limited to the coming on oneself or on persons dear to one of death or of a life of sorrow or of the loss of regal position. And these two are its appropriate ends.

[The end of comedy. 221, 37]

The end of comedy, as I say, in like manner is gladness or sadness, but not the same gladness nor the same sadness which we say pertains to tragedy. For the gladness which is the end of comedy consists in the covering up of some disgrace that has been brought on oneself or some person dear to one, or in the cessation of some shame which others did not think could cease, or in the recovery of a person or a precious possession that has been lost, or in the fulfilling of amorous desire. But the sadness of comedy consists in and is limited to the reception by oneself or persons dear to one of some disgrace or shame of a moderate sort, or in damage to property not very serious, or in the hindering of the enjoyment of the person loved, and in such things. These are the two ends proper to comedy.

[The persons of tragedy. 222, 5]

But it can be asked why tragedy or the plot of tragedy does not receive or cannot receive that gladness or sadness for its end that comedy receives, and why on the other hand comedy or the plot of comedy does not receive or is not able to receive that gladness or sadness for its end that tragedy receives. To this question we can answer that the persons of tragedy are of one sort and those of comedy of another. Those of tragedy are royal and have greater souls and are proud and have a strong desire for what they desire, and, if injury is done to them or they think it is going to be done to them, they do not run to the magistrates to make complaint of that injury nor do they bear it patiently, but they make a law for themselves according as their passions speak to them and kill for vengeance those who are distant and those united to them by blood, and in their desperation not merely those united to them by blood but sometimes themselves. To such persons, when they are put in a royal position, which is thought the summit of human felicity, and have the power to revenge themselves for any outrages done to them, injuries or insults of a moderate sort are not done, nor do they suffer or have done to them injuries in property of a trivial sort. Nor is their happiness increased by marriages or fulfilment of amorous desires, for they live, it can truly be said, in perpetual marriages and in continual amorous satisfactions to such an extent that if they are to be happy it is needful that they be removed from felicity, or at least that they fall into manifest peril which it is happiness to escape from, and to make sadness arise it is necessary that they fall into misery or into a low state with a spectacular plunge.

[The persons of comedy. 222, 27]

But the persons of comedy are of poor spirit and inclined to obey the magistrates and to live under the laws and to endure injuries and damage and to run to the officers of the law and to beg that by means of the statutes their honor may be restored to them or the damage they have suffered made good. They do not make laws unto themselves nor rush into murders of relatives or of themselves or of others for the reasons for which kings rush into them. And because they are in a poor and humble state it is not necessary, to make happiness come to them, that their felicity should abandon them, since it can increase through many steps and through some moderate happening, such as a wedding that is desired and similar things. On the other side, moderate injury and disgrace can produce melancholy in them. And these are the reasons why the happy and sad ends of tragedy are different from the happy and sad ends of comedy.

[Political influence on dramatic subjects. 222, 39]

And if it should be asked why it is not possible to introduce into comedy a private person who in a prosperous course of events will become a king, since we know through history that some from a lowly private condition have been elevated to kingship, I say first of all that such a story would be a subject not for comedy, but for tragedy, nor would it be possible reasonably to imagine such a plot, but it would be fitting to take it from history, for the reasons that have been given. Then a drama on that theme would not delight nor be pleasing if it were acted in a state with a popular government where people live in equality, for those who love liberty and wish to maintain it do not wish examples to be set before the citizens of private persons who have occupied the lordship over them. And it would be much less delightful and pleasing if represented in a state governed by a king, where the people live under the rule of one man, for a king is very jealous of his royal condition, and is careful about putting before the humble and before individuals examples that may arouse and direct their spirits toward innovations and a change of rulers. On the contrary, because the king knows that the common people delight in and enjoy the evil fortunes of the great, they do not ever have tragedies produced in public. Tragedies never appear on the stage except among people who are subject to no individual ruler.[48]

[Summary of tragic qualities. 223, 14]

The end of a tragedy is then, either happy or sad, and since when it has a happy end a regal person must of necessity fall into great peril, it generates fear and compassion along with the gladness which, because of the peril mingled with it, is not without sadness, as one may say, though to a greater extent it may generate similar passions with its final sadness. Then the end of the fable of the tragedy is gladness and sadness produced as we have said.

[The persons of tragedy. 223, 20]

Now it follows that we may speak of the second idea, which is the kind of person who is suitable for tragedy and chief in it, and of the plot of tragedy, on which is founded the final sadness or happiness of which we have spoken. In tragedy, then, there are three sorts of persons, those who act, those who suffer, and those who act and suffer together. For example, Jephthah acts, sacrificing his daughter for his rash vow, and his daughter suffers, being sacrificed.[49] Ajax acts and suffers at the same time, killing himself.[50] And since on account of the act or the suffering of each of

---

[48] Such a passage suggests why in Ben Jonson's day English politicians feared what they interpreted as political references in the drama. Heywood, as a friend of the drama, thought it might be of advantage to rulers. See the selections from Heywood and Jonson below.

[49] Judges 11.   [50] Sophocles, *Ajax.*

these persons, sadness arises, either greater sadness or less, according as the action or the suffering is the result of causes more or less reasonable, it is fitting for us to reason not merely of the acts and sufferings of the aforesaid persons, but also of the causes by reason of which they act or suffer.

[Causes of tragic suffering. 223, 33]

And speaking first of cause, I say that the cause that moves one to act is of two sorts, one of which has to do with the good or what is reputed to be good, and the other with the evil or what is thought to be evil. That which has to do with the good is likewise of two sorts, since one is moved to act either to acquire the good one does not have, or to maintain the good one has. For example, Clytemnestra, to acquire the good she did not have, which was to enjoy Egisthus, acted wickedly according to her corrupt appetite, committing adultery with breach of faith to her husband and incest by uniting herself with a relative. And to maintain the good that she had, she acted wickedly, killing Agamemnon, her husband, and driving Orestes, her son, from his paternal kingdom. That which has to do with evil is equally of two kinds, since anyone is influenced to act either to escape future evil or to remove the evil that is present. Phaedra, after she had in vain solicited the love of Hippolytus, fearing that if the fact became known infamy and injury would follow, acted wickedly to avoid those evils, falsely accusing Hippolytus to his father Theseus and inflaming her husband with wrath against his son. Phaedra, on her own part, rid herself of her immediate sufferings, namely sorrow of mind and seemingly insupportable pangs of conscience for the sins she had committed, by allowing herself to rush into so dishonorable and wicked a love, by accusing an innocent man as though he were guilty, by inducing Theseus with a lie to kill his son as a very wicked man when he was altogether good, and by causing the death of a young man so strong, courteous, and beautiful.[51] Now a present evil is removed with revenge, with pain, and with change, that is, with a less evil, and a future evil is got rid of either in an unjust way or in a way apparently rational. Likewise the good is acquired and maintained equally in a way that is unjust and in a way that is apparently reasonable. The present evil is removed with revenge, as when Medea kills her children to revenge herself on Jason;[52] with penalty, as when

[51] Euripides, *Hippolytus*.   [52] Euripides, *Medea*.

Torquatus puts to death his son;[53] with change or with a lesser evil, as when Phaedra hangs herself. A future evil is removed in an unjust way, as when Phaedra falsely accuses Hippolytus of attempting violence against her in order that she may not be defamed; in a way apparently reasonable, as when Hercules kills his wife and his sons, believing them wild beasts. The good is acquired unjustly, as when Clytemnestra, making herself free to Egisthus against her honor, has what she desires. The good is maintained in an unjust manner, as when Clytemnestra secures herself by the death of Agamemnon, her husband, and by driving her son Orestes from his paternal kingdom. The good is acquired in a way apparently reasonable, as when Oedipus by taking as his wife Jocasta, whom he thinks unrelated to him, acquires the sovereignty of Thebes. The good is maintained in a way apparently reasonable, as when Canace, sending away from home her son who has been born secretly, seeks to cover up her dishonorable action.[54] It may suffice to have said so much on the cause.

[Tragic activity. 224, 32]

And going on to speak of the doing, I say that activity can be divided in five ways. There is wicked activity, as was that of Phaedra when she sought the love of her stepson. There is that which is wicked and horrible together, as was that of Medea when she killed her innocent children. There is that which is painful, as for Peleus to go miserably through the world after being driven from home for killing Phocus, his brother.[55] Then there is one that can be called excusable, as the act of Lucretia when she consented to the licentious desires of Tarquin against her will in order not to die in dishonor.[56] Last comes the horrible, which is divided in four ways. A horrible act can be committed through necessity or what amounts to necessity; for example, one can see the necessity or almost necessity that induced Cato to inflict death on himself and induced Orestes to kill his mother; these are men not at all wicked and therefore both are constrained to do what they do. There is also found the horrible act unaccompanied by wicked-

---

[53] T. Manlius Imperiosus Torquatus, when general, executed his son who disobeyed orders (540 B.C.).

[54] Sperone Speroni, *Canace*. By sending away the child, Canace, daughter of Eolus, hoped to conceal her incestuous union with her brother Macareus. See the next section and 247, 33, below.

[55] Probably not a reference to any extant play, but to Horace, *Art of Poetry*, 96.

[56] A story often told, as by Shakespeare in his *Rape of Lucrece*.

ness because of ignorance of the persons concerned, as in the death of Laius at the hands of Oedipus and the marriage of Jocasta contracted with Oedipus, since he did not know that they were his father and mother nor did they know that he was their son. Likewise the horrible can appear without wickedness on the part of the person causing it, as when Hercules in insanity killed his wife and his children, and Athamas also in insanity killed his son. Finally the horrible can be separated from wickedness because of an error in the instrument, as happened when Peleus, thinking he was striking a wild animal, struck Eurytion, his dearest friend, and killed him, and in the same way Adrastus, thinking he was striking a wild beast, struck Atys, his master, the son of Croesus, and killed him.

[Kinds of tragic suffering. 225, 14]

It remains that we speak of suffering. Suffering first may be considered as pain or as anxiety. I call suffering painful when a person is killed, as Laius was; wounded, as was Philoctetes; or bound in a distressing manner, as was Prometheus on Mount Caucasus; or has violence done to him, as it was to Tamar,[57] and similar things. And I call suffering anxiety when it is like that which Theseus underwent when he believed that his son Hippolytus had done violence to his stepmother, and like that which Eolus suffered when he knew of the wicked union of Macareus and Canace, his children. Then suffering can be considered either as deservedly coming on a person who suffers, as death is deservedly inflicted on Canace, or as it comes on a person without desert, as death is undeservedly inflicted on the innocent child of Canace and Macareus. Or it can be wickedly substituted for some good that is deserved, as death was wickedly substituted for the good that Hippolytus deserved. Now it must be known that the cause generates the act and the act generates the suffering; this suffering can become the cause of another action, which generates further suffering, in such a way that in a plot there can be several causes and several instances of suffering which follow one after another. For example, hope to satisfy her burning desires was the cause that moved Phaedra to act wickedly by asking the love of Hippolytus her stepson. He because of this action underwent the suffering of anxiety, and that was the cause that moved him to an act revealing anxiety, the abandonment of his native land

[57] II Samuel 13.

and his father's royal house. His departure generated the suffering of anxiety in Phaedra and became the cause why she acted wickedly by accusing him, though he was innocent, as the destroyer of her honor. This act caused the suffering of anxiety in Theseus, and this suffering changed into cause forced him to curse horribly a son who deserved every blessing. From this action rose the suffering of Hippolytus's cruel death. This suffering was the cause why Phaedra carried out against herself the horrible act of hanging herself by the neck with her own hands, whence she received suffering according to her deserts.

[Agents in tragedy. 226, 2]

Now having seen these things in order to know of what sort are the persons fit for tragedy and the chief actors in it, from whom, because of their actions, there arise sufferings, fear, and compassion in those who see and hear, it is needful to look separately at those who act and those who suffer. Those who act and are moved to action by an unjust cause which they know to be unjust cannot excite compassion or fear in the minds of others, since it does not appear to anyone that desire to act unjustly against another man can come to him. But those who act when moved to action by a just cause arouse fear and compassion in the minds of the others. Such a one is Torquatus, who ordered the beheading of his son who was disobedient to his orders when he was captain of the army. But they produce much more fear and are much more worthy of compassion who, through error of mind, act horribly when they believe they are acting fitly, as the insane Hercules who killed his wife and his children thinking they were wild animals. And still more he arouses compassion and fear who through error in his instrument does something horrible, as did Peleus and Adrastus, who killed the one Eurytion, his friend, and the other Atys, his lord, through an accident in the use of the javelin, for each one intended to kill a wild beast. And greater terror and greater fear will proceed from the acts of those who through ignorance of persons commit horrible acts, such as Cinyras committed by lying with his daughter.[58] This fear and this compassion rise to their highest point when men, because of their ignorance of persons, draw near to the horrible and fall into it through the very means by which they think to escape it or be far from it. Such is Oedipus, who, getting away, as he believed, from his

[58] See 229, 11, below.

father and his mother to escape the horrible, drew near to it, and because of ignorance of persons did what he hated. And why this condition is more worthy of compassion and more terrifying than the others will be explained soon. Then there are five kinds of persons who bring to pass something horrible which moves compassion and fear in others, but not equally, for those who act with deliberation and with just cause move it less, and those who bring it about through error of mind excite in others a higher degree of the compassion already mentioned. And those who cause it through some error in the use of an instrument excite fear and compassion somewhat more than the second sort. And still more than by these, fear and compassion are caused by those who commit some horrible action in ignorance of the persons involved; and among them they are especially deserving of compassion and cause the greatest horror who fall into some frightful state through the very means by which they strive to avoid it.

[Those who suffer in tragedy. 226, 40]

Compassion and fear arise also from the persons who suffer, but not from all of them, since it does not rise from those who suffer because they have deserved to suffer, as in the instance of Clytemnestra's death, because if suffering is deserved it appears to ordinary men that they will never do things because of which they can deserve some punishment. But not all those who are undeserving of suffering move terror and compassion, for some are found who are led to kill themselves without having at all merited death, as in a story told by Valerius Maximus of an event that took place in his presence, and that of Sextus Pompeius, a noble citizen of Rome: in Giulide, a city of the island of Cea, an excellent and intelligent lady who had lived happily a long time drank poison of her own will in order to die. Such sufferings do not produce compassion or fear, for no one believes that a similar thing can happen to himself, since it could not come about without his own will, and those who kill themselves of their own accord without being forced, or as good as forced, or deceived, appear in a certain way to merit death since they do not esteem life as they should. There are also some who do not merit suffering, but rather merit reward instead, because of their ardent love for their country. Such persons do not terrify us with their suffering, for example, Curtius, who willingly leaped armed into the cavity in the earth for the good of his country, and the Decii, who spontaneously offered themselves to death for the safety of the others. Then some sufferings can produce terror without compassion, and some can produce compassion without terror, for terror excited by the sufferings of another enters our hearts because we think of the ease with which similar suffering can come on ourselves, and compassion enters our hearts because the afflictions of another seem undeserved, for we do not think the sufferer merits such suffering. Therefore, the suffering of Curtius or of the Decii does not terrify us, because such suffering cannot easily come to us, for it cannot come about against our wills, but we have great compassion for them because they did not deserve death, being brave and lovers of their country. And the suffering of a wicked man because a tree has fallen on him, let us say, could cause us terror without any compassion for the victim, because the wicked man merits that evil and worse, and because another tree can likewise fall on us, though we are not so wicked as he is. Now those persons who do not merit suffering, as the innocent do not, are worthy of compassion. And because these are of two sorts (one that does not deserve this suffering, such as the children of Medea and the son of Canace, and another sort that not merely does not deserve this suffering, but rather reward, as Hippolytus) when that kind of man suffers who does not merit suffering and does merit reward, it causes greater compassion than that which merely does not deserve suffering, since the first is less deserving of suffering than is the latter. Besides, those persons who suffer in a way that is less difficult excite greater fear than do those who suffer in a more difficult way. Because, though the children of Medea and the children of Hercules are equally undeserving of suffering, nevertheless the killing of his children by Hercules is more terrifying than the killing of hers by Medea. For it is a much easier thing that an insane person should kill his children than that one who is in his senses and realizes what he does should kill them. Now from what has been said, anyone, if I am not mistaken, will be able fully to understand not merely what persons cause fear and compassion by their acts and sufferings, but also which of them are more or less fitted to do this, and consequently who are the persons especially adapted to tragedy and most excellent in it.

[The marvelous and horrible. 228, 9]

Therefore let us go on to speak of the third and last thing indicated above, which was what sort of marvelous thing increases fear and compassion. And to understand this matter fully we must divide the marvelous into three types according as it is found in three diverse subjects, that is, as it can be found in animals without reason and things without sensation, in men who do something horrible deliberately and as the result of a plan, and in men who involuntarily do something horrible as the result of an accident. The last are divided into those who furnish a cause for the horrible in ways in which it is believed hardly possible to furnish it, and into those who without reason bring about the horrible because they are deceived. The marvelous in animals without reason and in things without sensation is greater in proportion as such animals or insensate things carry on, or appear to carry on, their acts according to reason and in the way in which men are in the habit of working according to a plan. It is narrated as a miracle in the story of a stallion that he did not wish to mate with a mare that was his mother, but being deceived in the darkness did mate with her; then on learning of it he was so sorrowful that he struck his head on a rock until he died. . . . It is among men a horrible and terrible thing that the son should join carnally with his mother, knowing her as his mother, and it is a great wonder when this in any age comes about once among men, but among horses such a happening causes no marvel at all. Therefore Myrrha says in Ovid:

> The other animals come together without any wickedness, and it is not held base for a heifer to bear her father on her back, and the daughter of a horse is made his mate.[59]

Yet more, if a stallion is found that avoids it, he causes amazement because he does something surpassing his nature that man does through the direction of his intellect. Similarly it would be esteemed a yet greater wonder that a statue of marble, falling by chance, should kill the murderer or enemy of the original of the statue, than that another statue, likewise falling by chance, should kill a person neither an enemy nor a friend of the original of the statue. And likewise it is a greater wonder among men that one should kill his friend or one not his enemy than that he should kill his enemy. And the reason is manifest, namely that the statue, which has no mind, does by chance and as though it were not without a mind what the reasoning man would do after reflection. The marvelous among men who do something horrible

---

[59] Ovid, *Metamorphoses*, x, 324–6.

with deliberate intention is much greater in proportion as the cause is less able to bring it about. For we wonder not at all or but little if one kills an enemy, but we marvel greatly if he kills a non-enemy or a friend. And however marvelous his act may be, it does not produce compassion for him but a great deal for the sufferer, who has not merited death at the hands of one not his enemy, and much less from his friend; and it tends to make us fear that something like it may come to us from the hand of one of our friends. But not so much fear is inspired in us by the death of an enemy, since it seems to us a thing that easily can come about and there is aroused in us less compassion for the sufferer, for it appears to us that the enemy because of his enmity is not altogether undeserving of death.

[The horrible and marvelous contrary to human will. 229, 11]

In the instance of men who do something horrible against their will, the marvelous, by furnishing them a cause for their acts in ways in which they believe it could not be given, receives a second distinction according to the methods they use, which are of three sorts. For either their actions are directly opposed to arrival at something horrible, or they are not wholly contrary but diverse, or they are common and can indifferently conduct to what is horrible or not. The examples make clear what perhaps seems to be said obscurely. Oedipus, having learned that he was going to kill his father and lie with his mother, in order that this might not come about, departed from Corinth, where he thought his father and his mother lived, and went far away. He thought his departure the way directly opposed to arrival at the horror that was predicted and yet this very departure was the direct and the single way that led him to kill Laius, his father, and to lie with Jocasta, his mother. Cinyras arranged with the nurse of Myrrha, his daughter, that she in the night should bring a young woman, his neighbor, to lie with him.[60] This was a way very distant or diverse from arriving at something horrible, yet in that way he came to it, since the nurse in place of the young neighbor conducted Myrrha, his daughter, to lie with him. Jephthah, fighting against his enemies, bound himself by a vow to God that if he obtained the victory, he would sacrifice that person who first met him as he returned to his home.[61] This vow was a way common

---

[60] Ovid, *Metamorphoses*, x, 298 ff. Myrrha was punished with a passion for her father by the angry Aphrodite, whose worship she had neglected.   [61] Judges 11, 30–40.

and indifferent for making him fall or not making him fall into something horrible. For if a servant had first come out to meet him he would not, by sacrificing him, have fallen into that horrible deed that he did fall into when his daughter first came out to meet him, and was horribly offered by him to God in sacrifice. Now a greater marvel is found to be in the first way than in the second or in the third, and more in the second than in the third, since it is little strange that the common way should lead us to the place where the horrible can happen. And it is somewhat strange that the diverse way and much more strange that the contrary way should lead us to the place where the horrible action can reasonably come to pass. And in occurrences of this type the terror and the compassion are equal to the marvel, since they are greater in the first than in the second and the third, and greater in the second than in the third, since a man merits more compassion in proportion as he has shown a more open desire to flee the horrible, and causes more terror when with all his diligence he has been unable to escape it. There was not much of this in Jephthah, nor so much in Cinyras as in Oedipus.

[Tragic deceptions. 230, 5]

The marvelous in the instances of men who do something horrible against their will without their giving any cause for it is of two kinds, according as the men are of two kinds, that is, either deceived by men or deceived by something other than men. These deceived by men are like Theseus, who when deceived by Phaedra cursed his son Hippolytus, and was the cause of his being cruelly killed, and like Lot, who lay with his daughters when by making him drunk they had taken away from him ability to recognize them. Those deceived by something else than by men are represented by Hercules, who in insanity killed his wife and his children, and by Iphigenia, who, because she did not recognize her brother nor he her, was about to kill him by sacrificing him. This quality of the marvelous cannot be looked on as equal in all the deceptions woven by men, nor likewise in all the deceptions that come on men through some other means than the work of men, since sometimes one is very different from the other. We can merely affirm that deceptions woven by men appear, generally speaking, less marvelous than are those which come about through deceptions resulting from other things, because the latter do not come about so frequently as the former, and it appears that by means of wise foresight some protection can be found against the deceptions devised by men, nor do they terrify so much or produce so much compassion as do these that come about in some other way, against which every remedy appears vain.

Chapter XI (and XVI; see below)

[Artistic use of ignorance. 246,12]

Now Aristotle speaks of the recognition by means of which the plot is made beautiful and says nothing of the ignorance which nonetheless can have a place and a principal place in the plot and makes it become beautiful; at present we may treat this ignorance in two ways, one called ignorance of fact, the other ignorance of persons. Ignorance of fact is divided in two ways, according as there are two ignorant persons; to one of them the deed pertains, to the other it does not. If those chiefly concerned in the deed are ignorant, the plot has an attractive end and gives great delight because of the deception that comes about. There are many examples of this in the *novelle* of Boccaccio, as in the stories of Gianni Lotteringhi,[62] the husband of Peronella,[63] the husband of Madonna Agnese,[64] the husband of Madonna Isabella,[65] Egano de Gallucci,[66] the jealous husband,[67] and Nicostrato.[68] Though all these are husbands and those to whom more than to any others pertain the adulteries of their wives, they are ignorant of them and by their ignorance provide amusing material for the plot.

Ignorance of the fact in those persons to whom the deed does not pertain or pertains less than to all the others is also a cause of pleasure in the plot, as in Boccaccio it may be seen how much pleasure is given by the ignorance of the neighbors and relatives about the action of the wife of Tofano, for being deceived by the words of the lady they believe what they should not, speak insultingly to Tofano, and give him blows.[69] And how pleasant the story is made by ignorance of the deed of Monna Sigismonda on the part of her mother and brothers, for being ignorant of what has happened they think her husband is drunk.[70]

Ignorance of the persons has part in the story and sometimes brings consolation to the ignorant and sometimes sorrow. It

---

[62] *Decameron*, VII, 1.   [65] VII, 6.   [68] VII, 9.

[63] VII, 2.   [66] VII, 7.   [69] VII, 4.

[64] VII, 3.   [67] VII, 5.   [70] VII, 8.

brings consolation when the ignorant person suffers, after having obtained what he desired through a person unknown and believed by him to be of adequate station or higher, as, in Plautus, ignorance of the vile woman with whom was found Pyrgopolynices, the bragging soldier, did not permit him to grieve because he had paid so much money, since he believed her noble and was consoled because he made payment for a woman that he really enjoyed and who, as he was given to understand, deserved the payment.[71] It brings sorrow when the ignorant person is so impeded that he is not able to enjoy the person who being vile is reputed noble, being made to believe that a great felicity is denied to him, as in Boccaccio when Calandrino, believing himself to be with the wife of Philippo, and being with the woman without taking any pleasure with her, is let go with this false belief so that he may not temper his sorrow at not being able to enjoy her by knowing that she was a harlot.[72] This ignorance on the part of Calandrino is perhaps the result of skillful planning by Boccaccio and makes the plot very good, but it was not brought in so skillfully by Plautus in the case of Pyrgopolynices, nor does it cause the plot to come out so well, since he completes his enjoyment and is able to console himself for the injury and the scorn he suffers by means of the pleasure he has with the woman, for because of his ignorant love for her he would have no reason for regret if he had suffered something still greater. For after the injury of the payment of the money Plautus should take away the soldier's ignorance of the person in order to take away also his consolation, as Boccaccio does, for the latter takes away from the provost of Fiesole his ignorance of the person of Ciutazza, with whom he has lain, in order to remove the consolation he might have if he continued to suppose that he had been with the widow he was in love with.[73]

[Defects in the *Poetics*. 247, 18]

Now it is to be known, as we have said, that Aristotle does not say a word on ignorance of persons or ignorance of the deed, nor does he speak at all of the recognitions of which we have spoken, but he speaks merely of three kinds of recognition, that is, of the chief recognition of an unknown person, of the recognition that appears to be made by things without intelligence and the power of perception, and of the recognition of the act; of these three he speaks in such a way that his speech cannot easily be understood

[71] Plautus, *Miles Gloriosus*.   [72] *Decameron*, x, 5.   [73] VIII, 4.

by everyone. By the words *either to love or hate*[74] he means that the principal recognition of unknown persons generates amity or enmity, as we have said above, that is, hate or love. Brotherly love is caused by the recognition of Iphigenia and Orestes. The recognition of Myrrha excites hate in Cinyras against her. The recognition of Oedipus and of Jocasta excites in each of them hate against himself. And because here Aristotle speaks only of the recognition of unknown persons, he does not need to give an example of the recognition of an unknown act. . . .

[Why recognition of persons is superior. 247,33]

In saying that the best recognition is accompanied by a peripety, Aristotle indicates by the word *accompanied* that he has in mind the recognition of the chief persons who are unknown, . . . and that he does not have in mind the recognition of incidental persons, such as Orestes and Electra.[75] Now it is evident why Aristotle calls this recognition of unknown persons who play a chief part the best sort of recognition, when compared with the recognition of accessory unknown persons. But it is not evident why a little later he prefers it to the other recognitions and especially to the recognition of a fact, unless it is explained by means of other reasons than those he brings forward. For since he wishes to prove that such recognitions and reversals are more suitable to the plot than all the other recognitions and reversals, he says that they generate compassion and fear, and in them is found happiness or misery, and still the recognition of the unknown fact and the reversal in those actions that can be matter for tragedy generate compassion and fear, and in them is found happiness or misery neither to a more nor a less extent. Eolus through his recognition of the abominable union of Canace and Macareus, his children, passed from happiness to unhappiness; this can arouse in other fathers, to whom such misadventures might happen, compassion toward him and fear for themselves. The recognition of unknown persons is not therefore better nor more suitable for the story, for the reasons given, than the recognition of the unknown fact, but it should be considered better and set ahead of the other recognitions because the ignorance of persons comes about more seldom than

[74] *Poetics*, XI, 52a29, above.
[75] The recognition of these two, in the *Electra* of Sophocles, does not in itself cause tragic feeling, but merely leads toward the main tragic action, the murder of Clytemnestra.

the ignorance of a deed, because it is not usual to lose knowledge of persons closely joined in blood, and if it is lost or ignorance comes about through some accident, it is close to a miracle that among so many thousands of persons in the world a horrible deed should involve just these unknown persons, and besides it is not less a marvelous thing that they should be recognized by chance and through the indications given by words or things intended for some other purpose. And these are the causes that set this recognition ahead of the others. . . .

[Discovery of an action. 249,2]

Aristotle says: "It can also be discovered whether a person has or has not done something." The sentence refers to the discovery of an unknown action. This . . . is divided into two classes; in one, what another has done is learned, as when Eolus learns what his children, Macareus and Canace, have done, namely their incest; in the other, it is learned that someone has not done something, as when Theseus learns what his son Hippolytus has not done, namely, that he has not done violence to his stepmother, nor done any deed or said any word to her that was not fitting for a modest stepson. Since it is to be observed that Aristotle said in his definition that, as the name signifies, the recognition is a change from ignorance to knowledge producing friendship or enmity in those who are ordained for happiness or unhappiness, it clearly appears that he did not mean that the recognition of which he speaks should be limited merely to those who have first had knowledge of the person or of the deed, and then through some accident have lost this knowledge, which they then regain; for example, Hercules, first having the clearest knowledge of Megara, his wife, and his children, when he became insane lost it, and because he did not know them killed them, but when he became sane once more he recovered the knowledge he had lost.[76] But Aristotle also extends this knowledge to those who had not first had any knowledge, but there is complete ignorance both of the person and the deed until the recognition. Hence it does not appear to be wrong to make a distinction between the recognition of unknown persons and that of unknown actions, and it may be said that there is a knowledge that is acquired and a knowledge that is recovered.

[76] See *Hercules Furens* by either Euripides or Seneca. The latter's Hercules arrives at the truth by process of reasoning; he sees his own bloody arrow and realizes that he alone was able to bend the bow that drove it (ll. 1196-1200). Cf. also Aristotle, *Poetics*, p. 93, above.

[Acquired and recovered knowledge. 249, 25]

The knowledge that is acquired must be of those persons and actions of which there is complete ignorance up to the point when they become known. For example, Alexander in Boccaccio was completely ignorant that the abbot was a woman until by touching her breasts he knew her to be one.[77] And in the same Boccaccio the unchastity of Ghismonda was wholly unknown to Tancred until the time when with his own eyes he saw Guiscard sporting with her.[78] Knowledge that is recovered has to do with those persons and deeds of which a person has in the past had knowledge, which through some accident he has lost and which later he recovers. An example of recovered knowledge may be seen in Hercules, who, as we said, having at one time clear knowledge of Megara, his wife, and his children, when he became insane forgot them and not knowing them killed them; then having become sane he recovered the knowledge he had lost. Another instance is found in Boccaccio, in the widow who, foolishly forgetting the injury done by her to the scholar, trusted him, but when she received the punishment due her she recovered what had passed from her memory.[79] It seems, then, that it is well to make the aforesaid distinction between knowledge that is acquired and knowledge that is recovered, because they are very different from each other; and perhaps superior ability is demanded from the poet if he will handle one of them well than if he will handle the other well, in accordance with necessity or probability.

[Three kinds of ignorance. 250, 2]

It also appears that each recognition of a person or of an unknown fact can and should receive a classification into three parts, according as there are three kinds of ignorance of persons or of facts, wholly separate and distinct one from the other in the mode in which the knowledge arising from ignorance has been concealed; without this preceding concealment there can be no recognition. The persons or the facts may be unknown because they do not appear in their own forms or those of anything else, or they may be unknown because they appear in the form of something else, or they may be unknown because they appear in their own forms as modified in some secondary way. The person of Guiscard, in Boccaccio's story, was unknown to Tancred while he was in the

[77] *Decameron*, II, 3.   [78] IV, I.   [79] VIII, 7.

cave, not because he appeared in his own form changed in some secondary way or in the form of something else, but because he did not appear in any form at all, being in a place where he could not be perceived by the sight or by any other sense of Tancred.[80] Buffalmacco was represented to Master Simone under the form of a horned beast and was not recognized.[81] Lodovico, who kept his appearance and changed his secondary quality of being a gentleman into that of a servant, was not known by Egano de Gallucci.[82] An adultery, in order that we may give example of ignorance of a fact, is not recognized by the husband in question, since it is not apparent to the husband because it is in the form of some other action, and not in the form of adultery, because of some secondary change, as that of the lady of Master Francesco Vergellesi with Zima, in Boccaccio's story.[83] And some other adultery, or rather some other adulteries, are unknown to the husband, as are those of Madonna Isabella with Leonetto and with Master Lambertuccio, since it is presented to the husband under the form of another action, that is, of a fight between the adulterers.[84] Further, an adultery may not be recognized by the husband as adultery, even though it is presented under the appearance of adultery, since it has some secondary modification, like that of Lucretia with Tarquin, for neither her husband nor her parents looked on it as adultery because of the menaces of Tarquin which modified its character.

[Comparison of ignorance of person and of action. 250, 31]

And it is to be considered that in the first case, when the person or the fact is unknown, because they do not appear in their form nor in the form of something else, ignorance of the person is not at all different from ignorance of the fact in the ease with which it is introduced. This is not true in the second case in which the person or the fact is unknown, because, when their aspect is concealed, they show themselves under the aspect of something else, and the person who conceals his aspect can make it appear in few forms of other things and with much difficulty, but the fact, when its true appearance is concealed, can be shown in the form of many things with little difficulty. And in order not to abandon the example I have taken of adultery, it can be seen how the adultery or the adulteries of Madonna Isabella with Leonetto and with Master Lambertuccio appear in the form of a fight between the adulterers,[85]

---

[80] *Decameron*, IV, 1.   [81] VIII, 9.   [82] VII, 7.   [83] III, 5.   [84] VII, 6.
[85] See the preceding note.

and the adultery of the godmother with Brother Rinaldo in the form of an enchantment,[86] and the adultery of Peronella with her lover in the form of the sale of a cask,[87] and the adultery of Goody Belcolore with the priest of Varlungo in the form of the loan of a stone mortar,[88] and the adultery of the avaricious Milanese lady with Gulfardo in the form of the loan of money.[89] But why should I go to the length of giving more examples of this action of adultery alone, since there are innumerable forms of other things in the form of which it can appear in such a way that it has been and can be unknown?

[Easy concealment of identity. 251,10]

But in the third instance the contrary comes about because the person who retains his own form is well supplied with means of concealing himself and bringing about ignorance through unessential changes, but an action is very poor in such means. Thus the fact of adultery, which in the form of other things finds many ways of concealing itself, when it appears in its own shape finds scarcely two methods of bringing about that it should not be recognized as adultery; one of these is force and the other the fear of death which is obviously impending. But a person, appearing in his own form, produces ignorance in others by means of so slight a thing as a change of costume; for example, the abbot, though really a woman, is supposed to be a man by Alexander,[90] and Achilles, though a man, is by Lycomedes supposed to be a woman.[91] And by the external change of a large number of attendants into a small number, great lords escape recognition, as in the instance of Saladin, who without being recognized came to see all the country of the Christians,[92] and Giglietta, who went from Roussillon to Florence without being known.[93] And merely by means of changing his garb from the secular to the religious, Tedaldo talks with his lady and is unknown.[94] And through so slight and external a thing as a change from Italian clothing to that of the Saracens, Master Torello remains unknown. Because of the external change from good light to bad through the coming of night, Tito is not known by Sophronia,[95] and since the windows of the chamber are closed, Catella does not recognize Ricciardo even at noon.[96] The

---

[86] *Decameron*, VII, 3; not strictly correct, for the characters are mother and godfather.
[87] VII, 2.   [88] VIII, 2.   [89] VIII, 1.   [90] II, 3.
[91] Achilles, disguised as a maiden to keep him from participation in the Trojan war, lived at the court of Lycomedes.
[92] *Decameron*, X, 9.   [93] III, 9.   [94] III, 7.   [95] X, 8.   [96] III, 6.

changes brought about by time alone prevent Madam Beritola from recognizing her son,[97] nor does Fineo recognize Teodoro.[98] By reason of a change in belief that does not affect the reality, Lady Catalina, the wife of Nicoluccio Caccianemico, is not recognized by him because he thinks her dead,[99] just as Tedaldo is not recognized by his brothers. . . .[100]

[The best recognition. 252, 9]

In order that we may know which recognition is most worthy of praise, we must understand that when one person knows and the other does not, the recognition can come about in two ways, either with the desire of the one who knows or against his desire. If a recognition comes about through the desire of the person who knows, the recognition has nothing marvelous in it, for it is an easy thing for one who knows to cause himself to be recognized, if he wishes to, by the one who does not know, but if the recognition is against the will of the one who knows, it cannot be other than wonderful, since the one who knows makes an effort not to be recognized. But when both persons do not know, it is likely that the first recognition will be very excellent and new, because it can come about only by chance, but the second, because it can come about either with the desire or against the desire of the one who knows, is of slight excellence if it is according to his wish, and of great excellence if it is against his will; it can be seen in the *Iphigenia among the Taurians* how much more marvelous is the first recognition, that of Iphigenia by Orestes, which came about through chance, than the second, that of Orestes by Iphigenia, which came about by his desire after he recognized his sister.

Chapter XIII

[Tragedy exists for pleasure, not for utility. 275, 19]

Now whether it is true or false that tragedy can have no other material than the terrifying or the piteous, I will not now speak further on it. But it surely appears to me that this has not been proved by Aristotle by means of the things he has said up to now, even though he presupposes that they are proved. Since he has set out to contradict Plato, who had said that tragedy was injurious to the morals of the people, he does not wish to approve any other sort of tragedy than that which according to him is of value

---

[97] *Decameron*, II, 6.　　[98] V, 7.　　[99] X, 4.　　[100] III, 7.

in giving the people good morals and purging with fear and compassion those passions and driving them from the minds of the people in the manner we have mentioned above. Aristotle was so intent on this that he did not take care not to contradict himself and the things he had said before. If it is true that poetry was invented chiefly for the sake of pleasure and not for the sake of utility, as he has shown when he speaks of the origin of poetry in general, why does he hold that in tragedy, which is one part of poetry, utility should chiefly be sought? Why is not pleasure chiefly sought for without any regard for utility? Either Aristotle should pay no attention to utility or he should at least pay so little that he would not reject all the other kinds of tragedy which do not have it, and he should limit utility to one kind alone, namely the bringing about of the purgation of terror and compassion.[101] And nonetheless, if utility is to be considered, it would be possible to present other kinds of tragedy, as, for example, those that contain the changes of good men from misery into happiness, or the change of the wicked from felicity into misery, in order that the people may be assured by the examples that are presented, and confirm themselves in the holy belief that God takes care of the world and exercises special providence over his own, defending them and confounding their enemies and his. . . .[102]

[Experience versus reason in literary criticism. 289, 25]

It is necessary to know that there are some things that reason shows to be of great efficacy in producing the effect of the art but which experience shows are of little efficacy, and indeed destroy the effect. For the sake of example and in order that we may not depart from the art of poetry, reason shows us that we are more moved by the sense of sight than by the sense of hearing, that is, that we are more moved when we see things with the eyes than when we hear them narrated and take them in with the ears, and that therefore poets should cause homicides and horrible things to be represented on the stage to be seen by the people, striving with all their power to cause the people to feel terror and compassion. Yet poets do not do so, and if they do so they are blamed, but they

---

[101] It is strange that Castelvetro, with his certainty that Aristotle did not on the whole stand for utility rather than pleasure in poetry and with his own belief that it exists for delight rather than profit, should have felt so sure that the catharsis was a moral matter. Possibly he is an early instance of the critic misled by assuming a violent opposition between Plato and Aristotle.

[102] Cf. Sidney, *Defense*, sect. 25, below.

introduce either a messenger or another person who by way of
narrative makes them hear merely, for experience has shown that
such cruelty and horror cannot with verisimilitude be made to appear in action, and that when they do, they make people rather
laugh than weep and that they produce the effect not of tragedy
but of comedy. [Here a * indicates that something is omitted by
the editor of 1576.] And there are some other things that reason
shows should be of great efficacy in producing the effect of art,
which experience likewise shows to be of the efficacy that has been
mentioned, for through their power the effect that is desired is
secured in an extraordinary fashion. Of this sort is the sad end of
tragedy, which by reason is proved to be of great value in generat-
ing terror and compassion, and through experience the same thing
is found to be true. Still further, in tragedy without a sad end reason does not suggest that there is generated nor is there generated,
according to what experience shows, terror or compassion. Then,
says Aristotle, since this is shown by experience, which is the
strongest proof that can be brought forward in the arts and the
one to which in dealing with the arts we should alone give heed, we
ought not to doubt at all, even though reason induces us to believe
otherwise. In this instance, however, as has been said, reason is in
conformity with experience.

Chapter XIV

[Tragic pleasure. 299, 5]

The pleasure especially belonging to tragedy is, then, that which
is derived from the terror and the compassion coming from the
change from happiness to misery, because of an error, of a person
neither good nor bad. But anyone can ask what the pleasure is
that is derived from seeing a good man undeservedly hurled from
prosperity into misery, for according to reason we would derive
from it not pleasure but displeasure. Now there is no doubt that
Aristotle understood by the word *pleasure* the purgation and the
removal of fear from human minds by the means of those same
passions in the way which we have above set forth at length. This
purgation and this driving away, if they proceed, as he affirms,
from those same passions, are seen to be capable of being with the
utmost propriety called *hedone*, that is, pleasure or delight, and it
ought properly to be called utility, since it is health of mind acquired through very bitter medicine. Then pleasure arising from

compassion and fear, which is truly pleasure, is that which we have already called indirect pleasure. This appears when, feeling displeasure from the misery of another that has come on him unjustly, we realize that we ourselves are good, since unjust things displease us; this realization is a very great pleasure to us because of the natural love that we have for ourselves. To this pleasure is joined another that is not at all small, namely, that on seeing the tribulations beyond what is reasonable that have come on someone else and which can possibly come on us and others like us, we learn silently and without realizing it that we are subject to many misfortunes and that we cannot believe that the current of human events runs smoothly. This delights us much more than if some other man, acting as a teacher and openly presenting the subject, taught us the same thing. For experience of things that have happened impresses instruction more on our minds than does the mere voice of a teacher, and we take more pleasure in a little that we learn for ourselves than in much that we learn from others, for we cannot learn from others if we do not admit ourselves ignorant of that which we learn and under obligation to our teachers for what we learn from them. And perhaps the wise man had these things in mind when he said that it is better to go to the house of mourning than to go to the house of feasting.[103]

Chapter XVI

[The means of recognition. 349, 3]

Means of recognition
- Marks
  - Apart from the body
  - On the body
    - Adventitious
    - Congenital
      - Shared with others
      - Individual
- Action
  - With respect to others
  - With respect to oneself
    - Voluntary
    - Natural
    - Accidental
- Words spoken
  - By the one to be recognized
    - Intentionally
    - Unintentionally
  - By a third person
    - Intentionally
    - Unintentionally

[103] Ecclesiastes 7, 4.

Chapter XVII

[Poetic inspiration. 374, 6]

[Comment on "Poetic art is the affair of the gifted man more than of the madman."] It has been concluded that he who well understands how to transform himself into an impassioned person will know how to represent such a person properly; that is, he will know how to say and do well, without the aid of art, what is fitting to such a one. And yet not everyone is fitted to do that, but merely he who is of great ability; moreover it is possible to represent a person affected by strong feeling not in this way alone but also in another way, namely to consider diligently that which men under the influence of feeling do and say in expressing their passion, but this is not a method to be used by everyone but merely by a man of high ability. Therefore it follows that poetry is devised and produced by the man of ability and not by the madman, as some say, for the madman is not in a position to put himself into various states of feeling nor is he a careful investigator of the sayings and acts of those under excitement. But it is to be observed that in my opinion there is an error in the text, since the words *or of the madman* ought to be written *not of the madman*.[104] It is not strange that *not* should be made *or* by those who have already absorbed that opinion of the *furor poeticus*[105] which . . . is here by this argument refuted by Aristotle. It is true that it is possible to retain the reading *or of the madman* without departing far from the

---

[104] Castelvetro renders it *non da furioso* in his Italian translation. For opinion at present see Aristotle's *Poetics*, xvii, 55a22, and the note on it in the appendix, above. Faustino Summo, in his *Discorsi poetici* (Padova, 1600) disagrees with Castelvetro (*Disc.* viii, p. 57 r).

Dryden, said to be following Rapin, accepts Castelvetro's reading (Preface to *Troilus and Cressida*, in Ker, *Essays of Dryden*, I, 221–2, 319).

[105] On page 65, l. 11, commenting on *Poetics*, iv, Castelvetro writes: "From this can be understood that Aristotle did not think poetry a special gift of God conceded to one man sooner than to another, as is the gift of prophecy and other like privileges not natural and not common to all. And without doubt he intends, though he does not do it openly, to censure the opinion that some attribute to Plato, that poetry is infused into men by divine inspiration (*furore divino*)." Continuing, he declares that the notion of poetic fury should not be attributed to Plato, but is an invention of the ignorant, impressed by the powers of the poet. In commenting on Aristotle's praise of Homer's skill in constructing the plot (chap. viii), Castelvetro writes: "Aristotle does not recognize in Homer any poetic fury to which he attributes such skill in planning his poem, and if he does not recognize it in Homer, much less does he recognize it in any other poet" (180, 9).

On the *furor poeticus* see also Patrizi, *La deca disputata*, Bk. i.

opinion just expressed if we interpret *or of the madman* as *rather than of the madman*, as is suggested by that verse of Homer:

> I wish your people to live rather than to perish.

That is, Aristotle says poetry is the product of a man of natural ability rather than of a madman, but because *than* instead of *rather than* seems suitable to verse rather than to prose, we rest on what we first said.

Chapter XXIII

[Delight, the end of tragedy. 505, 38]

Those who hold that poetry was invented chiefly for the sake of giving benefit, or to give benefit and delight together, should beware of opposing the authority of Aristotle, who here and elsewhere does not seem to assign any other end than delight;[106] if indeed he consents to some profit, he grants it incidentally, as in the purgation of terror and compassion by means of tragedy.

Chapter XXIV

[The realism of tragedy. 533, 23]

Now in order to understand fully what is being talked about, one must remember that Aristotle said above that there were two measures of tragedy, one obvious to the senses and external, which he thought did not pertain to art, and was measured by the clock, and the other intellectual and internal, and comprehended with the mind; the latter is the end of the process of passing from misery into felicity or from felicity into misery. The termination which is obvious to the senses and is measured with the clock cannot endure more than one course of the sun over the earth for the reasons that were spoken of above; this termination, though it is not that of art, as Aristotle says, yet properly is determined by and receives its measure from the time of the intellectual limit, since the two measures cannot be diverse in relation to time. As we said above, in presenting before spectators in tragedy an action that passes from misery to happiness or from happiness to misery, as much time is spent as is occupied in the actual occurrence of the same action in reality or in imagination.

---

[106] Castelvetro repeats that "the end of poetry is delight" (552, 42). See also 29, 37; 275, 30; 592, 14; 696, 34.

[Temporal limits of the epic. 533, 38]

But in the epic, though it has both limits, that is, one obvious to the senses and another intellectual, the sensible limit is not determined by and does not receive its measure of time from the intellectual limit, but is now longer, now shorter than that. Sometimes an action that took place in a brief space of time is narrated in a long time and the poet devotes many verses to it, and an action that occupied many years is narrated in a very short time and disposed of in a few words. Now if tragedy is limited for the senses to the measure of one revolution of the sun above the earth without passing beyond that, in order to prevent discomfort to the spectators and expense to the producers, so the limit of the epic is set for the senses by its capacity for being drawn out over a number of days, since neither discomfort to the spectators nor damage nor expense to the one reciting prevents it. But the limit for the senses of the epic, if it is an epic that is recited on the public square for the delight of the people, should not be shorter than some hours of one day . . . and according to Aristarchus it can be lengthened to many days, for he thought the wrath of Achilles, of which Homer wrote, had the length required by twenty-four days, and divided the poem into twenty-four books. . . . The internal or intellectual limit of the epic should come at the end of the action that embraces a change from misery to happiness and from happiness to misery, just as does the action of a tragedy.

[Tragedy and epic compared. 535, 32]

Aristotle says that the epic when compared with the tragedy is of greater size because the epic is able to represent several things that are finished in one time in various places, and tragedy can exhibit only that thing which comes about in one place, and appears in action on the stage and concerns certain actors. But he is silent about the other way through which the size of the epic comes to surpass that of tragedy, namely, that not merely can it present several things brought to an end in diverse places at one time, but that it can present diverse things, or one happening of great length, which came about in the course of a long time in one or in diverse places. Tragedy cannot do this because it cannot represent any action except such as occurs in one place and within the space of twelve hours, as has been said.[107] What Aristotle says, namely,

---

[107] Sect. 57, 1, above. Cf. Jonson's *Every Man out of His Humor*, below.

that it is not permissible to present many actions that happen at one time in diverse places, we must take rationally as applied only to what is brought upon the stage and is presented by the actors, for by means of messengers and prophecies it is possible to present in a drama things done in diverse places at the same time, according to what is said above. But because when a messenger or a prophet is introduced, one passes into the field of the epic, and into the narrative method, perhaps for that reason Aristotle has not made mention of this or thought of it as something that naturally pertains to tragedy and to the method of tragic presentation.

[The unreasonable in poetry. 567, 10]

It is here demonstrated by means of three examples how the improbable part of a play may be tolerable when it is not within the action or presented on the stage. The first example is in the *Oedipus Tyrannus* of Sophocles, in which there is the improbability that when he was set over the kingdom of Thebes and took as his wife Jocasta, who was a widow because of the death of Laius, king of Thebes, he did not inquire at the beginning how Laius came to his death, but so acted that he delayed to ask about it and to understand it until the day when he found out that Laius was his father and that he had killed him, and learned that Jocasta was his mother and that with her he had committed abominable incest; these things he learned years after the events. This improbability, namely, that Oedipus did not ask and find out how Laius his predecessor in the kingdom was killed, is tolerable because it is not presented on the stage but is silently presupposed by the reader or the intelligent spectator. But if into the stage presentation Oedipus should be introduced on his arrival at Thebes and should be ignorant how Laius was killed, and, though he was to succeed him in his kingdom and in his matrimonial bed, should not ask about it, the improbability of his conduct would appear more plainly than at present, since this part of the story is not now presented on the stage. We should carefully observe that Aristotle does not charge it to Sophocles as an improbability that the Thebans have given no attention to the death of their king nor sought for the murderers to take vengeance on them, nor does he remove the improbability by saying that it was excusable and tolerable, because committed outside the plot . . . because Aristotle does not blame the *Oedipus* of Sophocles for anything improbable except that Oedipus did not know at the beginning and had not inquired how Laius was killed, and Aristotle excuses Sophocles because this was outside the plot. . . .

[The improbability in the *Electra*. 567, 43]

The second example is in the *Electra* of Sophocles, where there is an improbable part, namely, that those who first come from the Pythian games and narrate how things have gone say nothing in Argos of the death of Orestes, as is presupposed by the indications made by Electra and Clytemnestra at the coming of the old servant and Orestes and Pylades, who pretend that they are bringing the ashes of the body of Orestes, which has been burned; yet certainly these three were not the first to bring news of the Pythian games.[108] But this improbable part—I call it improbable because it makes the coming of the old servant, Orestes, and Pylades improbable—is outside the presentation on the stage and because it is not mentioned is tolerable. . . . But that what is here discussed may be fully understood, it must be observed that there are some deeds that can be done at the time when they should be and also at the time when they should not be. For example, if Oedipus, when he was established in the dignity of the kingdom and the royal bed, had asked how Laius was killed, he would have asked it at the time when he should have asked it; he might also have asked it again perhaps twenty years later, at a time when it was possible for him to recognize Laius as his father and Jocasta as his mother, that is, at a time when he should not have asked it. And because he asked it at a time when he should not have asked it, this second action is faulty in being performed at a time not opportune, and because the question has already been asked the first time, it is faulty in being superfluous. Hence the repeated action has two faults. There are also some actions that are not done at the time when they should be done.

[Anachronism. 569, 15]

There are some actions that are done at the time when they should be done and are done truthfully, and again are done at a time when they should not be done and are done falsely. For example, we may say that those who first came to Argos from the Pythian games related what events had happened there and related them truthfully, just as they had happened, and related them at the time when they should and in every way as they ought to.

---

[108] That is, Castelvetro believes they could not have been the first.

Then after some days other men, namely, the old servant, Pylades, and Orestes, pretending they were others than they were and giving the appearance of coming from the Pythian games, recited anew how things went there, and did it falsely, reporting that Orestes was killed there. . . . But if the first true action did not take place . . . the second would have one defect only, that of occurring at a time when it should not occur. . . . Now it is to be observed that to the example from the *Electra* used by Aristotle one can object not merely that others, before the old servant, Orestes, and Pylades, would probably have given in Argos an account of the events at the Pythian games, and in another fashion, but also that the three men narrated impossible things which they knew to be impossible, that is, that Orestes was killed in the chariot race. Yet at that time the chariot race was not among the contests at the Pythian games. But Aristotle does not speak of this objection, but of the other, as we have shown. Because this race was to be seen at the Pythian games in the time of Sophocles, perhaps he allowed himself to think that it was permitted to him to feign that it was also one of the contests at a time when history makes evident that it was not. I do not believe that it was allowable for him to do this, as I do not believe that such a mistake can be excused by means of the figure called anachronism.[109]

Chapter XXV

[Is learning necessary to the poet? 591, 30]

There have been many in the past and also at present there are many well versed in letters and known to fame, who hold the belief that the poet should be excellently instructed in all the sciences and all the arts, and that without full knowledge of these he cannot be truly a poet. From this opinion Aristotle is far distant, so far as we can judge from the words he writes here. If he says there is one kind of correctness for poetry and another for every other art, and afterwards expresses the opinion that error and transgression in another art is another thing, and that therefore the poet should be unpunished for faults committed in other arts, it follows he believes poetry can be perfect and worthy of praise without depending on extraordinary or even moderate knowledge of the sciences and the arts.

[109] See the index.

JACOPO MAZZONI

oᗡ°oᗡo

DISTRESSED AT THE ATTACKS on Dante by Castravilla, an Italian noble-man applied to his friend Jacopo Mazzoni to defend the poet. Though deeply immersed in the philosophical studies from which issued a work in which the differences between Plato and Aristotle, and other philosophical matters, are settled in five thousand one hundred and ninety-seven questions, Mazzoni undertook the task, and within a month produced a little volume called *The Discourse of Giacopo Mazzoni in Defense of the Comedy of the Divine Poet Dante*, first published in 1572. Some years later he undertook a much longer work, *On the Defense of the Comedy of Dante*, directed in part against the objections of Belisario Bulgarini; the first three books were published in 1587.[1] The last four were not, however, printed until 1688.

In the earlier book Mazzoni announces that he has attempted to keep within the bounds set by Aristotle, though he does not pronounce them ultimate for poetry. In the later work he announces no such purpose; Aristotle is treated with respect, yet Mazzoni is not in bondage to him. Plato seems to have been the strongest influence on his thought. By setting out from a great poet whom he loved, and to whom the rules of poetry must yield, Mazzoni gained for his ideas a vigor and good sense less easily attained by those who made Aristotle their point of departure.

Milton mentions Mazzoni with respect as a teacher of the art of poetry in his tractate *Of Education*, and there are a number of passages in the work *On the Defense of the Comedy* that probably would have interested him. It is, however, difficult to find indications of direct and strong influence on the English poet.

The translations are by the editor.

BIBLIOGRAPHY

Barbi, Michele, *La fortuna di Dante nel secolo XVI*. Firenze, 1890.

Mazzoni, Jacopo, *Discorso in difesa della "Commedia" del divino poeta Dante*, ed. Mario Rossi. Citta di Castello, 1898.

——, *Della difesa della "Commedia" di Dante*. Cesena, 1688.

[1] The work seems actually to have been composed by Tuccio dal Corno, from material supplied by Mazzoni (*Modern Language Notes*, XLI [1926], 261). Tuccio dal Corno's name does not appear in the edition of 1688.

DISCOURSE IN DEFENSE OF THE *COMEDY* (*selection*)

1572

Section 10 (*in part*)

[Revolt against Aristotle]

Perhaps . . . I shall show that even when the laws of the Lyceum[1] have been broken and destroyed, it is still possible to write poetry legitimately in another fashion; from this demonstration will result an easier way to defend Dante and some of our other poets. And certainly as we see that gardens with various leafy trees are not less but more beautiful than groves in which we see oaks only, in like manner I think the beautiful and attractive variety of our epic poets (speaking of those who are not unworthy of that name) is much more to be commended than the severe and rigid simplicity of the ancients.[2]

ON THE DEFENSE OF THE *COMEDY* (*selections*)

1587

Introduction (*in part*)

[Imitation]

[1] Those arts that have as their object the image, or idol, have an object for the construction of which there is no other end than to represent and to imitate; hence they are properly called imitative. . . . The imitative arts are so called not because they use imitation, for in this sense all the arts in small or great measure use some sort of imitation, but because they imitate objects that have no being or use except from imitation and in imitation. I believe Plato wished to demonstrate this when he said in the second of the *Laws:* "The rightness of an imitation consists, as we said, in this, namely, that it is made so large and of such a sort that there is expressed by the imitation the size and quality of the thing in itself." And Proclus almost at the end of the *Poetical Questions*, founded on the authority of Plato, said: "Each imitator has as his end to make something like his example, whether it is or is not for

[1]The Lyceum was the school of Aristotle.　　[2]See *variety* in the index.

the delight of anyone." . . . It can be concluded that the imitative arts were so named because they have objects that are suitable for no end or use other than to represent and imitate, and that they are distinguished from the other arts that are not called imitative in that the latter have objects that are good for some other use and some other end than to represent alone and to imitate alone. In this way, then, the image is the object of the imitative arts. But to understand fully the nature of this image, which is the true and worthy object of the imitative arts, . . . it is necessary to commence at some distance. The image then, as I have said, is a figure and a similitude of some other thing, through which, as Plato has taught us in the *Sophist* and in the sixth of the *Republic*, it can come into being, either with our artifice or without it. And that which comes into being without human artifice has its origin from corporeal or from spiritual things. . . . Now coming to our subject, I say that when we concluded above that the image is the object of the imitative arts we did not mean that sort of image that comes into being without human artistic activity . . . but that which has its origin from our art, which usually springs from our phantasy and our intellect by means of our choice and will, as an image in pictorial art or in sculpture, and similar things. I conclude then that this species of image is that which is an adequate object of human imitation, and that when Aristotle said in the beginning of the *Poetics* that all the species of poetry were imitative, he meant that imitation which has for its object the image that springs entirely from human artifice in the method that is explained. . . . Plato in the *Sophist* has left a statement that imitation is of two sorts. One of these he has named icastic; it represents things that are truly derived from some work already existing, or at least are derived. The other, which he called phantastic, is exemplified in pictures that are made by the caprice of the artist. And indeed he himself says in the tenth of the *Republic* that the image is the subject of every imitation.[3] Then the image will be common to phantastic imitation as well. . . . I believe then that now everyone can know what imitative art is and how it is distinguished from the other arts that are not imitative, and what the image is that is the subject of imitation.

[3]"One [of the divisions of the imitative art] is the art of making likenesses. A likeness of anything is made by turning out a copy in the proportions of the originals, the same in length and breadth and depth, and with each part in its proper color" (*Sophist* 235). In painting there is some deception for the sake of appearance. See also pp. 42ff., above.

[Poetic imitation]

[2] Now I add that poetry should be placed among the imitative arts and in this class of imitation, as a species subordinate to its genus. Hence on beginning to define poetry one can say it is imitation. But here arises a new and very important difficulty. For full understanding of it we should remember that poems can be of three sorts, that is, either representing the persons themselves who speak, as do comedy and tragedy, or merely relating the things in the person of the poet, as dithyrambic poetry usually does and as is done in the first three books of the *Georgics* of Vergil, or partly narrating and partly introducing other speakers, as is seen in the *Iliad* and the *Odyssey*, and the *Aeneid* of Vergil.[4] Now it may be clearly seen that imitation is found in that sort of poem in which are introduced other persons as speakers. But it does not appear that there is imitation in those other sorts of poems in which something is narrated through the mouth of the poet. It seems then that imitation is the genus containing only the poetry that Aristotle called dramatic, and that imitation can by no means be the genus of narrative poetry. And this difficulty is the greater because it appears to be founded both on the reason immediately apparent and on the authority of Plato, who in the beginning of the third book of the *Republic* says clearly that dramatic poetry alone is imitative and that narrative poetry has nothing to do with imitation. . . .

[The kinds of poetic imitation]

[3] Now with respect to Aristotle I believe he sets up poetic imitation as a suitable genus which contains four species.

The first and most important is the dramatic-phantastic, which is an imitation because it necessarily contains two sorts of idols and images. The first image is that of the person represented. The other is the false but verisimilar image which the actor presents; since he does not represent the true but the verisimilar, he consequently represents the image and the simulacrum of the truth.

The second species is that of dramatic-icastic imitation, which necessarily contains the image of the person.

The third is that of narrative-phantastic imitation, which always certainly presents the image and the simulacrum of the truth and

---

[4] Plato, *Republic*, III, 392 f., above; Aristotle, *Poetics*, III, above.

can have another as well, which is always found in narrative-icastic poetry, of which we shall next speak.

The fourth and last species is that of narrative-icastic poetry, which ought to contain the idol and the image which consists in particularization. . . . I add that although Aristotle has called all four of these species of poetry imitations, that nonetheless when he compared dramatic imitation with narrative he thought dramatic imitation much more worthy of the name than narrative, to such a degree that at times he calls the narrative part the otiose part of the poem and not imitation; but this ought always to be understood of it in comparison with dramatic poetry and not absolutely. . . .

Now coming to Plato, I say he too has in some places denied that narrative poetry is imitation. . . . Yet he also has said that narrative poetry is not imitation when compared with dramatic poetry, but one should not conclude from this that, speaking absolutely, he did not believe narrative poetry to be imitation. On the contrary I insist that he himself in the *Sophist*[5] has identified narrative with imitation. . . . With respect to the narrative-icastic I say the poet is obliged to imitate in this also, and that he does it well if he sets himself to describe everything to the smallest detail. In that way are made the idols and the images proper to narrative. . . . Because Homer was excellent at it he was said by Longinus to describe images.[6] For this reason Lucian, giving minutely in one of his dialogues the beauties of Phanta, named the work *Images*. . . .[7] He shows a little farther on that Homer in describing the qualities and the beauty of Penelope made an image . . .[8] and finally at the end of the dialogue he concludes that poetic narrative makes im-

---

[5] Almost at the end.   [6] Chap. ix of *On Literary Excellence*, above.

[7] *Images* 6–9: "The hair, the forehead, the exquisite eyebrows, reason will keep as Praxiteles has rendered them; the eyes, too, those soft, yet bright-glancing eyes, she leaves unaltered. But the cheeks and the front of the face are taken from the 'Garden' Goddess; and so are the lines of the hands, the shapely wrists, the delicately tapering fingers. Phidias and the Lemnian *Athene* will give the outline of the face, and the well-proportioned nose, and lend new softness to the cheeks; and the same artist may shape her neck and closed lips, to resemble those of his *Amazon*. . . . For the flesh-tints, which must be neither too pale nor too highly coloured, Apelles shall copy his own *Campaspe*. And lastly, Aëtion shall give her Roxana's lips. Nay, we can do better: Have we not Homer, best of painters, though a Euphranor and an Apelles be present? Let him colour all like the limbs of Menelaus, which he says were 'ivory tinged with red.' He too shall paint her calm 'ox-eyes,' and the Theban poet shall help him to give them their 'violet' hue. Homer shall add her smile, her white arms, her rosy finger-tips, and so complete the resemblance to golden Aphrodite, to whom he has compared Briseus's daughter with far less reason" (*The Works of Lucian*, trans. by H. W. and F. G. Fowler [Oxford, 1905], III, 16–7).

[8] *Odyssey*, xviii, 187–96.

ages that are worthy to be preferred to those of Apelles, Parrhasius, and Polygnotus. . . . Because of this exact particularization suited to poets, I believe, Philostratus wrote in the first book of *Images* that poetry was like a picture.[9] Horace said: "Poetry will be like a picture,"[10] and Plutarch, in the book in which he explains how the poets should be listened to, writes plainly that poetry is a speaking picture,[11] and adds that as in a picture one does not blame the ugliness of the things represented, if they are well imitated, so likewise in poetry the ugliness of the characteristics of men should not be blamed, if they are artistically expressed. . . . Cicero writes in the fifth *Tusculan:* "It is reported that Homer was blind. But we see that he has given us a picture rather than a poem. What country, what shores, what place in Greece, what kind of form, what battles, what armies, what rowing of a ship, what motion of men or of wild beasts—which of these has he not so painted that what he did not see himself he has made us to see?" After making many other comments on this passage, Philip Beroaldus finally says: "It is the glory of the greatest poet so graphically to describe or rather to depict everything that he seems to spread it out before the eyes of the reader to be looked at. . . ." [In a book by Cardinal Paleotti] there are apposite references to some beautiful images produced by poets in narrative, among others one from Vergil, through which he wishes to show that the image in the poetic narrative surpasses in distinctness and clarity that of a picture itself; he quotes these verses:

> There, too, he had portrayed the mother-wolf stretched in Mars's green cavern; around her teats were the twin boys in play climbing and clinging, and licking their dam without dread; while she, her lithe neck bent back, was caressing them by turns and with her tongue molding their young limbs (*Aeneid*, VIII, 630–4).

I believe it can with probability be said that when Plato distinguished narrative poetry from imitation, he wished to say that, in comparison with dramatic poetry, narrative did not merit the name of imitation. . . . But still it should not be said that, speaking absolutely, narrative poetry is not in some way imitation, even according to the idea of Plato. It can, then, be taken as a firm and sure conclusion that the genus of poetry is imitation, and conse-

---

[9] *Images*, Bk. I, introd.   [10] *Art of Poetry*, 361, above.
[11] Plutarch, *How a Young Man Should Study Poetry*, sect. 3. Sidney uses the phrase in his *Defense*, sect. 12, immediately below.

quently that every species of poetry makes idols and images in the manner that has already been indicated. And because the truth of imitation, as has been said above on the authority of Plato, consists in representing things exactly as they are, it therefore follows that it is an essential mistake in poetry to represent them differently and with dissimilitude. . . . For this reason it appears that Plato, in the second of the *Republic*, thought Homer erred essentially in imitation when he represented many repulsive vices of the gods and the heroes, for he should have done the very opposite when attempting to represent with correct imitation divine and heroic nature. . . .

[Falsehood as the subject of poetry]

[4] Now let us consider the subject and matter suited to poetry. It is the opinion of many that the false and lying, though still verisimilar, is the proper subject for poetry.[12] They allow themselves to be induced to believe this because they think the poet is certainly the man who makes up within himself the invention of his poem, adding that he who takes from any other place than his own invention does not merit the name of poet. They think such was the opinion of Aristotle, who said Empedocles was rather a natural philosopher than a poet, because he intended to set forth in verse not his inventions but the truth of natural things. . . .[13] Plato appears to have favored this opinion in the *Phaedo*, with these words: "He who wishes to be a poet should compose not discourses but stories."[14] Plutarch, in the little book in which he inquires whether the Athenians have gained greater glory with arms or with letters, writes to this effect: "They say too that one of the friends of Menander said to him: 'The feasts of Bacchus draw near, and have you not composed your comedy?' He answered: 'I have composed the comedy, because I have obtained the plot and arranged it. I have only to add the verses to it.'" For the poets themselves think fables are more necessary to them than words. Corinna said to Pindar, when he was a young man and boldly made use of his power over words, that he was ignorant of poetics because he did not put fables in his writings, for that is the proper function of the poet. Because of all these and other authorities, one could easily fall in with the idea of whoever chances to think that poetry has no other subject than the fabulous and the false, but still joined with

---

[12] Varchi held that the "feigned and fabulous" was the proper field for the poet (*Della poetica in generale*, I, 2). [13] *Poetics*, I. [14] *Phaedo*, 61.

the verisimilar, since verisimilitude according to the rules of Aristotle is required in the fables of the poets. Yet I say this opinion does not conform to the truth for many reasons, of which I shall select some. . . . If this were the true subject of poetry, it would of necessity be in no way capable of truth, and yet Plato writes and Aristotle confirms and reason persuades that the contrary is true. Then Plato, having in the *Republic* and in the *Laws* approved that species of poetry that deals with the gods in conformity with the truth,[15] has gone on to demonstrate that the truth is not irreconcilable with poetry. Aristotle himself has confirmed this in three places in the *Poetics*. . . .[16]

But in addition to the authority of Plato and of Aristotle, reason also proves to us that the poet sometimes says what is true, for in recounting the wanderings of some heroes, he would often not be able to do other than describe the positions of cities. It must be said that when he follows the truth of geography either he for the time being loses the name of poet—something altogether ridiculous[17]—or it is necessary to confess that the truth can sometimes be a poetic subject. And we have already shown it is possible for idols and images to be made from truth, both in narrative and dramatically. For all these reasons it seems to me we should affirm two conclusions as true. The first is that the false is not always of necessity the subject of poetry. The second is that since the subject of poetry is sometimes true and sometimes false, it is consequently necessary to constitute a poetic subject that of itself can be sometimes true and sometimes false. . . .

[The credible as the subject of poetry]

[5] Because already with the authority of Aristotle it has been concluded that the credible is the subject of the arts of the poets, it seems to me that from what has been said we can lay down three conclusions. First, since the poet always has to do with the credible, he should of necessity treat all things in a manner suited to the credible, that is, he should always avail himself of individual and perceptible means in representing the things of which he speaks, whatever they are. Therefore when he treats things pertaining to contemplative teaching he should make every effort to represent

---

[15] *Republic*, x, 607; *Laws*, vii, 801, above.
[16] Chaps. ix, 51b19; xxv, 60b10 and 60b32.
[17] Yet it has not in our day seemed ridiculous to Croce that at times even Dante should lose the name of poet; see *The Poetry of Dante*, p. 84.

them with sensible images—something Empedocles did not do.
For that reason he was called rather a physicist than a poet. But
in this Dante is certainly marvelous, . . . as when in speaking of the
most holy and ineffable Trinity he writes thus:

> In the deep and pure substance of the lofty light there appeared
> to me three circles of three colors and of one content, and one
> appeared reflected from another as rainbow from rainbow, and
> the third appeared a flame that breathed equally from both the
> others (*Paradise*, XXXIII, 115–20).

For this same reason it comes about that the poet often uses comparisons and long detailed similitudes. He who asks why the poet
is obliged at least in narrative to use this type of the credible should
be satisfied with the reason I give, namely, that the poet needs to
speak to the people, among whom are many who are unpolished
and of little education; for that reason if the poets should speak in
the method suitable to science of things that are to be known, it
would not be understood by the people.[18] Hence the poet treats of
such matters in a credible fashion, that is, he teaches them by
means of comparisons and similitudes taken from things obvious
to the senses, and the common people, knowing that in such things
the truth exists in the fashion presented by the poet, therefore
easily believe poetry is also true in intelligible things.

From this we can conclude it is not forbidden to the poet to treat
things pertaining to the sciences and to the speculative intellect, if
only he treats them in a credible manner, making idols and poetic
images, as Dante surely has done with marvelous and noble artifice, in representing with idols and beautiful images before the eyes
of everyone all intellectual being and the intelligible world itself.
I remember that Plato in the *Phaedrus*, exalting his invention,
wrote as follows: "But the place that is above the heavens no one
of the poets ever has treated or ever will treat as it should be
done." . . .[19] But if he had seen the third *Cantica* of Dante he would
without any doubt have looked on his own invention as inferior
and given the palm to Dante and consequently to the poets for
knowing how to make idols and images fitted for making the people understand the quality of the supercelestial world. . . .

The second conclusion is that the poet having as his subject the
credible ought as a result to prefer credible things to true, to false,
to possible, to impossible—I mean that he should give more atten-

---

[18] Cf. Castelvetro on *Poetics*, I, 30, 7, immediately above.   [19] *Phaedrus*, 247.

tion to the credible than to any of all the others that can be mentioned. Therefore if it should happen that two things should be presented to him, one of them false but credible, the other true but incredible or at least little credible, the poet should wholly abandon the true and follow after the credible. . . .

[Poetry as a division of the rational or sophistic faculty[20]]

[6] The third and last conclusion, a corollary of the two preceding, is that poetry, because of paying more attention to the credible than to the true, ought to be classed as a subdivision of the rational faculty, called by the ancients sophistic.[21] For a complete understanding of this truth, which, if I do not deceive myself, has been up to now hidden, it must be realized that the poetic art can be regarded in two ways, namely, according to whether it treats of the law of the poetic image, or whether it builds up and forms the image.

In the first sense I say that it should be called poetic, and in the second poetry. In the first the art rules over and uses the image, and falls within the theory of the state, as I shall soon explain. In the second it is the art that forms and constructs the image, and is a species of the rational capacity, and as I have said should be put under sophistic, since it has no regard for the truth. But I see I have offended the poets, since I have given to the art until now reputed as divine the name of sophistic, which is thought ugly and infamous. And in order in some measure to console them, I wish to linger a while over this art of the sophists and to show how it has or does not have an evil suggestion. . . . Sophistic was that which treated of all things rhetorically, namely, in such a way that they might be believed, and that reasoned surely with some boast of its propositions, and that took feigned subjects, as of Orestes and Alcmaeon, imitating together the one and the other, and representing them through images. That this representing through idols and images was proper to the sophistic art, Plato has clearly

[20] Benedetto Varchi gives the following classification: "The logician uses as his means the most noble of instruments, that is, demonstration or the demonstrative syllogism; the dialectician uses the topic syllogism; the sophist uses the sophistic syllogism, namely, that which is apparent and deceptive; the orator uses the enthymeme; and the poet the example, which is the least worthy of all. Hence the subject of poetics is feigned and fabulous speech, and its means or instrument is the example" (*Della poetica in generale*, I, 2).

See also Tasso, *The Heroic Poem*, sect. 8, below, and *example* in the index.

[21] Scaliger writes: "It is not true, as is said, that poetry belongs to sophistic" (*Poetice*, VII, 2, p. 347B2).

shown in the *Sophist*,[22] where he calls it the maker of images, as that which represents what appears to be true. . . . Philostratus, . . . wishing to prove that Prodicus of Ceos was a sophist, shows that he wrote a book where he treated of a thing pertaining to moral philosophy, that is, of the appetites for virtue and for vice that combat in young men, making idols and images of it. He says then: "For this reason a pretty speech was written by Prodicus of Ceos, in which virtue and vice appeared to Hercules in female forms. Vice was ornamented and diversely colored, and Virtue was as chance found her. They made open offers to the young Hercules, the first ease and softness, the second troubles and fatigues."[23] It seems to me, then, it can reasonably be said that poetry deserves to be classified under the ancient sophistic, since poetry too deals with all things according to the credible, and speaks of them with great pride, as professing to know all things through the aid of Apollo and the Muses. Indeed Hesiod, as a poet, has the consummate arrogance to indicate that in an instant he learned all things, past, present, and future. For this reason the opinion of a learned commentator on the *Poetics* is pleasing to me: he thinks that it is in no way fitting for the poet to use words and modes of speech that throw doubt on the things he speaks of, for since he above all professes to deal with the credible he should say everything with much assurance and boldness. Hence for this reason too the poet merits the name of sophist. But he merits it much more because he is a maker of idols and represents all things with images. . . .

Philostratus also speaks of another kind of sophistic which he calls second sophistic, writing of it thus: "It took for its subject the poor, the rich, lords, and tyrants, giving his own name to each one, as history does." . . .[24] From these words of Philostratus we learn that old sophistic was not different from the second except in that the old used feigned names and the second real names. It can therefore be said that icastic poetry is a species of the second sophistic and phantastic poetry a species of the old sophistic.

Now I think everyone can understand that Philostratus was of the opinion the sophistic art was that which abandoned the true and concerned itself with the credible, and that he has thought it

---

[22] Secs. 236, 239, and elsewhere.

[23] *Lives of the Sophists*, sect. 483. See Erwin Panofsky, *Hercules am Scheidewege und andere antike Bildstoffe in der neueren Kunst* (Leipzig, 1930).

[24] *Lives of the Sophists*, sect. 481.

worthy and noble, not vile and infamous, as Boethius has preferred to call it,[25] and perhaps also Plato and Aristotle. But to reconcile the authors who have blamed and those who have praised sophistic, it must be understood that sophistic has been looked on as that which in some way parts from the law of true philosophy. Now true philosophy is accustomed to order the intellect by means of the false, and the will by means of evil. This was the sort of sophistic blamed by Plato, by Aristotle, and by all his followers, and it appears Plato wished to class with this species of sophistic the poetry of Homer, as that which disorders the intellect by representing false things of the gods and the heroes, and which disorders the will with the variety of its imitation and by immoderately increasing our affections. . . . Therefore it can be said that every other poem which is similar to that of Homer is to be classified under the sophistic blamed by that philosopher. Such sophistic was banished not merely from the republic of Plato but also from that of the Athenians, as Philostratus has written in the following words: "Seeing the eloquence of the sophists, the Athenians drove them away from the judges, as those who with unjust speech exercised power over justice and became too powerful over the law."[26]

The species of sophistic blamed by the philosophers, then, is that which disorders the intellect with the false, and the will with injustice. As a subdivision of it they also classify that sort of poetry productive of the same disorders, because it does not truly merit the name of poetry, since it does not form its idols in conformity with the laws of the poetic art as that which uses and commands. . . .

The second species of sophistic is that called by Philostratus the old sophistic,[27] which, though indeed it propounds to the intellect things that are feigned, yet does not disorder the will, but rather in every way and wholly attempts to make it conformable with the just; this species of sophistic was never blamed by the ancients. And if it should appear to anyone that it does merit blame because of disordering the intellect with falsity, I say that such an one should know that the ancient gentile philosophers (departing in this from the truth of sacred theology) praise this disorder of the intellect in certain things, when it was directed to a proper end. For this reason Plato holds that the magistrate should be able to lie to his citizens for the sake of some public good.[28] I omit the fact

---

[25] Boethius translated Aristotle's work entitled *Elenchorum sophisticorum libri duo*, or *Two Books on Unsound Proofs*.
[26] *Lives of the Sophists*, sect. 483.   [27] *Ibid*, sect. 481.   [28] *Republic*, II, 382, above.

that this species of sophistic almost always contains some truth beneath the husk of the first appearance. Now I say phantastic poetry regulated by the proper laws is part of this ancient sophistic, since it also propounds feigned things to our intellect in order to regulate the appetite, and many times contains beneath the husk of the fiction the truth of many noble conceptions.

The third species of sophistic is that called by Philostratus the second sophistic, which does not propound feigned names and acts, but true names and real events, of which it discourses according to the law of justice. . . . This species is called sophistic because though indeed it treated of true things for the sake of justice, it still dealt with them in a credible way, and therefore sometimes abandoned the truth when it looked on the false as more credible or as a more effective instrument in persuading men as was desired. . . . In this third species of sophistic, according to my judgment, icastic poetry should be placed, as representing real actions and persons, but yet always in a credible manner.

By means of all I have said on sophistic, then, I believe every one can understand the basis for our belief that poetry is a rational capacity, and that among the rational capacities it ought not to be classified under that which sets out to teach the truth and opposes it to all other things, but it should be classed under that which gives all its effort to investigating what is credible and apparent and sets it over against the truth; for that reason the second was by the ancients called sophistic. . . . I conclude then with certainty that poetry is a sophistic art, because of imitation, which is its proper genus, because of the credible, which is its subject, and because of delight, which is its end; because it is within that genus, is concerned with that subject, and moves toward that end, it is many times obliged to admit the false. . . . The credible is, then, the subject of poetry.

[The marvelous]

[7] But because it is also the subject of rhetoric, we must needs see in what way it can be the proper subject of poetry and the proper subject of rhetoric. . . . I say, then, the credible as credible is the subject of rhetoric and the credible as marvelous is the subject of poetry, for the poet should utter not merely credible things but marvelous things as well.[29] For this reason, when he can do so with credibility he falsifies human and natural history and goes on

[29] Cf. Aristotle's *Poetics*, chap. xxiv, 60a26, above.

to impossible things. . . . If there were set before the poet two things equally credible, one of which was more marvelous than the other, though it was false, so long as it was not impossible, the poet ought to take it over and give up the less marvelous one. . . .[30]

[Truth and falsehood in poetry]

[8] But perhaps it is possible to doubt whether this credible marvelous can be found in company with the truth, and therefore someone might think it was badly said above that poetry is sometimes capable of the truth. I answer that we find some true things more marvelous than the false, not merely in natural things . . . but also in human history. . . . Pliny explains to Caninius that the war in Dacia carried on by Trajan the emperor, though it was true, was a fit subject for a poem, because it was marvelous. These are his words: "You are doing very well in that you are preparing to write of the Dacian war, for how recent, how abundant, how sweeping the matter is, and yet how poetical and, though dealing with things that are perfectly true, how fabulous!" . . .[31] How well Pliny shows that the true can sometimes be consistent with the marvelous![32]

On this subject, then, we have left only to show the authorities by whom apparently it can be proved that the false, in so far as it is verisimilar, is the poetical subject. I say first, then, it is true that Aristotle calls Empedocles a physicist rather than a poet,[33] and he was confirmed by Plutarch in his book on listening to poems, in these words: "We do not know any poetry that is without fables and fictions. For the verses of Empedocles and Parmenides, the *Theriaca* of Nicander, and the sentences of Theognis are rather essays, which, to escape the lowliness of prose, took the greatness and the measure of poetry as a vehicle." . . .[34] With respect to Plutarch I say either he speaks truly of the true and perfect poet, who, as I have said, ought to be connected with phantastic rather

[30] Milton was possibly somewhat influenced by Mazzoni when he wrote that in education "poetry would be made subsequent, or rather indeed precedent [to rhetoric], as being less subtle and fine, but more simple, sensuous, and passionate" (*Of Education*). Mazzoni is mentioned in the context as teaching the sublime art of poetry. While there is no verbal similarity, Milton's "sensuous and passionate" perhaps suggests Mazzoni's "marvelous." [31] *Letters*, VIII, 4.
[32] Cf. Aristotle's "it is probable that things will happen contrary to probability" (*Poetics*, chap. XXV, 61b9, above). See *marvelous* in the index.
[33] *Poetics*, I, 47a28, above.
[34] Sect. 2, 53–4, in *Essays on the Study and Use of Poetry by Plutarch and Basil the Great*, trans. by F. M. Padelford (New York, 1902).

than with icastic imitation, or he was actually of an opinion opposed to that of Aristotle and Plato, namely, that poetry should in no way be composed of true matter. . . . To the text of Aristotle, in which he writes that the history of Herodotus set out in verse would always be history, and consequently not worthy of the name of poetry,[35] we answer that it is true, but it does not therefore follow that a poem cannot in some way be made of history, if it were represented as the credible marvelous in an idol and a particularized image, but if it were narrated in the method proper to history without making an idol or an image of it, even though it were set forth in verse, it would always remain history. . . . The true can also be made beautiful by narrating it in a fashion in harmony with the credible and making idols and images of it. For this reason I believe icastic poetry, which takes a true subject from history, is able nevertheless in many things to add something of its own in order to make that history particularized. Without any doubt this is more clearly recognized in icastic dramatic poetry than in narrative. . . .

[Poetry defined]

[9] Summarizing, then, this discourse on the poetic subject, one may say it should be credible and at the same time marvelous, and joining this subject to the form that has already been made clear, we can now say poetry is an imitation, made with harmony, with rhythm, and with verse, accompanied or joined with matter that is credible and marvelous.

[The causes of poetry]

[10] For full completion of this definition, it remains to find the efficient cause and the final cause of poetry. As to the efficient cause we can dispose of it quickly by saying it is the human intellect. But this is the common cause of all the arts; hence we should like to find a cause more nearly special to poetry, and that when united with its end will make clear the specific origin and legitimate use of poetry.

[Poetry and the state]

[11] To do this with some foundation, I believe there is no more certain mode than to consider what the art is that discovered the use of poetry, for this, if I am not mistaken, will reveal to us

---

[35] *Poetics*, IX, first par., above.

the origin and the end of poetry. I then think the civil faculty[36] is that which not merely found out the use of poetry, but afterwards should consider the norm and the rule of the poetic image. The following considerations force me to this belief, namely, that all the natural powers and the arts which spring from human reason are normally directed toward contrary objects. For example, medicine understands not only health and health-bringing beverages, but also sickness and deadly poisons. And so we can say that the legal faculty in the same way professes to know not merely the just but also the unjust. Now from these considerations I say the civil faculty professes to understand not alone the right ordering of human actions but also the right ordering of the cessation of these operations, which is opposed to the first rectitude as privation to habit. But because someone could object that the habits of our intellect and the human arts consider merely the positive contraries and not the privatives, I therefore add that positive contrariety and depriving contrariety are always considered by one and the same art. So, for example, the natural philosopher not merely considers the contrariety of movements in so far as it is positive, namely the contrariety that is found in movement as it is, whether toward the high part or toward the low, but he also considers the depriving contrariety which is between movement and its cessation, namely, quiet. . . . But the cessation of activity . . . should dispose and prepare men in such a way that they are more apt and more zealous for activity. Then the same faculty will give the law of operation and of cessation. And observe I do not understand cessation as a total privation and extinction of activity, but merely as a cessation of hard and fatiguing operations. Hence in the use of the word *cessation* we include the operations of play and of amusement which we indulge in for recreation and for pastime. Therefore it can be said that contrariety either of activity or of cessation is not merely negative, as has been said above, but positive as well. It is privative in so far as cessation means lack of weighty activities. It is positive in so far as cessation of serious activities should contain some pleasant activities fit to restore spirits fatigued in more important operations. . . .[37]

[36] That is the capacity that deals with the organization of society, with man as a civil or social animal, as the Renaissance learned it from Aristotle. The didactic theory common in the period was a recognition of the poet's social responsibility.

[37] Mazzoni justifies his opinion by reference to Aristotle, *Ethics*, x, 6 and 7; *Politics*, viii, 3, 1337b30.

[Poetry and recreation]

[12] So it appears to me possible to say with certainty that because this contrariety of cessation and of operation is negative and positive, it necessarily can be thought of in connection with the same art and the same faculty. But the civil faculty is that which considers the legality of actions; hence it is also that which considers the legality of cessation. In the latter are contained all the actions done for the sake of pastime, to wit, all those done in play. Hence the consideration of the lawfulness of recreations will be without doubt something pertinent to the civil faculty and to moral philosophy. But among all the recreations none is found more worthy, more noble, or more important than that which is made through the labors of the poets. Hence the civil faculty should take care to consider among all other recreations chiefly the norm and the law of poetry. Now that poetry was by the ancients esteemed a recreation is shown . . . by the authority of Vergil, Horace, Timocles the comic poet, Plato in the tenth of the *Republic* and the fifth of the *Laws*, and Eusebius of Caesarea in the twelfth book of his *Evangelic Preparations*. . . .[38]

For all these reasons it seems to me it can logically be said that the civil faculty should be divided into two chief parts, of which one considers the lawfulness of actions, and has received the general name of politics or civil affairs. The other deals with the lawfulness of cessation, or the lawfulness of actions for pastime, and has been named poetics. For this reason I think the *Poetics* is the ninth book of the *Politics*, and my belief seems to me so much the more probable because I find Aristotle in the eighth book of the

[38] Vergil, *Eclogues*, I, 10; Horace, *Art of Poetry*, 405; *Epistles*, II, 1, 180, *To Augustus;* Plato, in *Republic*, X, makes reference to poetry as recreation; *Laws*, V, is perhaps an error for *Laws*, VII, 813; Eusebius, *Evang. Prep.*, XII, 5, 4 (576d). Athenaeus (VI, 223b) writes as follows: "The comic poet Timocles, speaking of the many ways in which tragedy is useful in the conduct of life, says, in *Women at the Dionysia:* 'Good sir, harken, if haply I shall tell you the truth. Man is a creature born to labour, and many are the distresses his life carries with it. Therefore he has contrived these respites from his cares; for his mind, taking on forgetfulness of its own burdens, and absorbed in another's woe, departs in joy, instructed withal. Look first at the tragedians, if it please you, and see what a benefit they are to everybody. The poor man, for instance, learns that Telephus was more beggarly than himself, and from that time on he bears his poverty more easily The sick man sees Alcmeon raving in madness. One has a disease of the eyes—blind are the sons of Phineus. One has lost his son in death—Niobe is a comfort. One is lame—he sees Philoctetes. One meets with misfortune in old age— he learns the story of Oeneus. For he is reminded that all his calamities, which are greater than mortal man has ever borne, have happened to others, and so he bears his own trials more easily" (Gulick's translation).

Politics has already begun to treat music and the first principles of poetry, in order that in succession he may come to discourse of the management of the civil faculty. Therefore I say the first seven books of the *Politics* speak of the civil faculty in action and the last two speak of it as at rest; the latter I not long ago called poetics.

[Poetry and poetic theory defined]

[13] Poetics is then part of the civil faculty, and is that which prescribes the norm, the rule, and the laws of the poetic image to poetry. Its method is such that one may say poetics considers the idea of the image and poetry makes it. Hence poetics will be in its genus the art commanding and using the image made by the poets to that end of which we shall soon speak. And poetry will be in its genus the fabricating art, and a maker of the image, which then is to be used by poetics and the civil faculty. It is then possible to add to the words written above on the definition of poetry the efficient cause and to write as follows: Poetry is an imitation made with harmony, with number, and with verses that are accompanied or joined with credible and marvelous things that have been found out by the civil faculty.

[The end or final cause of poetry]

[14] Up to the present the form, the material, and the maker of poetry have been discovered. It remains only that there should be taken in hand the discussion of the final cause. In this the ancients and the moderns have stirred up the greatest tumults, not well understanding how to decide whether they ought to take as the end of poetry the useful, or the delightful, or both of them, or neither. And if I must freely confess the truth, it appears to me that until now men have proceeded in this matter with great obscurity, especially the moderns, who have not in any way known how (or I deceive myself) to illuminate this dark and intricate way with the light of dialectic; yet in Plato, Aristotle, and other ancient writers are found some scattered sparks of this truth, from which sufficient light can be gained.

Now in order that we may more easily find it, I believe it would be well first to make clear the cause that makes this discourse appear dark, intricate, and difficult. For if we know the difficulty, we know at the same time that from its solution depends entirely the settled and full doctrine pertaining to this affair. I say then it would appear strange, and with good reason, if one should seek to discover from writers whether delight or something useful is the end of poetry. For if it is true that poetry is an imitative art and each imitative art has the image as its object, and that the image, as I have already said, is good for nothing except to represent and to imitate,[39] it appears as a consequence that poetry has no other end than to represent and to imitate. Then it is unreasonably asked if the end of poetry is the useful or the delightful. I add that if the useful or the delightful were the end of poetry it would not be an imitative art.

[Poetry primarily neither useful nor delightful but imitative]

[15] I can prove my inference, for the imitative arts are different from the others that are not imitative through this alone, that the object of the imitative arts is not good for any other use than to represent alone. But the object of the other arts, that are not imitative, is good for some other use, either profitable or pleasant. Then if the object of poetry has as its end either the useful or the pleasant, of necessity it would be good for something else than merely to represent, and in this mode poetry would not be an imitative art. These two objections become more important in proportion as on the authority of three famous writers it appears one may conclude that poetry, so far as it is an imitator, has no other end than to represent and to imitate suitably. The first is Plato in the second book of the *Laws*. . . .[40] The second is Proclus,[41] who in his *Poetical Questions* says that the end of poetry is to imitate correctly, and proves it by quoting the same passage from Plato. . . . The third is Maximus Tyrius, who in his sixteenth *Sermo* clearly says that poetry, so far as it is an imitator, has no other end than to represent and to imitate. To prove this opinion of his he says first of all that the poets are properly compared with painters: "That I may speak briefly, the poetry of Homer is of the same sort as a picture by Polygnotus or Zeuxis." And then speaking of the end of painting he says this: "It is in conformity with art that the figures and the bodies shall preserve the appearance of truth." And a little further on, discussing the end of the poetic art, he adds the words next quoted in which he shows that the end of poetry is

---

[39] The Italian word is *rassomigliare*, literally *to resemble*, now obsolete in English in this sense. [40] Secs. 667, 668.
[41] A Neoplatonic philosopher in the fifth century A. D. Among his works are commentaries on Plato.

the perfect imitation of the fable: "That which has to do with poetry has as its purpose the effigy of the fable. . . ."

[Pleasure follows imitation]

[16] Now it should be known that, as Aristotle has said in the tenth book of the *Ethics*, pleasure is an accident naturally joined to some operations, and among the others it is without doubt very appropriate to imitation, since it is in such a way joined with it that no sort of imitation can be found that does not also give delight and pleasure. Of this many ancient writers give full and authentic testimony, among others Aristotle[42] and Plutarch. . . . Plutarch writes in the book in which he has shown how poets should be listened to: "We are disgusted to hear the grunting of the hog, the squeak of the pulley, the roaring of the wind and the dashing of the sea, but if anyone imitates these things excellently, as Parmenio did the hog and Theodore the pulley, we take delight in it. From sick men or those who are suspected of having some disease we flee as from an unpleasant spectacle, but we see with pleasure the *Philoctetes* of Aristophontes, and the *Jocasta* of Silamone, who represent persons who are dying, such as consumptives."[43] Since, then, imitation is always joined with delight, it has therefore come about that all who have wished to devise plays and pastimes have done so by means of some kind of imitation, as we show in dealing with the ancient games of backgammon and chess.[44] . . . And we are now able to add . . . the game of *primero*, in which is set forth the figure of the ochlocracy, that is, the state in which the common people have more power than the nobles. For as in this sort of state the nobles are weak and the common people powerful, so in this game the nobler cards, commonly called court cards, are of less value and less highly estimated than the other cards, which because of their ignobility are by the common people called *cartaccie*.[45] Now as in this game of *primero* it is possible to consider the imitation for itself, and in this way it has no other end

[42] *Poetics*, IV, first par., above.

[43] *On Listening to the Poets*, sect. 3, pp. 59–60, ed. by Padelford.

[44] He explains in Bk. II, chap. VI, that backgammon represents the movements of the heavenly bodies, and that chess imitates war. For example: "The rooks without doubt represent to us the high towers of wood that were placed on the backs of elephants employed in war by the ancients. They were placed in the game behind the footmen in the two corners, to show that in the battle array of the ancients they were put where they easily could aid the infantry." Cooper, in *The Deerslayer*, tells of rooks in the form of castles on the backs of elephants.

[45] Cards of little value.

than to present the figure of an ochlocracy, and as it is also possible to consider the game and pastime for itself in such a way that we recognize no other end than delight and pleasure, so in my opinion poetry in itself can be considered as an imitative art and as a game and pastime. In the first mode of consideration it has as its end the exactness of the image, that is, that things should be imitated in a suitable mode. But in the second it holds up to itself, as its end, delight and the pleasure that is joined with a good and perfect imitation. I conclude, then, that poetry as an imitative art has the exactness of the image as its end, but as a thing to be used for play and pastime and to secure some cessation of graver and more serious business, it proposes as its end the delight that rises from suitable imitation. Now this delight that is brought about by poetry can be considered in two ways, that is, either for itself alone, free and untrammeled by all laws, or as subordinated to and ruled by the civil faculty. Of the first sort is the end of that poetry that was subordinated to sophistic, and therefore deserves censure, for it is such as disorders the appetite with immoderate pleasure and renders it in every way a rebel to reason, and causes infinite injury and harm to virtuous life.

This is the kind of poetry that was driven out of the republic by Plato. . . .[46]

[Poetry and the state]

[17] If then we are to reason of the end of poetry, it can be said with certainty that as an imitative art it should have for its end exactness of the image, but that as a recreation it should have for its end pleasure alone. But if this pleasure is considered as regulated and qualified by the civil faculty, one must needs say that it should be directed to the useful, consequently that the species of poetry which was classed under praiseworthy sophistic—that is, under the sophistic which arranges the appetite and subjects it to reason—would be considered as recreation controlled by the civil faculty and would have utility as its end. It is, however, true that in this way I do not decide that this kind of poetry should be so harsh and so austere as Proclus shows it in his first *Poetic Question*, where he distinguishes two species of poetry, that is, the good and the bad, with the following words:" . . . It especially pertains to

---

[46] In *Sermo* VII, *Whether Plato Did Well in Dismissing Homer from His Republic*, Maximus Tyrius decides that because Plato's state was perfect it did not need poetry either as a medicine or as a bringer of pleasure.

the laws that govern the youth to deal carefully with such poetry, as that which is certainly pleasing, but is not useful to teach virtue, and as that which is exceedingly pleasant but in equal measure injurious. And to the same laws it pertains to choose an austere muse, who will guide us to virtue by the direct roads. For we do not marvel at a pleasant medicine but at one that cures." From these words of Proclus we see he believes poetry should be rather a medicine than a pastime, and consequently that in order to give it utility as its end he does not object to separating it from every sort of delight. But there is no doubt that in this he has departed from Plato, who has clearly confessed in many places that poetry is the bringer of the useful to our spirits by means of the delight it gives under the appearance of play and pastime.

[The moral value of poetry]

[18] Fully to understand this opinion of Plato's, we need to know there are three kinds of men, to whom, it appears, Plato believes the civil faculty, or we may say moral philosophy, can be of some avail. The three sorts of men are, first, those who are disposed and habituated to the good; second, the wicked, habituated to evil; third, those who are not disposed or at least habituated to either good or evil. The first sort are men who have learned to bridle the disordered movements of the appetite. For these I think moral philosophy is a good thing (as Plato writes in the *Protagoras* and the *Gorgias*) in so far as it is legal, that is, in so far as it gives laws and precepts, without any sort of emotion, on living well and blessedly. Of the second sort are wicked men, accustomed to despise the decrees of the laws; in the *Gorgias* he demonstrates at length that to such men moral philosophy is very profitable, in so far as it is judicial, that is, in so far as malefactors are castigated with the penalties determined in the decrees. Of the third sort are the boys and the young men, and all those who are subject to the tumult of the passions, but yet who are not habituated either to good or to evil, for they can still be instructed in the way of virtue as well as taught the way of vice. And because these (as Aristotle has written in the first book of the *Ethics*) are much agitated by whirling passions and by strong feelings, Aristotle believes they would not be fit auditors of the teachings of moral philosophy.[47] But Plato thinks that to these also it is possible to give moral instruction flavored with poetic sweetness. Hence it appears that

[47] *Ethics*, I, 1095a.

Plato believes, according to what he writes in the second, the third, and the tenth books of the *Republic*, and yet more clearly in the second of the *Laws*, that poetic is a civil faculty, or moral philosophy, which should be taught to those who are not capable of bare instruction, whether through age or because of the violence of their passions. Therefore I conclude with Proclus that Plato has sometimes called poetics a medicine, as that which seeks to render souls healthy, and consequently has the useful as its end.

[Delightful teaching]

[19] But I differ from him because Proclus does not recognize any sort of delight in poetics, and yet Plato thinks that by means of delight it introduces also the useful, and for this reason praises the habit of calling it play and desires that it should be thought of as play.[48]. . . Lucretius avails himself of the same comparison in the same connection:

> Even as healers, when they essay to give loathsome wormwood to children, first touch the rim all round the cup with the sweet golden moisture of honey, so that the unwitting age of children may be beguiled as far as the lips, and meanwhile may drink the bitter draught of wormwood, and though charmed may not be harmed, but rather by such means may be restored and come to health; so now, since this philosophy full often seems too bitter to those who have not tasted it, and the multitude shrinks back away from it, I have desired to set forth to you my reasoning in the sweet-tongued song of the muses, as though to touch it with the pleasant honey of poetry, if perchance it might avail by such means to keep your mind set upon my verses, while you take in the whole nature of things, and are conscious of your profit.[49]

. . . This opinion has been followed by many other famous writers. Eustathius, Athenaeus, and Suidas have written with the same words on this subject as follows: "That singers and poets were in ancient times modest and philosophers appears from Agamemnon's leaving of Clytemnestra under the direction of a man of that sort, who, singing above all the virtues of women, kindled in her desire of virtue. Then being pleasant in his conversation he diverted her

---

[48] He quotes from *Laws*, II, 659–60, given above.

[49] *On the Nature of Things*, IV, 11–25, trans. by Cyril Bailey (Cambridge University Press, 1910). For other references to this idea, see the index under *poetry as a sweet medicine*.

mind from evil thoughts. And therefore Egisthus was unable to bend her to his wishes until he had killed the poet. Demodocus sang the adultery of Venus and Mars not to give pleasure or because he approved that wickedness, but to fill them with fear, so that having been reared in softness they should not give themselves over to injurious pleasures.[50] And because they always had their minds on banquets and music, he sought therefore to please them with a kind of delight that would be in harmony with their habits. That Phemius sang to the senate of these matters has the same significance. And the Sirens sang to Ulysses those things in which he took great delight and which were in conformity with his desire and his great knowledge. And they say whoever has heard the song of the Sirens goes away with greater learning received into himself by means of delight."[51] Basil the Great says in one of his *Homilies:* "Though some use the residue of flowers for odor or color, the bees know how to extract honey from them; thus those who continue diligent in reading not merely seek out what is sweet and pleasant in their books, but are eager to gain from them something useful to the spirit."[52] This is confirmed by Strabo, Pausanias, and a thousand other writers.

Now with respect to the end I think this is beyond doubt the true opinion, that is, perfect poetry concerns itself with delight for the sake of utility. And for proof of this my opinion I am wont to speak as follows, differing little from Plato. I say then true poetry is a pastime, and receives its quality from the civil faculty and in so far as it is play it has delight as its end, but in so far as it gets its tone from moral philosophy and is, so to speak, given character by it, it puts delight first in order, and gives us benefit afterwards. Hence it appears the civil faculty should endeavor to give all the people opportunity to enjoy the pleasure that comes from poetry. And so Plato and other legislators have determined in their laws. I say further that the Athenian state estimated so high the pleasure given to the people by the poets that it did not feel ashamed to give every year large sums of money to its citizens, to enable them to buy seats in the theater where they could conveniently see comedies and tragedies acted. . . . Now it is unlikely that Athens would have attempted, with so great a drain on the treasury, to enable the people easily to enjoy the pleasure conferred by poetry if it had

[50] *Odyssey*, VIII, 266–369.   [51] *The Deipnosophists*, 14 a-c.
[52] *To the Young Men, on the Way in Which They May Get Profit from Heathen Books*, sect. 3 (in Migne, *Patrologia Graeca*, XXXI, p. 570 BC).

not believed that by means of that pleasure some profit was introduced into the minds of those who received it gladly.

[The value of different types of poetry]

[20] And if it should appear to anyone that it was necessary to expound the mode of it more in detail, I will make an effort to satisfy his desire by saying briefly something about it. Plato holds that the state should be composed of three sorts of persons, that is, of artificers, soldiers, and magistrates. Proclus adds that among the artificers Plato includes all the citizens of low and middle rank, and that among the magistrates are rated all the more powerful, who have the conduct of the state in their hands. Now if that is granted I say that through the foresight of the civil faculty there originated in the city three principal kinds of poetry, namely the heroic, the tragic, and the comic, each of which, even though it availed itself of pleasure in order to benefit all the people, nevertheless was chiefly applied to the benefit of one of the three parts, which, according to Plato, are necessary to the civil unit. Therefore we say that heroic poetry was chiefly directed to soldiers, since they may be encouraged to imitate the virtuous actions of the heroes presented in it as though by the sharp stimulus of glory.[53] Tragedy is concerned chiefly with what is useful and helpful to princes, magistrates, and powerful persons, and for this reason, in order to hold them always subject to the justice of the laws, it prefers to present the horrible and terrifying accidents of the great; this acts as a bridle which tempers and moderates the greatness of their fortune.[54] Comedy has as its chief purpose to benefit persons of low or middle estate, and in order to console them for their low fortune was in the habit of presenting actions that conclude happily. In this way the civil faculty intended to give men to understand that the humble life of the people is much more pleasant and fully satisfied than is the life of the great and regal. . . . We think it will not be disagreeable if we now prove this conclusion with some other authority. . . . Euripides, then, in his *Medea*, has spoken as follows on this subject:

[53] Cf. Sidney's remark that "Orlando Furioso, or honest King Arthur, will never displease a soldier" (*Defense*, sect. 42, below).

Milton admitted that this had been the notion of heroic poetry, but felt that military courage had been superseded by a superior heroic subject, "the better fortitude of patience and heroic martyrdom" (*Paradise Lost*, IX, 31–32). Cf. *Paradise Regained*, in which the patience of Job is several times mentioned.

[54] For Sidney's expression of this idea, see the *Defense*, sect. 32, below.

BETTER LIFE'S LEVEL WAY

Be it mine, if in greatness I may not,
In quiet and peace to grow old.
Sweeter name than "The Mean" shall ye say not,
And to taste it is sweetness untold.
But to men never weal above measure
Availed: on its perilous height
The gods in their hour of displeasure
The heavier smite.[55]

The civil faculty, then, wishing to put into the minds of the humble citizens obedience to their superiors, so that through the desire of new things they should not be moved to disobedience and rebellion,[56] and that they might always remain content with their state, had comedy invented, in which humble life is revealed as happy and fortunate and capable of infinite consolations. On the other side, in order that the more powerful and all those raised to authority over others should not confide too much in their fortune and consequently become insupportable and insolent in their dominion, the civil faculty desired tragedy to be presented, as a sufficient counterpoise to the insolence of prosperous fortune. Hence all who find themselves enjoying the fortune of high position can obtain useful instruction to moderate the pride normal to that condition.[57] This utility of tragedy, I believe, is clearly indicated to us by Dion Chrysostom in these words: . . . "There was never a poor man who was to be taught by the events of tragedy. But on the contrary all tragedies are concerned with Atreuses, Agamemnons, and Oedipuses, who possessed great stores of gold and silver and lands and animals. . . ."[58] Now from what has already been said on the utility of comedy and tragedy, it seems to me it can reasonably be concluded that these two poems were designed by the civil faculty for the extinction of sedition and for the preservation of peace. And because the civil faculty must needs think on military knowledge, in order that in time of war the state may be fitted to defend itself, it seems to me it can with probability be thought that the same faculty caused the origin of the heroic poem for that purpose, for in it is celebrated the overpowering strength of

---

[55] *Medea*, 123–30, trans. by A. S. Way, in the Loeb Classical Library (Cambridge, 1922).   [56] Cf. Heywood, *Apology*, sect. 4, below.
[57] Cf. Sidney, *Defense*, sect. 32, immediately below.   [58] *Oration* 13.

heroes and especially of those who courageously despised death for their native land, in order that our soldiers, looking on such examples, should as a result be more ready to despise the perils of death, for the sake of the safety and prosperity of the state. In this way we see that the three species of poetry I have mentioned, when regulated by the civil faculty, bring to the state, in addition to pleasure, utility and profit as well, by teaching as though secretly the three kinds of men of whom, according to Plato, the perfect group of citizens is wholly made up. . . .

[Poetry defined]

[21] But now to come to the end of this definition, I think it well to gather together in a brief epilogue all that has been written before of the final cause of poetry. I say then that . . . poetry is always an imitative art and, so far as it is, has always as its end the correct representation of the images of things, but all the same when it is considered as play it has pleasure as its end, and considered as play regulated by the civil faculty it has for its immediate end delight, but delight directed to benefit. From these premises it seems it can be concluded that poetry is capable of three definitions according as it is considered in three different manners, that is, as imitation, as play simply, or as play regulated by the civil faculty.[59] In the first mode it can be defined thus: Poetry is an imitative art composed with verses, number, and harmony which are accompanied or joined with the credible marvelous; it was devised by the human intellect to represent the images of things in a fitting manner. In the second mode perhaps this other definition would fit it: Poetry is an imitative play, made with verses, number, and harmony accompanied and joined with the credible marvelous; it was devised by the human intellect for the sake of delight. Now when poetry is considered in the first mode we should have in mind all the authorities who recognize correct imitation as the end of poetry, and similarly when it is considered in the second mode, one should expound all the other authorities who accept delight alone

[59] The possibility of varying definitions for poetry, each one correct under certain conditions, has frequently been overlooked by modern critics, who tend to ask: What one thing is poetry? They might learn from Mazzoni to ask rather: What are the diverse things that can be called poetry?

Varchi (1553) defined as follows: "Poetic is a faculty which teaches in what ways any action, feeling, or habit should be imitated with verse, number, and harmony, either mingled or separately, for the purpose of removing men from vices and kindling them to virtue, in order that their perfection and beatitude may follow" (*Della poetica in generale*, Pt. II, first par.).

as the end of poetry, and especially the words of Plato in the *Gorgias:*

> *Socrates.* Now think, does not all skill on the lyre and in dithyrambs and in poetry seem to you invented for the sake of pleasure?
>
> *Cal.* It does seem so to me.
>
> *Soc.* But what does this same famous tragedy and poetry that is so much to be wondered at attempt to do? Do not its desire and effort tend merely to the pleasure of the hearers? Or shall I be told that if there is something delightful and pleasant, but at the same time bad, poetry will avoid that thing? On the contrary if there is something unpleasant, but useful, will it speak and sing that even though the hearers object? Or what is it the poetry of the tragic writers seems to labor for?
>
> *Cal.* It surely seems to deviate from the useful toward the enjoyment and pleasure of the spectators.[60]

Considered in the third mode, perhaps poetry will be capable of this last definition: Poetry is an imitative amusement with verses, number, and harmony accompanied and joined with the credible marvelous; it was devised by the civil faculty to delight the people profitably. When poetry is considered in this way we must keep in mind all the authorities who set as its end the useful reached by means of pleasure. In this light should be understood the following words by Proclus, in which he speaks of poetry as concerned with erudition rather than imitation: ". . . Now if, as we have said, there must be imitation, it must have to do with some noble thing. For we say of all virtuous exercises, whether produced with imitation or without imitation, that they have no other end superior to the good."

From these three definitions follow of necessity four corollaries. The first of these is that poetry taken in the first two modes is not ruled or governed by the civil faculty. The second is that only poetry of the third mode is ruled and governed by moral philosophy and by the civil faculty. · The third is that the poetic which considers the image of the first poetry and that also which considers the image of the second poetry ought in no manner to be called part of moral philosophy. The fourth and last is that the name of part of the civil faculty is justly applied only to the poetic which considers the image of the third poetry; and according to the rules of

[60] *Gorgias,* 502. Mazzoni uses the Latin rendering of Marsilio Ficino.

the third sort each good poet should compile his poems, as surely Dante has done better than any of the others. . . .

[Imitation and moral philosophy]

[22] From what has been said up to this point I believe everyone can understand that the two objections mentioned above have now been explained and made clear, since it is true that the arts called imitative when considered as such always have as their end the correctness of the image, or the fitting similitude of the things they take for imitation. And this is necessary, since their object in and for itself is good for nothing else than for them to imitate. But for this reason one should not conclude that when they are considered not as imitative, but in some different way, as recreations or as parts of the civil faculty, they cannot have different ends than imitation, namely, the end of the pastime and the end of the civil faculty. . . . This seems to me what Proclus wished to say in the words cited above, namely, that poetry as an imitator has as its end to represent correctly, but as an instrument of virtue or of moral philosophy it has as its end the benefit of others. This was also said by Maximus Tyrius in the following words:

> That I may speak briefly, the poetry of Homer is of the same mode as were the pictures of Polygnotus and Zeuxis, if indeed you think these painters were philosophers and did not rashly engage in painting. The business of these was double, one part depending from art, the other from virtue; it is a matter of art that the figures and bodies should keep the appearance of truth, but it is a matter of virtue that the decorous arrangement of the lines should give an imitation of beauty. In about the same manner I think you should consider the Homeric poetry, in which equally there is a double activity. So far as it considers poetic, it is concerned with the imitation of the story; but so far as it is concerned with philosophy, it is given over wholly to the love of virtue and the knowledge of the truth.[61]

Book I, Chapter LXVII

[The phantasy or fancy]

I say, then, that the phantasy is the common power of the mind for dreams and for poetic verisimilitude. But because my adversaries express no doubt of what I also believe, namely, that the

[61] *Serm.* 16.

phantasy is the power on which dreams depend, something Aristotle has often said and his followers have often repeated, it will therefore be well to demonstrate that poetic verisimilitude is also founded on the same power of the mind. The verisimilitude, then, sought after by the poets is of such a nature that it is feigned by them according to their wish. Then it is necessary for it to be fabricated by the power that has the capacity for forming conceptions in harmony with the will. Now this power can in no manner be the intellective power, which is indispensable in producing conceptions in conformity with the nature of the objects. Therefore the subtle Scotus properly remarks in many places in his *Sentences* that the intellect is rather a natural than a free capacity. Then of necessity the power fitted to generate is the phantastic power called by the Latins *Imaginative*. All that we have just said was first set forth by Aristotle in the second of *De anima:* "It is in our power to imagine not merely things that can be but those that cannot be, as men with three heads and three bodies, such as in the fables Geryon is said to have been, and as winged men, such as Zetes and Calais the sons of Boreas, and Charybdis and Scylla.[62] For in whatever way it is possible for the painters to put in a picture an animal of any form whatever, in the same way it is possible to devise and form it in the mind. Besides when we think some formidable and terrible calamity is likely to come on us, we immediately restrict and lower our courage, our whole bodies shudder, we tremble, we grow pale; on the other hand, when we believe some special desire or some great gain is tending toward us and coming on us, we are made again bold, happy, and ready to shout for joy. But when we construct these things merely in our imaginations (as when we set before ourselves terrifying earthquakes and the grim aspects of savage wild beasts) no feeling of consternation follows, and as pictures do not deter us, neither do visions nor those figments which by our will we bring together and mingle. Thus we can distinguish imagination from thought and apprehension."[63]

We clearly see, then, if I am not wrong, that phantasy is the true power over poetic fables, since she alone is capable of those fictions which we of ourselves are able to feign and put together. From this of necessity it follows that poetry is made up of things feigned and imagined, because it is founded on phantasy.

[62] Cf. Sidney's similar remark, *Defense*, sect. 9, below.
[63] Mazzoni quotes a Latin translation of the comment of Themistius on *De anima*.

Book III, Chapter III

[Poetry and truth: the marvelous]

A striking objection comes up . . . namely, that rhetoric cannot be distinguished from poetry, since the two have the same object [i.e., the credible]. I say then by way of reply that the credible can be considered in two different ways. The first is when the credible is dealt with in so far as it is credible and persuasive; then it is the proper subject of rhetoric. The second is when it is considered as the marvelous, and thus becomes the proper subject of poetry, since poetry always seeks for a marvelous subject, as Aristotle has testified in many places in his *Poetics*[64] . . . . Poetics is directed to the credible marvelous by means of sonorous and dignified verse, and of fables and conceptions that are new and extraordinary. From these conclusions so set forth we can understand that Pontanus has not said badly in his dialogue entitled *Actius* . . . that the end of the poet and of poetry is to speak in such a way as fill the hearers with wonder.[65] This comes about when the hearers accept what they did not believe could happen. Hence, as it has been already said that poetry as an imitative art has for its end the presentation of an image, and as a pastime has delight as its end, and as a pastime under the control of the civil faculty has utility as its end, it appears to me I can now add that as a rational faculty it has the marvelous as its end.

Book III, Chapter VI

[Feigned geography]

[Without using any name, Mazzoni quotes from a commentator on the *Poetics* of Aristotle:][66] "If it is permitted to a poet to write of a king who has never existed and to imagine kings performing acts that have never happened, it will also be permitted to imagine new mountains, new rivers . . . new kingdoms, and to move the old rivers from one country to another." . . . [He then continues:] But against this commentator there is the authority of Aristotle, who praises the *Flower* of Agathon,[67] which was a story of a regal

---

[64] See *marvelous* in the index.
[65] Joannes Jovianus Pontanus, *Opera* (Basel, 1556), p. 1328.
[66] Castelvetro. This whole chapter deals with his comment on *Poetics*, IX, 189, 13, immediately above.   [67] *Poetics*, IX, 51b19.

action all feigned, and adds that always to look for a well-known plot is a ridiculous thing, because the things that are known are known to few and yet please everyone. Aristotle means that among the people who are capable of listening to poetic fables there are many simple and little-educated persons, who look on stories as credible even though they are really the inventions of the poet, and those who know stories are feigned are pleased with the imitation by means of which the false appears to be rendered credible. In this manner it is seen by experience that the *Education of Cyrus* delights equally the ignorant who hold it true and the learned who take it as false.[68] In addition, I say this commentator contradicts himself, for in other parts of his *Poetics* he shows he thinks the fit hearer of the fables of the poets should be ignorant or at least little skilled in letters.[69] For this reason he holds the poet should not set forth in his poems the subtle ideas of philosophy, of the sciences, and of the arts, since it appears to him that they cannot be understood by persons little educated,[70] such as he thinks are the fit hearers of the efforts of the poets. In addition, the commentator asserts that if the poet represents a story dealing with a king that is wholly feigned, he will go outside the limits of the credible, because the fiction will be apparent to the hearer. But it is necessary for the auditor to be well equipped in letters if he is to perceive that the plot is entirely made up by the brain of the poet, and especially if it is devised about the actions of a king who ruled peoples very distant and little known to us. Finally I add that the things he considers unsuitable, namely, the feigning of new countries, new peoples, and new kingdoms, and the altering and falsifying of the source and course of rivers, the site of countries, and the quality of other things in nature, are in our opinion wholly proper and fitting to the poet, since they are credible and marvelous. . . . I conclude, then, that the poet is able to feign a complete story dealing with a king, if only he feigns it of a country strange and remote.[71] Besides this, I say the opposite opinion is repugnant to reason, to the authority of Aristotle, and to the practice of good poets. There is another particular class of

[68] See the index under Xenophon, *Education of Cyrus*.

[69] On *Poetics*, I, 29, 32 and 30, 7, just above.

[70] The text here reads *introdotte*, but the sense seems to require *poco introdotte*, which occurs, in the singular, a few lines above (translated *little skilled*).

[71] This type of subject is exemplified by many Elizabethan plays, such as Beaumont and Fletcher's *Maid's Tragedy*, *Philaster*, and *Loyal Subject*, and Shakespeare's *The Winter's Tale*. Cf. Tasso, *The Heroic Poem*, sect. 20, below.

the incredible possible with respect to the things that happen, when the poet takes something from history and then goes on to add many things from his own invention. This can come about in two ways. The first is when the history is not known in detail. In this instance the poet has before him a wide field in which he can enlarge and particularize the history by introducing his own inventions without fear of transgressing the credible. This sort of regal story is better and more perfect than all the others. The second kind of this impossible credible taken from history appears when the poet transmutes and falsifies history that is true or at least recorded in some writer; this procedure is also according to my opinion fitting to the poetically credible.

[The Bible]

Among the Hebrews the false as credible could have no place, because of the great diligence and painstaking care they gave to the truth of history. Josephus, having discussed this subject in detail, ... at length concludes: "It is evident from our deeds in what way we believe in our own writings, for in all the time now gone by no one has presumed to add anything, to take anything away, or to change anything."[72] From this it appears to me that the ancient Hebrews did not know the kind of poetry that deals with the false, but only that which deals with the true, and by Plato is called icastic. Therefore I say they were all icastic poets who flourished among the ancient Hebrew people. But it is possible to doubt whether this is true of the Song of Solomon, which is full of the most beautiful poetic phantasies. To this objection I believe that it is possible to respond that the purely phantastic poem, which by its nature looks on the false in the way that has been explained, was not known to the Hebrews, and the poem of the Song of Solomon is not of that kind, but is one of those which under the husk of the literal sense conceals pure and complete truth. Hence it can be called phantastic with respect to the literal sense, but icastic with respect to the allegorical sense. ...

[Biblical poetry in the Renaissance]

Any poet who takes for the subject of his poem some ancient Hebrew story must of necessity be an icastic poet, since by its nature that history is in no way capable of alteration. ... For this reason I cannot praise Sannazaro nor Vida nor other similar poets

[72] *Against Apion*, I, 8, 4.

who, in spite of having taken from the sacred books a subject that is inalterable for the reasons just given, yet have wished to add to it, and certainly too boldly, many phantasies.[73]

Book III, Chapter XLII

[Aristotle's *Poetics* imperfect]

As to the authority of Aristotle . . . I say first of all that Aristotle has not spoken fully of all the things pertaining to the poetic art, and that we can see this clearly whenever we read the splendid *Decades* of Patricius,[74] in which everyone can easily learn how far from perfect is the little book by Aristotle called the *Poetics*. Hence according to my judgment it is not possible to conclude that if Aristotle has not spoken of a thing in his *Poetics* it therefore cannot legitimately be used by the poets.

Book III, Chapter LV

[Against unity]

I say, then, that in all the places in which Aristotle has mentioned several ends which nature proposes to herself in the fabric of some unit, he has also used some words through which we can understand that he has wished to say nature proposes to herself one of them as a principal end and the other as accessories. If then according to this last idea nature is able to set for herself one principal end and other accessory ends, in the same way poetry can have one principal end and other accessory ends, and further if by the agreement of Averroes and other opponents the action is the end of poetry, the poet will be able to set before himself for imitation several actions, provided one is principal and the others accessory. Thus can be defended those poets who have sung of the actions of Hercules and of Theseus, since we may say they have sung of one principal action and all the others are accessory to that. And in the same way the other poets defend

---

[73] Milton must have been interested in this passage on the theory of Biblical poetry. He doubtless supposed that his own additions to the sacred narrative were not too bold.

[74] *Della poetica* by Francesco Patrizi was published at Ferrara in 1586. The second section is called *La deca disputata*, or *Ten Books of Debate*. Four of the books deal with imitation, and the theories of Aristotle are minutely examined, with the conclusion that "Aristotle has not treated completely or truly of the modes of imitation" (Bk. X, p. 210).

themselves who include in their poems several actions, even though this is repugnant to Aristotle.

Book IV, Chapter XXXII[75]

[The poet may give his own judgment]

My adversaries go on with the intention of showing that the poet should not bring in his own judgment as follows: "To do that takes away from the reader the power of considering and judging about the things narrated by the very poet who gives his judgment, and in a certain way he seems to show he has little respect for the ability of his reader, since he reveals that he does not think the reader able to judge correctly without his aid." If this argument is true, the conclusion follows that in writing no one would be able to teach, because he would thus show himself to esteem his reader lightly, and therefore it would be necessary to condemn all the teachings that are found in instructive books, and all the precepts pertaining to civil life to be found in historians. To this argument I say the reader will be either ignorant or learned. If he is ignorant, he will be glad to learn some precepts useful to living well and happily; if he is well educated, he will likewise be able to learn, if perhaps the thing is explained by the writer with more efficacy than the learned man has been able to do it himself. There is no doubt, as Aristotle says, that words the better imprint a conception in our minds in proportion as it is better presented; moreover, the learned man would be able to take pleasure in hearing someone say well the things he knows.[76] This is the way in which Aristotle thinks we should take great pleasure in the pictures of things we know,[77] when they are well and ingeniously made. Who is there, indeed, who does not know that Pompey the Great would have been more famous if he had died before the Civil War? Yet Lucan expresses his judgment in such a manner that every ignorant man who understands his words will take great pleasure in it, but much more the learned and discerning man will take pleasure in seeing this judgment so

[75] Bks. IV–VII were first printed in 1688. Possibly they were circulated in manuscript. Otherwise they could have had no influence until they were published. They would still, however, represent literary discussion in the latter part of the sixteenth century. Here, as before, I often do not give the chapters in full.

[76] Cf. Pope's "oft was thought, but ne'er so well expressed" (*Essay on Criticism*, 298).

[77] *Poetics*, IV, first par.

well expressed, and in being able from the poet to obtain a splendid moral precept of great use to human life:

> So too long age great'st happiness destroyes,
> And life surviving Empires; former joyes
> Breede griefe, unlesse with them our end be sent,
> And grimly death ensuing woes prevent.[78]

Dante understood this utility that can be obtained from the judgment of poets when he introduced Statius, who confessed that he had abandoned avarice because he had many times read those words of Vergil:

> To what do you not drive the hearts of men, O sacred thirst for gold? (*Aeneid*, III, 56–7).

Dante puts it thus:

> If I had not corrected myself when I understood the passage where you, as though in pain, call out to human nature, "Why do you not control, O sacred thirst for gold, the appetite of mortals?" turning and returning I would understand the bitter jousts.[79]

Finally I say the judgment given by the author can be a matter of controversy. And perhaps there is no less utility derived from raising the question whether the writer has judged well and whether the precept that can be obtained from his judgment is the best one.

Book IV, Chapter XXXVI

[Extra-dramatic lines; the credible]

It is then evident that all historians of reputation have been in the habit of bringing in their own judgment . . . of the actions of persons introduced in their histories. . . . So if my adversaries will allow that the historian and the poet are here on equal footing, it is necessary to say that the poets also can boldly introduce their own belief, and the more as they have an evident reason that does not apply to the historians. It is that Aristotle in his *Poetics* has praised Homer as the one who taught the other poets how to tell falsehoods. To do this they should base themselves on things later

---

[78] Lucan, *Pharsalia, or the Civil Wars of Rome between Pompey the Great and Julius Caesar*, VIII, 27–32, trans. by May.

[79] That is, would be in hell (*Inferno*, VII, 35). Mazzoni quotes *Purgatorio*, XXII, 37–42.

than the credible thing they imitate, in order that with the allowance as true of the later thing there may come also that of the earlier thing.[80] . . . It necessarily follows that the poet should seek things coming after the credible in order that when they are received by his readers and hearers, the credible itself may be received and thought of as true. Hence the poet should not merely judge but also move the feelings[81] . . . in order that if this judgment and this passion are communicated to those who hear and read the poem there may also be communicated to them a belief in all the poet has said, since it is not possible to agree in judgment and feeling with something not reputed true. . . . I believe Vergil has enlarged this poetic privilege of judgment to include also the moving of the feelings, as appears in the following:

> O happy pair! if aught my verse can do, no day shall ever take you from the memory of time, so long as the house of Aeneas dwells hard by the immovable rock of the Capitol, and the Father of Rome holds his imperial sway.[82]

In these verses he judges and moves the feelings over the deaths of Nisus and Euryalus in such a way that if the judgment and the feeling are taken over by the readers of the poem, the fabulous antecedents are accepted as true. . . . It is not strange, then, if Dante has also sometimes wished not merely to judge but also to move the feelings, as is seen in these verses:

> Even if Count Ugo was supposed to have given up your castles by treachery, you should not have inflicted such sufferings on his sons. O new Thebes! Uguccione and Brigata and the other two that my poem mentions above were made innocent by their youth (*Inferno*, XXXIII, 85–90).

It seems, then, it has been the custom of all the good Latin poets not merely to judge but also to move the affections.[83]

The last reason given by my adversaries on this matter is that the poet . . . should not arrogate so much to himself as to wish to

[80] *Poetics*, XXIV, 60a18, above.   [81] Cf. Sidney, *Defense*, sect. 26, immediately below.
[82] *Aeneid*, IX, 446–9, trans. by Lonsdale and Lee.
[83] Milton carries the practice even further, by giving the general moral application; for example, after telling of the council of Satan and his followers he writes:

> For neither do the spirits damned
> Lose all their virtue; lest bad men should boast
> Their specious deeds on earth, which glory excites,
> Or close ambition varnished o'er with zeal.
> *Paradise Lost*, II, 482–5.

give his opinion as a definitive pronouncement, rather than leave free judgment to others. To which we answer that this argument, if it has validity, would silence all the noble writers we have mentioned above as presumptuous and arrogant.

Book IV, Chapter XLII

[Extra-dramatic speeches gain the reader's confidence]

It has been demonstrated with good reasons that the poet should pronounce judgment . . . because in judging he reveals that he is a good man and for that reason more deserving of our faith. . . . If then, according to Aristotle, the bad man does not merit belief because of his wickedness,[84] the good man necessarily merits it because of his goodness. But this goodness cannot be made clear in any way except by means of the judgment of things well or badly made. Speaking of the same thing, Cicero writes as follows: "It can be brought about by two things that men have confidence in us, namely, if we are thought to possess prudence united with justice."[85] And a little further he says: "Justice joined to intelligence will have great power for faith in men. Justice without prudence will have much power; without justice prudence avails nothing." Then according to the opinion of Cicero easy credence is found with hearers and readers only by means of justice and prudence, which cannot be shown by the poet except by his just judgments on actions that are just and unjust. . . . Hence the epic poet should sometimes resort to the judgment of things just and unjust, in order that revealing himself as a good man he may be reputed such as does not allow himself to be moved by passions or emotions, and to that extent merits belief in what he says. Now with respect to what they say about Homer, namely that he has judged less than all the rest, I believe they must be content if I say I do not believe it, because I say so with the authority of a great author, namely Plutarch, who writes of this as follows: ". . . Homer used this method best of all, giving reprehension to wrong words and commendation to good words, as in the following:

He spake a sweet and cunning word (*Odyssey*, VI, 148).

He stood by his side and restrained him with gentle words (*Iliad*, II, 189).

[84] *Rhetoric*, II, I. [85] *De officiis*, II, 33.

In doing this he does not so much protest that he himself does not
say and approve these things as indicate they are inept and wrong.
For example, when he is about to narrate the manner in which
Agamemnon treated the priest cruelly, he prefaces these words:

> It did not please the heart of Agamemnon, son of Atreus, but he
> sent him away insultingly and spoke roughly to him (*Iliad*, 1, 387).

That is, savagely and proudly and against fitness. Homer attributes to Achilles this fierce speech:

> Drunkard, with the eyes of a dog and the heart of a deer (*Iliad*,
> 1, 225).

Then he adds his own judgment upon it:

> The son of Peleus again spoke with baneful words and did not
> lay aside his wrath (*Iliad*, 1, 223).

For it is agreed that nothing can be rightly said in wrath and
vehemence. And so for actions as well:

> Thus having spoken, he devised foul treatment for noble Hector,
> stretching him prone on the ground by the bier of the son of
> Menoitios (*Iliad*, xxiii, 24–5).

With great skill he also gives at the end some saying as though it
were a decision about the deeds and acts. He does this when he
has the gods speak about the adultery of Mars and Venus, saying:

> Evil deeds prosper not; the slow catcheth the swift (*Odyssey*, viii,
> 329).

And on the pride and boasting of Hector:

> So he spake boasting, and Juno waxed wroth (*Iliad*, viii, 198).

And on the shooting of the arrow by Pandarus:

> With these words Athene persuaded the heart of the fool (*Iliad*,
> iv, 104).

Whoever clearly apprehends speeches and ideas of this sort at once
understands the poet's spirit."[86] . . . Servius in his comment on the
fourth book of the *Aeneid* expresses the opinion that the poet is
under obligation to judge. . . . The words of Servius may be read
in his exposition of that verse of Vergil:

> Wicked Love, to what do you not force the hearts of men! (*Aeneid*,
> iv, 412.)

[86] Plutarch, *On Listening to the Poets*, sect. 4, p. 62 (ed. by Padelford).

Servius remarks: "An exclamation against love." . . . Such is also:

> To what do you not drive the hearts of men, O cursed thirst for
> gold! (*Aeneid*, III, 56–7.)

From what I have said I believe it appears clearly enough that
Homer has judged many things, and that the poets better observe the laws of poetry and fulfill the obligations laid on them—
thus gaining much to establish the credible in their work—when
they judge properly than when they assume some license or abandon the precepts ordained for the correct writing of poetry.

Book IV, Chapter XLIII

[Ariosto does not deserve blame because he has often introduced
his judgments at the beginnings of his cantos.]

Bulgarini adds that Ariosto more than any other is to be
blamed for pronouncing judgment in the discourses he gives at the
beginnings of his cantos, where he certainly thrusts in his judgment at length.[87] To this we say in response that . . . the poems of
the ancients were normally sung by one man on the stage or elsewhere to an audience. On this matter we give . . . the following
testimony from Juvenal:

> When Statius has gladdened the city by promising to read, how
> people rush to hear his pleasant voice and the words of their favor-
> ite *Thebais;* with such sweetness does he hold their souls prisoner,
> and with such eagerness does the crowd listen (*Satires*, VII, 83–6).

Now it is probable that these heroic poems were divided and sung
in several books, which the poets in our language have called
cantos. Hence I say that I shall never bring an accusation against
poets who in the beginnings of books use the prefaces to which
poets are entitled. Giving the rule for such poetical introductions,
Aristotle speaks thus:

> In fables and heroic verses the beginning is a sort of oration on
> what is to come, that the hearers may foresee with what things
> the poem is to deal, that their minds may not be kept in sus-
> pense. For what is indefinite forces the mind to wander here and
> there. Therefore he who puts the matter as though in the hand
> of the hearer causes him to follow and understand what is said.[88]

---

[87]Bulgarini was the chief critic against whom Mazzoni's work is directed.
The habit of Ariosto is that of Spenser and Milton (*Paradise Lost*, III, 1–55; VII,
1–39; IX, 1–47).   [88] *Rhetoric*, III, 14, 1415a.

I do not know, then, why the poet should not follow the example of Ariosto in using these prefaces, approved by Aristotle as the opening lines of the books that are successively recited in the course of reading an epic poem. The poet, however, must not use such prefaces in the space he should give to imitation. Yet at the beginning of a book the poet always or for the most part ought to speak in his own person. And even when he should imitate . . . the poet would not deserve blame for using such prefaces at the beginnings of the books, since though he does not imitate he prepares the minds of his auditors for the credible which he wishes to sing, by revealing himself as a just and good man, and this preparation is perhaps more necessary in such a place than is imitation. In addition he can in this way better attain his end, for there is no doubt that in this manner he gives more delight to his hearers or readers than he otherwise would, since these prefaces serve for variety and for digression, and so give greater delight. . . . We cannot condemn Ariosto because he has placed prefaces at the beginnings of his cantos. Rather we should give him the highest praise, because, not departing from the matter before him, as poetical prefaces require, he has still mingled variety and morality in order to attain the two chief ends suitable to poetry, namely, to give profit and to give delight.

Book IV, Chapter LI

[Wicked characters in poetry]

There are two things the poet should guard against in his imitation of wicked customs—something that is conceded to him for the sake of the variety of the imitation. One is that he should avoid imitating wicked customs with the words of his own mouth,[89] since for this no excuse is valid, except those that are also fit to defend the evil customs of others that are imitated. . . . The other is that the poet should guard himself from attributing evil customs to persons who exceed in their goodness the condition of men. Now with these two cautions let us enter on the discussion of this variety which was the first head mentioned by us above. I know that Plato has blamed this variety in poets, and that he has not been willing to have poetry imitate habits other than good ones, as can

---

[89] Cf. Chaucer's words in the Prologue of "The Miller's Tale":

This Millere . . .
Tolde his cherles tale in his manere.

be seen from many places in the *Republic*. . . . And Proclus thinks that this variety is so far from excusing the poets that it has rather been the cause why Plato drove them from the state. According to Proclus, variety appears when the poet imitates indifferently good and wicked customs; he thinks such a mixture is not approved by Plato, since he thinks men more inclined to evil than to good would be quicker to follow the example of an evil habit than of a good one. Therefore he confesses that this varied imitation is certainly pleasing but not suited for use in education. Now it has been shown above . . . that vice placed in comparison with virtue appears more ugly and is more likely to be avoided.[90] . . . Aristotle in his *Ethics* says that, if this variety in itself alone is not enough to defend the imitation of evil habits when they are put in contrast with good ones, we are able to limit the discussion to three heads: the first is the addition made to wicked habits by something good; the second is ambiguity of idea; the third is that there are some causes that excuse an author for imitating wicked customs.

[Wickedness shown for moral ends]

The poet then can imitate wicked habits when his work falls under the three heads just mentioned, among which the first is the addition of something good to the wicked custom that is imitated. This can be divided into three heads. The first of these appears when after a time punishment and pain come upon the wicked custom. Under the second head the evil is corrected. According to the third, the judgment is explained because of which the wickedness of the custom is hated. Now turning to the first I say we have an example of it in Homer in the suitors who were all killed by Ulysses, and in Vergil in Mezentius,[91] though many believe the punishment with which they castigated the great sins of those wicked men was too pleasant and too honorable. So in Ariosto we have examples in Martano, Odorico, Pinabello, and others.[92] Now in this manner without any further reasoning we can say that if Dante has imitated wicked habits in the *Inferno*, he has still imitated them with the addition of punishment and penalty, and that to that extent he merits no condemnation at all but rather he

---

[90] Cf. Sidney, *Defense*, sect. 31, immediately below.   [91] *Aeneid*, VII, 648; VIII, 7.

[92] Martano is a coward who pretends to be the brave Grifone, whose arms he has stolen. He is discovered and punished (*Orlando Furioso*, XV–XVIII). Odorico was a traitor to his benefactor, Zerbino, who had intrusted Isabella to him (*ibid*, XIII). Pinabello, the worst man alive (*ibid*, XXII, 47), tried to kill Bradamante by treachery (II, 75), and established a wicked custom of despoiling knights and ladies at his castle.

should be praised instead of blamed. . . . It then appears from reason and authority that the poet does not sin in morality by imitating wicked customs if he adds to them the punishment they deserve.

Book IV, Chapter LV

[Evil intentions corrected]

The second head laid down above by means of which the poet can without any injury to morality imitate wicked customs is the correction of which . . . Plutarch has spoken in the book where he has taught the manner in which we ought to listen to poets, where he writes as follows: "This indicates the more that poetry is an imitation of manners and of the lives of men who are not perfect or sound, as immune from every censure, but rather in whom there is a great place for perturbations, opinions, and ignorance, which still they generally correct on account of the goodness of their nature."[93] We have an example of this same thing in the second book of the *Aeneid*, where Aeneas, after resolving to kill Helen, is impeded by Venus, who amends and corrects his wicked intention. And because I know the verses that speak of this were deleted by Tucca and Varius as showing an unworthy quality on the part of such a hero as Aeneas, I cannot keep from saying that I am greatly astonished at the decision of these correctors of Vergil, because in that passage Vergil represents the power of a passion, not wholly removed from propriety, leading to the proper punishment of the misdeed of Helen, which was then impeded and corrected by Venus, who signifies here the reason, since she is a goddess. . . . Now if this wrong disposition of Aeneas is founded on a passion that wishes to take vengeance for this offense and is corrected by reason, I do not know why those verses should be deleted that deal so cautiously with this wrong intention. The passions of this just vengeance are shown in the following passage:

A flame blazed up in my soul; indignation prompts me to avenge my falling fatherland, and exact the penalty of her crimes. . . . It will be a pleasure to have filled my soul with the fire of revenge, and satisfied the ashes of my people.

The improvement and correction of them appears in the following:

[93] Sect. 8.

My son, what is this anguish so great, that wakes the wildness of your wrath? Why are you maddened with rage? or whither has vanished your affection for me?[94]

But the finest example of all we find in the *Girone* of Luigi Alamanni, where Girone is allured by the great beauty of the wife of Danaino his best friend, and is determined to deface the honor of his friend and the chastity of the lady, but in the course of carrying out his wicked intention, he bethinks himself before he does it and corrects his wicked intention, as is seen in the following words:

> Unfitting desires of love, how is it that you come against my duty, against every law, to spot this heart which, I am certain, has until now been white and pure?[95]

Book V, Chapter IV

[Poetry for the few] [96]

If only those poems are to be thought good that are understood by the common people, it will consequently be necessary to say that no one now thought a clever poet will be worthy of the name of poet, if in Italy he has written in Latin or Greek, since the common people of Italy do not understand Latin or Greek, and so it will be necessary to confess that neither Vergil in the *Aeneid* nor Homer in the *Iliad* and the *Odyssey* are any longer poets, because they are not understood by the common people, which is so proper to say that there is nothing more so. Then if Vergil and Homer still remain poets and excellent ones, we are forced to admit that the good poet may be good even if he is not understood by the rude multitude. This truth was known to Cicero, who, speaking of the difference between the poet and the orator, writes as follows: "Not even Demosthenes himself can truly say what they report Antimachus Clusius the poet to have said. He was reading to a multitude that had come together that great volume of his you are familiar with, and as he read all left except Plato. Yet he said, 'I shall read on just the same, for to me Plato alone is worth all the rest.' He was right, for a poem should be reserved for the approbation of a few, but a popular oration ought to be adapted to the understanding of the multitude."[97] We have it then from Cicero

---

[94] *Aeneid*, II, 575–95, trans. by Lonsdale and Lee. Tucca and Varius were the literary executors of Vergil.   [95] Bk. V, st. 108. For other references to this poem, see the index.
[96] Directed against Castelvetro, *Poetics*, I, 30, 7, just above.   [97] *Brutus*, LI.

that those poems are thought good that are approved by a few, that is, by the learned and the understanding (whatever the ignorant say about it), but that the popular oration should be approved by all the people. It is not true, then . . . that the poet should fix his attention on the rude multitude, but on the lettered, who are few in comparison with the multitude. Horace has shown in many verses that good poets should give every effort to the pleasing of the learned, not taking any account of the untaught multitude: "You must not strive to catch the crowd, but be content with the few as your readers.". . .[98]

Book V, Chapter V

[Poetry should be fitted for both uneducated and educated]

It appears, then, the poet should not put in his fable conceits so trivial as my adversaries think, but on the other hand it also appears that if the poet is allowed to conceal his ideas without any distinction under the veil of enigmas, he will not be in a position to give any delight to the people. Yet, as has been said, he ought to consider this, if it is true that the credible poetical is what is credible to the people. Now it appears that this question can be settled in the method with which Plutarch, with the apologue of the stork and the fox, decided another interesting debate, that is, whether the talk at a banquet should be adapted to the learned or only to those who are ignorant. He shows here that if the talk at the banquet is adapted to those who do not know, it will be nothing else than chattering and emptiness, and since educated men cannot with pleasure be present at such recreations, they will be like the stork forced by the fox to take liquid foods from the table on which they were poured out. But on the other side he makes plain also that if the conversation is so learned that it can be understood only by lofty intellectuals, ordinary men would get little profit and less pleasure from the conversation at the banquet, and would be in the position of the fox invited by the stork to eat from vases with a mouth and neck so narrow that one who did not have the bill of the stork would not be able in any way to get the food. And therefore Plutarch concludes that the best mingling would be to take the middle course and proceed in such a way that both kinds of men would be satisfied and contented with the conversation.

---

[98] *Satires*, I, 10, 73–4. He continues the subject by naming worthy and unworthy readers. Cf. Milton's "Fit audience find, though few" (*Paradise Lost*, VII, 31).

So we can say on our topic that the good poet should labor in such a way at the composition of his poem that the common people and the learned may both be satisfied by his labors. This, if I do not deceive myself, will be fully carried out by the poet if in attending to the idea of his fable he is careful to make sure he can be understood by the common people, and if at the same time he embellishes his poem in places with some noble idea taken from the schools of the philosophers, in order that he may also delight that part of the people more noble than the rest. In this manner it will be true that the poet will be likely to please the common people and at the same time what Plato, Cicero, and Horace . . . have said will be true.

SIR PHILIP SIDNEY

∘◡∘∘◡∘

THE DEFENSE OF POESIE

1583

MANY OBJECTIONS can be urged against Sir Philip Sidney's *Defense of Poesie*. It does not appear to be an especially mature work; it is not deeply learned; it does not point forward by stating ideas to be accepted in the future; its thought is not original; it is unfortunate even in its time of composition, so early that Sidney did not know most of the literature that made Elizabeth's reign great. Yet in spite of all qualifications, it is still, so far as I have seen, the greatest of Renaissance works on its subject. If not original in ideas, it is original in its conception as a brief and independent essay on poetry, not following anything in English or continental tradition, not a commentary, not an assembly of directions to authors, not a study of versification, but an attempt to set forth what poetry is. If it has nothing for the future in idea, it states with clarity the dominant conception of its own age. It does offer to succeeding ages a belief in the importance and beauty of poetry that is more than any theory, didactic or hedonistic. Stating a classical theory, yet it is by the author of the *Arcadia*, a work in the spirit of the Renaissance rather than of ancient Rome. Poetry for Sidney is of the breath of life for soldier and statesman, not the possession of the scholar only. If the ideas are usually taken from other men, they are intermingled and new-molded in Sidney's own mind. The length and pedantry frequent in works on poetry has disappeared; here is a man who can bring into small compass the contents of many volumes. Above all, he writes as poet, producing in many passages a charm hardly attained in works less avowedly logical. If we could have but one sixteenth-century book on poetry, it should be that of Sidney.

It has been suggested that the work is a combination of the ideas of the Renaissance drawn from many sources. Still the number of actual sources identified is relatively small, partly, perhaps, because the author made what he took from others his own to such an extent that it is not recognizable as borrowed. Some of his material, indeed, may have come from conversation, in England or Italy, rather than from reading. At any rate his chief ideas appeared to him so important that they could hardly retain the individuality of their sources. The age speaks, rather than a collection of its books. And indeed it probably is easy to overestimate the amount of Sidney's reading. His spirit had a happy immunity from the diseases of his time. The *Poetice* of Julius Caesar Scaliger he used so evidently that scholars can point out passages he drew from it. There is no hint that Sidney was impatient with his master's weaknesses, as was Chapman when he called him "soul-blind Scaliger" for preferring Vergil to Homer. Yet the pedantry that led Scaliger to neglect all vernacular literature did not dampen Sir Philip's spirits; he can add Rinaldo and Orlando to a list of classical heroes without a qualm, without seeing that he is destroying Scaliger.

As he tells us, he was "a piece of a logician"; a reader might have learned that for himself, for as Mr. Myrick has recently made clear, the *Defense* has an admirable structure, within which Sidney works with freedom, just as he could manage his horse and weapons with grace and skill and yet according to the rules of the jousts.

If he had written twenty years later, what would he have said of the *Faerie Queene* and the Shakespearean drama? At least his willingness to declare that he has seen few English works "that have poetical sinews in them" shows he might have been a severe critic. He demands reason as well as verbal skill, and not too evident display of the latter. Yet in one respect he is of the future, utterly rejecting the position of Scaliger and predicting English achievement by saying that his native language is equal to any other tongue in the world "for the uttering sweetly and properly the conceits of the mind."

The *Defense* was first published after Sidney's death, in 1595, when there appeared two editions, one bearing the title of *An Apology for Poetry*. I have followed Mr. Feuillerat in preferring the earlier of the two as the basis for my modernized text, though I have adopted many obvious corrections from the other, especially when it is supported by some of the other early texts. For the large divisions of the work I accept, with slight modification, the analysis given by Mr. Kenneth O. Myrick in the second chapter of his *Sir Philip Sidney as a Literary Craftsman*. Those who wish to study the work minutely will find notes in the various editions mentioned in the bibliography. I am indebted for much to the notes of Albert S. Cook and Gregory Smith. From the latter I have taken over many of his references to Scaliger, Minturno, and other Renaissance critics, verifying, translating, and sometimes extending them; I have also added a few references. Sidney's quotations from the classics are translated in the notes, except when he himself supplies a translation. Otherwise most of the notes are by way of addition to those of Cook and Smith.

BIBLIOGRAPHY

Baroway, Israel, "Tremellius, Sidney, and Biblical Verse" in *Modern Language Notes*, XLIX, 145–9.

Goldman, Marcus Selden, *Sir Philip Sidney and the Arcadia*. Urbana, 1934.

Myrick, Kenneth O., *Sir Philip Sidney as a Literary Craftsman*. Cambridge, 1935.

Sidney, Sir Philip, *Works*, ed. by Albert Feuillerat. Cambridge, 1922–1926.

——, *Defense of Poesy*, ed. by Albert S. Cook. Boston, 1890.

Sidney's Apologie for Poetrie, ed. by J. Churton Collins. Oxford, 1907.

Admirable notes on the *Apologie* are to be found in Gregory Smith's *Elizabethan Critical Essays* (see the general bibliography, just preceding the index).

THE DEFENSE OF POESIE

[PART I. POETRY TO BE DEFENDED]

[1] WHEN the right virtuous Edward Wotton and I were at the Emperor's court together, we gave ourselves to learn horsemanship of John Pietro Pugliano, one that with great commendation had the place of an esquire in his stable. And he, according to the fertileness of the Italian wit, did not only afford us the demonstration of his practice but sought to enrich our minds with the contemplations therein which he thought most precious. But with none I remember mine ears were at any time more loaden, than when (either angered with slow payment, or moved with our learner-like admiration) he exercised his speech in the praise of his faculty. He said soldiers were the noblest estate of mankind, and horsemen the noblest of soldiers. He said they were the masters of war and ornaments of peace, speedy goers and strong abiders, triumphers both in camps and courts. Nay, to so unbelieved a point he proceeded, as that no earthly thing bred such wonder to a prince as to be a good horseman. Skill of government was but a *pedanteria* in

comparison.[1] Then would he add certain praises by telling what a peerless beast the horse was, the only serviceable courtier without flattery, the beast of most beauty, faithfulness, courage, and such more, that if I had not been a piece of a logician before I came to him I think he would have persuaded me to have wished myself a horse. But thus much at least with his no few words he drave into me, that self-love is better than any gilding to make that seem gorgeous wherein ourselves be parties. Wherein, if Pugliano's strong affection and weak arguments will not satisfy you, I will give you a nearer example of myself, who (I know not by what mischance) in these my not old years and idlest times having slipped into the title of a poet, am provoked to say something unto you in the defense of that my unelected vocation, which if I handle with more good will than good reasons, bear with me, since the scholar is to be pardoned that followeth the steps of his master. And yet I must say that, as I have just cause to make a pitiful defense of poor poetry, which from almost the highest estimation of learning is fallen to be the laughing-stock of children, so have I need to bring some more available proofs; since the former is by no man barred of his deserved credit, the silly latter hath had even the names of philosophers used to the defacing of it, with great danger of civil war among the Muses.

[Part II. The Character and Reputation of Poetry]

[2] And first, truly to all them that professing learning inveigh against poetry may justly be objected that they go very near to ungratefulness, to seek to deface that which, in the noblest nations and languages that are known, hath been the first light-giver to ignorance, and first nurse, whose milk by little and little enabled them to feed afterwards of tougher knowledges.[2] And will they now play the hedgehog that, being received into the den, drave out his host, or rather the vipers that with their birth kill their par-

---

[1] *Pedanteria:* pedantry, something to be found in a schoolmaster.

[2] Minturno writes that he has esteemed poetry the mother of the sciences, and the Muses inventors of the arts and directors of all things (*L'arte poetica*, preface).

Daniello writes: "Who first divided and separated private from public affairs? The poet. Who divided sacred and divine matters from wicked and profane ones? The poet. Who found the way to unite men and women with an indissoluble knot, though at first they conducted themselves like the animals, with whom they were on a level, if not the poets? With their verses they built cities. When they were built, they gave them laws. They taught man how he ought to rule and govern them" (*Poetica*, p. 12). In this connection he speaks of Amphion and Orpheus. Further he writes: "The ancients called poetry the first philosophy" (p. 21).

ents? Let learned Greece in any of her manifold sciences be able to show me one book before Musaeus, Homer, and Hesiod, all three nothing else but poets. Nay, let any history be brought that can say any writers were there before them, if they were not men of the same skill, as Orpheus, Linus,[3] and some other are named, who, having been the first of that country that made pens deliverers of their knowledge to their posterity, may justly challenge to be called their fathers in learning. For not only in time they had this priority (although in itself antiquity be venerable) but went before them as causes to draw with their charming sweetness the wild untamed wits to an admiration of knowledge, so as Amphion was said to move stones with his poetry to build Thebes, and Orpheus to be listened to by beasts—indeed stony and beastly people.[4] So among the Romans were Livius Andronicus and Ennius. So in the Italian language the first that made it aspire to be a treasure-house of science were the poets Dante, Boccace, and Petrarch. So in our English were Gower and Chaucer, after whom, encouraged and delighted with their excellent foregoing, others have followed, to beautify our mother tongue as well in the same kind as in other arts.

[Philosophers as poets]

[3] This did so notably show itself that the philosophers of Greece durst not a long time appear to the world but under the masks of poets. So Thales, Empedocles,[5] and Parmenides sang their natural philosophy in verses; so did Pythagoras and Phocylides their moral counsels; so did Tyrtaeus in war matters, and Solon in matters of policy,[6] or rather, they, being poets, did exercise their delightful vein in those points of highest knowledge which before them lay hid to the world. For that wise Solon was directly a poet it is manifest, having written in verse the notable fable of the Atlantic Island which was continued by Plato. And truly even Plato whosoever well considereth shall find that in the

---

[3] This passage on the antiquity of poetry is perhaps derived from Minturno, *De poeta* (Venice, 1559), pp. 9, 13, 15. Something of the sort also appears in the dedication of *L'arte poetica*, where "Orpheus, Linus, and some other are named." See also Goldman, p. 69.

[4] See Horace, *Art of Poetry*, 391 ff., above.   [5] See Aristotle, *Poetics*, I, 47a28, above.

[6] Daniello writes: "Solon, who was the one who first gave the Athenians the laws set out in verse, was the cause of their revoking and abolishing a law that had been made with the agreement of the whole city, namely, that no one should be permitted to mention the war of Salamis nor to exhort the people to it. Feigning that he was mad, he read publicly in the public squares and streets the verses he had made in favor of that war, and was elected general by the citizens" (*Poetica*, pp. 21, 22).

body of his work, though the inside and strength were philosophy, the skin as it were and beauty depended most of poetry;[7] for all stands upon dialogues, wherein he feigns many honest burgesses of Athens speak of such matters, that if they had been set on the rack they would never have confessed them, besides his poetical describing the circumstances of their meetings, as the well ordering of a banquet, the delicacy of a walk, with interlacing mere tales, as Gyges' Ring, and others, which who knows not to be flowers of poetry did never walk into Apollo's garden.

[Historians as poets]

[4] And even historiographers (although their lips sound of things done, and verity be written in their foreheads) have been glad to borrow both fashion and perchance weight of the poets. So Herodotus entitled his history by the name of the nine Muses; and both he and all the rest that followed him either stole or usurped of poetry their passionate describing of passions, the many particularities of battles which no man could affirm, or, if that be denied me, long orations put in the mouths of great kings and captains, which it is certain they never pronounced. So that truly neither philosopher nor historiographer could at the first have entered into the gates of popular judgments, if they had not taken a great passport of poetry, which in all nations at this day where learning flourisheth not is plain to be seen; in all which they have some feeling of poetry.[8]

[7] For other passages in which appears this dualism of body and skin, see sect. 16, below, and the index under *content and language*. Daniello says: "I cannot but marvel at the ability and the profound teaching of Plato. While he labors with the intent of blaming the poets, he is held in estimation as a very great poet by everybody who understands about him. There is not one of his *Dialogues* . . . in which he does not express his conceptions under a fabulous veil and a mystery, but with the brightest and most splendid flames of words and with the grandest numbers" (p. 22).

Owen Felltham wrote: "The words being rather the drossy part, conceit I take to be the principal. And here, though it digresseth from truth, it flieth above her, making her more rare by giving curious raiment to her nakedness" (*Resolves*, "Of Poets and Poetry").

Even the Biblical narratives were thought to observe the principles of poetry: "The single parts of a parable are not always to be adjusted to the thing signified by the parable, for many things are said to fill up and ornament the narrative" (Ioannes Maldonatus, *In quatuor evangelistas commentarii* [Mainz, 1622] on John 15, 6).

[8] Minturno writes: "Since for these reasons poetry was so profitable and so pleasing, there was never any nation or any people that did not gladly receive it into its bosom and embrace. . . . What race of men then is so barbarous, so savage, that poetry is alien to it?" (*De poeta*, I, 9). In the Argument to "October," in the *Shepherd's Calendar*, Spenser writes of poetry that it has "been in all ages and even amongst the most barbarous always of singular account and honor."

[Poetry among barbarians]

[5] In Turkey, besides their law-giving divines they have no other writers but poets. In our neighbor country Ireland, where truly learning goes very bare, yet are their poets held in a devout reverence. Even among the most barbarous and simple Indians where no writing is, yet have they their poets, who make and sing songs, which they call *areytos*, both of their ancestors' deeds and praises of their gods—a sufficient probability that, if ever learning come among them, it must be by having their hard dull wits softened and sharpened with the sweet delights of poetry. For until they find a pleasure in the exercise of the mind, great promises of much knowledge will little persuade them that know not the fruits of knowledge. In Wales, the true remnant of the ancient Britons, as there are good authorities to show the long time they had poets, which they called bards, so through all the conquests of Romans, Saxons, Danes, and Normans, some of whom did seek to ruin all memory of learning from among them, yet do their poets even to this day last; so as it is not more notable in soon beginning than in long continuing.

[Poetry among the Greeks and Romans]

[6] But since the authors of most of our sciences were the Romans, and before them the Greeks, let us a little stand upon their authorities, but even so far as to see what names they have given unto this now scorned skill. Among the Romans a poet was called *vates*, which is as much as a diviner, foreseer, or prophet, as by his conjoined words *vaticinium* and *vaticinari* is manifest; so heavenly a title did that excellent people bestow upon this heart-ravishing knowledge, and so far were they carried into the admiration thereof, that they thought in the chanceable hitting upon any such verses great foretokens of their following fortunes were placed. Whereupon grew the word of *Sortes Vergilianae*, when by sudden opening Vergil's book they lighted upon some verse of his, as it is reported by many; whereof the histories of the emperors' lives are full, as of Albinus, the governor of our island, who in his childhood met with this verse,

Arma amens capio nec sat rationis in armis;[9]

and in his age performed it. Although it were a very vain and

---

[9] *Aeneid*, II, 314: "I seize arms in a frenzy, nor is there sufficient reason for arms."

godless superstition, as also it was to think that spirits were commanded by such verses—whereupon this word charms, derived of
carmina, cometh—so yet serveth it to show the great reverence those
wits were held in. And altogether not without ground, since both
the oracles of Delphos and Sibylla's prophecies were wholly delivered in verses; for that same exquisite observing of number and
measure in words, and that high flying liberty of conceit proper to
the poet did seem to have some divine force in it.

[Sacred poetry]

[7] And may not I presume a little further, to show the reason-
ableness of this word *vates,* and say that the holy David's Psalms
are a divine poem?[10] If I do, I shall not do it without the testimony of great learned men, both ancient and modern. But even
the name of Psalms will speak for me, which being interpreted is
nothing but Songs; then that it is fully written in meter, as all
learned Hebricians agree, although the rules be not yet fully found;
lastly and principally, his handling his prophecy, which is merely
poetical. For what else is the awaking his musical instruments, the
often and free changing of persons, his notable *prosopopeias,* when
he maketh you, as it were, see God coming in his majesty, his telling of the beasts' joyfulness, and hills' leaping, but a heavenly
poesy, wherein almost he showeth himself a passionate lover of
that unspeakable and everlasting beauty to be seen by the eyes of
the mind, only cleared by faith? But truly now having named him,
I fear I seem to profane that holy name, applying it to poetry,
which is among us thrown down to so ridiculous an estimation.
But they that with quiet judgments will look a little deeper into it,
shall find the end and working of it such as being rightly applied
deserveth not to be scourged out of the Church of God.

[The poet is the maker]

[8] But now let us see how the Greeks have named it, and how
they deemed of it. The Greeks named him poet, which name
hath, as the most excellent, gone through other languages. It
cometh of this word *poiein,* which is *to make;* wherein, I know not
whether by luck or wisdom, we Englishmen have met with the
Greeks in calling him a maker;[11] which name, how high and in-

---

[10] Cf. Milton's opinion, *The Reason of Church Government,* sect. 1, below.

[11] Scaliger regretted that the Latins had not used the word *factor,* as the equivalent
of poet (*Poetice,* 1, 1, p. 3D1).

comparable a title it is, I had rather were known by marking the scope of other sciences than by any partial allegation.

[Poetry and nature]

[9] There is no art delivered unto mankind that hath not the works of nature for his principal object, without which they could not consist, and on which they so depend as they become actors and players, as it were, of what nature will have set forth.[12] So doth the astronomer look upon the stars, and by that he seeth, set down what order nature hath taken therein. So doth the geometrician and arithmetician in their diverse sorts of quantities. So doth the musician in times tell you which by nature agree, which not. The natural philosopher thereon hath his name, and the moral philosopher standeth upon the natural virtues, vices, or passions of man; and "follow Nature" (saith he) "therein, and thou shalt not err." The lawyer saith what men have determined; the historian what men have done. The grammarian speaketh only of the rules of speech; and the rhetorician and logician, considering what in nature will soonest prove and persuade thereon, give artificial rules, which still are compassed within the circle of a question according to the proposed matter. The physician weigheth the nature of man's body, and the nature of things helpful or hurtful unto it. And the metaphysic, though it be in the second and abstract notions, and therefore be counted supernatural, yet doth he indeed build upon the depth of nature. Only the poet, disdaining to be tied to any such subjection, lifted up with the vigor of his own invention, doth grow in effect into another nature, in making things either better than nature bringeth forth, or, quite anew, forms such as never were in nature, as the heroes, demigods, cyclops, chimeras, furies, and such like; so as he goeth hand in hand with nature, not enclosed within the narrow warrant of her gifts but freely ranging within the zodiac of his own wit.[13] Nature never set forth the earth in so rich tapestry as divers poets have done,

---

[12] Gregory Smith (see bibliography) thinks the illustrative details of this paragraph were suggested by Minturno's *De poeta*, pp. 87–99.

[13] Giraldi suggests that the poet is a "maker" because he produces marvelous tales (*On the Romances*, sect. 56, above). Mazzoni attributes to the poet the capacity "of feigning new species and such as are not actually to be found, as Centaurs, Chimeras, Hydras of many heads, Geryons, Pegasuses, Sirens, and others of the sort, which (as Lucretius has learnedly shown) cannot in truth come into being or live or exist" (*Defense of Dante*, III, 8). Though Sidney does not use the word *variety*, this passage seems to imply the idea, as it is exemplified in the *Arcadia*. For Tasso's treatment, see sect. 31, below.

neither with so pleasant rivers, fruitful trees, sweet-smelling flowers, nor whatsoever else may make the too much loved earth more lovely.[14] Her world is brazen, the poets only deliver a golden.

[Poetry and man]

[10] But let those things alone, and go to man—for whom as the other things are, so it seemeth in him her uttermost cunning is employed—and know whether she have brought forth so true a lover as Theagenes, so constant a friend as Pylades, so valiant a man as Orlando, so right a prince as Xenophon's Cyrus, so excellent a man every way as Vergil's Aeneas.[15] Neither let this be jestingly conceived, because the works of the one be essential, the other in imitation or fiction; for every understanding knoweth the skill of each artificer standeth in that *idea* or fore-conceit of the work, and not in the work itself. And that the poet hath that *idea* is manifest, by delivering them forth in such excellency as he had imagined them; which delivering forth also is not wholly imaginative, as we are wont to say by them that build castles in the air; but so far substantially it worketh, not only to make a Cyrus, which had been but a particular excellency, as nature might have done, but to bestow a Cyrus upon the world to make many Cyruses, if they will learn aright why and how that maker made him.

[The poet as creator]

[11] Neither let it be deemed too saucy a comparison to balance the highest point of man's wit with the efficacy of nature; but rather give right honor to the heavenly maker of that maker, who, having made man to his own likeness, set him beyond and over all the works of that second nature; which in nothing he showeth so much as in poetry, when with the force of a divine breath he bringeth things forth far surpassing her doings,[16] with no small

[14] Cf. Dryden, *Of Dramatic Poesy*, sect. 38, below.
[15] See secs. 16, 21, 23, 34, below, and notes.
[16] This view of the superiority of art to nature, though it would be acceptable to some modern students of aesthetics, is opposed to the superficial one stated in the popular lines by Joyce Kilmer:

> Poems are made by fools like me,
> But only God can make a tree.

Scaliger writes: "But the poet makes another nature and other outcomes for men's acts, and finally in the same way makes himself another God, as it were. The other sciences are as it were users of what the maker of them all produced; but poetry, when it so splendidly gives the appearance of the things that are and of those that are not, seems not to narrate the events, as others, like the historian, do, but as a God to produce them" (*Poetice*, 1, 1, p. 3D1). See also sect. 23, below.

argument to the incredulous of that first accursed fall of Adam, since our erected wit maketh us know what perfection is, and yet our infected will keepeth us from reaching unto it. But these arguments will by few be understood, and by fewer granted. Thus much, I hope, will be given me, that the Greeks with some probability of reason gave him the name above all names of learning.

[PART III. POETRY DEFINED]

[12] Now let us go to a more ordinary opening of him, that the truth may be the more palpable; and so I hope, though we get not so unmatched a praise as the etymology of his names will grant, yet his very description, which no man will deny, shall not justly be barred from a principal commendation. Poesy therefore is an art of imitation, for so Aristotle termeth it in the word *mimesis*, that is to say, a representing, counterfeiting, or figuring forth—to speak metaphorically, a speaking picture;[17] with this end, to teach and delight.[18] Of this have been three general kinds.[19]

[PART IV. THREE KINDS OF POETRY. 1. Religious]

[13] The chief, both in antiquity and excellency, were they that did imitate the inconceivable excellencies of God. Such were David in his Psalms; Solomon in his Song of Songs, in his Ecclesiastes, and Proverbs; Moses and Deborah in their Hymns; and the writer of Job, which, beside other, the learned Emanuel Tremellius and Franciscus Junius do entitle the poetical part of the Scripture. Against these none will speak that hath the Holy Ghost in due holy reverence. In this kind though in a full wrong divinity,

[17] See Horace, *Art of Poetry*, 361, above; Mazzoni, *Of the Defense of the "Comedy,"* sect. 3, immediately above; the index under *picture*.

[18] Horace, *Art of Poetry*, 333, above. Scaliger says that an end of poetry is imitation, but imitation "is a means to the last end, which is teaching with delight. For the poet certainly teaches; he does not merely delight, as some think" (*Poetice*, I, I, p. 1B2); "the end of the poet is to teach with jocundity" (*ibid*, VII, 2, p. 347D2). According to Varchi (1553) "the poet does not ordinarily have the purpose of delighting for the sake of delight alone, but of delighting for the sake of benefiting" (*Della poetica in generale*, I, 3).

As one who benefits, the poet may be compared with the physician, of whom Philippus Beroaldus writes: "It is the business of the medical man, as Asclepiades says, . . . to cure quickly, safely, and with jocundity" (*De optimo statu libellus*, in *Varia opuscula* [Basel, 1513], folio 128 verso). See *poet as physician*, in the index.

[19] The division and some of the examples are taken from Scaliger, *Poetice*, I, 2, p. 5D1 ff. Sidney omits some and adds others, as Manilius, Pontanus, and Lucan, though the last is discussed by Scaliger in the same chapter. Pontanus is discussed by Scaliger in Bk. VI, chap. II.

were Orpheus, Amphion, Homer in his Hymns, and many other, both Greeks and Romans. And this poesy must be used by whosoever will follow St. James's counsel in singing psalms when they are merry, and I know is used with the fruit of comfort by some, when in sorrowful pangs of their death-bringing sins they find the consolation of the never-leaving goodness.

[2. Philosophical poetry]

[14] The second kind is of them that deal with matters philosophical: either moral, as Tyrtaeus, Phocylides, and Cato; or natural, as Lucretius and Vergil's *Georgics*; or astronomical, as Manilius and Pontanus; or historical, as Lucan;[20] which who mislike, the fault is in their judgment quite out of taste, and not in the sweet food of sweetly uttered knowledge.

[3. Right poets]

[15] But because this second sort is wrapped within the fold of the proposed subject and takes not the free course of his own invention, whether they properly be poets or no let grammarians dispute; and go to the third, indeed right poets,[21] of whom chiefly this question ariseth. Betwixt whom and these second is such a kind of difference as betwixt the meaner sort of painters, who counterfeit only such faces as are set before them, and the more excellent, who having no law but wit, bestow that in colors upon you which is fittest for the eye to see, as the constant though lamenting look of Lucretia, when she punished in herself another's fault, wherein he painteth not Lucretia whom he never saw but painteth the outward beauty of such a virtue. For these third be they which most properly do imitate to teach and delight, and to imitate borrow nothing of what is, hath been, or shall be; but range, only reined with learned discretion, into the divine consideration of what may be and should be.[22] These be they that, as the first and most noble sort may justly be termed *vates*, so these are waited on in the excellentest languages and best understandings, with the fore-described name of poets; for these indeed do merely make to imitate, and

[20] See *Lucan* in the index.
[21] True poets. Sidney's friend Henri Estienne, in the preface of his *Poesis philosophica*, makes somewhat the same distinction as does Sidney, speaking of works called poems when they are not truly (*vere*) poems (Marcus S. Goldman, *Sir Philip Sidney and the Arcadia*, pp. 69–70).
[22] Men as they should be formed one of Aristotle's classes: see *Poetics*, xxv, 60b32, above.

imitate both to delight and teach, and delight to move men to take that goodness in hand, which without delight they would fly as from a stranger, and teach to make them know that goodness whereunto they are moved; which being the noblest scope to which ever any learning was directed, yet want there not idle tongues to bark at them.

[Verse]

[16] These be subdivided into sundry more special denominations. The most notable be the heroic, lyric, tragic, comic, satiric, iambic, elegiac, pastoral, and certain others, some of these being termed according to the matter they deal with, some by the sort of verse they liked best to write in; for indeed the greatest part of poets have appareled their poetical inventions in that numbrous kind of writing which is called verse—indeed but appareled, verse being but an ornament and no cause to poetry,[23] since there have been many most excellent poets that never versified, and now swarm many versifiers that need never answer to the name of poets.[24] For Xenophon, who did imitate so excellently as to give us *effigiem justi imperii*, the portraiture of a just Empire, under the name of Cyrus, as Cicero saith of him, made therein an absolute heroical poem.[25] So did Heliodorus in his sugared invention of that picture of love in Theagenes and Chariclea;[26] and yet both these wrote in prose—which I speak to show that it is not rhyming and versing that maketh a poet, no more than a long gown maketh an advocate, who though he pleaded in armor should be an advocate and no soldier. But it is that feigning notable images of vir-

---

[23] Cf. sect. 3, above.

[24] Scaliger writes: "Those who can attain but little glory, since they tell simple narratives in verse, are called merely versifiers; those who gain for themselves the care and oversight of the Muses, in the spirit of whom they find out what escapes others, are called poets" (*Poetice*, I, 2, p. 3B2). In Jonson's *Timber* we read that "a rimer and a poet are two things" (p. 76, ed. Schelling). Sidney repeats the idea in sect. 37, below.

[25] Xenophon's *Cyropaedia*, or *Education of Cyrus*, is written in prose. In his letter to Sir Walter Raleigh on the *Faerie Queene*, Spenser seems to accept the *Cyropaedia* as a poem (Letter to Raleigh, below). Machiavelli and other Renaissance writers looked on the work as highly instructive.

[26] The *Aethiopica* of Heliodorus, the chief characters of which are Theagenes and Chariclea. Scaliger praises its arrangement and adds: "I hold the opinion that this book should be very carefully read by the epic poet and that he should set it before himself as a most excellent example" (*Poetice*, III, 96, p. 144D1). Gregory Smith indicates that Sidney's reference comes from Scaliger, but the tone of Sidney's remarks (cf. also sect. 10, above) and the opinions of other scholars suggest that he is speaking from his own knowledge. See Kenneth O. Myrick, *Sidney as a Literary Craftsman*, and the index under *Heliodorus*.

tues, vices,[27] or what else, with that delightful teaching, which must be the right describing note to know a poet by, although indeed the senate of poets hath chosen verse as their fittest raiment, meaning, as in matter they passed all in all, so in manner to go beyond them, not speaking table-talk fashion or like men in a dream, words as they chanceably fall from the mouth, but peizing[28] each syllable of each word by just proportion according to the dignity of the subject.

[PART V. TRUE POETRY DISCUSSED IN ITS EFFECTS AND ITS KINDS]

[17] Now therefore it shall not be amiss first to weigh this latter sort of poetry by his works and then by his parts, and if in neither of these anatomies he be condemnable, I hope we shall obtain a more favorable sentence. This purifying of wit, this enriching of memory, enabling of judgment, and enlarging of conceit, which commonly we call learning, under what name soever it come forth, or to what immediate end soever it be directed, the final end is to lead and draw us to as high a perfection as our degenerate souls, made worse by their clay lodgings, can be capable of.[29] This, according to the inclination of man, bred many-formed impressions. For some that thought this felicity principally to be gotten by knowledge, and no knowledge to be so high or heavenly as acquaintance with the stars, gave themselves to astronomy; others, persuading themselves to be demigods if they knew the causes of things, became natural and supernatural philosophers; some an admirable delight drew to music; and some the certainty of demonstration to the mathematics. But all one and other having this scope: to know, and by knowledge to lift up the mind from the dungeon of the body to the enjoying his own divine essence. But when by the balance of experience it was found that the astronomer looking to the stars might fall into a ditch, that the inquiring philosopher might be blind in himself, and the mathematician

---

[27] Gregory Smith observes that these words seem as though taken from Minturno, since the latter writes that dramatists "feign either the vices or the virtues" of their characters (*De poeta*, p. 27). In the dedication of Minturno's *L'arte poetica* we read "Verse does not make the writer a poet, but he is made a poet by feigning and giving to the matter he treats that form which is necessary for poetry." Cf. also Giraldi, *Romances*, sect. 56, above, and Aristotle, *Poetics*, 1, above.   [28] Weighing.

[29] Milton wrote in his tractate *Of Education:* "The end then of learning is to repair the ruins of our first parents by regaining to know God aright, and out of that knowledge to love him, to imitate him, to be like him, as we may the nearest by possessing our souls of true virtue, which being united to the heavenly grace of faith makes up the highest perfection."

might draw forth a straight line with a crooked heart, then, lo, did
proof, the overruler of opinions, make manifest that all these are
but serving sciences, which, as they have each a private end in
themselves, so yet are they all directed to the highest end of the
mistress knowledge, by the Greeks called *architectonike*, which
stands, as I think, in the knowledge of a man's self, in the ethic and
politic consideration, with the end of well doing and not of well
knowing only; even as the saddler's next end is to make a good sad-
dle, but his further end to serve a nobler faculty, which is horsemanship; so the horseman's to soldiery, and the soldier not only to
have the skill, but to perform the practice of a soldier.[30] So that
the ending end of all earthly learning being virtuous action, those
skills that most serve to bring forth that have a most just title to be
princes over all the rest. Wherein we can show the poet is worthy
to have it before any other competitors, among whom principally
to challenge it step forth the moral philosophers, whom methinks
I see coming towards me with a sullen gravity, as though they
could not abide vice by daylight, rudely clothed for to witness
outwardly their contempt of outward things, with books in their
hands against glory, whereto they set their names, sophistically
speaking against subtlety, and angry with any man in whom they
see the foul fault of anger. These men, casting largesse as they go
of definitions, divisions, and distinctions, with a scornful interroga-
tive do soberly ask whether it be possible to find any path so
ready to lead a man to virtue as that which teacheth what virtue
is, and teacheth it not only by delivering forth his very being, his
causes, and effects, but also by making known his enemy, vice,
which must be destroyed, and his cumbersome servant, passion,
which must be mastered, by showing the generalities that contain
it, and the specialities that are derived from it; lastly, by plain setting down, how it extends itself out of the limits of a man's own
little world to the government of families and maintaining of public societies.

[How history teaches]

[18] The historian scarcely gives leisure to the moralist to say
so much, but that he, laden with old mouse-eaten records, author-
izing himself for the most part upon other histories, whose greatest
authorities are built upon the notable foundation of hearsay, having much ado to accord differing writers and to pick truth out of
partiality, better acquainted with a thousand years ago than with

[30] Cf. Plato, *Republic*, x, 600E, above.

the present age and yet better knowing how this world goes than how his own wit runs, curious for antiquities and inquisitive of novelties, a wonder to young folks and a tyrant in table talk, denieth, in a great chafe, that any man for teaching of virtue and virtuous actions is comparable to him: "I am *testis temporum, lux veritatis, vita memoriae, magistra vitae, nuncia vetustatis,* etc.[31] The philosopher," saith he, "teacheth a disputative virtue, but I do an active. His virtue is excellent in the dangerless Academy of Plato but mine showeth forth her honorable face in the battles of Marathon, Pharsalia, Poitiers, and Agincourt. He teacheth virtue by certain abstract considerations, but I only bid you follow the footing of them that have gone before you. Old-aged experience goeth beyond the fine-witted philosopher but I give the experience of many ages. Lastly, if he make the song-book, I put the learner's hand to the lute, and if he be the guide, I am the light." Then would he allege you innumerable examples, confirming story by stories, how much the wisest senators and princes have been directed by the credit of history, as Brutus, Alphonsus of Aragon, and who not if need be? At length the long line of their disputation makes a point in this, that the one giveth the precept and the other the example.

[The poet as moderator]

[19] Now, whom shall we find, since the question standeth for the highest form in the school of learning, to be moderator? Truly, as me seemeth, the poet; and if not a moderator, even the man that ought to carry the title from them both, and much more from all other serving sciences. Therefore compare we the poet with the historian and with the moral philosopher; and if he go beyond them both no other human skill can match him. For as for the divine, with all reverence it is ever to be excepted, not only for having his scope as far beyond any of these as eternity exceedeth a moment but even for passing each of these in themselves. And for the lawyer, though *Jus* be the daughter of Justice, and Justice the chief of virtues, yet because he seeks to make men good rather *formidine poenae* than *virtutis amore,*[32] or, to say righter, doth not endeavor to make men good, but that their evil hurt not others, having no care, so he be a good citizen, how bad a man he be;

---

[31] Cicero, *On the Orator,* II, 9, 36: "I am the witness of time, the light of truth, the life of memory, the master of life, the messenger of antiquity."

[32] By fear of punishment rather than by love of virtue.

therefore, as our wickedness maketh him necessary and necessity
maketh him honorable, so is he not in the deepest truth to stand
in rank with these who all endeavor to take naughtiness away and
plant goodness even in the secretest cabinet of our souls. And
these four are all that any way deal in the consideration of men's
manners, which being the supreme knowledge, they that best
breed it deserve the best commendation.

[Philosopher and historian]

[20] The philosopher therefore and the historian are they
which would win the goal, the one by precept, the other by example. But both, not having both, do both halt. For the philosopher,
setting down with thorny arguments the bare rule, is so hard of
utterance and so misty to be conceived,[33] that one that hath no
other guide but him shall wade in him till he be old before he shall
find sufficient cause to be honest. For his knowledge standeth so
upon the abstract and general that happy is that man who may
understand him, and more happy that can apply what he doth
understand. On the other side, the historian, wanting the precept,
is so tied not to what should be but to what is, to the particular
truth of things and not to the general reason of things, that his
example draweth no necessary consequence, and therefore a less
fruitful doctrine.

[Both precept and example in poetry]

[21] Now doth the peerless poet perform both; for whatsoever
the philosopher saith should be done, he gives a perfect picture
of it in some one by whom he presupposeth it was done; so as he
coupleth the general notion with the particular example.[34] A

---

[33] Daniello says: "The poet often expresses with gravity and in pleasing fashion
what the philosopher generally treats in his arguments with few and subtle words. . . .
The speech of the philosopher is usually dry, without force in itself, and always without
any poetic power to rouse, without anything causing anger or sorrow or anything
pleasant, sweet, wonderful, or astute" (*Poetica*, pp. 19–20).
  Minturno indicates that the "philosophers debate more severely and harshly than
they need to" (*De poeta*, 39).
  Sidney's use of the word *bare* suggests the Latin *nudus* and the Italian *nudo* in similar
connections (Quintilian, v, 12, 6; viii, 6, 41; Heinsius, *De tragoediae constitutione*, chap.
xvii, p. 165; Minturno, *L'arte poetica*, dedication, p. 2; pp. 30, 450).
[34] On teaching by example cf. Spenser's letter to Raleigh, below. Horace was
aware of this aspect of the didactic theory, writing of the poet that "he forms the
heart with friendly precepts, corrects harshness, envy, and wrath, tells of noble
deeds, and instructs the ages as they come on with famous examples" (*Epistles*, ii, 1
128–31).

perfect picture, I say, for he yieldeth to the powers of the mind an image of that whereof the philosopher bestoweth but a wordish description, which doth neither strike, pierce, nor possess the sight of the soul so much as that other doth.[35] For as in outward things, to a man that had never seen an elephant or a rhinoceros, who should tell him most exquisitely all their shapes, color, bigness and particular marks; or of a gorgeous palace an architector,[36] who declaring the full beauties might well make the hearer able to repeat, as it were by rote, all he had heard, yet should never satisfy his inward conceit with being witness to itself of a true lively knowledge; but the same man, as soon as he might see those beasts well painted, or the house well in model, should straightways grow without need of any description to a judicial comprehending of them; so no doubt the philosopher with his learned definitions—be it of virtues, or vices, matters of public policy or private government—replenisheth the memory with many infallible grounds of wisdom, which notwithstanding lie dark before the imaginative and judging power, if they be not illuminated or figured forth by the speaking picture of poesy. Tully taketh much pains, and many times not without poetical helps, to make us know the force love of our country hath in us. Let us but hear old Anchises speaking in the midst of Troy's flames, or see Ulysses in the fullness of all Calypso's delights bewail his absence from barren and beggarly Ithaca. Anger, the Stoics said, was a short madness; let but Sophocles bring you Ajax on a stage, killing and whipping sheep and oxen, thinking them the army of Greeks with their chieftains Agamemnon and Menelaus, and tell me if you have not a more familiar insight into anger than finding in the

[35] Leon Battista Alberti writes in his *Momus:* "Do they prefer to learn from poets rather than from philosophers the rules and modes of life? . . . Those things that are learned from the poets with pleasure are understood more easily . . . and remain more firmly fixed in the memory" (IV, 105.17ff., in *Opuscoli morali* [Venice, 1586]).

Minturno writes: "The populace is to be taught and moved toward virtue not by the precepts of the philosophers but by examples brought forward not by the historians but by the poets. . . . They should feign and set forth those fables that please the people, and nothing else than what is approved by the people, for the philosophers in their dreams remove the powers of the mind from the normal course of life or, to put it more correctly, they are in their speculations so removed from ordinary matters that they do not see that unless speech is fitted to the opinions of those who listen nothing can be accomplished by orators of any sort. . . . But the poet does not so serve the people nor judge himself so under the control of the masses that he is unable to present anything except that which the multitude approves" (*De poeta*, pp. 38–39). This may be compared with Sidney's whole presentation of the philosopher.

[36] Architect. The early editions read *architecture.* I have adopted a conjecture by Albert S. Cook.

schoolmen his genus and difference.[37] See whether wisdom and temperance in Ulysses and Diomedes, valor in Achilles, friendship in Nisus and Euryalus,[38] even to an ignorant man carry not an apparent shining, and contrarily the remorse of conscience in Oedipus, the soon-repenting pride of Agamemnon, the self-devouring cruelty in his father Atreus, the violence of ambition in the two Theban brothers, the sour sweetness of revenge in Medea, and to fall lower, the Terentian Gnatho and our Chaucer's Pandar so expressed that we now use their names to signify their trades; and finally, all virtues, vices, and passions so in their own natural states laid to the view, that we seem not to hear of them, but clearly to see through them. But even in the most excellent determination of goodness, what philosopher's counsel can so readily direct a prince, as the feigned Cyrus in Xenophon; or a virtuous man in all fortunes, as Aeneas in Vergil; or a whole commonwealth, as the way of Sir Thomas More's *Utopia?* I say the way, because where Sir Thomas More erred, it was the fault of the man and not of the poet, for that way of patterning a commonwealth was most absolute, though he perchance hath not so absolutely performed it.

[Philosophy and poetry]

[22] For the question is, whether the feigned image of poetry or the regular instruction of philosophy hath the more force in teaching; wherein if the philosophers have more rightly showed themselves philosophers than the poets have attained to the high top of their profession, as in truth,

Mediocribus esse poetis,
Non di, non homines, non concessere columnae;[39]

it is, I say again, not the fault of the art, but that by few men that art can be accomplished. Certainly, even our Saviour Christ could as well have given the moral commonplaces of uncharitableness and humbleness as the divine narration of Dives and Lazarus, or of disobedience and mercy, as that heavenly discourse of the lost child and the gracious father, but that his through-searching wisdom knew the estate of Dives burning in hell, and of Lazarus in

---

[37] Myrick (see bibliography) holds that this reference comes not from Sidney's own reading of the *Ajax*, but from an account in Minturno's *De poeta*, p. 41. He suggests further that the references to Greek heroes in the remainder of the paragraph come from the tragedies of Seneca (see the index), not from the Greek dramatists.

[38] *Aeneid*, IX. The story is used as an example by Peter Ramus in his *Logic* (I, 4), presumably well-known to Sidney.   [39] Horace, *Art of Poetry*, 372–3, above.

Abraham's bosom, would more constantly, as it were, inhabit both the memory and judgment. Truly, for myself, meseems I see before mine eyes the lost child's disdainful prodigality turned to envy a swine's dinner; which by the learned divines are thought not historical acts, but instructing parables.[40] For conclusion, I say the philosopher teacheth, but he teacheth obscurely, so as the learned only can understand him; that is to say, he teacheth them that are already taught. But the poet is the food for the tenderest stomachs, the poet is indeed the right popular philosopher. Whereof Aesop's tales give good proof; whose pretty allegories, stealing under the formal tales of beasts, make many, more beastly than beasts, begin to hear the sound of virtue from those dumb speakers.

[History and poetry]

[23] But now may it be alleged that, if this imagining of matters be so fit for the imagination, then must the historian needs surpass, who brings you images of true matters, such as indeed were done, and not such as fantastically or falsely may be suggested to have been done. Truly, Aristotle himself in his discourse of poesy plainly determineth this question, saying that poetry is *philosophoteron* and *spoudaioteron*, that is to say, it is more philosophical and more studiously serious than history.[41] His reason is, because poesy dealeth with *katholou*, that is to say, with the universal consideration, and the history with *kathekaston*, the particular. "Now," saith he, "the universal weighs what is fit to be said or done, either in likelihood or necessity, which the poesy considereth in his imposed names, and the particular only marks whether Alcibiades did or suffered this or that." Thus far Aristotle; which reason of his, as all his, is most full of reason. For indeed if the question were whether it were better to have a particular act truly or falsely set down, there is no doubt which is to be chosen, no more than whether you had rather have Vespasian's picture right as he was, or at the painter's pleasure nothing resembling. But if the question be for your own use and learning, whether it be better to have it set down as it should be, or as it was, then certainly is more doctrinable the feigned Cyrus in Xenophon than the true Cyrus in Justin, and the feigned Aeneas in Vergil than the right Aeneas in Dares Phrygius; as to a lady that desired to fashion her countenance to the best grace, a painter should more

[40] Minturno in the dedication of his *L'arte poetica* speaks of the parables as poetic.
[41] *Poetics*, IX, first par., above.

benefit her to portrait a most sweet face, writing Canidia upon it, than to paint Canidia as she was, who Horace sweareth was foul and ill favored. If the poet do his part aright, he will show you in Tantalus, Atreus, and such like, nothing that is not to be shunned; in Cyrus, Aeneas, Ulysses, each thing to be followed; where the historian, bound to tell things as things were, cannot be liberal, without he will be poetical, of a perfect pattern, but, as in Alexander or Scipio himself, show doings, some to be liked, some to be misliked.[42] And then how will you discern what to follow but by your own discretion, which you had without reading Quintus Curtius? And whereas a man may say, though in universal consideration of doctrine the poet prevaileth, yet that the histor[ian], in his saying such a thing was done, doth warrant a man more in that he shall follow, the answer is manifest: that if he stand upon that *was*—as if he should argue, because it rained yesterday, therefore it should rain today—then indeed it hath some advantage to a gross conceit. But if he know an example only informs a conjectured likelihood, and so go by reason, the poet doth so far exceed him, as he is to frame his example to that which is most reasonable, be it in warlike, politic, or private matters; where the historian in his bare *was* hath many times that which we call fortune to overrule the best wisdom. Many times he must tell events whereof he can yield no cause; and, if he do, it must be poetically.

[The feigned and the true example]

[24] For that a feigned example hath as much force to teach as a true example (for as for to move, it is clear, since the feigned may be tuned to the highest key of passion), let us take one example wherein a poet and a historian do concur. Herodotus and Justin do both testify that Zopyrus, King Darius's faithful servant, seeing his master long resisted by the rebellious Babylonians, feigned himself in extreme disgrace of his king; for verifying of which he caused his own nose and ears to be cut off, and so flying to the Babylonians, was received, and for his known valor so far credited that he did find means to deliver them over to Darius. Much like matter doth Livy record of Tarquinius and his son. Xenophon excellently feigneth such another stratagem performed

---

[42] Minturno speaks of the poet's power to modify facts for the sake of his function as teacher: "The poets increase, amplify, and exaggerate, showing what is shocking as much more shocking, and what is humane as much more humane, that they may deter the minds of those who read from the shocking and encourage them to humanity" (*De poeta*, p. 38). Cf. sect. 11, above, on the power of the poet to modify nature and fact.

by Abradates in Cyrus's behalf. Now would I fain know, if occasion be presented unto you to serve your prince by such an honest dissimulation, why you do not as well learn it of Xenophon's fiction as of the other's verity, and truly so much the better, as you shall save your nose by the bargain; for Abradates did not counterfeit so far. So then the best of the historian is subject to the poet; for whatsoever action, or faction, whatsoever counsel, policy, or war stratagem the historian is bound to recite, that may the poet, if he list, with his imitation make his own, beautifying it both for further teaching, and more delighting, as it please him,[43] having all, from Dante's heaven to his hell, under the authority of his pen. Which if I be asked what poets have done so, as I might well name some, so yet say I, and say again, I speak of the art, and not of the artificer.

[Poetry always exalts virtue]

[25] Now to that which commonly is attributed to the praise of history, in respect of the notable learning is got by marking the success, as though therein a man should see virtue exalted and vice punished—truly that commendation is peculiar to poetry, and far off from history. For indeed poetry ever sets virtue so out in her best colors, making Fortune her well-waiting handmaid, that one must needs be enamored of her.[44] Well may you see Ulysses in a storm and in other hard plights, but they are but exercises of patience and magnanimity, to make them shine the more in the near-following prosperity. And of the contrary part, if evil men come to the stage, they ever go out (as the tragedy writer answered to one that misliked the show of such persons) so manacled as they little animate folks to follow them.[45] But history,

[43] Sidney exemplifies this in the *Arcadia*, I, 6 (ed. Feuillerat, pp. 39–41). Scaliger writes: "When the poet narrates the plans of generals, whether they are evident to all or of the subtle kind the Greeks call stratagems, . . . he imitates that he may teach" (*Poetice*, I, I, p. 1C2). Cf. Elyot, *The Governor*, sect. 2, above.

[44] Cf. Dryden, sect. 31, below.

[45] Plutarch writes: "Euripides is said to have replied to those who found fault with his Ixion as an impious and dirty fellow: 'Nay, but I did not take him off the stage until I had fastened him in to a torturing wheel' " (*How a Young Man Should Study Poetry*, in F. M. Padelford, *Essays on the Study and Use of Poetry*, Yale Studies in English [New Haven, 1902], sect. 4, p. 62).

Benedetto Varchi writes: "For the sake of example the poet introduces now a vicious man, who receives the proper punishment for his evil deeds; now a virtuous man, to whom come from either God or men proper rewards for his virtues" (*Della poetica in generale*—1553—parte I, particella 3).

Guarini held that the wicked characters of tragicomedy should not be punished (*Tragicomedy*, 38, below). Cf. Dryden, *Of Dramatic Poesy*, sect. 24, below.

being captived to the truth of a foolish world, is many times a terror from well doing, and an encouragement to unbridled wickedness.[46] For see we not valiant Miltiades rot in his fetters; the just Phocion and the accomplished Socrates put to death like traitors; the cruel Severus live prosperously; the excellent Severus miserably murdered; Sylla and Marius dying in their beds; Pompey and Cicero slain then when they would have thought exile a happiness? See we not virtuous Cato driven to kill himself, and rebel Caesar so advanced that his name yet after 1,600 years lasteth in the highest honor? And mark but even Caesar's own words of the forenamed Sylla (who in that only did honestly, to put down his dishonest tyranny), *Litteras nescivit,*[47] as if want of learning caused him to do well. He meant it not by poetry, which, not content with earthly plagues, deviseth new punishments in hell for tyrants, nor yet by philosophy, which teacheth *occidendos esse;*[48] but no doubt by skill in history, for that indeed can afford you Cypselus, Periander, Phalaris, Dionysius, and I know not how many more of the same kennel, that speed well enough in their abominable injustice or usurpation. I conclude, therefore, that he excelleth history not only in furnishing the mind with knowledge, but in setting it forward to that which deserves to be called and accounted good; which setting forward and moving to well doing, indeed setteth the laurel crown upon the poet as victorious, not only of the historian, but over the philosopher, howsoever in teaching it may be questionable.

[The poet moves men]

[26] For suppose it be granted (that which I suppose with great reason may be denied) that the philosopher, in respect of his methodical proceeding, doth teach more perfectly than the poet, yet do I think that no man is so much *philophilosophos*[49] as to compare the philosopher, in moving, with the poet. And that moving is of a higher degree than teaching, it may by this appear, that it is well-nigh both the cause and the effect of teaching.[50] For who will be taught, if he be not moved with desire to be taught, and what so much good doth that teaching bring forth (I speak still of moral doctrine) as that it moveth one to do that which it doth teach?

---

[46] Cf. Giraldi, *Romances*, sect. 58, above.   [47] "He was ignorant of letters."
[48] "They are to be slain." Sidney evidently believed in tyrannicide. Cf. the reference to tyrants in sect. 32, below.
[49] A lover of the philosopher.
[50] On moving, see the appendix immediately following the *Defense.*

For, as Aristotle saith, it is not *gnosis* but *praxis*[51] must be the fruit. And how *praxis* cannot be, without being moved to practise, it is no hard matter to consider. The philosopher showeth you the way, he informeth you of the particularities, as well of the tediousness of the way, as of the pleasant lodging you shall have when your journey is ended, as of the many by-turnings that may divert you from your way. But this is to no man but to him that will read him, and read him with attentive studious painfulness; which constant desire whosoever hath in him, hath already passed half the hardness of the way, and therefore is beholding to the philosopher but for the other half. Nay truly, learned men have learnedly thought that where once reason hath so much overmastered passion as that the mind hath a free desire to do well, the inward light each mind hath in itself is as good as a philosopher's book; since in nature we know it is well to do well, and what is well and what is evil, although not in the words of art which philosophers bestow upon us. For out of natural conceit the philosophers drew it; but to be moved to do that which we know, or to be moved with desire to know, *Hoc opus, hic labor est.*[52]

[The poet entices]

[27] Now therein of all sciences (I speak still of human, and according to the human conceit) is our poet the monarch. For he doth not only show the way, but giveth so sweet a prospect into the way, as will entice any man to enter into it. Nay, he doth, as if your journey should lie through a fair vineyard, at the very first give you a cluster of grapes, that full of that taste you may long to pass further. He beginneth not with obscure definitions, which must blur the margent with interpretations,[53] and load the memory with doubtfulness; but he cometh to you with words set in delightful proportion, either accompanied with, or prepared for, the well-enchanting skill of music; and with a tale forsooth he cometh unto you, with a tale which holdeth children from play, and old men from the chimney corner. And pretending no more, doth intend the winning of the mind from wickedness to virtue; even as the child is often brought to take most wholesome things by hiding them in such other as have a pleasant

---

[51] "Not knowledge but action." See Goldman, *Sir Philip Sidney*, pp. 153–4, 210.

[52] *Aeneid*, VI, 129: "This is the task, this the labor."

[53] In Renaissance books the notes were put in the margins rather than at the bottoms of the pages.

taste,[54] which, if one should begin to tell them the nature of the aloes or rhubarb they should receive, would sooner take their physic at their ears than at their mouth. So is it in men (most of which are childish in the best things, till they be cradled in their graves); glad they will be to hear the tales of Hercules, Achilles, Cyrus, and Aeneas; and hearing them, must needs hear the right description of wisdom, valor, and justice, which if they had been barely,[55] that is to say philosophically, set out, they would swear they be brought to school again. That imitation whereof poetry is, hath the most conveniency to nature of all other, insomuch that, as Aristotle saith, those things which in themselves are horrible, as cruel battles, unnatural monsters, are made in poetical imitation delightful.[56] Truly, I have known men, that even with reading *Amadis de Gaule* (which God knoweth wanteth much of a perfect poesy) have found their hearts moved to the exercise of courtesy, liberality, and especially courage. Who readeth Aeneas carrying old Anchises on his back, that wisheth not it were his fortune to perform so excellent an act? Whom do not those words of Turnus move, the tale of Turnus having planted his image in the imagination?

> *Fugientem haec terra videbit?*
> *Usque adeone mori miserum est?*[57]

Where the philosophers, as they think, scorn to delight, so must they be content little to move, saving wrangling whether *virtus* be the chief or the only good, whether the contemplative or the active life do excel; which Plato and Boethius well knew, and therefore made Mistress Philosophy very often borrow the masking raiment of Poesy.[58] For even those hard-hearted evil men who think virtue a school name, and know no other good but

---

[54] Cf. the end of the paragraph, and the index under *poetry, a pleasant medicine*.

[55] Milton speaks of those who will not "look upon Truth herself, unless they see her elegantly dressed" (*Reason of Church Government*, sect. 2, below). Truth was allegorically represented as naked. Sidney's word *bare* translates the Latin *nudus* or Italian *nudo*, naked, unadorned. Minturno speaks of writing "or con semplice e nudo parlare, or con ornato e di lumi vestito" (*L'arte poetica*, p. 450)—"now with simple and naked language, now with language ornamented and clothed with splendor." Cf. Sidney's use of the word *bare* in secs. 20, 23, above. Spenser speaks of "good discipline delivered plainly in way of precepts" (*Letter to Raleigh*, immediately following this selection).

[56] *Poetics*, IV, first par., above.

[57] *Aeneid*, XII, 645–6: "Shall this land see Turnus in flight? Is it so miserable to die as this?"

[58] Spenser speaks of good discipline as by the poet "enwrapped in allegorical devices" (*Letter to Raleigh*, immediately below). Allegory was frequently employed in masques.

indulgere genio,[59] and therefore despise the austere admonitions of the philosopher, and feel not the inward reason they stand upon, yet will be content to be delighted—which is all the good fellow poet seems to promise—and so steal to see the form of goodness, which seen they cannot but love ere themselves be aware, as if they took a medicine of cherries.

[Examples of poetic effects]

[28] Infinite proofs of the strange effects of this poetical invention might be alleged; only two shall serve, which are so often remembered as I think all men know them. The one of Menenius Agrippa, who, when the whole people of Rome had resolutely divided themselves from the senate, with apparent show of utter ruin, though he were for that time an excellent orator, came not among them upon trust either of figurative speeches or cunning insinuations, and much less with far-fet[60] maxims of philosophy, which (especially if they were Platonic) they must have learned geometry before they could well have conceived; but forsooth he behaves himself like a homely and familiar poet. He telleth them a tale, that there was a time when all the parts of the body made a mutinous conspiracy against the belly, which they thought devoured the fruits of each other's labor; they concluded they would let so unprofitable a spender starve. In the end, to be short (for the tale is notorious, and as notorious that it was a tale), with punishing the belly they plagued themselves. This applied by him wrought such effect in the people, as I never read that only words brought forth but then so sudden and so good an alteration; for upon reasonable conditions a perfect reconcilement ensued. The other is of Nathan the Prophet, who, when the holy David had so far forsaken God as to confirm adultery with murder, when he was to do the tenderest office of a friend in laying his own shame before his eyes, sent by God to call again so chosen a servant, how doth he it but by telling of a man whose beloved lamb was ungratefully taken from his bosom? The application most divinely true, but the discourse itself feigned; which made David (I speak of the second and instrumental cause) as in a glass see his own filthiness, as that heavenly Psalm of mercy well testifieth.

---

[59] Persius, *Satires*, v, 151: "to indulge one's nature."

[60] Far-fetched. Milton refers to food brought from various lands by Satan for his temptation of Jesus by a splendid banquet as "far-fet spoil" (*Paradise Regained*, II, 401). The words were often used proverbially by the Elizabethans.

[Conclusion in favor of poetry]

[29] By these, therefore, examples and reasons, I think it may be manifest that the poet, with that same hand of delight, doth draw the mind more effectually than any other art doth. And so a conclusion not unfitly ensueth, that, as virtue is the most excellent resting place for all worldly learning to make his end of, so poetry, being the most familiar to teach it, and most princely to move towards it, in the most excellent work is the most excellent workman.

[The kinds of poetry]

But I am content not only to decipher him by his works (although works in commendation and dispraise must ever hold a high authority), but more narrowly will examine his parts, so that, as in a man, though all together may carry a presence full of majesty and beauty, perchance in some one defectious piece we may find a blemish. Now in his parts, kinds, or species, as you list to term them, it is to be noted that some poesies have coupled together two or three kinds, as the tragical and comical, whereupon is risen the tragi-comical.[61] Some, in the like manner, have mingled prose and verse, as Sannazaro and Boethius. Some have mingled matters heroical and pastoral.[62] But that cometh all to one in this question, for, if severed they be good, the conjunction cannot be hurtful. Therefore perchance forgetting some, and leaving some as needless to be remembered, it shall not be amiss in a word to cite the special kinds, to see what faults may be found in the right use of them.

[Pastoral]

Is it then the pastoral poem which is misliked? For perchance where the hedge is lowest they will soonest leap over. Is the poor pipe disdained, which sometimes out of Melibaeus' mouth can show the misery of people under hard lords and ravening soldiers?[63] and again by Tityrus, what blessedness is derived to them that lie lowest from the goodness of them that sit highest? sometimes, under the pretty tales of wolves and sheep, can include the whole

---

[61] See Guarini's *Compendium of Tragicomic Poetry*, below.

[62] As did Sidney himself in the *Arcadia*. This passage shows his theoretical acceptance of the literature of his time. Contrast his objection to the contemporary drama, sect. 48, below.

[63] Sidney is interested in the political and social ideas often expressed in pastoral poetry. The attack on the corrupt clergy in Milton's *Lycidas* is a well-known example.

considerations of wrongdoing and patience; sometimes show that contentions for trifles can get but a trifling victory; where perchance a man may see that even Alexander and Darius, when they strave who should be cock of this world's dunghill, the benefit they got was that the afterlivers may say,

Haec memini et victum frustra contendere Thirsim.
Ex illo Coridon, Coridon est tempore nobis.[64]

[Elegiac, iambic, satiric]

[30] Or is it the lamenting elegiac? which in a kind heart would move rather pity than blame, who bewails with the great philosopher Heraclitus the weakness of mankind and the wretchedness of the world; who surely is to be praised either for compassionate accompanying just causes of lamentations or for rightly painting out how weak be the passions of woefulness. Is it the bitter but wholesome iambic? which rubs the galled mind, in making shame the trumpet of villainy with bold and open crying out against naughtiness. Or the satiric? who

Omne vafer vitium ridenti tangit amico;[65]

who sportingly never leaveth till he make a man laugh at folly, and, at length ashamed, to laugh at himself, which he cannot avoid, without avoiding the folly; who, while

circum praecordia ludit,[66]

giveth us to feel how many headaches a passionate life bringeth us to; how, when all is done,

Est Ulubris animus si nos non deficit aequus.[67]

[Comedy]

[31] No, perchance it is the comic, whom naughty play-makers and stage-keepers have justly made odious. To the arguments of abuse I will after answer. Only thus much now is to be said, that the comedy is an imitation of the common errors of our life,

---

[64] Vergil, *Eclogue*, VII, 69–70: "I remember these things and that the vanquished Thyrsis strove in vain. From that time Corydon is Corydon for us."

[65] Condensed from Persius, *Satires*, I, 116–7: "The rogue touches every vice while making his friend laugh."

[66] Part of the same passage: "He plays about the heart-strings."

[67] Horace, *Epistles*, I, 11, 30: "Happiness is to be found at Ulubrae, if a well-balanced mind does not fail us." Sidney changes the *you* of the original to *us*. Ulubrae was a "dead" town.

which he representeth in the most ridiculous and scornful sort that may be,[68] so as it is impossible that any beholder can be content to be such a one. Now, as in geometry the oblique must be known as well as the right, and in arithmetic the odd as well as the even, so in the actions of our life who seeth not the filthiness of evil wanteth a great foil to perceive the beauty of virtue.[69] This doth the comedy handle so in our private and domestical matters, as with hearing it we get as it were an experience, what is to be looked for of a niggardly Demea, of a crafty Davus, of a flattering Gnatho, of a vainglorious Thraso; and not only to know what effects are to be expected, but to know who be such, by the signifying badge given them by the comedian.[70] And little reason hath any man to say that men learn evil by seeing it so set out; since, as I said before, there is no man living but, by the force truth hath in nature, no sooner seeth these men play their parts, but wisheth them in *pistrinum;*[71] although perchance the sack of his own faults lie so behind his back that he seeth not himself dance the same measure; whereto yet nothing can more open his eyes than to see his own actions contemptibly set forth.[72]

[Tragedy]

[32] So that the right use of comedy will (I think) by nobody be blamed; and much less of the high and excellent tragedy, that openeth the greatest wounds, and showeth forth the ulcers that are covered with tissue, that maketh kings fear to be tyrants, and tyrants manifest their tyrannical humors; that with stirring the affects of admiration and commiseration[73] teacheth the uncertainty of this world, and upon how weak foundations gilden roofs are builded,[74] that maketh us know,

[68] Cf. sect. 50, below, for scornful laughter.

[69] Spenser apologizes as follows for presenting a wanton lady:
Good by paragon
Of evil, may more notably be rad,
As white seems fairer, matched with black attone.
Faerie Queene, III, 9, 2.
For contraries, see the index. Minturno deals with the subject in *De poeta*, p. 42.

[70] Cf. Elyot, *The Governor*, sect. 7, above.

[71] The *pistrinum* is the mill, where Roman slaves were punished with heavy labor.
Minturno says the poets describe things not commendable that they may be avoided (*De poeta*, p. 38).

[72] Cf. Trissino's view of comedy, *Poetica*, VI, sect. 120a ff., above.

[73] See the appendix to the *Defense*, immediately following it.

[74] The uncertainty of this life and the overthrow of the prosperous, so important in tragedy, was in the Renaissance assigned to Fortune; hence the theory of Fortune is important in estimating tragedy. See *fortune*, in the index.

Qui sceptra saevus duro imperio regit,
Timet timentes, metus in auctorem redit.[75]

But how much it can move, Plutarch yieldeth a notable testimony of the abominable tyrant Alexander Pheraeus, from whose eyes a tragedy, well made and represented, drew abundance of tears, who without all pity had murdered infinite numbers, and some of his own blood, so as he that was not ashamed to make matters for tragedies yet could not resist the sweet violence of a tragedy.[76] And if it wrought no further good in him, it was that he, in despite of himself, withdrew himself from hearkening to that which might mollify his hardened heart. But it is not the tragedy they do mislike; for it were too absurd to cast out so excellent a representation of whatsoever is most worthy to be learned.

[Lyric]

[33] Is it the lyric that most displeaseth, who with his tuned lyre and well-accorded voice giveth praise, the reward of virtue, to virtuous acts, who giveth moral precepts and natural problems, who sometimes raiseth up his voice to the height of the heavens, in singing the lauds of the immortal God? Certainly, I must confess mine own barbarousness: I never heard the old song of Percy and Douglas that I found not my heart moved more than with a trumpet; and yet is it sung but by some blind crowder, with no rougher voice than rude style; which, being so evil apparelled in the dust and cobwebs of that uncivil age, what would it work trimmed in the gorgeous eloquence of Pindar? In Hungary I have seen it the manner at all feasts and other such like meetings to have songs of their ancestors' valor, which that right soldierlike nation think one of the chiefest kindlers of brave courage. The incomparable Lacedemonians did not only carry that kind of music ever with them to the field, but even at home, as such songs were made, so were they all content to be singers of them, when the lusty men

---

[75] Seneca, *Oedipus*, 705–6: "The savage tyrant who sways his scepter with a heavy hand fears the subjects that fear him, and fear returns upon its creator."

Like Sidney's notion of tragedy is that of Jason Denores: "To tragedy they assign the actions of powerful men and tyrants, so arranged that though these men are at first prosperous, they finally come to ruin, exile, and death; these sufferings come with probability to those who depart from just and lawful government and rule others with violence" (*Discorso intorno a . . . la comedia, la tragedia*, etc. [Padua, 1587], p. 3).

Note Sidney's reference to tyrants in sect. 25, above.

[76] The word *sweet* (*hadus*) and its derivatives is several times used by Aristotle, as in his definition of tragedy in *Poetics*, VI, par. 1, above.

were to tell what they did, the old men what they had done, and the young men what they would do. And where a man may say that Pindar many times praiseth highly victories of small moment, rather matters of sport than virtue; as it may be answered, it was the fault of the poet, and not of the poetry, so indeed the chief fault was in the time and custom of the Greeks, who set those toys at so high a price that Philip of Macedon reckoned a horse-race won at Olympus among his three fearful felicities. But as the unimitable Pindar often did, so is that kind most capable and most fit to awake the thoughts from the sleep of idleness to embrace honorable enterprises.

[Heroic poetry]

[34] There rests the heroical, whose very name I think should daunt all backbiters; for by what conceit can a tongue be directed to speak evil of that which draweth with it no less champions than Achilles, Cyrus, Aeneas, Turnus, Tydeus, and Rinaldo?[77] who doth not only teach and move to a truth, but teacheth and moveth to the most high and excellent truth; who maketh magnanimity and justice shine through all misty fearfulness and foggy desires; who, if the saying of Plato and Tully be true, that who could see Virtue would be wonderfully ravished with the love of her beauty, this man sets her out to make her more lovely in her holiday apparel to the eye of any that will deign not to disdain until they understand. But if anything be already said in the defense of sweet poetry, all concurreth to the maintaining the heroical, which is not only a kind, but the best and most accomplished kind of poetry.[78] For as the image of each action stirreth and instructeth the mind, so the lofty image of such worthies most inflameth the mind with desire to be worthy, and informs with counsel how to be worthy. Only let Aeneas be worn in the tablet of your memory, how he governeth himself in the ruin of his country, in the preserving his old father, and carrying away his religious ceremonies, in obeying the god's commandment to leave Dido, though not only all passionate kindness but even the human consideration of virtuous gratefulness would have craved other of him, how in storms, how in sports, how in war, how in peace,

---

[77] Cyrus, from Xenophon's *Cyropaedia*, is again classed with characters from Homer and Vergil. Rinaldo, from the *Orlando Furioso* of Ariosto, represents modern literature —seldom neglected by Sidney.

[78] Aristotle decided for tragedy as the superior form (*Poetics*, XXVI, sect. 62a14, above); the Renaissance generally held for the epic.

how a fugitive, how victorious, how besieged, how besieging, how to strangers, how to allies, how to enemies, how to his own, lastly, how in his inward self, and how in his outward government, and I think, in a mind most prejudiced with a prejudicating humor, he will be found in excellency fruitful; yea, as Horace saith,

Melius Chrysippo et Crantore.[79]

But truly I imagine it falleth out with these poet-whippers as with some good women who often are sick but in faith they cannot tell where. So the name of poetry is odious to them, but neither his cause nor effects, neither the sum that contains him nor the particularities descending from him, give any fast handle to their carping dispraise.

[Summary of the virtues of poetry]

[35] Since then poetry is of all human learnings the most ancient and of most fatherly antiquity, as from whence other learnings have taken their beginnings; since it is so universal that no learned nation doth despise it, nor no barbarous nation is without it; since both Roman and Greek gave divine names unto it, the one of prophesying, the other of making, and that indeed that name of *making* is fit for him, considering that whereas other arts retain themselves within their subject and receive, as it were, their being from it, the poet only bringeth his own stuff and doth not learn a conceit out of a matter but maketh matter for a conceit; since neither his description nor his end containeth any evil, the thing described cannot be evil; since his effects be so good as to teach goodness and delight the learners of it; since therein (namely in moral doctrine, the chief of all knowledges) he doth not only far pass the historian, but, for instructing, is wellnigh comparable to the philosopher, and for moving leaves him behind him; since the Holy Scripture (wherein there is no uncleanness) hath whole parts in it poetical, and that even our Savior Christ vouchsafed to use the flowers of it; since all his kinds are not only in their united forms but in their severed dissections fully commendable, I think (and think I think rightly) the laurel crown

[79] Horace, *Epistles*, I, 2, 4. Sidney had in mind the whole passage, which runs thus: "I have been rereading the author of the Trojan war, who tells us what is fair and what is base, what is useful and what is not, better than do Chrysippus and Crantor." Homer is a better teacher than the two philosophers.
Scaliger devotes some pages to the virtues of Aeneas (*Poetice*, III, 12, pp. 90–5).

appointed for triumphant captains doth worthily (of all other learnings) honor the poet's triumph.[80]

[PART VI. ANSWERS TO OBJECTIONS]

[36] But because we have ears as well as tongues, and that the lightest reasons that may be will seem to weigh greatly if nothing be put in the counterbalance, let us hear and, as well as we can, ponder what objections may be made against this art, which may be worthy either of yielding or answering. First, truly I note not only in these *mysomousoi*, poet-haters, but in all that kind of people who seek a praise by dispraising others, that they do prodigally spend a great many wandering words in quips and scoffs, carping and taunting at each thing, which, by stirring the spleen, may stay the brain from a thorough beholding the worthiness of the subject. Those kind of objections, as they are full of a very idle easiness, since there is nothing of so sacred a majesty but that an itching tongue may rub itself upon it, so deserve they no other answer but instead of laughing at the jest to laugh at the jester. We know a playing wit can praise the discretion of an ass, the comfortableness of being in debt, and the jolly commodities of being sick of the plague.[81] So of the contrary side, if we will turn Ovid's verse,

Ut lateat virtus proximitate mali,

that "good lie hid in nearness of the evil," Agrippa will be as merry in showing the vanity of science as Erasmus was in commending of folly. Neither shall any man or matter escape some touch of these smiling railers. But for Erasmus and Agrippa, they had another foundation than the superficial part would promise. Marry, these other pleasant faultfinders, who will correct the verb before they understand the noun, and confute others' knowledge before they confirm their own, I would have them only remember that scoffing cometh not of wisdom; so as the best title in true English they get with their merriments is to be called good fools, for so have our grave forefathers ever termed that humorous kind of jesters.

---

[80] A triumph like that of a Roman general was awarded to the poet Petrarch; as part of the ceremony he was crowned with laurel.

[81] Such paradoxes were somewhat popular in Sidney's time and later. For example, John Donne, in his *Paradoxes and Problems* (about 1600) writes "That Women Ought to Paint," "That Only Cowards Dare Dye," etc.

[Objection to verse refuted]

[37] But that which giveth greatest scope to their scorning humor is rhyming and versing. It is already said (and, as I think, truly said) it is not rhyming and versing that maketh poesy. One may be a poet without versing, and a versifier without poetry.[82] But yet presuppose it were inseparable (as indeed it seemeth Scaliger judgeth)[83] truly it were an inseparable commendation. For if *oratio* next to *ratio*, speech next to reason, be the greatest gift bestowed upon mortality, that cannot be praiseless which doth most polish that blessing of speech; which considers each word, not only (as a man may say) by his forcible quality but by his best measured quantity, carrying even in themselves a harmony, without, perchance, number, measure, order, proportion be in our time grown odious. But lay aside the just praise it hath, by being the only fit speech for music (music, I say, the most divine striker of the senses), thus much is undoubtedly true, that if reading be foolish without remembering, memory being the only treasure of knowledge, those words which are fittest for memory are likewise most convenient for knowledge. Now that verse far exceedeth prose in the knitting up of the memory, the reason is manifest: the words (besides their delight, which hath a great affinity to memory) being so set as one cannot be lost but the whole work fails, which accusing itself, calleth the remembrance back to itself, and so most strongly confirmeth it. Besides, one word so as it were begetting another, as, be it in rhyme or measured verse, by the former a man shall have a near guess to the follower. Lastly, even they that have taught the art of memory have showed nothing so apt for it as a certain room divided into many places well and thoroughly known. Now, that hath the verse in effect perfectly, every word having his natural seat, which seat must needs make the word remembered. But what needeth more in a thing so known to all men? Who is it that ever was scholar that doth not carry away some verses of Vergil, Horace, or Cato, which in his youth he learned, and even to his old age serve him for hourly lessons? as

Percontatorem fugito, nam garrulus idem est.[84]

[82] See sect. 16, note 24, above.

[83] "The name of the poet is not, as they think, derived from feigning, since he uses fictions, but at the beginning from making verse" (Scaliger, *Poetice*, 1, 2, p. 3A2).

[84] Horace, *Epistles*, 1, 18, 69: "Avoid an inquisitive man; he is sure to be talkative." Quoted by Heinsius, *De tragoediae constitutione*, chap. XVI.

Dum sibi quisque placet, credula turba sumus.[85]

But the fitness it hath for memory is notably proved by all delivery of arts; wherein for the most part, from grammar to logic, mathematic, physic, and the rest, the rules chiefly necessary to be borne away are compiled in verses. So that verse being in itself sweet and orderly and being best for memory, the only handle of knowledge, it must be in jest that any man can speak against it.

[Objections to poetry]

[38] Now then go we to the most important imputations laid to the poor poets. For aught I can yet learn, they are these. First, that there being many other more fruitful knowledges, a man might better spend his time in them than in this. Secondly, that it is the mother of lies. Thirdly, that it is the nurse of abuse, infecting us with many pestilent desires, with a siren's sweetness drawing the mind to the serpent's tale of sinful fancies (and herein especially comedies give the largest field to ear, as Chaucer saith), how both in other nations and in ours, before poets did soften us we were full of courage, given to martial exercises, the pillars of manlike liberty, and not lulled asleep in shady idleness with poets' pastimes. And lastly and chiefly, they cry out with open mouth, as if they had overshot Robin Hood, that Plato banished them out of his commonwealth.[86] Truly, this is much, if there be much truth in it.

[The poet moves to virtue]

[39] First to the first, that a man might better spend his time is a reason indeed, but it doth, as they say, but *petere principium*,[87] for if it be, as I affirm, that no learning is so good as that which teacheth and moveth to virtue, and that none can both teach and move thereto so much as poesy, then is the conclusion manifest that ink and paper cannot be to a more profitable purpose employed. And certainly though a man should grant their first assumption, it should follow (methinks) very unwillingly, that good is not good because better is better. But I still and utterly deny that there is sprung out of earth a more fruitful knowledge.

---

[85] Ovid, *Remedy of Love*, 686: "While each flatters himself, we are a credulous company." [86] Discussed in sect. 43, below.

[87] Beg the question, or ask that the decision be given in their favor before it is argued. If a man had better spend his time in other things than poetry, poetry is esteemed as not valuable, and the case is decided against it. But if poetry moves to virtue, time may well be spent on it.

[The poet not a liar]

[40] To the second therefore, that they should be the principal liars, I answer paradoxically, but truly I think truly, that of all writers under the sun the poet is the least liar and, though he would, as a poet can scarcely be a liar. The astronomer with his cousin the geometrician can hardly escape, when they take upon them to measure the height of the stars. How often, think you, do the physicians lie, when they aver things good for sicknesses, which afterwards send Charon a great number of souls drowned in a potion before they come to his ferry? And no less of the rest which take upon them to affirm. Now, for the poet, he nothing affirms and therefore never lieth. For as I take it, to lie is to affirm that to be true which is false. So as the other artists, and especially the historian, affirming many things, can in the cloudy knowledge of mankind hardly escape from many lies. But the poet, as I said before, never affirmeth. The poet never maketh any circles about your imagination, to conjure you to believe for true what he writes. He citeth not authorities of other histories, but even for his entry calleth the sweet Muses to inspire into him a good invention; in troth, not laboring to tell you what is or is not but what should or should not be. And therefore, though he recount things not true, yet because he telleth them not for true, he lieth not, without we will say that Nathan lied in his speech, before alleged, to David; which as a wicked man durst scarce say, so think I none so simple would say that Aesop lied in the tales of his beasts; for who thinks that Aesop wrote it for actually true were well worthy to have his name chronicled among the beasts he writeth of. What child is there that coming to a play and seeing *Thebes* written in great letters upon an old door doth believe that it is Thebes?[88] If then a man can arrive to the child's age, to know that the poets' persons and doings are but pictures what should be and not stories what have been, they will never give the lie to things not affirmatively but allegorically and figuratively written. And therefore as in history, looking for truth, they may go away full fraught with falsehood, so in poesy, looking but for fiction, they shall use the narration but as an imaginative ground-plot of

---

[88] We should not assume from this that scenes were indicated by signboards on the stage of Shakespeare and Jonson. In fact, Sidney himself remarks that on the English stage the player on entering "must ever begin with telling where he is"; otherwise the audience would not know the locality of the scene (sect. 48, below).

a profitable invention. But hereto is replied that the poets give names to men they write of, which argueth a conceit of an actual truth, and so, not being true, proves a falsehood. And doth the lawyer lie then, when under the names of John of the Stile and John of the Noakes he putteth his case? But that is easily answered. Their naming of men is but to make their picture the more lively, and not to build any history; painting men, they cannot leave men nameless. We see we cannot play at chess but that we must give names to our chessmen; and yet methinks he were a very partial champion of truth that would say we lied for giving a piece of wood the reverend title of a bishop. The poet nameth Cyrus or Aeneas no other way than to show what men of their fames, fortunes, and estates should do.

[Poetry does not teach lustful love]

[41] Their third is how much it abuseth men's wit, training it to wanton sinfulness and lustful love; for indeed that is the principal, if not the only abuse I can hear alleged. They say the comedies rather teach than reprehend amorous conceits. They say the lyric is larded with passionate sonnets, the elegiac weeps the want of his mistress, and that even to the heroical, Cupid hath ambitiously climbed. Alas, Love, I would thou couldst as well defend thyself as thou canst offend others. I would those on whom thou dost attend could either put thee away or yield good reason why they keep thee. But grant love of beauty to be a beastly fault, although it be very hard, since only man and no beast hath that gift to discern beauty; grant that lovely name of Love to deserve all hateful reproaches, although even some of my masters the philosophers spent a good deal of their lamp-oil in setting forth the excellency of it; grant, I say, what they will have granted, that not only love, but lust, but vanity, but, if they list, scurrility, possess many leaves of the poets' books; yet think I, when this is granted they will find their sentence may with good manners put the last words foremost, and not say that poetry abuseth man's wit, but that man's wit abuseth poetry. For I will not deny but that man's wit may make poesy, which should be *eikastike*,[89] which some learned have defined, *figuring forth good things*, to be *phantastike*, which doth contrariwise infect the fancy with unworthy objects, as the painter, that should give to the eye either some excellent perspective, or some fine picture fit for

---

[89] See Mazzoni, *Of the Defense of the "Comedy,"* Introduction, sect. 1, above.

building or fortification, or containing in it some notable example, as Abraham sacrificing his son Isaac, Judith killing Holofernes, David fighting with Goliath, may leave those and please an ill-pleased eye with wanton shows of better hidden matters. But what, shall the abuse of a thing make the right use odious? Nay truly, though I yield that poesy may not only be abused, but that being abused, by the reason of his sweet charming force it can do more hurt than any other army of words, yet shall it be so far from concluding that the abuse should give reproach to the abused, that contrariwise it is a good reason that whatsoever, being abused, doth most harm, being rightly used (and upon the right use each thing receives his title), doth most good. Do we not see skill of physic (the best rampire to our often-assaulted bodies), being abused, teach poison, the most violent destroyer? Doth not knowledge of law, whose end is to even and right all things, being abused, grow the crooked fosterer of horrible injuries? Doth not (to go to the highest) God's word abused breed heresy, and his name abused become blasphemy? Truly, a needle cannot do much hurt, and as truly (with leave of ladies be it spoken) it cannot do much good. With a sword thou mayest kill thy father, and with a sword thou mayest defend thy prince and country. So that as in their calling poets fathers of lies they said nothing, so in this their argument of abuse they prove the commendation.

[Poetry the companion of camps]

[42] They allege herewith, that before poets began to be in price our nation had set their heart's delight upon action, and not imagination, rather doing things worthy to be written, than writing things fit to be done. What that before-time was, I think scarcely Sphinx can tell, since no memory is so ancient that hath the precedence of poetry. And certain it is that, in our plainest homeliness, yet never was the Albion nation without poetry. Marry, this argument, though it be leveled against poetry, yet is it indeed a chain-shot against all learning, or bookishness as they commonly term it. Of such mind were certain Goths, of whom it is written that, having in the spoil of a famous city taken a fair library, one hangman, belike fit to execute the fruits of their wits who had murdered a great number of bodies, would have set fire on it. "No," said another very gravely, "take heed what you do, for while they are busy about those toys, we shall with more leisure conquer their countries." This indeed is the ordinary doctrine

of ignorance, and many words sometimes I have heard spent in it; but because this reason is generally against all learning as well as poetry, or rather all learning but poetry; because it were too large a digression to handle it, or at least too superfluous, since it is manifest that all government of action is to be gotten by knowledge, and knowledge best by gathering many knowledges, which is reading, I only, with Horace, to him that is of that opinion,

Iubeo stultum esse libenter;[90]

for as for poetry itself, it is the freest from this objection. For poetry is the companion of camps.[91] I dare undertake, Orlando Furioso or honest King Arthur will never displease a soldier, but the quiddity of *ens* and *prima materia* will hardly agree with a corslet. And therefore, as I said in the beginning, even Turks and Tartars are delighted with poets. Homer, a Greek, flourished before Greece flourished. And if to a slight conjecture a conjecture may be opposed, truly it may seem that as by him their learned men took almost their first light of knowledge, so their active men received their first motions of courage. Only Alexander's example may serve, who by Plutarch is accounted of such virtue that Fortune was not his guide but his footstool; whose acts speak for him though Plutarch did not—indeed the Phoenix of warlike princes. This Alexander left his schoolmaster, living Aristotle, behind him, but took dead Homer with him. He put the philosopher Callisthenes to death for his seeming philosophical, indeed mutinous, stubbornness, but the chief thing he was ever heard to wish for was that Homer had been alive. He well found he received more bravery of mind by the pattern of Achilles than by hearing the definition of fortitude. And therefore if Cato misliked Fulvius for carrying Ennius with him to the field, it may be answered that, if Cato misliked it, the noble Fulvius liked it or else he had not done it; for it was not the excellent Cato Uticensis, whose authority I would much more have reverenced, but it was the former, in truth a bitter punisher of faults, but else a man that had never sacrificed to the Graces. He misliked and cried out

---

[90] Adapted from Horace, *Satires*, I, 1, 63: "I bid him be a fool as much as he will."

[91] George Gascoigne, who died in 1577, had as his motto *Tam Marti quàm Mercurio*, to indicate that he was in the service of Mars as well as of Mercury, both a soldier and a poet. The frontispiece of *The Tale of Hemetes the Hermit* shows him presenting a book to the Queen with one hand, while in the other he holds a spear. His gown, the garment of the literary man, is "half off," to indicate that he could easily be ready for military activity.

against all Greek learning, and yet being four score years old began to learn it, belike fearing that Pluto understood not Latin. Indeed, the Roman laws allowed no person to be carried to the wars but he that was in the soldier's roll; and therefore, though Cato misliked his unmustered person, he misliked not his work. And if he had, Scipio Nasica, judged by common consent the best Roman, loved him. Both the other Scipio brothers, who had by their virtues no less surnames than of Asia and Afric, so loved him that they caused his body to be buried in their sepulchre. So as Cato's authority being but against his person, and that answered with so far greater than himself, is herein of no validity.

[Plato did not expel the poets]

[43] But now indeed my burthen is great,[92] that Plato's name is laid upon me, whom I must confess of all philosophers I have ever esteemed most worthy of reverence, and with good reason, since of all philosophers he is the most poetical. Yet if he will defile the fountain out of which his flowing streams have proceeded, let us boldly examine with what reasons he did it. First truly a man might maliciously object that Plato, being a philosopher, was a natural enemy of poets.[93] For indeed after the philosophers had picked out of the sweet mysteries of poetry the right discerning true points of knowledge, they forthwith, putting it in method and making a school art of that which the poets did only teach by a divine delightfulness, beginning to spurn at their guides, like ungrateful prentices were not content to set up shop for themselves, but sought by all means to discredit their masters; which by the force of delight being barred them, the less they could overthrow them the more they hated them. For indeed, they found for Homer seven cities strave who should have him for their citizen, where many cities banished philosophers as not fit members to live among them. For only repeating certain of Euripides' verses, many Athenians had their lives saved of the Syracusans, where the Athenians themselves thought many philosophers unworthy to live. Certain poets, as Simonides and Pindarus, had so prevailed with Hiero the First that of a tyrant they made him a just king; where Plato could do so little with Dionysius,

<hr/>

[92] Sidney takes up the debate suggested in sect. 38, above. See Plato, *Republic*, x, 606E, above.

[93] "Formerly there was no small disagreement between poetry and philosophy" (Minturno, *De poeta*, p. 36). Plato speaks of "an ancient quarrel between philosophy and poetry" (*Republic*, x, 607, above).

that he himself of a philosopher was made a slave. But who should do thus, I confess should requite the objections made against poets with like cavillations against philosophers; as likewise one should do that should bid one read *Phaedrus* or *Symposium* in Plato, or the discourse of love in Plutarch, and see whether any poet do authorize abominable filthiness as they do.[94] Again, a man might ask out of what commonwealth Plato doth banish them. In sooth, thence where he himself alloweth community of women. So as belike this banishment grew not for effeminate wantonness, since little should poetical sonnets be hurtful when a man might have what woman he listed. But I honor philosophical instructions, and bless the wits which bred them, so as they be not abused, which is likewise stretched to poetry. St. Paul himself, who yet for the credit of poets allegeth twice two poets, and one of them by the name of a prophet, setteth a watchword upon philosophy, indeed upon the abuse. So doth Plato upon the abuse, not upon poetry. Plato found fault that the poets of his time filled the world with wrong opinions of the gods, making light tales of that unspotted essence; and therefore would not have the youth depraved with such opinions. Herein may much be said; let this suffice: the poets did not induce such opinions but did imitate those opinions already induced. For all the Greek stories can well testify that the very religion of that time stood upon many and many-fashioned gods, not taught so by the poets, but followed according to their nature of imitation. Who list may read in Plutarch the discourses of Isis and Osiris, of the cause why oracles ceased, of the divine providence, and see whether the theology of that nation stood not upon such dreams which the poets indeed superstitiously observed, and truly since they had not the light of Christ did much better in it than the philosophers, who, shaking off superstition, brought in atheism. Plato therefore (whose authority I had much rather justly construe than unjustly resist) meant not in general of poets, in those words of which Julius Scaliger saith: *Qua authoritate barbari quidam atque hispidi abuti velint ad poetas e republica exigendos.*[95]

[94] Scaliger writes: "Plato should look to himself, to see how many inept and how many vile stories he introduces, what opinions stinking of Greek vice he frequently inculcates. Certainly it would have been worth one's while never to have read the *Symposium*, the *Phaedrus*, and other monsters" (*Poetice*, I, 2, p. 5B1).

[95] "An authority which certain barbarous and rude fellows wish to abuse in order to drive the poets out of the state" (Scaliger, *Poetice*, I, 2, p. 5A1). The authority is that of Plato in the *Republic*, which Scaliger thought of less esteem than the *Ion*, apparently because it seemed less favorable to poetry.

But only meant to drive out those wrong opinions of the deity whereof now, without further law, Christianity hath taken away all the hurtful belief, perchance as he thought nourished by the then esteemed poets. And a man need go no further than to Plato himself to know his meaning, who in his Dialogue called *Ion* giveth high and rightly divine commendation unto poetry.[96] So as Plato, banishing the abuse, not the thing, not banishing it but giving due honor to it, shall be our patron and not our adversary. For indeed I had much rather, since truly I may do it, show their mistaking of Plato, under whose lion's skin they would make an asslike braying against poesy, than go about to overthrow his authority; whom, the wiser a man is, the more just cause he shall find to have in admiration; especially since he attributeth unto poesy more than myself do, namely to be a very inspiring of a divine force, far above man's wit, as in the afore-named Dialogue is apparent.[97]

[Great men have approved poetry]

[44] Of the other side, who would show the honors have been by the best sort of judgments granted them, a whole sea of examples would present themselves: Alexanders, Caesars, Scipios, all favorers of poets; Laelius, called the Roman Socrates, himself a poet, so as part of *Heautontimorumenos* in Terence was supposed to be made by him; and even the Greek Socrates, whom Apollo confirmed to be the only wise man, is said to have spent part of his old time in putting Aesop's fables into verses. And therefore, full evil should it become his scholar Plato to put such words in his master's mouth against poets. But what needs more? Aristotle writes the Art of Poesy; and why, if it should not be written? Plutarch teacheth the use to be gathered of them, and how, if they should not be read? And who reads Plutarch's either history or philosophy shall find he trimmeth both their garments with guards of poesy.

[Summary of the case for poetry]

[45] But I list not to defend poesy with the help of her underling historiography. Let it suffice to have showed it is a fit soil for

---

[96] For the *Ion*, see the beginning of the present volume.

[97] It is difficult to feel that Sidney's discussion of Plato is based on knowledge of the *Republic*, for Plato surely makes his speaker banish most of the poets from the ideal state. Sidney is, I believe, right in his feeling that Plato is not an enemy of art, though his reasons are not good ones. See Gilbert, "Did Plato Banish the Poets or the Critics?" in *Studies in Philology*, XXXVI (1939), 1–19.

praise to dwell upon; and what dispraise may set upon it is either easily overcome or transformed into just commendation. So that since the excellencies of it may be so easily and so justly confirmed, and the low-creeping objections so soon trodden down, it not being an art of lies but of true doctrine, not of effeminateness but of notable stirring of courage, not of abusing man's wit but of strengthening man's wit, not banished but honored by Plato, let us rather plant more laurels for to engarland the poets' heads (which honor of being laureate, as besides them only triumphant captains were, is a sufficient authority to show the price they ought to be held in) than suffer the ill-savored breath of such wrong-speakers once to blow upon the clear springs of poesy.

[PART VII. POETRY IN ENGLAND]

[46] But since I have run so long a career in this matter, methinks, before I give my pen a full stop, it shall be but a little more lost time to inquire why England, the mother of excellent minds, should be grown so hard a stepmother to poets, who certainly in wit ought to pass all other, since all only proceeds from their wit, being indeed makers of themselves, not takers of others. How can I but exclaim,

Musa, mihi causas memora, quo numine laeso![98]

Sweet poesy, that hath anciently had kings, emperors, senators, great captains, such as, besides a thousand others, David, Adrian, Sophocles, Germanicus, not only to favor poets, but to be poets; and of our nearer times can present for her patrons a Robert, king of Sicily, the Great King Francis of France, King James of Scotland; such cardinals as Bembus and Bibbiena; such famous preachers and teachers as Beza and Melanchthon; so learned philosophers as Fracastorius and Scaliger; so great orators as Pontanus and Muretus; so piercing wits as George Buchanan; so grave counsellors as, besides many but before all, that Hospital of France, than whom I think that realm never brought forth a more accomplished judgment, more firmly builded upon virtue. I say these, with numbers of others, not only to read others' poesies, but to poetize for others' reading. That poesy, thus embraced in all other places, should only find in our time a hard welcome in England, I think the very earth laments it, and therefore decks

---

[98] Vergil, *Aeneid*, I, 8: "Bring to my mind, O Muse, the causes—what was the injury to her godhead?"

our soil with fewer laurels than it was accustomed. For heretofore poets have in England also flourished, and, which is to be noted, even in those times when the trumpet of Mars did sound loudest. And now that an overfaint quietness should seem to strew the house for poets, they are almost in as good reputation as the mountebanks at Venice. Truly even that, as of the one side it giveth great praise to poesy, which like Venus, but to better purpose, had rather be troubled in the net with Mars than enjoy the homely quiet of Vulcan, so serveth it for a piece of a reason why they are less grateful to idle England, which now can scarce endure the pain of a pen. Upon this necessarily followeth that base men with servile wits undertake it, who think it enough if they can be rewarded of the printer. And so as Epaminondas is said with the honor of his virtue to have made an office, by his exercising it, which before was contemptible to become highly respected, so these men no more but setting their names to it by their own disgracefulness disgrace the most graceful poesy. For now, as if all the Muses were got with child to bring forth bastard poets, without any commission they do post over the banks of Helicon, till they make the readers more weary than posthorses, while, in the meantime, they,

Queis meliore luto finxit praecordia Titan,[99]

are better content to suppress the outflowings of their wit than, by publishing them, to be accounted knights of the same order. But I that, before ever I durst aspire unto the dignity, am admitted into the company of the paper-blurrers, do find the very true cause of our wanting estimation is want of desert, taking upon us to be poets in despite of Pallas. Now wherein we want desert were a thankworthy labor to express, but if I knew, I should have mended myself. But as I never desired the title, so have I neglected the means to come by it. Only, overmastered by some thoughts, I yielded an inky tribute unto them. Marry, they that delight in poesy itself should seek to know what they do and how they do, and especially look themselves in an unflattering glass of reason, if they be inclinable unto it. For poesy must not be drawn by the ears; it must be gently led, or rather it must lead; which was partly the cause that made the ancient learned affirm it was a divine gift and no human skill, since all other knowledges lie

[99] Compressed from Juvenal, XIV, 34-5; it means: "Whose hearts Titan formed from better earth."

ready for any that have strength of wit; a poet no industry can make, if his own genius be not carried unto it; and therefore is an old proverb, *Orator fit, poeta nascitur*.[100] Yet confess I always that as the fertilest ground must be manured,[101] so must the highest-flying wit have a Daedalus to guide him. That Daedalus, they say, both in this and in other hath three wings to bear itself up into the air of due commendation, that is, art, imitation,[102] and exercise. But these neither artificial rules nor imitative patterns we much cumber ourselves withal. Exercise indeed we do, but that very forebackwardly; for where we should exercise to know, we exercise as having known: and so is our brain delivered of much matter which never was begotten by knowledge. For, there being two principal parts—matter to be expressed by words and words to express the matter—in neither we use art or imitation rightly.[103] Our matter is *quodlibet* indeed, though wrongly performing Ovid's verse,

> *Quicquid conabor dicere, versus erit;*[104]

never marshalling it into any assured rank, that almost the readers cannot tell where to find themselves.

[Chaucer, Spenser, and others]

[47] Chaucer, undoubtedly, did excellently in his *Troilus and Cressida;* of whom truly I know not whether to marvel more, either that he in that misty time could see so clearly, or that we in this clear age go so stumblingly after him. Yet had he great wants, fit to be forgiven in so reverent an antiquity. I account the *Mirrour of Magistrates* meetly furnished of beautiful parts; and in the Earl of Surrey's *Lyrics* many things tasting of a noble birth, and worthy of a noble mind. The *Shepheard's Calendar* hath much poetry in his eclogues, indeed worthy the reading, if I be not deceived. That same framing of his style to an old rustic language I dare not allow, since neither Theocritus in Greek, Vergil

---

[100] The orator is made, the poet is born.

[101] *Tilled*, etymologically, *cultivated by hand.*

[102] See Minturno's treatment of imitation, *L'arte poetica*, Bk. IV, 445a, above, and the index.

[103] For this clear separation between words and matter see also sect. 3, above.

[104] Sidney is apparently either quoting from memory or deliberately modifying *Tristia*, IV, 10, 26:
> *Et quod tentabam dicere, versus erat.*
> Whatever I endeavored to say, it was verse.

As the line stands, the verbs are in the future.

in Latin, nor Sannazaro in Italian did affect it. Besides these, I do not remember to have seen but few (to speak boldly) printed, that have poetical sinews in them. For proof whereof, let but most of the verses be put in prose, and then ask the meaning; and it will be found that one verse did but beget another, without ordering at the first what should be at the last; which becomes a confused mass of words, with a tingling sound of rhyme, barely accompanied with reason.

[English drama faulty in time and place]

[48] Our tragedies and comedies not without cause cried out against, observing rules neither of honest civility nor skillful poetry, excepting *Gorboduc* (again, I say, of those that I have seen), which notwithstanding, as it is full of stately speeches and well-sounding phrases, climbing to the height of Seneca's style,[105] and as full of notable morality, which it doth most delightfully teach, and so obtain the very end of poesy,[106] yet in truth it is very defectious in the circumstances, which grieves me, because it might not remain as an exact model of all tragedies. For it is faulty both in place and time, the two necessary companions of all corporal actions.[107] For where the stage should always represent but one place, and the uttermost time presupposed in it should be, both by Aristotle's precept and common reason, but one day,[108] there is both many days and many places, inartificially imagined. But if it be so in *Gorboduc*, how much more in all the rest, where you shall have Asia of the one side and Afric of the other, and so many other under-kingdoms, that the player, when he comes in, must ever begin with telling where he is, or else the tale will not be conceived? Now ye shall have three ladies walk to gather flowers, and then we must believe the stage to be a garden. By and by we hear news of shipwreck in the same place, and then we are to blame if we accept it not for a rock. Upon the back of that comes out a hideous monster, with fire and smoke, and then the miserable beholders are bound to take it for a cave. While in the mean-

---

[105] For other opinions on Seneca, see the index. In contrast to Sidney, Trissino, perhaps the best equipped of all the critics in knowledge of Greek drama, said that Seneca's plays "are for the most part fragments of Greek things, put together with very little art" (*Poetica*, sect. 5, p. 101).

[106] See sect. 12, above, and the note. Benedetto Varchi wrote in 1553 that the end of poetry is "to remove men from vices and stimulate them to virtue, that their perfection and blessedness may follow" (*Della poetica in generale*, part II, first par.).

[107] See *unity of time* and *unity of place* in the index.

[108] *Poetics*, v, 49b9, above.

time two armies fly in, represented with four swords and bucklers, and then what hard heart will not receive it for a pitched field? Now of time they are much more liberal,[109] for ordinary it is that two young princes fall in love. After many traverses, she is got with child, delivered of a fair boy; he is lost, groweth a man, falleth in love, and is ready to get another child; and all this in two hours' space; which how absurd it is in sense, even sense may imagine, and art hath taught, and all ancient examples justified, and, at this day, the ordinary players in Italy will not err in. Yet will some bring in an example of *Eunuchus* in Terence, that containeth matter of two days, yet far short of twenty years.[110] True it is, and so was it to be played in two days, and so fitted to the time it set forth. And though Plautus have in one place done amiss, let us hit with him, and not miss with him. But they will say, How then shall we set forth a story, which contains both many places and many times? And do they not know that a tragedy is tied to the laws of poesy, and not of history; not bound to follow the story, but having liberty either to feign a quite new matter or to frame the history to the most tragical conveniency?[111] Again, many things may be told which cannot be showed, if they know the difference betwixt reporting and representing.[112] As for example, I may speak (though I am here) of Peru, and in speech digress from that to the description of Calicut; but in action I cannot represent it without Pacolet's horse. And so was the manner the ancients took, by some *Nuntius* to recount things done in former time or other place. Lastly, if they will represent an history, they must not (as Horace saith) begin *ab ovo*,[113] but they must come to the principal point of that one action which they will represent. By example this will be best expressed. I have a story of young Polydorus, delivered for safety's sake, with great riches, by his father Priam to Polymnestor, king of Thrace, in the Trojan war time. He, after some years, hearing the overthrow of Priam, for to make the treasure his own, murdereth the child. The body of the child is taken up by Hecuba. She, the same day, findeth a slight to be

[109] On the whole passage cf. Lope de Vega, *New Art of Making Comedies*, sect. 3, below. Cf. also George Whetstone's dedication to *Promos and Cassandra* (1578).

[110] Sidney apparently means not the *Eunuchus* but the *Heautontimorumenos* of Terence (see the index). His belief that it was played in two days probably comes from Scaliger, *Poetice*, VI, 3, p. 297 AB 1. See *unity of time* in the index.

[111] Aristotle allowed a plot invented by the poet (*Poetics*, IX, 51b19, above). The subject was much discussed in the Renaissance. See the index under *poet, liberty of.*

[112] See Castelvetro on *Poetics*, III, 57, 1, above, and the index under *nuntius*, and *imitation.* [113] *Art of Poetry*, 147, above.

revenged most cruelly of the tyrant. Where now would one of our tragedy writers begin, but with the delivery of the child? Then should he sail over into Thrace, and so spend I know not how many years, and travel numbers of places. But where doth Euripides? Even with the finding of the body, leaving the rest to be told by the spirit of Polydorus. This needs no further to be enlarged; the dullest wit may conceive it.

[Tragicomedy]

[49] But besides these gross absurdities, how all their plays be neither right tragedies nor right comedies, mingling kings and clowns, not because the matter so carrieth it, but thrust in the clown by head and shoulders to play a part in majestical matters, with neither decency nor discretion,[114] so as neither the admiration and commiseration[115] nor the right sportfulness is by their mongrel tragicomedy obtained.[116] I know Apuleius did somewhat so, but that is a thing recounted with space of time, not represented in one moment:[117] and I know the ancients have one or two examples of tragicomedies, as Plautus hath *Amphitryo*. But if we mark them well we shall find that they never, or very daintily, match hornpipes and funerals. So falleth it out that, having indeed no right comedy, in that comical part of our tragedy we have nothing but scurrility unworthy of any chaste ears, or some extreme show of doltishness, indeed fit to lift up a loud laughter, and nothing else; where the whole tract of a comedy should be full of delight, as the tragedy should be still maintained in a well-raised admiration.[118]

[The nature of laughter]

[50] But our comedians think there is no delight without laughter; which is very wrong, for though laughter may come with delight, yet cometh it not of delight, as though delight should be the cause of laughter; but well may one thing breed both together. Nay rather in themselves they have, as it were, a kind of contrariety; for delight we scarcely do but in things that have a

---

[114] *Decency* has no moral reference here, but rather is *fitness, suitability, decorum;* see the index under *decorum*.   [115] Cf. sect. 32 above, and the appendix to the *Defense*.

[116] Sidney perhaps allows the mixture in sect. 29 above. Guarini objected to a mere mixture of the tragic and the comic and demanded proper selection of material (*Tragicomedy*, sect. 13b, below).

[117] It is a narrative rather than a drama. For discussion see Castelvetro, on *Poetics*, III, 57, 1, above.

[118] For delight and admiration as the effects of comedy and tragedy, see also sect. 50, just below.

conveniency to ourselves or to the general nature; laughter almost ever cometh of things most disproportioned to ourselves and nature. Delight hath a joy in it, either permanent or present. Laughter hath only a scornful tickling.[119] For example, we are ravished with delight to see a fair woman, and yet are far from being moved to laughter. We laugh at deformed creatures, wherein certainly we cannot delight. We delight in good chances, we laugh at mischances; we delight to hear the happiness of our friends and country, at which he were worthy to be laughed at that would laugh. We shall, contrarily, laugh sometimes to find a matter quite mistaken and go down the hill against the bias, in the mouth of some such men as for the respect of them one shall be heartily sorry, yet he cannot choose but laugh; and so is rather pained than delighted with laughter. Yet deny I not but that they may go well together. For as in Alexander's picture well set out we delight without laughter, and in twenty mad antics we laugh without delight, so in Hercules, painted with his great beard and furious countenance, in woman's attire, spinning at Omphale's commandment, it breeds both delight and laughter. For the representing of so strange a power in love procures delight; and the scornfulness of the action stirreth laughter. But I speak to this purpose, that all the end of the comical part be not upon such scornful matters as stir laughter only, but mix with it that delightful teaching which is the end of poesy. And the great fault even in that point of laughter, and forbidden plainly by Aristotle, is that they stir laughter in sinful things, which are rather execrable than ridiculous;[120] or in miserable, which are rather to be pitied than scorned. For what is it to make folks gape at a wretched beggar or a beggarly clown; or against law of hospitality to jest at strangers, because they speak not English so well as we do? What do we learn? since it is certain

> *Nil habet infelix paupertas durius in se,*
> *Quam quod ridiculos homines facit.*[121]

But rather a busy loving courtier, a heartless threatening Thraso, a self-wise-seeming schoolmaster, a wry transformed traveller— these if we saw walk in stage names, which we play naturally,

---

[119] Cf. sect. 31, above, and Dryden, *Of Dramatic Poesy*, sect. 59, below. See *laughter* and *comedy* in the index.

[120] At the beginning of *Poetics*, v, above, Aristotle excludes from comedy laughter painful or harmful to others.

[121] Juvenal, III, 152–3: "Unhappy poverty has nothing worse in itself than this, that it makes men ridiculous."

therein were delightful laughter, and teaching delightfulness;[122] as in the other, the tragedies of Buchanan do justly bring forth a divine admiration. But I have lavished out too many words of this play matter. I do it because, as they are excelling parts of poesy, so is there none so much used in England, and none can be more pitifully abused; which, like an unmannerly daughter showing a bad education, causeth her mother Poesy's honesty to be called in question.

[Lyric poetry]

[51] Other sorts of poetry almost have we none but that lyrical kind of songs and sonnets; which, Lord, if he gave us so good minds, how well it might be employed and with how heavenly fruits, both private and public, in singing the praises of the immortal beauty, the immortal goodness of that God who giveth us hands to write and wits to conceive; of which we might well want words, but never matter; of which we could turn our eyes to nothing, but we should ever have new budding occasions. But truly many of such writings as come under the banner of unresistible love, if I were a mistress would never persuade me they were in love; so coldly they apply fiery speeches, as men that had rather read lovers' writings and so caught up certain swelling phrases— which hang together like a man that once told me the wind was at northwest and by south, because he would be sure to name winds enough—than that in truth they feel those passions, which easily, as I think, may be betrayed by that same forcibleness, or *energia* as the Greeks call it, of the writer.[123] But let this be a sufficient though short note that we miss the right use of the material point of poesy.

[Diction]

[52] Now for the outside of it, which is words, or (as I may term it) diction, it is even well worse. So is that honey-flowing matron Eloquence apparelled, or rather disguised, in a courtesan-like painted affectation:[124] one time with so far-fet words that they

---

[122] Cf. Trissino's treatment of the comic (*Poetica*, 120a ff., above), and see the index under *comic*.

[123] *Energia* is especially dealt with by Demetrius of Phalerum (*On Style*, IV, 209–20). A translation is given in the Loeb Classical Library, in the same volume with Aristotle's *Poetics*. Sidney perhaps drew his information from Scaliger (*Poetice*, III, 27, p. 116B2).

[124] Minturno, in the dedication of *L'arte poetica*, speaks of those who have changed poetry "from a chaste virgin to a shameless, mocking, and lascivious harlot."

may seem monsters, but must seem strangers, to any poor Englishman; another time with coursing of a letter, as if they were bound to follow the method of a dictionary; another time with figures and flowers extremely winter-starved. But I would this fault were only peculiar to versifiers and had not as large possession among prose-printers, and (which is to be marvelled) among many scholars, and (which is to be pitied) among some preachers. Truly I could wish, if at least I might be so bold to wish in a thing beyond the reach of my capacity, the diligent imitators of Tully and Demosthenes, most worthy to be imitated, did not so much keep Nizolian paper-books of their figures and phrases, as by attentive translation (as it were) devour them whole, and make them wholly theirs. For now they cast sugar and spice upon every dish that is served to the table, like those Indians not content to wear earrings at the fit and natural place of the ears, but they will thrust jewels through their nose and lips, because they will be sure to be fine.[125] Tully, when he was to drive out Catiline, as it were with a thunderbolt of eloquence, often used the figure of repetition, *Vivit et vincit, imo in senatum, venit imo, in senatum venit* &c.[126] Indeed, inflamed with a well-grounded rage, he would have his words, as it were, double out of his mouth, and so do that artificially which we see men in choler do naturally.[127] And we having noted the grace of those words, hale them in sometimes to a familiar epistle, when it were too much choler to be choleric. How well store of *similiter* cadences[128] doth sound with the gravity of the pulpit I would but invoke Demosthenes' soul to tell, who with a rare daintiness useth them. Truly they have made me think of the sophister that with too much subtlety would prove two eggs three, and though he might be counted a sophister had none for his labor. So these men bringing in such a kind of eloquence, well may they obtain an opinion of a seeming fineness but persuade few, which should be the end of their fineness.

[125] Elizabethan taste permitted earrings to men. Likewise a literary style that to us appears overornamented would to Sidney have seemed in good taste.

[126] If Sidney's words are correctly preserved, he did not quote accurately but modified to strengthen the effect he was speaking of. The meaning is: "He lives and conquers; even into the senate, he comes even, into the senate he comes." But the text is probably corrupt.

[127] *Artificially* in this sentence has none of the derogatory meaning we usually give the word; it is rather equivalent, as usually in Renaissance language, to *artistically*.

[128] From the Latin *similiter cadentia* (Quintilian, *Institutes*, IX, 4, 42), final sounds or cadences produced by corresponding forms of oblique cases of nouns or parts of verbs.

[Similitudes]

[53] Now for similitudes in certain printed discourses, I think all herbarists, all stories of beasts, fowls, and fishes are rifled up, that they may come in multitudes to wait upon any of our conceits, which certainly is as absurd a surfeit to the ears as is possible. For the force of a similitude not being to prove anything to a contrary disputer, but only to explain to a willing hearer, when that is done, the rest is a most tedious prattling, rather over-swaying the memory from the purpose whereto they were applied than any whit informing the judgment, already either satisfied or by similitudes not to be satisfied. For my part I do not doubt when Antonius and Crassus, the great forefathers of Cicero in eloquence, the one (as Cicero testifieth of them) pretended not to know art, the other not to set by it, because with a plain sensibleness they might win credit of popular ears; which credit is the nearest step to persuasion; which persuasion is the chief mark of oratory—I do not doubt, I say, but that they used these knacks very sparingly; which, who doth generally use, any man may see doth dance to his own music,[129] and so to be noted by the audience, more careful to speak curiously than truly.

[Courtly and pedantic styles]

[54] Undoubtedly (at least to my opinion undoubtedly) I have found in divers small-learned courtiers a more sound style than in some professors of learning; of which I can guess no other cause but that the courtier, following that which by practice he findeth fittest to nature, therein (though he know it not) doth according to art, though not by art; where the other, using art to show art, and not hide art (as in these cases he should do), flieth from nature, and indeed abuseth art.

[The English language]

[55] But what? Methinks I deserve to be pounded for straying from poetry to oratory;[130] but both have such an affinity in this

129 Cf. Puttenham on anaphora: "We make one word begin and as they are wont to say lead the dance to many verses in suite" (*Art of English Poesy*, Bk. iii, chap. xix).
130 Such straying was almost inevitable in view of the influence of Cicero and other rhetorical writers, such as Quintilian. Even in a recent work such as Professor Atkins's *Literary Criticism in Antiquity* we read, in the preface of the second volume: "As before, much of the theorizing is concerned with oratory and prose style, though poetry as well comes in for some amount of treatment." It is good to keep Sidney's distinction in mind.

wordish consideration that I think this digression will make my
meaning receive the fuller understanding—which is not to take
upon me to teach poets how they should do, but only, finding
myself sick among the rest, to show some one or two spots of the
common infection grown among the most part of writers, that
acknowledging ourselves somewhat awry we may bend to the
right use both of matter and manner. Whereto our language
giveth us great occasion, being indeed capable of any excellent
exercising of it. I know some will say it is a mingled language.
And why not so much the better, taking the best of both the other?
Another will say it wanteth grammar. Nay truly, it hath that
praise that it wanteth grammar;[131] for grammar it might have but
it needs it not, being so easy in itself and so void of those cumbersome differences of cases, genders, moods, and tenses, which I
think was a piece of the Tower of Babylon's curse, that a man
should be put to school to learn his mother-tongue. But for the
uttering sweetly and properly the conceits of the mind, which is
the end of speech, that hath it equally with any other tongue in
the world; and is particularly happy in compositions of two or
three words together, near the Greek, far beyond the Latin; which
is one of the greatest beauties can be in a language.[132]

[Versification]

[56] Now of versifying there are two sorts, the one ancient, the
other modern: the ancient marked the quantity of each syllable
and according to that framed his verse; the modern observing only
number, with some regard of the accent, the chief life of it standeth
in that like sounding of the words which we call rhyme. Whether
of these be the more excellent would bear many speeches. The
ancient no doubt more fit for music, both words and time observing quantity, and more fit lively to express divers passions by
the low or lofty sound of the well-weighed syllable. The latter
likewise with his rhyme striketh a certain music to the ear; and in
fine since it doth delight, though by another way, it obtaineth the
same purpose; there being in either sweetness, and wanting in
neither majesty. Truly the English, before any other vulgar

---

[131]All texts give *not* before *grammar*, but the sense seems to exclude the negative.

[132] Sidney's praise of the English language sets him on the side of modern literature,
as opposed to those who imitated the classics and wrote only in Latin. Scaliger (see
the index) does not recognize that there is a vernacular literature but discusses only
Neo-Latin writers. The passage also shows Sidney's independence of the Italian critics
from whom he learned so much.

language I know, is fit for both sorts; for, for the ancient, the Italian is so full of vowels that it must ever be cumbered with elisions; the Dutch so, of the other side, with consonants that they cannot yield the sweet sliding fit for a verse; the French, in his whole language, hath not one word that hath his accent in the last syllable saving two, called *antepenultima*, and little more hath the Spanish; and, therefore, very gracelessly may they use dactyls. The English is subject to none of these defects.

[Rhyme]

[57] Now for rhyme, though we do not observe quantity, yet we observe the accent very precisely; which other languages either cannot do, or will not do so absolutely. That *caesura*, or breathing place in the midst of the verse, neither Italian nor Spanish have; the French and we never almost fail of. Lastly, even the very rhyme itself the Italian cannot put in the last syllable, by the French named the masculine rhyme, but still in the next to the last, which the French call the female, or the next before that, which the Italians term *sdrucciola*. The example of the former is *buono, suono;* of the *sdrucciola* is *femina, semina*. The French, of the other side, hath both the male, as *bon, son,* and the female, as *plaise, taise,* but the *sdrucciola* he hath not. Where the English hath all three, as *due, true; father, rather; motion, potion*, with much more which might be said, but that already I find the triflingness of this discourse is much too much enlarged.

[PART VIII. THE READER EXHORTED TO BELIEVE IN POETRY]

[58] So that since the ever-praiseworthy poesy is full of virtue-breeding delightfulness, and void of no gift that ought to be in the noble name of learning; since the blames laid against it are either false or feeble; since the cause why it is not esteemed in England is the fault of poet-apes, not poets; since, lastly, our tongue is most fit to honor poesy, and to be honored by poesy; I conjure you all that have had the evil luck to read this ink-wasting toy of mine, even in the name of the Nine Muses, no more to scorn the sacred mysteries of poesy, no more to laugh at the name of poets, as though they were next inheritors to fools, no more to jest at the reverent title of a rhymer; but to believe, with Aristotle, that they were the ancient treasurers of the Grecians' divinity; to believe, with Bembus, that they were first bringers-in of all civility; to believe, with Scaliger, that no philosopher's precepts can sooner

make you an honest man than the reading of Vergil;[133] to believe, with Clauserus, the translator of Cornutus, that it pleased the heavenly Deity, by Hesiod and Homer, under the veil of fables, to give us all knowledge, logic, rhetoric, philosophy, natural and moral, and *quid non?*[134] to believe, with me, that there are many mysteries contained in poetry, which of purpose were written darkly lest by profane wits it should be abused;[135] to believe, with Landino,[136] that they are so beloved of the gods that whatsoever they write proceeds of a divine fury; lastly, to believe themselves when they tell you they will make you immortal by their verses. Thus doing, your name shall flourish in the printers' shops. Thus doing, you shall be of kin to many a poetical preface. Thus doing, you shall be most fair, most rich, most wise, most all; you shall dwell upon superlatives. Thus doing, though you be *libertino patre natus*,[137] you shall suddenly grow *Herculea proles*,[138]

Si quid mea carmina possunt.[139]

Thus doing, your soul shall be placed with Dante's Beatrix or Vergil's Anchises. But if (fie of such a but) you be born so near the dull-making cataract of Nilus that you cannot hear the planet-like music of poetry, if you have so earth-creeping a mind that it cannot lift itself up to look to the sky of poetry, or rather, by a certain rustical disdain, will become such a mome as to be a Momus of poetry; then, though I will not wish unto you the ass's ears of Midas, nor to be driven by a poet's verses, as Bubonax was, to hang himself, nor to be rhymed to death as is said to be done in Ireland; yet thus much curse I must send you, in the behalf of all poets, that while you live, you live in love, and never get favor for lacking skill of a sonnet, and, when you die, your memory die from the earth for want of an epitaph.

[133] "You cannot turn out better or more adapted to society by learning the precepts of any of the philosophers than by reading Vergil" (Scaliger, *Poetice*, VI, 20, p. 104A2).

[134] What not?

[135] Spenser refers to the *Faerie Queene* as a "dark conceit" (*Letter to Raleigh*, below).

[136] Prefixed to Cristoforo Landion's edition of Dante (Venice, 1596) are discourses on poetry; one section is headed "divine fury." He says the poet is "stimulated by the divine spirit. Poetry sets forth exalted and divine thoughts and feeds the mind with heavenly ambrosia. This divine fury . . . proceeds from the Muses. Hence he who attempts to become a poet without this divine fury labors in vain."

[137] Horace, *Satires*, I, 6, 6: "The son of a freedman," that is, of a former slave.

[138] "Herculean offspring." Perhaps from Ovid, *Fasti*, II, 237.

[139] *Aeneid*, IX, 446: "If aught my songs can do" to make you famous.

(secs. 26, 32, and 49, above)

Admiration and commiseration (secs. 32, 49) are apparently
Aristotle's fear and pity (*Poetics*, VI);[1] admiration may be terror caused
by the astonishing (*Poetics*, IX; XXIV). Milton speaks of passion and admiration (*Reason of Church Government*, sect. 2, below), and Heinsius of
terror and commiseration, and horror and commiseration (*De tragoediae
constitutione*, chap. VIII).

Gregory Smith connects admiration with the moving power of all
poetry, placing it with "instruction and delight in the general definition
of the purpose of poetry" (p. 392). Sidney combines "teach and move"
in his discussion of heroic poetry (sect. 34, above).

Castelvetro speaks of *meraviglia* (astonishment) which is closely connected with tragic fear, since terror is caused by the marvelous and the
striking (on *Poetics*, IX, 228, 9, above); *meraviglia* "generates and increases terror and compassion" (221, 18). A passage in Boccaccio runs:
"This thing excited in his spirit *meraviglia* and terror at once, and finally
compassion for the ill-fated lady" (*Decameron*, V, 8). Minturno (*L'arte
poetica*, sect. 76, above) indicates that the tragic poet moves to *meraviglia*
with terror and pity. The person who is so moved has his mind purged
from the *affetti* (Sidney's *affects*) or passions. The word *passioni* in
Minturno's margin is apparently a synonym of *affetti*. The moving
power of tragedy of which Sidney immediately speaks, instancing the
tyrant Alexander, is exerted to produce pity. Gregory Smith quotes
Minturno (*De poeta*, pp. 102, 106) and Scaliger (*Poetice*, III, 97, p. 145A2)
on poetry as moving, teaching, and delighting.[2] Similarly in his *Arte
poetica* (p. 76) Minturno makes the function of the tragic poet "so to
speak in verse that he may teach, delight, and move in such a way as to
purge the minds of the spectators from the passions." The three purposes are numbered in the margin. In *De poeta* (pp. 179–80) he speaks

---

[1] *Compassione* seems the more usual word in the Italian critics, though Giraldi uses
commiseratione in his *Discourse on Comedies and Tragedies*, p. 222.

[2] Cf. Giovanni Pontano: "The function of the poet, if I mistake not, is directed to
these three ends: that it may teach, that it may delight, that it may move. Though
these seem rightly to be diverse, and really are, yet while he teaches and moves, it is
necessary that he also delight. How can you teach an auditor or move him, if you
employ discourse that is unlearned, confused, and badly connected, if your words are
awkward, your gestures ridiculous and wild, your voice rough, inharmonious, and
dissonant? So it is above all needful that a writer should be especially mindful of
charm, attractiveness, and grace" (*Aegidius, a Dialogue* [in *Opera*, Basel, 1556], pp.
1481–2).

a second time to the same effect; it is the business of the tragic poet "to demonstrate, to delight, and to move," ("ut probet, ut delectet, ut moveat"). This is apparently from Cicero: "Erit igitur eloquens . . . is, qui . . . ita dicet, ut probet, ut delectet, ut flectat" (*Orator*, 21).[3] This passage is perhaps enough to explain the Italian critic's formula. Minturno continues that the poet "moves vehemently when he excites admiration, whether he influences to terror or to commiseration or to both." The function of the tragic poet is to cause admiration, and "those things are to be admired that rouse pity or excite to terror."

As the quotation from Cicero suggests, the added element of moving comes from the theory of oratory. For example, Alessandro Lionardi, in his *Dialogues on Poetic Invention*, indicates that the poet must be something of an orator and that one of the orator's chief functions is to move.[4] He speaks of matters in poems that "move, delight, and persuade," and discusses the subject, with much dependence on the theory of oratory, for some pages (pp. 51–8). Similarly Scaliger in *Poetice*, I, 1. Ben Jonson writes in his *Discoveries:* "The poet is the nearest borderer upon the orator and expresseth all his virtues. . . . And, of the kind, the comic comes nearest, because in moving the minds of men and stirring of affections (in which oratory shows and especially approves her eminence) he chiefly excels" (sect. 130, Castelain's ed., p. 128). Note Sidney's word *affects*.[5] Perhaps the emphasis on moving in poetry was supported by a variant reading of Horace, *Art of Poetry*, 344; it usually appears as

Lectorem delectando pariterque monendo,

but some mss (Horace,*Works*, Delphine ed. [London, 1825]) give as a variant *movendo*. I do not know how widely this reading was circulated. Ben Jonson, for example, translates *monendo*, but *movendo* apparently underlies the paraphrase of Horace by Fabricius, who writes: "Utile est quod animos incitat doctrina et sapientia" (sect. 28).[6] The word *incitat* suggests *movendo*.

---

[3] Used by St. Augustine in his *Christian Doctrine*, IV, 12, but instead of *probet* he gives the word *doceat*, also found in Minturno, *De poeta*, pp. 102, 106.

[4] "*Muovere, conciliare, et provare*" (p. 10, ed. of 1554). See also Bundy's introduction to Fracastoro's *Naugerius* [Urbana, 1924], pp. 17–20.

[5] Sect. 32, above. Sforza Oddi has Tragedy say to Comedy: "As to compassion and the affects, which are especially mine, with what authority do you so often usurp them, and by using them strive to make your dramas almost tragic?" (Prologue to *Prigione d'amore, commedia nuova* [Venice, 1591]).

[6] Vincentius Madius keeps *monendo* in his text, but explains that the poem that is to be generally commended must "at the same time both move and delight" (*In Horatii lib. de arte poet. interpretatio* [Venice, 1550], p. 362).

Admiration may be distinguished from and set over against moving.
Scaliger writes: "The subject matter of poetry is to be so arranged and
disposed that it may approach as nearly as possible to the truth; nor
should the poet give his attention merely to causing the spectators to
admire or be astounded, as the critics say Aeschylus did, but he should
think of teaching, moving, and delighting" (*Poetice*, III, 96, p. 145A2).[7]
Minturno will have the admiration of the reader or hearer follow the
teaching, delighting, or moving of the poet (*De poeta*, p. 106); this
section pertains to poetry in general, not to tragedy alone. The word
admiration is sometimes used in its most obvious sense, as when Scaliger
says that in the *Frogs* of Aristophanes the question was put to Euripides:
"What virtue is especially able to excite us to admiration of a poet?"
(*Poetice*, I, I, p. 1C2.)

Sidney once asserts that moving is "of a higher degree than teaching"
(sect. 26); this apparently is not founded on the doctrine of Minturno.
Likewise the Italian does not put admiration and commiseration on a
level, or make them, as Sidney seems to, equivalent to the pity and fear
of Aristotle. So far as admiration and commiseration are equivalent to
pity and fear, Sidney either is not following Minturno, or he has neglected, misunderstood, forgotten, or deliberately modified the theory
of his predecessor.

Influence of Sidney's formula perhaps appears in Dryden's "admiration, compassion, or concernment" (see *admiration* in the index).

[7] Boileau wrote in 1700: On the stage "one should not hope to excite pity and fear,
like the poets of ancient tragedy, but, by sublimity of thought and beauty of idea, to
excite in the souls of the spectators a certain admiration. Many persons, especially the
young, are often better suited with this than with the true passions of tragedy" (Letter
to Perrault, quoted by Gregory Smith in *Elizabethan Critical Essays*, I, 392-3).

EDMUND SPENSER

o○oo○o

ONE OF THE GREAT LOSSES to English criticism is the disappearance of Spenser's *English Poet*. It is true that he composed it early in his career, since it seems to have been finished when the *Shepherd's Calendar* was printed,[1] yet even then his reflections on the long narrative poem must have been sufficiently influenced by his plan and probable labors on the *Faerie Queene* to link his critical work with the great poem. After he had actually published part or all of his epic as we now have it, he would have been still better fitted to explain it. It seems that he might, like Tasso, have defended his methods, or have written somewhat in the strain that Giraldi employed in explaining Ariosto. Obviously Spenser was familiar with the issue between the classical epic and the romance, and clearly too, though like Giraldi he valued Homer and Vergil, he was still nearer to Tasso; with respect to structure his affinity with Ariosto is very close, though his use of twelve separate heroes is unparalleled among romantic epics, as he must have well understood. Possibly, however, his plan was not developed quite to that state when he produced the *English Poet*. He may not have been in so good a position for explaining the English epic as was Jonson for apologizing for the English drama, but it may still be supposed that something would have been said calculated to restrain the worst excesses of classical critics during the next two centuries.

Indications of what he wrote we probably can gather from the letter to Raleigh (which in various respects may be compared with Dante's letter to Can Grande). Something more is furnished by the Eclogue for October in the *Shepherd's Calendar*, with its accompanying matter. Especially we learn from the argument and the emblem that poetry is "a divine gift and heavenly instinct not to be gotten by labor and learning, but adorned with both, and poured into the wit by a certain ἐνθουσιασμός and celestial inspiration," or that it is "divine instinct and unnatural rage passing the reach of common reason." Little of this is apparent from the letter to Raleigh, which gives the didactic theory for which the beauty of poetry is but a means to the end of instruction. Spenser shows little of Sidney's zeal for "right poetry," being apparently content that art should serve a didactic end.

[1]*Shepherd's Calendar*, Argument to "October."

BIBLIOGRAPHY

Jones, H. S. V., *A Spenser Handbook*. New York, 1930. An encyclopedia of Spenser.

Langdon, Ida, *Materials for a Study of Spenser's Theory of Fine Art*. Ithaca, 1911. Introduction and illustrative passages.

Spenser, Edmund, *Works*. Baltimore, 1932–1936.

LETTER TO SIR WALTER RALEIGH (*in part*)

1589

Sir: Knowing how doubtfully all allegories may be construed, and this book of mine, which I have entitled the *Faerie Queene*, being a continued allegory or dark conceit, I have thought good as well for avoiding of jealous opinions and misconstructions,[1] as also for your better light in reading thereof (being so by you commanded) to discover unto you the general intention and meaning which in the whole course thereof I have fashioned, without expressing of any particular purposes or by-accidents therein occasioned. The general end therefore of all the book is to fashion a gentleman or noble person in virtuous and gentle discipline.[2] Which for that I conceived should be most plausible and pleasing being colored with an historical fiction—the which the most part of men delight to read rather for variety of matter than for profit of the ensample—I chose the history of King Arthur as most fit for the excellency of his person, being made famous by many men's former works and also furthest from the danger of envy and suspicion of present time. In which I have followed all the antique poets historical: first, Homer, who in the persons of Agamemnon and Ulysses hath ensampled a good governor and a virtuous man, the one in his *Iliad*, the other in his *Odyssey;* then Vergil, whose like intention was to do in the person of Aeneas; after him Ariosto comprised them both in his *Orlando*; and lately Tasso dissevered them again and formed both parts in two persons, namely, that

---

[1] Perhaps by the spies of the statesmen of the time, and even by the statesmen themselves, who gave political interpretations to literature. The "suspicion of the present time," mentioned a few lines further, perhaps has the same suggestion.

[2] Jonson, in the dedication of *Volpone* to the universities, speaks of the poet as "able to inform young men to all good disciplines, inflame grown men to all great virtues, keep old men in their best and supreme state."

part which they in philosophy call ethice, or virtues of a private man, colored in his Rinaldo, the other named politice in his Godfredo.[3] By ensample of which excellent poets I labor to portray in Arthur before he was king the image of a brave knight perfected in the twelve private moral virtues as Aristotle hath devised, the which is the purpose of these first twelve books. Which if I find to be well accepted I may be perhaps encouraged to frame the other part of politic virtues in his person after that he came to be king. To some I know this method will seem displeasant, which had rather have good discipline delivered plainly in way of precepts or sermoned at large, as they use, than thus cloudily enwrapped in allegorical devices. But such, me seem, should be satisfied with the use of these days, seeing all things accounted by their shows and nothing esteemed of that is not delightful and pleasing to common sense. For this cause is Xenophon preferred before Plato, for that the one in the exquisite depth of his judgment formed a commonwealth such as it should be, but the other in the person of Cyrus and the Persians fashioned a government such as might best be;[4] so much more profitable and gracious is doctrine by example than by rule.[5] So have I labored to do in the person of Arthur, whom I conceive after his long education by Timon, to whom he was by Merlin delivered to be brought up so soon as he was born of the Lady Igraine, to have seen in a dream or vision the Faerie Queen. With whose excellent beauty ravished, he awaking resolved to seek her out, and so being by Merlin armed and by Timon thoroughly instructed, he went to seek her forth in Faerie Land. In that Faerie Queen I mean glory in my general intention, but in my particular I conceive the most excellent and glorious person of our sovereign the Queen, and her kingdom in Faerie Land.[6] And yet in some places else I

[3] Cf. Sidney's opinion (Defense, sect. 10, above). Scaliger devotes a chapter to the high qualities of Aeneas, concluding: "We therefore have in Aeneas alone a sort of Socratic idea of any person; his perfection seems to emulate Nature herself in genus, and in special and private instances even to surpass her" (Poetice, III, 12, p. 95C2).

In the preface to Alaric, a heroic poem (1654) by Georges de Scudéry, we read: "One sees in the person of Aeneas perfect piety, in Achilles high valor, in Ulysses the nicest, most exquisite prudence. And it is in accordance with these high originals that I have tried to show in the person of Alaric, to form the idea of an accomplished prince, both the piety of the first, the valor of the second, and the prudence of the third."

[4] For Xenophon's Cyropaedia see Sidney's Defense, secs. 16, 21, 23, 24, above.

[5] The rules or precepts of the philosophers. See Sidney, Defense, sect. 21, above.

[6] Cf. Dante's allegorical method explained in his letter to Can Grande, above. The Faerie Queen is literally Elizabeth, figuratively she is glory. The second is obviously the more important.

do otherwise shadow her.[7] For considering she beareth two persons, the one of a most royal queen or empress, the other of a most virtuous and beautiful lady, this latter part in some places I do express in Belphoebe, fashioning her name according to your own excellent conception of Cynthia (Phoebe and Cynthia being both names of Diana). So in the person of Prince Arthur I set forth magnificence in particular, which virtue, for that (according to Aristotle and the rest) it is the perfection of all the rest and containeth in it them all, therefore in the whole course I mention the deeds of Arthur appliable to that virtue which I write of in that book. But of the twelve other virtues I make twelve other knights the patrons, for the more variety of the history,[8] of which these three books contain three. The first of the Knight of the Redcrosse, in whom I express holiness; the second of Sir Guyon, in whom I set forth temperance; the third of Britomartis, a lady knight, in whom I picture chastity. But because the beginning of the whole work seemeth abrupt and as depending upon other antecedents, it needs that ye know the occasion of these three knights' several adventures. For the method of a poet historical is not such as of an historiographer. For an historiographer discourseth of affairs orderly as they were done, accounting as well the times as the actions; but a poet thrusteth into the midst even where it most concerneth him,[9] and there recoursing to the things forepast and divining of things to come maketh a pleasing analysis of all. . . .

Thus much, Sir, I have briefly overrun to direct your understanding to the well-head of the history, that from thence gathering the whole intention of the conceit ye may as in a handful grip all the discourse, which otherwise may haply seem tedious and confused.

[7] Picture her.   [8] See *variety* in the index.   [9] Horace, *Art of Poetry*, 148, above.

TORQUATO TASSO

୦◯୦୦◯୦

DISCOURSES ON THE HEROIC POEM

1594

TORQUATO TASSO is still considered one of the greatest of Italian poets, being mentioned with Dante, Petrarch, and Ariosto. His chief work is the *Jerusalem Delivered*, an epic in twenty books on the first Crusade. Next in renown is the *Aminta*, a pastoral drama, in its day the most popular of Tasso's works. Perhaps no poet of a high order has ever been more concerned with criticism or more susceptible to the influence of critical opinion than Tasso. The chief evidence is to be found in the two versions of his epic. When the work appeared, it was attacked as too little in conformity with the rules for heroic poetry as derived from Aristotle, Homer, and Vergil, and too much like the great romantic poem of Ariosto, the *Orlando Furioso*. Yielding to this opinion, or more probably because he came to feel that the critics were right, he revised according to classical principles, giving to the new version the name of *Jerusalem Conquered*. The verdict of history is that the revision was not a success; while there have been various editions of it, the earlier form is that which has been generally circulated. Is this to be taken as a practical demonstration that poetical inspiration is stifled by continual attention to the laws of the critics?

A number of Tasso's minor writings are concerned with critical and aesthetic problems, such as his dialogue entitled *Il Minturno, or Of Beauty*, and the *Apology in Defense of His Jerusalem Delivered*. In his letters he also discusses literary matters; for example, he writes to Scipio Gonzaga that he has just been rereading the *Poetics* of Aristotle.

The translation of the *Discourses* is by the editor.

BIBLIOGRAPHY

Boulting, William, *Tasso and His Times*. London, 1907.

Tasso, Torquato, *Jerusalem Delivered*, translated by Edward Fairfax. London, 1890. This edition gives at the back Tasso's Account of the Allegory of the Poem, which is to be found also in other editions; it should be read by every student of criticism.

——— , *Opere*. Milano, 1826.

DISCOURSES ON THE HEROIC POEM (*selections*)

Book I

[Poetry defined]

[1] Since each definition should have in view the best, in defining poetry we should set before ourselves a most excellent end; and that is to give profit to men through the example of human actions, because the example of the animals cannot be of equal profit and that of divine beings is not fitted to us. . . . Poetry, then, is an imitation of human actions, produced for giving instruction on life. And because every act is performed with some reason and some choice, character and thought, which the Greeks call *dianoia*,[1] must accordingly be treated. And though when this imitation is made it produces the greatest delight, it cannot be said that there are two ends, one that of delight, the other that of profit, as it appears that Horace indicates in that verse

The poets aim either to profit or to delight.[2]

A single art cannot have two ends unless one is subordinate to the other, but it should either lay aside the profit that comes from admonition and advice (as Isocrates says)[3] and following the example of Homer and the tragic poets direct all the force of its words toward delight; or if profit is to be retained, the pleasure should be directed to this end. And perhaps delight is the end of poetry, and an end arranged with a view to profit. Hence we read in the second oration of the same Isocrates that the ancient poets left us a heritage of teaching about life, through which men might become better,[4] and in the Panathenaic oration that poetry diverts

---

[1] Aristotle, *Poetics*, XIX, 56a33, above.   [2] *Art of Poetry*, 333, above.

[3] "This much, however, is clear, that those who aim to write anything in verse or prose which will make a popular appeal should seek out, not the most profitable discourses, but those which most abound in fictions; for the ear delights in these just as the eye delights in games and contests. Wherefore we may well admire the poet Homer and the first inventors of tragedy, seeing that they, with true insight into human nature, have embodied both kinds of pleasure in their poetry; for Homer has dressed the contests and battles of the demigods in myths, while the tragic poets have rendered the myths in the form of contests and action, so that they are presented, not to our ears alone, but to our eyes as well. With such models, then, before us, it is evident that those who desire to command the attention of their hearers must abstain from admonition and advice, and must say the kind of things which they see are most pleasing to the crowd" (Isocrates, *To Nicocles*, 48–9, trans. by George Norlin [New York, 1928]).   [4] *To Nicocles*, 43.

us from many sins.[5] Hence no other employment is better fitted to youth.

[Pleasure and profit]

[2] But profit is considered chiefly with respect to that art which is as it were architect of all others. Therefore, it is the statesman's duty to consider what poetry and what delight should be prohibited, since pleasure, which should correspond to that honey with which the lip of the cup is smeared when medicine is given to children,[6] should not produce the effect of injurious poison and should not keep the mind occupied in vain reading. The poet should not, then, set for himself pleasure as his end, as Eratosthenes seems to have thought, for he is rebuked by Strabo, who defended Homer from such imputations.[7] But profit should be the poet's end, because poetry, as the same author thinks, following the opinions of the ancients, is a first philosophy which even from early youth instructs us in morals and in the truths of life. But later authors are of the opinion that the poet should merely be wise. At least it should be believed that not every pleasure is the end of poetry but only the pleasure which is joined with goodness; because just as the delight that rises from reading of inhuman and disgraceful acts is unworthy of the good poet, so the pleasure of learning many things, joined with goodness, is suitable to him. Hence it may be that this end is not so much to be despised as appears to Fracastoro in his *Dialogue on Poetry;*[8] rather, if compared to the useful, pleasure is the nobler end, for pleasure is desired for itself and other things are desired because of it. In this respect it is so like felicity, which is the end of man in society, that nothing can be found more similar. In addition, pleasure is the friend of virtue, because it makes the nature of man magnificent, as may be read in Athenaeus;[9] therefore, those who

[5] Apparently an error by Tasso. In the *Panathenaicus* (35) there is a promise to discuss poetry, but it is not kept.

[6] See the index, *poetry as pleasing medicine.*

[7] "Eratosthenes is wrong in his contention that the aim of every poet is to entertain, not to instruct; indeed the wisest of the writers on poetry say, on the contrary, that poetry is a kind of elementary philosophy" (Strabo, *Geography*, I, 1, 10, trans. by H. L. Jones [New York, 1917]). See also I, 2, 3. The earlier part of Strabo's work is an expansion of this assertion by means of examples from the geographical knowledge of Homer.

[8] Girolamo Fracastoro, *Naugerius sive de poetica dialogus*, University of Illinois Press, 1924, with translation by Ruth Kelso: "Teaching is in a measure the concern of the poet, but not in his peculiar capacity" (p. 56).

[9] *The Deipnosophists*, xii, 512.

love pleasure are likely to become both magnanimous and splendid. But the useful is not sought for itself alone, but for some other reason. Therefore, it is a less noble end than pleasure and has less similarity with the final end. If the poet then in so far as he is poet has this end, he will not widely miss that mark to which he should direct all his thoughts as an archer does his arrows. But in so far as he is a man in society and part of a city, or at least in so far as his art is subordinate to that which is queen of the others, profit is proposed as an end, as something that is rather decorous than useful. Of the two ends, then, that a poet sets for himself, one is especially that of his own art, the other that of the superior art. But when he is intent on that which is especially his own, he should guard against the opposite excess, because virtuous pleasures are contrary to dishonorable ones. For this reason they merit no praise who have described amorous embracings in such a way as Ariosto does those of Ruggiero with Alcina, or of Ricciardetto with Fiordispina.[10]. . .

[Imitation]

[3] Anyone who, in defining the poet, makes him a good man and a good imitator of the actions and habits of men for the purpose of giving profit by means of delight will not perhaps offer a definition that fits all poets; yet he will define the best and most excellent poet. Then if the poet is an imitator of human actions and habits, poetry will be an imitation of the same thing, and if the poet is a good imitator, his poetry will be an imitation equally well done. But some have thought the poet should consider not so much the goodness as the beauty of his subjects. Among these is Fracastoro, who in the *Naugerius* proves that the end of the poet should be to concern himself with the idea of the beautiful.[11]

[Poetry and philosophy]

[4] Now it does not appear to me that the opinion of Maximus Tyrius ought to be despised; he thought that philosophy and poetry were one thing, double in name but single in essence, as is the light with respect to the sun, and therefore he defines poetry as a philosophy of ancient standing, metrical in sound, in subject

---

[10] *Orlando Furioso*, VII, 23–29; XXV, 50–70.

[11] "The aim of the poet is to please and to instruct, by imitating in every individual object the most excellent and most beautiful elements, in a style which is appropriate and simply beautiful" (*Naugerius*, concluding par.).

fabulous.[12] But philosophy is, it seems to him, poetry that is younger and more independent of meter, and more obvious in its reasoning. But I think its method of considering things makes one different from the other, for poetry considers things so far as they are beautiful, and philosophy considers them so far as they are good, as the same author points out in another place,[13] saying that Homer had two things to do, one of them pertaining to philosophy, the other to poetry; in the first he had virtue to consider, in the other the figures set forth by the plot. Poetry is then a searcher for and as it were a lover of beauty, and in two ways seeks to show it and to put it before our eyes; one way is narration, the other representation; both methods are included under imitation, as under its genus, but sometimes it gets its name from a particular kind of imitation. Those then who have defined poetry as the narration of a human action that is memorable and possible have not given a definition appropriate to all the species of poetry, but merely to the epic poem, or the heroic as we wish to call it, and have excluded comedy and tragedy.

[Profit and delight]

[5] I say that a heroic poem is an imitation of illustrious actions, grand and perfect, composed in narrative form in the loftiest verse, having as its end to profit by delighting, that is, delight is the cause why no one fails to obtain benefit, because delight induces him to read the more gladly. But to profit through delight is perhaps the end of all poetry, for tragedy profits by delighting, and so does comedy. . . . The epic, however, ought to produce its special kind of delight with its own special method of working, and this perhaps is to move the reader to wonder;[14] yet this does not seem wholly confined to the epic, for tragedy also moves to wonder, as may be gathered from those words of Isocrates which I not long ago referred to. . . .

Book II

[The matter of poetry]

[6] No forest was ever so crowded with a great variety of trees as poetry is with a great diversity of subjects. The matter of

---

[12] Near the beginning of the essay entitled "Whether the Poets or the Philosophers Treat Better of the Gods."

[13] In the essay on "What Homer Chose to Do."

[14] See the appendix to Sidney's *Defense*, just above.

poetry then appears more varied than that of any other subject, for it includes things high and low, serious and comic, sad and laughable, public and private, the unknown and known, modern and ancient, native and foreign, sacred and secular, civilized and primitive, human and divine; hence its boundaries are not the mountains or seas that separate Italy from Spain; not the Taurus, not Atlas, not Bactria, not Thule, not the south or the north or the east or the west, but the sky and the earth, indeed the highest part of the sky and the deepest of the heavier elements, for Dante, ascending from the center, rosé above all the fixed stars and above all the circles of the heavens,[15] and Vergil and Homer described not merely the things beneath the earth but also those the intellect can scarcely comprehend, but they covered them with a charming veil of allegory. The variety then of the things treated by them and by the others who have written before and after them is very great; and great too is the diversity of opinions, or rather the contrariety of judgments, the mutations of words, of customs, of laws, of ceremonies, of republics, of kingdoms, of emperors, and as it were of the world itself, which appears to have changed its appearance and to be represented to us as though in another form and under another aspect. Therefore if anyone is able to select, among such a multitude of things doubtful and uncertain, the best and what is most fitted to receive ornament and beauty, he will show art and wisdom above all others; for art should not be dissociated from wisdom, but, as some think, is wisdom itself, since its activities are not carried on and its judgments made without choice and the advice of others, though some have thought the taking of advice has no place in the most exact arts. But I write these things as a man who utters his opinion and asks for that of others, as though wishing to kindle a great light from the many sparks that light up the shades that darken the immense forest of poetic matter. . . .

[Truth and feigning]

[7] Though we read in the *Poetics* of Aristotle that feigned stories please because of their novelty, as among the ancients the *Flower* of Agathon and among the modern Tuscans the heroic stories of Boiardo and Ariosto and the tragedies of some still more

---

[15] Sidney, *Defense*, sect. 24, above: "the poet . . . having all, from Dante's Heaven to his Hell, under the authority of his pen." Cf. also Vauquelin de la Fresnaye, *Art poétique*, Bk. i.

recent poets,[16] we should not allow ourselves to be persuaded that any feigned story is worthy of greater commendation, for the contrary has already been established by many proofs; two of the most important may be cited here. One of them is by Aristotle himself, to the effect that those things are credible that can be done, but if we are not sure they have been done we think them hardly possible.[17] The last is, as it were, a fruit of the same seed, sprung, I say, from his opinion that the novelty of the poem does not consist chiefly in the falsity of the subject that has not been heard of before, but in the clever entanglement and in the solution of the story.[18] The subjects of Thyestes, Medea, and Oedipus were treated by various ancients in Greek and in Latin, but by a different weaving of the threads they made something specific of what was general and something new of what was old. Therefore, Robertello is badly deceived when he assigns the false as the material of a poem,[19] for the reason that the false, in the judgment of Plato and Aristotle, is the matter of the sophist, who labors on that which does not exist. The poet, however, bases his work on some true action and considers it as like the truth. Hence his matter is something having verisimilitude that can be true or false, though it tends to be true, since it is not at all reasonable that what possesses verisimilitude should tend toward the false, for the probable is very unlike the false, because where there is dissimilitude there cannot be identity, so to speak; but similar things can be the same, if not in substance at least in quality. Hence Monsignor Alessandro Piccolomini was little less wrong in holding the opinion that the subject of a poem should be false rather than true. . . .[20]

---

[16] Perhaps Giraldi Cinthio is one of the tragic poets.   [17] *Poetics*, IX, 51a36, above.
[18] *Poetics*, XVIII, first par., above.   [19] See *Robertello* in the index.
[20] "It is not then necessary that a poetic imitation in itself should deal with what is false or with what is true, but it is necessary that a thing should be imitated according to verisimilitude; from this follows that as not merely the false but the true as well can be combined with what is suitable and has verisimilitude, so equally it can come about by accident that not merely the false but the true as well can become the subject and the matter for poetry, but this comes to pass, as I have said, by accident. For it must be admitted that nature and art seldom reach the height of their powers, because of the various impediments that are opposed to them; and so likewise man in his acts and passions and habits is infrequently able to rise to the greatest heights. If, for example, anyone, as enraged, or envious, or fearful, or strong, or pious, or avaricious, or prodigal, or as under the sway of any other habit or desire, should perform some action, it will rarely happen that his actions will result from these habits or desires in their most extreme form. That is, very rarely will be found in him wrath, envy, timidity, fortitude, piety, prodigality, avarice, or any other passion or habit in the greatest force or in the greatest excess that is possible. Consequently, the actions

[Poetry and logic]

[8] I cannot concede that poetry is to be placed among the arts of the sophists or that the most excellent species of poetry is the phantastic. Though I concede that poetry is a maker of images, as is sophistry, and not merely of idols but of gods (since it is necessary to the highest renown of the poets that they deify just and valorous princes and place them in the number of the immortals and consecrate their memory to endless ages), yet I do not concede that the art of the sophists and that of the poets is the same. I say then that without doubt poetry is to be classified under dialectic with rhetoric, which, as Aristotle says, is the other scion of the dialectic power, to which appertains the consideration not of the false but the probable; hence rhetoric treats the false not in so far as it is false but in so far as it is probable; but the probable in so far as it has verisimilitude pertains to the poet. The poet, however, uses proof less efficiently than does the dialectician; indeed the imitation and the example and the comparison are the weakest kinds of proof, as Boethius teaches in his *Topics*.[21]. . . Since the poet, like the dialectician, differs from the sophist rather through choice than through faculty, it thence results that the good poet ought to labor more gladly than any other on subjects probable in themselves, as Homer did, who in the person of Hector wished to show

resulting from such false habits and passions will usually not be so intense and so full as according to verisimilitude they ought to be if they were derived from and issued out of such habits or feelings on the highest level. This is the reason why human actions that actually are performed by one individual or another are far different from those that the poets attribute to them, since the poets view the actions of men, and with them their habits and their feelings, in their universal aspect, and not in accord with their exact truth, except in the cases we have alluded to when the exact truth is accidentally united with the universal. Thence it comes about that the false is more often found in poetic imitation than is the true, not because falsehood is the matter most suitable for poetry, but because though not merely the false but the true as well can by accident be joined with the universal and with what has verisimilitude, yet the false is more often joined with it than is the true" (Alessandro Piccolomini, *Annotationi nel libro della poetica d'Aristotele* [Venice, 1575], sig. †† 6 recto).

Tasso refers also to Mazzoni, *On the Defense of the "Comedy,"* Introduction, sect. 4, above.

[21] See *topics* and *example* in the index. Such use of logic in literary criticism is frequent in the sixteenth century. See, for example, Bernardino Parthenio, *Della imitatione poetica* (Vinega, 1560), pp. 34, 78, 82, and the last note in the selections from Minturno, above. In France the union of logic and rhetoric appears in the *Logic* of Peter Ramus (1515–72). Ramus had great influence in England, as on Sir Philip Sidney and Milton. The latter issued in 1672 a *Logic* based on that of Ramus and reproducing his quotations from the poets. For text and translation see the *Works* of Milton, Columbia University Press, XI.

it was a very laudable thing to defend one's native land, and in
that of Achilles that vengeance was very laudable and the act of
a magnanimous man and consequently just and approved by the
gods. These opinions, being certainly probable in themselves,
have verisimilitude, and because of the art of Homer become very
probable or certain and very like to the truth. Or I should say
that poetry is not a subdivision of dialectic but rather of logic,
which contains three parts, the demonstrative, the probable, and
the apparently probable, which is the sophistic; hence, in some
things the poet demonstrates, as did Parmenides and Empedocles
among the ancient Greeks, Lucretius and Boethius among the
Latins, Dante among the Tuscans;[22] in some other matters the poet
gives probable syllogisms, and this he does more often, because in
doing so he attends properly to his own function; in some matters
he uses a paralogism, and this he does more rarely. If I am right,
the latitude of poetry is as great as that of logic, and it has three
parts subordinate and correspondent with the three superior parts
of logic, sometimes demonstrating with philosophers and using the
philosopheme, at other times following verisimilitude and making
use of the example and the enthymeme, as did Homer and Vergil,
and at other times, like the sophist, the poet applies himself to the
apparently probable, and with equivocation and other sorts of falla-
cious arguments, which consist in words and things, he captivates
his auditors at his pleasure. This sophistic artifice was first used
by the Tuscan poets in the poetry of love more than in any other,
and perhaps many of them were not conscious of it. Nevertheless
the most nearly perfect imitation or the best species of poetry
does not rest on sophistry, whether new or old, but on dialectic.

[Phantasy]

[9] Much less is true what is said by Mazzoni,[23] that the best
poetry is the phantastic imitation, for such an imitation is of things
that are not and never were, but the best poetry imitates the
things that are, that were, and that can be, such as the war at

---

[22] Mazzoni in his *Discourse in Defense of Dante* points out Dante's use of logic in the
following passage: "He cannot be absolved who does not repent, and it is not possible
at once to repent and to wish to sin, because of the contradiction that does not allow
it" (*Inferno*, xxvii, 118–20).

For a discussion of contradictories in logic, with examples from Latin literature, see
Milton's *Art of Logic*, i, 16 (ed. cit., pp. 136 ff.). In this chapter Milton quotes from the
Topics of Boethius, mentioned by Tasso just above.

[23] *On the Defense of the "Comedy,"* Introduction, sect. 3, above.

Troy, the wrath of Achilles, the piety of Aeneas, the battles between the Trojans and the Latins, and other things that were or
can be done.   But the Centaurs, the Harpies, and the Cyclopes are
not the adequate or principal subject of poetry, nor the flying
horses and the other monsters that fill the romances.[24] But because
the poet, according to the opinion of Aristotle, imitates things
either as they are or as it is possible for them to be, or as report
makes them, or as they are believed to be, the principal subject of
poetry is what is, or what can be, or what is believed to be, or what
is told of; or as Aristotle held,[25] all of these together, since they can
be imitated by the poet, furnish matter fit for poetry according to
this requirement of verisimilitude.   One of the classes mentioned
is not, then, the sole subject fitted for poetry, as Mazzoni thinks,
nor does he present a conclusive argument, namely, "poetry is a
maker of idols, sophistic is a maker of idols, therefore poetry is
sophistic."[26]   The argument does not hold, not merely because in
the second figure of the syllogism the two affirmative propositions
are unsound, but also because the term *idols* has various meanings,
and as it is variously defined the making of idols pertains either to
the poet or to the sophist.   Favorinus, as Mazzoni himself says,
defines an idol as a shadowy similitude or a thing feigned that
truly is not, a form that has no substance, like the forms that appear in water and in mirrors. . . . But idols, as Suidas defines them,
are effigies of things that do not subsist, as Tritons, Sphinxes, and
Centaurs; and the similitudes are images of existing things, as
animals and men.[27] Hesychius, giving with another word the
meanings of the word *idol,* says: "An idol is an image, and a
similitude, and a sign,"[28] as though it might be of the things that
are and those that are not, as appears also to Ammonius and to
Plato himself.   When we say, then, that the sophist is a maker of
idols, we refer to the idols that are images of things that do not
subsist, for the subject of the sophist is that which is not, and in
this meaning Saint Paul says: "An idol is nothing."[29]   But when
we affirm that the poet is a maker of idols, we do not mean merely
the idols of things not subsisting, for the poet imitates things that
subsist and chiefly produces a resemblance of them.

[24] Cf. Sidney's apparently opposed opinion, *Defense,* sect. 9, above.
[25] *Poetics,* xxv, 60b32, above.
[26] *On the Defense of the "Comedy,"* Introduction, sect. 6, above.
[27] Suidas, *Lexicon, s. v.* εἴδωλον.
[28] Hesychius of Alexandria, author of a Greek lexicon; an edition was issued in 1514.
See εἴδωλον.   [29] I Corinthians 8, 4.

[Poetry and theology]

[10] Then in so far as the poet is a maker of idols, this should not be understood in the same sense in which it is said that the sophist is a maker of idols; but we ought rather to say that he is a maker of images in the guise of a speaking picture,[30] and in this like to the divine theologian who forms the ideas of things and commands that they be realized, and if dialectic and metaphysic, which were the divine philosophy of the Gentiles, have such conformity that they were by the ancients thought of as the same, it is not strange that the poet should be almost the same as the theologian and the dialectician. But divine philosophy, or theology as we prefer to call it, has two parts, and each of them is adapted and fitted to one part of our mind, which is composed of the divisible and the indivisible, not merely according to the opinion of Plato and of Aristotle, but of the Areopagite, who wrote in the epistles to Pope Titus in the *Mystic Theology*, and elsewhere, that that part of occult theology that is contained in the signs, and has the power of making one perfect, is fitting to the indivisible part of our soul, which is the intellect at its purest.[31] The other, eager for wisdom, which brings proofs, he attributes to the divisible part of the soul, much less noble than the indivisible. Thence it leads to the contemplation of divine things; and to move readers in this way with images, as do the mystic theologian and the poet, is a much more noble work than to teach by means of demonstrations, which is the function of the scholastic theologian. The mystic theologian and the poet, then, are far more noble than any of the others, even though Saint Thomas in the first part of the *Summa* put poetry in the lowest order of teaching,[32] but he is dealing with those parts of poetry that teach with weak proofs, such as examples and comparisons used for demonstrations; and yet he does not class it with the art of the sophists, which is not a genuine branch of learning but a deceitful appearance and an art like that of the jugglers. Then the poet as a maker of images is not a phantastic imitator, as appears to Mazzoni. . . .[33]

---

[30] Cf. Sidney, *Defense*, sect. 12, above.

[31] Dionysius the Areopagite, *Epistle* ix, sect. 1 (in Migne, *Patrologia Graeca*, iii, 1107).

[32] Part I, q. 1, art. 9: "It is objected that sacred teaching should not use metaphors. . . . But to proceed by various similitudes and representations is proper to poetry, which is the humblest branch of knowledge. . . . I answer that it is proper for Sacred Scripture to set forth in metaphors divine and spiritual things under the similitude of corporeal things." [33] *On the Defense of the "Comedy."* Introduction, sect. 1, above.

[Images]

[11] But if the images are of subsisting things, this imitation pertains to the icastic imitator. But what sort of things shall we say subsist? Are they the intelligible or the visible? Certainly they are the intelligible, and this is the judgment of Plato, who puts things visible in the genus of not-being, and puts the intelligible only in the genus of being. Then the images of the angels, described by Dionysius,[34] are of things superior to all the human subsistances, and the winged lion too, and the eagle, and the ox, and the angel, which are the images of the Evangelists, do not then pertain chiefly to phantasy and are not its special object, because the phantasy is in the divisible part of the soul, and not in the indivisible, which is the intellect in its purest form, if indeed besides the phantasy which is a capacity of the sensitive soul there is not also another which is the capacity of the intellective. This appears likely enough, because phantasy among the Greeks had its name from the light (this may be read in the book *On the Dogmas of the Philosophers* by Plutarch)[35] as being that power which is similar to light in making things plain and in revealing itself; this is wholly fitting to the intellectual phantasy. Yet this power, though it is posited by our theologians who concede the intellective memory and by the Platonic philosophers, was not recognized and admitted by Aristotle nor by Plato in the *Sophist;* otherwise he would not distinguish icastic from phantastic imagination, since the icastic can also fit with the intellectual imagination. Perhaps Dante had this in mind when he wrote:

To my lofty phantasy here power failed (*Paradiso*, xxxiii, 142),

and elsewhere:

Next rained down within my deep phantasy one crucified, despiteful and proud in his visage (*Purgatory*, xvii, 25-7).

The poet, then, though he is a maker of images, is like the dialectician and the theologian rather than the sophist, though not only among the ancients, according to the opinion of Aristotle, were poets and theologians the same, as Linus, Orpheus, and Musaeus, but also among the moderns, as Boccaccio writes in the

---

[34] Dionysius the Areopagite (see Acts 17, 34), formerly supposed to be the author of the work on the celestial hierarchies from which was derived much of the Renaissance theory of angels.   [35] *De plac. phil.* IV, 12.

Life of Dante.[36] Therefore the poet's imitation is icastic rather than phantastic; if it was merely an operation of the phantasy, an intellectual imagination would be understood, but this cannot be distinguished from the icastic.

[Poetry and truth]

[12] We can give another proof that the subject of the poem is rather the true than the false; it is derived from the teaching of Saint Thomas in his *Summa* and in his other works. He says that the good and the true and the one are convertible, and that the true is the good of the intellect.[37] Besides this, he thinks that evil is not a natural being.[38] Hence if it is not in any natural being, it is founded on something good, or on some good thing, for there is nothing wholly evil and bad. In this same way every multitude is based on unity, nor is there any multitude that does not participate in unity,[39] and every falsehood is founded on the truth. Hence what is wholly false cannot be the subject of poetry; indeed it does not exist. Hesiod, an old Greek poet, in his *Genealogy of the Gods* writes that the Muses know how to utter lies similar to the truth, and also know how to speak the truth, if they so desire, but absolutely he calls them daughters of Jove and tellers of the truth.[40] Hence I conclude that poetry is an art or faculty of speaking what is true or what is false, but chiefly what is true. Among the theologians, Athanasius holds an opinion not unlike what I think the best, for, writing against the Gentiles, who thought it was the function of the poet to feign what does not exist, he shows the opposite and proves it with the example of poets who uttered lies, but more about the gods than about men, for when writing of human actions they were not deceivers in everything; and he brings forward the authority of Homer himself, who if he had written falsely of everything, would have attributed timidity to Achilles and courage to Thersites.[41] Then the poet is in some ways a friend of the truth, which he renders splendid and beautiful with new colors and, so to speak, makes it new instead of old and antique. . . .[42]

---

[36] See the end of the selection from Boccaccio, above.

[37] A simplification of the teaching of Aquinas, perhaps founded on *Summa theologica,* I, 16, *De veritate* (Of Truth). Cf. Dante, *Inferno,* III, 18.

[38] *Summa,* I, 48, 1. *Utrum malum sit natura quaedam* (Is Evil an Existing Thing?).

[39] *Summa,* I, 11, 2.   [40] Hesiod, *Theogony,* 26–9.   [41] *Iliad,* II, 243–77.

[42] Cf. Shelley: "Poetry lifts the veil from the hidden beauty of the world, and makes familiar objects be as if they were not familiar." And some pages further: "It repro-

[The marvelous]

[13] However that may be, the argument of the best epic should be founded on history. But history is concerned either with false religion or with true, nor do I think the actions of pagans give us a very fitting subject on which to base an epic poem, for in such poems we determine either to have recourse to the deities that were adored by the pagans or we decide not to do so. If we do not do so, the marvelous will be lacking; if we do have recourse to the same ones as were invoked by the ancients, by that plan we are deprived of the probable and the credible. . . . I speak of the enchanted rings, the flying horses, the ships turned into nymphs, the ghosts that interpose in battles, the burning sword, the garland of flowers, the forbidden chamber . . . and other inventions that please even in prose and are gladly read and reread without the charm of verse. But if these miracles, or prodigies rather, cannot be brought about by the power of nature, it is necessary that the cause be some supernatural force or some diabolical power, and if we turn to the deities of the pagans, we for the most part give up the lifelike and the probable, or rather I would say the credible. . . . How wholly without probability, without verisimilitude, without credibility, without charm, and without authority is the marvelous that Joves and Apollos give rise to, anyone of moderate judgment can easily see on reading the modern authors, but in the ancient poets these things should be read in another frame of mind and with another taste, as it were, not merely as things received by the people but as those approved by their religion. Therefore Robertello has no reason for blaming that beauteous story and learned allegory of the branch of gold, yet he condemns it as a thing impossible.[43] If what is impossible to nature were also impossible to the gods, . . . the opinion of Robertello would be sound, but if nothing is impossible to the gods, this marvel should not be thought more nearly impossible than the others, nor does it merit more censure than the fleece of gold and the apples of gold, whose

duces the common universe of which we are portions and percipients, and it purges from our inward sight the film of familiarity which obscures from us the wonder of our being" (*Defense of Poetry*). Wordsworth also wrote: "The principal object, then, proposed in these poems was to choose incidents and situations from common life, and . . . to throw over them a certain coloring of imagination, whereby ordinary things should be presented to the mind in an unusual aspect" (Preface to the second edition of *Lyrical Ballads*).

[43] Robertello or Robortelli, Italian commentator on Aristotle's *Poetics* (1548) and editor of Longinus, *On the Sublime*. For the branch of gold, see *Aeneid*, VI, 137.

stories are told in so many poems with so much praise for the storytellers and so much delight for the readers. These things would be thought impossible by students of physics, but since to the theologians of the pagans they did not appear so, to the poets was granted this daring and free range in feigning. In fact the theologians and the ancient poets were the same, as Aristotle says in his *Metaphysics*,[44] which Robertello does not pay much attention to, for there he could have read what the theologians might write of ambrosia and other things censured by him; yet he does not censure them as a Christian theologian, whom alone this office would befit, but as a critic of the pagan poets. . . .

[Truth and the marvelous]

[14] But now let us go on with our inquiry into how what is true to life can be joined with the marvelous, without relying on the grace and the charm of verses, which are as it were enticements to persuade the ear. The natures of these two things, the marvelous and the lifelike, are very different, and different in such a way that they are like contraries, yet both of them are necessary in a poem, though the art of an excellent poet is required to couple them. The fact has, however, been performed by many, though, so far as I know, no one has taught how it is to be done. Some men of great learning, seeing the mutual repugnance of these two kinds of things, have judged that the lifelike parts of poems cannot be marvelous, and the marvelous cannot be lifelike; but since both are necessary, one should give attention part of the time to what is true to fact, part of the time to the marvelous, in such a manner that one will not yield to the other, but the one may be tempered by the other. But I do not approve this opinion, nor do I think there should be any part of the poem that does not represent the truth. The reason that moves me to this belief is as follows: Poetry is nothing else than imitation; this cannot be called in question; imitation cannot be separated from verisimilitude, for imitation is nothing else than giving a resemblance; no part, then, of poetry can be other than true to fact. In short, truth is not one of the conditions demanded from poetry for its greater beauty and ornament, but it is intrinsic to its very essence and in every part is necessary above anything else. But though I hold the epic poet to a perpetual obligation to keep to the truth, I do not therefore exclude the other quality, that is, the marvelous; rather I hold that

---

[44] Bk. III, chap. IV.

the same action can be both marvelous and true. I believe there are many modes of joining these discordant qualities; so . . . we shall speak here of what is most important for this matter. Some actions which greatly exceed the power of men the poet attributes to God, to his angels, to devils, or to those to whom God or the devils have conceded this power, such as the saints, magicians, and fairies. These actions, if they are considered of themselves, appear marvelous; in fact, they are called miracles in ordinary speech. If one regards the virtue and power of the doer, these same things will be judged true to life, because the men of the present age drank in this opinion with their milk when they were in their swaddling clothes and were confirmed in it by the teachers of our holy faith, namely that God and his ministers, and by his permission the demons and the magicians, are able to do wondrous things exceeding the force of nature; by reading and observation they seem every day to get new instances; therefore not merely what they believe is possible but what they think has often happened and can happen many times again will not seem beyond the limits of verisimilitude, just as the ancients who lived in the error of their vain religion saw no improbability in the miracles that not the poets alone but the historians as well fabled of their gods. But if learned men give us little credit, the opinion of the multitude is enough for the poet in this as in many other things, and leaving the exact truth, he does and should attend to it. The same action, then, can be both marvelous and according to verisimilitude, marvelous when thought of for itself and circumscribed within the limits of nature, true to life when considered apart from those limits and with respect to its cause, which is a force, supernatural, powerful, and accustomed to bring about similar marvels. But this method of joining the true with the marvelous is not open to those poems in which the deities of the pagans are introduced, as the *Ercole* of Giraldi,[45] and the *Costante* of Bolognetto.[46]. . .

[Good examples]

[15] And in addition if anyone wishes to form the idea of a perfect knight, I do not see that we can by any means deny him the right to praise piety and religion; for this purpose I should

---

[45] An epic on the life of Hercules.

[46] Francesco Bolognetti published his *Costante*, on the heroic adventures of the great-grandfather of Constantine the Great, in 1565–6.

greatly prefer the person of Charles or Arthur[47] to that of Theseus
or Jason. Finally, since the poet should be much concerned for
the profit of his readers, he can much better set on fire the souls
of our knights with the example of Christians than of infidels,
since the authority of those like ourselves is always more influential
than that of those unlike us, and that of those we know than of
strangers. . . . The subject of a heroic poem should then be derived
from true history and from religion that is not false. But histories
and writings are sacred or not sacred, and of the sacred some have
greater authority, if it is permitted to say so, for all spiritual things
are sacred, as it appears to Saint Thomas, but not all sacred
things are spiritual; the others without doubt have less authority.
The poet hardly dares put his hand to histories of the first quality;
but they can be left in pure and simple truth, for there is no labor
in obtaining the subject, and it appears that feigning is hardly to
be allowed in this matter; and he who may not feign and may not
imitate, since he is tied down to the exact particulars that are contained there, would not be a poet but rather a historian. In these
same histories another distinction can be made, namely, that they
contain events of our days or of very remote times or else things
neither very new or very old. In some ways the history of an age
or a nation very distant from us appears a subject well-suited for a
heroic poem, because, since those things are so buried in antiquity
that there scarcely remains a weak and obscure memory of them,
the poet is able to change them and change them again and tell of
them as he pleases.[48]

[Anachronism]

[16] But this convenience is perhaps accompanied by an inconvenience and not a small one, for with the antiquity of time it
is almost necessary that antiquity of manners be introduced into
the poem, but the manner of carrying on war used by the ancients,
their banquets, ceremonies, and other usages of a remote age
sometimes seem to our contemporaries tedious and distasteful
rather than not, as happens to some persons of little education who
read the divine works of Homer translated into another language.
The cause of a good part of this is the antiquity of the customs,
which, to those whose taste is accustomed to the refinement and

---

[47] Charlemagne appears in the *Orlando Furioso* and in many other romances. King
Arthur and his knights, well known to English readers, appear also in continental
romances.   [48] See also sect. 20, below.

propriety of the present time, are despised as old fashioned and obsolete. But one who determined to combine ancient times with modern customs would perhaps sometimes appear similar to a painter of little judgment who presents a figure of Cato or Cincinnatus clothed according to the fashions of the young men of Milan or Naples, or takes away from Hercules his club and lion's skin and equips him with a doublet and helmet, as Giraldi did in his poem,[49] though not without an important precedent, for long ago Hesiod described the arms and the shield of Hercules as though competing with Homer and told of his combat with Cycnus the son of Mars.[50] Modern histories are very convenient and easy for a poet in this matter of customs and usages, but they deprive him almost wholly of the opportunity for feigning and imitating, which is indispensable to poets, especially epic poets. Besides this, it appears that Aristotle for another reason denies to the tragic poet a subject taken from modern times, because tragedy is the imitation of men more excellent than are the moderns, and for this reason events in the present or those that happened but a short time ago should not be the subject of a heroic poem. . . .

[Tragedy and epic]

[17] If the epic and the tragic actions were of the same nature, they would produce the same effects, for from the same causes the same effects are derived, but since they produce diverse passions it follows that they are diverse in nature. Tragic actions excite horror and compassion, and if the piteous and the horrifying are lacking the tragic no longer remains. But epics do not generally in the same way produce a feeling of sadness nor is it a necessity of their nature that they should. Aristotle says that the taking of pleasure in the suffering of the wicked, though pleasing to the spectators, is not of the essence of the tragic plot, but in the heroic poem it is certainly praiseworthy. If sometimes in heroic poems there is seen something horrible or worthy of pity, horror or compassion is not sought for in all the weaving of the plot, in which we take pleasure in the victory of friends and the overthrow of enemies, but for enemies, since they are barbarians or infidels, we should not have the same pity. Nor do the actions of the tragedy and the epic present high matters in the same fashion; for their

---

[49] The *Ercole*. For Giraldi's theory on the subject see *On the Composition of Romances*, sect. 57, above. See *anachronism* in the index.
[50] Hesiod, *Shield of Hercules*, 57–end.

concern with great affairs is diverse in nature and form. In tragedy it appears in an unexpected and sudden change of fortune, and in the greatness of the happenings that produce pity and terror, but the splendid action of the heroic poem is founded on lofty military virtue and on a magnanimous resolution to die, on piety, on religion, and on actions in which these virtues are resplendent, which are in harmony with the nature of the epic and not fitting in a tragedy. Thence it comes about that the persons introduced in the two types of poem are not of the same nature, though both types deal with kings and great princes. Tragedy demands persons neither good nor wicked, but of a middle sort; such as Orestes, Electra, Jocasta, Eteocles, and Oedipus, who were judged by Aristotle very suitable for a tragic plot. The epic poet, on the contrary, requires the highest degree of virtue; therefore the persons are heroic, as their virtue is. In Aeneas is found the excellence of piety, in Achilles that of military courage, in Ulysses that of prudence. And if sometimes the tragic and the epic poet both take the same person as their subject, he is considered diversely by them and from different points of view. The epic writer considers in Hercules, Theseus, Agamemnon, Ajax, and Pyrrhus their valor and ability in arms; the tragedian is concerned with them in so far as they have fallen into infelicity through some error. Epic poets, however, run much less risk than tragedians do in taking as their subject not only the highest attainment of virtue in the persons described by them but the utmost of vice as well. Such are Mezentius, Busiris, Procrustes, Diomede, Thersites, and others of the sort; of the same kind, or not much different, are the Cyclops and the Laestrygonians, in whom savagery stands in the place of vice, though it is much more terrible than vice and more horrifying. . . .

[Love as a poetic subject]

[18] Some are of the opinion that love is not suitable material for the heroic or the tragic poet and say that in his two poems, the *Iliad* and the *Odyssey*, Homer scarcely speaks of love. . . . They assign love rather to comedy. But I have ever been of the contrary opinion, since it seems to me that the most beautiful things are well adapted to heroic poetry, and love is very beautiful, as Phaedrus thought, according to Plato.[51] But if it is neither beautiful nor ugly, as on the other hand Diotima thought,[52] it is not

---

[51] See Plato's *Symposium*, 178–80. [52] *Ibid.*, 202.

therefore fitting to comedies, which delight their audiences with
ugly things and those that move to laughter. For this reason the
old comedy ought perchance to be more praised, as Maggi believed,[53] for the new comedy has many times presented to us love
as so beautiful that it could hardly be described with more colors
in heroic poetry. But it cannot be denied that love is a passion
suitable to heroes. . . . If love is not merely a passion and a movement of the sensitive appetite but also a noble habit of the will, as
Saint Thomas thought, love will be praiseworthy in heroes and
consequently in the heroic poem. The ancients did not know this
love, or did not wish to describe it in heroes. But if they did not
honor love as a human virtue, they adored it as divine; therefore
they should have esteemed no other virtue more fitting to heroes.
Hence those actions resulting from love, in addition to the others,
could appear to them heroic. But modern poets, if they do not
wish to describe the divinity of love in those who exposed their
lives for Christ, are yet able in creating a knight to describe love
as a constant habit of the will; and so, more clearly than any of the
others, those Spanish authors have formed it who write in their
own mother tongue without any necessity for rhyme, and with so
little ambition that the name of scarcely one of them has come
down to posterity. But whoever he was who described to us
Amadigi the lover of Oriana, he merits more fame than any of the
French writers, and I do not make an exception of Arnaut
Daniel, who wrote of Lancelot, though Dante says of him:

> All verses of love and prose of romance he excelled; and let the
> fools talk who believe that he of Limoges surpasses him.[54]

But if he had read *Amadis of Gaul*, or *Amadis of Greece*, or *Primaleón*,[55]
perhaps he would have changed his opinion, for loves are described
by Spanish poets more nobly and with greater constancy than by
the French, except that *Girone il Cortese* merits to be excepted from
this number,[56] because it so severely punishes the hero's amorous
incontinence at the fountain, but certainly it deserves greater

---

[53] Author, with Lombardi, of a commentary on the *Poetics* of Aristotle (1550).

[54] *Purgatorio*, xxvi, 118–20. He of Limoges is Gerard of Borneuil.

[55] *Amadis of Gaul* was one of the romances saved from the bonfire described in
Don Quixote, i, 6; *Amadis of Greece* was burned. *Primaleón*, or *La historia de Primaleón y
Polendos*, was first published in 1548, a romance following that of *Palmerin de Oliva*, and
dealing with the sons of Palmerin.

[56] A poem of chivalry by Luigi Alamanni, first published in 1548. The reference
is to Bk. v.

praise to have produced such a disposition in the soul that no passion is able to take up arms against the reason. Hence the friendship of Girone with Danaino would have been more perfect if it had not been disturbed by love. Yet the fault of Girone is rather less serious than that of Odorico of Biscay in the *Orlando Furioso*,[57] or rather no comparison can be made between them, and if Girone had not been so near to committing a fault, his virtue doubtless would appear greater to us, but the poem would not seem so pleasing in that portion. But the virtue of Leone in the *Orlando Furioso* surpasses all the other instances that I have read of.[58] It appears to me, however, that the dispute over which is the more courteous, Leone or Ruggiero, is a foolish one, for that is not courtesy that is done against honor and justice. But it was not honest for Ruggiero to deceive Bradamante.[59] Ruggiero therefore did not show courtesy; hence his courtesy cannot vie with that of Leone, the Greek prince. . . . In short, love and friendship form a most fitting subject for a heroic poem, and if we wish to give the name of friendship to the attachment of Achilles and Patroclus, no other theme can give matter for writing in a more heroic strain. But the opinion of Dante should not be neglected, for his authority in this tongue, which is not small, can be used as the foundation of our opinion. He says in his book *On the Vulgar Tongue* that there are three things that should be sung in the most elevated style: salvation, love, and virtue,[60] salvation because it is profitable, love because it is delightful, virtue because it is noble. But if the highest style is the tragic in so far as it is the same as the epic or in so far as it includes it, there is no doubt that love should be sung in the heroic poem. But such a poem considers love delightful, and love can also be considered as noble, or as a knightly virtue, that is, as a habit of the will. Let it be admitted, then, that a heroic poem can be formed with an amorous subject, such as the love of Leander and Hero, of which Musaeus,[61] a very ancient Greek poet, wrote, and that of Jason and Medea, of which Apollonius wrote among the Greeks and Valerius Flaccus among the Latins,[62] . . . and the

---

[57] XIII, 12 ff.

[58] *Orlando Furioso*, XLV, 41 ff. Leone resigned Bradamante, whom he hoped to marry, to his friend Ruggiero.

[59] By disguising himself to fight in Leone's interests.

[60] Dante, *On the Vulgar Tongue*, II, 4.

[61] Musaeus (sixth century B. C.), *Hero and Leander*.

[62] Apollonius Rhodius, *Argonautica*, Bks. III and IV. Valerius Flaccus, *Argonautica*, Bks. V–VIII.

loves of Theagenes and Chariclea, and of Leucippe and Clitophon, which were written of in the same language by Heliodorus[63] and Achilles Tatius;[64] or the others of Arcite and Palamon, and of Florio and Biancofiore, of whom Boccaccio wrote poems in our language;[65] or the adventures of Pyramus and Thisbe, who gave matter for a little poem by Tasso my father;[66] or the madness of Narcissus, from which Alamanni took a subject.[67]

[The noble action]

[19] But in this idea of the perfect poem that we now go searching for, it is needful for us to consider nobility and excellence more than everything else. Therefore we should select actions in which there is the greatest possible amount of nobility, as in the undertaking of the Argonauts who went for the golden fleece, of which first Orpheus[68] and then Apollonius[69] wrote their poems. This requirement is equally satisfied by the Trojan war and the wanderings of Ulysses sung by Homer, the siege of Thebes and the youth of Achilles written by Statius,[70] the *Civil War* put in verse by Lucan, and the second African war versified by Silius Italicus[71] and Petrarch, who in the loves of Massinissa surpassed the first by a great distance.[72] But an action noble beyond all the others is the coming of Aeneas into Italy, because the subject is in itself great and splendid, and yet more great and splendid because the Roman Empire took origin from it, as in the beginning of the *Aeneid* the divine poet writes:

So great a labor was it to lay the foundations of the Roman people.

[63] The *Aethiopica* of Heliodorus, the most famous of Greek romances, tells of the loves of Theagenes and Chariclea. A Latin translation appeared in 1552. See the index.

[64] Achilles Tatius, *Leucippe and Clitophon*, a Greek romance of the fifth or sixth century. A Latin translation appeared in 1554.

[65] Boccaccio (1313–75) in the *Teseide*, or poem on Theseus, presents Palamon and Arcite. Chaucer retold their story in "The Knight's Tale." The *Filocolo* gives the story of Florio and Biancofiore.

[66] Bernardo Tasso, *The Story of Pyramus and Thisbe*.

[67] Alamanni, *The Fable of Narcissus*, published in 1532.

[68] To him was attributed an epic poem, called *Argonautica*, on his own exploits during the voyage of the Argonauts.

[69] Apollonius Rhodius, *Argonautica*, a Greek epic composed in the third century B. C.

[70] Statius, *The Thebaid*, the story of the strife at Thebes between the children of Oedipus; *The Achilleid*.

[71] Lucan (first century A.D.), *The Pharsalia*. Silius Italicus (died in 102 A.D.), *Punica*.

[72] Petrarch (1304–74) left unfinished the *Africa*, an epic poem in Latin on the second Punic war.

Such was the liberation of Italy from the Goths, which furnished material for the poem of Trissino;[73] such are those enterprises for the confirmation of the Christian faith or for the exaltation of the Church and the Empire that were fortunately and gloriously accomplished.[74] These actions in themselves win over the souls of the readers and produce expectation and marvelous pleasure, and when the art of an able poet is added there is nothing they cannot accomplish in our souls.

[The perfect subject]

[20] The poet should then avoid feigned subjects, especially if it is feigned that something has come about in a land near at hand and well known and among a friendly people, for among distant peoples and in unknown countries we can easily feign many things without taking away authority from the story.[75] Therefore from the land of the Goths and from Norway and Sweden and Iceland or from the East Indies or the countries recently discovered in the vast ocean beyond the pillars of Hercules, the subjects of such poems should be taken.[76] The poet should not touch those subjects that cannot be treated poetically and in which there is no place for fiction and artistry, and he should reject subjects too rude, to which he cannot add splendor, and should remember that precept of Horace:

> Abandon a subject if you fear you cannot make it splendid by
> your treatment.[77]

He should reject what is badly arranged as though it were a stick of timber too crooked to be good for building; he should refuse materials too dry and arid, which do not give much scope to the ability and art of the poet, and above all those that are unpleasant and annoying, and those that end unhappily, as the death of the Paladins and the defeat at Roncesvalles.[78] . . . The

[73] The *Italy Liberated from the Goths;* see the index under *Trissino.*

[74] Apparently a reference to the Crusades, the first of which Tasso dealt with in his epic of *Jerusalem Delivered.*

[75] On this subject cf. Mazzoni, *On the Defense of the "Comedy,"* Bk. III, chap. VI, above.

[76] The *Lusiad* of Camoens, the national epic of Portugal, deals with the East Indies, and *La Araucana,* by Alonso de Ercilla, with South America. Both authors were contemporaries of Tasso. The curate in *Don Quixote* pronounced the *Araucana* one of the three best heroic poems in Spanish, able to compete with the most famous of Italy (*Don Quixote* I, 6).

[77] Modified from Horace, *Art of Poetry,* 149–50.

[78] The defeat of part of Charlemagne's army on its retirement from Spain is the subject of *The Song of Roland.* Tasso looked on it as an overthrow of Christians by pagans.

poet should not become fascinated with material too subtle, and
fitted for the schools of the theologians and the philosophers rather
than the palaces of princes and the theaters, and he should not
show himself ambitious in the questions of nature and theology,[79]
and should not forget what Horace says in praise of Homer, putting him higher than many philosophers who have written of
virtue and nobility, as may be read in the second epistle to Lollius:

> While you, Lollius Maximus, declaim at Rome, I have been
> reading afresh at Praeneste the writer of the Trojan War; who
> tells us what is fair, what is foul, what is helpful, what is not,
> more plainly and better than Chrysippus or Crantor (ll. 1–4).

Nor should the poet show himself too curious in the knowledge of
antiquity that is obscure and as it were forgotten, when the obscurity is not that of things that are very great and worthy of
knowledge; he should despise trifles rather than not; in the witty
he should be magnificent, in the hidden he should be clear, and
in all he should excite wonder; he should not be too lengthy in
describing sacred or secular ceremonies; in games he should be
ornate, and vigorous, and put events before our eyes, and not
describe all that is done, but the more famous and splendid, and
those that are imitations of war or warlike exercises, as Homer and
Vergil did, one in the obsequies of Patroclus, the other in the
burial of Anchises. But now the place of games has been taken by
tournaments and jousts, which have been splendidly described by
our poets, as by Ariosto that of Damascus and by Tasso that of
Cornwall with more propriety,[80] for in England they were accustomed to conduct them but it was not the custom of the Turks and
Saracens to joust; hence Gemma, the brother of Bajazet II, when
he was a prisoner in Rome was in the habit of saying that there
was too much play and too little reality. The poet should also have
in mind the glory of the nation, the origin of cities, famous families,
and princes of kingdoms and empires, as did Vergil beyond all the
others. But he should not be too free in feigning things that are
impossible, monstrous, supernatural, and unfitting, as did the man
who wished to imitate the fable of Tiresias, who struck the serpents
twice and was first transformed from a man to a woman and then

---

[79] Cf. Castelvetro on *Poetics*, I, sect. 29, 10 ff., above.
[80] For Damascus, see Ariosto, *Orlando Furioso*, XVIII, 132. But these jousts are not
fully described; we are merely told that they were held and that Sansonetto won the
prize. Bernardo Tasso tells of jousts in Cornwall in his *Amadigi*.

from a woman to a man, for it was not a happy thought to transform Rinaldo into a woman. The author should consider the
power of the magic art and of nature itself, as though inclosed
within certain limits and confined by certain laws, and ancient
and forgotten prodigies, and the occasions of marvels and miracles
and monstrous events, and the diversity of religions, and the dignity of the persons, and should seek as much as he can to increase
faith in the marvel without diminishing the pleasure. He should
therefore not reject incantations or hunting scenes, though they
show the pursuit of terrible animals such as have seldom been
seen. . . . In this matter we may follow the authority of the
ancients in the hunt of the boar killed by Atalanta, which supplied
the cause for the unhappiness of Meleager, celebrated by the
Greek and Latin poets, and in that of the bull overcome by
Theseus, and of the serpents killed by Hercules. He describes
tempests, great fires, voyages, countries and particular places; he
takes pleasure in the description of battles by land and by sea, of
assaults on cities, of the drawing up of an army, and of the method
of encamping it. But in this he avoids excess and tempers the
unpleasantness of too detailed instruction. . . . The poet should be
similarly careful in his descriptions of hunger, thirst, sickness, the
sunrise, the sunset, midday, midnight, the seasons of the year, the
quality of the months or of the days, whether rainy, or clear, or
calm, or stormy. But in councils and assemblies he can confidently write at greater length with the authority of the ancient
poets. And in describing arms, impresses,[81] horses, ships, temples,
pavilions, tents, paintings, and statues and other similar things, he
should always have in mind what is fitting, and avoid the irritation that too great length always causes. In deaths he should seek
for variety, effectiveness, pathos; in encounters with the lance,
and in blows with the sword, for verisimilitude, not passing too far
beyond what has come about or can come about or is believed or
told of. In menaces he should be lofty and bitter, in laments short
and full of feeling, in jests playful and gracious. He should not
conceal things that are true in antiquity and as though in the
clouds; he should not show feigned things in the light of the sun,
but rather in the darkness, like goods that in that way are more
easily sold. Of the ages between our times and high antiquity he

[81] Individual symbolic devices worn on the shield and elsewhere. Sidney describes
a number in the *Arcadia*, e.g., III, II. Milton declared he was "not sedulous by nature
. . . to describe . . . impresses quaint" (*Paradise Lost*, IX, 27–35).

should select those removed from our memory a convenient distance, like a painter who does not put his picture close before our faces nor yet so distant that it cannot be made out, but suitably disposes it in the light in a high place. He chooses the most beautiful among beautiful things, the grandest among the grand, the most marvelous among the marvelous, and to the most marvelous he seeks to add novelty and greatness. Necessary things, such as eating and preparing food, he leaves out or describes briefly, as Vergil describes them in the following passage:

> They gird themselves to deal with the game, their forthcoming meal; strip the hide from the ribs, and lay bare the flesh—some cut it into pieces and impale it yet quivering on spits, others set up the caldrons on the beach, and supply them with flame. Then with food they recall their strength, and, stretched along the turf, feast on old wine and fat venison to their hearts' content.[82]

But such descriptions are pleasing in proportion as they are more distant from us in place and their methods are different from ours. Our poet should also disdain all low things, all that are popular, all that are indecent, like the story of Fiametta and that of the Doctor.[83] Things not on a high level he should elevate; to the obscure he should give the effect of being generally known and illustrious, he should supply art to the simple, ornament to the true, authority to the false. If he sometimes makes use of shepherds, goatherds, swineherds, and other persons of that sort, he should have regard not merely to fitness of person but also to that of the poem, and show them as they are in royal palaces and on occasions of ceremony.[84]

[Summary of Book II]

[21] Here are the conditions that the judicious poet should seek in his matter. Briefly summarizing what has already been

---

[82] *Aeneid,* I, 210–15, trans. by Conington. Tasso quotes also the similar passages I, 637–42; 701–6.   [83] *Orlando Furioso,* XXVIII, 57–74; XLIII, 72–144.

[84] This whole section may be illustrated by the practice of Tasso in his *Jerusalem Delivered,* for example, a battle VII, 106–21; an army arrayed XX, 8–10; a city assaulted XVIII, 68–105; sunrise III, 1; IX, 74; XVIII, 12; assemblies I, 20–34; IV, 4–17; a helmet IX, 25; an impress VIII, 49; decorated doors XVI, 2–7; deaths IX, 32–8; XIX, 26; blows with the sword IX, 31–9; IX, 68–70; XX, 120. Similar examples can be found in Spenser's *Faerie Queene.* Milton, according to a reference in his tractate *Of Education,* had read Tasso's advice and perhaps profited by it, as in the description of the council in *Paradise Lost,* II, 1–506, of a battle in VI, 189–866, of dawn in V, 1–2, of an army in *Paradise Regained,* III, 299–336.

said, they are the authority of history, the truth of religion, opportunity to feign new stories, attention to the nature of the times, and greatness in the events represented.

Book III

[The divinity of art]

[22] Let us go on to consider the idea of things formed by art, for the operations of art appear to us as though divine and in imitation of God, the first artist. . . .

[The universal]

[23] When the poet has selected material in itself capable of every perfection, there remains to him the other still more difficult task of giving it poetic form and disposition; this is a procedure on which, as its most appropriate object, art expends its utmost strength. Because what chiefly constitutes the nature of poetry and makes it different from history is not verse, as Aristotle says,[85] . . . but is the consideration of things not as they are but as they ought to be—with regard rather to the universal than to the truth of particulars—the poet before anything else should consider whether in the matter he is to treat there is any event which, if it happened otherwise, would be more marvelous, or more true to life, or for any other reason would cause greater delight. Everything he can find of that sort, that is, anything that would have been better if it had happened in some other way, he may, without any regard to truth or history, alter and change as he wishes, arranging, rearranging, and modifying the circumstances as he thinks best, and mingling the false with the true, but in such a way that the true will be the foundation of the plot. . . . Vergil in the wanderings of Aeneas and in the war fought between him and Latinus did not write merely things he thought true, but what he judged better and more excellent, for not merely are the love and death of Dido false, and the story of Polyphemus and the descent of Aeneas to the lower world fabulous, but the battles between Aeneas and the people of Latium are described otherwise than as they truly came about. . . . And in the story of Dido he makes great confusion in the order of time by means of that figure the Greeks call anachronism,[86] or rather with that license first used by Plato and the Greek poets who introduce as speaking together men

---

[85] *Poetics*, I.　　　　　　[86] See the index.

who lived in different ages, as Athenaeus notes in the *Banquet of the Deipnosophists*.[87] This license was likewise used by Ovid in his *Metamorphoses*, at the end of which Pythagoras, an Italian philosopher, gives instruction to Numa, king of the Romans, though it is certain that Pythagoras was born some hundreds of years later than Numa. The same theory or the same artistic practice of mingling the true with the false or with the feigned can be learned from Horace[88] and from Plutarch at the beginning of his *Life of Theseus*[89] . . . and from Plato himself, and by Xenophon in his *Cyropaedia*, and though the last was not a poet, but a philosopher and a historian, yet, in his outlook on the universal and the ideal, he was more like the poets than like the historians.[90]. . . With this authority of old and new writers Vergil can be defended, but he perhaps sought occasion for mingling with the severity of other matters some pleasant discourses of love, though the death of Dido, a terrible and unhappy event, might follow; or rather he wished to assign a noble and inherited cause to the enmity between Romans and Carthaginians. . . .

[Poetic license]

[24] The license of the poet should not extend so far that he dares to change the outcome of the actions he undertakes to treat, or to narrate anything contrary to the issue of some of the principal and best-known events which are accepted as true by the opinion of the world. . . . Our epic poet, then, should retain, with little or no change, the truth about the origin and the end of the action and the other things best known and accepted in common report; he may change, if it appears well to him, the means and the circumstances, and may confuse the temporal connections and the relations of the other things, and in short may show himself a poet, working artistically, rather than a veracious historian, keeping ever in mind what was said by Plutarch in his book *On the Fortune of the Romans*, that is, that the man who conceals falsehood in the antiquity of the ages is like him who escapes from brightly lighted places into those that are dark and shady.[91]

[87] Bk. v, 216c.   [88] *Art of Poetry*, 119–30, 240–3, above.
[89] "Let us hope that fable may, in what shall follow, so submit to the purifying processes of reason as to take the character of exact history. In any case, however, where it shall be found contumaciously slighting credibility, and refusing to be reduced to anything like probable fact, we shall beg that we may meet with candid readers, and such as will receive with indulgence the stories of antiquity" (Dryden and Clough's trans. [Boston, 1916]).   [90] See the index, under *Xenophon*.   [91] Sect. 2.

[Poetry and fact]

[25] But if in the material he has chosen there are some actions that happened just as the poet wishes, what shall he do? Can he relate them in his poem? Most certainly, if his narrative is poetical, and he does not despoil himself of the person of the poet to put on that of the historian, for at times it can happen that one man as poet, another as historian may deal with the same matter, though they will look at it differently, for the historian narrates it as true, the poet imitates it as like the truth. . . . If Lucan is not a poet, this is because he is in bondage to the truth of particulars rather than attending to the universal, and, as it seems to Quintilian,[92] is more like an orator than a poet. In addition, the order followed by Lucan is not the order appropriate to the poet but the true and natural order in which are narrated things that have already happened; he has this in common with the historian.[93]

[Suspense]

[26] But in the artistic order, which Castelvetro calls the perturbed order,[94] some of the early events should be first narrated, and others postponed, others should be passed over for the present and reserved for a better time, as Horace teaches.[95] The author should give first those without which there would be no knowledge of the present state of affairs, but if possible should remain silent about many, for to tell them would diminish the expectation and the astonishment of the reader, who should always be kept in suspense and desirous of reading further.

[Unity]

[27] Unity is the topic which has given to our times occasion for various and long contests among those "whom the fury of letters leads into war." Some have judged unity necessary; others, on the contrary, have thought a multitude of actions more suitable for heroic poetry, and "each one considers himself a great judge." The defenders of unity, making a shield of the authority of Aristotle and the majesty of the ancient Greek and Latin poets, and not lacking the arms that are given by reason, have as adversaries

[92] x, 1, 90. See also *Lucan* in the index.

[93] In his letter to Sir Walter Raleigh (above) Spenser explains that in the *Faerie Queene* he does not follow the chronological order, as would a "historiographer."

[94] *Commentary* on the *Poetics* of Aristotle, 156, 19 ff.

[95] *Art of Poetry*, 148, above.

the habit of the present age, the universal agreement of ladies, knights, and courts, and, as it seems, experience as well, an infallible touchstone of the truth. It is evident that Ariosto, who, leaving the path trod by the ancient writers and the rules of Aristotle, has included in his poem many and diverse actions, is read and reread by persons of all ages and by both sexes, is known to speakers of all languages, pleases all, is praised by all, lives, and ever renews the youth of his fame, and flies in glory over the tongues of mortals. Yet Trissino, on the contrary, who determined to imitate religiously the poems of Homer and to observe the precepts of Aristotle, is named by few, and read by very few, is mute in the theater of the world and dead to the light,[96] and can hardly be found buried in the libraries and in the study of some scholar. Nor are there lacking in favor of this plan, in addition to experience, solid and striking arguments, since some men both learned and ingenious, either because they truly think so or merely to show the force of their ability and to make themselves acceptable to the world, which flatters this universal agreement as though it were a tyrant (for such it truly is), have found new and subtle reasons with which they have confirmed it and made it stronger. . . .

[Unity a general law]

[28] But against this virtual law of poetry, that of unity (which was accepted as good by Horace when he said: Let what is treated be simple and one),[97] various men have directed opposition supported with various reasons, excluding unity of plot from those heroic poems that are called romances, not merely as unnecessary but even as damaging.[98] [He then proceeds to show that the romance is of the same kind as the epic.] If then the romance and the epic are of the same species, they should be confined by the same bonds of law, especially when these laws are absolutely necessary not merely to the heroic poem, but to every poem. Such a law is unity of plot, which Aristotle prescribes for every species of poem, not more for the heroic than for the tragic and the comic.[99] Therefore if what is said of the romance is true [that it differs from the epic] it would not therefore follow that unity of plot would not according to the idea of Aristotle be necessary to it. . . .

---

[96] Cf. Lope de Vega, *New Art of Making Comedies*, sect. 1, below.
[97] *Art of Poetry*, 23, above.
[98] For Giraldi's opinion see his *Discourse on the Romances*, sect. 44, above.
[99] Cf. Castelvetro on *Poetics*, VIII, 178, 39, above.

[Unity not fitted to classical languages only]

[29] The second reason was that every tongue has some individual quality, and that a number of actions is appropriate to Tuscan poetry, as is unity to Greek and Latin poetry. I do not deny that each language has some forms peculiar to itself. . . . But what is the particular property of one language is either a matter of speech, and not of importance in this matter, since we are speaking of actions, not of words, or we should make the peculiar property of a language these matters that are better treated by it than by any other, as is war by the Latin language and love by the Tuscan. But it is plain that if the Tuscan speech is fitted to set forth many amorous happenings, it is equally fitted to set forth one, and if the Latin tongue is fitted to deal with one warlike event, it will be equally fitted to deal with many. So for my part I cannot understand the reason why unity of action is appropriate for Latin poems and multiplicity of action for those in the vulgar tongue. . . .

[Unity and nature]

[30] It is not more difficult to deal with the third reason, which was that those poems are most excellent that are most approved in practice; the romance would therefore be more excellent than the epic, being more approved in practice. Wishing to contradict this reason, it is necessary that for greater intelligibility and clearness of the truth I should derive my reasoning from a remote beginning. Some things in their nature are neither good nor bad, but, since they depend on custom, are good or bad as custom determines. Such is clothing, which is commendable in proportion as it is accepted by custom. . . . There are other things the quality of which is determined by their nature; that is, they are either good or evil in themselves and custom has no rule or authority over them. Of this sort are vice and virtue; vice is evil in itself; virtue is admirable in itself; virtuous and vicious actions are in themselves commendable and blameworthy. And what has this characteristic in itself, though customs may vary, always has this characteristic. Hence the eating of human flesh will always be reputed savage, though it was practiced by some nations. Chastity always has been and always will be a virtue, though the Spartan women were not esteemed chaste. If at any time the man deserved praise who refused the gold of the Samnites, or that man

who bound himself when he was alive and released his father who was dead, they will never be blamed for such noble acts. Of the same kind are the acts of nature, for in spite of the instability of custom, what was once excellent will always be excellent. Nature is very stable in its operations and ever proceeds with a certain and perpetual tenor, even if it sometimes seems to vary because of the weakness and inconstancy of the matter it works on, for, directed by a light and guide that are infallible, it considers always the good and the perfect; and since the good and the perfect are always the same, it is needful that its mode of working always be the same. Beauty is a work of nature, and since it consists in a certain proportion of limb with a fitting size and beautiful and pleasing coloring,[100] these conditions that once were beautiful in themselves will ever be beautiful, nor can custom bring about that they will appear otherwise; as on the contrary custom cannot bring about that pointed heads and goitres will appear beautiful even among those nations where they are seen in the majority of men and women. But if such in themselves are the works of nature, such must needs be the works of that art which without any intermediary is an imitator of nature. Thence it is reasonable for Cicero in his *Topics*[101] to enumerate nature and art among the causes that are unchangeable, for their effects are invariable, as Boethius says in his commentary on that passage. And to linger over the example that has been given, if the proportion of the members in itself is beautiful, it will be in itself beautiful when imitated by the painter and the sculptor, and if something in nature is worthy of admiration, the artificial thing that is similar to the natural will also be admirable. Thence it happens that those statues by Praxiteles and Phidias that have survived the attacks of envious Time appear as beautiful in our eyes as they did in those of the ancients, nor has the flight of so many ages or the alterations of so many customs been able to lessen their dignity. Having made this distinction, I can easily answer the argument that those poets are most excellent who are most approved in practice, for every piece of poetry is composed of words and things. In respect to the words it may be conceded (since they have nothing to do with our contention) they are the best that are most approved by practice, for in themselves they are neither beautiful nor ugly, but they appear such as custom makes them, so that some words that were highly regarded by the Emperor Frederick and King

[100] Cf. Aristotle, *Poetics*, VII, 50b34, above.　　　　[101] Sect. 16.

Enzio and other old writers have in our ears I do not know what that is displeasing. Things then that depend on custom, as the manner of jousting, the customs of sacrifices and banquets, ceremonies, the decorum and dignity of persons can, I believe, be arranged as befits the customs that exist and rule the world today. It would therefore be unfitting to the majesty of our times that the daughter of a king, with her maiden companions, should go to wash clothes in the river, yet in the time of Nausicaa, told of by Homer, it was not deserving of reprehension.[102] Equally he who instead of jousts should describe combats with chariots would merit little praise. But the things that in themselves are good do not have any regard for custom nor does the tyranny of convention extend over them in any respect. Such is unity of plot, which carries in its nature goodness and perfection for the poem, as in every age, past and future, it has carried and will carry it. Such are human traits, not those that are called by the name of customs, but those by which we may form the habits that can be put among constant causes. . . . Of them Horace speaks in these verses:

> The child who now knows how to speak and to walk with a firm step delights in play with other children, and easily gets angry and easily forgets his anger, and changes from one hour to the other.[103]

And Aristotle at length in the *Rhetoric*.[104] Any of these characteristics of the boy, the old man, the rich man, the powerful man, the noble and ignoble man that are suitable in one age will be suitable in every age. Were this not so, Aristotle would not have spoken of it, for he professes to teach only those things that fall within the realm of art, and since art is fixed and determined, nothing can be comprehended within its rules which, being dependent on the instability of custom, is mutable and uncertain. Similarly he would not have discussed unity of plot if he had not thought it necessary in every age. But while some wish to found a new art on new custom, they destroy the nature of art and show that they do not know that of custom. . . .

[Variety][105]

[31] The last reason against unity remains, which was that since the end of poetry is delight, those poems are most excellent

---

[102] *Odyssey*, vi.
[104] Bk. ii, chaps. 12–17.

[103] *Art of Poetry*, 158–60, above.
[105] See the index.

which most nearly attain this end, but the romance arrives nearer
to it than does the epic, as experience shows. Let us concede what
we could deny, namely, that delight is the end of poetry. I concede also what experience shows us, to wit, that greater delight is
given to men of our day by the *Orlando Furioso* than by the *Italy
Liberated*[106] or even by the *Iliad* or the *Odyssey*. But I deny that the
concession is of great importance or applies at all to our argument,
that is, that a number of actions are more fitted to delight than unity,
for the opposite can be proved on the authority of Aristotle and
with the proof he gives in the *Problems*.[107] And though the *Orlando
Furioso*, which contains a number of plots, is more delightful than
any other Tuscan poem, or even than the poems of Homer, that is
not the result of unity or of number, but of two reasons that have
no application to our theme. The one is that in the *Furioso* one
can read of loves, knighthood, adventure, and incantations, and in
short, inventions very delightful and well suited to our ears; the
other is that in the propriety of action and in the decorum of persons Ariosto is more excellent than any of the others.[108] These
causes are accidental to the multiplicity and the unity of the plot,
and not in such a fashion fitted to the one type that they are not
fitted to the other as well. Thence it should not be concluded that
multiplicity is more pleasing than unity. But perhaps it can be
proved by another reason, for, since our humanity is composed of
natural qualities rather different among themselves, it is necessary
that it should not always be delighted by one and the same thing, but
by means of diversity should contrive to satisfy now one, now
another of its parts. Since then variety is very delightful to our
nature, it can be said that much greater delight is found in multiplicity than in unity of plot. I do not deny that variety gives
pleasure, for the denial would contradict experience and our perceptions, since we see that things displeasing in themselves through
their variety become pleasant to us, and that the sight of deserts
and the roughness and severity of the mountains please us after
the softness of lakes and gardens. I say that variety is pleasing just
so long as it does not pass over into confusion, and unity is quite
capable of variety up to that point, for to unity . . . multiplicity is
accidental, and if such diversity is not seen in a poem of one action,

---

[106] By Trissino. Cf. Tasso's remarks in sect. 19, above.

[107] *Problems*, xviii, 9: "Why do we take more pleasure in listening to narratives in
which the attention is concentrated on a single point than in hearing those concerned
with many subjects?"   [108] See the index under *decorum*.

we can believe it comes rather from the lack of skill of the artists than from a defect inherent in art itself, for artists, perhaps to excuse their own insufficiency, attribute their own faults to art. Perhaps this variety was less necessary in the times of Vergil and Homer,[109] since the men of that age were less sated in their tastes; at any rate they did not attain so much, though more is found in Vergil than in Homer. Variety is especially pleasing to our times,[110] and therefore our poets have to season their poems with this spice of variety if they wish not to be rejected by our delicate palates, and if some of them do not attempt to introduce it, either they do not understand the need for it or they despair of it as impossible. I too think it very pleasant in a heroic poem and possible of introduction there, for in this admirable realm of God called the world, the sky is seen to be scattered over and beautified with a great variety of stars, and descending lower from region to region, the air and the sea are full of birds and fishes, and the earth harbors many animals both fierce and gentle, and in it we can see many streams, fountains, lakes, fields, plains, forests, and mountains, here fruits and flowers, there ice and snow, here dwellings and cultivation, there solitude and wild places. Yet for all that, the world, which includes in its bosom so many and so diverse things, is one, one in its form and essence, one the knot with which its parts are joined and bound together in discordant concord; and while there is nothing lacking in it, yet there is nothing there that does not serve either for necessity or ornament. I judge that in the same way the great poet (who is called divine for no other reason but that, because he resembles in his works the supreme architect, he comes to participate in his divinity) is able to form a poem in which as in a little world can be read in one passage how armies are drawn up, and in various others there are battles by land and sea, attacks on cities, skirmishes, duels, jousts, descriptions of hunger and thirst, tempests, conflagrations, prodigies; there are a variety of celestial and infernal councils, and the reader encounters seditions, discords, wanderings, adventures, incantations, works of cruelty, audacity, courtesy, and generosity, and actions of love, now unhappy, now happy, now pleasing, now causing compassion. Yet in spite of all,

---

[109] Cf. Giraldi's presentation of the variety of Vergil especially (*On the Romances*, sect. 42, above).

[110] Julius Caesar Scaliger writes: "Variety, which we have so often advised, is the greatest of all poetic virtues" (*Poetice*, IV, 48, near the end, p. 212D2; see also III, 25, p. 113D1; III, 27, p. 116D2; III, 28 is devoted to variety in the *Aeneid*). See *variety* in the index.

the poem that contains so great variety of matter is one, one is its form and its soul; and all these things are put together in such a way that one has relation to the other, one corresponds to the other, the one necessarily or apparently so depends on the other that if one part is taken away or changed in position the whole is destroyed. And if this is true, the art of composing a poem is like the nature of the universe, which is composed of contraries, such as appear in the law of music, for if there were no multiplicity there would be no whole, and no law, as Plotinus says.

[Unity difficult]

[32] But this variety will be so much the more marvelous in proportion as it carries with it more difficulty and as it were impossibility, for contrary qualities cannot be found together except in ascending order, as in the heavens, or at least abated as in the elements. In a poem then in which tragedy is joined with comedy, laughter should not be laughter except blunted. It surely is an easy thing to bring it about that in many and separate actions there should be a variety of events, but that the same variety should be furnished by one sole action, *hoc opus, hic labor est.*[111] In that variety which arises from the multitude of the plots in themselves, no art or ingenuity of the poet is to be observed, and it is common to both learned and ignorant. Variety in the unified plot depends on the skill of the poet, and when it is attained is recognized as the result of his skill and as not to be achieved by any moderate capacities. The multiple plot will delight the less in proportion as it is more confused and less intelligible; the unified plot because of its arrangement and the binding together of its parts will not merely be more clear and distinct but will appear much more novel and marvelous. The plot and the form should then be one in every sort of poem, including those that treat of arms and the loves of heroes and of errant knights, which generally are called heroic poems. . . .

[Qualities of heroic poetry]

[33] The heroic style is not remote from the gravity of tragic style nor from the beauty of lyric style, but it exceeds both the one and the other in the splendor of its wonderful majesty. Yet it is not inappropriate to the epic poet that issuing sometimes from the

---

[111] Vergil, *Aeneid*, VI, 129: "this the task, this the labor." Cf. Castelvetro on *Poetics*, VIII, 179, 14, above.

limits of his splendid magnificence, he should cause his style to approach the gravity of the tragic writer, as he often does; at other times, though more rarely, he can cause it to approach the flowery ornament of lyric style. But the style of a tragedy, though it describes glorious events and royal personages, for two reasons should be less sublime than the heroic. The first is that it normally deals with matter of a more passionate sort, and passion demands purity and simplicity, for it is likely that in that manner a person would speak who is full of anxiety, fear, pity, or some similar disturbance.[112] The other cause is that in a tragedy the poet never speaks, but only those who carry on the action of the play, to whom should be assigned a manner of speaking less strange and less unlike that of ordinary life than epic diction. But the chorus perhaps should speak more loftily, for, as Aristotle says in the *Problems*,[113] it is a sort of guardian that is additional and separate, and for the same reason the poet speaks more loftily in his own person and discourses as though with another tongue, like one who feigns to be rapt out of himself by divine inspiration. . . .

Book VI

[Comedy]

[34] Many have thought the delight that springs from things full of grace is the same as laughter; therefore they have sought to move this delight everywhere, and all their writings are full of their attempt to do it; they have wished to sprinkle as it were with this salt their stories, letters, orations, satires and other burlesque poems, comedies, heroic poetry, and even tragedy itself, which gladly receives grace but is the enemy of laughter, as Demetrius of Phalerum says.[114] And according to my opinion heroic poetry is of the same nature, though it may move a terrible laugh by means of the Cyclops; but in the same way the tragedy of Euripides called by that name can move laughter, if indeed it is a tragedy, and not a satyr drama as some have believed; yet if it is a tragic poem it is

---

[112] See *tragedy, language of*, in the index.

[113] The chorus "takes no active part" (*Problems*, trans. by E. S. Forster [Oxford, 1927], XIX, 48, 922b26). But in 922b20, Aristotle says that a quiet musical mode is suited to the chorus.

[114] "There is, indeed, one place in which the arts of laughter and of charm are found together, in the satyric drama and in comedy. It is different, however, with tragedy, which often welcomes charm, but finds in laughter a sworn foe" (*On Style*, trans. by Rhys Roberts [New York, 1927], sect. 169).

of the less perfect sort, for laughter would probably have no place in the more perfect, as it does not have in the heroic poem, except in the manner that has been mentioned, full of bitterness and terror and far from the immodest; indeed this is not properly laughter, for laughter arises from ugly things without pain. The words, then, that put ugliness before our eyes can move us to laughter, for they, being as it were images of ugly things, are ugly words. But beautiful words are the cause of that gracious delight that is fitting for the heroic and the lyric poet beyond all others, and is also fitting to tragedy, but less so. Laughter and the gracious, then, arise from two opposite causes, that is, one from the beautiful and one from the ugly, and they are as different as are Thersites and Cupid. But both of them arise with astonishment, because astonishment is in the habit of accompanying both. Therefore we marvel at dwarfs and at an ugly old woman who has the face of a monkey as did Gabrina,[115] and we marvel also at the beauty of a girl; for that reason Laura was called a monster by her gentle poet:

O proud and rare monster among ladies.[116]

But though astonishment arises from either kind of poetry, that is, from that which imitates ugly things and from that which resembles beautiful things, yet it is not so suited to one as to the other, for astonishment rapidly disappears from ugly things, which as they lose their novelty lose the power to astonish us, but our astonishment at beautiful things is more durable and of higher value. And beautiful beyond all other poems is the heroic; hence this delight is its peculiar property. The heroic is also the most magnificent of poems; this is another reason why such astonishment is appropriate to it. . . .

[Teaching by example]

[35] There are two modes of teaching by example, one that of inciting to good works by showing the reward of the noblest virtue and of well-nigh divine valor, the other that of frightening us from evil with a punishment. The first is that of the epic, the second that of tragedy, which for that reason is less beneficial and also causes less delight, for man is not of so fierce and wicked a nature as to put his greatest pleasure in sorrow and in the unhappiness of those who through some human error have fallen into misery.

[115] *Orlando Furioso*, xx, 120.   [116] Petrarch, *Donna, che lieta col principio nostro*.

GIAMBATTISTA GUARINI

❍◯ooo◯o

THE COMPENDIUM OF TRAGICOMIC POETRY

1599

By 1585 GUARINI had finished his play entitled *The Pastor Fido, a Pastoral Tragicomedy;* it was printed for the first time in 1590. Its popularity was so great that the edition of 1602, supervised as definitive by the author, was the twentieth. Such wide circulation did not result from approval alone; the play was vigorously attacked in works that themselves acquired some circulation. For example, a tiny volume of objections by Malacreta was in its second edition in 1600. The most important opponent was Giasone di Nores, who published his censures in 1587. Guarini replied in 1590 and again in 1593. His two replies were then combined and revised to appear in 1601, as the *Compendium of Tragicomic Poetry,* which is here translated in part. Obviously it should represent the mature thought of its author.

The nature of the most important objections may be gathered from the defense against them. Essentially they are that the author has flown in the face of the Aristotelian tradition by writing a pastoral drama; such a work was not discussed by Aristotle, who authorized only tragedy and comedy. Still further, the tragicomedy, pastoral or not, is illegitimate, since it mingles parts peculiar to both tragedy and comedy.

The problem concerns the rights of the artist. Is it proper for him to attempt new ways of doing things, or shall he be held to the patterns of ancient Greece and Rome? Is there to be a new, modern literature such as Aristotle or even Horace had never seen? Is the richness and variety of the Renaissance to be allowed expression in literary art, or is classicism to be ever in control?

Guarini had declared his independence on the title page of his play, and vigorously asserts it in the *Compendium.* He is, however, not an extremist. With knowledge of Aristotle equal to that of his opponents, he sets out to show that what he has done is countenanced by the very letter of the *Poetics,* or at least that his methods follow directly in the course of development from hints in the exposition of the Greek philosopher. Latin comedy, too, offers him justification. His process reminds one of the use of the Bible by sectaries, even by such a man as Milton. They show how everything in their doctrine is supported by Sacred Scripture, and there is no reason to doubt their sincerity; yet one can hardly suppose that in forming their opinions they really set out from a Scriptural basis. They followed their own reason or their own liking, and they sought for justification of what was already accomplished and seemed good to them.

For the highest development of the new Renaissance drama one must go to the England of Marlowe, Shakespeare, Jonson, and Fletcher; none of them has left us such a defense of his methods as Guarini attempted. If we had such a discussion from their pens, we may suppose it would not have been essentially different from that of Guarini. With Fletcher we can feel almost certain of this, for in the address to the reader prefixed to the *Faithful Shepherdess* in 1609 he apparently repeats some of the ideas of Guarini, as he has obviously learned from him much that he used in the play itself, also called "a pastoral tragicomedy."

The translation is by the editor.

BIBLIOGRAPHY

Guarini, Giambattista, *Il Pastor Fido e il compendio della poesia tragicomica.* Bari, 1914. This reproduces, with corrections, the text of the edition of 1601.

——, *Il Pastor Fido, tragicommedia pastorale . . . con un compendio di poesia.* Venice, 1602. The *Compendio* in this edition is, I understand, that of 1601 with a change in the date only.

THE COMPENDIUM OF TRAGICOMIC POETRY

(*in part*)

[Imitation. 2[1]]

To poetry alone the name of imitator is especially appropriate, as that which for the most part does not, like other objects of man's attention, present concepts, thoughts, or forms, but human activities which are highly valued by all. And truly what is making something resemble the truth if it is not imitation? It is not strange that this marvelous and truly divine activity is so delightful and highly valued, because there is nothing of any sort in this world subject to perception and alteration which does not participate in

---

[1] The figures refer to pages in the edition of 1602; when more than one section begins on a page, letters are also used.

some way in this rare gift of imitation. Beginning with the creation of the world, does it not appear that when the divine workman produced it he wished in some sense to imitate? and not merely because he produced it in conformity with the divine idea that had been in his breast from all eternity, but because in the celestial production he made it in the semblance of eternity, in that it could not be injured or altered; this condition is the sign of a nature that does not perish. Hence it is not strange if Aristotle, seeing the world to be of such a nature, deceived himself by thinking it eternal. Then in forming man as a little world,[2] the divine voice of the same divine artist indicated that he was pleased with the work of imitation, saying: Let us make man in our image, after our own likeness. And further, he was so desirous to see imitation carried on that he wished man to obtain nothing except by imitation. What teaches us to speak? Imitation. What to live well? Imitation. How is human felicity acquired? By making oneself like to God. When sciences discuss the truth, what else do they do than show the way to set forth and imitate, with the intellect and the tongue, the thing that has been learned, by retracing the true form of it like a picture either on paper or by the voice? Finally, everything that is active and directs itself toward its natural and true perfection in some mode partakes in imitation, whether more or less. It is no wonder, then, that imitation is so delightful, when through it man learns to know what is the first desire of human nature, its dearest delight, and the thing most fitted to it. In addition, imitation is a sort of producing what is new—an operation in itself very dear to nature, who avails herself of it to preserve herself in her species, every day supplying all that has been lost. Now poetry, among all the arts that give their effort to imitation, succeeds marvelously, not merely because she imitates human actions—for in that she is not alone—but because she imitates with speech. In this she is a unique imitator, because all the others carry on imitation with other means and other instruments, but no other art with speech, which is peculiar to poetry. . . .

[Types of plot. 5]

There are two ways in which it can be said that the precept of unity is not preserved in the poem[3] of the *Pastor Fido:* one is that it

---

[2] The microcosm.

[3] In England also in the Elizabethan period it was customary to speak of dramas as poems.

contains two forms, the tragic and the comic; the other is that it has more than one subject, like almost all the plays of Terence. In order that we may make our discourse more convenient and clear, we shall call the first of these by the usual name of mixed and the second "grafted." As to the first, it must be considered that tragicomedy is not made up of two entire plots, one of which is a perfect tragedy and the other a perfect comedy, connected in such a way that they can be disjoined without doing injury to either. Nor should anyone think that it is a tragic story vitiated with the lowliness of comedy or a comic fable contaminated with the deaths of tragedy, for neither of these would be a proper component; for he who makes a tragicomedy does not intend to compose separately either a tragedy or a comedy, but from the two a third thing that will be perfect of its kind and may take from the others the parts that with most verisimilitude can stand together. Therefore, in judging it, one does not need to confound the terms *mixed* and *double*, as do those of little understanding who do not realize that nothing can be mixed if it is not one and if its parts are not so mingled that one cannot be independently recognized or separated from the other. . . .

[Components common to tragedy and comedy. 6]

Let us consider the parts of these two poems that are both opposed and in harmony with each other, in order to see that the mixed tragicomic is reasonable. Tragedy shares with comedy presentation on the stage, and all the rest of the apparatus, rhythm, harmony, limited time, dramatic plot, probability, recognition, and reversal. I mean that each makes use of the same things, though in the method of use there is some difference between them. Other qualities are then peculiar to one and to the other, and these qualities not only vary in their use, as do the other things that have been mentioned, but they diversify the species in such a way that they become differences between them. And I have no doubt that he who would think of making one of these pass entire into the confines of the other, and of using in tragedy what belongs to comedy alone, or *vice versa*, would produce an unseemly and monstrous story. But the point is that one should see whether these specific differences cause so much opposition that it is in no way possible to form a third species that can be a legitimate and reasonable poem.

[Comic characters in tragedy. 7a]

In tragedy these differences are the character of high rank, the serious action, terror and commiseration. In comedy they are private character and affairs, laughter, and witty speeches. As to the first, I confess, and admit it is the doctrine of Aristotle, that characters of high rank are fitting to tragedy, and those of humble station are suited to comedy;[4] but I deny that it is contrary to nature and to poetic art in general that persons great and those not great should be introduced into one plot. What tragedy has there ever been that did not have many more servants and other persons of similar station than men of great consequence? Who unfastens the admirably tied knot in the *Oedipus* of Sophocles? Not the king, not the queen, not Creon, not Tiresias, but two servants, guardians of herds. Then it is not contrary to the nature of the stage that there should be united in a play persons of high rank and those of low station, not merely under the name of a mixed poem, such as is tragicomedy, but also under that of pure tragedy, and comedy as well, if Aristophanes is alluded to, who mixes men and gods, citizens and countrymen, and even brings in beasts and clouds to speak in his plays.

[Grave and light are to be reconciled. 7b]

With respect to actions that are great and not great, I cannot see for what reason it is unfitting that they should appear in one same plot, not entirely tragic, if they are inserted with judgment. Can it not be that amusing events intervene between serious actions? Are they not many times the cause of bringing perils to a happy conclusion? But then, do princes always act majestically? Do they not at times deal with private affairs? Assuredly they do. Why, then, cannot a character of high importance be presented on the stage at a time when he is not dealing with important matters? Certainly Euripides did this in his *Cyclops*, where he mixed grave danger for the life of Odysseus, a tragic character, with the drunkenness of the Cyclops, which is a comic action. And among the Latins, Plautus did the same thing in the *Amphitryo*, mingling

---

[4] This is rather the Renaissance Aristotle than the Greek himself; see *Poetics*, II, end, above. For example, the Latin grammarian Diomedes (fourth century A.D.) wrote: "Comedy differs from tragedy in that heroes, generals, and kings are introduced into tragedy, into comedy humble and private persons" (Keil, *Grammatici Latini*, I, 488). Diomedes was known in the middle ages and there were several editions of his work in the sixteenth century. See the index for further quotations

the laughter and the jests of Mercury with persons of importance, not merely Amphitryo, but the king of the gods. It is, then, not unreasonable that in one story for the stage there can be at the same time persons of high rank and those not of high rank.

[Pity and laughter not inharmonious. 8a]

The same can be said of commiseration and laughter, qualities of which one is tragic and the other comic. And indeed to me they do not appear so completely opposite that the same story cannot include them under diverse occasions and persons. On reading in Terence the fate of Menedemus,[5] who willingly mortified himself because of the severity he adopted toward his son, what man is not moved to pity, and does not with Chremes, who does not restrain his tears, weep over it? And in the same play there is laughter at the art with which the astute Syrus mocks and deceives Chremes. I do not say that there can be happiness and sorrow in the same story, but there can be pity with laughter. Thus all the sum of this contradiction is seen to be reduced to a single difference, that is, the terrible, which can never occur except in a tragic plot, nor can any comedy ever be mixed with it, since terror is never introduced except by means of serious and mournful dramas; where it is found, there is never any room for laughter and sport.

[Are tragedy and comedy too diverse for union? 8b]

All the things I have said above can be brought forward in defense of tragicomic poetry. But I do not wish to avail myself of them, and am content to hand over to tragedy kings, serious actions, the terrible, and the piteous; to comedy I assign private affairs, laughter, and jests; in these things are the specific differences between the two. I wish for the present to concede that one may not enter into the jurisdiction of the other. Will it follow from this that, since they are of diverse species, they cannot be united to make up a third poem? Certainly it cannot be said that this is in opposition to the practice of nature, and much less to that of art.

[Nature joins diverse things. 8c]

Speaking first of nature, are not the horse and the ass two distinct species? Certainly, and yet of the two is made a third, the mule, which is neither one nor the other. . . . But perhaps it will be said that these third natures spring from the mixture of seeds and

[5] In the *Heautontimorumenos.*

not of bodies, and that they are works of nature and not of art, though we are treating of works of art. Therefore, we may pass to the arts and to their mixtures, made of bodies that are solid and diverse by nature. Bronze is made of copper and tin, and the body of both of them enters into the mixture, and they and their natures are so well mingled that the third which results from them is neither tin nor copper. Into gunpowder enter sulphur and nitre and as a third carbon, all complete bodies and wholly different in their characteristics; the powder is not any one of them. But someone may say that these examples are not appropriate, for the mixture is brought about by means of fire, which alters the qualities of bodies in such a way that nature can be said to have a part in the process; but this is not true of poetic mixtures, which are dependent on the skill of the worker, without any intervention of the work of nature.

[Painting and music unite diversities. 9a]

We may concede this and speak of painting, which is blood-cousin to poetry;[6] does not painting make various mixtures of her colors without the employment of any other means? The same can be said of music, born at the same birth with poetry. Does it not mix the diatonic with the chromatic, and the chromatic with the enharmonic, and does it not mix what the Philosopher calls harmonies? And it is indeed a single work of music. But anyone who still wishes to contradict would be able to say in reply that the painter manages colors and the musician sounds, but the poet sets in motion human deeds and persons. Yet this may be made good and in the end a mixture may be found so similar to poetry that there will be no difference between them except that between the true and the feigned. This is so fitting to our condition that the figure is as it were the same thing as that which it sets forth, since poetry is nothing other than the verisimilar imitated.

[Contraries in politics. 9b]

Has it not been said before that poetry employs actions and persons? We may give, then, an example of them. Do not Marcus Tullius and Horace say comedy is the mirror of human relations?[7]

[6] For other references to painting, see the index.
[7] Cicero's saying is given in full by Heywood, *Apology*, Bk. III, sect. 3, below. Horace does not speak of the mirror in this connection; Guarini perhaps has in mind such remarks as that the characteristics of various ages are to be observed (*Art of Poetry*, 158 ff., above).

We may give an example from human relations. Does not Aristotle say that tragedy is made up of persons of high rank and comedy of men of the people? Let us give an example of men of rank and men of the people. The republic is such a thing. I do not say this in respect to its material, for every city is of necessity composed of nobles and those who are not noble, of rich and poor, and, as the Philosopher himself says, of greater and less; but I speak of the forms that spring from the diversity of these two, that is, the power of the few and the power of the masses. Are not these two species of government very different among themselves? If we believe Aristotle, or even pure reason, there is no doubt of it; yet the Philosopher puts them together and makes of them the mixture of the republic. But in the republic are not the citizens human persons and the acts of government human operations? If these, that work practically, can be mixed, cannot the art of poetry do it in those things that are done for sport? In an oligarchy do not the few alone govern? Are not these contraries? Yet they join in a single mixed form. Is not tragedy an imitation of the great and comedy an imitation of the humble? Are not the humble opposite to the great? Why cannot poetry make the mixture if politics can do it? . . .

[Tragic and comic elements that cohere. 12]

He who composes tragicomedy takes from tragedy its great persons but not its great action, its verisimilar plot but not its true one, its movement of the feelings but not its disturbance of them, its pleasure but not its sadness, its danger but not its death; from comedy it takes laughter that is not excessive, modest amusement, feigned difficulty, happy reversal, and above all the comic order, of which we shall speak in its place. These components, thus managed, can stand together in a single story, especially when they are handled in a way in accord with their nature and the kind of manners that pertains to them. We conclude, then, that the ability of the tragic poet, naturally fitted to produce tragedy, will not produce either comedy or tragicomedy when the parts other than I have mentioned appear in their vigor and entirety, but only when they are not all present. And if instead of tragic components we speak of those of comedy, the comic power will never work toward the formation of a tragic poem; on the contrary the contest between the tragic parts and the comic will render that power very weak and destroy its capacity for being put into practice. . . .

[Selection by art. 13a]

Art observes that tragedy and comedy are composed of hetero-
geneous parts, and that therefore if an entire tragedy and an entire
comedy should be mixed, they would not be able to function properly together as in a natural mixture, because they do not have a
single intrinsic natural principle, and it would then follow that in
a single subject two forms contrary to each other would be included. But art, a most prudent imitator of nature, plays the part
of the intrinsic principle, and while nature alters the parts after
they are united, art alters them before they are joined in order
that they may be able to exist together and, though mixed, produce
a single form.

[Tragicomedy the highest form. 13b]

But it would be possible here to raise a new question, namely,
what actually is such a mixture as tragicomedy? I answer that it
is the mingling of tragic and comic pleasure, which does not allow
hearers to fall into excessive tragic melancholy or comic relaxation.
From this results a poem of the most excellent form and composition, not merely fully corresponding to the mixture of the human
body, which consists entirely in the tempering of the four humors,[8]
but much more noble than simple tragedy or simple comedy, as
that which does not inflict on us atrocious events and horrible and
inhumane sights, such as blood and deaths, and which, on the
other hand, does not cause us to be so relaxed in laughter that we
sin against the modesty and decorum of a well-bred man. And
truly if today men understood well how to compose tragicomedy
(for it is not an easy thing to do), no other drama should be put on
the stage, for tragicomedy is able to include all the good qualities
of dramatic poetry and to reject all the bad ones; it can delight all
dispositions, all ages, and all tastes—something that is not true of
the other two, tragedy and comedy, which are at fault because
they go to excess.[9] For this reason one of them is today abhorred
by many great and wise men, and the other is little regarded.

---

[8] The psychology and physiology of the time believed that in a healthy body the
four humors—blood, phlegm, black bile, and yellow bile—were mixed in the right
proportions.

[9] A bold declaration of the superiority of the new Renaissance drama to that of
antiquity.

Tragicomedy is also defended by Tirso de Molina in *The Orchards of Toledo*. For a
translated selection see Barrett H. Clark, *European Theories of the Drama*, p. 94.

[The end of tragicomedy. 14]

But I should not appear to have completed my task if, after I have made known the parts or forms, as it were, that tragicomedy ought to have as a good and legitimate poem, I should fail to prove the same thing of its end. Someone, perhaps, may wish to know what its end is, whether tragic or comic or mixed, as it seems that he might ask its function, since it is a mixed story. This cannot be explained without much difficulty, for each art has its end, toward which it is directed as it works; and if it has two of them, one of them is dependent on the other, in such a way that one thing alone is the chief end toward which the art is directed. Now if we concede that tragicomedy is a reasonable mixture, what does it attempt to do? what end has it? does it wish laughter or tears? for the two cannot be done at once. Then what does it do first? what next? what is of less importance? what of chief importance? what is subaltern? To such questions one can hardly give answers without first determining what the end of tragedy is and what the end of comedy. To understand those matters one must realize that each art, in addition to the principal end of which we have spoken before, has another end. One of them is that by means of which the artist as he works introduces into the matter which he has in hand the form that is the end of the work. The other is that for the good and advantage of which he labors at the work he wishes to carry to its end. In that sense Aristotle says that man is the end of all things. We call one of these ends instrumental, and the other, using Aristotle's own word, architectonic. Both of these appear in both tragic and comic art.

[The ends of comedy. 15a]

Beginning with comedy, its instrumental end is to imitate those actions of private men which by their deficiency move us to laughter; this is Aristotle's notion.[10] But the architectonic end is not mentioned in his extant writings, for we lack the discussion of comedy in that treatise of his called the *Poetics*, though it may be supposed that there he gave an end for comedy as he did for tragedy. But from the instrumental end we are able to conjecture what he would assign as the architectonic end, since this is the exemplar which the artist sets before himself. Hence, if we con-

---

[10] *Poetics*, v, above. Guarini gives us a very Renaissance Aristotle, when he changes Aristotle's "men worse than the average" to private citizens as opposed to men of rank.

sider that the Bacchic songs, all full of drunkenness and phallic license, gave rise to comedy, and, besides this, seeing that the same Aristotle distinguishes it from tragedy by means of its plebeian persons, assigning laughter to it as its specific difference, it appears to me that it can have no end other than that of purging men's minds of those passions that are caused in us by labors both private and public. It purges melancholy, an emotion so injurious that often it leads a man to grow mad and to inflict death on himself, in the same way as, according to Aristotle's teaching, melody purges the feeling the Greeks call enthusiasm; the Sacred Scriptures in dealing with it say that David, with the harmony of his music, drove away the evil spirits from Saul, the first king of the Hebrews. And just as one part of music, as the Scriptures teach us, is necessary to recreate us and enable us to gain that restoration of which human life has so great need, so comedy, with its gay and ridiculous presentations, refreshes our spirit. As a breeze is wont to drive away the thickened air, comedy by moving us to laughter shakes off that gloomy and foggy humor, generated in us by too much mental concentration, which often renders us slow and obtuse in our activities. For this reason comedy represents only private persons, with defects evoking laughter, mocks, sports, intrigues of little importance, covering but a short time and ending happily. Such is the architectonic end of comedy.

[The ends of tragedy. 15b]

But tragedy, on the other hand, calls back the relaxed and wandering soul; it has, therefore, ends wholly diverse, both of them demonstrated by Aristotle in the *Poetics*, where he defines tragedy, more fortunate in this matter than comedy. One end is the imitation of some horrible and pitiable action, and this is the instrumental; the other is the purgation of terror and compassion, the architectonic end. It is very necessary to understand how this purgation is carried on if one wishes to lay one's hand on what is sought after. I know that the passage on the catharsis is one of the most difficult in all the *Poetics* of Aristotle.[11] For that reason I intend to treat it with great modesty toward those who have been the first men of their time, who, in my opinion, have rather obscured it than made it clear. Everything in it that raises serious doubt can, in my opinion, be reduced to two points.

---

[11] Guarini's words are still true. See *Poetics*, VI, 49b20, above, and the bibliography for the *Poetics;* also the index under *purgation* and *catharsis.*

[Why is compassion to be purged away? 16a]

One point, required by Aristotle, is that a man should be freed from compassion, a feeling, as Boccaccio says, altogether human. And in fact that terror should be purged, as a disordered feeling that corrupts the virtue of fortitude, is much more reasonable or, to put it better, more necessary. But to rid ourselves of pity, who can do it without ridding himself of humanity? For this alone tragedy would deserve to be abhorred as a savage and offensive spectacle.

[Do terrors purge fear? 16b]

The other point is how it can be that terrible things purge fear, since it does not appear that choleric matters purge anger but rather make it worse, and so with the phlegmatic and other humors. Therefore, by means of the sight of things horrible and alarming there would rather come fear to a person who is by nature easily frightened. Yet some say that habituation to the sight of horrible things, as blood, wounds, and deaths, renders the spirit intrepid, and from the example of the soldier they conclude that in such a fashion tragedy purges terror.[12] This perhaps could be conceded if tragedy presented gladiators or assassins. But tragedy is so far from this that even the deaths that appear in it rarely occur before the eyes of the spectators, but are narrated, though sometimes the dead bodies are produced on the stage, as Euripides did in the *Phoenician Women*. It is altogether certain that Sophocles never did it, as some say who have thought that the death of Ajax happened in the sight of the audience, but anyone who understands the passage and considers it well knows that that is not so. Tragedy, then, cannot wish to purge in this fashion, since scenes of ferocity surely make men more cruel but not more brave. Nor can the courage of the soldier, when it comes from the habit of seeing dead bodies, be called virtue, and he who is not brave in some other way is improperly called brave, as even the virtue of the sailor, since he is habituated to storms at sea, cannot according to the teaching of Aristotle be called true courage.[13] If a man sees death often, it gives him assurance in working where death is, and for this reason executioners and, in times of pestilence, gravediggers, who are persons of the lowest sort, are more intrepid in their duties than are others; but the sight of death does not make the spirits valiant or purge away the fear of death. And this is true,

---

[12] Apparently a reference to Castelvetro on *Poetics*, VI, 116, 34.   [13] *Ethics*, III, 6.

for even though soldiers see blood every day, yet there are few of them who will stand in firm order of battle and not turn their backs when the peril of death is no longer in the hands of Fortune but in those of a strong enemy, and they see themselves overcome. And the few who do resist and forge ahead are not strong through the habit of seeing terrifying and horrid sights, but because they are fixed upon an honored, virtuous, and praiseworthy object.

[To lose compassion is to lose humanity. 17a]

Now I come to compassion, of which I can say that the continual sight of actions that arouse compassion would cause the destruction of the feeling. But I do not see how anyone can be divested of this feeling without divesting himself of humanity, that is, by making himself cruel; nor do I see how Aristotle could have meant it, since he teaches in the *Ethics* that he who has a friend must sympathize with his afflictions.[14] Now these are the difficulties which one must first resolve if he wishes to understand correctly the way in which the tragic poem purges.

[The word *purge* has two senses. 17b]

First of all, it must be realized that the word *purge* has two meanings. One means *to blot out completely;* in this sense Boccaccio uses it, in the passage where he writes: "The sins which you have committed up to the hour of repentance will all be purged." The other meaning is *to purify and cleanse;* in this sense Petrarch says: "Virgin, I consecrate and purge to your name both thought and ability and style." Yet here he does not mean to blot out his own ability, as Boccaccio meant to blot out the sins, but to rid it of all vileness and make it perfect in its nature. In this second sense is to be taken the *purge* of tragedy, as also the physicians take it; when, for example, they wish to purge bile, they do not have the intention of blotting it out or eradicating it wholly from the human body, for that would be to wish not to heal but to kill by completely depriving nature of a humor she uses to keep the proper proportion among the others; to purge is merely to take away the parts which by passing their natural bounds corrupt the symmetry of life and so cause disease. A tragic poem, then, does not purge the affections in stoic fashion, by removing them totally from our hearts, but by moderating and reducing them to that proper consistency which can contribute to a virtuous habit. It rather avails

---

[14] *Ethics,* ix, 10–11.

itself of one affection as medicine for the other, since it is so far from true that all fears are vicious that rather there are some of them which naturally kindle virtue, as for example fear of infamy. Equally pity is not all good, because, if the proper modes are not preserved, it passes into softness and effeminacy which deprive the spirits of their proper strength.

[Purgation correctly explained. 18]

These two feelings then need to be purged, that is, reduced to a proper mixture,[15] and this is done by tragedy. But if purging is considered as the effect of the thing that purges, we shall say these feelings are purged in the first meaning, for good has as its purpose to blot out and entirely uproot the bad. If then fear and compassion purge feelings similar to themselves, and some fears and some feelings of pity are good and others not, it must needs be that we see what things in tragedy are purging and what are purged; thence it will appear that it is not contradictory to their nature to purge and be purged. And beginning at the beginning, I say that as man has two lives, one of the intellect and the other of the senses, so he can fear two deaths, on which, according to Aristotle,[16] the terrible for the most part depends. What is, then, the purging terror of tragedy? It is terror of internal death, which, excited in the spirit of the spectator by the image of what is represented, interprets the injurious evil tendency as a calamity because of the likeness that one fear has with another. Then reason, which is the nature and first principle of the life of the spirit, abhorring the bad tendency as its capital enemy and opponent, drives it out, leaving behind only the beneficial fear of infamy and of internal death, which is the foundation of virtue. When then terror purges terror, it is not as though wrath were joined to wrath, but the terror acts like rhubarb, which, though it has an occult likeness to the humor that it purges,[17] yet in respect to its end is wholly opposed, for one heals and the other corrupts. Thus terror purges terror, since no way can be found more valid nor more certain of not fearing death than to give vigor and spirit to the life of the spirit, which is the perception of reason. All the other arguments are less effective, for, if of the two lives the internal is the more appropriate to man,

---

[15] The Italian is "ridotti a vertuoso temperamento," which suggests "to temper and reduce them to just measure" in Milton's preface to the *Samson Agonistes* below.

[16] Apparently a reference to *Poetics*, xiv.

[17] Cf. in Milton's preface to *Samson Agonistes* below, "sour against sour" etc. Milton and Guarini hold a homeopathic theory.

there is no doubt that he who perceives it as active in himself will prefer not to exist rather than to be wicked. In this, then, consists all the business of tragedy, which, presenting before us the terrible as it may appear in the death of the spirit, teaches us to have no fear of that of the body, and makes us perceive within ourselves the force of justice, because of which we see that the persons of tragedy, when they are tormented in spirit, are unaware of the torments of the body and have no fear of death. For this reason the wicked have no place in tragedy, for they have completely killed the internal perceptions of reason. But let us come to examples. For what does Oedipus sorrow in the *Tyrannus* of Sophocles, the queen and exemplar of tragedies? For what, I say, does that unhappy king sorrow after the recognition of the parricide and incest he has committed? Is it that he is going to be deprived of his kingdom? of his native land? that he has fallen from his royal estate and been made a beggar instead of a king? No. And yet these are the greatest and heaviest blows that can come on one who is nobly born. But he does not feel this, but prays that as soon as possible he may be led out of the city, leaving the kingdom to Creon by a death that is legal rather than natural. Nothing torments him but his parricide and his incest, for he sees that he has fallen into a sin so horrible and so greatly abhorred that, according to internal justice, he preferred to die rather than commit it. This horror, this infamy occupies him so much that he forgets every other evil; this sorrow he so lays to heart that he does not perceive the loss of his eyes nor of his native land nor of his regal scepter, and speaks of his internal pains as if he perceived no external pain or loss. This is a spectacle that makes us consider and repent of our sins and makes those who fear to die realize clearly that there is something more terrible to human nature than death, for if death is to be feared at all, only that of the spirit should be feared, since in comparison with it that of the body becomes as it were unfelt. Sophocles gives us the same teaching in the *Ajax*, where the hero is tormented by infamy alone, into which he appears to have fallen by a madness that is the death of the spirit; this infamy drives him to take his own life, since he does not wish to live in the flesh when he is dead to honor. . . .

[The function of tragedy to purge, not to teach. 20a]

But at this point can arise a question that should be dealt with, since in his discussion of courage Aristotle does not accept suicide as a virtuous action;[18] this permits us to think that tragedy, teaching us to fall into sin, would not purge our spirits, but rather would corrupt them. Answer can be made in two ways. One is that the Philosopher does not rebuke those who are brought to kill themselves to flee infamy or because they have knowledge of their sin, but those who do it because they cannot bear poverty or other bodily annoyance. And though our holy and true religion teaches that it is always a sin when a man brings about his own death, yet paganism, which did not have this light, judged it a noble deed to commit suicide, as did Cato, Brutus, and others, and above all Lucretia, who not for glory but to prove her chastity inflicted death on herself.[19] The other answer is that tragedy is not brought about by the voluntary action of a man who kills himself to imitate a virtuous act, but exists to show that so great is the sorrow of the spirit that he who kills himself does not perceive the suffering of the body, and that our humanity suffers things which are more grievous and terrible than death, and finally that a tragedy is a story and does not have as its function the teaching of virtue, but that its function is to purge—so far as a story can—those two perturbations of the spirit which are an obstacle to fortitude, which in all human actions is so noble and necessary a virtue.

[Compassion. 20b]

Now let us go on to the other feeling, that of compassion, which is nothing other than sorrow for the affliction of someone else. But this evil can be of two sorts, either of the body or of the spirit; thence spring the two kinds of compassion, good and ill; the good kind is present when we are sorrowful for someone who is afflicted in spirit because he has had too great pleasure in the body; and the bad kind is present when we feel sorrowful for someone who injures his body that he may have peace in his spirit. In this consists the true understanding of this feeling, which is most useful, indeed necessary, to all human life; for there is no other difference between the continent and the incontinent, who can be called the soldiers of virtue, except that one does not have pity for his body and afflicts it that he may not have torment in his spirit, while the other is so tender of his body that he permits himself to fall into an offense of the spirit, which causes him the anxiety of repentance.

---

[18] Aristotle discusses courage in *Ethics*, III, 6–9. Suicide is mentioned at the end of chap. 7.

[19] For Lucretia cf. Heywood, *Apology*, Bk. III, sect. 13, below.

Thence comes the proverb that the compassionate physician makes a wound maggoty, for if he used the knife and did not have such foolish pity that he is unwilling to pain the injured man, he would save him from death by giving him a little pain. The same is true of the soldier, who, if he is too careful of himself, flies fatigues and perils, whence it easily comes about that by leaving the ranks or turning his back or doing something else unworthy of him, he falls into infamy and then suffers and is worthy of true compassion. . . .

[Two kinds of compassion. 21a]

It is not necessary, then, to have compassion for any pain of body when it is just, but rather for a fault which when known and perceived by the sinner becomes pain for his sin. The first weakens the spirit of him who has compassion and the second strengthens it; the first disintegrates it and the second unites it; the first relaxes it and the second makes it firm. There is no doubt that without suffering and hardening himself against the flatteries and injuries of the body, by abstaining and enduring, man cannot follow the virtuous course suitable to his nature. Whoever suffers in this way disposes himself to suffer in body in order not to have anxiety of mind. What then is the compassion that purges and what is that which ought to be purged can be understood from what has been said. Not to give up the celebrated example of Oedipus, consider his troubles, which were of two sorts, some of the body and some of the reason. On seeing that king, once so great but now deprived of rank, blind, and banished—ills that he had not foreseen but rather that he had guarded against—who is there who would not have more compassion for the internal cause of that blindness and that sad fortune than for its external effect? Who does not see the same thing in the *Ajax*, and in the *Iphigenia* of Euripides and, contemplating the fortitude of that maiden in preparing herself to die for the benefit of the public, does not purge his spirit of that softness and baseness which excites selfishness? Who does not learn to expose his life to the perils of death for the sake of virtue and of great and striking works? In proportion, then, as a story has more of the terrible and the piteous it will be the more tragic.

[Varying tragic quality. 21b]

For this reason, if to be tragic is a quality that can be altered and increased and diminished, as may be gathered from the words of Aristotle, it will be in the hand of the poet to make the story more and less tragic, according as he endows it with more and less of terror and compassion. Stories that are exceedingly tragic will have great characters, true names, a serious action, and magnificent manners, stage appliances, decorum, language and ideas; there will be a recognition, a change of fortune, and a calamitous end. Such is the *Oedipus Tyrannus* of Sophocles. Less tragic plays do not have either recognition or change of fortune; those much less tragic lack an unhappy conclusion; the least perfect are the double, of which I shall speak in their proper place, the episodic, and those that are not true. Hence the terrible and the piteous, in various degrees of purgative power, determine the classes of tragedy.

[The difficulty solved. 22a]

If, as has been said, tragic quality can be raised and lowered in degree, there is no doubt it can also be injured and diluted in such a way it will no longer be tragic, but will pass into another species. Therefore, if in its changes it receives anything which is not repugnant to the feelings of the terrible and the miserable, it will continue to be tragic, though more and less so. But if with the two qualities that have been named are mingled those repugnant and contrary to them, such as laughter, corruption of the species will result, and when the end is changed the form will also be changed, since where laughter is desired there can be neither pity nor terror, for the feelings are opposite, and one destroys the other. If then laughter corrupts tragic form, when laughter is found in a subject that is not vile and plebeian, and that possesses those parts of tragedy that are not repugnant to the ridiculous, what sort of poem shall we have? Not tragedy, because the tragic form is destroyed by reason of the laughter; and not comedy either, which does not receive a noble subject and does nothing but represent to us the defects of men who are vile and deserve to be laughed at. What will the poem be if not a third sort participating in those qualities both tragic and comic that can be united? But what end will it have? We have come to the solution of that difficulty that has moved us to so long a discourse.

[Tragicomedy does not purge pity and terror. 22b]

Though tragicomedy, like the others, has two ends, the instrumental, which is the form resulting from the imitation of tragic and comic affairs mixed together, and the architectonic, which is to purge the mind from the evil affection of melancholy, an end which is wholly comic and wholly simple, yet I say that tragicomedy can be connected in no way with tragedy. The effects of the purging in the two types are truly opposite; one gladdens and the other saddens, one relaxes and the other constrains; these are mutually repellent motions of the spirit, since one goes from the center to the circumference, the other travels in the opposite direction; these are the ends that in a drama can be called contradictory. But the instrumental end can be a mixed one, since tragedy has many parts which, when the terrible is removed, have with the other comic parts the power of producing comic pleasure. Therefore, since Aristotle concedes pleasure in tragedy, pleasure is easily reconciled with pleasure. And what is tragic pleasure? The imitation of serious actions of persons of rank with new and unexpected accidents. Now if terror is removed and the work is reduced to pleasure alone, a new story and new names may be feigned and all may be made harmonious with laughter; the delight in the imitation will remain, which will be tragic in possibility but not in fact, and only the outside of it will remain, but not the tendency for purging that resides in the terrible; purgation can be produced only by means of all the tragic parts; if it could be done otherwise the story would still be a tragedy. There is a great difference between the two types; for one, with its simple narrative, does not wish to purge; but the other, with its gravity, and its stage setting, with harmony, numbers, magnificent and sumptuous diction and other tragic sights and devices, wishes to excite the terrible and the piteous, in order to purge them. This is the reason why, when Aristotle says that stories with sad endings are especially tragic, he thinks it well to add "when they are well handled,"[20] meaning that all dramas do not produce a tragic effect, but merely those accompanied by all the other parts that belong with them. Tragic pleasure consists, then, in the imitation of horrible and pitiable actions, which in itself, according to Aristotle,[21] is delightful. But that is not enough; it is also necessary that the other parts also be of a similar sort, if the end of purging is to be attained; otherwise it will be a tragedy only equivocally, that is, outside the terms of the definition given by the Philosopher. If a poet wishes to make use of any subject in such a way as not to purge terror, he must temper it with laughter and other comic qualities in such a manner that, though it is by nature terrible and pitiable, yet it has not

[20] *Poetics*, XIII, 53a12, above.　　　　　[21] *Poetics*, XIV, 53b1, above.

the power of producing either terror or compassion, and much less of purging them, but remains with the single virtue of delighting by imitating. And just as every terrible action is not fit to purge terror (something that is proved in pictures, though they may be horrible and terrifying, and in things of similar quality which are merely narrated without any dramatic art), so every imitation of the terrible does not produce tragedy, if it is not united with other parts that agree with it. . . .

[Purgation no longer needed. 24]

If then tragedy delights, it does it by imitating, and does it in the way in which men deceive a child who dislikes medicine, by smearing the edge of the glass, as Lucretius says, with some sweet thing to make easy for him the drinking of the medicine.[22] Tragic sights delight, but then they leave at the end a great sadness in the spirit, and that is what has a purgative effect. Hence, to many the tragic poem is not pleasing in nature, since all do not have need of what purges. And just as the age changes, habits change. . . . And to come to our age, what need have we today to purge terror and pity with tragic sights, since we have the precepts of our most holy religion, which teaches us with the word of the gospel? Hence these horrible and savage spectacles are superfluous, nor does it seem to me that today we should introduce a tragic action for any other reason than to get delight from it.

[The decay of comedy. 25]

On the other side comedy has come to be so tedious and is so little valued that if she is not accompanied with the marvels of the intermezzi, there is today no one who can endure her. This is because of mercenary and sordid persons who have contaminated her and reduced her to a vile state, carrying here and there for vile pay that excellent poem which was once accustomed to crown its makers with glory. In order to raise comic poetry from such a state of disgrace, that it may be able to please the unwilling ears of a modern audience, the makers of tragicomedy—following the steps of Menander and Terence, who raised it to dignity graver and more entitled to respect—have undertaken to mingle with the

---

[22] Lucretius, *On the Nature of Things*, iv, 11-17. The figure is used also by Tasso in the *Jerusalem Delivered*, i, 3. It admirably expresses a view of poetry important in the Renaissance. Cf. Sidney, *Defense*, sect. 27, above; and Tasso, *Discourses*, sect. 2, above.

pleasing parts of comedy those parts of tragedy that can suitably accompany comic scenes to such an extent that they strive for the purgation of sadness. They defend themselves, and not badly, by explaining that as the ancient Romans, according to the testimony of Horace,[23] introduced satyrs, who were ridiculous persons, into the severity of the tragic poem, as will be shown below, for no other reason than the solace and recreation of their hearers, so, in order to remove the dislike and distaste which the world today has for simple and ordinary comedies, we should be permitted to temper them with such tragic gravity as is not repugnant to the architectonic end of purging sadness.

[Description of tragicomedy. 26]

But to conclude once for all that which it was my first intention to show, I say that to a question on the end of tragicomedy I shall answer that it is to imitate with the resources of the stage an action that is feigned and in which are mingled all the tragic and comic parts that can coexist in verisimilitude and decorum, properly arranged in a single dramatic form, with the end of purging with pleasure the sadness of the hearers. This is done in such a way that the imitation, which is the instrumental end, is that which is mixed, and represents a mingling of both tragic and comic events. But the purging, which is the architectonic end, exists only as a single principle, which unites two qualities in one purpose, that of freeing the hearers from melancholy. And as in mixed bodies found in nature, though in these all four of the elements are found in an abated state,[24] as has been said, yet each of them retains a peculiar quality of either one or another of the elements that is dominant and surpasses the others and toward which especially that which is most like it is directed, so in the mixed form of which I speak, though its parts are altogether tragic and comic, it is still not impossible for the plot to have more of one quality than of another, according to the wish of him who composes it, if only he will remain within the bounds that have been mentioned above. The *Amphitryo* of Plautus has more of the comic, the *Cyclops* of Euripides more of the tragic. Yet it is not true that the first or the second is not a tragicomedy, since neither of them has as its end the purging of terror and compassion, for this purgation cannot exist where there is laughter, which disposes

---

[23] *Art of Poetry*, 220–4, above.
[24] The reference is to the four elements, earth, air, fire, and water.

the spirits to expand, and not to restrain themselves. . . . No one has described tragicomedy better than has Horace in his poetic *Epistle to the Pisos.* . . .[25]

[The style of tragicomedy. 27]

Now having sufficiently proved that the mixed tragicomedy is reasonable in its parts and its end, it remains that this should also be proved of the style, which, since it should be suited to the story, must if that is mixed also be mixed, in order to be a unit. And as Demetrius of Phalerum,[26] a complete master of styles, teaches us that the two forms he calls humble and magnificent cannot mix, so he affirms that the other two, the polished and the dignified, can mingle, even when accompanied by one or other of those first mentioned; hence the composer of tragicomedy, though he may grant that the first two do not mix, would be unable to deny that the other two properly can. The normal and chief style of tragicomedy is the magnificent, which, when accompanied with the grave, becomes the norm of tragedy, but when mingled with the polished, makes the combination fitting to tragicomic poetry. Since it deals with great persons and heroes, humble diction is unfitting, and since it is not concerned with the terrible and the horrible, but rather avoids it, it abandons the grave and employs the sweet, which modifies the greatness and sublimity that is proper to pure tragedy. So Donatus praised the judgment and art of Terence,[27] because he so well understood to take a middle course between these two forms that are so completely contrary. Still further, the styles are not like bells, which beyond the ordinary, crude tone the artificer gave them, are unfitted to make any sound more or less sharp than they have always done; but styles are like the sensitive and pliant cords of a musical instrument, which, though they all have their proper tone, still are normally more or less intense or relaxed according as it pleases the musician. The *ipate*[28] certainly will never be the *nete*,[29] nor will the second ever be deep or the first sharp. Either one sounds more or less deep or

---

[25] He here quotes from the *Art of Poetry*, 221-9.

[26] Demetrius's work *On Style*, trans. by Rhys Roberts, may be found in the same volume of the Loeb Classics as Aristotle's *Poetics*. Milton speaks of the work as valuable in his tractate *Of Education*.

[27] Donatus was a Latin grammarian of the middle of the fourth century A.D. For his comment on Terence see Thomas Heywood, *Apology for Actors*, sect. 3, below.

[28] The lowest chord or note in the earliest Greek musical scale.

[29] The highest note.

sharp as is necessary, yet in these pleasing alterations they never issue from their bounds to such an extent that the *ipate* is not always a chord of the deep and the *nete* of the sharp. In the same way the styles are handled, nor because the magnificent is relaxed will it cease therefore to be magnificent, nor because the humble becomes more strong will it therefore pass into the confines of the grand. And as the deep and sharp chords in their greater and lesser extensions run through grades which are called tones, so the styles pass through some parts of a composition which receive them and modify them. These parts are the sentence, the method, the figure, the locution, the texture, and the number.[30] From these parts the styles emerge in the same way as from the forehead, the eyes, the mouth, the chin, and the other parts of the human face emerges an expression that in one man is virile and severe, in another soft, delicate, and humble, and in another temperate. Now how does the tragicomic poet proceed in giving the right effect to his style? Certainly he will not compose a sentence or a figure in the sublime manner, and a locution and a number in the humble style, but, moderating the gravity of the sentence with those methods that normally make it humble, and in other ways sustaining the humility of some person or subject of which he treats, and using a little of that nobility of speech that is proper to the magnificent style, he proceeds to turn out an idea in harmony with his subject matter, not so grand that it rises to the tragic nor so humble that it approaches the comic. And so in dealing with the other parts he will proceed pleasingly to temper their texture with the contrary quality. This is not my doctrine but that of Hermogenes, the famous artist in ideas.[31] Speaking of the attractive and beautiful mixture that Demosthenes and Xenophon and Plato knew how to produce, he says that the styles are mixed in the same way as colors, and as of black and white, which are wholly contrary, there is formed a third that is called gloomy, so from the opposite forms of speech spring the mixed forms, which render discourse beautiful and striking. It may be added that it is no wonder if one idea touches another at some point and in some other does not harmonize with it; an example is that of man, who as a whole is very different from the other animals, yet in being

---

[30] Giraldi, *Discourse on Tragedy and Comedy*, p. 205, speaks of a "measured movement of the body that is called number."

[31] Hermogenes, a Greek rhetorician of the second century A.D. He is mentioned by Milton in his tractate *Of Education* as one from whom rhetoric is to be learned.

mortal is similar to many of them, and in having intellect has something in common with the gods. This mixture, then, so much praised by two famous Greek rhetoricians, ought not to be unsuitable to tragicomic poetry, since, according to the testimony of Hermogenes, the most famous tongues and the best chosen pens of all Greece have used it with such pleasure. . . .

[New poetry truly Aristotelian. 34]

Up to this point we have proved with the precepts of the Aristotelian art in general that even though it may be conceded that in the *Poetics* of Aristotle there is found no particular poem like the tragicomedy, nevertheless, since it is composed according to those rules of nature on which the Philosopher has based the other poems, it is not to be called a phantastic poem; this is confirmed by the example of the *Comedy* of Dante, the *Triumphs* of Petrarch, and the romances of our times, which are all new forms of writing poetry derived from the springs of poetic nature marked out to us by the Philosopher.[32] It now remains to be proved, if I am not to omit anything bearing on the perfection of such a poem, that poetry mingled of tragic and comic parts is composed not merely according to the universal rules of Aristotle, but is so like one of the particular species he mentions that tragicomedy is not merely its daughter, as we have proved, but its legitimate daughter. [He then attempts to show that the tragedy with a double conclusion, happy for the good and unhappy for the bad (*Poetics*, XIII, end, above), is the mother of tragicomedy.]

[No punishment in tragicomedy. 38]

Punishment, which in the double form of tragedy comes upon the malefactors, is unfitting to tragicomic poetry, in which according to comic custom, the bad characters are not chastised. . . .[33] Comedy ordinarily desires to give a prosperous end to its worst characters. . . .

[Terence and the double plot. 41a]

I will first tell what cause moved Terence to graft one story into another and then I will defend him, to the confusion of those who

---

[32] The spirit of this passage appears in Milton's question whether he should follow the rules or nature (*Reason of Church Government*, sect. 1, below).

[33] Guarini here abandons the highly moral position usual among Renaissance critics, who expected wickedness to be punished (see Sidney, *Defense*, sect. 25, above).

have been forward in blaming him, and to the consolation of those who, following him, have written or think to write in this genus. That man of genius, that judicious poet, says that simple comedy was rather a poor thing. . . . And because episodes are needed in all stories, he thought to make essential parts not of speeches and persons outside the theme, but of the action and subject itself. He reasoned well, as follows: Since the principal duty of the poet and the delight of poetry are founded in the representation of the deeds and performances of men, no episode can be joined to comedy that is more fitting and more delightful and more artistic than that which contains not words alone, but actions, which are handled and knit together with such art and judgment that the unity of the subject is not impaired, and—that which is all-important and cannot come from other episodes—the story is more firmly knotted and in consequence is made more beautiful and more delightful. These were the causes of the comedy in which one plot is grafted on another, and this its origin. But such grafting of secondary stories is unsuitable to a tragic poem, as something that would tend directly to injure the parts of it that are most its own and most necessary.

[The sub-plot of the *Andria*. 41b]

It now remains to defend this grafting in of subordinate stories. In order to do this I shall consider four agents indispensable to the plot of the *Andria*, the first, not merely in date but in beauty, of the comedies of Terence: Pamphilus the first, Glycerium the second, Philumena the third, and Charinus the fourth; the love of Pamphilus and Glycerium is the chief thing, and that of Charinus and Philumena is episodic and grafted to the other. That this is so, he who has but a little understanding of the dramatic art cannot doubt, since all the difficulties arise because of Pamphilus and Glycerium. With the person of Glycerium is concerned the recognition through which the plot is turned in an opposite direction, and in her marriage it has its happy end. Concerning the marriage of Charinus there is but a little sport at the end, and that with admirable artistry. Hence the principal subject is nothing else than the love of Pamphilus and Glycerium, not interrupted by that of Charinus, but greatly aided. And if that love alone had been represented, with the pregnancy of Glycerium and the displeasure of Simo, the father of Pamphilus, how insipid the story would have been! A young man fallen under the displeasure of his father because he has married a woman of no standing, who at last, when she is discovered to be a free woman, is given to him as his wife—what is there in that to make a plot? The plot might indeed have been pathetic and have displayed character, but there would have been no activity, which is the strength of the dramatic art. How would the plot have come to a crisis? From the indignation of the father and the love of the son strong feelings could have resulted, but not intrigues. The knot is tied by the marriage that Simo arranges, for it causes Pamphilus a great deal of trouble in his need for escaping it, since he has pledged his faith to Glycerium that he will take her as his wife, and causes the astute Davos to set about his clever plans. If this marriage then is so necessary that without it the drama would have little or no action, how can the person of Philumena be passed over? Pamphilus would not have believed his father when he said that he wished that day, all of a sudden, to give him a wife, if the wife had not been selected, named, and known by Pamphilus, and if the marriage had not a little before been negotiated. So the necessity of the third agent is obvious. Now that girl who was going to be that day a wife and who had been announced as such in the house of her father, was she then to remain disappointed because of the marriage of Glycerium? Was she to be all that day in the belief and hope of being a wife and then to be left high and dry? It would be very unwise and unfitted to a comic poem that, whenever there is introduced a person so necessary to tying the knot and to such an extent an accessory in untying it, no account should be made of her at the end of the story and she should not share in the common rejoicing. Hence it was necessary to prepare her a husband and to make him her lover, that he might be dearer to her and the end of the story might be more joyous, and—what is still more important—that there might be more intrigue and continual enrichment of the subject with new incidents. This makes clear the necessity of the fourth agent and the second love. It is false then that the action of Charinus and Philumena does not depend on that of Pamphilus and Glycerium, and that the dependence is not necessary; consequently it is also true to life. On the defense of the *Andria* necessarily follows that of the *Pastor Fido*. . . .[34]

[34] Guarini proceeds to show that his play is constructed on the Terentian model. I feel that the analysis of the *Andria*, more accessible in English translation than the *Pastor Fido*, is sufficient to illustrate the idea. It should be recalled, however, that Guarini's drama, first published in 1590, was very popular in Italy and known in other countries. Perhaps the clearest sign of its influence in England is the *Faithful Shepherdess* of John Fletcher.

[The pastoral. 45]

Now having fully and sufficiently proved that the *Pastor Fido*, in so far as it is a story in which tragic and comic parts are mixed, and in so far as it contains two subjects grafted together in the manner of Terence, is a poem reasonable, properly proportioned, and capable of every artifice that pertains to a well-knit story, and finally that it is a true son of the art and legitimate according to the rules of Aristotle, it remains for us to make clear the scope of a pastoral drama and the word *pastoral*, which appears on the title page of the work. This word, either not being well understood or not very plainly interpreted, was the cause of scandal to some and to its defenders a cause of much praise, since they had an occasion and field sufficiently large to enable them to gather such new and curious things about life, nobility, and pastoral poetry that to neglect them will be a great fault, considering our labor and the end we have in view.

[Pastoral characters. 46]

In order to understand better, one must know that the ancient shepherds, in that first age the poets call golden, were not distinguished from persons of rank by the distinction which exists today between countrymen and citizens, since all were surely shepherds, but, as happens in the classes of society in a city, some were important, some poor, some rich, and, to speak in the manner of Aristotle, some better and others worse. Neither were they all servants of the citizens, for in that age there were no cities, but they ruled themselves and he who was of most worth was governor; but not for that reason was he who governed any the less a shepherd than was some other man who obeyed him, nor was it unfitting to say "the shepherd who is master," "the shepherd who rules the others"; nor because he was ruler did he cease to be shepherd, just as in an army he who is called a captain or a colonel does not for that reason cease to be a soldier. And so in all organizations it is found that the importance of one's duties changes the name but not the profession. In the same way in those early times the pastoral life was conducted; they were all shepherds, but some of them governed and others were governed; some took the flocks afield and others did not. [The author continues to develop the dignity possible to shepherds, referring to Aristotle's *Politics*, instancing Moses and King David, and quoting Basil the Great.]

[The pastoral drama a new form. 49]

It must always be recognized that though, in respect to the persons introduced, pastoral poetry[35] recognizes its origin in the eclogue and the satyr drama of the ancients, yet as to form and method it can be called something modern, since we have from antiquity no example of such a drama in either Greek or Latin. The first of the moderns who had the courage to do it and succeeded was Agostin de' Beccari, a respected citizen of Ferrara, to whom alone the world should assign the happy invention of such a poem. He saw certainly with excellent judgment, that the eclogue is not other than a short, and, as it were, selected discourse by two shepherds, in nothing unlike that scene that the Latins call dialogue, except in being united, independent, with its beginning and end in itself. Moreover Theocritus, a very famous Greek and master of the great Vergil, departing from the general practice of those who speak in compositions of the sort, made one of them not merely of many persons, but also on a subject more dramatic than is usual and notable for length beyond the others, with five interlocutors, some of whom speak without the intervention of the others and the others then enter in and take their parts; above all, he made use of that distinction of times and places and actions that is suitable to the dramatic poem. . . . Examining all these things, Beccari decided that he could much more easily do the same thing with the eclogue, since without doubt it has more conformity with pastoral than comedy and tragedy have with their own weak beginnings, for according to the testimony of Aristotle himself they were nothing else than rude and, as reason persuades us, rather short improvisations.[36] And so occupying this beautiful situation, not yet touched by a Greek or a Latin pen, and arranging many pastoral speeches within the single form of a dramatic story, and separating it into acts, with a beginning, middle, and end sufficient and properly proportioned, with a knot, with a reversal, with its setting, and with the other necessary parts—apart from the chorus, which was added by Tasso—he gave origin to a comedy, except that the persons introduced are shepherds; for this reason he called it a pastoral drama. In this way, if the life of citizens has its drama, which is called comedy, so, through the work of Beccari, pastoral life also has its drama, which is called pastoral alone, though composed in comic form. The invention

[35] I.e., pastoral drama.   [36] *Poetics*, IV.

has been acclaimed by the world with so great applause and so happily received as genuine on Parnassus that the first composers of our age, and especially Torquato Tasso, who undeniably was in his *Aminta* an imitator of Beccari, have had the honor not merely of giving their efforts to it but of obtaining from it, or at least hoping for, great renown and fame in poetry.

[What pastoral is. 51]

Now this epithet of pastoral drama does not mean other than actions by the sort of men who are called shepherds. And since every dramatic action must be either comic or tragic or mixed, there is no doubt that the *Sacrificio* of Beccari is thrown into the form of a comedy, dealing with characters in a private station, causing laughter, and having a knot, a solution, and an end that are wholly comic. Yet he does not wish to call it comedy, but takes the generic rather than the specific name, and says *fable*[37] rather than *comedy* in order not to use the latter name improperly, for though it would be very suitable to the form and other parts of the work, yet because the action is without the city and does not represent citizens, it would be called a comedy with less than the usual reason. And then there is this adjective *pastoral*, which has with time acquired the force and meaning of a substantive, such that when one says *pastoral*, without anything further, drama dealing with shepherds is understood. This word is today so received and understood everywhere when it is alone, as "the pastoral of Beccari," "the pastoral of Tasso." And so too of all the others, though when their authors have joined it to *fable* they have availed themselves of it as an adjective signifying quality and not as a substantive signifying an action distinct from that story. The word *pastoral* can then be taken in two ways, either as an adjunct meaning pastoral quality, or as that particular substantive that today signifies action and story of shepherds, when it stands by itself. The word pastoral applied to the *Pastor Fido* should not be taken for a substantive signifying a fable separated from the tragicomedy, but for an adjective relating to tragicomedy, signifying that it differs from those that represent citizens by being composed of pastoral persons. The word *tragicomedy* shows us the quality of the drama and the word *pastoral* that of the persons who are presented in it, for since they could be citizens the poet wishes to show that

---

[37] In the Italian *favola;* the word in this connection, like the Latin *fabula*, means *play* or *drama*.

they are shepherds. And since some of the shepherds are noble and others are not, the first produce the tragedy and the second the comedy, and both together the tragicomedy, which is pastoral because of the persons represented in it. There are not then in the *Pastor Fido* three dramas, one of private persons who cause a comic action, a second of men of high rank who sustain the tragic part, and a third of shepherds who compose the pastoral action; there is only one drama of pastoral characters, made up of mingled tragedy and comedy, but constructed in comic fashion; this poem is a unit. And truly who is so stupid that he does not see that when this word *pastoral* is accompanied by *comedy* or *tragedy* or *tragicomedy*, it refers to a drama of shepherds in a form comic or tragic or tragicomic, and not to a play bringing in both citizens and shepherds? As *tragicomedy* refers to the quality of the story, so *pastoral* adds to it that of the persons, from which issues a single conception of this sort: an action of shepherds, composed of tragic and comic parts mixed together, and not three actions, one of private persons, the second of persons of rank, the third of shepherds; there is one action that at the same time is kingly and private and pastoral. Thus the parts that are kingly, private, and pastoral produce a single subject, just as the reasonable animal, in virtue of his specific differences, forms the single human being, and not an animal and a man distinct by nature and then joined together.

BEN JONSON

oᗣooᗣo

WE LEARN from one of Jonson's poems[1] as well as from the report of his conversations with William Drummond of Hawthornden[2] that the translation of Horace's *Art of Poetry* made by Jonson was to be accompanied by a preface and a commentary in the form of a dialogue. The commentary, according to Jonson's own account, was Aristotelian. The preface, so Drummond says, was read to him by the author; unhappily the only thing he tells us about its content is that it contained "an apology of a play of his, *St. Bartholomew's Fair.*" In the address "To the Readers," prefixed to *Sejanus,* Jonson speaks of the work as "Observations upon Horace's *Art of Poetry.*" He says he would show in them that the classical rules need not and perhaps could not be applied in his day by a dramatist who hoped for popularity. We have, then, some notion of the sort of work Jonson produced. It was based on Horace and made use of Aristotle, whose theories probably were studied at first hand;[3] it dealt specifically with at least one and probably two of Jonson's own works, one a tragedy, the other a comedy, apologizing for and justifying them against any who held they were not in harmony with the best principles of dramatic writing. The question is then: What were the principles that Jonson held to?

The answer, sufficient for tentative reconstruction of the dialogue intended to accompany the translation of Horace, may be gained from Jonson's *Timber* or *Discoveries,*[4] a sort of notebook in which he recorded and to some extent commented on his reading in literary theory, from the prologues and addresses prefixed to his plays, from passages in the plays themselves, notably the *Poetaster,* and from his practice as poet.

As a comic writer he stood for the didactic theory, mentioning "profit and delight" in Horatian terms, and hoping diseased spirits will be pleased with his "fair correctives." Human follies, rather than crimes, are his theme, though Asper, in *Every Man out of His Humor,* speaks in a fiercer tone of "public vice." Like Massinger he sometimes

---

[1] "An Execration upon Vulcan," *Underwoods,* XLIII.

[2] Jonson's *Works,* ed. by Herford and Simpson, I, 134, 144.

[3] But in the *Timber* one of the references to Aristotle is a quotation from Seneca, *On Tranquillity of the Mind,* 15.   [4] *Timber,* ed. Schelling, pp. 81–5.

disclaims attacks on individuals of public importance, though in the *Poetaster* contemporary poets are attacked in person. The subjects are men as they are and not "monsters." The needful rules of comedy, such as "the laws of time, place, persons," are observed. He looked on himself as having set an important example, writing to Richard Brome

> of those comic laws
> Which I, your master, first did teach the age.
> *To My Old Faithful Servant.*

This perhaps refers to satisfaction both in the proper application of classical rules on the one hand and in any advances he had made on the other. For Jonson believed in the independence of his own time, as may be inferred from several passages in the *Discoveries*, such as: "Let Aristotle and others have their dues; but if we can make further discoveries of truth and fitness than they, why are we envied?" Most striking of all is the passage on the evolution of comedy which appears in *Every Man out of His Humor*, below. This, it seems, must be Jonson's own opinion, for Cordatus, the speaker, is described in the *dramatis personae* as "the author's friend; a man inly acquainted with the scope and drift of his plot, of a discreet and understanding judgment." Its assertion of the rights of modern comedians to independence from "strict and regular forms" is as vigorous as one could wish. The play to which it is prefixed is sufficiently unclassical to deserve what Jonson says; how much more vigorous he might have been in his apology for *Bartholomew Fair* fifteen years later! that play, as Jonson's latest editors remark, shows "glaring disregard of classical structure."[5] Yet how many of his comedies surpass it?

In tragedy Jonson's attitude is much as in comedy, though perhaps somewhat less extreme. Certain things from classical theory he wishes to retain, such as a plot taken from history, characters of high rank, dignified language, and proper use of sentences,[6] but otherwise he has not thought it "needful" to make use of the "forms." This, too, he set forth in the dialogue accompanying the translation of Horace.

It seems, then, though Jonson might have censured some of his contemporaries, that his lost work on poetry not merely defended his own productions, but would have been also a manifesto of the rights of the Elizabethan dramatists. If it had been preserved from the flames, we might have been spared much mistaken and irrelevant criticism of Shakespeare and his contemporaries.

[5] Herford and Simpson, I, 70. [6] See the index.

As a learned poet of rational rather than emotional genius, Jonson accepted the theory of poetic imitation (see the index). An example of his imitation of Sappho appears above.[7] To what extent may Jonson be said to have carried out the principles of imitation presented in his *Timber*, where he speaks of the ability "to convey the substance or riches of another poet to his own use," and indicates that the poet must be able to "handle, place, or dispose" the matter he imitates "with elegancy?"[8] He has put his adaptation, as Sappho did her original, in the mouth of a woman possessed by love, but it is difficult to feel that the Englishwoman's passion is comparable to the Greek's in violence, being but recently awakened after indifference, and occurring in a comic play; Sappho's feeling is suited only for a tense atmosphere. As Jonson's lady speaks, the modern reader has almost a feeling that she is conscious that she appears comic in her sudden shift from the part of cold pursued to that of hot pursuer. Perhaps Jonson intended some such feeling; if so, he has exemplified the theory he suggests by mastering his model and shifting it to a different purpose. He has also given an Elizabethan tone to the passage, largely by adding to its stark description the figures dear to the age, such as the fantastic one of the lake of fire curled with the wind of sighs. He has truly imitated rather than borrowed or merely translated.

BIBLIOGRAPHY

Castelain, Maurice, *Ben Jonson, l'homme et l'œuvre*. Paris, 1907.

Jonson, Ben, *Works*, ed. by Herford and Simpson. Oxford, 1925 ff. Six volumes have been issued.

———, *Timber*, ed. by Felix E. Schelling. Boston, 1892.

———, *Discoveries*, ed. by Maurice Castelain. Paris, 1906.

———, *Conversations with Drummond of Hawthornden*, ed. by R. F. Patterson. London, 1923.

———, *Poems*, ed. by Bernard H. Newdigate. Oxford, 1936.

Palmer, John, *Ben Jonson*. New York, 1934.

Reinsch, Hugo, *Ben Jonsons Poetik und seine Beziehungen zu Horaz*. Erlangen, 1899.

Snuggs, Henry L., *Classical Theory and Practice in the Comedies of Ben Jonson*. 1928. A typed thesis in the Library of Duke University.

---

[7] In the note to Dionysius or Longinus, *On Literary Excellence*, chap. x, above.

[8] *Timber*, ed. Schelling, p. 77. For a long discussion of imitation, see Roger Ascham's *Scholemaster*, Bk. II (reprinted in Gregory Smith's *Elizabethan Critical Essays*, I,5-45). Ascham gives a survey, as it were, of opinion on the subject before 1570. Erasmus, for example, is alluded to.

EVERY MAN OUT OF HIS HUMOR

1600

After the second sounding (lines 228–86)

Mitis. You have seen his play, Cordatus; pray you, how is it?

Cordatus. Faith, sir, I must refrain to judge; only this I can say of it, 'tis strange, and of a particular kind by itself, somewhat like *Vetus Comoedia;*[1] a work that hath bounteously pleased me; how it will answer the general expectation, I know not.

Mit. Does he observe all the laws of comedy in it?

Cor. What laws mean you?

Mit. Why, the equal division of it into acts and scenes,[2] according to the Terentian manner; his true number of actors; the furnishing of the scene with Grex or Chorus; and that the whole argument fall within compass of a day's business.[3]

Cor. O no, these are too nice observations.

Mit. They are such as must be received, by your favor, or it cannot be authentic.[4]

Cor. Troth, I can discern no such necessity.

Mit. No?

Cor. No, I assure you, signior. If those laws you speak of had been delivered us *ab initio,* and in their present virtue and perfection, there had been some reason of obeying their powers; but 'tis extant that that which we call *Comoedia* was at first nothing but a simple and continued song sung by one only person, till Susario invented a second; after him, Epicharmus a third; Phormus and Chionides devised to have four actors, with a prologue and chorus; to which Cratinus, long after, added a fifth and sixth; Eupolis, more; Aristophanes, more than they; every man in the dignity of his spirit and judgment supplied something. And though that in him this kind of poem appeared absolute and fully perfected, yet how is the face of it changed since! in Menander, Philemon, Cecilius, Plautus, and the rest, who have utterly excluded the

---

[1] Old Comedy. Aristophanes is its most famous representative.

[2] For the division into acts, see Horace, *Art of Poetry,* 189, above.

[3] This speech gives much that the Elizabethans thought necessary for the "authentic" play. The emphasis on the chorus, something that seems strange to us, is normal. The "day's business," or so-called unity of time, found support in Aristotle's *Poetics,* v, 49b9, and was developed by Castelvetro. See *chorus* and *unity of time* in the index.

[4] *Authentic:* in harmony with classical practice as interpreted by the Italian critics. See the index.

chorus, altered the property of the persons, their names, and natures, and augmented it with all liberty, according to the elegancy and disposition of those times wherein they wrote.[5] I see not then, but we should enjoy the same license or free power to illustrate and heighten our invention as they did; and not be tied to those strict and regular forms which the niceness of a few, who are nothing but form, would thrust upon us.[6]

Mit. Well, we will not dispute of this now; but what's his scene?

Cor. Marry, *Insula Fortunata*, sir.

Mit. O, the Fortunate Island! mass, he has bound himself to a strict law there.

Cor. Why so?

Mit. He cannot lightly alter the scene without crossing the seas.[7]

Cor. He needs not, having a whole island to run through, I think.

Mit. No? how comes it then that in some one play we see so many seas, countries, and kingdoms passed over with such admirable dexterity?

Cor. O, that but shows how well the authors can travel in their vocation,[8] and outrun the apprehension of their auditory.

SEJANUS

1605

To the Readers (*a selection*)

First, if it be objected that what I publish is no true poem in the strict laws of time, I confess it; as also in the want of a proper

[5] Jonson gives here the evolution of comedy, and suggests the fitness of different types to different ages.

[6] A strong declaration of independence from classical practice and precept.

[7] In the chorus of *Every Man in His Humor*, Jonson objects to plays in which the "chorus wafts you o'er the seas." Perhaps he had in mind Shakespeare's *Henry V*, the chorus of Act II:

> The king is set from London; and the scene
> Is now transported, gentles, to Southampton:
> There is the playhouse now, there must you sit:
> And thence to France shall we convey you safe,
> And bring you back, charming the narrow seas
> To give you gentle pass.

[8] Perhaps Jonson intends a double satire, both of the authors who put scenes of the same play in various continents, and of those who stuck too strictly to one place. Jonson was willing to allow events within one city as adequate for unity of place; perhaps an entire island seemed to him large enough to make the idea comic. He plays on *travel* in the senses of *journey* and *labor;* Elizabethan spelling did not distinguish the two.

chorus, whose habit and moods are such and so difficult as not any whom I have seen since the ancients (no, not they who have most presently affected laws) have yet come in the way of. Nor is it needful or almost possible in these our times and to such auditors as commonly things are presented, to observe the old state and splendor of dramatic poems with preservation of any popular delight. But of this I shall take more seasonable cause to speak in my observations upon Horace's *Art of Poetry*, which (with the text translated) I intend shortly to publish. In the meantime if in truth of argument, dignity of persons, gravity and height of elocution, fullness and frequency of sentence,[1] I have discharged the other offices of a tragic writer, let not the absence of these forms be imputed to me, wherein I shall give you occasion hereafter (and without my boast) to think I could better prescribe than omit the due use for want of a convenient knowledge.[2]

The next is, lest in some nice nostril the quotations might savor affected, I do let you know that I abhor nothing more, and have only done it to show my integrity in the story and save myself in those common torturers that bring all wit to the rack, whose noses are ever like swine spoiling and rooting up the Muses' gardens and their whole bodies like moles as blindly working under earth to cast any the least hills upon virtue.[3]

---

[1] Evidently the prime requirements of a tragedy.

[2] A further statement of Jonson's independence, combined with an assertion that his departure from the rules is not the result of ignorance. Cf. the similar assertions of Lope de Vega (p. 541, below) and Webster (p. 551, below).

[3] Jonson's opinion of the source-hunters of his time.

LOPE DE VEGA

o◯ooo◯o

THE NEW ART OF MAKING COMEDIES

1609

In this poem Lope de Vega gives a summary of classical theories on the drama and defends his own lawless procedure in writing three-act comedies, regardless of the unities, by pointing out the irreconcilable differences between the ruling of tradition and the public taste of his day. *The New Art of Making Comedies* must not be considered an authentic exposition of Lope's theories. He asserts that he desired to follow the precepts of Aristotle but was forced to compromises by the crude and barbaric demands of the amusement-loving crowd. In reality he was not confronted with so rational a choice, as his robust rooting in his own age, his natural distaste for elaboration, and his unbelievably prolific and rapid production all gravitated against the smoothness and regularity of classical forms.

Perhaps the tone of the essay is more revealing than its substance. It shows the blend of respect and contempt for learning typical of Lope, who deprecated Cervantes because he was not versed in academic traditions but has Diocleciano (in *Lo fingido verdadero*) say:

> Give me a new plot which has more invention [than the *Andria* of Terence and the *Miles Gloriosus* of Plautus] though it be lacking in art; for in this respect I have the Spaniard's taste and if you give me the lifelike I care nothing for theory. On the contrary, its inflexibility wearies me and I have observed that they who devote themselves to concentrating on art fail to seize upon the natural.

The value and charm of the essay are in its picture of the theater of the sixteenth and early seventeenth century in Spain. Where Lope breaks away from theorizing, with its premise of scholarly analysis usually incompatible with the creative mind, he furnishes us with sketches of actors, stage sets, and spectators that are stamped with the truth of what is real and what has been seen.

The introduction and translation are by Dr. Olga Marx Perlzweig.

BIBLIOGRAPHY

Lope de Vega, *El arte nuevo de hacer comedias*, ed. by A. Morel-Fatio,
Bulletin Hispanique, tomo III, pag. 365 y sigs.

Rennert, Hugo, and Castro, Americo, *Vida de Lope de Vega*. Madrid,
1919.

Schevill, Rudolph, *The Dramatic Art of Lope de Vega together with La
Dama Boba*. University of California Press. Berkeley, 1918.

Vossler, Carlos, *Lope de Vega y su tiempo*, traduccion del Aleman por
Ramon de la Serna, Revista del Occidente. Madrid, 1933.

THE NEW ART OF MAKING COMEDIES

[Popular comedy ignores rules]

[1] You order me, lofty spirits, flower of Spain—who in this
society and illustrious academy will in a brief space of time exceed
in excellence not only those of Italy which Cicero, envying Greece,
made renowned by his own name, near the Lake of Avernus,[1] but
Athens too, where in Plato's Lyceum was seen so noble a gathering
of philosophers—to write you a treatise on the art of making comedies which may be acceptable for the use of the public.

This subject appears easy and it would be easy for any one of
you who has written but few plays and knows more than I do
about the art of writing them and about everything; for in this
matter I am at a disadvantage, since I have written them without
art. Not that I was unaware of the rules; I thank God that even
as an apprentice to grammar I had already read the books which
treated of these subjects before I had seen the sun run its course
ten times from the Ram to the Fishes. But I finally found that the
plays in Spain at that time were not as their early makers in the
world thought they should be written, but as many untutored
writers treated them who worked for the public according to its
own rude ways, and thus insinuated themselves into favor to such
an extent that whoever now writes plays with art dies without
fame or reward; for among those who lack fire, custom can accomplish more than reason or force.

It is true that occasionally I have written in accordance with the
art that few know, but later when from others I saw proceed monstrous things full of theatrical apparatus, to which the crowd and

[1] An allusion to Cicero's *Puteolanum*, where he wrote his *Academic Questions*.

the women who canonize this sad business came running, I returned to the barbarous manner, and when I have to write a play I lock the rules away with six keys; I remove Terence and Plautus from my study that they may not cry out at me, for the truth in silent books is wont to scream, and I write in the manner of those devisers who aspired to the acclaim of the crowd; for since it is the crowd that pays, it is proper to speak to it stupidly in order to please.[2]

[Goal and history of comedy]

[2] The true play like every kind of poetic composition has its proposed goal, and that has been to imitate the actions of men and to paint the customs of their age.[3] Any poetic imitation is made up of three things: speech, rhythm, harmony or music. In this it is like tragedy, different from it only in that it treats of the actions of the humble and plebeian, and tragedy of the royal and lofty. See whether there be few faults in our comedies!

They were called *autos*[4] because they imitate the actions and business of the crowd. In Spain, Lope de Rueda[5] was the example of these principles, and today his prose comedies are printed, and so crude are they that he introduces in them the affairs of mechanics and the love of a blacksmith's daughter. From that time on the custom of calling the old comedies *entremeses* has remained, for there the art is at its height, being one action and that among common people, since never has there been seen an *entremés* with a king. And so it is made manifest that the art, because of its low style, came to be held in contempt and the king in the comedy to be for the ignorant.

Aristotle depicts the beginning of comedy in his *Poetics*, although obscurely: the quarrel between Athens and Megara as to which of them was the first inventor. The people of Megara say it was Epicharmus, while the Athenians hold it was Magnetes. Aelius Donatus says that they originated in the sacrifices of old;[6] as the author of tragedy he names Thespis, following Horace,[7] as Aris-

---

[2] In a letter dated August 14, 1604, Lope de Vega writes to a friend: "If some people who think I am writing for pleasure complain of my comedies, disillusion them and tell them I am writing for money."

[3] Literally translated from Robortello: "Finem habet sibi propositum comoedia eum, quem et alia poematum genera, imitari mores et actiones hominum" (*Paraphrasis in librum Horatii: De comoedia*).

[4] *Auto* or *acto*, a term first applied to any kind of dramatic composition.

[5] Lope de Rueda (1520–1566), Spanish playwright. His *Armelina* is alluded to here.

[6] Donatus, *Euanthius de fabula*, I, 2–5.   [7] Horace, *Art of Poetry*, 276, above.

tophanes is of comedy. Homer composed the *Odyssey* in imitation of comedy, but the *Iliad* is a famous example of tragedy, in imitation of which I gave the name of epic to my *Jerusalem*[8] and added "tragic." Likewise the *Hell, Purgatory,* and *Heaven* of the celebrated poet Dante Alighieri everybody habitually calls comedy and this Manetti[9] recognizes and regrets in his prologue.

Everyone already knows that for a while comedy, held suspect, was silent, and that then the satire was born, which being cruel came sooner to an end and permitted the new comedy to arise. First came the choruses, later the right number of characters was introduced. But Menander, whom Terence followed, held the choruses in contempt as tiresome. Terence was more versed in the rules and never raised the comic style to tragic grandeur,[10] which many criticized as vicious in Plautus, for in this Terence was more wary.

For a subject tragedy has history and comedy has feigning; for this reason comedy was called flat-footed, of humble plot, since the actor played without buskin or stage. There were comedies of the *pallium*, pantomimes, Roman and Athenian comedies and comedies of the tavern, which, as now, were varied. The men of Athens with Attic elegance condemned vice and low customs in their comedies and gave their prizes to authors both of verse and of action. For this reason Tully called them "a mirror of customs and a vivid image of truth,"[11] a very high tribute which puts it on a par with history. See if it is worthy of this crown and this glory!

But already I seem to hear you say that this is merely translating books and wearying you by painting for you this confused matter. Believe me that I was forced to recall to your memory some of these things, because, you see, you asked me to write on the art of making comedies in Spain, where whatever is written is against art; and to tell you how comedies are now written, contrary to the ancient art and the foundation of reason, is to ask me to give my experience rather than art, since art tells the truth which the ignorant crowd contradicts. If it is art that you desire, I implore you, men of genius, to read the learned Robertello of Udine, and you will see in *On Aristotle* and in the part where he has written *On*

---

[8] *Jerusalem conquistada*, epopea tragica (Madrid, 1609).

[9] Antonio di Tuccio Manetti, a Florentine mathematician and architect, wrote a commentary on Dante's *Divine Comedy*. But he wrote no prologue such as Lope refers to. Lope seems to have confused him with some earlier commentator on Dante.

[10] Horace, *Art of Poetry*, 89, 94, above.

[11] See *Cicero, his description of comedy*, in the index.

Comedy, as much as is scattered through many books: for everything today is confusion.

[Rules appropriate for current dramatic composition]

[3] If you ask an opinion concerning those that now hold sway and whether it is necessary that the public with its laws establish the vile chimera of this monster of comedy, I shall tell you what is essential and—pardon me—since I have to obey those who can command me, that, gilding the error of the mob, I wish to tell you how I would have them, since, in following the rules of the art, there is no help save to observe the mean between the two extremes.

Let the subject be chosen and do not be surprised—pardon these rules—if it be of kings. I understand that the prudent Philip, King of Spain and our lord, was annoyed to see a king appear in them, either because he realized that this was a contradiction of art or because royal power should not be feigned among the common people.[12] This is merely a return to ancient comedy, where we see that Plautus introduced gods, as in his *Amphitryo* he shows Jupiter. God knows that it is difficult for me to approve of this, for Plutarch, speaking of Menander, does not express himself favorably on ancient comedy. But since we have strayed so far from art and in Spain violate it in a thousand ways, let the learned here close their lips.

The tragic mixed with the comic, Terence with Seneca, although it be like another Minotaur of Pasiphae, will make one part grave, the other absurd: and this variety gives much delight. Nature gives us a good example, for because of such variety it has beauty.[13]

The subject should have one action; the plot should be in no wise episodic, I mean to say interspersed with other things that deviate from the original plan, and one should not be able to remove any part of it without destroying the whole context. It is not necessary to prescribe that it take place within the limits of one day, though this is a precept of Aristotle's,[14] because we already cease to show respect to him when we mix tragic sublimity with the simple and low comic. Let the action take place in the least time possible, unless the poet is writing history in which several years must elapse; these may be put between the acts,[15] or, if it is necessary, a character can go on some journey, a thing which greatly offends him who perceives it. But who is offended, let him not go to see comedies!

---

[12] Cf. Castelvetro, *On Poetics*, IX, 222, 39, above.   [13] See *variety* in the index.

[14] *Poetics*, v, 49b9, above.   [15] Cf. Dryden, *Of Dramatic Poesy*, sect. 12, below.

O! how many in these days cross themselves to see the years that must elapse in a matter which ends in one artificial day; for this, though, they would not allow the mathematical day. But considering that the anger of a seated Spaniard is not calmed unless he sees within two hours a representation from Genesis to the Last Judgment, I consider it most proper here, if our purpose is to please, to arrange all so that it be a success.

After the subject has been chosen, let it be written in prose and divided into three acts of time, bringing about, if possible, that in each one the limits of one day are not interfered with. Captain Virués,[16] an excellent mind, divided comedy, which before had gone on all fours like a small child, into three acts, for then comedies were in their infancy. At the age of eleven and twelve, I myself wrote them in four acts and on four sheets of paper, for each sheet contained an act. And in the three interludes there were three little *entremeses*, while today there is scarcely one, and later a dance, for the dance means so much in comedy that Aristotle approves it, and Athenaeus, Plato, and Xenophon treat of it, but the last named disapproves of improper dancing and is annoyed therefore with Callipides when he seems to be imitating the ancient chorus. After the subject matter has been divided into two parts, connect everything well from the beginning to the waning of the action, but do not permit the denouement until you arrive at the last scene: for when the crowd knows the end, it turns its face to the door and its back on the conclusion it has awaited three hours face to face; for there is no more to be known in what appears.

Rarely should the stage be left without a character who is speaking, for in these intervals the crowd becomes unquiet and the story spreads itself out at length. And apart from the fact that this is a grave fault, the avoidance of it increases grace and artifice.

[Speech and form appropriate for different characters]

[4] Begin then and do not waste thought or ideas on family matters which are only supposed to represent the chatter of two or three people. But when the character who is introduced advises or dissuades, then it is necessary to have thought and ideas, for this

---

[16] Cristobal de Virués, born at Valencia about 1550, wrote in the prologue to his tragedy *La Gran Semiramis*, claiming to have originated the division into three acts:

advierto
que esta tragedia, con estilo nuevo
que ella introduze, viene in tres jornadas.

He was mistaken, as the division had been tried by Francisco de Avendaño in 1553.

without doubt is imitating the truth, since a man speaks in a style different from the ordinary when he counsels, persuades, or discusses something. Aristides the rhetorician gave us assurance of this, for he wishes the language of comedy to be pure, clear, and simple, and he adds that it should be taken from common usage and differ from that of high society; for then the diction will be splendid, high sounding, and ornamented. Let not your style of composition offend with out-of-the-way words, nor your language offend with them, for if you are to imitate people who speak, the language should not be of Panchaia,[17] of the Metaurus, of hippogriffs, demigods, and centaurs.

If a king is to speak, imitate as much as possible royal gravity; if an old man is to speak, observe thoughtful modesty; describe lovers with those emotions which greatly move the listener; paint monologues in such a way that the speaker is transformed and with the change in himself changes the one who hears. Let him ask questions of himself and answer them, and if he complains of his mistress' cruelty let him maintain the decorum owing to women. Let ladies be in keeping with their characters, and if they change their costume let it be in a manner that can be excused, for male disguise is very pleasing. Avoid the impossible, for it is of the greatest importance that only the truth should be imitated. The lackey should not treat of lofty matters nor express the ideas we have seen in some foreign plays; and in no way let the character contradict himself in what he has already said, I mean to say, forget, as in Sophocles it is to be blamed that Oedipus does not remember having killed Laius with his own hand. Let the scenes terminate with cleverness, with charm, and with elegant verse, so that at his exit he who is speaking does not leave the audience displeased. In the first act state the case; in the second entangle the incidents in such a way that until the middle of the third act no one can even guess at the solution. Always deceive anticipation, and so it may come about that something quite remote from what is intended may be left to the understanding. Adjust your verses wisely to the subjects you treat of. *Décimas* are good for laments, the sonnet is good for those who are in a state of anticipation, narrative passages call for *romances*, though they are very brilliant in *octavas*. Tercets are good for serious matters, and for affairs of love *redondillas*. Rhetorical figures are desirable, such as repetition or

---

[17] See Vergil, *Georgics*, II, 139. The fabulous island of Panchaia is celebrated for its perfumes.

anadiplosis, and in the beginning of the same verses the different forms of anaphora and irony, questions, apostrophes, and exclamations.

[How to win the audience]

[5] To trick with truth is a device which has seemed good, and Miguel Sánchez, worthy of a memorial for this invention, used it in all his comedies. Equivocal speech and the uncertainty arising from the ambiguous has always held a great place with the crowd, for it thinks that it alone understands what the other man is saying. Subjects concerned with honor are the best, since they move everyone forcefully; and with them acts of virtue, for virtue is beloved everywhere. So it must be seen to that if an actor is portraying a traitor, he is so hateful to everybody that what he wants to buy is not sold to him, and that the crowd flees him when it encounters him; but if he is loyal, they lend to him and invite him, and even the chief personages honor and love him, seek him out, entertain him, and give him approval.

Let each act have only four folios,[18] for twelve are correct for the time and the patience of him who is listening. In the satirical part, be not too clear and open, for it is known that because of this comedies were forbidden by law in Greece and Italy; wound without hate, for if by chance there be slander, look for no applause and aspire to no fame.

[Stage apparatus and costume]

[6] These words you may take for aphorisms with which ancient art does not supply you and to which the present occasion can give no further space. What has to do with the kind of stage apparatus that Vitruvius speaks of, is the business of the impresario. Valerius Maximus, Petrus Crinitus, Horace in his *Epistles*, and others describe it with drops, trees, cabins, houses, and feigned marbles. If it were needful Julius Pollux would tell us about costume, for in Spain today comedy is full of barbarous things: a Turk wearing a Christian's neckgear and a Roman in tight breeches.[19]

But no one more than myself can I call barbarous, since contrary to art, I venture to give precepts, and I allow myself to glide with the common current, wherefore Italy and France call me

---

[18] Four folios of four sheets each composed one act. Hence twelve folios or forty-eight sheets composed the whole comedy. For fuller information see Morel-Fatio, *Comedia espagnole du XVII siècle*, p. 37.

[19] Doubtless some of the Elizabethans held the same opinion. See *anachronism* in the index.

ignorant. But what can I do if I have written, including the one I have finished this week, four hundred and eighty-three comedies? For all except six of them sin grievously against art. But after all, I defend what I have written, and I know that though they might have been better in another manner, they would not have found the favor they have; for sometimes that which is contrary to correctness for that very reason pleases the taste.

> Why should comedy be a mirror of human life,
> Or what benefits does it give to a young man or to an old man?
> What do you ask from it besides pleasing and smart sayings
>   and finished words
> And a purer kind of diction?
> What important things occur in the midst of its sports, and what
> Serious things have been mingled in its jests?
> How deceptive the servants are, how shameless the lady always
> Is, full of fraud and wiles of every sort!
> How wretched, unhappy, foolish and inept the lover!
> How hardly do those things come to an end that you think well
>   begun.

Listen attentively and do not dispute about art, for in comedy everything will be found of such a sort that if you listen to it everything is apparent.

GEORGE CHAPMAN

oᴑooᴑo

THIS DEDICATION gives a glimpse at the theory of an important English dramatist, George Chapman. Apparently his play had been censured by those who held that poetry must be historically true, and he wished to defend himself. Otherwise Chapman shows less knowledge of classical theory than Webster and Heywood, alluding only to the requirement that poetry should teach.

BIBLIOGRAPHY

Chapman, George, *The Tragedies*, ed. with introductions and notes by Thomas M. Parrott. London, 1910.

THE REVENGE OF BUSSY D'AMBOIS

About 1611

The Dedication[1] (*in part*)

Since works of this kind have been lately esteemed worthy the patronage of some of our worthiest nobles, I have made no doubt to prefer this of mine to your undoubted virtue and exceeding true noblesse, as containing matter no less deserving your reading, and excitation to heroical life,[2] than any such late dedication.[3] Nor have the greatest Princes of Italy and other countries conceived it any least diminution to their greatness to have their names winged with these tragic plumes, and dispersed by way of patronage through the most noble notices of Europe.[4]

Howsoever therefore in the scenical presentation it might meet with some maligners, yet considering even therein it passed with approbation of more worthy judgments, the balance of their side (especially being held by your impartial hand) I hope will to no grain abide the out-weighing. And for the authentical truth of

---

[1] To the right virtuous and truly noble knight, Sir Thomas Howard.
[2] Perhaps meaning that his play is no less a stimulus or excitation to heroic life than other recent tragedies.　　　　　　　　　　　[3] Dedicated matter.
[4] For example, the *Orbecche* of Giraldi Cinthio was dedicated to Ercole, the fourth duke of Ferrara.

either person or action, who (worth the respecting) will expect it
in a poem, whose subject is not truth, but things like truth?[5] Poor
envious souls they are that cavil at truth's want in these natural
fictions; material instruction, elegant and sententious excitation
to virtue, and deflection from her contrary, being the soul, limbs,
and limits of an authentical tragedy.[6]

Act I, scene i, ll. 319–51

Guise.   I would have these things
Brought upon stages, to let mighty misers[7]   320
See all their grave and serious miseries play'd,
As once they were in Athens and old Rome. . . .

Clermont.   And stages too
Have a respect due to them, if but only
For what the good Greek moralist says of them:[8]   335
"Is a man proud of greatness, or of riches?
Give me an expert actor, I'll show them all
That can within his greatest glory fall.
Is a man fray'd with poverty and lowness?
Give me an actor, I'll show every eye   340
What he laments so, and so much doth fly,
The best and worst of both." If but for this then,
To make the proudest outside that most swells
With things without him, and above his worth,
See how small cause he has to be so blown up,   345
And the most poor man to be griev'd with poorness,
Both being so easily borne by expert actors,
The stage and actors are not so contemptful
As every innovating Puritan,
And ignorant sweater-out of zealous envy,   350
Would have the world imagine.

[5] See the index under *truth* and *verisimilitude*.
[6] For *authentic* see Jonson, *Every Man out of His Humor*, above. For a similar use of
sententious see Webster, *The White Devil*, below. Cf. Sidney's praise of *Gorboduc, Defense*,
sect. 48, above.
[7] *Misers:* wretched persons, not necessarily covetous.
[8] Epictetus, *Discourses*, IV, vii, 13.

JOHN WEBSTER

oᴑooᴑo

THE REQUIREMENTS for tragedy here suggested are those of Jonson (above), but the tone is different. Webster regrets that he is unable to use the rules he knows, while Jonson independently says he knows them and does not care to observe them.

BIBLIOGRAPHY

Webster, John, *Complete Works,* ed. by F. L. Lucas. Boston, 1928.

THE WHITE DEVIL

1612

To the Reader (*in part*)

If it be objected this is no true dramatic poem,[1] I shall easily confess it; *non potes in nugas dicere plura meas ipse ego quam dixi.*[2] Willingly, and not ignorantly, in this kind have I faulted. For should a man present to such an auditory the most sententious tragedy that ever was written,[3] observing all the critical laws, as height of style, and gravity of person, enrich it with the sententious chorus, and, as it were, liven death in the passionate and weighty nuntius,[4] yet, after all this divine rapture, *O dura messorum ilia,*[5] the breath that comes from the uncapable multitude is able to poison it. And, ere it be acted, let the author resolve to fix to every scene this of Horace:

Haec porcis hodie comedenda relinques.[6]

[1] That is, an "authentic" tragedy. See Jonson's use of the words *authentic* (*Every Man out of His Humor,* above) and *true poem* (*Sejanus,* above).

[2] Martial, XIII, 2, 4–5: "You cannot say anything about these trifles of mine beyond what I have said myself."

[3] The word *sententious* is used as though it expressed the principle and representative virtue of tragedy. See Jonson's opinion in *Sejanus,* above, and *sentence* in the index.

[4] See the index.

[5] Horace, *Epodes,* 3, 4: "O strong stomachs of mowers!" The public likes and can digest bad literature.

[6] "You are leaving these to be eaten by the swine today" (Horace, *Epistles,* I, 7, 19). The dramatist is casting pearls before swine.

THOMAS HEYWOOD

oʘ₀₀ʘo

AN APOLOGY FOR ACTORS

1612

HEYWOOD WAS both actor and dramatist. Though he was perhaps the most prolific of the Elizabethan playwrights, he was sufficiently able to merit from Charles Lamb the praise of a "prose Shakespeare." His *Apology* is the longest formal work in defense of the stage by any dramatist of the period. It is concerned more with actors than with the nature of the drama; only the parts dealing with the latter subject are here presented. It appears that his theory is like that of his fellow dramatists, including Shakespeare. The tone of the essay is not unlike that of Thomas Nashe's "Defense of Plays" in "The Complaint of Sloth" in *Pierce Penniless' Supplication to the Devil*, where we read that plays are "a rare exercise of virtue," and furnish "sour pills of reprehension, wrapped up in sweet words."

BIBLIOGRAPHY

Cromwell, Otelia, *Thomas Heywood*. New Haven, 1928.

Clark, Arthur M., *Thomas Heywood*. Oxford, 1931.

Heywood, Thomas, *A Woman Killed with Kindness* and *The Fair Maid of the West*, ed. (with introduction, notes, and bibliography) by Katharine Lee Bates. Boston, 1917.

——, *An Apology for Actors*, in Somers's *Second Collection of Scarce . . . Tracts*, I. London, 1750.

——, *An Apology for Actors*, in *A Collection of Scarce . . . Tracts . . .* selected from [the library of] the late Lord Somers, the second edition, III, 574–600. London, 1810.

——, *An Apology for Actors*, reprinted for the Shakespeare Society. London, 1841.

I have taken the text from the last two editions; errors in the Greek and Latin quotations have been corrected; corrections in English words are indicated by footnotes. When the editions differ, my modernized version follows the one that apparently is correct.

AN APOLOGY FOR ACTORS (*selections*)

Book I

[The tragic muse defends herself]

[1] *Nox erat et somnus lassos submisit ocellos.*[1] It was about that time of the night when darkness had already overspread the world and a hushed and general silence possessed the face of the earth, and men's bodies, tired with the business of the day, betaking themselves to their best repose, their never-sleeping souls labored in uncouth dreams and visions—when suddenly appeared to me the tragic Muse Melpomene

> —*animosa Tragaedia*[2]
> —*et movit pictis innixa cothurnis*
> *Densum cesarie terque quaterque caput,*[3]

her hair rudely disheveled, her chaplet withered, her visage with tears stained, her brow furrowed, her eyes dejected, nay her whole complexion quite faded and altered; and perusing her habit, I might behold the color of her fresh robe all crimson breathed,[4] and with the envenomed juice of some profane spilled ink in every place stained, nay more, her buskin of all the wonted jewels and ornaments utterly despoiled, about which in manner of a garter I might behold these letters written in a plain and large character:

> Behold my tragic buskin rent and torn,
> Which kings and emperors in their times have worn.

This I no sooner had perused but suddenly I might perceive the enraged Muse cast up her scornful head; her eyeballs sparkle fire, and a sudden flash of disdain intermixt with rage purples her cheek. When pacing with a majestic gait and rousing up her

---

[1] Ovid, *Amores*, III, 5, 1. "It was night and sleep overcame my tired eyes."

[2] *Ibid.*, III, 1, 35: "Spirited Tragedy."

[3] *Ibid.*, III, 1, 32: "Standing in her embroidered buskins she moved thrice and four times her head thick with hair."

[4] The meaning at this point is not clear. Some lines later her robe is said to have been "of the deepest crimson," and still farther on is the line:

> Such with their breath have blasted my fresh robe.

The present passage, perhaps misprinted, suggests that the fresh crimson robe has been blasted by the breath of detraction.

fresh spirits with a lively and quaint action, she began in these or the like words:

Grande sonant tragici; tragicos decet ira cothurnos.[5]

[Tragedy a moral teacher]

[2] Am I Melpomene, the buskined Muse,
That held in awe the tyrants of the world
And played their lives in public theaters,
Making them fear to sin,[6] since fearless I
Prepared to write their lives in crimson ink
And act their shames in eye of all the world?
Have I not whipped Vice with a scourge of steel,
Unmasked stern Murder, shamed lascivious Lust,
Plucked off the visor from grim Treason's face,
And made the sun point at their ugly sins?
Hath not this powerful hand tamed fiery Rage,
Killed poisonous Envy with her own keen darts,
Choked up the covetous mouth with molten gold,
Burst the vast womb of eating Gluttony,
And drowned the Drunkard's gall in juice of grapes?
I have showed Pride his picture on a stage,
Laid ope the ugly shapes his steel-glass hid
And made him pass thence meekly. In those days
When emperors with their presence graced my scenes
And thought none worthy to present themselves
Save emperors, to delight ambassadors,
Then did this garland flourish, then my robe
Was of the deepest crimson, the best dye.
Cura ducum fuerant olim regumque poetae
Praemiaque antiqui magna tulere chori.[7]
Who lodge[d] then in the bosom of great kings
Save he that had a grave cothurnate Muse?
A stately verse in an iambic style
Became a Kesar's mouth. Oh! these were times
Fit for you bards to vent your golden rhymes.
Then did I tread on arras; cloth of tissue

---

[5] Ovid, *Remedy of Love*, 375: "Grand is the speech of tragic actors; rage befits the tragic buskins."

[6] Cf. Sidney, *Defense*, sect. 25, above.

[7] Ovid, *Art of Love*, III, 405–6: "Poets once were the charge of rulers and kings, and the old choruses obtained great rewards."

Hung round the fore-front of my stage; the pillars
That did support the roof of my large frame
Double appareled in pure Ophir gold;
Whilst the round circle of my spacious orb
Was thronged with princes, dukes, and senators.
Nunc hederae sine honore jacent.[8]
But now's the iron age, and black-mouthed curs
Bark at the virtues of the former world.
Such with their breath have blasted my fresh robe,
Plucked at my flowery chaplet, towsled my tresses;
Nay, some, whom, for their baseness hissed and scorned,[9]
The stage as loathsome hath long-since spued out,
Have watched their time to cast envenomed ink
To stain my garments with. Oh! Seneca,
Thou tragic poet, hadst thou lived to see
This outrage done to sad Melpomene,
With such sharp lines thou wouldst revenge my blot
As armed Ovid against Ibis wrot.

With that, in rage she left the place and I my dream, for at the instant I awaked.

Book III

[Tragedy and comedy defined]

[3] Tragedies and comedies, saith Donatus,[10] had their beginning *a rebus divinis*, from divine sacrifices. They differ thus: in comedies *turbulenta prima, tranquilla ultima;*[11] in tragedies *tranquilla prima, turbulenta ultima;* comedies begin in trouble and end in peace; tragedies begin in calms and end in tempest. . . . The definition of the comedy according to the Latins: a discourse consisting of divers institutions comprehending civil and domestic things, in which is taught what in our lives and manners is to be followed, what to be avoided. The Greeks define it thus: Κωμῳδία ἔστιν ἰδιωτικῶν καὶ πολιτικῶν πραγμάτων ἀκίνδυνος

---

[8] *Ibid.*, III, 411: "Now ivies lie without honor in the dust."

[9] Could the reference be to Gosson, who after writing plays attacked the stage in his *School of Abuse?* Gosson's date, 1579, perhaps fits with "long-since."

[10] Aelius Donatus, a Latin grammarian and commentator on Terence and Vergil. From the prefatory matter of his comment on Terence, the *De fabula* of Euanthius, and the *Excerpta de comoedia*, Heywood took the material of the present paragraph.

[11] The beginning troubled, the end tranquil.

περιοχή.[12] Cicero saith a comedy is the imitation of life, the glass of custom, and the image of truth.[13] . . .

[All things have their abuses]

[4] I hope there is no man of so unsensible a spirit that can inveigh against the true and direct use of this quality.[14] Oh but, say they, the Romans in their time and some in these days have abused it, and therefore we volley out our exclamations against the use. Oh shallow! because such a man hath his house burned we shall quite condemn the use of fire; because one man quaffed poison we must forbear to drink; because some have been shipwrecked no man shall hereafter traffic by sea. Then I may as well argue thus: he cut his finger, therefore must I wear no knife; yond man fell from his horse, therefore must I travel a foot; that man surfeited, therefore I dare not eat. What can appear more absurd than such a gross and senseless assertion? I could turn this unpointed weapon against his breast that aims it at mine, and reason thus: Roscius[15] had a large pension allowed him by the senate of Rome; why should not an actor of the like desert have the like allowance now? Or thus:[16] The most famous city and nation in the world held plays in great admiration. *Ergo*[17]—but it is a rule in logic, *ex particularibus nihil fit.*[18] These are not the bases we must build upon nor the columns that must support our architecture.

> *Et latro et cautus precingitur ense viator;*
> *Ille sed insidias, hic sibi portat opem.*[19]

[12] "Comedy is a portion, involving no danger, of the affairs of ordinary men and citizens." The same description of comedy, with a slight exception indicated, below, is given also by the grammarian Diomedes, Bk. III (Keil, *Grammatici Latini*, I, 488). Theophrastus is supposed to be the source. Cf. Horace, *Art of Poetry*, 90, above. The word πολιτικῶν does not occur in Keil's text, though it is found in the text followed by Egger, *L'histoire de la critique chez les Grecs*, p. 344. It seems to underlie *civilia* in Minturno's description: "Comedia . . . cum civilia tum privata negotia sine periculo comprehendat" (*De poeta*, p. 280).

[13] This saying by Cicero is known only from Donatus, whom Heywood is here following. It is quoted by Jonson in *Every Man out of His Humor*, III, vi, 206-7, by Minturno in *De poeta*, p. 280, and by many others. Perhaps its influence appears in Hamlet's remark on "playing, whose end, both at the first and now, was and is to hold, as 'twere, the mirror up to nature, to show virtue her own feature, scorn her own image, and the very age and body of the time his form and pressure" (*Hamlet*, II, ii, 21–5).   [14] The profession of the actor.

[15] A famous Roman comic actor of the time of Cicero. Cf. *Hamlet*, II, ii, 396: "When Roscius was an actor in Rome,—"   [16] Printed *this* in both editions.

[17] "Therefore." He is about to draw a conclusion but breaks off.

[18] "Nothing can be concluded from single instances." He cannot draw general conclusions from the single instance of Rome.   [19] Ovid, *Tristia*, II, 271-2.

Both thieves and true men weapons wear alike;
The one to defend, the other comes to strike.

Let us use fire to warm us, not to scorch us, to make ready our
necessaries, not to burn our houses; let us drink to quench our
thirst, not to surfeit; and eat to satisfy nature, not to gourmandize.

> *Comaedia, recta si mente legatur,*
> *Constabit nulli posse nocere.*[20]

Plays are in use as they are understood,
Spectators' eyes may make them bad or good.

Shall we condemn a generality for any one particular miscon-
struction? Give me then leave to argue thus. Among kings have
there not been some tyrants? Yet the office of a king is the image of
the majesty of God. Among true subjects have there not crept in
some false traitors? Even among the twelve there was one Judas,
but shall we for his fault censure worse of the eleven? God forbid.
Art thou prince or peasant? Art thou of the nobility or common-
alty? Art thou merchant or soldier? Of the city or country? Art
thou preacher or auditor? Art thou tutor or pupil? There have
been of thy function bad and good, profane and holy. I adduce
these instances to confirm this common argument that the use of
any general thing is not for any one particular abuse to be condemned, for if that assertion stood firm we should run into many
notable inconveniences.

> *Quis locus est templis augustior? haec quoque vitet,*
> *In culpam si qua est ingeniosa suam!*[21]

[Playing an ornament to the city]

[5] To proceed to the matter. First, playing is an ornament to
the city, which strangers of all nations repairing hither report of in
their countries, beholding them here with some admiration; for
what variety of entertainment can there be in any city of Christendom more than in London? But some will say this dish might
be very well spared out of the banquet. To him I answer: Diog-
enes, that used to feed on roots, cannot relish a marchpane.[22]

---

[20] *Ibid.*, 275–6. The usual reading is *carmen* rather than *comaedia.*
[21] Ovid, *Tristia*, II, 287–8: "What place more sacred than the temples? yet these too
should be shunned by any woman inclined by nature to fault."
[22] A sweet dessert.

[Playing improves the language]

[6] Secondly, our English tongue, which has been the most harsh, uneven, and broken language of the world, part Dutch, part Irish, Saxon, Scotch, Welsh, and indeed a gallimaufry of many but perfect in none, is now by this secondary means of playing continually refined, every writer striving in himself to add a new flourish unto it, so that in process from the most rude and unpolished tongue it is grown to a most perfect and composed language, and many excellent works and elaborate poems written in the same, that many nations grow enamored of our tongue (before despised). . . . Thus you see to what excellency our refined English is brought, that in these days we are ashamed of that euphony and eloquence which within these sixty years the best tongues in the land were proud to pronounce.

[Plays are instructive]

[7] Thirdly, plays have made the ignorant more apprehensive, taught the unlearned the knowledge of many famous histories, instructed such as cannot read in the discovery of all our English chronicles, and what man have you now of that weak capacity that cannot discourse of any notable thing recorded even from William the Conqueror, nay from the landing of Brute, until this day? being possessed of their true use; for or because plays are written with this aim and carried with this method: to teach subjects obedience to their king, to show the people the untimely ends of such as have moved tumults, commotions, and insurrections; to present them with the flourishing estate of such as live in obedience, exhorting them to allegiance, dehorting them from all traitorous and felonious stratagems.

[The value of tragedy]

[8] *Omne genus scripti gravitate tragedia vincit.*[23]

If we present a tragedy, we include the fatal and abortive ends of such as commit notorious murders, which is aggravated[24] and acted with all the art that may be, to terrify men from the like abhorred practices. If we present a foreign history, the subject is so intended that in the lives of Romans, Grecians, or others,

[23] Ovid, *Tristia*, II, 381: "Tragedy surpasses in seriousness every sort of writing."
[24] Made more striking for greater moral effect. Cf. Sidney, *Defense*, sect. 23, above.

either the virtues of our countrymen are extolled or their vices reproved, as thus by the example of Caesar to stir soldiers to valor and magnanimity, by the fall of Pompey that no man trust in his own strength; we present Alexander killing his friend in his rage, to reprove rashness; Mydas choked with his gold, to tax covetousness; Nero against tyranny; Sardanapalus against luxury; Ninus against ambition; with infinite others by sundry instances either animating men to noble attempts or attacking the consciences of the spectators, finding themselves touched in presenting the vices of others.

[Moral plays]

[9] If a moral, it is to persuade men to humanity and good life, to instruct them in civility and good manners, showing them the fruits of honesty and the end of villany.[25]

> *Versibus exponi tragicis res comica non vult.*[26]

Again Horace, *Arte poetica,*

> *At vestri proavi Plautinos et numeros et*
> *Laudavere sales.*[27]

[The value of comedy]

[10] If a comedy, it is pleasantly contrived with merry accidents and intermixt with apt and witty jests to present before the prince at certain times of solemnity, or else merrily fitted to the stage. And what is then the subject of this harmless mirth? Either in the shape of a clown to show others their slovenly and unhandsome behavior, that they may reform that simplicity in themselves which others make their sport, lest they happen to become the like subject of general scorn to an auditory; else it entreats of love, deriding foolish enamorates who spend their ages, their spirits, nay themselves, in the servile and ridiculous employments of their mistresses; and these are mingled with sportful acci-

---

[25] The moral, in which, as in *Everyman*, personified virtues and vices were presented, was old-fashioned when Heywood wrote. In the first folio of the plays of Beaumont and Fletcher, however, appeared a work called *Four Plays or Moral Representations in One.* The four are *The Triumph of Honor, The Triumph of Love, The Triumph of Death,* and *The Triumph of Time.* In the last are such characters as Time, Poverty, Vain Delight, and Honesty. Moral intention is prominent throughout. In *The Gull's Hornbook* (1609) Dekker refers to the plays then on the stage as "pastoral or comedy, moral or tragedy" (chap. VI).

[26] Horace, *Art of Poetry,* 89: "Comic matter should not be set forth in tragic verses."

[27] *Ibid.,* 270-1: "Your fathers praised the verses of Plautus for both meter and wit."

dents to recreate such as of themselves are wholly devoted to melancholy, which corrupts the blood, or to refresh such weary spirits as are tired with labor or study, to moderate the cares and heaviness of the mind, that they may return to their trades and faculties with more zeal and earnestness after some small, soft and pleasant retirement. Sometimes they discourse of pantaloons, usurers that have unthrifty sons, which both the fathers and sons may behold to their instruction, sometimes of courtezans, to divulge their subtleties and snares in which young men may be entangled, showing them the means to avoid them.[28]

[Pastoral plays]

[11] If we present a pastoral we show the harmless love of shepherds diversely moralized, distinguishing between the craft of the city and the innocence of the sheep-cote.

[Moral value of the drama reiterated]

[12] Briefly there is neither tragedy, history, comedy, moral, or pastoral[29] from which an infinite use cannot be gathered. I speak not in the defense of any lascivious shows, scurrilous jests, or scandalous invectives. If there be any such I banish them quite from my patronage, yet Horace, Sermon I, satyr iv, thus writes:

> *Eupolis atque Cratinus Aristophanesque poetae*
> *Atque alii, quorum comoedia prisca virorum est,*
> *Si quis erat dignus describi, quod malus aut fur,*
> *Quod moechus foret aut sicarius aut alioqui*
> *Famosus, multa cum liberatate notabant.*[30]

Eupolis, Cratinus, Aristophanes, and other comic poets in the time of Horace, with large scope and unbridled liberty, boldly and plainly scourged all such abuses as in their ages were generally practised to the staining and blemishing of a fair and beautiful commonweal. Likewise a learned gentleman in his *Apology for*

---

[28] Cf. Massinger, *The Roman Actor*, I, iii, 60–3, below, and Elyot, *The Governor*, sect. 7, above; and Thomas Randolph, *The Muses' Looking-Glass*, I, iv.

[29] With these, except for the moral, Polonius begins his list of types of play (*Hamlet*, II, ii, 402 ff.).

[30] "The poets Eupolis and Cratinus and Aristophanes, and the others to whom Old Comedy belongs, pointed out with great freedom anyone who deserved to be described because he was a bad man or a thief or a whoremaster or a cutthroat or infamous in any other way."

Poetry speaks thus:[31] Tragedies well handled be a most worthy kind of poesie. Comedies make men see and shame at their faults, and proceeding further among other university plays he remembers the Tragedy of Richard the Third[32] acted in St. John's in Cambridge so essentially that had the tyrant Phalaris beheld his bloody proceedings, it had mollified his heart and made him relent at sight of his inhuman massacres. Further he commends of comedies the Cambridge *Pedantius*[33] and the Oxford *Bellum grammaticale*[34] and leaving them passes on to our public plays, speaking liberally in their praise and what commendable use may be gathered of them. If you peruse *Margarita poetica*[35] you may see what excellent uses and sentences[36] he hath gathered out of Terence's *Andria, Eunuchus,* and the rest; likewise out of Plautus's *Amphitryo, Asinaria.*

[Plays teach by example]

[13] Is thy mind noble and wouldst thou be further stirred up to magnanimity? Behold, upon the stage thou mayst see Hercules, Achilles, Alexander, Caesar, Alcibiades, Lysander, Sertorius, Hannibal, Antigonus, Philip of Macedon, Mithridates of Pontus, Pyrrhus of Epirus, Agesilaus among the Lacedemonians, Epaminondas among the Thebans, Scaevola alone entering the armed tents of Porsenna, Horatius Cocles alone withstanding the whole army of the Etrurians, Leonidas of Sparta choosing a lion to lead a band of deer rather than one deer to conduct an army of lions, with infinite others in their own persons, qualities, and shapes, animating thee with courage, deterring thee from cowardice. Hast thou of thy country well deserved and art thou of thy labor evil requited? To associate[37] thee thou mayst see the valiant Roman Marcellus pursue Hannibal at Nola, conquering Syracusa, vanquishing the Gauls at Padua, and presently (for his reward) banished his country into Greece. There thou mayest see Scipio Africanus, now triumphing for the conquest of all Africa and

---

[31] The remainder of the paragraph is taken, and in part quoted, from Sir John Harington's *Apologie of Poetry*, prefixed to his translation of Ariosto's *Orlando Furioso*, published in 1591. For other quotations see the index under *Harington*.

[32] A Latin tragedy by Thomas Legge, 1579.

[33] A Latin comedy by Edward Forsett, acted in Trinity College, Cambridge.

[34] *Bellum grammaticale, sive Nominum verborumque discordia civilis*, acted in Christ Church, Cambridge, in 1592. The title means *Grammatical War, or Civil Strife between Nouns and Verbs.*

[35] An anthology compiled by Albertus de Eyb, circulated in the fifteenth, sixteenth, and seventeenth centuries.   [36] See the index.   [37] Accompany.

immediately exiled the confines of Romania. Art thou inclined to lust? Behold the falls of the Tarquins in the rape of Lucrece;[38] the guerdon of luxury in the death of Sardanapalus; Appius destroyed in the ravishing of Virginia; and the destruction of Troy in the lust of Helena.[39] Art thou proud? Our scene presents thee with the fall of Phaeton; Narcissus pining in the love of his shadow; ambitious Haman now calling himself a god, and by and by thrust headlong among the devils. We present men with the ugliness of their vices to make them the more to abhor them, as the Persians use, who, above all sins loathing drunkenness, accustomed in their solemn feasts to make their servants and captives extremely overcome with wine and then call their children to view their nasty and loathsome behavior, making them hate that sin in themselves which showed so gross and abominable in others. The like use may be gathered of the drunkards so naturally imitated in our plays, to the applause of the actor, content of the auditory, and reproving of the vice. Art thou covetous? Go no further than Plautus's comedy called *Euclio*.

> *Dum fallax servus, durus pater, improba lena*
> *Vixerit, et meretrix blanda, Menandros erit.*

While there's false servant, or obdurate sire,
Sly baud, smooth whore, Menandros we'll admire.[40]

To end in a word, art thou addicted to prodigality, envy, cruelty, perjury, flattery, or rage? Our scenes afford thee store of men to shape your lives by, who be frugal, loving, gentle, trusty, without soothing, and in all things temperate. Wouldst thou be honorable, just, friendly, moderate, devout, merciful, and loving concord? Thou mayest see many of their fates and ruins who have been dishonorable, unjust, false, gluttonous, sacrilegious, bloody-minded, and broachers of dissention. Women likewise that are chaste are by us extolled and encouraged in their virtues, being instanced by Diana,[41] Belphoebe, Matilda, Lucrece,[42] and the Countess of Salisbury. The unchaste are by us shown their errors in the persons of Phryne, Lais, Thais, Flora, and among us Rosa-

---

[38] Heywood's own play of *The Rape of Lucrece* shows the punishment of Tarquin.

[39] Helen's guilt is emphasized in Heywood's *Iron Age*, Part II. Other plays, both before and after the publication of the present work, may be instanced in illustration of this passage, such as *Appius and Virginia*, traditionally ascribed to Webster, but held by some to be by Heywood.   [40] Ovid, *Amores*, I, xv, 17-18.

[41] She appears in Heywood's play of *The Golden Age*.

[42] In Heywood's *Rape of Lucrece*.

mond and Mistress Shore.[43] What can sooner print modesty in the souls of the wanton than by discovering unto them the monstrousness of their sin?

[Plays catch the conscience]

[14] It follows that we prove these exercises to have been the discoverers of many notorious murders long concealed from the eyes of the world. To omit all far-fetched instances, we will prove it by a domestic and home-born truth which within these few years happened. At Lynn, in Norfolk, the then Earl of Sussex' players acting the old History of Fair Francis[44] and presenting a woman who, insatiately doting on a young gentleman, the more securely to enjoy his affection, mischievously and secretly murdered her husband; whose ghost haunted her, and at divers times, in her most solitary and private contemplations, in most horrid and fearful shapes appeared and stood before her. As this was acted, a town's-woman (till then of good estimation and report), finding her conscience (at this presentment) extremely troubled,[45] suddenly screeched and cried out: "Oh, my husband, my husband! I see the ghost of my husband fiercely threatening and menacing me." At which shrill and unexpected outcry, the people about her, moved to a strange amazement, inquired the reason of her clamor, when presently, un-urged, she told them that seven

[43] In Heywood's *King Edward IV*.

[44] The Shakespeare Society's edition gives Feyer Frances, often interpreted as Friar Francis. *Fair* seems to fit the story better; certainty seems impossible.

[45] Cf. Hamlet's remarks:

> I have heard
> That guilty creatures sitting at a play
> Have by the very cunning of the scene
> Been struck so to the soul that presently
> They have proclaimed their malefactions;
> For murder, though it have no tongue, will speak
> With most miraculous organ. I'll have these players
> Play something like the murder of my father
> Before mine uncle; I'll observe his looks;
> I'll tent him to the quick. If he but blench,
> I know my course.
>
> *Hamlet*, ii, ii, 596–606.

Massinger has an actor say:

> I once observed
> In a tragedy of ours, in which a murder
> Was acted to the life, a guilty hearer
> Forced by the terror of a wounded conscience
> To make discovery of that which torture
> Could not wring from him.
>
> *The Roman Actor*, ii, i, 90–5.

years ago she, to be possessed of such a gentleman (meaning[46] him), had poisoned her husband, whose fearful image personated itself in the shape of that ghost. Whereupon the murderess was apprehended, before the justices further examined, and by her voluntary confession after condemned. That this is true, as well by the report of the actors as the records of the town, there are many eyewitnesses of this accident yet living vocally to confirm it.

[46] Indicating, setting forth. No examples of the word in this sense since the fifteenth century are given by the *New English Dictionary*. Cf. Shakespeare, *Midsummer Night's Dream*, v, i, 322: "And thus she means, videlicet." Sidney, *Astrophel and Stella*, xxxv, ii: "Meaning my Stella's name."

MARTIN OPITZ

oᎾooᎾo

IN THE SEVENTEENTH CENTURY various associations were formed among literary men in Germany whose purpose it was to delete foreign words and locutions from the language and to recommend a cultivation and love of the native tongue. In his *Buch von der deutschen Poeterei* Opitz expands this general tendency to direct attention specifically to the study and writing of German poetry. He pleads for the production of verse freed from the mechanics of counting syllables without regard for natural word stress and based on inner rather than on external incidents. Although his own verse, which was largely translation or imitation of the classics, Dutch, and French, tended to neutralize the effect of the book, and although the Swabian poet Weckherlin had actually preceded him in his theories, Opitz is accorded an important position in the development of German literature and his name is almost synonymous with the beginning of a new epoch.

The introduction and translation are by Dr. Olga Marx Perlzweig.

BIBLIOGRAPHY

Berghoeffer, W., *Martin Opitz Buch von der deutschen Poeterei* (Göttinger Dissertation). Frankfurt a/M., 1886.

Opitz, Martin, *Buch von der deutschen Poeterei*. Halle, 1913.

THE BOOK CONCERNING GERMAN POETRY (*selections*)

1624

Chapter II

In the beginning poetry was nothing but disguised theology and instruction in matters pertaining to God. Then because this first rough world was too crude and coarse to grasp and understand aright the teaching of wisdom and of the things of heaven, wise men, to further the fear of God, good morals, and conduct, had to hide and conceal what they had evolved in rhymes and fables, which the common people like to hear.

Eumolpus, Musaeus, Orpheus, Homer, Hesiod, and others, the first fathers of wisdom, as Plato called them, and of all good order, instructed the uncouth, almost comparable to cattle, in a more polished and better mode of living. They related many delightful things and put together their words in certain rhymes and rhythms, so that they neither stepped beyond bounds nor contained too little, but presented, as it were, the balanced scales of speech and told many things which gave forth a glamour of prophecies and secrets, so that the simple and ignorant thought they must contain something godly, and thus through the charm of lovely poems, allowed themselves to be led to all virtue and good conduct.

Chapter III

From the above it may be seen how foolishly they behave who make I know not what small matter of poetry and, while they do not actually reject it, hold it in little esteem. They also claim that the poet can be used little or not at all in public offices, since he is so immersed in his agreeable foolishness and serene delight that he usually neglects the other arts and sciences from which we derive real use and honor. Yes, when they wish to show scorn for a man they call him a poet. In this way it happened that common people applied this epithet to Erasmus of Rotterdam, but he answered that he considered himself unworthy of such praise, since even a mediocre poet should be more highly rated than ten philosophers. Furthermore they have much to say about their lies and obnoxious writing and living, and believe that no one can be a good poet without being a bad man, an unbased prejudice which I deem unworthy of a reply.

There is nothing more absurd than to believe that poetry consists only in itself; it includes all arts and sciences. Apuleius calls Homer a man knowing much and versed in all matters. Tertullian calls him the father of the liberal arts. Plato, who became so proficient in writing tragedies that he could compete with others, mixed, as Proclus said of him, the Pythagorean and Socratic quality. He learned geometry from Theodorus Cyrenaeus and the science of the stars from the Egyptian priests and had knowledge of all things. It used to be the custom to paint our Muses dancing a roundelay with joined hands. The name given to them, Muses, as though derived from a word meaning together, meant to suggest the common bond and interrelation of all the arts. Even though verses are but words (albeit that is as impossible as it would be for the body to subsist without the soul) is it not true that Eratosthenes wrote a poem describing the world, that Parmenides and Empedocles wrote concerning the nature of things, that Servilius and Heliodorus, whom Galen mentions, wrote about medicine? Or who can deny that Vergil was a good farmer, Lucretius an excellent naturalist, Manilius an astronomer, Lucanus a historian, Oppianus a hunter, and all of them distinguished philosophers although they were nothing but poets? I must admit, however, that those who wish undeservedly to be considered poets are not a little to blame for this contempt of poetry, for they seek to hide their ignorance under the laurel wreath as Julius Caesar hid his bald head under it. . . .

To write words and syllables according to rules and to write verses is the least one seeks in a poet. He must be euphantastic, that is, full of significant ideas and inventions; he must have a great and fearless mind and he must be able to beget lofty thoughts within himself if his speech is to have value and rise above the earth.

They who demand verses about all they do and plan to do, damage the good name of poetry considerably. No wedding or funeral can take place without us.[1] Just as if no one could die alone, so our verses perish with him. We appear on all bowls and pitchers, on walls and stones, and if a man has acquired a house by cheating, we are supposed to make it honorable with our verses. One wants a poem about another man's wife, another dreamed of his neighbor's daughter, one desires a poem because his sweetheart has smiled at him, or rather in all probability laughed at him—there is no end to their silly demands. We either have to refuse and incur their enmity, or agree and do a decided injury to poetry. For a poet cannot write when he wants to, but when he is able, that is, when the urge of that spirit that Ovid and others say comes from heaven drives him. . . .

I cherish the consoling hope, that not only Latin poetry, which many great men have revived after the barbarism of its long exile, may remain unshaken in its values in spite of these dull times and the scorn of the erudite, but that German poetry also, for which I have unfurled the banner to the best of my poor ability, will be produced by worthy spirits, so that our Fatherland may not lag behind France and Italy.

---

[1] An epithalamium or marriage poem was usual at fashionable weddings in the early seventeenth century, and funeral elegies are found in the complete works of most of the poets of the time.

PHILIP MASSINGER

oᴗooᴗo

THE ROMAN ACTOR

1626

In this play Massinger gives us the most spirited defense of the stage that came from the pen of any Elizabethan dramatist. In fact, he goes even further than logical defense, for he also presents a play within a play, called *The Cure of Avarice*, which exemplifies the principles set forth in the speeches here reproduced. Parthenius laments the avarice of his father, and the Roman actor, Paris, suggests:

> Nor can it appear
> Like an impossibility but that
> Your father looking on a covetous man
> Presented on the stage as in a mirror
> May see his own deformity and loathe it.[1]

The plan is carried out but fails to produce the desired effect on the old miser, who stoutly declares:

> An old fool to be gulled thus! had he died
> As I resolve to do, not to be altered,
> It had gone off twanging.[2]

In spite of this comic failure, however, I do not doubt the seriousness of Massinger's defense of the stage. While he is one of the more moral of the playwrights of his age, it seems likely that he represents current opinion. Probably even Shakespeare, if forced to defend his profession, would have said pretty much what Massinger puts in the mouths of his characters and doubtless believed himself. At least Massinger presents respectable and current opinion, since, as the notes indicate, various passages come from Horace, one of the chief lawgivers to the dramatists of the age.

The accusation of libeling great men brought against the quality or profession of actors, and with them dramatic authors, appears through-

---

[1] II, i, 95–99. For the context see Thomas Heywood, *Apology*, sect. 14, note 45, above. For the mirror see the index under *Cicero, his description of comedy.*
[2] II, i, 407–9.

out the speeches of Aretinus; Paris, apparently speaking for Massinger, vigorously disclaims any intention of immediate political reference by the dramatist. The matter is one of much interest to any interpreter of Elizabethan and Jacobean literature for two reasons, namely (1) Elizabethan public men seem to have believed in it; (2) many students at present attempt to give political interpretations to Elizabethan works of art. If Elizabethan authors were continually making cryptic political references, any effective literary criticism must take their political purpose into account; on the other hand, if their allusions to politics are open and clear, and for the most part obvious to us, the critic must conduct himself quite differently.

The present writer takes the disclaimer of Massinger—and there are others that might be brought forward in its support—as a serious statement, and believes that they who search zealously for what is called historical allegory are likely to make literature, whether a poem like the *Faerie Queene* or a drama like *King Lear,* into something other and less important than it is, that, as Massinger phrases it,

> they make that a libel which the poet
> Writ for comedy.

BIBLIOGRAPHY

Sandidge, William L., A Critical Edition of Massinger's *The Roman Actor.* Princeton University Press, 1929. See the introduction, pp. 17–24.

THE ROMAN ACTOR (*selections*)

[Act I, scene i, ll. 1–26]

Aesopus. What do we act today?
Latinus.   Agave's frenzy,
With Pentheus' bloody end.
Paris.   It skills not what;
The times are dull, and all that we receive
Will hardly satisfy the day's expense.
The Greeks, to whom we owe the first invention,
Both of the buskined scene and humble sock,[1]
That reign in every noble family,
Declaim against us; and our amphitheater,
Great Pompey's work, that hath given full delight

[1] See Horace, *Art of Poetry,* 275–81, above.

Both to the eye and ear of fifty thousand   10
Spectators in one day, as if it were
Some unknown desert, or great Rome unpeopled,
Is quite forsaken.
    Lat.   Pleasures of worse natures
Are gladly entertained; and they that shun us,
Practise, in private, sports the stews would blush at.
A litter borne by eight Liburnian slaves,
To buy diseases from a glorious strumpet,
The most censorious of our Roman gentry,
Nay, of the guarded robe, the senators,
Esteem an easy purchase.
    Par.   Yet grudge us   20
That with delight join profit,[2] and endeavor
To build their minds up fair, and on the stage
Decipher to the life what honors wait
On good and glorious actions, and the shame
That treads upon the heels of vice, the salary
Of six sestertii. . . .

[Act I, scene iii, ll. 31–141]

    Aretinus   Stand forth.
In thee, as being the chief of thy profession,
I do accuse the quality of treason,[3]
As libellers against the state and Caesar.
    Par. Mere accusations are not proofs, my lord:
In what are we delinquents?
    Aret.   You are they
That search into the secrets of the time,
And, under feigned names, on the stage, present
Actions not to be touched at; and traduce
Persons of rank and quality of both sexes,   40
And, with satirical and bitter jests,
Make even the senators ridiculous
To the plebeians.
    Par.   If I free not myself,
And, in myself, the rest of my profession,
From these false imputations, and prove
That they make that a libel which the poet

[2] *Ibid.*, 334, above.   [3] *The quality:* actors generally.

Writ for a comedy,[4] so acted too,
It is but justice that we undergo
The heaviest censure.
   Aret.   Are you on the stage,
You talk so boldly?
   Par.   The whole world being one,   50
This place is not exempted; and I am
So confident in the justice of our cause,
That I could wish Caesar, in whose great name
All kings are comprehended, sat as judge,
To hear our plea, and then determine of us.
If to express a man sold to his lusts,
Wasting the treasure of his time and fortunes
In wanton dalliance, and to what sad end
A wretch that's so given over does arrive at;
Deterring careless youth, by his example,[5]   60
From such licentious courses; laying open
The snares of bawds, and the consuming arts
Of prodigal strumpets, can deserve reproof;
Why are not all your golden principles,
Writ down by grave philosophers to instruct us
To choose fair virtue for our guide, not pleasure,
Condemned unto the fire?
   Sura.   There's spirit in this.
   Par. Or if desire of honor was the base
On which the building of the Roman empire
Was raised up to this height; if to inflame   70
The noble youth with an ambitious heat
To endure the frosts of danger, nay, of death,
To be thought worthy the triumphal wreath
By glorious undertakings, may deserve
Reward or favor from the commonwealth;
Actors may put in for as large a share
As all the sects of the philosophers:
They with cold precepts—perhaps seldom read—

---

[4] Cf. Jonson, prologue to the *Epicoene:* "They make a libel, which he made a play."
In the dedication of *Volpone* to the universities he warns public men against "these
invading interpreters."

[5] Edmund Spenser, in his letter to Sir Walter Raleigh explaining the *Faerie Queene*,
emphasizes the power of poetry to teach by example, saying: "So much more profitable and gracious is doctrine (i.e., teaching) by ensample than by rule." Sidney
(*Defense*, sect. 21, above) refers to poetry as teaching by example.

Deliver what an honorable thing
The active virtue is;[6] but does that fire   80
The blood, or swell the veins with emulation,
To be both good and great, equal to that
Which is presented on our theaters?
Let a good actor, in a lofty scene,
Show great Alcides honored in the sweat
Of his twelve labors; or a bold Camillus,
Forbidding Rome to be redeemed with gold
From the insulting Gauls; or Scipio,
After his victories, imposing tribute
On conquered Carthage; if done to the life,   90
As if they saw their dangers, and their glories,
And did partake with them in their rewards,
All that have any spark of Roman in them,
The slothful arts laid by, contend to be
Like those they see presented.
   Rusticus.   He has put
The consuls to their whisper.
   Par.   But 'tis urged
That we corrupt youth, and traduce superiors.
When do we bring a vice upon the stage,
That does go off unpunished? Do we teach,
By the success of wicked undertakings,   100
Others to tread in their forbidden steps?
We show no arts of Lydian panderism,
Corinthian poisons, Persian flatteries,
But mulcted so in the conclusion that
Even those spectators that were so inclined
Go home changed men.[7] And, for traducing such
That are above us, publishing to the world

[6] For poet *versus* philosopher see Sidney's *Defense*, sect. 22, above.
[7] Poets and critics felt there was moral value in the presentation of wicked actions.
Spenser writes in preface to a tale of evil characters:
            Redoubted knights, and honorable dames,
              To whom I level all my labor's end, .
              Right sore I fear, lest with unworthy blames
              This odious argument my rhymes should shend,
              Or aught your goodly patience offend,
            Whiles of a wanton lady I do write,
              Which with her loose incontinence doth blend
              The shining glory of your sovereign light,
           And knighthood foul defaced by a faithless knight.
            But never let th'ensample of the bad
              Offend the good; for good by paragon

Their secret crimes, we are as innocent
As such as are born dumb. When we present
An heir that does conspire against the life 110
Of his dear parent, numbering every hour
He lives, as tedious to him; if there be,
Among the auditors, one whose conscience tells him
He is of the same mould, we cannot help it.
Or, bringing on the stage a loose adulteress,
That does maintain the riotous expense
Of him that feeds her greedy lust, yet suffers
The lawful pledges of a former bed
To starve the while for hunger; if a matron,
However great in fortune, birth, or titles, 120
Guilty of such a foul unnatural sin,
Cry out, 'Tis writ by me, we cannot help it.
Or, when a covetous man's expressed, whose wealth
Arithmetic cannot number, and whose lordships
A falcon in one day cannot fly over;
Yet he so sordid in his mind, so griping,
As not to afford himself the necessaries
To maintain life; if a patrician—
Though honored with a consulship—find himself
Touched to the quick in this, we cannot help it. 130
Or, when we show a judge that is corrupt,
And will give up his sentence as he favors
The person, not the cause; saving the guilty,
If of his faction, and as oft condemning
The innocent, out of particular spleen;
If any in this reverend assembly,
Nay, e'en yourself, my lord, that are the image
Of absent Caesar, feel something in your bosom,
That puts you in remembrance of things past,
Or things intended, 'tis not in us to help it. 140
I have said, my lord; and now, as you find cause,
Or censure us, or free us with applause.

> Of evil, may more notably be rad,
> As white seems fairer, matched with black attone.
> *Faerie Queene*, III, ix, 1–2.

Sir John Harington, in his *Apologie of Poetry*, prefixed to his translation of the *Orlando Furioso* of Ariosto, exhorts the reader of licentious parts of the poem "to read them as my author meant them, to breed detestation and not delectation."

Cf. Sidney's reference to evil men sent off the stage "manacled" (*Defense*, sect. 25).

PIERRE CORNEILLE

o◯oo◯o

CORNEILLE SHOWS how a great dramatist looked upon the "rules" derived from Aristotle at a period when they were fully and strictly formulated. In the first selection he does not use the expression *unity of place*, but speaks rather in the manner of Castelvetro; in the *Discourses* the formula occurs.

The translation is by Dr. Clara W. Crane.

BIBLIOGRAPHY

Bray, René, *La tragédie cornélienne devant la critique classique d'après la querelle de Sophonisbe (1663)*. Paris, 1927.

Fisher, Dorothea F., *Corneille and Racine in England*. New York, 1904.

Corneille, Pierre, *Œuvres*. Paris, 1862.

Faguet, Émile, *En lisant Corneille*. Paris, 1913.

DEDICATORY EPISTLE TO *LA SUIVANTE* (*in part*)

1634

[Not a slave to the rules]

We pardon many things to the ancients; we often admire in their writings what we should not tolerate in our own; we make mysteries of their imperfections, and hide their mistakes under the name of poetic licenses. The learned Scaliger noted faults in all the Latins, and men less learned than he have pointed them out in the Greeks, and even in Vergil, whose altars he adorned with the scorn of others. I leave you then to reflect whether it would not be ridiculous presumption to claim that close criticism could not touch our works, when those of these great geniuses of antiquity could not stand up under rigorous examination. . . .

To come to this *Suivante* which I dedicate to you, it is of a genre which requires a style naïve rather than pompous. The intrigues and ruses are chiefly those of comic interplay; the passions enter only accidentally. The rules of the ancients are quite religiously observed in it. There is only one principal action, and to it all the others converge; the place is no more extensive than the stage itself; and the time is no longer than the representation, if you except the dinner hour, which passes between the first and the second acts. Even the linking of scene to scene, which is only an embellishment and not a requirement, is observed; and if you will take the trouble to count the verses, you will find no more in one act than another. Not that I am a slave to these strict exactions; I love to follow the rules, but far from being their slave, I enlarge them or narrow them down according to the demands of my subject, and I break without scruple even that which concerns the duration of the action, when its severity seems to me absolutely incompatible with the beauties of the events I am describing. To know the rules and to understand the secret of skillfully adjusting them to our stage are two very different sciences; and perhaps to make a play succeed nowadays it is not enough to have studied the books of Aristotle and Horace. I hope one day to discuss these matters more fundamentally, and to show the nature of this verisimilitude which the great masters of the other centuries have followed even while they were giving speech to animals, and things which had no existence. But my opinion is that of Terence: that since we are making poems to be represented, our first aim should be to please the court and the people, and to attract a great crowd to our performances. We should then, if possible, add the rules, so as not to displease the learned,[1] but to get applause from everyone. But, first of all, we should gain the public voice; otherwise, however fine and regular our play may be, if it is hissed off the stage, the learned will not dare speak in our favor, but will prefer to say that we have misunderstood the rules rather than to praise us when we are cried down by the general consent of those who go to a comedy only to be amused.

DISCOURSE I

On Dramatic Poetry (*in part*)

1660

[Verisimilitude]

It is necessary to observe unity of action, place, and time; that no one doubts. But there is no small difficulty in knowing what

---

[1] A suggestion that the rules were not a matter of interest to the public generally but only to those educated to demand them. Compare the attitude of Lope de Vega in the selection given above.

unity of action is, or how far one can extend this unity of time and place. The poet must treat his subject with regard for necessity and verisimilitude. . . . . The great tragic subjects which vigorously move the passions and oppose their impetuosity to the laws of duty or the tendernesses of kinship must always run counter to verisimilitude; and they would find no belief among their audiences if they were not supported either by the authority of history . . . or by the acceptations of common opinion, which give us an audience already persuaded. There is no verisimilitude in Medea's killing her children, in Clytemnestra's murder of her husband, in Orestes's stabbing of his mother; but history says they did so, and the representation of these great crimes meets no incredulity. It is neither true nor in accord with verisimilitude that Andromeda, exposed and at the mercy of a sea-monster, should have been rescued by a flying knight with winged feet; but that is a fiction which antiquity accepted, and as it has been transmitted to us, no one is offended at seeing it on the stage. But it would not be acceptable to invent new stories on these models. What truth or opinion has made acceptable would be rejected if it had no other foundation than likeness to truth or opinion. That is why our learned doctor said that *subjects come by chance*, which makes things happen, *and not by art*, which imagines them. Chance is mistress of events, and the choice she gives us among those she presents to us involves a secret prohibition to interfere with her and produce any event on the stage which is not in accordance with her ways. Thus *the ancient tragedies were centered in a few families only, because only to a few do things happen which are worthy of tragedy.*[1] Succeeding ages have given us material enough to permit us to break away from the narrow limits of these stories and to follow no longer in the steps of the Greeks, but they have not given us the liberty to set aside their rules. We must still, as we can, adjust ourselves to them and accept them. Cutting out the chorus has obliged us to introduce more episodes than the ancients used . . . ; but we need not go beyond their rules in going outside their practice.

[The utility of drama]

We must, then, know what these rules are. . . . The assertion I have made from the beginning, *that dramatic poetry aims only to please the spectators*, does not contradict those who think to ennoble

---

[1] Aristotle, *Poetics*, XIII and XIV.

art by giving it the aim of profiting as well as pleasing. The very dispute is useless, for it is impossible to please according to the rules, without including much that is useful. . . . Thus, though the useful enters only under the form of the delightful, it does not cease to be necessary, and there is more value in investigating how it is to be introduced, than in raising . . . a vain question about its usefulness. I think, then, that there are four kinds of utility.

The first consists in sentences and moral teachings, which can be scattered throughout; but they must be soberly employed and rarely in general discourse. . . .

The second lies in the natural painting of the vices and virtues, which never fails to achieve its end when it is well done and when the traits are recognizable, and not to be confounded, vice with virtue. This character is always to be loved, though unfortunate, and this one always hated, though triumphant. . . .

It is the interest we like to take in the virtuous which has brought about the fashion of ending a dramatic poem by the punishment of evil actions and the rewarding of good, which is not a precept of art, but a custom we have adopted and which we depart from at our peril. . . . The success of virtue, in spite of perils and obstacles, excites us to embrace it; and the failure of crime or injustice is capable of adding to our natural horror a fear of like misfortune. . . . [This will be discussed in *Discourse III.*]

DISCOURSE III

On the Three Unities (*in part*)

1660

I hold then, as I have said already, that unity of action consists, in comedy, in unity of intrigue, or of the obstacles to the designs of the principal characters, and in tragedy, in unity of peril, whether the hero succumbs or escapes it. . . .

Further, unity of action does not mean that one may not display more than one action on the stage. What the poet chooses for his subject must have a beginning, a middle, and an end; and not only are these three parts as many separate actions which contribute towards the principal one, but also each of them may contain others in the same subordination to it. . . .

[As for the unity of time] for me I find that there are subjects so difficult to compress within so short a time, that not only will I grant them their entire twenty-four hours, but I will even use the license the Philosopher gives to exceed that time a little, and unscrupulously extend it to thirty hours.[2]. . . I find that a writer is somewhat inconvenienced by this constraint, which, indeed, forced some of the ancients to commit the impossible. . . .

Many cry out against this rule, which they call tyrannical, and they would be justified if it were founded only on the authority of Aristotle; but what should lead to its acceptance is that natural reason which supports it. A dramatic poem is an imitation, or rather, a portrait of human action; and it is beyond question that portraits are more excellent as they better resemble the original. The representation lasts two hours, and it would be a perfect resemblance if the action which it represented did not require more time in reality. Thus let us not stop at twelve or at twenty-four hours, but compress the action of the poem into the least time possible so that the representation shall be more like and more perfect. . . .

But do not mark the time. When we take a longer time, as for example ten hours, I should prefer that the eight which must be lost should be used up in the intervals between the acts. . . . Nevertheless, I believe that the fifth act, by a particular privilege, may force time a little, so that the part of the action it represents may include a little more than it requires for the presentation. The reason for that is that the spectator is then impatient for the end. . . .

As for unity of place, I find no precept concerning it in either Aristotle or Horace.[3] This has led some to think that the rule was established only in consequence of that of unity of time, and so to extend it to admit any place to which a man can go and return in twenty-four hours. That opinion is somewhat free; if one were to represent an actor riding post, the two sides of the theater might represent Paris and Rouen. I should prefer, so as not to incommode the spectator in any way, that what one represented before him in two hours and what one displayed to him on a stage that did not change should be kept within a room or a hall, whichever one might choose. But often that is so difficult, not to say impossible, that one must of necessity find some extension in place as well as in time. . . . We cannot take kings from their private

[2] Aristotle, *Poetics*, v, 49b9, above.
[3] Butcher says unity of place "is nowhere even hinted at in the *Poetics*" (p. 291); see Aristotle, *Poetics*, xxiv, 59b17, above.

apartments, for instance, to discuss their affairs in public places.

I believe, then, that we must seek to make this unity as exact as possible, but as it does not fit with every sort of subject, I should willingly grant that everything taking place in the same city possessed unity of place. Not that I should wish the stage to represent the entire city—that would be rather too large—, but only two or three particular places enclosed within the compass of its walls.[4] Thus the scene of *Cinna* does not leave Rome, and is now the apartment of Augustus in his palace, now Emilia's house. . . . The *Cid* further increases the number of particular places without leaving Seville. And as the linking of scene to scene is not observed in that play, the stage in the first act is the house of Chimène, the apartment of the princess in the king's palace, and the public square. The second act adds to these the king's chamber. And surely there is some excess in this freedom. In some way to correct the multiplying of scenes when it is unavoidable, I should like to make two conditions: one, that the scene should never be changed within the act, but only between the acts, as is done in the first three acts of *Cinna;* the other, that the two places should not have different scenery, and that neither should be given a name, but only the general place in which the two are included, as Paris, Rome, Lyons, or Constantinople.[5]

It is easy for the speculative critics to be severe, but if they would give ten or twelve dramatic poems to the public, they might perhaps enlarge their rules even more than I have done, as soon as they realized by experience what constraint their precision required and how many beauties it banned from the stage. However that may be, these are my opinions, or, if you will, my heresies, on the principal points of dramatic art; and I do not know how better to harmonize ancient rules and modern taste.

[4] Cf. Dryden, *Essay of Dramatic Poesy*, sect. 13, p. 607, below.

[5] "Often there is no need of specifying a scene's location or hour. It is needful for two characters to converse; it makes no difference where they talk—upstairs, downstairs, or in my lady's chamber, or in her garden, or on a city square. In such scenes the painstaking tags of the editors are really an impertinence. Few of the scenes are definitely placed by headings in the original texts. Many are deftly fixed by allusions in the dialogue, but some should be frankly tagged in modern editions 'unlocated'" (Hazelton Spencer, *The Art and Life of William Shakespeare* [New York, 1940], pp. 100–1).

GEORGES DE SCUDÉRY

o◯ooo◯o

THE ROMANCE is by Madeleine de Scudéry, but the preface by Georges.
It is here included as an early discussion of what we now call the novel.
The work is, however, thought of according to the epic tradition,
founded on Homer. The same confusion, if it be that, was in the minds
of Sidney and Scaliger, who thought of *Theagenes and Chariclea* (see the
index) as an epic.

The translation is by Dr. Clara W. Crane.

BIBLIOGRAPHY

Georges de Scudéry, *Works*. Paris, 1641.

THE PREFACE TO *IBRAHIM* (*selections*)

1641

[The rules of art]

I do not know what sort of praise the ancients thought they were
giving to the painter who, when he could not finish his picture,
threw his sponge at it to let chance do his work; but I know very
well that I could not have been pleased with such praise, and that
I should have taken it for satire rather than commendation. The
works of the spirit are too significant to be left to chance; and I
had rather be accused of having failed consciously, than of having
succeeded without knowing what I was about. . . . Every art has
certain rules which by infallible means lead to the ends proposed;
and if an architect makes his plans carefully he can be certain of
the beauty of his building. Do not think, reader, that I expect
my work to succeed because I have followed the rules by which
it might succeed. I know that in this work as in the mathematical
sciences there may be a failure in the execution, though the art be
sound. Thus I am undertaking this discussion only to demonstrate that if there are faults in my work they come from my weakness, not from my negligence. Let me then . . . show you . . . what
I have been trying to do.

[Ancient example]

As we can be learned only through what others teach us, and as it is for the last comer to follow those who go before, I have concluded that in drawing up a plan for this work I must consult the Greeks . . . , and to try by imitating them to arrive at the same end which these great men proposed to themselves. I have observed that in the famous romances of antiquity, in imitation of the epic poem, there is one principal action, to which all the others are bound, which rules the whole work, and to whose perfection all the others only contribute. This action in the *Iliad* is the ruin of Troy . . . ; in Vergil, the death of Turnus, or better, the conquest of Italy; nearer us, in Tasso,[1] the taking of Jerusalem; and to pass from the poem to the romance, which is my chief concern, in Heliodorus, the marriage of Chariclea and Theagenes.[2] Not that epic episodes and the various stories of the romances are not rather beauties than faults, but the skill of the user must always bind them in some way to the main action, so that through his ingenious linking all the parts make but one body, and none seems useless and separate. Thus the marriage of my Justinian and his Isabelle being the end proposed, I have taken every care that each part of my work leads to that end, that there is a close connection between the parts, and that except for the obstacles that fortune puts in the way of my hero's desires, everything advances, or attempts to advance, the marriage which is the conclusion of my work. Now the great geniuses of antiquity whose light I borrow, knowing arrangement to be one of the chief parts of a picture, have so successfully endowed with it their speaking pictures, that it would be as stupid as arrogant not to wish to imitate them. They have not done as those painters do who display on the same canvas a prince in his cradle, on his throne, and in his shroud, and who by this confusion embarrass their spectators; but with incomparable skill they have begun their story in the middle, so as to create suspense for their reader from the very opening of the book, and in order to keep the story within reasonable limits they have (and I following them) made it last only a year,[3] and given all the rest in indirect narration, so that everything is ingeniously placed and of a reasonable length. The result is indubitable pleasure for the reader and glory for the author. But among all the

---

[1] Cf. Milton's list of epics in the *Reason of Church Government*, sect. 1, below.
[2] See the index. [3] Cf. Minturno, *Arte poetica*, 1, 24, above.

rules which must be observed in composing these works, verisimilitude is certainly the most necessary. It is like the foundation stone of the building; on that alone the whole stands. Without it nothing can touch, nothing can please. And if its enticing deception does not deceive in the romances, to read them can only disgust the mind instead of pleasing it. I have, then, tried never to depart from verisimilitude; for it I have observed manners and morals, the laws, the religions, the bents of various peoples; and to increase verisimilitude, I have wished the foundation of my work to be historical, my principal personages distinguished in true history as illustrious, and my wars such as have actually taken place.[4] There is no doubt that one can in this way achieve his end; for when truth and falsehood are confounded by a skillful hand, the mind has difficulty in distinguishing them; nor does it easily destroy what it finds pleasing. But when invention does not avail itself of this artifice, and when falsehood is easily discoverable, the great untruth makes no impression upon the soul and gives no pleasure. Indeed, how shall I be touched by the misfortunes of the Queen of Guindaye and the King of Astrobacia, if I know that their very realms are not on the map of the world? . . . But that is not the only fault through which a work can depart from verisimilitude. We have seen romances which offered us monstrosities; their authors, wishing to show us miracles and holding too much to the marvelous, have made grotesques much like the visions of a fevered brain. We might with much more reason than the Duke of Ferrara have asked these gentlemen what he asked Ariosto after he had read the *Orlando:* "Mr. Lodovico, where the devil did you find so much nonsense?" As for me, I hold that the more natural events are, the more they satisfy us; and the ordinary course of the sun seems more wonderful to me than the strange and awful rays of comets. For this reason I have not in my story caused so many shipwrecks as there are in some of the old romances. And to speak seriously, Du Bartas might say of their authors, that "their words tighten and loose the reins of the charioteers of Aeolus." You might think that God had given them the winds done up in a bag as they were given to Ulysses, so freely do these gentlemen loose them to create shipwreck. Authors make tempest and shipwreck at will; they stir them up on a peaceful sea; they find reefs and rocks in places where the most experienced pilots have never noticed them. But those who make so

[4] See *history*, in the index.

free with the winds do not know that the prophet has told us that God keeps them in his treasury, and that philosophy, with all her clairvoyance, has not discovered their hiding place. I do not say that shipwrecks must be banished from romances; I approve of them in the works of others, and I use them in my own; I even recognize that the sea is the most fitting scene for great changes, and that some have called it the theater of inconstancy. But as all excess is bad, I use it only with moderation to preserve verisimilitude. For the same purpose I do not overwhelm my hero with the prodigious number of accidents which happen to some others, for I feel they depart from verisimilitude; no man has ever lived a life so thwarted. It is better, in my opinion, to separate the adventures, to make different stories of them, to give them several heroes; and so to appear fertile and judicious at the same time, and to be always true to the verisimilitude which is so necessary. Indeed, those who so often undo whole armies by a single man's exploits have forgotten the proverb which says, *Nul contre deux;* and they do not realize that antiquity shows us that even Hercules's strength could not have achieved so much.[5] It is beyond question that to represent the true heroic ardor you must make it do something extraordinary, as if by a transport of the hero, but you must not continue with the same force, for, if you do, the incredible actions will degenerate into ridiculous stories and will not touch the spirit. This fault carries another along with it; for those who do nothing but heap adventure on adventure, without ornament and without rousing the passions by the artifices of rhetoric, are tedious when they think they are amusing. Such dry and artless narrative is more like an old chronicle than a romance, which may well adorn itself with rhetorical decorations, since history, wholly severe and scrupulous as it is, will not permit their use.

[Character]

After having described an adventure, a bold design, or some surprising event capable of giving rise to the finest sentiments in the world, certain authors content themselves with assuring us that such a hero thought of very fine things, without telling us of them; and it is only those fine things that I should desire to know. For how do I know that in these events fortune has not played as large a part as he? that his valor is not a brutal valor? How do I

---

[5] *Ne Hercules quidem adversus duos.* "Two are enough to encounter Hercules" (Chapman, *The Revenge of Bussy D'Ambois,* III, iii, 24).

know that he has endured like a man and a gentleman the evils that have befallen him? It is not by external things, it is not by the caprices of destiny, that I can judge of him; it is by the movements of his soul and by the things that he says. I honor all those who are writing today, I recognize their personality, their work, their merit, but as apotheosis is only for the dead, they will not take it amiss that, since they are still alive, I do not deify them, and that on this occasion I propose for example only the great and incomparable d'Urfé.[6] Certainly it must be admitted that he has deserved his reputation, that the love the entire world has for him is just, and that so many different nations who have translated his book into their various languages had a reason for doing so. The truth is, he is admirable in every way: he is fertile in adventures, reasonable in inventions; everything in him is marvelous, everything is beautiful; and what is most important, everything is natural and full of verisimilitude. But among so many rare things, what I esteem most is that he knows how to touch the passions so delicately that one can call him the painter of the soul. He goes searching in the depth of the heart for its most secret feelings; and in the diversity of natures he represents, each man finds his own portrait.

And so, if among mortals, any deserves an altar, only d'Urfé has a right to claim one.

In this sort of composition there is certainly nothing more important than to impress very strongly on the mind of the reader the *idea*, or better, the *image*, of the heroes, but to impress it so that the reader may feel he knows these heroes, for that is what interests him in their adventures and from that comes his pleasure. Now to make him know them perfectly, it is not enough to tell how many times they have been shipwrecked, or how many times they have fallen among thieves; they must be judged by their discourse, their inclinations. Otherwise, one has a right to say of these mute heroes the apt word of antiquity: *Parle afin que je te voye.*[7]

[6] Honoré d'Urfé published the first and second parts of *L'Astrée*, a pastoral romance, in 1610; a third part followed. Boileau wrote that the author sustained his plan "with a narrative at once lively and flowery, with ingenious fictions, and with characters that are as finely imagined as they are agreeably varied and well developed. Altogether he composed a romance that gained him a high reputation and was much esteemed, even by persons of the most exquisite taste" (quoted by Louis Mercier, in the preface to *L'Astrée* [Lyon, 1925] p. xxiv).

[7] Speak that I may know what you are.

[Manners and customs]

Now if from verisimilitude and inclinations expressed in words, we wish to go on to manners and customs, to pass from the pleasing to the useful and from diversion to example, I must tell you, reader, that here virtue appears always rewarded and vice punished, if by a just and sensible repentance he who has transgressed has not obtained his pardon from Heaven. Thus I have observed, in this matter, a sameness of manners and morals in all the persons who act, except when passion brings them to transgress, or when remorse touches them. I have even taken care that the faults committed in my story should be caused by love or ambition, which are the most noble of the passions, and that they should be rejected if suggested by the evil counsels of flatterers, in order to preserve the respect due to kings.[8] You will see in this, reader, if I am not deceived, that the decorum of things and of the conditions of men is rather exactly observed; and I have put nothing into my book which ladies may not read without lowering their eyes and blushing.

[8]The ideal prince is not subject to flattery. See Machiavelli's *The Prince*, chap. xxiii.

JOHN MILTON

oᎤooᎤo

THE CHIEF INTEREST in Milton's poetic theories is that reflected from his poetic accomplishment. Some of his critical utterances are rather obvious apologies by a poet moved as much by the work immediately before him as by any philosophical views. An instance is his violent attack on rhyme in the paragraph on the Verse prefixed to *Paradise Lost*—an attack that goes beyond objection to rhyme in the epic. Yet Milton had himself used rhyme in sonnets not many years before, and was later to use it in the choruses of the *Samson Agonistes* (unless an early date be assigned to that work). Even the introductory remarks to the *Samson* are still apologetic in tone, though in idea not dissimilar to other expressions of their author's views. The passages least apparently related to his own poetry are those in the *Reason of Church Government*, given here, and a few lines in the tractate *Of Education*, in which he indicates he would have his pupils learn "that sublime art which in Aristotle's *Poetics*, in Horace, and the Italian commentaries of Castelvetro, Tasso, Mazzoni,[1] and others teaches what the laws are of a true epic poem, what of a dramatic, what of a lyric. This would make them soon perceive what despicable creatures our common rhymers and play-writers be." In the context he speaks also of Longinus and other rhetorical writers.

It would appear, then, that Milton had an excellent knowledge of classical and Renaissance theory. There is inaccuracy, however, in his manner of speaking of the Italians; Castelvetro's work is a commentary, but those of Tasso and Mazzoni are not; perhaps Milton has in mind their dependence on Aristotle; at any rate, the word probably should not suggest lack of acquaintance with them. Clearly, the writers that came first to Milton's mind are primarily conservative. Castelvetro is not without independence, yet he is after all a commentator. Tasso, though he wrote the *Jerusalem Delivered*, also rewrote it in closer accord with the ruling Aristotelianism of his time.[2] Mazzoni defended Dante as one who had observed the ancient rule of structure. Of those who

---

[1] All represented in the present volume. For quotations from Milton in addition to those here given, see the selection from Edward Phillips below, and the index under Milton. [2] See the introduction to Tasso's *Discourses on the Heroic Poem*, above.

asserted the rights of modern literature Milton says nothing. Perhaps this means no more than that he thought their writings relatively unsuitable for his young pupils.

Milton's practice is primarily classical. The *Samson Agonistes* is written with Aristotle in mind; he is quoted on the title page, mentioned in the preface, and virtually quoted in the concluding lines of the drama itself. Yet "the best rule to all who endeavor to write tragedy" is to be found not so much in Aristotle as in the three tragic poets themselves, Aeschylus, Sophocles, and Euripides. And the plays the *Samson* most resembles are not among those selected for praise by Aristotle; they are rather the *Prometheus Bound* and the *Oedipus at Colonus*. Milton worked from Greek practice rather than Aristotelian precept. Nor in spite of its obvious classicism is the play without romantic elements, even comic ones, as in the elaborate description of the fully dressed Dalilah as a ship (ll. 710–21), a figure frequent in the dramatists earlier in the century.

In the epic Milton moves in some sense closer to Aristotle than to the obvious models. Though an admirer of Homer, the Stagirite dared to suggest that the Homeric poems were too long (*Poetics*, XXIV, 59b17). In *Paradise Regained*, Milton gave an example of epic compression that might be supposed to satisfy the most extreme demands. *Paradise Lost* is much shorter than the *Iliad*, and shorter than the *Odyssey* by over 1500 lines; English, moreover, tends to be more diffuse than Greek and the Homeric verse is hexameter, while that of Milton is pentameter. Further, most readers will probably consider *Paradise Lost*, though it includes the long episode of the creation, more compact than either the *Iliad* or the *Odyssey*. Even the *Aeneid*, allowing for the hexameter and the greater compactness of Latin, must be reckoned as longer than *Paradise Lost*. But Milton is not to be set down as a mere classicist in the long poem; he admired the *Orlando Furioso* and the *Faerie Queene*, both stumbling blocks to the Aristotelians, and various marks of his interest in the romances appear even in *Paradise Regained* (III, 338–43) where he draws one of his most extensive ornamental comparisons from Boiardo's *Orlando Innamorato*, the sort of passage the classicist Bentley was to reject from *Paradise Lost*. If it is difficult to say that Milton followed nature rather than the rules of Aristotle, a procedure he commends in our first selection, he can at least be said to have enriched his classical models. The departure of Milton from orthodox precept is most apparent when his work is contrasted with the Vergilian Biblical epic of Vida, the *Christiad*. The theological exposition in the third book of *Paradise Lost* is a philosophical element foreign to the classical epic.

The seventh book, on the creation, is in the current of the Biblical expansion of Du Bartas, and hardly to be ranked as Aristotelian. In the eighth book the debate on astronomy seems inspired rather by Lucretius than by Homer. The great episode of the poem (books six and seven) does not deal with the exploits of the human hero, as in the *Odyssey* and the *Aeneid*, but with actions only later to be connected with him. Such a method fits with the idea of art suggested by Milton in the *Areopagitica:*

> Neither can every piece of the building be of one form; nay rather the perfection consists in this, that out of many moderate varieties and brotherly dissimilitudes that are not vastly disproportional arises the goodly and the graceful symmetry that commends the whole pile and structure.

Variety is not unknown in Greek theory and practice, yet seems to have been especially developed by the opponents of strict classicism, as is indicated even in presentations of the variety of the *Aeneid* itself.[3] Variety, in fact, is both natural and divine,

> For earth hath this variety from heaven
> Of pleasure situate in hill and dale.
> *Paradise Lost*, vi, 640–1.

In the variety of *Paradise Lost*, Milton is following nature and the spirit of modern literature rather than strictly keeping the rules of Aristotle.

BIBLIOGRAPHY

Fletcher, Harris, *Contributions to a Milton Bibliography, 1800–1930, being a List of Addenda to Stevens's Reference Guide to Milton.* Urbana, 1931.

Jebb, Sir Richard, *"Samson Agonistes" and the Hellenic Drama.* London, 1908. (*Proceedings* of the British Academy, pp. 341–8.)

Langdon, Ida, *Milton's Theory of Poetry and Fine Art.* New Haven, 1924.

Milton, John, *Samson Agonistes*, ed. by A. W. Verity. Cambridge, 1912.

——, *Paradise Regained*, the *Minor Poems*, and *Samson Agonistes*, ed. by Merritt Y. Hughes. New York, 1937.

Stevens, David H., *Reference Guide to Milton from 1800 to the Present Day.* Chicago, 1930.

Thompson, Elbert N. S., *John Milton. A Topical Bibliography.* New Haven, 1916.

[3] See *variety* in the index.

THE REASON OF CHURCH GOVERNMENT

Introduction to Book II (*in part*)

1641-42

[Types of poetry]

[1] Time serves not now, and perhaps I might seem too profuse to give any certain account of what the mind at home in the spacious circuits of her musing hath liberty to propose to herself, though of highest hope and hardest attempting, whether that epic form wherof the two poems of Homer, and those other two of Vergil and Tasso are a diffuse, and the book of Job a brief model;[1] or whether the rules of Aristotle herein are strictly to be kept, or nature to be followed,[2] which in them that know art and use judgment is no transgression, but an enriching of art. And lastly, what king or knight before the conquest might be chosen in whom to lay the pattern of a Christian hero.[3] And as Tasso gave to a prince of Italy his choice whether he would command him to write of Godfrey's expedition against the infidels, or Belisarius against the Goths, or Charlemagne against the Lombards; if to the instinct of nature and the emboldening of art aught may be trusted, and that there be nothing adverse in our climate, or the fate of this age, it haply would be no rashness from an equal diligence and inclination to present the like offer in our own ancient stories. Or whether those dramatic constitutions wherein Sophocles and Euripides reign shall be found more doctrinal and exemplary to a nation. The Scripture also affords us a divine pastoral drama in the Song of Solomon, consisting of two persons and a double chorus, as Origen rightly judges. And the Apocalypse of St. John is the majestic image of a high and stately tragedy, shutting up and intermingling her solemn scenes and acts with a sevenfold chorus of hallelujahs and harping symphonies; and this my opinion the

---

[1] The Book of Job has no episodes or partially extraneous matter. Milton's *Paradise Regained* is often thought of as a brief epic, while *Paradise Lost* is diffuse.

[2] This and the following clauses indicate that Milton is not a strict classicist. Giraldi (*On the Romances*, sect. 43, above) had asserted that there were two forms, the classical and the romantic, and that the romantic is not inferior, as Milton here indicates that classical principles can be "enriched."

[3] Milton had thought of an epic on King Arthur. He seems to have in mind here a character made perfect by the poet, such as Sidney advised (*Defense*, sect. 23, above).

grave authority of Pareus commenting that book is sufficient to confirm.[4] Or if occasion shall lead to imitate those magnific odes and hymns wherein Pindarus and Callimachus are in most things worthy, some others in their frame judicious, in their matter most an end faulty. But those frequent songs throughout the law and prophets beyond all these, not in their divine argument alone, but in the very critical art of composition, may be easily made appear over all the kinds of lyric poesy to be incomparable.[5]

[The poet's function]

[2] These abilities, wheresoever they be found, are the inspired gift of God rarely bestowed, but yet to some (though most abuse) in every nation; and are of power, beside the office of a pulpit, to inbreed and cherish in a great people the seeds of virtue and public civility, to allay the perturbations of the mind, and set the affections in right tune; to celebrate in glorious and lofty hymns the throne and equipage of God's almightiness, and what he works, and what he suffers to be wrought with high providence in his church; to sing the victorious agonies of martyrs and saints, the deeds and triumphs of just and pious nations doing valiantly through faith against the enemies of Christ; to deplore the general relapses of kingdoms and states from justice and God's true worship. Lastly, whatsoever in religion is holy and sublime, in virtue amiable or grave, whatsoever hath passion or admiration in all the changes of that which is called fortune from without,[6] or the wily subtleties and refluxes of man's thoughts from within—all these things with a solid and treatable smoothness to paint out and describe. Teaching over the whole book of sanctity and virtue through all the instances of example, with such delight to those especially of soft and delicious temper, who will not so much as look upon Truth herself,[7] unless they see her elegantly dressed,

[4] The passage suggests how Milton's age looked on the Bible as literature and subject to criticism according to literary principles. For earlier instances see the views of Dante, above, and Boccaccio, above, and St. Augustine, *Christian Doctrine*, Bk. IV.

David Pareus published in 1618 his commentary on the Apocalypse of St. John. He makes it a tragic drama divided into four acts and seven visions. In support of his procedure Pareus quotes the opinion of Origen to which Milton alludes just above.

[5] See *Paradise Regained*, IV, 347, below, and note. The quality of the Biblical lyrics was evidently a settled opinion of Milton's.

[6] See *admiration* and *fortune* in the index.

[7] For a similar theory see Spenser's letter to Raleigh above, and *delightful teaching* in the index.

The allegorical figure of Truth was represented as naked, for example, on the title page of Raleigh's *History of the World*.

that whereas the paths of honesty and good life appear now rugged and difficult, though they be indeed easy and pleasant, they would then appear to all men both easy and pleasant though they were rugged and difficult indeed.

[Practical application of poetry]

[3] And what a benefit this would be to our youth and gentry may be soon guessed by what we know of the corruption and bane which they suck in daily from the writings and interludes of libidinous and ignorant poetasters, who having scarce ever heard of that which is the main consistence of a true poem, the choice of such persons as they ought to introduce and what is moral and decent to each one,[8] do for the most part lap up vicious principles in sweet pills to be swallowed down and make the taste of virtuous documents harsh and sour.[9] But because the spirit of man cannot demean itself lively in this body without some recreating intermission of labor and serious things, it were happy for the commonwealth if our magistrates, as in those famous governments of old, would take into their care not only the deciding of our contentious law cases and brawls, but the managing of our public sports and festival pastimes; that they might be not such as were authorized a while since, the provocations of drunkenness and lust, but such as may inure and harden our bodies by martial exercises to all warlike skill and performance; and may civilize, adorn, and make discreet our minds by the learned and affable meeting of frequent academies, and the procurement of wise and artful recitations sweetened with eloquent and graceful enticements to the love and practice of justice, temperance, and fortitude, instructing and bettering the nation at all opportunities, that the call of wisdom and virtue may be heard everywhere, as Solomon saith: "She crieth without, she uttereth her voice in the streets, in the top of high places, in the chief concourse, and in the openings of the gates." Whether this may not be not only in pulpits, but after another persuasive method, at set and solemn paneguries,[10] in theaters, porches, or what other place or way may win most upon the people to receive at once both recreation and instruction,[11] let them in authority consult.

[8] What is in accord with the habits of each one and appropriate to him. See *decorum* in the index.

[9] The reverse of the method suggested by Lucretius; see the index.

[10] General assemblies.

[11] Like the delight and profit of Horace, *Art of Poetry*, 333, above.

[Inspiration and labor]

[4] The thing which I had to say, and those intentions which have lived within me ever since I could conceive myself anything worth to my country, I return to crave excuse that urgent reason hath plucked from me, by an abortive and foredated discovery. And the accomplishment of them lies not but in a power above man's to promise; but that none hath by more studious ways endeavored and with more unwearied spirit that none shall,[12] that I dare almost aver of myself, as far as life and free leisure will extend, and that the land had once enfranchised herself from this impertinent yoke of prelaty, under whose inquisitorious and tyrannical duncery no free and splendid wit can flourish. Neither do I think it shame to covenant with any knowing reader that for some few years yet I may go on trust with him toward the payment of what I am now indebted, as being a work not to be raised from the heat of youth, or the vapors of wine, like that which flows at waste from the pen of some vulgar amorist, or the trencher fury of a rhyming parasite; nor to be obtained by the invocation of Dame Memory and her siren daughters, but by devout prayer to that eternal Spirit who can enrich with all utterance and knowledge, and sends out his seraphim with the hallowed fire of his altar to touch and purify the lips of whom he pleases. To this must be added industrious and select reading, steady observation, insight into all seemly and generous arts and affairs; till which in some measure be compassed, at mine own peril and cost I refuse not to sustain this expectation from as many as are not loth to hazard so much credulity upon the best pledges that I can give them.

THE PREFACE TO *SAMSON AGONISTES*

1671

OF THAT SORT OF DRAMATIC POEM WHICH IS CALLED TRAGEDY

[Apology for tragedy]

Tragedy, as it was anciently composed, hath been ever held the gravest, moralest, and most profitable of all other poems; therefore said by Aristotle to be of power by raising pity and fear

---

[12] For Milton's emphasis on labor, see Phillips's *Theatrum Poetarum*, sect. 9, below, and Horace, *Art of Poetry*, 409, and the note, above.

or terror to purge the mind of those and such like passions, that is, to temper and reduce them to just measure with a kind of delight stirred up by reading or seeing those passions well imitated. Nor is Nature wanting in her own effects to make good his assertion; for so in physic things of melancholic hue and quality are used against melancholy, sour against sour, salt to remove salt humors.[1] Hence philosophers and other gravest writers, as Cicero, Plutarch, and others, frequently cite out of tragic poets, both to adorn and illustrate their discourse. The Apostle Paul himself thought it not unworthy to insert a verse of Euripides into the text of Holy Scripture, I Corinthians 15,33; and Pareus, commenting on the Revelation, divides the whole book as a tragedy into acts, distinguished each by a chorus of heavenly harpings and song between.[2] Heretofore men in highest dignity have labored not a little to be thought able to compose a tragedy. Of that honor Dionysius the elder was no less ambitious than before of his attaining to the tyranny. Augustus Caesar also had begun his *Ajax*, but unable to please his own judgment with what he had begun, left it unfinished. Seneca, the philosopher, is by some thought the author of those tragedies (at least the best of them) that go under that name.[3] Gregory Nazianzen, a Father of the Church, thought it not unbeseeming the sanctity of his person to write a tragedy, which he entitled *Christ Suffering*. This is mentioned to vindicate tragedy from the small esteem or rather infamy which in the account of many it undergoes at this day with other common interludes, happening through the poet's error of intermixing comic stuff with tragic sadness and gravity, or introducing trivial and vulgar persons, which by all judicious hath been counted absurd and brought in without discretion, corruptly to gratify the people.[4]

[1] See *catharsis* in the index. Milton's wording implies that the pity and fear are imitated by the actors rather than felt by the audience; it seems that he must have had in mind the imitation of actions that would produce such passions. Milton's theory is apparently medical to such an extent that it does not contemplate the complete expulsion of pity and fear, just as it would not be well to expel from the human body any of its natural fluids or humors. These humors should, however, be in proper quantity and adjustment, that is, should be tempered and reduced to just measure if the body is to be in good health. Cf. the theory of Guarini, *Tragicomic Poetry*, sect. 17b, above. [2] See the *Reason of Church Government*, note 4, just above.

[3] Possibly Milton did not admire Seneca so much as some earlier authors had (see *Seneca* in the index). Doubts about authorship go hand in hand with unfavorable remarks on quality, as in the remarks by Thomas Farnaby prefixed to *L. et M. Senecae . . . Tragoediae*, London, 1613.

[4] Cf. Sidney's opinion, *Defense*, sect. 49, above. On the mixture of tragedy and comedy, see Guarini, *Tragicomic Poetry*, above.

[Explanation of Milton's practice]

And though ancient tragedy use no prologue, yet using sometimes in case of self-defense or explanation that which Martial calls an epistle, in behalf of this tragedy coming forth after the ancient manner, much different from what among us passes for best, thus much beforehand may be *epistled*, that chorus is here introduced after the Greek manner, not ancient only but modern and still in use among the Italians. In the modeling therefore of this poem, with good reason the ancients and Italians are rather followed as of much more authority and fame. The measure of verse used in the chorus is of all sorts, called by the Greeks monostrophic or rather *apolelymenon*,[5] without regard had to strophe, antistrophe, or epode, which were a kind of stanzas framed only for the music then used with the chorus that sung, not essential to the poem and therefore not material; or being divided into stanzas or pauses they may be called *allaeostropha*. Division into act and scene, referring chiefly to the stage (to which this work never was intended), is here omitted. It suffices if the whole drama be found not produced beyond the fifth act.[6] Of the style and uniformity, and that commonly called the plot, whether intricate or explicit[7]—which is nothing but such economy or disposition of the fable as may stand best with verisimilitude and decorum[8]—they only will best judge who are not unacquainted with Aeschylus, Sophocles, and Euripides, the three tragic poets unequaled yet by any and the best rule to all who endeavor to write tragedy. The circumscription of time wherein the whole drama begins and ends is, according to ancient rule and best example, within the space of twenty-four hours.[9]

PARADISE REGAINED

[Book IV, lines 254–352]

1666

There thou shalt hear and learn the secret power
Of harmony in tones and numbers hit
By voice or hand, and various-measured verse,

[5] Literally, *set free* or *released;* in free verse, as it were. See Phillips, *Theatrum Poetarum,* sect. 5, below.

[6] See Horace, *Art of Poetry,* 189, above. [7] Aristotle, *Poetics,* x, above.

[8] Milton often refers to *decorum;* see the index. [9] See *unity of time,* in the index.

Aeolian charms and Dorian lyric odes,
And his who gave them breath, but higher sung,
Blind Melesigenes, thence Homer called,
Whose poem Phoebus challenged for his own.   260
Thence what the lofty grave tragedians taught
In chorus or iambic, teachers best
Of moral prudence, with delight received
In brief sententious precepts,[1] while they treat
Of fate, and chance,[2] and change in human life,
High actions and high passions best describing. . . .
To whom our Saviour sagely thus replied: . . .
    If I would delight my private hours
With music or with poem, where so soon
As in our native language can I find
That solace? All our Law and Story strewed
With hymns, our Psalms with artful terms inscribed,
Our Hebrew songs and harps in Babylon,
That pleased so well our victor's ear, declare
That rather Greece from us these arts derived—
Ill imitated, while they loudest sing
The vices of their deities, and their own   340
In fable, hymn, or song, so personating
Their gods ridiculous, and themselves past shame.[3]
Remove their swelling epithets thick-laid
As varnish on a harlot's cheek, the rest,
Thin-sown with aught of profit or delight,[4]
Will far be found unworthy to compare
With Zion's songs, to all true tastes excelling,[5]
Where God is praised aright, and godlike men,
The Holiest of Holies, and his Saints;   349
Such are from God inspired, not such from thee;
Unless where moral virtue is expressed
By light of Nature not in all quite lost.

[1] For Chapman's similar opinion, see the selection from him, above.

[2] Theophrastus spoke of tragedy as a "reversal of heroic chance," as is reported by the grammarian Diomedes (Keil, *Grammatici Latini*, I, 487).

[3] Cf. Plato's opinion, *Republic*, II, above.

[4] From Horace, *Art of Poetry*, 333, above.

[5] Guarini writes: "The poetry of David surpasses, in my judgment, all the other lyric poetry that ever has been written" (*Compendium of Tragicomic Poetry* [Bari, 1914], p. 250; ed. of 1602, p. 30).

Note Milton's earlier expression of this belief, in the *Reason of Church Government*, sect. 1, above.

PIERRE NICOLE

o◯ooo◯o

THESE SELECTIONS serve to remind us that in most times there has been a body of opinion hostile to the stage and the writing of fiction. However much ignorance such attacks show, they at least raise the problem of the social relations of literature, one that the critic should not neglect. As furnishing an unphilosophical discussion of the problem of censorship, Nicole may be contrasted with Plato. He is, it appears, much like the unsophisticated person who in our time wishes to censor literature he does not understand. Yet even such a critic need not be wholly rejected, for the student who would understand the various effects of poetry can learn something from its enemies.

The translations are by Dr. Clara W. Crane.

BIBLIOGRAPHY

Nicole, Pierre, *Œuvres*. Cologne (chez Pierre Marteau), 1683.
_____, *Œuvres*. Paris (chez G. Desprez), 1781.

LES VISIONNAIRES

Letter I (*a selection*)

1664

The qualities necessary [for the writer of plays and romances], which are not very honorable in the judgment of respectable men, are horrible when they are considered according to the principles of religion and the rules of the Gospel. A maker of romances and a poet of the stage is a public poisoner—not a poisoner of bodies, but of the souls of the faithful; he must be regarded as guilty of an infinity of spiritual homicides, whether he has caused them in literal fact, himself, or whether he has been able to cause them through his pernicious writings. The more care he takes to cover with a veil of respectability the criminal passions he describes in these writings, the more dangerous he makes them, the more capable of taking simple and innocent souls by surprise and corrupting them.

OF COMEDY (*selections*)

1671

Chapter I
[Comedy as it really is]

[Very few have tried to justify comedy in this age; men have been either too simple in their piety, or too conscious that their passion for the theater did not harmonize with it.] But we discover some who in this matter have pretended to find an alliance possible between the worldly spirit and piety. They are not content to follow vice; they must see it honored, not dishonored by the shameful name of vice, for that troubles their pleasure a little by its connotation of horror. . . . The means the most subtle of these men employ to this end is to form a certain metaphysical idea of comedy, and to purge this idea of every sin. Comedy, they say, is a representation of words and actions as if they were present: what harm is there in that? And after they have justified this general idea of comedy, they think they have proved that there is no offense in ordinary comedies. But the way to avoid this deception is to consider comedy, on the contrary, not as an unreal abstraction, but as a common and ordinary practice. . . . We must consider the life of actors and actresses, the subjects and the purpose of our comedies, the effects they ordinarily bring about in those who play them and in those who see them played, the impressions they leave; and we must then decide if all that has any connection with the life, the feelings, and the duties of a true Christian. . . . But as most of the reasons we can urge against comedy extend naturally to the reading of romances, we shall often include them here; and we beg those who read to understand them when we do not expressly mention them.

Chapter II
[Evil passions in comedy]

There is nothing more unworthy a child of God than this occupation [of acting]. . . . It is an occupation in which men and women represent passions of hate, anger, ambition, vengeance, and especially love. They must express these passions in as natural and lively a way as they can. . . . Those who represent the passion of love must be to some extent touched by it while they are representing it. Now it is impossible to think that anyone can efface from his mind an impression voluntarily excited. . . . Hence comedy by its very nature is a practical school of vice. . . .

Chapter III

The second reason is drawn from the danger of the passion of love, which rules in all comedies.

[Our good education bridles this passion and gives it "a certain horror" for us. Comedies and romances, on the other hand, instead of rendering it horrible, make us love it, try to render it honorable. But there is no use in arguing that they deal with honorable passion, for] though marriage makes good use of concupiscence, this passion is nevertheless in itself wholly evil and immoderate. . . . We should always regard it as . . . a source of poison.

Chapter IV

What makes the danger greater is that comedy removes all the remedies which might prevent the evil impression it makes; the heart is softened by the pleasure of seeing it; and the mind is wholly occupied with externals and drunk with the follies it sees represented, and consequently beyond the state of Christian vigilance. . . .

Chapter V

That whatever care we take to dissociate comedy from indecent objects, we cannot render it acceptable, because it inspires the pleasure of loving and being loved, and teaches the language of the passions. . . .

Chapter VI

It is so true that comedy is almost always a representation of vicious passions, that the greater part of the Christian virtues cannot be presented on the stage. Silence, patience, moderation, wisdom, poverty, penitence are not virtues the representation of which can divert the spectators; and, above all, men will not hear of humility and the suffering of injury. . . .

Not only must we have passions in comedies but we must have them vigorous and violent. . . .

In short, the very end of comedy engages the poets to represent only the evil passions.[1] For the end they propose is to please the spectators; and they could not please without putting into the mouths of their actors words and sentiments conformable to the personages they cause to speak or before whom they speak. Now they represent only evil men, and they speak only before worldly persons whose hearts and minds are corrupted by immoderate passions and evil maxims.

This means that there is nothing more pernicious than the morals of poetry and romance, for they are only a mass of false opinions born of concupiscence and only pleasing because they flatter the corrupt inclinations of readers or spectators.[2]

[1] This suggests the belief that the *Inferno* of Dante, since it deals with the wicked, is necessarily more poetical and more interesting than the *Paradiso*. See Croce, *The Poetry of Dante* (New York, 1922), pp. 35–7.

[2] The problem of what is or seems to be pernicious in literature of high artistic quality has exercised many critics, as Elyot (p. 240, above), Sidney (p. 432, above), and Mazzoni (p. 398, above). Sir John Harington writes as follows of Ariosto's *Orlando Furioso:* "But now it may be and is by some objected that although he write Christianly in some places, yet in other some he is too lascivious, as in that of the bawdy friar, in Alcina and Rogero's copulation, in Anselmo's Giptian, in Richardetto's metamorphosis, in mine host's tale of Astolfo, and some few places beside. Alas, if this be a fault, pardon him this one fault, though I doubt too many of you (gentle readers) will be too exorable in this point; yea, methinks, I see some of you searching already for those places of the book, and you are half offended that I have not made some directions that you might find out and read them immediately. But I beseech you stay a while, and as the Italian saith, *pian piano,* fair and softly, and take this caveat with you, to read them as my author meant them, to breed detestation and not delectation. Remember, when you read of the old lecherous friar, that a fornicator is one of the things that God hateth; when you read of Alcina, think how Joseph fled from his enticing mistress; when on mine host's tale (if you will follow my counsel) turn over the leaf and let it alone, although even that lewd tale may bring some men profit (*A Brief Apology for Poetry,* in Smith's *Elizabethan Critical Essays,* II, 214).

JOHN DRYDEN

oꙨooꙨo

AN ESSAY OF DRAMATIC POESY

1668 (revised in 1684)

THIS ESSAY is in the form of a dialogue in which various speakers present their opinions on dramatic theory. The form is used less to present various sides of the truth than to make clear wrong positions to be refuted. Neander is commonly supposed to represent Dryden himself.

French ideas form the basis of much that is said, especially the passages on the three unities and dramatic construction. So well does Dryden represent Corneille that his essay almost serves as a substitute for the original. The most vigorous ideas appear in the defense of modern dramatists against the ancients and in the support of the English drama against all rivals, ancient or modern. The presentation of richness and variety as determining characteristics of the Elizabethan and Jacobean drama may be further developed but remains fundamental, not to be superseded. In spite of that, Dryden is on the whole on the side of regularity, and regrets the errors, as he thinks them, of Shakespeare. He can apologize for his English predecessors and show that at times they are almost regular; he cannot attain such a position as Giraldi Cinthio held with respect to the modern epic, insisting that the romantic drama may be put over against that on the classical model as another type, having its own principles of construction. One set of principles is all he can imagine. As a result his appreciation of Shakespeare, Jonson, and Beaumont and Fletcher remained an individual matter, and could have little influence in aiding the development of principles for the judgment of Elizabethan literature. The opportunity for putting the criticism of the English drama on a firm basis and forestalling much of the misdirected effort of his successors was before him, but Dryden could not grasp it.

Even his assertion of the greatness of Shakespeare had its dangers. He had already arrived at the essentials of the idolatry of Shakespeare, which represents him as towering unique above the other poets. That

Dryden was clear-sighted enough also to find fault with Shakespeare has been forgotten, because the criticism was overpowered by such praise as he quotes with apparent approval: "That there was no subject of which any poet ever writ, but he would produce it much better treated of in Shakespeare."[1]

If Dryden's principles are granted, his example of specific criticism in the Examen of *The Silent Woman* has so much to commend it that it should be read by all who aspire to give opinions on the drama. Perhaps its faults may also serve as a warning to those who feel secure in their own theories.

BIBLIOGRAPHY

Dryden's Essays on the Drama, edited by William Strunk. New York, 1898. Valuable introduction, notes, and descriptive index of plays cited. The later editors were unfortunate in being ignorant of this edition, in which are explained some difficulties which they pass over.

The Essays of John Dryden, ed. by W. P. Ker, 2 vols. Oxford, 1926 (a reimpression of the edition of 1900). The text of the first edition with notes giving the variants of the later editions. Introduction and explanatory notes. The modernized text which follows is derived from this edition and that of Professor Strunk.

Dryden's Essay of Dramatic Poesy, edited by Thomas Arnold and revised by William T. Arnold. Oxford, 1903. The text of the second edition, with variants. Good notes.

AN ESSAY OF DRAMATIC POESY (*in part*)

[1] It was the fortune of Eugenius, Crites, Lisideius, and Neander to be in company together; three of them persons whom their wit and quality have made known to all the town; and whom I have chose to hide under these borrowed names, that they may not suffer by so ill a relation as I am going to make of their discourse. . . .

[The ancients and the moderns]

[2] "If your quarrel," said Eugenius, "to those who now write, be grounded only on your reverence to antiquity, there is no man more ready to adore those great Greeks and Romans than I am; but on the other side, I cannot think so contemptibly of the age

[1] See p. 637, below.

in which I live, or so dishonorably of my own country, as not to judge we equal the ancients in most kinds of poesy, and in some surpass them; neither know I any reason why I may not be as zealous for the reputation of our age, as we find the ancients themselves were in reference to those who lived before them. For you hear your Horace saying:

> *Indignor quidquam reprehendi, non quia crasse*
> *Compositum, illepideve putetur, sed quia nuper.*[1]

And after:

> *Si meliora dies, ut vina, poemata reddit,*
> *Scire velim, pretium chartis quotus arroget annus?*[2]

"But I see I am engaging in a wide dispute, where the arguments are not like to reach close on either side; for poesy is of so large an extent, and so many both of the ancients and moderns have done well in all kinds of it, that in citing one against the other, we shall take up more time this evening than each man's occasions will allow him; therefore I would ask Crites to what part of poesy he would confine his arguments, and whether he would defend the general cause of the ancients against the moderns, or oppose any age of the moderns against this of ours."

[The drama]

[3] Crites, a little while considering upon this demand, told Eugenius that, if he pleased, he would limit their dispute to Dramatic Poesy; in which he thought it not difficult to prove, either that the ancients were superior to the moderns, or the last age to this of ours.

[English dramas superior]

[4] Eugenius was somewhat surprised when he heard Crites make choice of that subject. "For aught I see," said he, "I have undertaken a harder province than I imagined; for though I never judged the plays of the Greek or Roman poets comparable to ours, yet, on the other side, those we now see acted come short of many which were written in the last age. But my comfort is, if we are

---

[1] "I dislike to have anything censured not because it is clumsily or ungracefully composed but because it is new" (Horace, *Epistles*, II, 1, 76–7).

[2] "If age makes poems, like wine, better, I should like to know how many years are required to make manuscripts valuable" (Horace, *Epistles*, II, 1, 34–5).

overcome, it will be only by our own countrymen; and if we yield to them in this one part of poesy, we more surpass them in all the other; for in the epic or lyric way, it will be hard for them to show us one such amongst them as we have many now living, or who lately were; they can produce nothing so courtly writ, or which expresses so much the conversation of a gentleman as Sir John Suckling; nothing so even, sweet, and flowing as Mr. Waller; nothing so majestic, so correct as Sir John Denham; nothing so elevated, so copious, and full of spirit as Mr. Cowley. As for the Italian, French, and Spanish plays, I can make it evident that those who now write surpass them; and that the drama is wholly ours."

[English verse]

[5] All of them were thus far of Eugenius's opinion, that the sweetness of English verse was never understood or practiced by our fathers; even Crites himself did not much oppose it; and everyone was willing to acknowledge how much our poesy is improved by the happiness of some writers yet living, who first taught us to mold our thoughts into easy and significant words,— to retrench the superfluities of expression,—and to make our rhyme so properly a part of the verse, that it should never mislead the sense, but itself be led and governed by it.

[The definition of a play]

[6] Eugenius was going to continue this discourse, when Lisideius told him that it was necessary, before they proceeded further, to take a standing measure of their controversy; for how was it possible to be decided who writ the best plays before we know what a play should be? But this once agreed on by both parties, each might have recourse to it, either to prove his own advantages or to discover the failings of his adversary.

He had no sooner said this, but all desired the favor of him to give the definition of a play; and they were the more importunate, because neither Aristotle nor Horace nor any other who had writ of that subject, had ever done it.

Lisideius, after some modest denials, at last confessed he had a rude notion of it; indeed, rather a description than a definition; but which served to guide him in his private thoughts, when he was to make a judgment of what others writ: that he conceived a play ought to be *a just and lively image of human nature*,[3] *representing its*

³ Cf. Heywood's quotation from Cicero (*Apology*, Bk. III, sect. 3, above).

passions and humors, and the changes of fortune[4] *to which it is subject,
for the delight and instruction of mankind.*[5]

This definition (though Crites raised a logical objection against
it, that it was only *a genere et fine,* and so not altogether perfect)
was yet well received by the rest; and after they had given order
to the watermen to turn their barge and row softly, that they
might take the cool of the evening in their return, Crites, being
desired by the company to begin, spoke on behalf of the ancients,
in this manner:

[The ancients defended]

[7] "If confidence presage a victory, Eugenius, in his own
opinion, has already triumphed over the ancients; nothing seems
more easy to him than to overcome those whom it is our greatest
praise to have imitated well; for we do not only build upon their
foundations, but by their models. Dramatic Poesy had time
enough, reckoning from Thespis (who first invented it) to Aristophanes, to be born, to grow up, and to flourish in maturity. It has
been observed of arts and sciences that in one and the same century they have arrived to great perfection; and no wonder, since
every age has a kind of universal genius, which inclines those that
live in it to some particular studies; the work then being pushed
on by many hands must of necessity go forward.

[Modern science]

[8] "Is it not evident in these last hundred years, when the
study of philosophy has been the business of all the virtuosi in
Christendom, that almost a new nature has been revealed to us?
that more errors of the school have been detected, more useful
experiments in philosophy have been made, more noble secrets in
optics, medicine, anatomy, astronomy discovered, than in all
those credulous and doting ages from Aristotle to us?—so true it
is that nothing spreads more fast than science, when rightly and
generally cultivated.

[The ancients honored poetry]

[9] "Add to this the more than common emulation that was in
those times of writing well; which though it be found in all ages
and all persons that pretend to the same reputation, yet poesy,

---

[4] See *fortune* in the index.
[5] Horace, *Art of Poetry,* 334. This definition would have been acceptable to Sidney.

being then in more esteem than now it is, had greater honors decreed to the professors of it, and consequently the rivalship was more high between them. They had judges ordained to decide their merit, and prizes to reward it; and historians have been diligent to record of Aeschylus, Euripides, Sophocles, Lycophron, and the rest of them, both who they were that vanquished in these wars of the theater, and how often they were crowned; while the Asian kings and Grecian commonwealths scarce afforded them a nobler subject than the unmanly luxuries of a debauched court, or giddy intrigues of a factious city; *Alit aemulatio ingenia* (says Paterculus), *et nunc invidia, nunc admiratio incitationem accendit:* 'emulation is the spur of wit; and sometimes envy, sometimes admiration, quickens our endeavors.'

[Modern sloth]

[10] "But now since the rewards of honor are taken away, that virtuous emulation is turned into direct malice; yet so slothful that it contents itself to condemn and cry down others, without attempting to do better; 'tis a reputation too unprofitable, to take the necessary pains for it; yet wishing they had it, that desire is incitement enough to hinder others from it. And this in short, Eugenius, is the reason why you have now so few good poets and so many severe judges. Certainly, to imitate the ancients well, much labor and long study is required;[6] which pains, I have already shown, our poets would want encouragement to take, if yet they had ability to go through the work. Those ancients have been faithful imitators and wise observers of that nature which is so torn and ill represented in our plays; they have handed down to us a perfect resemblance of her; which we, like ill copiers, neglecting to look on have rendered monstrous and disfigured.[7] But that you may know how much you are indebted to those your masters, and be ashamed to have so ill requited them, I must remember you that all the rules by which we practice the drama at this day (either such as relate to the justness and symmetry of the plot, or the episodical ornaments, such as descriptions, narrations, and other beauties, which are not essential to the play) were delivered to us from the observations which Aristotle made of those poets who either lived before him, or were his contempo-

---

[6] See *imitation* in the index.

[7] Pope later wrote: "Nature and Homer were, he found, the same" (*An Essay on Criticism*, 135).

raries; we have added nothing of our own, except we have the confidence to say our wit is better; of which none boast in this our age but such as understand not theirs. Of that book which Aristotle has left us, περὶ τῆς Ποιητικῆς, Horace's *Art of Poetry* is an excellent comment, and I believe restores to us that second book of his concerning comedy, which is wanting in him.

[The three unities]

[11] "Out of these two have been extracted the famous rules, which the French call *Des Trois Unités*, or the Three Unities, which ought to be observed in every regular play; namely, of time, place, and action.[8]

[Unity of time]

[12] "The unity of time they comprehend in twenty-four hours, the compass of a natural day, or as near as it can be contrived; and the reason of it is obvious to everyone[9]—that the time of the feigned action, or fable of the play, should be proportioned as near as can be to the duration of that time in which it is represented; since, therefore, all plays are acted on the theater in the space of time much within the compass of twenty-four hours, that play is to be thought the nearest imitation of nature, whose plot or action is confined within that time. And by the same rule which concludes this general proportion of time, it follows that all the parts of it are (as near as may be) to be equally subdivided; namely, that one act take not up the supposed time of half a day, which is out of proportion to the rest; since the other four are then to be straitened within the compass of the remaining half; for it is unnatural that one act which being spoke or written is not longer than the rest should be supposed longer by the audience; 'tis therefore the poet's duty to take care that no act should be imagined to exceed the time in which it is represented on the stage; and that the intervals and inequalities of time be supposed to fall out between the acts.[10]

[8] It has commonly been supposed that the three unities are those of Aristotle, though he does not mention unity of place, and only hints at what is called unity of time (*Poetics*, v, 49b9, above).

[9] See *unity of time* in the index.

[10] Alessandro Piccolomini explains that since a play represents the events of twelve hours, verisimilitude requires that its presentation take an entire day. The inconvenience of this has been avoided by the use of the five acts: "The poets give the space of three or four hours to the presentation and arrange that four times the actors rest and remain off the stage for a while, that the spectators may be able to imagine

"This rule of time, how well it has been observed by the ancients, most of their plays will witness. You see them in their tragedies (wherein to follow this rule, is certainly most difficult) from the very beginning of their plays falling close into that part of the story which they intend for the action or principal object of it, leaving the former part to be delivered by narration; so that they set the audience, as it were, at the post where the race is to be concluded; and saving them the tedious expectation of seeing the poet set out and ride the beginning of the course, they suffer you not to behold him till he is in sight of the goal and just upon you.

[Unity of place]

[13] "For the second unity, which is that of place, the ancients meant by it that the scene ought to be continued through the play in the same place where it was laid in the beginning; for the stage on which it is represented being but one and the same place it is unnatural to conceive it many, and those far distant from one another.[11] I will not deny but by the variation of painted scenes the fancy, which in these cases will contribute to its own deceit, may sometimes imagine it several places with some appearance of probability; yet it still carries the greater likelihood of truth, if those places be supposed so near each other as in the same town or city, which may all be comprehended under the larger denomination of one place; for a greater distance will bear no proportion to the shortness of time which is allotted, in the acting, to pass from one of them to another. For the observation of this, next to the ancients, the French are to be most commended. They tie themselves so strictly to the unity of place that you never see in any of their plays a scene changed in the middle of an act; if the act begins in a garden, a street, or chamber, 'tis ended in the same place; and that you may know it to be the same, the stage is so supplied with persons that it is never empty all the time; he

that some things are done by the actors while they are not on the stage; these actions would take too long if they were actually presented on the stage. The actors assume, then, and wish the spectators to allow that such interims, though very short, occupy more time than they do. Hence the actors, returning to the stage, can indicate they have carried on business that actually would have required more time." He explains further that if the day is of twelve hours, and four are given to the action on the stage, eight hours remain at the disposal of the imagination, or two hours for each interval between the acts. Hence without damage to verisimilitude actions occupying two hours can be supposed to take place between the acts (*Annotations on the Poetics of Aristotle* [Venice, 1575], pp. 180–1).

[11] See *unity of place*, in the index.

who enters second has business with him who was on before; and before the second quits the stage, a third appears who has business with him. This Corneille calls *la liaison des scènes*, the continuity or joining of the scenes; and 'tis a good mark of a well-contrived play when all the persons are known to each other and every one of them has some affairs with all the rest.

[Unity of action]

[14] "As for the third unity, which is that of action, the ancients meant no other by it than what the logicians do by their *finis*, the end or scope of any action—that which is the first in intention, and last in execution. Now the poet is to aim at one great and complete action, to the carrying on of which all things in his play, even the very obstacles, are to be subservient; and the reason of this is as evident as any of the former. For two actions, equally labored and driven on by the writer, would destroy the unity of the poem; it would be no longer one play, but two; not but that there may be many actions in a play, as Ben Jonson has observed in his *Discoveries*;[12] but they must be all subservient to the great one (which our language happily expresses in the name of *under-plots*); such as in Terence's *Eunuch* is the difference and reconcilement of Thais and Phaedria, which is not the chief business of the play but promotes the marriage of Chaerea and Chremes's sister, principally intended by the poet.[13] There ought to be but one action, says Corneille,[14] that is, one complete action, which leaves the mind of the audience in a full repose; but this cannot be brought to pass but by many other imperfect actions which conduce to it and hold the audience in a delightful suspense of what will be.

[Modern plays inferior]

[15] "If by these rules (to omit many other drawn from the precepts and practice of the ancients) we should judge our modern plays, 'tis probable that few of them would endure the trial; that which should be the business of a day takes up in some of them an age; instead of one action, they are the epitomes of a man's life; and for one spot of ground which

---

[12] Section 135, "What by one and entire."
[13] Cf. the discussion of the *Andria* by Guarini, sect. 41b, above.
[14] *Discourse* III, 99.

the stage should represent we are sometimes in more countries than the map can show us.

[The ancients wrote well]

[16] "But if we allow the ancients to have contrived well, we must acknowledge them to have written better. Questionless we are deprived of a great stock of wit in the loss of Menander among the Greek poets, and of Caecilius, Afranius, and Varius among the Romans; we may guess at Menander's excellency by the plays of Terence, who translated some of them; and yet wanted so much of him, that he was called by C. Caesar the half-Menander; and may judge of Varius, by the testimonies of Horace, Martial, and Velleius Paterculus. 'Tis probable that these, could they be recovered, would decide the controversy; but so long as Aristophanes and Plautus are extant, while the tragedies of Euripides, Sophocles, and Seneca are in our hands, I can never see one of those plays which are now written but it increases my admiration of the ancients. And yet I must acknowledge farther that to admire them as we ought we should understand them better than we do. Doubtless many things appear flat to us, the wit of which depended on some custom or story which never came to our knowledge; or perhaps on some criticism in their language, which being so long dead and only remaining in their books, 'tis not possible they should make us understand perfectly. To read Macrobius, explaining the propriety and elegancy of many words in Vergil which I had before passed over without consideration as common things, is enough to assure me that I ought to think the same of Terence; and that in the purity of his style (which Tully so much valued that he ever carried his works about him) there is yet left in him great room for admiration, if I knew but where to place it. In the meantime I must desire you to take notice that the greatest man of the last age, Ben Jonson, was willing to give place to them in all things; he was not only a professed imitator of Horace, but a learned plagiary of all the others; you track him everywhere in their snow. If Horace, Lucan, Petronius Arbiter, Seneca, and Juvenal had their own from him, there are few serious thoughts which are new in him; you will pardon me, therefore, if I presume he loved their fashion when he wore their clothes. But since I have otherwise a great veneration for him, and you, Eugenius, prefer him above all other poets, I will use no farther argument to you than his example; I will produce before you

Father Ben, dressed in all the ornaments and colors of the ancients; you will need no other guide to our party, if you follow him; and whether you consider the bad plays of our age or regard the good plays of the last, both the best and worst of the modern poets will equally instruct you to admire the ancients."

[Modern poetry, like the other arts, is better]

[17] Crites had no sooner left speaking, but Eugenius, who had waited with some impatience for it, thus began:

"I have observed in your speech that the former part of it is convincing as to what the moderns have profited by the rules of the ancients; but in the latter you are careful to conceal how much they have excelled them. We own all the helps we have from them, and want neither veneration nor gratitude, while we acknowledge that to overcome them we must make use of the advantages we have received from them; but to these assistances we have joined our own industry; for had we sat down with a dull imitation of them, we might then have lost somewhat of the old perfection but never acquired any that was new. We draw not therefore after their lines but those of nature; and having the life before us, besides the experience of all they knew, it is no wonder if we hit some airs and features which they have missed. I deny not what you urge of arts and sciences, that they have flourished in some ages more than others; but your instance in philosophy makes for me; for if natural causes be more known now than in the time of Aristotle, because more studied, it follows that poesy and other arts may, with the same pains, arrive still nearer to perfection,[15] and that granted, it will rest for you to prove that they wrought more perfect images of human life than we; which seeing in your discourse you have avoided to make good, it shall now be my task to show you some part of their defects, and some few excellencies of the moderns. And I think there is none among us can imagine I do it enviously or with purpose to detract from them; for what interest of fame or profit can the living lose by the reputation of the dead? On the other side, it is a great truth which Velleius Paterculus affirms: *Audita visis libentius laudamus; et praesentia invidia, praeterita admiratione prosequimur; et his nos obrui, illis instrui*

---

[15] The assumption here is that poetry is like other classes of human knowledge. For the opposite view, see Phillips, sect. 12, below. Dryden did not believe in the madness of the poet (Preface to *Troilus and Cressida*, in Ker, *Essays*, I, 221–2); Phillips did believe in the poet's inspiration; hence the difference in their opinions of the nature of poetry, if the present passage is to be taken as Dryden's own opinion.

credimus; [16] that praise or censure is certainly the most sincere, which unbribed posterity shall give us.

[Changes in ancient practice]

[18] "Be pleased then in the first place to take notice that the Greek poesy, which Crites has affirmed to have arrived to perfection in the reign of the old comedy, was so far from it that the distinction of it into acts was not known to them; or if it were, it is yet so darkly delivered to us that we cannot make it out.

"All we know of it is from the singing of their chorus; and that too is so uncertain that in some of their plays we have reason to conjecture they sung more than five times. Aristotle indeed divides the integral parts of a play into four.[17] First, the *protasis* or entrance, which gives light only to the characters of the persons, and proceeds very little into any part of the action. Secondly, the *epitasis* or working up of the plot; where the play grows warmer, the design or action of it is drawing on, and you see something promising that it will come to pass. Thirdly, the *catastasis*, called by the Romans *status*, the height and full growth of the play; we may call it properly the counterturn, which destroys that expectation, embroils the action in new difficulties, and leaves you far distant from that hope in which it found you; as you may have observed in a violent stream resisted by a narrow passage—it runs round to an eddy and carries back the waters with more swiftness than it brought them on. Lastly, the *catastrophe*, which the Grecians called λύσις, the French *le dénouement*, and we the discovery, or unraveling of the plot; there you see all things settling again upon their first foundations; and, the obstacles which hindered the design or action of the play once removed, it ends with that resemblance of truth and nature that the audience are satisfied with the conduct of it. Thus this great man delivered to us the image of a play; and I must confess it is so lively that from thence much light has been derived to the forming it more perfectly into acts and scenes; but what poet first limited to five the number of the acts I know not; only we see it so firmly established in the time of Horace that he gives it for a rule in comedy: *Neu brevior quinto, neu sit productior actu.*[18] So that you see the Grecians cannot be said to have

---

[16] "We praise what we hear more freely than what we see; we regard what is present with envy, what is past with admiration; we think ourselves injured by the first and instructed by the second" (II, 92, slightly modified).

[17] *Poetics,* XII.   [18] *Art of Poetry,* 189, above.

consummated this art, writing rather by entrances than by acts, and having rather a general indigested notion of a play than knowing how and where to bestow the particular graces of it.

"But since the Spaniards at this day allow but three acts, which they call *jornadas*, to a play, and the Italians in many of theirs follow them, when I condemn the ancients, I declare it is not altogether because they have not five acts to every play but because they have not confined themselves to one certain number; it is building a house without a model; and when they succeeded in such undertakings, they ought to have sacrificed to Fortune, not to the Muses.

[No novelty in ancient plots]

[19] "Next for the plot, which Aristotle called ὁ μῦθος, and often τῶν πραγμάτων σύνθεσις,[19] and from him the Romans *fabula;* it has already been judiciously observed by a late writer that in their tragedies it was only some tale derived from Thebes or Troy,[20] or at least something that happened in those two ages; which was worn so threadbare by the pens of all the epic poets, and even by tradition itself of the talkative Greeklings (as Ben Jonson calls them), that before it came upon the stage it was already known to all the audience; and the people, so soon as ever they heard the name of Oedipus, knew as well as the poet that he had killed his father by a mistake and committed incest with his mother before the play; that they were now to hear of a great plague, an oracle, and the ghost of Laius; so that they sat with a yawning kind of expectation till he was to come with his eyes pulled out and speak a hundred or more verses in a tragic tone, in complaint of his misfortunes. But one Oedipus, Hercules, or Medea had been tolerable; poor people, they escaped not so good cheap; they had still the *chapon bouillé* set before them, till their appetites were cloyed with the same dish, and the novelty being gone,[21] the pleasure vanished; so that one main end of Dramatic Poesy in its definition, which was to cause delight, was of consequence destroyed.

[19] Literally the *myth*, the story; and the arrangement of events (*Poetics*, VI, 49b31, above).
[20] Cf. Milton:

> Gorgeous tragedy . . .
> Presenting Thebes, or Pelops' line,
> Or the tale of Troy divine.
> *Il Penseroso*, 97–100.

[21] See *novelty* and *variety* in the index.

[The defects of Roman comic plots]

[20] "In their comedies the Romans generally borrowed their plots from the Greek poets; and theirs was commonly a little girl stolen or wandered from her parents, brought back unknown to the city, there got with child by some lewd young fellow, who, by the help of his servant, cheats his father; and when her time comes to cry *Juno Lucina, fer opem*,[22] one or other sees a little box or cabinet which was carried away with her, and so discovers her to her friends, if some god do not prevent it by coming down in a machine and taking the thanks of it to himself.

[The characters of Roman comedy]

[21] "By the plot you may guess much of the characters of the persons. An old father who would willingly, before he dies, see his son well married; his debauched son, kind in his nature to his mistress but miserably in want of money; a servant or slave who has so much wit to strike in with him and help to dupe his father; a braggadocio captain, a parasite, and a lady of pleasure.

"As for the poor honest maid on whom the story is built and who ought to be one of the principal actors in the play, she is commonly a mute in it; she has the breeding of the old Elizabeth way, which was for maids to be seen and not to be heard; and it is enough you know she is willing to be married when the fifth act requires it.

[Ancient narrowness]

[22] "These are plots built after the Italian mode of houses— you see through them all at once; the characters are indeed the imitation of nature, but so narrow as if they had imitated only an eye or a hand, and did not dare to venture on the lines of a face or the proportion of a body.

[The ancients do not keep the laws of drama]

[23] "But in how straight a compass soever they have bounded their plots and characters, we will pass it by if they have regularly pursued them and perfectly observed those three unities of time, place, and action, the knowledge of which you say is derived to us from them. But in the first place give me leave to tell you that the unity of place, however it might be practiced by them, was never any of their rules; we neither find it in Aristotle, Horace, or any

---

[22] "Juno Lucina [goddess of childbirth], help me."

who have written of it, till in our age the French poets first made it a precept of the stage.[23] The unity of time even Terence himself, who was the best and most regular of them, has neglected; his *Heautontimorumenos*, or *Self-Punisher*, takes up visibly two days, says Scaliger,[24] the two first acts concluding the first day, the three last the day ensuing; and Euripides, in tying himself to one day, has committed an absurdity never to be forgiven him, for in one of his tragedies he has made Theseus go from Athens to Thebes, which was about forty English miles, under the walls of it to give battle, and appear victorious in the next act; and yet from the time of his departure to the return of the Nuntius who gives the relation of his victory, Aethra and the chorus have but thirty-six verses, which is not for every mile a verse.

"The like error is as evident in Terence's *Eunuch*, when Laches, the old man, enters by mistake into the house of Thais; where, betwixt his exit and the entrance of Pythias, who comes to give ample relation of the garboyles he has raised within, Parmeno, who was left upon the stage, has not above five lines to speak. *C'est bien employer un temps si court*, says the French poet who furnished me with one of the observations;[25] and almost all their tragedies will afford us examples of the like nature.

"It is true they have kept the continuity, or, as you called it, *liaison des scènes*, somewhat better; two do not perpetually come in together, talk, and go out together; and other two succeed them, and do the same throughout the act, which the English call by the name of single scenes; but the reason is because they have seldom above two or three scenes, properly so called, in every act; for it is to be accounted a new scene, not only every time the stage is empty, but every person who enters, though to others, makes it so, because he introduces a new business. Now the plots of their plays being narrow, and the persons few, one of their acts was written in a less compass than one of our well-wrought scenes; and yet they are often deficient even in this. To go no farther than Terence; you find in the *Eunuch*, Antipho entering single in the midst of the third act, after Chremes and Pythias were gone off; in the same play you have likewise Dorias beginning the fourth act alone; and

---

[23] See *unity of place* in the index. Dryden apparently did not realize that the three unities were discussed long before Corneille. It seems, however, that the term was first used in Corneille's time.

[24] *Poetice*, VI, 3. Cf. Sidney, *Defense*, sect. 48, above.

[25] The example from Euripides is found in Corneille, *Discourse* III, 112, as also the comment: "That is making good use of so short a time."

after she had made a relation of what was done at the Soldier's entertainment (which by the way was very inartificial, because she was presumed to speak directly to the audience and to acquaint them with what was necessary to be known, but yet should have been so contrived by the poet as to have been told by persons of the drama to one another, and so by them to have come to the knowledge of the people), she quits the stage, and Phaedria enters next, alone likewise; he also gives you an account of himself and of his returning from the country in monologue; to which unnatural way of narration Terence is subject in all his plays. In his *Adelphi*, or *Brothers*, Syrus and Demea enter after the scene was broken by the departure of Sostrata, Geta, and Canthara; and indeed you can scarce look into any of his comedies where you will not presently discover the same interruption.

[Ancient drama not properly didactic]

[24] "But as they have failed both in laying of their plots and in the management, swerving from the rules of their own art by misrepresenting nature to us, in which they have ill satisfied one intention of a play, which was delight, so in the instructive part they have erred worse; instead of punishing vice and rewarding virtue, they have often shown a prosperous wickedness, and an unhappy piety:[26] they have set before us a bloody image of revenge in Medea, and given her dragons to convey her safe from punishment; a Priam and Astyanax murdered and Cassandra ravished, and the lust and murder ending in the victory of him who acted them. In short, there is no indecorum in any of our modern plays which, if I would excuse, I could not shadow with some authority from the ancients.

[Comic and tragic genius]

[25] "And one further note of them let me leave you: tragedies and comedies were not writ then as they are now, promiscuously by the same person; but he who found his genius bending to the one never attempted the other way. This is so plain that I need not instance to you that Aristophanes, Plautus, Terence, never any of them writ a tragedy; Aeschylus, Euripides, Sophocles, and Seneca never meddled with comedy; the sock and buskin were not worn by the same poet. Having then so much care to excel in one

---

[26] Cf. Sidney, *Defense*, sect. 25, above, for the poet's duty in representing the punishment of vice.

kind, very little is to be pardoned them if they miscarried in it; and this would lead me to the consideration of their wit, had not Crites given me sufficient warning not to be too bold in my judgment of it, because the languages being dead, and many of the customs and little accidents on which it depended lost to us, we are not competent judges of it. But though I grant that here and there we may miss the application of a proverb or a custom, yet a thing well said will be wit in all languages; and though it may lose something in the translation, yet to him who reads it in the original, 'tis still the same; he has an idea of its excellency, though it cannot pass from his mind into any other expression or words than those in which he finds it. . . .

[The passions in ancient drama]

[26] "But to return from whence I have digressed, to the consideration of the ancients' writing, and their wit, of which by this time you will grant us in some measure to be fit judges. Though I see many excellent thoughts in Seneca, yet he of them who had a genius most proper for the stage was Ovid; he had a way of writing so fit to stir up a pleasing admiration and concernment,[27] which are the objects of a tragedy, and to show the various movements of a soul combating betwixt two different passions, that, had he lived in our age or in his own could have writ with our advantages, no man but must have yielded to him; and therefore I am confident the *Medea* is none of his,[28] for, though I esteem it for the gravity and sententiousness of it, which he himself concludes to be suitable to a tragedy—*Omne genus scripti gravitate tragoedia vincit,*[29]—yet it moves not my soul enough to judge that he who in the epic way wrote things so near the drama as the story of Myrrha, of Caunus and Biblis, and the rest, should stir up no more concernment where he most endeavored it. The masterpiece of Seneca I hold to be that scene in the *Troades* where Ulysses is seeking for Astyanax to kill him; there you see the tenderness of a mother so represented in Andromache that it raises compassion to a high degree in the reader, and bears the nearest resemblance of anything in the tragedies of the ancients to the excellent scenes of passion in Shakespeare or in Fletcher. For love scenes, you will find few among them; their tragic poets dealt not with that soft passion, but with lust, cruelty, revenge, ambition, and those bloody actions they

---

[27] See also the end of sect. 30, below.
[28] The *Medea* written by Ovid is lost; Dryden is apparently referring to that of Seneca.
[29] Quoted by Heywood, *Apology*, sect. 8, above.

produced, which were more capable of raising horror than compassion in an audience; leaving love untouched, whose gentleness would have tempered them, which is the most frequent of all the passions and which, being the private concernment of every person, is soothed by viewing its own image in a public entertainment.

[Tenderness in ancient comedy]

[27] "Among their comedies, we find a scene or two of tenderness, and that where you would least expect it, in Plautus; but to speak generally, their lovers say little when they see each other but *anima mea, vita mea, ζωὴ καὶ ψυχῇ*,[30] as the women in Juvenal's time used to cry out in the fury of their kindness. Any sudden gust of passion (as an ecstasy of love in an unexpected meeting) cannot better be expressed than in a word and a sigh, breaking one another. Nature is dumb on such occasions, and to make her speak would be to represent her unlike herself. But there are a thousand other concernments of lovers, as jealousies, complaints, contrivances, and the like, where not to open their minds at large to each other were to be wanting to their own love and to the expectation of the audience, who watch the movements of their minds as much as the changes of their fortunes. For the imaging of the first is properly the work of a poet; the latter he borrows from the historian."

[The moderns are not better but different]

[28] Eugenius was proceeding in that part of his discourse when Crites interrupted him. "I see," said he, "Eugenius and I are never like to have this question decided betwixt us; for he maintains the moderns have acquired a new perfection in writing; I can only grant they have altered the mode of it. Homer described his heroes men of great appetites, lovers of beef broiled upon the coals, and good fellows; contrary to the practice of the French romances, whose heroes neither eat nor drink nor sleep for love. Vergil makes Aeneas a bold avower of his own virtues:

> *Sum pius Aeneas, fama super aethera notus,*[31]

which in the civility of our poets is the character of a fanfaron or Hector; for with us the knight takes occasion to walk out or sleep,

---

[30] "My soul, my life, my life and soul" (Juvenal, *Satires*, VI, 195).
[31] "I am the pious Aeneas, whose renown has risen above the skies" (an abridgment of *Aeneid*, I, 378–9).

to avoid the vanity of telling his own story, which the trusty squire is ever to perform for him. So in their love scenes, of which Eugenius spoke last, the ancients were more hearty, we more talkative; they writ love as it was then the mode to make it; and I will grant thus much to Eugenius, that perhaps one of their poets, had he lived in our age,

Si foret hoc nostrum fato delapsus in aevum,[32]

as Horace says of Lucilius, he had altered many things; not that they were not natural before, but that he might accommodate himself to the age in which he lived. Yet in the meantime we are not to conclude anything rashly against those great men, but preserve to them the dignity of masters, and give that honor to their memories, *quos Libitina sacravit,*[33] part of which we expect may be paid to us in future times."

[The rules of the French stage]

[29] This moderation of Crites, as it was pleasing to all the company, so it put an end to that dispute, which Eugenius, who seemed to have the better of the argument, would urge no farther; but Lisideius, after he had acknowledged himself of Eugenius's opinion concerning the ancients, yet told him he had forborne, till his discourse were ended, to ask him why he preferred the English plays above those of other nations, and whether we ought not to submit our stage to the exactness of our next neighbors.

"Though," said Eugenius, "I am at all times ready to defend the honor of my country against the French, and to maintain we are as well able to vanquish them with our pens as our ancestors have been with their swords, yet if you please," added he, looking upon Neander, "I will commit this cause to my friend's management; his opinion of our plays is the same with mine; and besides there is no reason that Crites and I, who have now left the stage, should re-enter so suddenly upon it, which is against the laws of comedy."

[The superiority of the French drama]

[30] "If the question had been stated," replied Lisideius, "who had writ best, the French or English, forty years ago, I should have been of your opinion, and adjudged the honor to our own nation; but since that time" (said he, turning towards Neander) "we

---

[32] "If fate had assigned him to this age of ours" (Horace, *Satires* I, 10, 68).

[33] "Whom Libitina [goddess of death] has consecrated" (Horace, *Epistles*, II, 1, 49).

have been so long together bad Englishmen that we had not leisure to be good poets. Beaumont, Fletcher, and Jonson (who were only capable of bringing us to that degree of perfection which we have) were just then leaving the world; as if, in an age of so much horror, wit and those milder studies of humanity had no farther business among us. But the Muses, who ever follow peace, went to plant in another country; it was then that the great Cardinal of Richelieu began to take them into his protection, and that, by his encouragement, Corneille and some other Frenchmen reformed their theater, which before was as much below ours as it now surpasses it and the rest of Europe. But because Crites in his discourse for the ancients has prevented me by observing many rules of the stage which the moderns have borrowed from them, I shall only, in short, demand of you whether you are not convinced that of all nations the French have best observed them. In the unity of time you find them so scrupulous that it yet remains a dispute among their poets whether the artificial day of twelve hours, more or less, be not meant by Aristotle, rather than the natural one of twenty-four;[34] and consequently whether all plays ought not to be reduced into that compass. This I can testify, that in all their dramas writ within these last twenty years and upwards I have not observed any that have extended the time to thirty hours; in the unity of place they are full as scrupulous, for many of their critics limit it to that very spot of ground where the play is supposed to begin; none of them exceed the compass of the same town or city. The unity of action in all plays is yet more conspicuous; for they do not burden them with underplots, as the English do, which is the reason why many scenes of our tragi-comedies carry on a design that is nothing of kin to the main plot, and that we see two distinct webs in a play, like those in ill-wrought stuffs, and two actions, that is, two plays, carried on together to the confounding of the audience; who, before they are warm in their concernments for one part, are diverted to another, and by that means espouse the interest of neither. From hence likewise it arises that the one half of our actors are not known to the other. They keep their distances as if they were Montagues and Capulets, and seldom begin an acquaintance till the last scene of the fifth act, when they are all to meet upon the stage. There is no theater in the world has anything so absurd as the English tragi-comedy; 'tis a drama of our own invention, and the fashion of it is enough to proclaim it so; here a course of mirth,

---

[34] *Poetics,* v, 49b9, above.

there another of sadness and passion, and a third of honor and a duel; thus in two hours and a half we run through all the fits of Bedlam. The French affords you as much variety on the same day, but they do it not so unseasonably or *mal à propos* as we; our poets present you the play and the farce together; and our stages still retain somewhat of the original civility of the Red Bull:

> *Atque ursum et pugiles media inter carmina poscunt.*[35]

The end of tragedies or serious plays, says Aristotle, is to beget admiration, compassion, or concernment,[36] but are not mirth and compassion things incompatible? and is it not evident that the poet must of necessity destroy the former by intermingling of the latter? that is, he must ruin the sole end and object of his tragedy to introduce somewhat that is forced into it and is not of the body of it. Would you not think that physician mad, who, having prescribed a purge, should immediately order you to take restringents?

[French plots are from history]

[31] "But to leave our plays and return to theirs. I have noted one great advantage they have had in the plotting of their tragedies; that is, they are always grounded upon some known history, according to that of Horace, *Ex noto fictum carmen sequar;*[37] and in that they have so imitated the ancients that they have surpassed them. For the ancients, as was observed before, took for the foundation of their plays some poetical fiction such as under that consideration could move but little concernment in the audience, because they already knew the event of it. But the French goes farther:

> *Atque ita mentitur, sic veris falsa remiscet,*
> *Primo ne medium, medio ne discrepet imum.*[38]

He so interweaves truth with probable fiction that he puts a pleasing fallacy upon us; mends the intrigues of fate, and dispenses with the severity of history, to reward that virtue which has been rendered to us there unfortunate.[39] Sometimes the story[40] has left the success so doubtful that the writer is free, by the privilege of a poet, to take that which of two or more relations will best suit with his

---

[35] "They call for the bear and the boxers in the midst of the songs" (Horace, *Epistles*, II, 1, 185–6, modified).

[36] *Poetics*, VI, par. 1, above. Cf. sect. 26, above, and Sidney's "admiration and commiseration" (*Defense*, sect. 32, and the appendix to Sidney).

[37] *Art of Poetry*, 240, above. [38] Horace, *Art of Poetry*, 151–2, above.

[39] Cf. Sidney, *Defense*, sect. 25, above. [40] History.

design: as for example in the death of Cyrus, whom Justin and some others report to have perished in the Scythian war but Xenophon affirms to have died in his bed of extreme old age. Nay more, when the event is past dispute, even then we are willing to be deceived, and the poet, if he contrives it with appearance of truth, has all the audience of his party, at least during the time his play is acting; so naturally we are kind to virtue, when our own interest is not in question, that we take it up as the general concernment of mankind. On the other side, if you consider the historical plays of Shakespeare, they are rather so many chronicles of kings or the business many times of thirty or forty years cramped into a representation of two hours and a half, which is not to imitate or paint nature, but rather to draw her in miniature, to take her in little, to look upon her through the wrong end of a perspective and receive her images not only much less but infinitely more imperfect than the life; this, instead of making a play delightful, renders it ridiculous:

> *Quodcunque ostendis mihi sic, incredulus odi.*[41]

For the spirit of man cannot be satisfied but with truth, or at least verisimility; and a poem is to contain, if not τὰ ἔτυμα, yet ἐτύμοισιν ὁμοῖα,[42] as one of the Greek poets has expressed it.

[French plots are limited]

[32] "Another thing in which the French differ from us and from the Spaniards is that they do not embarrass or cumber themselves with too much plot; they only represent so much of a story as will constitute one whole and great action sufficient for a play; we, who undertake more, do but multiply adventures, which, not being produced from one another as effects from causes, but barely following, constitute many actions in the drama and consequently make it many plays.

[English plots are confused]

[33] "But by pursuing closely one argument which is not cloyed with many turns, the French have gained more liberty for verse, in which they write; they have leisure to dwell on a subject which deserves it; and to represent the passions (which we have acknowl-

---

[41] Horace, *Art of Poetry*, 188, above.
[42] "Not true narratives," yet "narratives like true ones" (Hesiod, *Theogony*, 27). Cf. Chapman: "not truth but things like truth" (in the selection given above).

edged to be the poet's work) without being hurried from one thing to another, as we are in the plays of Calderon which we have seen lately upon our theaters under the name of Spanish plots. I have taken notice but of one tragedy of ours whose plot has that uniformity and unity of design in it which I have commended in the French; and that is *Rollo*,[43] or rather, under the name of Rollo, the story of Bassianus and Geta in Herodian; there indeed the plot is neither large nor intricate, but just enough to fill the minds of the audience, not to cloy them. Besides, you see it founded upon the truth of history,[44] only the time of the action is not reducible to the strictness of the rules; and you see in some places a little farce mingled, which is below the dignity of the other parts; and in this all our poets are extremely peccant; even Ben Jonson himself, in *Sejanus* and *Catiline*,[45] has given us this oleo of a play, this unnatural mixture of comedy and tragedy, which to me sounds just as ridiculously as the history of David with the merry humors of Golias. In *Sejanus* you may take notice of the scene betwixt Livia and the physician, which is a pleasant satire upon the artificial helps of beauty; in *Catiline* you may see the parliament of women, the little envies of them to one another, and all that passes betwixt Curio and Fulvia; scenes admirable in their kind but of an ill mingle with the rest.

[The parts of a French plot are properly related to each other]

[34] "But I return again to the French writers, who, as I have said, do not burden themselves too much with plot, which has been reproached to them by an ingenious person of our nation as a fault; for, he says, they commonly make but one person considerable in a play; they dwell on him and his concernments, while the rest of the persons are only subservient to set him off. If he intends this by it, that there is one person in the play who is of greater dignity than the rest, he must tax not only theirs but those of the ancients, and which he would be loth to do, the best of ours; for it is impossible but that one person must be more conspicuous in it than any other, and consequently the greatest share in the action must devolve on him. We see it so in the management of all affairs; even in the most equal aristocracy the balance cannot be

---

[43] *The Bloody Brother*, or *Rollo*, by John Fletcher, published in 1639.

[44] See the index under *truth*, and *history*.

[45] For Jonson's feeling of independence from the prescriptions of Aristotle, see the introduction to the selections from him above.

so justly poised but some one will be superior to the rest, either in parts, fortune, interest, or the consideration of some glorious exploit; which will reduce the greatest part of business into his hands.

"But, if he would have us to imagine that in exalting one character the rest of them are neglected, and that all of them have not some share or other in the action of the play, I desire him to produce any of Corneille's tragedies wherein every person, like so many servants in a well-governed family, has not some employment and who is not necessary to the carrying on of the plot or at least to your understanding it.

[Narrations in French plays]

[35] "There are indeed some protatic persons in the ancients,[46] whom they make use of in their plays either to hear or give the relation; but the French avoid this with great address, making their narrations only to or by such who are some way interested in the main design. And now I am speaking of relations, I cannot take a fitter opportunity to add this in favor of the French that they often use them with better judgment and more *à propos* than the English do. Not that I commend narrations in general—but there are two sorts of them. One, of those things which are antecedent to the play, and are related to make the conduct of it more clear to us. But 'tis a fault to choose such subjects for the stage as will force us on that rock, because we see they are seldom listened to by the audience, and that is many times the ruin of the play, for being once let pass without attention, the audience can never recover themselves to understand the plot; and indeed it is somewhat unreasonable that they should be put to so much trouble as that to comprehend what passes in their sight they must have recourse to what was done, perhaps, ten or twenty years ago.

[Tumults on the English stage]

[36] "But there is another sort of relations, that is, of things happening in the action of the play and supposed to be done behind the scenes; and this is many times both convenient and beautiful; for by it the French avoid the tumult to which we are subject in England by representing duels, battles, and the like; which renders our stage too like the theaters where they fight prizes. For

---

[46] Donatus in his comment on the *Andria* of Terence (Praefatio, 1, 8) defines a protatic character as one who is brought on once at the beginning of the play but is not employed in any later parts of it.

what is more ridiculous than to represent an army with a drum
and five men behind it; all which the hero of the other side is to
drive in before him; or to see a duel fought and one slain with two
or three thrusts of the foils, which we know are so blunted that we
might give a man an hour to kill another in good earnest with
them.[47]

[Death on the stage is comic]

[37] "I have observed that in all our tragedies the audience
cannot forbear laughing when the actors are to die; it is the most
comic part of the whole play.[48] All *passions* may be lively represented on the stage, if to the well-writing of them the actor supplies a good commanded voice and limbs that move easily and
without stiffness; but there are many *actions* which can never be
imitated to a just height; dying especially is a thing which none
but a Roman gladiator could naturally perform on the stage, when
he did not imitate or represent, but do it; and therefore it is better to omit the representation of it.

[Narration better than action]

[38] "The words of a good writer, which describe it lively, will
make a deeper impression of belief in us than all the actor can in-
sinuate into us when he seems to fall dead before us; as a poet in
the description of a beautiful garden, or a meadow, will please our
imagination more than the place itself can please our sight.[49] When
we see death represented, we are convinced it is but fiction; but
when we hear it related, our eyes, the strongest witnesses, are
wanting, which might have undeceived us; and we are all willing
to favor the sleight, when the poet does not too grossly impose on
us. They therefore who imagine these relations would make no
concernment in the audience are deceived, by confounding them
with the other which are of things antecedent to the play; those are
made often in cold blood, as I may say, to the audience; but these
are warmed with our concernments, which were before awakened
in the play. What the philosophers say of motion, that when it is

[47] Cf. Shakespeare, *Henry V*, IV, chorus:

> We shall much disgrace,
> With four or five most vile and ragged foils,
> Right ill-disposed in brawl ridiculous,
> The name of Agincourt.

See also Sidney, *Defense*, sect. 48, above.
[48] Cf. Castelvetro, *On Poetics*, XIII, 289, 25, above.
[49] Cf. Sidney, *Defense*, sect. 9, above.

once begun it continues of itself and will do so to eternity, without some stop put to it, is clearly true on this occasion; the soul, being already moved with the characters and fortunes of those imaginary persons, continues going of its own accord; and we are no more weary to hear what becomes of them when they are not on the stage than we are to listen to the news of an absent mistress. But it is objected that if one part of the play may be related then why not all? I answer, some parts of the action are more fit to be represented, some to be related. Corneille says judiciously that the poet is not obliged to expose to view all particular actions which conduce to the principal;[50] he ought to select such of them to be seen which will appear with the greatest beauty, either by the magnificence of the show or the vehemence of passions which they produce or some other charm which they have in them, and let the rest arrive to the audience by narration. 'Tis a great mistake in us to believe the French present no part of the action on the stage; every alteration or crossing of a design, every new-sprung passion and turn of it is a part of the action, and much the noblest, except we conceive nothing to be action till the players come to blows; as if the painting of the hero's mind were not more properly the poet's work than the strength of his body. Nor does this anything contradict the opinion of Horace, where he tells us,

> *Segnius irritant animos demissa per aurem,*
> *Quam quae sunt oculis subjecta fidelibus.*[51]

For he says immediately after,

> *Non tamen intus*
> *Digna geri promes in scenam;* multaque *tolles*
> *Ex oculis, quae mox narret facundia praesens.*[52]

Among which many he recounts some:

> *Nec pueros coram populo Medea trucidet,*
> *Aut in avem Progne mutetur, Cadmus in anguem; etc.*[53]

That is, those actions which by reason of their cruelty will cause aversion in us, or, by reason of their impossibility, unbelief, ought either wholly to be avoided by a poet or only delivered by narration. To which we may have leave to add such as, to avoid tumult (as was before hinted), or to reduce the plot into a more reasonable compass of time or for defect of beauty in them, are rather to be

---

[50] *Discourse* III, 100.
[51] Horace, *Art of Poetry*, 180–1, above.
[52] *Ibid.*, 182–4.
[53] *Ibid.*, 185, 187.

related than presented to the eye. Examples of all these kinds are frequent, not only among all the ancients but in the best received of our English poets. We find Ben Jonson using them in his *Magnetic Lady*, where one comes out from dinner and relates the quarrels and disorders of it, to save the undecent appearance of them on the stage and to abbreviate the story; and this in express imitation of Terence, who had done the same before him in his *Eunuch*, where Pythias makes the like relation of what had happened within at the soldier's entertainment. The relations likewise of Sejanus's death and the prodigies before it are remarkable, the one of which was hid from sight to avoid the horror and tumult of the representation, the other to shun the introducing of things impossible to be believed. In that excellent play, *The King and No King*, Fletcher goes yet farther, for the whole unraveling of the plot is done by narration in the fifth act, after the manner of the ancients, and it moves great concernment in the audience, though it be only a relation of what was done many years before the play. I could multiply other instances, but these are sufficient to prove that there is no error in choosing a subject which requires this sort of narrations; in the ill management of them there may.

[Other excellences of the French]

[39] "But I find I have been too long in this discourse, since the French have many other excellences not common to us, as that you never see any of their plays end with a conversion or simple change of will,[54] which is the ordinary way which our poets use to end theirs. It shows little art in the conclusion of a dramatic poem when they who have hindered the felicity during the four acts desist from it in the fifth, without some powerful cause to take them off their design; and though I deny not but such reasons may be found, yet it is a path that is cautiously to be trod, and the poet is to be sure he convinces the audience that the motive is strong enough. As, for example, the conversion of the usurer in *The Scornful Lady*[55] seems to me a little forced; for being an usurer, which implies a lover of money to the highest degree of covetousness—and such the poet has represented him—the account he gives for the sudden change is that he has been duped by the wild young fellow; which in reason might render him more wary another time, and make him punish himself with harder fare and coarser clothes, to get up again what he had lost; but that he should look

---

[54] Corneille, *Discourse* I, 27–8; III, 105.　　[55] By Beaumont and Fletcher.

on it as a judgment, and so repent, we may expect to hear in a sermon but I should never endure it in a play.

[A reason for an entrance or an exit]

[40] "I pass by this; neither will I insist on the care they take that no person after his first entrance shall ever appear but the business which brings him upon the stage shall be evident; which rule, if observed, must needs render all the events in the play more natural; for there you see the probability of every accident in the cause that produced it; and that which appears chance in the play will seem so reasonable to you that you will there find it almost necessary; so that in the exit of the actor you have a clear account of his purpose and design in the next entrance (though, if the scene be well wrought, the event will commonly deceive you), for there is nothing so absurd, says Corneille, as for an actor to leave the stage only because he has no more to say.[56]

[Verse]

[41] "I should now speak of the beauty of their rhyme, and the just reason I have to prefer that way of writing in tragedies before ours in blank verse; but because it is partly received by us and therefore not altogether peculiar to them, I will say no more of it in relation to their plays. For our own, I doubt not but it will exceedingly beautify them; and I can see but one reason why it should not generally obtain, that is, because our poets write so ill in it. This indeed may prove a more prevailing argument than all others which are used to destroy it, and therefore I am only troubled when great and judicious poets, and those who are acknowledged such, have written or spoken against it;[57] as for others, they are to be answered by that one sentence of an ancient author: *Sed ut primo ad consequendos eos quos priores ducimus, accendimur, ita ubi aut praeteriri, aut aequari eos posse desperavimus, studium cum spe senescit: quod, scilicet, assequi non potest, sequi desinit; . . . praeteritoque eo in quo eminere non possumus, aliquid in quo nitamur, conquirimus.*"[58]

---

[56] *Discourse* III, 108.

[57] Perhaps Milton, in the note on the Verse, prefixed to *Paradise Lost*, quoted in the note on sect. 6 of Phillips's *Theatrum Poetarum* below.

[58] "But as at first we are on fire to imitate those whom we consider of the highest rank, so when we despair to surpass or to equal them, our zeal grows weak in proportion as our hope does: what cannot be equalled is no longer imitated; . . . abandoning that in which we cannot secure fame, we seek for something in which we may gain glory" (Velleius Paterculus, I, 17).

[The English stage defended]

[42] Lisideius concluded in this manner; and Neander, after a little pause, thus answered him:

"I shall grant Lisideius, without much dispute, a great part of what he has urged against us; for I acknowledge that the French contrive their plots more regularly and observe the laws of comedy and decorum of the stage (to speak generally) with more exactness than the English. Farther, I deny not but he has taxed us justly in some irregularities of ours which he has mentioned; yet, after all, I am of opinion that neither our faults nor their virtues are considerable enough to place them above us.

[The lively imitation of nature]

[43] "For the lively imitation of nature being in the definition of a play, those which best fulfil that law ought to be esteemed superior to the others. 'Tis true, those beauties of the French poesy are such as will raise perfection higher where it is, but are not sufficient to give it where it is not; they are indeed the beauties of a statue but not of a man, because not animated with the soul of poesy, which is imitation of humor and passions; and this Lisideius himself or any other, however biassed to their party, cannot but acknowledge, if he will either compare the humors of our comedies or the characters of our serious plays with theirs. He who will look upon theirs which have been written till these last ten years, or thereabouts, will find it a hard matter to pick out two or three passable humors amongst them. Corneille himself, their arch-poet, what has he produced except *The Liar*?[59] and you know how it was cried up in France; but when it came upon the English stage, though well translated and that part of Dorant acted to so much advantage as I am confident it never received in its own country, the most favorable to it would not put it in competition with many of Fletcher's or Ben Jonson's. In the rest of Corneille's comedies you have little humor; he tells you himself his way is first to show two lovers in good intelligence with each other; in the working up of the play to embroil them by some mistake and in the latter end to clear it and reconcile them.[60]

[59] *Le menteur*, translated into English as *The Mistaken Beauty, or The Lyar*, printed in 1661. The translator is unknown.

[60] *Discourse* I, 27. He remarks that his comedies seldom have any other end than marriage, resulting not from a simple change of will but from a proper occasion.

[The French imitate the English]

[44] "But of late years Molière, the younger Corneille, Quinault, and some others have been imitating afar off the quick turns and graces of the English stage. They have mixed their serious plays with mirth, like our tragi-comedies, since the death of Cardinal Richelieu; which Lisideius and many others not observing have commended that in them for a virtue which they themselves no longer practice. Most of their new plays are, like some of ours, derived from the Spanish novels. There is scarce one of them without a veil, and a trusty Diego who drolls much after the rate of *The Adventures*.[61] But their humors, if I may grace them with that name, are so thin-sown that never above one of them comes up in any play. I dare take upon me to find more variety of them in some one play of Ben Jonson's than in all theirs together; as he who has seen *The Alchemist*, *The Silent Woman*, or *Bartholomew Fair* cannot but acknowledge with me.

[Tragicomedy]

[45] "I grant the French have performed what was possible on the groundwork of the Spanish plays; what was pleasant before, they have made regular; but there is not above one good play to be writ on all those plots; they are too much alike to please often; which we need not the experience of our own stage to justify. As for their new way of mingling mirth with serious plot, I do not, with Lisideius, condemn the thing, though I cannot approve their manner of doing it. He tells us we cannot so speedily recollect ourselves after a scene of great passion and concernment as to pass to another of mirth and humor and to enjoy it with any relish; but why should he imagine the soul of man more heavy than his senses? Does not the eye pass from an unpleasant object to a pleasant in a much shorter time than is required to this? and does not the unpleasantness of the first commend the beauty of the latter? The old rule of logic might have convinced him that contraries, when placed near, set off each other.[62] A continued gravity keeps the spirit too much bent; we must refresh it sometimes, as we bait in a journey that we may go on with greater ease. A scene of mirth, mixed with tragedy, has the same effect upon us which our music has between the acts; which we find a relief to us from the best

---

[61] *The Adventures of Five Hours*, by Sir Samuel Tuke.
[62] See Milton, *Art of Logic*, i, 12.

plots and language of the stage, if the discourses have been long. I must therefore have stronger arguments ere I am convinced that compassion and mirth in the same subject destroy each other; and in the meantime cannot but conclude, to the honor of our nation, that we have invented, increased, and perfected a more pleasant way of writing for the stage than was ever known to the ancients or moderns of any nation, which is tragi-comedy.[63]

[French plots barren]

[46] "And this leads me to wonder why Lisideius and many others should cry up the barrenness of the French plots above the variety and copiousness of the English. Their plots are single; they carry on one design which is pushed forward by all the actors, every scene in the play contributing and moving towards it. Our plays, besides the main design, have under-plots or by-concernments of less considerable persons and intrigues, which are carried on with the motion of the main plot: as they say the orb of the fixed stars and those of the planets, though they have motions of their own, are whirled about by the motion of the *primum mobile*, in which they are contained. That similitude expresses much of the English stage; for if contrary motions may be found in nature to agree, if a planet can go east and west at the same time—one way by virtue of his own motion, the other by the force of the first mover—it will not be difficult to imagine how the under-plot, which is only different, not contrary to the great design, may naturally be conducted along with it.

[Variety]

[47] "Eugenius has already shown us, from the confession of the French poets, that the unity of action is sufficiently preserved if all the imperfect actions of the play are conducing to the main design; but when those petty intrigues of a play are so ill ordered that they have no coherence with the other, I must grant that Lisideius has reason to tax that want of due connection; for co-ordination in a play is as dangerous and unnatural as in a state.[64] In the meantime he must acknowledge our variety,[65] if well ordered, will afford a greater pleasure to the audience.

---

[63] Cf. the discussion of tragicomedy in the selection from Guarini above.

[64] As a kingdom should have one ruler, so a play should have one dominant plot. Co-ordination or equality of several rulers or several plots is dangerous.

[65] See *variety* in the index.

[English superiority in passion and wit]

[48] "As for his other argument, that by pursuing one single theme they gain an advantage to express and work up the passions, I wish any example he could bring from them would make it good; for I confess their verses are to me the coldest I have ever read. Neither, indeed, is it possible for them, in the way they take, so to express passion as that the effects of it should appear in the concernment of an audience, their speeches being so many declamations which tire us with the length; so that instead of persuading us to grieve for their imaginary heroes, we are concerned for our own trouble, as we are in tedious visits of bad company; we are in pain till they are gone. When the French stage came to be reformed by Cardinal Richelieu, those long harangues were introduced to comply with the gravity of a churchman. Look upon the *Cinna* and the *Pompey*; they are not so properly to be called plays, as long discourses of reason of state;[66] and *Polyeucte* in matters of religion is as solemn as the long stops upon our organs. Since that time it is grown into a custom and their actors speak by the hourglass, like our parsons; nay, they account it the grace of their parts and think themselves disparaged by the poet if they may not twice or thrice in a play entertain the audience with a speech of an hundred lines. I deny not but this may suit well enough with the French; for as we, who are a more sullen people, come to be diverted at our plays, so they, who are of an airy and gay temper, come thither to make themselves more serious: and this I conceive to be one reason why comedies are more pleasing to us, and tragedies to them. But to speak generally, it cannot be denied that short speeches and replies are more apt to move the passions and beget concernment in us than the other; for it is unnatural for anyone in a gust of passion to speak long together, or for another in the same condition to suffer him without interruption. Grief and passion are like floods raised in little brooks by a sudden rain; they are quickly up; and if the concernment be poured unexpectedly in upon us, it overflows us; but a long sober shower gives them leisure to run out as they came in, without troubling the ordinary current. As for comedy, repartee is one of its chiefest graces; the greatest pleasure of the audience is a chase of wit, kept up on both sides and swiftly managed. And this our forefathers, if not we, have had in

---

[66] A transliteration of the Italian *ragione di stato*, principles or theories or important matters of government.

Fletcher's plays to a much higher degree of perfection than the French poets can reasonably hope to reach.

[The labyrinth of design]

[49] "There is another part of Lisideius's discourse in which he has rather excused our neighbors than commended them; that is, for aiming only to make one person considerable in their plays. 'Tis very true what he has urged, that one character in all plays, even without the poet's care, will have advantage of all the others, and that the design of the whole drama will chiefly depend on it. But this hinders not that there may be more shining characters in the play, many persons of a second magnitude, nay, some so very near, so almost equal to the first that greatness may be opposed to greatness, and all the persons be made considerable, not only by their quality but their action. 'Tis evident that the more the persons are, the greater will be the variety of the plot. If then the parts are managed so regularly that the beauty of the whole be kept entire and that the variety become not a perplexed and confused mass of accidents, you will find it infinitely pleasing to be led in a labyrinth of design where you see some of your way before you, yet discern not the end till you arrive at it. And that all this is practicable I can produce for examples many of our English plays, as *The Maid's Tragedy, The Alchemist, The Silent Woman;* I was going to have named *The Fox,* but that the unity of design seems not exactly observed in it, for there appear two actions in the play, the first naturally ending with the fourth act, the second forced from it in the fifth; which yet is the less to be condemned in him because the disguise of Volpone, though it suited not with his character as a crafty or covetous person, agreed well enough with that of a voluptuary; and by it the poet gained the end at which he aimed, the punishment of vice and the reward of virtue, both which that disguise produced. So that to judge equally of it, it was an excellent fifth act but not so naturally proceeding from the former.

[Fighting and death on the stage]

[50] "But to leave this and pass to the latter part of Lisideius's discourse, which concerns relations: I must acknowledge with him that the French have reason to hide that part of the action which would occasion too much tumult on the stage, and to choose rather to have it made known by narration to the audience. Farther, I think it very convenient, for the reasons he has given, that all in-

credible actions were removed; but whether custom has so insinuated itself into our countrymen or nature has so formed them to
fierceness, I know not; but they will scarcely suffer combats and
other objects of horror to be taken from them. And indeed, the
indecency of tumults is all which can be objected against fighting;
for why may not our imagination as well suffer itself to be deluded
with the probability of it as with any other thing in the play? For
my part, I can with as great ease persuade myself that the blows
are given in good earnest, as I can that they who strike them are
kings or princes or those persons which they represent. For objects
of incredibility, I would be satisfied from Lisideius whether we
have any so removed from all appearance of truth as are those of
Corneille's *Andromède*, a play which has been frequented the most
of any he has written. If the Perseus, or the son of an heathen god,
the Pegasus, and the Monster were not capable to choke a strong
belief, let him blame any representation of ours hereafter. Those
indeed were objects of delight; yet the reason is the same as to the
probability, for he makes it not a ballet or masque but a play,
which is to resemble truth.[67] But for death, that it ought not to be
represented, I have, besides the arguments alleged by Lisideius,
the authority of Ben Jonson, who has forborne it in his tragedies,
for both the death of Sejanus and Catiline are related; though in
the latter I cannot but observe one irregularity of that great poet:
he has removed the scene in the same act from Rome to Catiline's
army, and from thence again to Rome; and besides, has allowed a
very inconsiderable time after Catiline's speech for the striking of
the battle and the return of Petreius, who is to relate the event of it
to the senate; which I should not animadvert on him, who was
otherwise a painful observer of τὸ πρέπον or the *decorum* of the
stage,[68] if he had not used extreme severity in his judgment on the
incomparable Shakespeare for the same fault.[69] To conclude on
this subject of relations; if we are to be blamed for showing too
much of the action, the French are as faulty for discovering too

[67] The play must have verisimilitude. Ben Jonson, declaring that comedy should
"show an image of the times," concludes the prologue of *Every Man in His Humor* by
hoping that the audience, "that have so graced monsters, may like men." See
verisimilitude in the index. [68] See *decorum* in the index.

[69] Presumably a reference to the prologue to *Every Man in His Humor* in which Jonson
objects to the long space of time covered by plays that
Fight over York and Lancaster's long jars.
He may have had in mind *Henry IV*, *Henry V*, and *Henry VI*. In *Henry V* the
Chorus wafts you o'er the seas,
as Jonson puts it.

little of it; a mean betwixt both should be observed by every judicious writer, so as the audience may neither be left unsatisfied by not seeing what is beautiful, or shocked by beholding what is either incredible or undecent.

[Irregularity an aid to beauty]

[51] "I hope I have already proved in this discourse that though we are not altogether so punctual as the French in observing the laws of comedy, yet our errors are so few and little and those things wherein we excel them so considerable that we ought of right to be preferred before them. But what will Lisideius say if they themselves acknowledge they are too strictly bounded by those laws for breaking which he has blamed the English? I will allege Corneille's words as I find them in the end of his Discourse of the Three Unities: *Il est facile aux spéculatifs d'être sévères, etc.* ''Tis easy for speculative persons to judge severely; but if they would produce to public view ten or twelve pieces of this nature, they would perhaps give more latitude to the rules than I have done, when by experience they had known how much we are limited and constrained by them and how many beauties of the stage they banished from it.' To illustrate a little what he has said: by their servile observations of the unities of time and place and integrity of scenes, they have brought on themselves that dearth of plot and narrowness of imagination which may be observed in all their plays. How many beautiful accidents might naturally happen in two or three days which cannot arrive with any probability in the compass of twenty-four hours? There is time to be allowed also for maturity of design, which amongst great and prudent persons such as are often represented in tragedy cannot, with any likelihood of truth, be brought to pass at so short a warning. Farther, by tying themselves strictly to the unity of place and unbroken scenes, they are forced many times to omit some beauties which cannot be shown where the act began; but might, if the scene were interrupted and the stage cleared for the persons to enter in another place; and therefore the French poets are often forced upon absurdities; for if the act begins in a chamber, all the persons in the play must have some business or other to come thither or else they are not to be shown that act; and sometimes their characters are very unfitting to appear there. As suppose it were the king's bed-chamber; yet the meanest man in the tragedy must come and dispatch his business there rather than in the lobby or courtyard (which is fitter for him), for fear the

stage should be cleared and the scenes broken. Many times they
fall by it in a greater inconvenience; for they keep their scenes unbroken and yet change the place, as in one of their newest plays
where the act begins in the street.[70] There a gentleman is to meet
his friend; he sees him with his man, coming out from his father's
house; they talk together, and the first goes out; the second, who is
a lover, has made an appointment with his mistress; she appears at
the window, and then we are to imagine the scene lies under it.
This gentleman is called away and leaves his servant with his mistress; presently her father is heard from within; the young lady is
afraid the serving-man should be discovered and thrusts him into a
place of safety, which is supposed to be her closet. After this the
father enters to the daughter, and now the scene is in a house, for
he is seeking from one room to another for this poor Philipin, or
French Diego, who is heard from within, drolling and breaking
many a miserable conceit on the subject of his sad condition. In
this ridiculous manner the play goes forward, the stage being never
empty all the while; so that the street, the window, the houses, and
the closet are made to walk about and the persons to stand still.
Now what, I beseech you, is more easy than to write a regular
French play, or more difficult than to write an irregular English
one, like those of Fletcher, or of Shakespeare?

[English methods better]

[52] "If they content themselves, as Corneille did, with some
flat design which, like an ill riddle, is found out ere it be half proposed, such plots we can make every way regular, as easily as they;
but whenever they endeavor to rise to any quick turns and coun-
terturns of plot, as some of them have attempted since Corneille's
plays have been less in vogue, you see they write as irregularly as
we, though they cover it more speciously. Hence the reason is per-
spicuous why no French plays, when translated, have or ever can
succeed on the English stage. For if you consider the plots, our
own are fuller of variety; if the writing, ours are more quick and
fuller of spirit; and therefore 'tis a strange mistake in those who
decry the way of writing plays in verse, as if the English therein
imitated the French. We have borrowed nothing from them; our
plots are weaved in English looms; we endeavor therein to follow
the variety and greatness of characters which are derived to us

[70] Identified by Ker as Thomas Corneille's *L'amour à la mode*, confused in Dryden's
memory with Quinault's *L'amant indiscret*.

from Shakespeare and Fletcher; the copiousness and well-knitting of the intrigues we have from Jonson; and for the verse itself we have English precedents of elder date than any of Corneille's plays. Not to name our old comedies before Shakespeare, which were all writ in verse of six feet or Alexandrines, such as the French now use, I can show in Shakespeare many scenes of rhyme together, and the like in Ben Jonson's tragedies; in *Catiline* and *Sejanus* sometimes thirty or forty lines—I mean besides the chorus or the monologues; which, by the way, showed Ben no enemy to this way of writing, especially if you read his *Sad Shepherd*, which goes sometimes on rhyme, sometimes on blank verse, like an horse who eases himself on trot and amble. You find him likewise commending Fletcher's pastoral of *The Faithful Shepherdess*,[71] which is for the most part rhyme, though not refined to that purity to which it hath since been brought. And these examples are enough to clear us from a servile imitation of the French.

[Regular English plays]

[53] "But to return whence I have digressed, I dare boldly affirm these two things of the English drama: First, that we have many plays of ours as regular as any of theirs, and which besides have more variety of plot and characters; and secondly, that in most of the irregular plays of Shakespeare or Fletcher (for Ben Jonson's are for the most part regular) there is a more masculine fancy and greater spirit in the writing than there is in any of the French. I could produce, even in Shakespeare's and Fletcher's works, some plays which are almost exactly formed, as *The Merry Wives of Windsor*, and *The Scornful Lady;* but because (generally speaking) Shakespeare, who writ first, did not perfectly observe the laws of comedy, and Fletcher, who came nearer to perfection, yet through carelessness made many faults, I will take the pattern of a perfect play from Ben Jonson, who was a careful and learned observer of the dramatic laws, and from all his comedies I shall select *The Silent Woman*, of which I will make a short examen, according to those rules which the French observe."

[Ben Jonson]

[54] As Neander was beginning to examine *The Silent Woman,* Eugenius, earnestly regarding him: "I beseech you, Neander," said he, "gratify the company and me in particular so far as, be-

[71] In commendatory verses prefixed to the play, Jonson predicted immortality for it.

fore you speak of the play, to give us a character of the author; and tell us frankly your opinion, whether you do not think all writers, both French and English, ought to give place to him."

"I fear," replied Neander, "that in obeying your commands I shall draw some envy on myself. Besides, in performing them, it will be first necessary to speak somewhat of Shakespeare and Fletcher, his rivals in poesy; and one of them in my opinion at least his equal, perhaps his superior.

[Shakespeare]

[55] "To begin, then, with Shakespeare. He was the man who of all modern and perhaps ancient poets had the largest and most comprehensive soul. All the images of nature were still present to him, and he drew them not laboriously but luckily; when he describes anything, you more than see it, you feel it too. Those who accuse him to have wanted learning give him the greater commendation; he was naturally learned; he needed not the spectacles of books to read nature; he looked inwards and found her there. I cannot say he is everywhere alike; were he so, I should do him injury to compare him with the greatest of mankind. He is many times flat, insipid; his comic wit degenerating into clenches,[72] his serious swelling into bombast. But he is always great when some great occasion is presented to him; no man can say he ever had a fit subject for his wit and did not then raise himself as high above the rest of poets,

Quantum lenta solent inter viburna cupressi.[73]

The consideration of this made Mr. Hales of Eton say that there was no subject of which any poet ever writ but he would produce it much better done in Shakespeare; and however others are now generally preferred before him, yet the age wherein he lived, which had contemporaries with him Fletcher and Jonson, never equaled them to him in their esteem;[74] and in the last king's court, when

[72] Puns, of which the Elizabethans were fond. The modern objection to the pun seems to have started with Dryden. See the index.

[73] "As high as the cypresses that tower above the bending viburnums" (Vergil, *Eclogues*, 1, 25).

[74] Perhaps rather strong. John Webster writes: "I have ever truly cherished my good opinion of other men's worthy labors, especially of that full and heightened style of Master Chapman, the labored and understanding works of Master Jonson, the no less worthy composures of the both worthily excellent Master Beaumont and Master Fletcher, and lastly (without wrong last to be named) the right happy and copious industry of Master Shakespeare, Master Dekker, and Master Heywood" (To the Reader of *The White Devil*). See also Levin L. Schücking, *Shakespeare im literarischen Urteil seiner Zeit* (Heidelberg, 1908).

Ben's reputation was at highest, Sir John Suckling and with him the greater part of the courtiers set our Shakespeare far above him.

[Beaumont and Fletcher]

[56] "Beaumont and Fletcher, of whom I am next to speak, had, with the advantage of Shakespeare's wit, which was their precedent, great natural gifts improved by study, Beaumont especially being so accurate a judge of plays that Ben Jonson, while he lived, submitted all his writings to his censure, and 'tis thought used his judgment in correcting, if not contriving, all his plots. What value he had for him appears by the verses he writ to him;[75] and therefore I need speak no farther of it. The first play that brought Fletcher and him in esteem was their *Philaster*, for before that they had written two or three very unsuccessfully, as the like is reported of Ben Jonson before he writ *Every Man in His Humor*. Their plots were generally more regular than Shakespeare's, especially those which were made before Beaumont's death, and they understood and imitated the conversation of gentlemen much better, whose wild debaucheries and quickness of wit in repartees no poet before them could paint as they have done. Humor, which Ben Jonson derived from particular persons, they made it not their business to describe; they represented all the passions very lively, but above all love. I am apt to believe the English language in them arrived to its highest perfection; what words have since been taken in are rather superfluous than ornamental. Their plays are now the most pleasant and frequent entertainments of the stage, two of theirs being acted through the year for one of Shakespeare's or Jonson's; the reason is because there is a certain gaiety in their comedies and pathos in their more serious plays which suits generally with all men's humors. Shakespeare's language is likewise a little obsolete, and Ben Jonson's wit comes short of theirs.

[Ben Jonson]

[57] "As for Jonson, to whose character I am now arrived, if we look upon him while he was himself (for his last plays were but his dotages), I think him the most learned and judicious writer which any theater ever had. He was a most severe judge of himself as well as others. One cannot say he wanted wit, but rather that he was frugal of it. In his works you find little to retrench or alter. Wit and language and humor also in some measure we had before

---
[75] *Epigrams,* LV.

him; but something of art was wanting to the drama till he came. He managed his strength to more advantage than any who preceded him. You seldom find him making love in any of his scenes, or endeavoring to move the passions; his genius was too sullen and saturnine to do it gracefully, especially when he knew he came after those who had performed both to such a height. Humor was his proper sphere; and in that he was delighted most to represent mechanic people. He was deeply conversant in the ancients, both Greek and Latin, and he borrowed boldly from them; there is scarce a poet or historian among the Roman authors of those times whom he has not translated in *Sejanus* and *Catiline*. But he has done his robberies so openly that one may see he fears not to be taxed by any law. He invades authors like a monarch; and what would be theft in other poets is only victory in him. With the spoils of these writers he so represents old Rome to us, in its rites, ceremonies, and customs, that if one of their poets had written either of his tragedies, we had seen less of it than in him. If there was any fault in his language, 'twas that he weaved it too closely and laboriously, in his comedies especially; perhaps too, he did a little too much Romanize our tongue, leaving the words which he translated almost as much Latin as he found them; wherein, though he learnedly followed their language, he did not enough comply with the idiom of ours. If I would compare him with Shakespeare, I must acknowledge him the more correct poet but Shakespeare the greater wit. Shakespeare was the Homer or father of our dramatic poets; Jonson was the Vergil, the pattern of elaborate writing; I admire him, but I love Shakespeare. To conclude of him; as he has given us the most correct plays, so in the precepts which he has laid down in his *Discoveries* we have as many and profitable rules for perfecting the stage as any wherewith the French can furnish us.

"Having thus spoken of the author, I proceed to the examination of his comedy, *The Silent Woman*.

Examen of *The Silent Woman*

[The plot]

[58] "To begin first with the length of the action; it is so far from exceeding the compass of a natural day that it takes not up an artificial one. 'Tis all included in the limits of three hours and a half, which is no more than is required for the presentment on the

stage; a beauty perhaps not much observed; if it had, we should not have looked on the Spanish translation of *Five Hours* with so much wonder. The scene of it is laid in London; the latitude of place is almost as little as you can imagine; for it lies all within the compass of two houses, and after the first act in one. The continuity of scenes is observed more than in any of our plays except his own *Fox* and *Alchemist*. They are not broken above twice or thrice at most in the whole comedy; and in the two best of Corneille's plays, the *Cid* and *Cinna*, they are interrupted once. The action of the play is entirely one; the end or aim of which is the settling Morose's estate on Dauphine. The intrigue of it is the greatest and most noble of any pure unmixed comedy in any language.

[The humors; Morose and Falstaff]

[59] "You see in it many persons of various characters and humors, and all delightful, as first Morose, or an old man, to whom all noise but his own talking is offensive. Some who would be thought critics say this humor of his is forced; but to remove that objection, we may consider him first to be naturally of a delicate hearing, as many are, to whom all sharp sounds are unpleasant; and secondly, we may attribute much of it to the peevishness of his age or the wayward authority of an old man in his own house, where he may make himself obeyed; and to this the poet seems to allude in his name Morose. Besides this, I am assured from divers persons that Ben Jonson was actually acquainted with such a man, one altogether as ridiculous as he is here represented. Others say it is not enough to find one man of such a humor; it must be common to more, and the more common the more natural. To prove this, they instance in the best of comical characters, Falstaff; there are many men resembling him, old, fat, merry, cowardly, drunken, amorous, vain, and lying. But to convince these people, I need but tell them that humor is the ridiculous extravagance of conversation, wherein one man differs from all others. If then it be common or communicated to many, how differs it from other men's? or what indeed causes it to be ridiculous so much as the singularity of it? As for Falstaff, he is not properly one humor but a miscellany of humors or images drawn from so many several men; that wherein he is singular is his wit or those things he says *praeter expectatum*, unexpected by the audience, his quick evasions when you imagine him surprised, which as they are extremely diverting of themselves, so receive a great addition from his person; for the

very sight of such an unwieldy old debauched fellow is a comedy alone. And here, having a place so proper for it, I cannot but enlarge somewhat upon this subject of humor into which I am fallen. The ancients had little of it in their comedies; for the τὸ γελοῖον[76] of the old comedy, of which Aristophanes was chief, was not so much to imitate a man as to make the people laugh at some odd conceit which had commonly somewhat of unnatural or obscene in it. Thus when you see Socrates brought upon the stage, you are not to imagine him made ridiculous by the imitation of his actions, but rather by making him perform something very unlike himself; something so childish and absurd as by comparing it with the gravity of the true Socrates makes a ridiculous object for the spectators. In their new comedy which succeeded, the poets sought indeed to express the ἦθος,[77] as in their tragedies the πάθος[78] of mankind. But this ἦθος contained only the general characters of men and manners; as old men, lovers, serving-men, courtesans, parasites, and such other persons as we see in their comedies; all which they made alike; that is, one old man or father, one lover, one courtesan, so like another, as if the first of them had begot the rest of every sort; ex homine hunc natum dicas.[79] The same custom they observed likewise in their tragedies. As for the French, though they have the word humeur among them, yet they have small use of it in their comedies or farces; they being but ill imitations of the ridiculum or that which stirred up laughter in the old comedy. But among the English 'tis otherwise; where by humor is meant some extravagant habit, passion, or affection, particular (as I said before) to some one person, by the oddness of which he is immediately distinguished from the rest of men; which being lively and naturally represented, most frequently begets that malicious pleasure in the audience which is testified by laughter,[80] as all things which are deviations from customs are ever the aptest to produce it; though by the way this laughter is only accidental, as the person represented is fantastic or bizarre; but pleasure is essential to it, as the imitation of what is natural. The description of these humors, drawn from the knowledge and observation of particular persons, was the peculiar genius and talent of Ben Jonson, to whose play I now return.

[76] The laughable quality.   [77] Character.   [78] Suffering.
[79] "You would say that this man is his son" because he is so like him (Terence, Eunuchus, III, 2).
[80] Cf. Sidney's "scornful" laughter, Defense, secs. 31, 50, above, and Trissino, Poetica, sect. 127b, above.

[Skill in using other characters]

[60] "Besides Morose, there are at least nine or ten different characters and humors in *The Silent Woman*, all which persons have several concernments of their own, yet are all used by the poet to the conducting of the main design to perfection. I shall not waste time in commending the writing of this play; but I will give you my opinion that there is more wit and acuteness of fancy in it than in any of Ben Jonson's. Besides, that he has here described the conversation of gentlemen in the persons of True-Wit and his friends, with more gaiety, air, and freedom than in the rest of his comedies.

[The plot]

[61] "For the contrivance of the plot, 'tis extreme, elaborate, and yet withal easy; for the λύσις, or untying of it, 'tis so admirable that when it is done, no one of the audience would think the poet could have missed it; and yet it was concealed so much before the last scene that any other way would sooner have entered into your thoughts. But I dare not take upon me to commend the fabric of it, because it is altogether so full of art that I must unravel every scene in it to commend it as I ought. And this excellent contrivance is still the more to be admired because 'tis comedy, where the persons are only of common rank and their business private,[81] not elevated by passions or high concernments as in serious plays. Here everyone is a proper judge of all he sees; nothing is represented but that with which he daily converses, so that by consequence all faults lie open to discovery, and few are pardonable. 'Tis this which Horace has judiciously observed:

> Creditur, ex medio quia res arcessit, habere
> Sudoris minimum; sed habet Comedia tanto
> Plus oneris, quanto veniae minus.[82]

But our poet, who was not ignorant of these difficulties, has made use of all advantages; as he who designs a large leap takes his rise from the highest ground. One of these advantages is that which Corneille has laid down as the greatest which can arrive to any poem, and which he himself could never compass above thrice in all his plays: viz., the making choice of some signal and long-

---

[81] See *comedy, definition of*, in the index. Dryden is speaking according to Renaissance tradition.

[82] "Comedy, since it draws its themes from a middle walk of life, is believed to call upon its author for less severe exertion, but it is the heavier burden in proportion as the indulgence allowed it is less" (Horace, *Epistles*, II, 1, 168-70).

expected day whereon the action of the play is to depend.[83] This day was that designed by Dauphine for the settling of his uncle's estate upon him; which to compass, he contrives to marry him. That the marriage had been plotted by him long beforehand is made evident by what he tells True-Wit in the second act, that in one moment he had destroyed what he had been raising many months.

[Preliminary descriptions of characters]

[62] "There is another artifice of the poet which I cannot here omit, because by the frequent practice of it in his comedies he has left it to us almost as a rule; that is, when he has any character or humor wherein he would show a *coup de maître*, or his highest skill, he recommends it to your observation by a pleasant description of it before the person first appears. Thus in *Bartholomew Fair* he gives you the picture of Numps and Cokes, and in this those of Daw, Lafoole, Morose, and the Collegiate Ladies; all which you hear described before you see them. So that before they come upon the stage you have a longing expectation of them, which prepares you to receive them favorably; and when they are there, even from their first appearance you are so far acquainted with them that nothing of their humor is lost to you.

[The climactic quality of the play]

[63] "I will observe yet one thing further of this admirable plot; the business of it rises in every act. The second is greater than the first; the third than the second; and so forward to the fifth. There too you see, till the very last scene, new difficulties arising to obstruct the action of the play; and when the audience is brought into despair that the business can naturally be effected, then, and not before, the discovery is made. But that the poet might entertain you with more variety all this while, he reserves some new characters to show you, which he opens not till the second and third act; in the second Morose, Daw, the Barber, and Otter; in the third the Collegiate Ladies; all which he moves afterwards in by-walks, or under-plots, as diversions to the main design lest it should grow tedious, though they are still naturally joined with it and somewhere or other subservient to it. Thus, like a skillful chess-player, by little and little he draws out his men and makes his pawns of use to his greater persons.

---

[83] *Discourse* III, 116. Corneille indicates four of his plays: *Horace, Rodogune, Andromède, Don Sanche.*

[The revival of English poetry]

[64] "If this comedy and some others of his were translated into French prose (which would now be no wonder to them, since Molière has lately given them plays out of verse which have not displeased them), I believe the controversy would soon be decided betwixt the two nations, even making them the judges. But we need not call our heroes to our aid; be it spoken to the honor of the English, our nation can never want in any age such who are able to dispute the empire of wit with any people in the universe. And though the fury of a civil war, and power for twenty years together abandoned to a barbarous race of men, enemies of all good learning, had buried the muses under the ruins of monarchy, yet, with the restoration of our happiness, we see revived poesy lifting up its head and already shaking off the rubbish which lay so heavy on it. We have seen since his Majesty's return many dramatic poems which yield not to those of any foreign nation and which deserve all laurels but the English. I will set aside flattery and envy; it cannot be denied but we have had some little blemish either in the plot or writing of all those plays which have been made within these seven years (and perhaps there is no nation in the world so quick to discern them or so difficult to pardon them as ours), yet if we can persuade ourselves to use the candor of that poet who, though the most severe of critics, has left us this caution by which to moderate our censures—

> *ubi plura nitent in carmine, non ego paucis*
> *Offendar maculis*[84]—

if in consideration of their many and great beauties we can wink at some slight and little imperfections, if we, I say, can be thus equal to ourselves, I ask no favor from the French. And if I do not venture upon any particular judgment of our late plays, 'tis out of the consideration which an ancient writer gives me: *vivorum, ut magna admiratio, ita censura difficilis;*[85] 'betwixt the extremes of admiration and malice, 'tis hard to judge uprightly of the living.' Only I think it may be permitted me to say that as it is no lessening to us to yield to some plays, and those not many, of our own nation in the last age, so it can be no addition to pronounce of our present poets that they have far surpassed all the ancients and the modern writers of other countries."

[84] Horace, *Art of Poetry*, 351–2, above.　　　　[85] Velleius Paterculus, II, 36.

[Rhyme on the stage]

[65] This was the substance of what was then spoke on that occasion; and Lisideius, I think, was going to reply, when he was prevented thus by Crites: "I am confident," said he, "that the most material things that can be said have been already urged on either side; if they have not, I must beg of Lisideius that he will defer his answer till another time; for I confess I have a joint quarrel to you both, because you have concluded, without any reason given for it, that rhyme is proper for the stage.[86] I will not dispute how ancient it hath been among us to write this way; perhaps our ancestors knew no better till Shakespeare's time. I will grant it was not altogether left by him and that Fletcher and Ben Jonson used it frequently in their pastorals and sometimes in other plays. Farther, I will not argue whether we received it originally from our own countrymen, or from the French; for that is an inquiry of as little benefit as theirs who, in the midst of the late plague, were not so solicitous to provide against it as to know whether we had it from the malignity of our own air or by transportation from Holland. I have therefore only to affirm that it is not allowable in serious plays; for comedies, I find you already concluding with me. To prove this, I might satisfy myself to tell you how much in vain it is for you to strive against the stream of the people's inclination, the greatest part of which are prepossessed so much with those excellent plays of Shakespeare, Fletcher, and Ben Jonson which have been written out of rhyme that except you could bring them such as were written better in it, and those too by persons of equal reputation with them, it will be impossible for you to gain your cause with them who will still be judges. This it is to which, in fine, all your reasons must submit. The unanimous consent of an audience is so powerful that even Julius Caesar (as Macrobius reports of him), when he was perpetual dictator, was not able to balance it on the other side; but when Laberius, a Roman knight, at his request contended in the *Mime* with another poet, he was forced to cry out, *Etiam favente me victus es, Laberi.*[87] But I will not on this occasion take the advantage of the greater number, but only urge such reasons against rhyme as I find in the writings of those who have argued for the other way. First then, I am of opin-

---

[86] See *rhyme* in the index.

[87] Macrobius, *Saturnalia*, II, 7, slightly modified: "You are defeated, Laberius, even when I am on your side."

ion that rhyme is unnatural in a play, because dialogue there is presented as the effect of sudden thought; for a play is the imitation of nature, and since no man without premeditation speaks in rhyme, neither ought he to do it on the stage. This hinders not but the fancy may be there elevated to a higher pitch of thought than it is in ordinary discourse, for there is a probability that men of excellent and quick parts may speak noble things *ex tempore;* but those thoughts are never fettered with the numbers or sound of verse without study, and therefore it cannot be but unnatural to present the most free way of speaking in that which is the most constrained. For this reason, says Aristotle,[88] 'tis best to write tragedy in that kind of verse which is the least such, or which is nearest prose; and this amongst the ancients was the Iambic, and with us is blank verse, or the measure of verse kept exactly without rhyme. These numbers therefore are fittest for a play, the others for a paper of verses or a poem, blank verse being as much below them as rhyme is improper for the drama. And if it be objected that neither are blank verses made *ex tempore,* yet as nearest nature they are still to be preferred. But there are two particular exceptions which many besides myself have had to verse, by which it will appear yet more plainly how improper it is in plays. And the first of them is grounded on that very reason for which some have commended rhyme; they say the quickness of repartees in argumentative scenes receives an ornament from verse. Now what is more unreasonable than to imagine that a man should not only light upon the wit but the rhyme too upon the sudden? This nicking of him who spoke before both in sound and measure is so great a happiness that you must at least suppose the persons of your play to be born poets: *Arcades omnes, et cantare pares, et respondere parati;*[89] they must have arrived at the degree of *quicquid conabar dicere,*[90] to make verses almost whether they will or no. If they are anything below this, it will look rather like the design of two than the answer of one; it will appear that your actors hold intelligence together, that they perform their tricks like fortune-tellers, by confederacy. The hand of art will be too visible in it, against that maxim of all professions, *Ars est celare artem,* that it is the greatest perfection of art to keep itself undiscovered.[91] Nor will it serve you

---

[88] *Poetics,* IV, 49a9, above.
[89] Vergil, *Eclogues,* VII, 4: "Both Arcadians, prepared to sing on equal terms and to reply." Dryden has changed *both* to *all.*   [90] See Sidney, *Defense,* sect. 46, above.
[91] This maxim perhaps depends on Ovid, *Metamorphoses,* X, 252: *Ars adeo latet arte sua.* Cf. Dionysius or Longinus, *On Literary Excellence,* XXXVIII, above.

to object that however you manage it 'tis still known to be a play; and consequently the dialogue of two persons understood to be the labor of one poet. For a play is still an imitation of nature; we know we are to be deceived, and we desire to be so, but no man ever was deceived but with a probability of truth; for who will suffer a gross lie to be fastened on him? Thus we sufficiently understand that the scenes which represent cities and countries to us are not really such, but only painted on boards and canvas; but shall that excuse the ill painture or designment of them? Nay, rather ought they not to be labored with so much the more diligence and exactness, to help the imagination? since the mind of man does naturally tend to truth, and therefore the nearer anything comes to the imitation of it, the more it pleases.

[Verse circumscribes the fancy]

[66] "Thus, you see, your rhyme is uncapable of expressing the greatest thoughts naturally, and the lowest it cannot with any grace; for what is more unbefitting the majesty of verse than to call a servant or bid a door be shut in rhyme? and yet you are often forced on this miserable necessity. But verse, you say, circumscribes a quick and luxuriant fancy which would extend itself too far on every subject, did not the labor which is required to well-turned and polished rhyme set bounds to it. Yet this argument, if granted, would only prove that we may write better in verse, but not more naturally. Neither is it able to evince that; for he who wants judgment to confine his fancy in blank verse may want it as much in rhyme; and he who has it will avoid errors in both kinds. Latin verse was as great a confinement to the imagination of those poets as rhyme to ours; and yet you find Ovid saying too much on every subject. *Nescivit* (says Seneca) *quod bene cessit relinquere;*[92] of which he gives you one famous instance in his description of the deluge:

> *Omnia pontus erat, deerant quoque litora ponto.*[93]
> Now all was sea, nor had that sea a shore.

Thus Ovid's fancy was not limited by verse, and Vergil needed not verse to have bounded his.

[92] Marcus Annaeus Seneca, *Controversia*, IX, 5 (28), 17: "He did not know how to leave off what was well ended." A comment on *Metamorphoses*, XIII, 503–5.

[93] *Metamorphoses*, I, 292. Quoted as admirable by Lucius Annaeus Seneca (*Questiones naturales*, III, 27, 13); he does object to the next line which tells of the wolf and the sheep swimming together.

[Jonson's restraint]

[67] "In our own language we see Ben Jonson confining him-self to what ought to be said, even in the liberty of blank verse; and yet Corneille, the most judicious of the French poets, is still vary-ing the same sense a hundred ways and dwelling eternally on the same subject, though confined by rhyme. Some other exceptions I have to verse; but since these I have named are for the most part already public, I conceive it reasonable they should first be answered."

[The defense of rhyme]

[68] "It concerns me less than any," said Neander (seeing he had ended), "to reply to this discourse; because when I should have proved that verse may be natural in plays, yet I should always be ready to confess that those which I have written in this kind come short of that perfection which is required. Yet since you are pleased I should undertake this province, I will do it, though with all imaginable respect and deference both to that per-son from whom you have borrowed your strongest arguments and to whose judgment, when I have said all, I finally submit.[94] But before I proceed to answer your objections, I must first remember you that I exclude all comedy from my defense; and next that I deny not but blank verse may be also used; and content myself only to assert that in serious plays where the subject and charac-ters are great and the plot unmixed with mirth, which might allay or divert these concernments which are produced, rhyme is there as natural and more effectual than blank verse.

[Arguments from bad rhymes]

[69] "And now having laid down this as a foundation—to begin with Crites, I must crave leave to tell him that some of his argu-ments against rhyme reach no farther than from the faults or de-fects of ill rhyme to conclude against the use of it in general. May not I conclude against blank verse by the same reason? If the words of some poets who write in it are either ill chosen or ill placed, which makes not only rhyme but all kinds of verse in any language unnatural, shall I, for their vicious affectation, condemn

---

[94] Strunk suggests that this sentence should run "both *to you and* to that person." According to the usual explanation, Crites, to whom Neander (Dryden) is replying, is Sir Robert Howard, and according to Arnold "that person" is Sir Robert Howard. Did Dryden for an instant forget he was writing a dialogue?

those excellent lines of Fletcher which are written in that kind? Is there anything in rhyme more constrained than this line in blank verse? *I heaven invoke, and strong resistance make;* where you see both the clauses are placed unnaturally, that is, contrary to the common way of speaking, and that without the excuse of a rhyme to cause it; yet you would think me very ridiculous if I should accuse the stubbornness of blank verse for this, and not rather the stiffness of the poet. Therefore, Crites, you must either prove that words, though well chosen and duly placed, yet render not rhyme natural in itself, or that however natural and easy the rhyme may be yet it is not proper for a play. If you insist on the former part, I would ask you what other conditions are required to make rhyme natural in itself, besides an election of apt words and a right disposition of them? For the due choice of your words expresses your sense naturally, and the due placing them adapts the rhyme to it. If you object that one verse may be made for the sake of another,[95] though both the words and rhyme be apt, I answer it cannot possibly so fall out; for either there is a dependence of sense betwixt the first line and the second or there is none; if there be that connection, then in the natural position of the words the latter line must of necessity flow from the former; if there be no dependence, yet still the due ordering of words makes the last line as natural in itself as the other; so that the necessity of a rhyme never forces any but bad or lazy writers to say what they would not otherwise. 'Tis true, there is both care and art required to write in verse. A good poet never establishes the first line till he has sought out such a rhyme as may fit the sense already prepared to heighten the second; many times the close of the sense falls into the middle of the next verse or farther off, and he may often prevail himself of the same advantages in English which Vergil had in Latin: he may break off in the hemistich and begin another line. Indeed, the not observing these two last things makes plays which are written in verse so tedious, for though most commonly the sense is to be confined to the couplet, yet nothing that does *perpetuo tenore fluere,* 'run in the same channel,' can please always. 'Tis like the murmuring of a stream, which not varying in the fall, causes at first attention, at last drowsiness. Variety of cadences is the best rule; the greatest help to the actors and refreshment to the audience.

[95] Cf. Sidney, sect. 37, above. Milton, however, felt that rhyme made poets "express many things otherwise, and for the most part worse" (The Verse, prefixed to *Paradise Lost*).

[The realism of the stage]

[70] "If then verse may be made natural in itself, how becomes it unnatural in a play? You say the stage is the representation of nature, and no man in ordinary conversation speaks in rhyme. But you foresaw when you said this that it might be answered: neither does any man speak in blank verse or in measure without rhyme. Therefore you concluded that which is nearest nature is still to be preferred. But you took no notice that rhyme might be made as natural as blank verse by the well placing of the words, etc. All the difference between them, when they are both correct, is the sound in one which the other wants; and if so, the sweetness of it and all the advantage resulting from it, which are handled in the Preface to *The Rival Ladies*, will yet stand good. As for that place of Aristotle where he says plays should be written in that kind of verse which is nearest prose,[96] it makes little for you, blank verse being properly but measured prose. Now measure alone, in any modern language, does not constitute verse; those of the ancients in Greek and Latin consisted in quantity of words and a determinate number of feet. But when by the inundation of the Goths and Vandals into Italy new languages were introduced, and barbarously mingled with the Latin, of which the Italian, Spanish, French, and ours (made out of them and the Teutonic)[97] are dialects, a new way of poesy was practiced; new, I say, in those countries, for in all probability it was that of the conquerors in their own nations; at least we are able to prove that the eastern people have used it from all antiquity.[98] This new way consisted in measure or number of feet, and rhyme; the sweetness of rhyme and observation of accent supplying the place of quantity in words, which could neither exactly be observed by those barbarians, who knew not the rules of it, neither was it suitable to their tongues, as it had been to the Greek and Latin. No man is tied in modern poesy to observe any farther rule in the feet of his verse but that they be dissyllables; whether Spondee, Trochee, or Iambic, it matters not; only he is obliged to rhyme; neither do the Spanish, French, Italians, or Germans acknowledge at all, or very rarely, any such kind of poesy as blank verse amongst them.[99] Therefore,

---

[96] See sect. 65, just above.

[97] Dryden is impressed by the great number of Romance words in English.

[98] Here Dryden gives a note to Samuel Daniel's *Defence of Rime*.

[99] Milton, however, in the Verse, prefixed to *Paradise Lost*, says that "some both

at most 'tis but a poetic prose, a *sermo pedestris;* and as such, most fit for comedies, where I acknowledge rhyme to be improper. Farther, as to that quotation of Aristotle, our couplet verses may be rendered as near prose as blank verse itself by using those advantages I lately named—as breaks in an hemistich or running the sense into another line—thereby making art and order appear as loose and free as nature; or not tying ourselves to couplets strictly, we may use the benefit of the Pindaric way practised in *The Siege of Rhodes;* where the numbers vary and the rhyme is disposed carelessly and far from often chiming. Neither is that other advantage of the ancients to be despised, of changing the kind of verse when they please with the change of the scene or some new entrance; for they confine not themselves always to iambics, but extend their liberty to all lyric numbers and sometimes even to hexameter. But I need not go so far to prove that rhyme, as it succeeds to all other offices of Greek and Latin verse, so especially to this of plays, since the custom of nations at this day confirms it; the French, Italian, and Spanish tragedies are generally writ in it; and sure the universal consent of the most civilized parts of the world ought in this, as it doth in other customs, to include the rest.

[Verse to use the order of prose]

[71] "But perhaps you may tell me I have proposed such a way to make rhyme natural, and consequently proper to plays, as is unpracticable, and that I shall scarce find six or eight lines together in any play, where the words are so placed and chosen as is required to make it natural. I answer: no poet need constrain himself at all times to it. It is enough he makes it his general rule; for I deny not but sometimes there may be a greatness in placing the words otherwise; and sometimes they may sound better; sometimes also the variety itself is excuse enough. But if for the most part the words be placed as they are in the negligence of prose, it is sufficient to denominate the way practicable; for we esteem that to be such which in the trial oftener succeeds than misses. And thus far you may find the practice made good in many plays; where you do not, remember still that if you cannot find six natural rhymes together, it will be as hard for you to produce as many lines in blank verse, even among the greatest of our poets, against which I cannot make some reasonable exception.

Italian and Spanish poets of prime note have rejected rhyme." Among them are Trissino and Tasso in his *Aminta.*

[Can there be anything new in drama?]

[72] "And this, Sir, calls to my remembrance the beginning of your discourse, where you told us we should never find the audience favorable to this kind of writing till we could produce as good plays in rhyme as Ben Jonson, Fletcher, and Shakespeare had written out of it. But it is to raise envy to the living to compare them with the dead. They are honored and almost adored by us as they deserve; neither do I know any so presumptuous of themselves as to contend with them. Yet give me leave to say thus much without injury to their ashes; that not only we shall never equal them, but they could never equal themselves were they to rise and write again. We acknowledge them our fathers in wit; but they have ruined their estates themselves, before they came to their children's hands. There is scarce a humor, a character, or any kind of plot which they have not used. All comes sullied or wasted to us; and were they to entertain this age, they could not now make so plenteous treatments out of such decayed fortunes. This therefore will be a good argument to us either not to write at all, or to attempt some other way. There is no bays to be expected in their walks: *tentanda via est, qua me quoque possim tollere humo.*[100]

[To write in rhyme the only variety left]

[73] "This way of writing in verse they have only left free to us; our age is arrived to a perfection in it which they never knew and which (if we may guess by what of theirs we have seen in verse, as *The Faithful Shepherdess*, and *Sad Shepherd*) 'tis probable they never could have reached. For the genius of every age is different; and though ours excel in this, I deny not but to imitate nature in that perfection which they did in prose is a greater commendation than to write in verse exactly. As for what you have added—that the people are not generally inclined to like this way—if it were true, it would be no wonder that betwixt the shaking off an old habit and the introducing of a new there should be difficulty. Do we not see them stick to Hopkins and Sternhold's psalms and forsake those of David? I mean Sandys's translation of them. If by the people you understand the multitude, the οἱ πολλοί, 'tis no matter what they think; they are sometimes in the right, sometimes in the wrong; their judgment is a mere lottery. *Est ubi plebs recte*

---

[100] "I must explore a path by which I can raise myself from the ground" (Vergil, *Georgics*, III, 8–9).

putat, est ubi peccat.[101] Horace says it of the vulgar judging poesy. But if you mean the mixed audience of the populace and the noblesse, I dare confidently affirm that a great part of the latter sort are already favorable to verse, and that no serious plays written since the king's return have been more kindly received by them than *The Siege of Rhodes,* the *Mustapha, The Indian Queen,* and *Indian Emperor.*

[Rhyme cannot be extempore]

[74] "But I come now to the inference of your first argument. You said that the dialogue of plays is presented as the effect of sudden thought, but no man speaks suddenly, or *ex tempore,* in rhyme; and you inferred from thence that rhyme, which you acknowledge to be proper to epic poesy, cannot equally be proper to dramatic, unless we could suppose all men born so much more than poets that verses should be made in them, not by them.

[The representation of nature]

[75] "It has been formerly urged by you, and confessed by me that since no man spoke any kind of verse *ex tempore,* that which was nearest nature was to be preferred. I answer you, therefore, by distinguishing betwixt what is nearest to the nature of comedy, which is the imitation of common persons and ordinary speaking, and what is nearest the nature of a serious play; this last is indeed the representation of nature, but 'tis nature wrought up to a higher pitch. The plot, the characters, the wit, the passions, the descriptions are all exalted above the level of common converse, as high as the imagination of the poet can carry them with proportion to verisimility. Tragedy, we know, is wont to image to us the minds and fortunes of noble persons, and to portray these exactly; heroic rhyme is nearest nature, as being the noblest kind of modern verse.

> *Indignatur enim privatis et prope socco*
> *Dignis carminibus narrari coena Thyestae,*[102]

says Horace; and in another place,

> *Effutire leves indigna tragoedia versus.*[103]

---

[101] Horace wrote: *Interdum volgus rectum videt, est ubi peccat* (*Epistles,* II, 1, 63). Dryden's memory gave the Latin the verbal parallelism of his own translation, "sometimes in the right, sometimes in the wrong."

[102] *Art of Poetry,* 90–1, above. See *comedy, definition of,* in the index.

[103] *Art of Poetry,* 231, above.

Blank verse is acknowledged to be too low for a poem,[104] nay more, for a paper of verses; but if too low for an ordinary sonnet, how much more for tragedy, which is by Aristotle in the dispute betwixt the epic poesy and the dramatic, for many reasons he there alleges, ranked above it?[105]

[Is verse natural in the epic?]

[76] "But setting this defense aside, your argument is almost as strong against the use of rhyme in poems as in plays; for the epic way is everywhere interlaced in dialogue, or discursive scenes; and therefore you must either grant rhyme to be improper there, which is contrary to your assertion, or admit it into plays by the same title which you have given it to poems. For though tragedy be justly preferred above the other, yet there is a great affinity between them, as may easily be discovered in that definition of a play which Lisideius gave us. The *genus* of them is the same, a just and lively image of human nature in its actions, passions, and traverses of fortune; so is the end, namely, for the delight and benefit of mankind. The characters and persons are still the same, viz., the greatest of both sorts; only the manner of acquainting us with those actions, passions, and fortunes is different. Tragedy performs it *viva voce*, or by action in dialogue; wherein it excels the epic poem, which does it chiefly by narration and therefore is not so lively an image of human nature. However, the agreement between them is such that if rhyme be proper for one, it must be for the other. Verse, 'tis true, is not the effect of sudden thought; but this hinders not that sudden thought may be represented in verse, since those thoughts are such as must be higher than nature can raise them without premeditation, especially to a continuance of them, even out of verse; and consequently you cannot imagine them to have been sudden either in the poet or in the actors. A play, as I have said, to be like nature is to be set above it; as statues which are placed on high are made greater than the life, that they may descend to the sight in their just proportion.

[Repartee]

[77] "Perhaps I have insisted too long on this objection; but the clearing of it will make my stay shorter on the rest. You tell us,

---

[104] Strunk explains that this acknowledgment is found in Sir Robert Howard's Preface to *Four New Plays* (Arber's *English Garner*, III, 498).

[105] *Poetics*, xxvi, above.

Crites, that rhyme appears most unnatural in repartees, or short replies, when he who answers, it being presumed he knew not what the other would say, yet makes up that part of the verse which was left incomplete and supplies both the sound and measure of it. This, you say, looks rather like the confederacy of two than the answer of one.

"This, I confess, is an objection which is in every man's mouth who loves not rhyme; but suppose, I beseech you, the repartee were made only in blank verse, might not part of the same argument be turned against you? for the measure is as often supplied there, as it is in rhyme; the latter half of the hemistich as commonly made up, or a second line subjoined as a reply to the former; which any one leaf in Jonson's plays will sufficiently clear to you. You will often find in the Greek tragedians and in Seneca that when a scene grows up into the warmth of repartees, which is the close fighting of it, the latter part of the trimeter is supplied by him who answers; and yet it was never observed as a fault in them by any of the ancient or modern critics. The case is the same in our verse as it was in theirs, rhyme to us being in lieu of quantity to them. But if no latitude is to be allowed a poet, you take from him not only his licence of *quidlibet audendi*,[106] but you tie him up in a straiter compass than you would a philosopher. This is indeed *Musas colere severiores*.[107] You would have him follow nature, but he must follow her on foot; you have dismounted him from his Pegasus. But you tell us this supplying the last half of a verse or adjoining a whole second to the former looks more like the design of two than the answer of one. Suppose we acknowledge it: how comes this confederacy to be more displeasing to you than in a dance which is well contrived? You see there the united design of many persons to make up one figure; after they have separated themselves in many petty divisions, they rejoin one by one into a gross; the confederacy is plain amongst them, for chance could never produce anything so beautiful; and yet there is nothing in it that shocks your sight. I acknowledge the hand of art appears in repartee, as of necessity it must in all kinds of verse. But there is also the quick and poignant brevity of it (which is an high imitation of nature in those sudden gusts of passion) to mingle with it; and this, joined with the cadency and sweetness of the rhyme,

---

[106] "Poets and painters have always had an equal right to indulge their whims" (*Art of Poetry*, 10, above).
[107] "To cultivate the stricter muses" (Martial, IX, 11, 17).

leaves nothing in the soul of the hearer to desire. 'Tis an art which appears; but it appears only like the shadowings of painture, which being to cause the rounding of it, cannot be absent, but while that is considered, they are lost; so while we attend to the other beauties of the matter, the care and labor of the rhyme is carried from us or at least drowned in its own sweetness, as bees are sometimes buried in their honey. When a poet has found the repartee, the last perfection he can add to it is to put it into verse. However good the thought may be, however apt the words in which 'tis couched, yet he finds himself at a little unrest while rhyme is wanting; he cannot leave it till that comes naturally, and then is at ease and sits down contented.

[Commonplace language in verse]

[78] "From replies, which are the most elevated thoughts of verse, you pass to those which are most mean, and which are common with the lowest of household conversation. In these, you say, the majesty of verse suffers. You instance in the calling of a servant or commanding a door to be shut in rhyme. This, Crites, is a good observation of yours but no argument; for it proves no more but that such thoughts should be waived, as often as may be, by the address of the poet. But suppose they are necessary in the places where he uses them, yet there is no need to put them into rhyme. He may place them in the beginning of a verse and break it off as unfit, when so debased, for any other use; or granting the worst, that they require more room than the hemistich will allow, yet still there is a choice to be made of the best words and least vulgar (provided they be apt) to express such thoughts. Many have blamed rhyme in general for this fault, when the poet with a little care might have redressed it. But they do it with no more justice than if English poesy should be made ridiculous for the sake of the Water Poet's rhymes.[108] Our language is noble, full, and significant; and I know not why he who is master of it may not clothe ordinary things in it as decently as the Latin, if he use the same diligence in his choice of words. *Delectus verborum origo est eloquentiae.*[109] It was the saying of Julius Caesar, one so curious in his, that none of them can be changed but for a worse. One would think *unlock the door* was a thing as vulgar

---

[108] John Taylor, the "water poet," had been a boatman on the Thames.
[109] Quoted by Cicero in *Brutus*, LXXII, 253. "The choice of words is the source of eloquence."

as could be spoken; and yet Seneca could make it sound high and lofty in his Latin:

> Reserate clusos regii postes laris.[110]
> Set wide the palace gates.

"But I turn from this exception, both because it happens not above twice or thrice in any play that those vulgar thoughts are used, and then too, were there no other apology to be made, yet the necessity of them, which is alike in all kinds of writing, may excuse them. For if they are little and mean in rhyme, they are of consequence such in blank verse. Besides that the great eagerness and precipitation with which they are spoken makes us rather mind the substance than the dress, that for which they are spoken rather than what is spoke. For they are always the effect of some hasty concernment and something of consequence depends on them.

[Rhyme restrains the overluxuriant fancy]

[79] "Thus, Crites, I have endeavored to answer your objections; it remains only that I should vindicate an argument for verse which you have gone about to overthrow. It had formerly been said that the easiness of blank verse renders the poet too luxuriant, but that the labor of rhyme bounds and circumscribes an over-fruitful fancy; the sense there being commonly confined to the couplet and the words so ordered that the rhyme naturally follows them, not they the rhyme. To this you answered, that it was no argument to the question in hand; for the dispute was not which way a man may write best, but which is most proper for the subject on which he writes.

"First, give me leave, Sir, to remember you that the argument against which you raised this objection was only secondary; it was built on this hypothesis, that to write in verse was proper for serious plays. Which supposition being granted (as it was briefly made out in that discourse by showing how verse might be made natural), it asserted that this way of writing was an help to the poet's judgment, by putting bounds to a wild overflowing fancy. I think, therefore, it will not be hard for me to make good what it was to prove on that supposition. But you add that were this let pass, yet he who wants judgment in the liberty of his fancy may as well show the defect of it when he is confined to verse; for he who

[110] *Hippolytus*, 863.

has judgment will avoid errors, and he who has it not will commit them in all kinds of writing.

[Judgment the master-workman]

[80] "This argument, as you have taken it from a most acute person, so I confess it carries much weight in it; but by using the word *judgment* here indefinitely, you seem to have put a fallacy upon us. I grant he who has judgment, that is, so profound, so strong, or rather so infallible a judgment that he needs no helps to keep it always poised and upright, will commit no faults either in rhyme or out of it. And on the other extreme, he who has a judgment so weak and crazed that no helps can correct or amend it shall write scurvily out of rhyme, and worse in it. But the first of these judgments is nowhere to be found, and the latter is not fit to write at all. To speak therefore of judgment as it is in the best poets, they who have the greatest proportion of it want other helps than from it, within. As for example, you would be loath to say that he who is endued with a sound judgment has no need of history, geography, or moral philosophy to write correctly. Judgment is indeed the master-workman in a play; but he requires many subordinate hands, many tools to his assistance. And verse I affirm to be one of these; 'tis a rule and line by which he keeps his building compact and even, which otherwise lawless imagination would raise either irregularly or loosely. At least, if the poet commits errors with this help, he would make greater and more without it; 'tis, in short, a slow and painful, but the surest kind of working. Ovid, whom you accuse for luxuriancy in verse, had perhaps been farther guilty of it, had he writ in prose. And for your instance of Ben Jonson, who, you say, writ exactly without the help of rhyme; you are to remember, 'tis only an aid to a luxuriant fancy, which his was not; as he did not want imagination, so none ever said he had much to spare. Neither was verse then refined so much, to be an help to that age, as it is to ours. Thus then the second thoughts being usually the best, as receiving the maturest digestion from judgment, and the last and most mature product of those thoughts being artful and labored verse, it may well be inferred that verse is a great help to a luxuriant fancy; and this is what that argument which you opposed was to evince."

SAINT-ÉVREMOND

o☉ooo☉o

SAINT-ÉVREMOND is interesting for his clear expression of the liberty of modern authors, their right and even duty to act with independence, at a time and in a country popularly assumed to have held the classical rules sacred. Like Guarini and Ben Jonson, he acknowledged the ability of classical critics, but like them he also held that though "Aristotle's *Art of Poetry* is an excellent work . . . there is nothing so perfect in it as to be the standing rule of all nations and all ages."[1] Similarly the great artistic works of one age may be ill adapted to another time.

The translation of the last selection is by Dr. Olga Marx Perlzweig.

BIBLIOGRAPHY

Saint-Évremond, *Œuvres*, ed. by René de Planhol, 3 vols. Paris, 1927. ——, *Works*, tr. by Mr. des Maizeaux, 3 vols. (2nd edition; first English ed. by des Maizeaux, 1713). London, 1728. The first two selections are from this edition.

OF TRAGEDY, ANCIENT AND MODERN *(selections)*

1672

[Sacred things are not suited to the modern stage]

[1] The gods and goddesses amongst the ancients brought about everything that was great and extraordinary upon the theater, either by their hatred or their friendship, by their revenge or by their protection; and among so many supernatural things nothing appeared fabulous to the people, who believed there passed a familiar correspondence between gods and men. . . . But all these wonders are downright romance to us, at this time of day. The gods are wanting to us, and we are wanting to the gods; and if, in imitation of the ancients, an author would introduce angels and saints upon our stage, the devouter sort of people would be offended at it and look on him as a profane person; and the libertines would certainly think him weak. Our preachers would by

---

[1] "Of Tragedy, Ancient and Modern," *Works* (1728), II, 102.

no means suffer a confusion of the pulpit and the theater or that the people should go and learn these matters from the mouth of comedians, which they themselves deliver in their churches with authority to the whole people. Besides this, it would give too great an advantage to the libertines, who might ridicule in a comedy those very things they receive at church with a seeming submission. But let us put the case that our doctors should freely leave all holy matters to the liberty of the stage; let us likewise take it for granted that men of the least devotion would hear them with as great an inclination to be edified as persons of the profoundest resignation; yet certain it is that the soundest doctrines, the most Christian actions, and the most useful truths would produce a kind of tragedy that would please us the least of anything in the world. The spirit of our religion is directly opposite to that of tragedy. The humility and patience of our saints carry too direct an opposition to those heroical virtues that are so necessary for the theater. What zeal, what force is there which heaven does not bestow upon Nearchus and Polyeucte? . . . Nevertheless, this very subject, which would make one of the finest sermons in the world, would have made a wretched tragedy if the conversation of Paulina and Severus, heightened with other sentiments and other passions, had not preserved that reputation to the author, which the Christian virtue of our martyrs had made him lose.[1] The theater loses all its agreeableness when it pretends to represent sacred things; and sacred things lose a great deal of the religious opinion that is due to them, by being represented upon the theater.

[Only the human in tragedy]

[2] To say the truth, the histories of the Old Testament are infinitely better suited to our stage. . . . But I am apt to believe that the priests would not fail to exclaim against the profanation of these sacred histories, with which they fill their ordinary conversations, their books, and their sermons; and to speak soberly upon a point, the miraculous passage through the Red Sea, the sun stopped in his career by the prayer of Joshua . . . all these miracles, I say, would not be credited in a play because we believe them in the Bible; but we should be rather apt to question them in the Bible because we should believe nothing of them in a play. If what I have already delivered is founded on good and solid reasons, we ought to content ourselves with things purely natural, but

[1] The reference is to Corneille's *Polyeucte* (*Martyr*).

at the same time such as are extraordinary, and in our heroes to choose the principal actions which we may believe possible as human, and which may cause admiration in us as being rare and of an elevated character. In a word, we should have nothing but what is great, yet still let it be human; in the human we must carefully avoid mediocrity, and fable in that which is great. . . .

[Terror on the ancient stage]

[3] To give you my opinion freely, I believe that the tragedy of the ancients might have suffered a happy loss in the banishment of their gods, their oracles, and soothsayers. For it proceeded from these gods, these oracles, and these diviners that the stage was swayed by a spirit of superstition and terror, capable of infecting mankind with a thousand errors. . . . For as their tragedies wholly consisted in excessive motions of fear and pity, was not this the direct way to make the theater a school of terror and pity, where people only learnt to be affrighted at all dangers, and to abandon themselves to despair upon every misfortune. . . ?[2] Aristotle was sensible enough what prejudice this might do the Athenians; but he thought he sufficiently prevented it by establishing a certain purgation, which no one hitherto has understood, and which, in my opinion, he himself never fully comprehended. . . .[3]

[Terror and pity on the modern stage]

[4] Our theatrical representations are not subject to the same inconveniences as those of the ancients were, since our fear never goes so far as to raise this superstitious terror which has produced such ill effects upon valor. Our fear, generally speaking, is nothing else but an agreeable uneasiness which consists in the suspension of our minds; it is a dear concern which our soul has for these subjects that draws its affection to them. We may almost say the same of pity, as it is used on our stage. We divest it of all its weakness, and leave it all that we call charitable and human. I love to see the misfortune of some great unhappy person lamented; I am content, with all my heart, that he should attract our compassion, nay, sometimes command our tears; but then I would have these tender and generous tears paid to his misfortune and virtues together, and that this melancholy sentiment of pity be accompanied with vigorous admiration, which shall stir up in our souls a sort of amorous desire to imitate him.[4]

[2] Cf. Plato, *Republic*, III, above.   [3] See *purgation* in the index.   [4] Cf. P. 516, above.

[Love]

[5] We were obliged to mingle somewhat of love in the new tragedy, the better to remove those black ideas which the ancient tragedy caused us by superstition and terror. And in truth there is no passion that more excites us to everything that is noble and generous, than a virtuous love[5]. . . . I am in good hopes we shall one day find out the true use of this passion, which is now become too common; that which ought to sweeten cruel or calamitous accidents, that which ought to affect our very souls, to animate our courage, and raise our spirits will not certainly be always the subject of a little affected tenderness, or of a weak simplicity. Whenever this happens, we need not envy the ancients; and without paying too great a respect to antiquity, or being too much prejudiced against the present age, we shall not set up the tragedies of Sophocles and Euripides as the only models for the dramatic compositions of our times.

[Ancient tragedy not adapted to our time]

[6] However, I don't say that these tragedies wanted anything that was necessary to recommend them to the palate of the Athenians; but should a man translate even the *Oedipus*, the best performance of all antiquity, into French, with the same spirit and force as we see it in the original, I dare be bold to affirm, that nothing in the world would appear to us more cruel, more opposite to the true sentiments which mankind ought to have.

Our age has, at least, this advantage over theirs, that we are allowed the liberty to hate vice and love virtue. . . . For in our tragedies we neither introduce any villain who is not detested, nor any hero who does not cause himself to be admired. With us, few crimes escape unpunished, and few virtues go off unrewarded.[6] In short, by the good examples we publicly represent on the theater, by the agreeable sentiments of love and admiration, which are discreetly interwoven with a rectified fear and pity, we are in a capacity of arriving to that perfection which Horace desires:

Omne tulit punctum, qui miscuit utile dulci,[7]

which can never be affected by the rules of the ancient tragedy.

---

[5] Cf. Tasso's assertion of the propriety of love in the epic (*Discourses*, sect. 18, p. 484, above).
  [6] Cf. Sidney, *Defense*, sect. 25, above.   [7] *Art of Poetry*, 343, above.

[The effect of modern tragedy]

[7] I shall conclude with a new and daring thought of my own, and that is this: we ought in tragedy, before all things whatever, to look after a greatness of soul well expressed, which excites in us a tender admiration. By this sort of tender admiration our minds are sensibly ravished, our courage elevated, and our souls deeply affected.

ON THE IMITATION OF THE ANCIENTS (*selections*)

1678

[Divinities in poetry]

[1] No man pays a greater veneration to the works of the ancients than myself. I admire the design, the economy, the elevation of spirit, the extent of knowledge which are so visible in their compositions; but the differences of religion, government, customs, and manners have introduced so great a change in the world that we must go, as it were, upon a new system, to suit with the inclination and genius of the present age. And certainly my opinion must be accounted reasonable by all those who will examine it. For if we give opposite characters when we speak of the God of the Israelites and of the God of the Christians, though it be the same deity, if we speak otherwise of the Lord of Hosts, of that terrible God who commanded to destroy the enemy to the very last man, than we do of that God patient, meek, merciful who enjoins to love them, if the creation of the world is described with one genius and the redemption of men with another, if we want one kind of eloquence to set forth the greatness of the Father . . . , and another kind to express the love of the Son, . . . why should there not be a new art, a new genius to pass from the false gods to the true one . . . ? Take away the gods from the ancients, and you take away from them all their poems; the constitution of the fable is in disorder and the design is turned upside down. . . . These immortal leaders of parties among men contrived all, gave life to all, inspired force and courage, engaged themselves in fight, and if we except Ajax, who asked nothing of them but light,[1] there was no considerable warrior that had not his god upon his chariot, as well

[1] See Dionysius or Longinus, *On Literary Excellence*, IX, above.

as his squire, the god to conduct his spear, the squire to direct his horses. Men were pure machines whom secret springs put in motion; and those springs were nothing else but the inspiration of their gods and goddesses.[2] The Divinity we serve is more favorable to the liberty of men. We are in his hands, like the rest of the universe, by way of dependence; but in our own to deliberate and to act.

[Manners and customs]

[2] This great change is followed by that of manners, which by reason of their being civilized and softened at present, cannot suffer that wild and unbecoming freedom that was assumed in former times. It is this change that makes me nauseate the vile and brutal scolding between Achilles and Agamemnon [and other such inhumanities in Homer]. . . .

[3] Their customs differ no less from ours than their morals. . . . Truth was not the inclination of the first ages; a useful lie and a lucky falsehood gave reputation to impostors, and pleasure to the credulous. 'Twas the secret of the great and wise to govern the simple ignorant herd. The vulgar, who paid a profound respect to mysterious errors, would have despised naked truth, and it was thought a piece of prudence to cheat them. All their discourses were fitted to so advantageous a design, in which there was nothing to be seen but fictions, allegories, and similitudes. . . . The genius of our age is quite the opposite to this spirit of fables and false mysteries. We love plain truth; good sense has gained ground upon the illusions of fancy, and nothing satisfies us nowadays but solid reason. To this alteration of humor we may add that of knowledge; we have other notions of nature than the ancients had. The heavens, the eternal mansion of so many divinities, are nothing else with us but an immense fluid space. The same sun shines still upon us, but we assign it another course; and instead of hastening to set in the sea, it goes to enlighten another world. The earth, which was immovable in the opinion of the ancients, now turns round in ours, and is not to be equalled for the swiftness of its motion. In short, everything is changed, gods, nature, politics, manners, humors, and customs. Now is it to be supposed that so many alterations should not produce a mighty change in our writings? If Homer were now alive, he would undoubtedly write admirable poems; but then he would fit them to

---

[2] A suggestion of the notion still frequently repeated that the Greek drama is one of fate; it is hardly in harmony with Aristotle's discussion in the *Poetics*, XIII and XV, above.

the present age. Our poets make bad ones, because they model them by those of the ancients, and order them according to rules which are changed with things that time hath altered.

[Eternal rules]

[4] I know there are certain eternal rules, grounded upon good sense, built upon firm and solid reason, that will always last; yet there are but few that bear this character.[3] Those that relate to the manners, affairs, and customs of the ancient Greeks make but a weak impression upon us at present. We may say of them, as Horace has said of words, they have their certain period and duration. Some die with old age, *ita verborum interit aetas;*[4] others perish with their nation, as well as their maxims of government, which subsist not after the empire is dissolved. So it is plain there are but very few that have a right to prevail at all times; and it would be ridiculous to regulate matters wholly new by laws that are extinct. Poetry would do ill to exact from us what religion and justice do not obtain.

LETTER TO THE DUCHESS OF MAZARIN

1678

[On imitation of the ancients]

Our new productions are often extravagant and the sound sense found in our writings is the sound sense of the ancients rather than our own. I desire it to be inspired by the spirit of the ancients but not taken over from them. I desire them to teach us to think clearly but I do not like to avail myself of their thoughts. What we see in them had the charm of novelty when they wrote it; what we write today has grown old through the centuries and has reached the understanding of our authors after it has become dim.

What are we to do with a new author who puts forth only old productions; who uses the imaginings of the Greeks and presents their shining thoughts to the world as if they were his own? They bring us endless rules which were made three thousand years ago, to regulate everything that is done today; they do not consider in

[3] Cf. Tasso, *The Heroic Poem*, sect. 28, above.
[4] "The earliest-invented words are the first to fall: an elder generation passes away" (*Art of Poetry*, 61, above). Cf. Pope, *Essay on Criticism*, 482–3.

the least that the same subjects are not to be treated nor the same manner employed.[5]

If we made love like Anacreon and Sappho there would be nothing more absurd; if like Terence nothing more bourgeois; if like Lucian nothing more coarse. All ages have their own characteristic tone. They have their politics, their interests, their business; they have their morals of some sort or other, with their vices and virtues. Man is always man but nature is varied in man; and art which is nothing but a variation of nature must vary with it. Our absurdities are no longer the absurdities that Horace ridiculed; our vices are no longer the vices that Juvenal branded: we must employ another kind of ridicule and use another kind of censure.

[5] For shifts in manners as affecting literature see pp. 266, 498, 618, above, and 668, below.

EDWARD PHILLIPS

oʘooʘo

EDWARD PHILLIPS is known chiefly because he was closely associated with his uncle, John Milton. It is likely that his opinions on poetry were influenced by, perhaps wholly derived from, the author of *Paradise Lost*. If so, in Phillips's preface we have a view of the poetical theories of Milton more extensive than any he has given himself and supplementing the fragments collected from his own writings given above. Since Edward was one of the pupils in his uncle's school, parts of this theory may be as early as the 1640's, but he may also reproduce some of Milton's latest views and his reactions to the literary fashions of the Restoration.

The text is based on that printed by J. E. Spingarn in *Critical Essays*.

BIBLIOGRAPHY

Darbishire, Helen, *The Early Lives of Milton*. London, 1932.

Phillips, Edward, Preface to *Theatrum Poetarum*, in Spingarn, *Critical Essays*, II, 256–72. Oxford, 1908.

Wood, Anthony à, "The Life of Edward Phillips," *Athenae Oxonienses*, II, pp. 276–7. London, 1721.

See also the bibliography under Milton above.

THE PREFACE TO *THEATRUM POETARUM* (*in part*)

1675

[Inspiration]

[1] I pitched upon one faculty first which not more by chance than inclination falls out to be that of the poets, a science certainly of all others the most noble and exalted, and not unworthily termed divine, since the height of poetical rapture hath ever been accounted little less than Divine Inspiration. . . .

[Antiquity and the smooth style of the present]

[2] As for the antiquated and fallen into obscurity from their former credit and reputation, they are for the most part those that

have written beyond the verge of the present age. For let us look back as far as about thirty or forty years and we shall find a profound silence of the poets beyond that time, except of some few dramatics of whose real worth the interest of the now flourishing stage cannot but be sensible.[1] Is antiquity then a crime? No, certainly it ought to be rather had in veneration; but nothing, it seems, relishes so well as what is written in the smooth style of our present language, taken to be of late so much refined.[2] True it is that the style of poetry till Henry VIII's time, and partly also within his reign, may very well appear uncouth, strange, and unpleasant to those that are affected only with what is familiar and accustomed to them; not but there were even before those times some that had their poetical excellencies if well examined, and chiefly among the rest Chaucer, who, through all the neglect of former-aged poets, still keeps a name, being by some few admired for his real worth,[3] to others not unpleasing for his facetious way, which, joined with his old English, entertains them with a kind of drollery. However, from Queen Elizabeth's reign the language hath been not so unpolished as to render the poetry of that time ungrateful to such as at this day will take the pains to examine it well.

[Fashions in poetry]

[3] Besides, if no poetry should please but what is calculated to every refinement of a language, of how ill consequence this would be for the future, let him consider and make it his own case who, being now in fair repute and promising to himself a lasting fame, shall two or three ages hence, when the language comes to be double refined, understand (if souls have any intelligence after their departure hence what is done on earth) that his works are become obsolete and thrown aside. If then their antiquated style be no sufficient reason why the poets of former ages should be rejected, much less the pretense of their antiquated mode or fashion of poetry, which, whether it be altered for the better or not, I cannot but look upon it as a very pleasant humor that we should be so compliant with the French custom as to follow set fashions not only in garments but also in music (wherein the

---

[1] In his youth Milton was in the habit of going to the theater. Many passages in his writings suggest familiarity with the drama of the seventeenth century.

[2] Possibly a reference to such work as that of Waller, praised by Pope for his "sweetness" (*Essay on Criticism*, 361).

[3] Milton quotes Chaucer at the end of the first book of his work entitled *Of Reformation in England*, and elsewhere.

Lydian mood is now most in request) and poetry. For clothes I leave them to the discretion of the modish, whether of our own or the French nation. Breeches and doublet will not fall under a metaphysical consideration, but in arts and sciences as well as in moral notions I shall not scruple to maintain that what was *verum et bonum* once continues to be so always.[4] Now whether the trunk-hose fancy of Queen Elizabeth's days or the pantaloon genius of ours be best I shall not be hasty to determine, not presuming to call in question the judgment of the present age. Only thus much I must needs see, that custom and opinion ofttimes take so deep a root that judgment hath not free power to act.

[The classics]

[4] To the ancient Greeks and Latins the modern poets of all nations and for several ages have acknowledged themselves beholding for those, both precepts and examples, which have been thought conducing to the perfection of poetry;[5] for the manner of its garb and dress, which is verse, we in particular to the Italians, the first of the moderns that have been eminently famous in this faculty, the measure of the Greek and Latin verse being no way suitable to the modern languages.

[Imitation of the Italians]

[5] And truly, so far as I have observed, the Italian stanza in heroic poem and the sonnet, canzon, and madrigal in the lyric, as they have been formerly more frequently made use of by the English than by any, so except their own proper language they become none better than ours. And therefore having been used with so good success I see no reason why they should be utterly rejected. There is certainly a decency in one sort of verse more than another which custom cannot really alter, only by familiarity make it seem better. How much more stately and majestic in epic poems, especially of heroic argument, Spenser's stanza (which I take to be but an improvement upon Tasso's ottava rima) or the ottava rima

---

[4] With this assertion of the permanence of the true and good, cf. Dionysius or Longinus, *On Literary Excellence*, VII, above.

[5] Milton's practice and precept turn toward the classics, though not slavishly; see "nature to be followed" (*Reason of Church Government*, sect. I, above). In his tractate *Of Education* he recommends Aristotle's *Poetics* and Horace's *Art of Poetry*, as well as the works of Castelvetro, Tasso, and Mazzoni, all of whom appear in the present volume. He classes the last two with Castelvetro as commentators; they are not strictly that, though they do deal with Aristotelian and Horatian principles.

itself, used by many of our once esteemed poets, is above the way either of couplet or alternation of four verses only, I am persuaded, were it revived, would soon be acknowledged. And in like manner the Italian sonnet and canzon above Pindaric ode, which, whatever the name pretends, comes not so near in resemblance to the odes of Pindarus as the canzon, which though it answers not so exactly as to consist of stroph, antistroph, and epode, yet the verses which in the first stroph of the canzon were tied to no fixed number, order, or measure, nevertheless in the following strophs return in the same number, order, and measure as were observed in the first. Whereas that which we call the Pindaric hath a nearer affinity with the monostrophic or apolelymenon used in the choruses of Aeschylus's tragedies.[6] One thing more is to be observed between the Italian verse and ours, namely, that the dissyllable, which in that language is the only way of rhyming, is also in ours very applicable to rhyme and hath been very much used formerly;[7] I was going to say with as much grace sometimes, if not more, than the monosyllable, but that I am loath to appear too singularly addicted to that which is now so utterly exploded, especially since there are other things of much greater consequence than the verse, though it cannot be denied but that a poetical fancy is much seen in the choice of verse proper to the chosen subject.[8] Yet however let the fashion of the verse be what it will according to the different humor of the writer, if the style be elegant and suitable, the verse, whatever it is, may be the better dispensed with.

[Blank verse]

[6] And the truth is, the use of measure alone, without any rhyme at all, would give far more ample scope and liberty both to style and fancy than can possibly be observed in rhyme, as evidently appears from an English heroic poem which came forth

---

[6] Milton writes in the preface of *Samson Agonistes:* "The measure of verse used in the chorus is of all sorts, called by the Greeks monostrophic, or rather apolelymenon, without regard had to strophe, antistrophe, or epode."

[7] Ben Jonson has two poems wholly or largely in feminine rhyme, *A Fit of Rhyme against Rhyme* (*Underwoods*, XLVII), and *The Dedication of the King's New Cellar to Bacchus* (*ibid.*, LXVI). Milton used it in his very early verse (*The Death of a Fair Infant*, 1, 3), in his well-known minor poems (e.g., *Comus*, 859, 861), and seven times in the choruses of *Samson Agonistes* (172, 175; 303, 306; 622, 632; 668, 669; 688, 691; 1277, 1283; 1660, 1664).

[8] Cf. Dionysius or Longinus, *On Literary Excellence*, xxx, above. For the verse as secondary to the thought, see Sidney, sect. 16, above.

not many years ago,[9] and from the style of Vergil, Horace, Ovid, and other of the Latins, which is so pure and proper that it could not possibly have been better in prose.

[Poetic types]

[7] Another thing yet more considerable is conduct and design in whatever kind of poetry, whether the epic, the dramatic, the lyric, the elegiac, the epaenetic, the bucolic, or the epigram, under one of which all the whole circuit of poetic design is one way or other included,[10] so that whoever should desire to introduce some new kind of poem, of different fashion from any known to the ancients, would do no more than he that should study to bring a new order into architecture altogether different both from the Doric, Ionic, Corinthian, Tuscan, and Composite. Epigram is as it were the fag end of poetry, and indeed consists rather of conceit and acumen of wit than of poetical invention, yet it is more commendable to be a Martial in epigram than Juvenal's *Codrus* in heroic poetry. The epaenetic comprehends the hymn, the epithalamium, the genethliacon, or what else tends to the praise or congratulation of divine or on earth eminent persons. The bucolic or eclogue pretends only the familiar discourse of shepherds about their loves or such like concernments, yet under that umbrage treats ofttimes of higher matters thought convenient to be spoken of rather mysteriously and obscurely than in plain terms.[11] The elegiac seems intended at first for complaint of crosses in love or other calamitous accidents but became applicable afterwards to all manner of subjects and various occasions. The lyric consists of songs or airs of love or other the most soft and delightful subject, in verse most apt for musical composition, such as the Italian sonnet, but most especially canzon and madrigal before mentioned,

[9] *Paradise Lost.* In the note on the Verse, prefixed to the poem, Milton writes of rhyme as "graced indeed since by the use of some famous modern poets, carried away by custom, but much to their own vexation, hindrance, and constraint, to express many things otherwise, and for the most part worse, than else they would have expressed them." In his notes for the life of Milton, John Aubrey writes: "John Dryden, Esq., poet laureate, who very much admires him and went to him to have leave to put his *Paradise Lost* into a drama in rhyme. Mr. Milton received him civilly and told him he would give him leave to tagg his verses" (Helen Darbishire, *The Early Lives of Milton* [London, 1932], p. 7; also pp. 296, 335).

[10] Cf. the remark on "economy or disposition of the fable" in one of the last sentences of the preface to *Samson Agonistes* above.

[11] Cf. Milton's attack on "our corrupted clergy" in *Lycidas.* His reference to the "two-handed engine at the door" (l. 130) is so "mysteriously and obscurely" made that there is still much debate on it.

and the English ode, heretofore much after the same manner. The dramatic comprehends satyr and her two daughters, tragedy and comedy.

[Epic poetry]

[8] The epic is of the largest extent and includes all that is narrative either of things or persons, the highest degree whereof is the heroic,[12] as tragedy of the dramatic; both which consist in the greatness of the argument,[13] and this is that which makes up the perfection of a poet. In other arguments a man may appear a good poet, in the right management of this alone a great poet; for if invention be the grand part of a poet, or maker, and verse the least,[14] then certainly the more sublime the argument the nobler the invention and by consequence the greater the poet. And therefore it is not a mere historical relation spiced over with a little slight fiction, now and then a personated[15] virtue or vice rising out of the ground and uttering a speech, which makes a heroic poem, but it must be rather a brief, obscure, or remote tradition, but of some remarkable piece of story, in which the poet hath an ample field to enlarge by feigning of probable circumstances.[16] In which and in proper allegory, invention (the well management whereof is indeed no other than decorum[17]) principally consisteth, and wherein there is a kind of truth even in the

[12] A similar distinction between the epic and the heroic is found in Minturno, who speaks of the *puri* (genuine, undoubted) epics, "which narrate things of many persons and many years," and the *veri* (in the strict sense) epics, "which are called heroic; they use recognitions and peripeties, and depict manners and passions, and make choice of one man whom they intend to praise above all the others, and lengthen the poem with many episodes" (*Arte poetica*, Bk. I, p. 35). Similarly *De poeta*, pp. 26–7, 146.

[13] The subject. Cf. Milton's lines:

> That to the height of this great argument
> I may assert eternal providence,
> And justify the ways of God to men.
> *Paradise Lost*, I, 24–6.

Milton is aspiring to the highest place in poetry, if the words of Phillips may be applied to him.

[14] Apparently with this dualism of thought and expression in mind, Milton wrote: "I applied myself to . . . fix all the industry and art I could unite to the adorning of my native tongue, not to make verbal curiosities the end—that were a toilsome vanity—but to be an interpreter and relater of the best and sagest things" (*Reason of Church Government*, introd. to Bk. II).

[15] Personified.

[16] The themes of *Paradise Lost* and *Paradise Regained* are both brief and remote, though hardly obscure to a seventeenth-century theologian. This passage probably suggests how Milton looked on his poems; all is feigned except what actually reproduces the Biblical text. Cf. Castelvetro *On Poetics*, IX, 213, 38, above.

[17] For Milton's emphasis on decorum see the index. In *Of Education* he speaks of it as "the great master-piece to observe."

midst of fiction. For whatever is pertinently said by way of allegory is morally though not historically true,[18] and circumstances the more they have of verisimility the more they keep up the reputation of the poet,[19] whose business it is to deliver feigned things as like to truth as may be, that is to say, not too much exceeding apprehension or the belief of what is possible or likely or positively contradictory to the truth of history.[20] So that it would be absurd in a poet to set his hero upon romantic actions (let his courage be what it will) exceeding human strength and power, as to fight singly against whole armies and come off unhurt, at least if a mortal man and not a deity or armed with power divine.[21]

[Epic poetry requires learning]

[9] In like manner to transgress so far the compute of time as to bring together those that lived several ages asunder, as if Alexander the Great should be brought to fight a single duel with Julius Caesar, would either argue a shameful ignorance in chron-

---

[18] As the account of the birth of Sin in *Paradise Lost*, II, 746–67.

[19] See *verisimilitude* in the index. Milton mentions it along with *decorum* in the preface of the *Samson Agonistes*, as though it were of equal importance. One gathers from the present passage that the literal basis of an allegory should be true to life.

[20] Early in his career Milton thought of an epic on King Arthur (*Mansus*, 81; "king before the Conquest"—*Reason of Church Government*, sect. 1, above). But in his *History of Britain* he wrote: "But who Arthur was and whether ever any such reigned in Britain hath been doubted heretofore and may again with good reason. For the Monk of Malmsbury and others whose credit hath swayed most with the learneder sort, we may well perceive to have known no more of this Arthur five hundred years past, nor of his doings, than we now living, and what they had to say transcribed out of Nennius, a very trivial writer yet extant, which hath already been related. Or out of a British book, the same which he of Monmouth set forth, utterly unknown to the world till more than six hundred years after the days of Arthur, of whom (as Sigebert in his *Chronicle* confesses) all other histories were silent, both foreign and domestic, except only that fabulous book. Others of later time have sought to assert him by old legends and cathedral regests. But he who can accept of legends for good story may quickly swell a volume with trash, and had need be furnished with two only necessaries, leisure and belief, whether it be the writer or he that shall read" (Bk. III, in *Works*, Columbia University Press, X, 127–28). It is possible to guess that the vigor with which Milton speaks here is the result of a recent abandonment of an Arthurian subject as not in harmony with "the truth of history." The subject he chose, that of the Fall of man, was true on what he believed the highest authority.

Of Shakespeare's representation of Richard III as a tyrant, Milton writes: "The poet used not much license in departing from the truth of history" (*Eikonoklastes*, chap. 1).

[21] But of the divinely inspired Samson, Milton could write that he

Ran on embattled armies clad in iron,
And weaponless himself,
Made arms ridiculous.

Samson Agonistes, 129–31.

ology or an irregular and boundless license in poetical fiction. Which I reckon is allowed the poet chiefly upon this consideration because, being supposed as he ought to understand the ways of heroic virtue[22] and magnanimity from better principles than those of common and implicit opinion, he hath the advantage of representing and setting forth greater ideas and more noble examples than probably[23] can be drawn from known history.[24] And indeed there is no ingenuous or excellent quality either native or acquired wherewith he should not be fully acquainted, no part of learning in which he ought not to be exactly instructed, since, as a curious piece of history-painting, which is the highest perfection in the art of picture, is the result of several other arts, as perspective, proportion, the knowledge of history, morality, the passions of the mind, etc., so heroic poesie ought to be the result of all that can be contrived of profit, delight, or ornament,[25] either from experience in human affairs or from the knowledge of all arts and sciences[26]—it being but requisite that the same work which sets forth the highest acts of kings and heroes should be made fit to allure the inclinations of such like persons to a studious delight in reading of those things which they are desired to imitate.[27] They likewise very much err from probability of circumstance who go about to describe ancient things after a modern model, which is an untruth even in poetry itself, and so against all decorum[28] that it shows no otherwise than as if a man should read the ancient history of the Persians or Egyptians to inform himself of the customs and manners of the modern Italians and Spaniards. Besides that,

---

[22] In *Paradise Lost*, xi, 690, Milton speaks of "valor and heroic virtue," probably with some thought of what was admirable enough to be mentioned in poetry.

[23] With probability.

[24] Cf. Sidney's belief that the poet should heighten the truth, *Defense*, secs. 9, 10, above. Something of the sort is implied in Milton's "pattern of a Christian hero" (*Reason of Church Government*, sect. 1, above). Sir William Alexander wrote: "The praise of an epic poem is to feign a person exceeding nature, not such as all ordinarily be, but with all the perfections whereof a man can be capable" (*Anacrisis*, written about 1634).

[25] This word is partly or wholly synonymous with delight. It represents the dualism of the didactic theory of poetry; the poet must select good ideas and ornament them properly. Cf. Milton's "adorning of my native tongue" (sect. 8, note 14, just above), and Sidney, *Defense*, sect. 3, above.

[26] Cf. Milton's "insight into all seemly and generous arts and affairs" (*Reason of Church Government*, sect. 4, above). Milton obviously thought the poet should be as well informed as possible, though he adds a qualification, "till which in some measure be compassed."

[27] Cf. Spenser's letter to Raleigh above.

[28] *Decorum* here, as frequently, does not refer to morals. See the index.

our author should avoid as much as might be the making such descriptions as should any way betray his ignorance in ancient customs or any other knowledge in which he ought industriously to show himself accomplished.[29]

[The style of heroic poetry]

[10] There is also a decorum to be observed in the style of the heroic poem:[30] that is, that it be not inflate or jingling with an empty noise of words, nor creepingly low and insipid, but of a majesty suitable to the grandeur of the subject, not nice or ashamed of vulgarly unknown or unusual words—if either terms of art well chosen or proper to the occasion[31]—for fear of frighting the ladies from reading, as if it were not more reasonable that ladies who will read heroic poem should be qualified accordingly

[29] Anachronism is here condemned not so much because it teaches falsehood as because it will destroy the effect of verisimilitude that the poet should strive for. See Aristotle, *Poetics*, IX, above, Castelvetro, *On Poetics*, XXIV, 569, 15, above, and the index under *verisimilitude* for the choice of subjects that will appear probable. The paragraph perhaps also hints at the studious Milton's contempt for a poet who for lack of "intent study" appears ignorant. Indeed, this condemnation of poetic anachronism indicates that the poet cannot modify historical facts for poetic purposes (see *anachronism* in the index). Milton's practice seems not to confirm it as his belief; he may have known that the emperor's residence in Rome in the first century was not adorned

With gilded battlements, conspicuous far,
Turrets and terraces and glittering spires.
Paradise Regained, IV, 53–4,

and yet he may have felt that such a description would be more effective for his readers than one founded on archeological observations in the imperial city.

[30] Decorum here is concerned with the fitness of the language to the poem. Perhaps the following clause has some dependence on Dionysius or Longinus, *On Literary Excellence*, III and XLI, above.

[31] Milton has been censured for doing this by Addison: "A second fault in his language is that he often affects a kind of jingle in his words, as in the following passages and many others:

And brought into this world a world of woe.
Paradise Lost, IX, 11. . . .
This tempted our attempt.
Ibid., I, 642.

I know there are figures for this kind of speech, that some of the greatest ancients have been guilty of it, and that Aristotle himself has given it a place in his *Rhetoric* among the beauties of that art. But as it is in itself poor and trifling, it is, I think, at present universally exploded by all the masters of polite writing.

"The last fault which I shall take notice of in Milton's style is the frequent use of what the learned call technical words, or terms of art. . . . Milton makes use of *larboard* in the same manner. When he is upon building, he mentions *Doric pillars, pilasters, cornice, frieze, architrave*. When he talks of heavenly bodies, you meet with *ecliptic* and *eccentric*, the *trepidation*, stars dropping from the *zenith*, rays *culminating* from the *equator*" (*Spectator*, no. 297). The modern reader may exercise his taste in deciding between poet and critic.

than that the poet should check his fancy for such either men or ladies whose capacities will not ascend above *Argalus and Parthenia*.[32]

[Tragedy]

[11] Next to the heroic poem (if not, as some think, equal) is tragedy, in conduct very different, in height of argument alike, as treating only of the actions and concernments of the most illustrious persons, whereas comedy sets before us the humors, converse, and designs of the more ordinary sort of people. The chief parts thereof are the ἦθος and πάθος, by which latter is meant that moving and pathetical manner of expression which in some respect is to exceed the highest that can be delivered in heroic poesie, as being occasioned upon representing to the very life the unbridled passions of love, rage, and ambition, the violent ends or downfalls of great princes, the subversion of kingdoms and estates, or whatever else can be imagined of funest[33] or tragical; all which will require a style not ramping but passionately sedate and moving. As for the *ethos*, waiving farther large discourses, as intending a preface only, not poetical system, I shall only leave it to consideration whether the use of the chorus and the observation of the ancient law of tragedy, particularly as to limitation of time, would not rather, by reviving the pristine glory of the tragical, advance than diminish the present[34]—adding moreover this caution that the same indecorums are to be avoided in tragedy as have already been intimated in heroic poem, besides one incident to tragedy alone, as namely that linsie-woolsie intermixture of comic mirth with tragic seriousness, which being so frequently in use, no wonder if the name of play be applied without distinction as well to tragedy as comedy.[35] And for the verse, if it must needs be rhyme I am clearly of opinion that way of versifying which bears the name of Pindaric and which hath no necessity of being divided into strophs or stanzas would be much more suitable for tragedy than the continued rhapsody of rhyming couplets, which whoever shall mark it well will find it appear too stiff and of too

[32] A suggestion that Milton expected female readers to make up part of his "fit audience . . . though few." Argalus and Parthenia are characters in Sidney's *Arcadia;* possibly Phillips had in mind Quarles's poem with the title.

[33] Latin *funestus,* dreadful, fraught with misfortune.

[34] Cf. the preface to the *Samson,* above. See *chorus* in the index.

[35] Cf. Milton's preface to the *Samson,* above, as making clear his preference for the classical form of tragedy, and Sidney's "mongrel tragicomedy" (*Defense,* sect. 49, above).

much constraint for the liberty of conversation and the interlocution of several persons. . . .[36]

[True native poetry]

[12] Wit, ingenuity, and learning in verse, even elegancy itself, though that comes nearest, are one thing. True native poetry is another, in which there is a certain air and spirit which perhaps the most learned and judicious in other arts do not perfectly apprehend;[37] much less is it attainable by any study or industry. Nay, though all the laws of heroic poem, all the laws of tragedy were exactly observed, yet still this *tour entrejeant*, this poetic energy, if I may so call it, would be required to give life to all the rest; which shines through the roughest, most unpolished, and antiquated language, and may haply be wanting in the most polite and reformed.[38] Let us observe Spenser, with all his rusty, obsolete words, with all his rough-hewn clowterly verses; yet take him throughout and we shall find in him a graceful and poetic majesty.[39] In like manner Shakespeare, in spite of all his unfiled expressions,[40] his rambling and undigested fancies, the laughter of the critical, yet must be confessed a poet above many that go beyond him in literature some degrees.[41]

[36] The Pindaric mode is used in the choruses of the *Samson Agonistes*. Cf. Dryden's discussion of rhymed plays in *Of Dramatic Poesy*, secs. 41, 65–80, above.

[37] An academic fallacy now common is the assumption that the procedure of the poet is like that of the scholar. It is presumably fatal to good criticism. In the opinion of Sidney, the poet as a creator is set apart from other men (*Defense*, sect. 9, above). To Milton poetry is a divine gift (*Reason of Church Government*, secs. 2 and 4, above; *Paradise Regained*, 1, 8–12; *Paradise Lost*, 1, 17–23).

[38] This and the preceding sentences are obviously in harmony with Milton's theory that genius and inspiration are indispensable to the poet, though labor and study are also needed. See his *Reason of Church Government* above, and *inspiration* in the index.

[39] Perhaps this dispraise mingled with praise indicates that at some time Milton had objected to parts of Spenser. In one version of the interview with Dryden mentioned in note 9, above, Milton is made to designate his own verses as "awkward and old fashioned," obviously meaning that they were so in the eyes of the fashionable literary men of the Restoration.

[40] See Horace, *Art of Poetry*, 291, above.

[41] It is not difficult to imagine this as Milton's opinion; it is not unlike Ben Jonson's in his *Timber*; cf. that stated in Dryden's *Essay of Dramatic Poesy*, sect. 55, above. The influence of Shakespearean idolatry is still so powerful that it is difficult for us to see defects in the great dramatist. Enlightened criticism will, however, enable us to do so.

GENERAL BIBLIOGRAPHY

oᗯ○○ᗯo

Works listed here do not appear in the bibliographies that accompany each selection.

Anderson, Ruth L., "The Mirror Concept in the Drama of the Renaissance," in *The Northwest Missouri State Teachers College Studies*, III (1939), 45–74.

Andreoli, Aldo, *Antologia storica della critica letteraria Italiana*. Milan, 1926.

L'année philologique; bibliographie critique et analytique de l'antiquité greco-latine. Paris, 1924– . See the articles on individual authors and the section entitled "Histoire littéraire."

Atkins, J. W. H., *Literary Criticism in Antiquity, A Sketch of Its Development*. Cambridge, 1934.

Baker, Courtland D., "Certain Religious Elements in the English Doctrine of the Inspired Poet During the Renaissance," in *ELH, A Journal of English Literary History*, VI (1939), 300–23.

Baldwin, Charles Sears, *Ancient Rhetoric and Poetic, Interpreted from Representative Works*. New York, 1924.

——, *Medieval Rhetoric and Poetic* (to 1400) *Interpreted from Representative Works*. New York, 1928.

——, *Renaissance Literary Theory and Practice*. New York, 1939.

Borinski, Karl, *Die Poetik der Renaissance und die Anfänge der litterarischen Kritik in Deutschland*. Berlin, 1886.

Bullock, Walter L., "Italian Sixteenth-Century Criticism," in *Modern Language Notes*, XLI (1926), 254–63. A list of critical works supplementary to that by Ralph C. Williams given below.

——, "The Precept of Plagiarism in the Cinquecento," in *Modern Philology*, XXV (1928), 293–312.

Bundy, Murray W., "Invention and Imagination in the Renaissance," in the *Journal of English and Germanic Philology*, XXIX (1930), 535–45.

Chaytor, Henry John, *Dramatic Theory in Spain, Extracts from Literature before and during the Golden Age*. Cambridge, 1925.

Clark, Barrett, *European Theories of the Drama, An Anthology of Dramatic Theory and Criticism from Aristotle to the Present Day*. New York, 1930.

Clark, Donald L., *Rhetoric and Poetic in the Renaissance*. New York, 1922.

Cook, Albert S., *The Art of Poetry*. Boston, 1892. The poetical treatises of Horace, Vida, and Boileau, with translations, introductions, and notes.

Cooper, Lane, *Theories of Style*. New York, 1907. A collection of important works on style.

Cowl, Richard P., *The Theory of Poetry in England, Its Development in Doctrine and Ideas from the Sixteenth to the Nineteenth Century*. London, 1914.

Craig, Hardin, "The Shackling of Accidents: A Study of Elizabethan Tragedy," in the *Philological Quarterly*, XIX (1940), 1–19.

D'Alton, J. F., *Roman Literary Theory and Criticism*. London, 1931.

Denniston, J. D., *Greek Literary Criticism*. London, 1924. Translations, beginning with Aristophanes.

Ebner, J., *Beitrag zu einer geschichte der dramatischen einheiten in Italien*. Leipzig, 1898.

Egger, Émile, *Essai sur l'histoire de la critique chez les Grecs*. Paris, 1886.

Gayley, Charles M., and Scott, Fred N., *An Introduction to the Methods and Materials of Literary Criticism*. Boston, 1899.

Gilbert, Katharine, and Kuhn, Helmut, *A History of Aesthetics*. New York, 1939.

Hammond, William A., *A Bibliography of Aesthetics and of the Philosophy of the Fine Arts from 1900 to 1932*. New York, 1934.

Howard, William G., "Ut pictura poesis," in *Publications of the Modern Language Association*, XXIV (1909), 44–123.

Jones, Edmund D., editor, *English Critical Essays, Sixteenth, Seventeenth, and Eighteenth Centuries*. Oxford, 1922.

Kastner, L. E., and Charlton, H. B., "The Growth of the Senecan Tradition in Renaissance Tragedy," in *The Poetical Works of Sir William Alexander*, I, xvii—cc. Manchester, 1921.

Klein, David, *Literary Criticism from the Elizabethan Dramatists; Repertory and Synthesis*. New York, 1910.

Meres, Francis, "Poetrie," excerpted from *Palladis Tamia*, ed. by Don Cameron Allen. Urbana, Illinois, 1933. Introduction and notes.

Modern Humanities Research Association, *Annual Bibliography of English Language and Literature*. Cambridge, 1920– . A sub-section is devoted to literary criticism.

Padelford, Frederick Morgan, *Essays on the Study and Use of Poetry by Plutarch and Basil the Great*, translated from the Greek with an introduction. New York, 1902.

Patterson, Warner F., *Three Centuries of French Poetic Theory*. Ann Arbor, 1935.

Puttenham, George, *The Arte of English Poesie*, ed. by Gladys D. Willcock and Alice Walker. Cambridge, 1936.

Saintsbury, George, *A History of Criticism and Literary Taste in Europe from the Earliest Texts to the Present Day*. London, 1934.

———, *The History of English Criticism*. London, 1911.

Schelling, Felix E., *Poetic and Verse Criticism of the Reign of Elizabeth*. Philadelphia, 1891.

Smith, G. Gregory, editor, *Elizabethan Critical Essays*. Oxford, 1904. The chief critical writings, complete or in selections, with excellent notes.

Smith, James H., and Parks, Edd W., editors, *The Great Critics, an Anthology of Literary Criticism*. New York, 1939.

Spingarn, Joel E., *A History of Literary Criticism in the Renaissance*. New York, 1930.

———, *La critica letteraria nel rinascimento*. Bari, 1905. The author says that this Italian translation of the work mentioned above is "so much fuller and maturer than the original that the latter is completely superseded by it."

———, editor, *Critical Essays of the Seventeenth Century* (in England). Oxford, 1908. An anthology, with notes.

Studies in Philology. Chapel Hill, North Carolina. In April of each year a bibliography of Renaissance literature is published. No section is devoted to criticism, but works relating to criticism are listed.

Trabalza, Ciro, *La critica letteraria nel rinascimento* (Secoli XV–XVI–XVII). Milan, 1915.

Vial, Francisque, and Denise, Louis, editors, *Idées et doctrines littéraires du XVIIe siècle*. Paris, 1933. Selections from the critics, including some from the 16th century.

White, Harold O., *Plagiarism and Imitation during the English Renaissance*. Cambridge, Mass., 1935.

Williams, Ralph C., "Italian Critical Treatises of the Sixteenth Century," in *Modern Language Notes*, XXXV (1920), 506–7.

———, *The Theory of the Heroic Epic in Italian Criticism of the Sixteenth Century*. Baltimore, 1921.

INDEX

oᴑooᴑo

The primary purpose of the index is to present topics and names important in criticism. Such words as *profit, inspiration,* and *purgation* have independent headings and are not to be found under *poetry* and *tragedy.* Under such heads as the latter are to be found only topics occurring so infrequently as not to demand separate listing. The material of the notes is indexed. Names of recent scholars are not listed.

A

abuse, of comedy 556; of poetry 441
accident 83, as tragic subject 382. *See also* coincidence
Accius, tragic writer 136
acting, value of 557
action 76, author must visualize 91, 94, 216, 225; does not need explanation 98; end of *Divine Comedy* 205; and knowledge 442; multiplicity of 496; narrated 133; principal 581; on the stage 133; sentences in 300; in tragedy 77; unity of 496, 574; vulgar 114. *See also* plot
actors 16, 113–4, 328, 571, 597, 627; not to be imitated 53; excessive action of 113; expelled from state 41; number of 249, 250, 537; and poetry 12; regulated 39–40; tragic and comic 38
acts 260, 606; division into 251, 606; five 134, 594; four 545; function of 260–1, 546; intervals between 578; and scenes, 247, 248, 537, 594, 611; in tragedy 244; three, 545, 612
Addison, Joseph, *Spectator* 150, 154, 155, 163, 188, 675
admiration 226; definition of 461; in tragedy 432, 451-2, 459–61, 590, 616, 620, 662, 663. *See also* pity and fear, astonishment
adornment 674, function of episode 276. *See also* beauty, delight
adversity in tragedy, consolation for 291
Aeneas 317, 423, 428, 440, 464; perfect character 413, 422, 434; piety of 484; virtues of 435. *See also* Vergil
Aeneas Silvius, on Vergil, Ovid, Lucan, and Statius 237
Aeschylus 87, 93, 167, 460, 461, 587, 594, 605, 615, 670; erected first stage 136; false portrait of gods 29; increased number of actors 74; *Choephoroe* 93, 117; *Niobe* 35; *Oreithyia* 148; *Philoctetes* 102; *Prometheus* 120; *Seven against Thebes* 97, 166
Aesop 423, 439, 445
aesthetic criticism 144; problems discussed in Tasso's writings 466; view of poetry 6, 7
Aëtion the painter 362
affectation 453
affects (*affetti*) 432, 459–60
Agathon 82, 91, 97, 112, 321, 388, 471
ages, of man 510; characteristics of 133, 498; of history, vary 652; of history, have their own character 666. *See also* manners and customs, old age
Agrippa, H. Cornelius, paradoxes 436
Alamanni, Luigi, 246, 401, 485–6, 487

Alberti, Leon Battista, *Momus* 421
Alexander, Sir William, *Anacrisis* 674
allegory, adaptable to all men 208; advantages of 211; of Amphion and Orpheus 140, 408; basis true 673; in Bible 208; Boccaccio on 208–11; Dante on 202–6; disguised theology 565; examples of 209; fabulous veil 409, 428, 458, 471, 664; of gods 156; or hidden meaning 25; medieval 199; of poetry *frontispiece,* ii; Spenser on 463–5; Tasso on 466; and truth 439
Altobello 282
Amadis of Gaul 428, 485
Amadis of Greece 485
ambiguity, comic 229; popularity of 547
Ammonius 475; sources of Plato 164
Amphicrates 149, 151
Amphion 415; allegory of 140, 407, 408
amplification 161; defined 162
anachronism, Aristotle and Castelvetro on 122; classical instances of 492; condemned 357, 673–5; defended 266; discussed 270, 356, 482–3, 498; on Spanish stage 547. *See also* manners and customs, history
Anacreon 666
analysis, valuable 148
anaphora 173
ancient customs, distasteful in poetry 482; drama, not didactic 615; languages and poetry 401; plots, no novelty in 612; poets 479; practice, not followed by poets 243; tragedy not adapted to our time 662
ancients 664; Dante followed 403; defended 604; do not keep the laws of drama 613; economy of 663; imitation of 286, 663, 665, 669; and moderns 286, 601–18, 644
Ancroja 282
angels, in poetry 283; on the stage 659
anticipation 546
antidote, the knowledge of the true nature of poetry 52; against bad poetry 25, 42, 241
Antimachus Clusius 401
antiquity 490, 664, 667; in poetry 482, 489; as subject 482
Antonius 455
Apelles the painter 362
Apollonius Rhodius 185, 486–7
apostrophe 169
appeal, direct, to reader 177
Apuleius 232, 451, 566; plagiarized from by Boccaccio, himself a plagiarist 325
Aquinas 199, 206, 476, 478, 482, 485; on poetry 476
Aratus 160, 178, 287, 307
Archilochus 10, 12, 130, 161, 164, 185

278; easily deceived 664; in the epic 491; judgment of, in poetry 276; poor judges 551, 652; considered by Lope 540, 542, 544; poet should satisfy 403; poetry for 307–8, 389, 402; poetry not for 401; persuaded by poetry 366; taught by poet 423; as readers 284; speech of 204; tastes of 138, 565, 599, 620; in theater 135; in tragedy 249, 508; tragedy for 113. *See also* audience, spectators, comedy

common things, charm of 132

commonplace book 454

compassion, to be purged 520; not purged by tragedy 516; purges 520; tragic, discussed 519–23; two kinds of 520; unwise 520; why purged away 515. *See also* pity, pity and fear

complication of tragedy 95, 472

composition 192, law of, in language 303; by Scudéry 581

concentration, in art 114, 194; of tragic effect 315

concernment 616–7, 620. *See also* pity, pity and fear

consistency 128; of character 90, 131, 132

contemplation 406, 476

content and language. *See* dualism

contests, dramatic 80, 82

contraries 113, 123, 432, 474, 480, 629; in language 112; make each other clearer 432

conversion at end of comedy 626

Corneille, Pierre, 574–9, 619, 623, 625, 629, 636, 642, 643, 648; influenced Dryden 600; *Discourses* 575–9; *Discourse* I 626; *Discourse* III, of the three unities 608, 614, 625, 627, 634, 643; *Andromède* 633; *Cid* 579; *Cinna* 579; *The Liar* 628; *Polyeucte* 660; *La suivante* 574–5

Corneille, Thomas, *L'amour à la mode* 635

correctness 129, 189; in poetic art 108, 113, 123

costume on the stage 547

Cowley, Abraham 306, 603

creation 43–4; and imitation 506; by poet 412

creator, poet as 412, 413, 500, 677

credible, subject of poet 82, 365, 366, 367, 368, 370, 372, 375, 388, 389, 390, 393, 397, 472, 479, 661. *See also* possible, probability

critic 137; bad 111; blames poets 111; competent 12; and drama 579; function of 480; good 9, 56, 142; poet and 96; poet as 125

critical justifications, twelve 123

criticism 152; dishonest 198; effect of on poetry 466; fundamentals of 108; history of, its value 4; influence on poets 3, 466; influence on Tasso 466; of literature 152; problems in 108

Croce, Benedetto, 70, 206, 365, 599, 649

crowd. *See* common people

Curtius, Quintus, 424

custom 496, 497, 498, 669; effect on language 130; validity of 496. *See also* manners and customs

Cyrus. *See* Xenophon

D

dance 69, 74, 545, 655

Daniel, Arnaut, 485

Daniel, Samuel, *Defence of Rime* 650

Daniello, *Poetica* 407, 408, 409, 420

Dante 199–206, 214, 274, 408, 456, 466, 590; allegorical method compared with Spenser's 464; on allegory 199–206; allowed historical poetry 306; not Aristotelian 359; attacked by Bulgarini 358; attacked by Castravilla 358; Boccaccio's life of 207–11; both judges and moves 394; defended by Mazzoni 358; demonstrative poet 474; digressions in 272; expresses moral judgments 272, 393; followed ancient poets 403; followed Horace 125; greater than Plato 366; Italian romances later than 283; meaning of 202–4; methods of treating subject 203; not always poetic 365; poet of the highest order 215; poetry governed by civil faculty 386; praise of romances 485; quoted 223; representative of medieval theory 199; scope of 425, 471; subject of 471; too learned 308; use of logic 474; use of science 366; use of sentences 297; use of phantasy 477; wicked characters shown punished 399

Divine Comedy 527; Aristotelian 527; author 202; end of 202; form of 202; genus of its philosophy 202; instruction 202; subject of 202; title of 202, 543; *Inferno* 394, 474, 478, 599; *Purgatorio* 272, 393, 477, 485; *Paradiso* 206, 366, 394, 403, 477, 599. *Letter to Can Grande della Scala* 202–6, 462, 464; *On the Vulgar Tongue* 1, 129, 200, 206, 215, 486; *Convivio* 200

Dark ages 214, 567

Davenant, William, *The Siege of Rhodes* 651, 653

David, King, a poet 446

death, external, tragedy teaches not to fear 518; internal, tragedy teaches to fear 518; on the stage 85, 245, 257, 309, 349, 515, 624, 632, 633; on the stage, Castelvetro's interpretation of 258

deceptions, comic 312, tragic 340

decorum 133, 672–3; discussed 272–3; and verisimilitude 673; emphasized by Milton 672–77; essential to tragedy 521; immoderate laughter violates 512; in descriptions of gods 156; in *Dido* 247; in Horace's theory 133; of actions 585, 625; of Ariosto 499; of characters 546, 591; of French drama 628; of language 273; of plot 594; of stage observed by Jonson 633; in style 675; of tragedy 249, 261, 676; of tragicomedy 524; Seneca excels in 256; violated by classicism 674; violated by tragicomedy 451; violation of 615

deformity, of mind, comic 227; physical or mental, comic 228, 313

Dekker, Thomas, 559, 637

delight 459–61, 469–70; of audience 630; augmented by prefaces 398; in Bible 595; comic 87, 451–2, 522; distinguished from pleasure 378–9, 384; in *Divine Comedy* 206; in drama 53; enables poetry to teach 379; end of drama 576, 612, 615, 633; end of epic as of drama 654; end of games 378; end of poetry 6, 139, 307, 349, 370, 375, 378, 384, 388, 467, 498, 599; end of tragedy 56, 289, 348–50, 353, 385, 522; follows imitation 377; function of poet 297; and Jonson's theory 534; and laughter 452, 502; means to moral instruction 590; motive for epic 674; in poetry 61, 115, 213, 289, 307, 375–6, 381,

427, 443, 457; and profit in poetry 55, 237, 276, 570, 577, 591; and profit, end of poetry 385, 467-9; purpose of poetic imitation 415; of readers 447; in romances 271; romances superior in 499; studious 674; in suffering 377; and teach 416-7, 452; tragic 57, 87, 348, 350, 522, 523. *See also* pleasure, profit, instruction

delightful teaching 57, 380, 566, 590

Demetrius of Phalerum 525; *On Style* 453, 502

democracy, and literature 196, 592; and tragedy 331

Democritus, on poetic madness 137

Demodocus, song of Venus and Mars 381

Demosthenes 401; and Cicero compared 162; artistry of 526; energy of 163; faults of 188; faulty but great 186; ordering of words by 192; selection and arrangement in 161; translated by Cicero 284; use of figures 169, 177, 182; use of hyperbaton 175; use of rhetorical devices 173, 179; worthy of imitation 164, 454; *On the Crown* 182; *Philippics* 171; *Timocrates* 168

Denham, Sir John, praised 603

Denores, Jason, 433; attack on Guarini 504

denouement (catastrophe, solution) 95-6, 248, 254, 472, 545, 611, 642; spectator's uncertainty about 257

description, metaphorical 183; in Milton, Spenser, Tasso 491

design 632; poetic 671

details, excessive 195; finish of, and greatness 153

deus ex machina 90, 126, 134, 248, 613

dialectician. *See* logician

dialogue 409, 600; how used 5

dianoia. See thought

diatyposis 173

diction. *See* (1) language

didactic theory 462, 534; of poetry 3, 139, 201, 373; important in Spenser 462. *See also* profit, instruction

difficulty, and artistic merit 501; of poet 319

dignity, lack of 194, 195; in words 196

digressions 326, 398; in the epic 264, 272; in romances 272, 288. *See also* episodes

Diomedes 556, 595; on comedy and tragedy 508

Dion Chrysostom on tragedy 383

Dionysius (Greek painter) 71

Dionysius the Areopagite 476-7

Dionysius of Halicarnassus 215, 217

Dionysius or Longinus. *See* Longinus

discovery 121, 611; of an action 344. *See also* recognition

distant places, as subjects 482, 488, 491

diversity. *See* multiplicity, variety

divinity, of art 492; of poet 500; of poetry 458

Donatus, Aelius, 525, 542, 555, 556, 623

Donne, John, *Paradoxes and Problems* 436

double, form of tragedy 259; plot 254, 292, 521, 527; plot not effective 630

drama, ancient and modern 602; and action, Greek words for, related 72; and the Church 660; corrupts morals 596; English 449; French 618-36; moral value of 550, 568; morally superior to reality 572; origins of 72, 604; and narrative 309; as poem 506; problem of, in Renaissance 242; Puritan criticism of 550; Roman, censured 615; and

society 663; and the state 564, 631; modern 605. *See also* comedy, etc.

dramatic method 309-10; in the epic 36

Dryden, John, 130, 600-58; on admiration 461; on ancients and moderns 286; on Aristotle 144; as a critic 64; rhymed *Paradise Lost* 671; on greatness of Milton 286; on Longinus 144; poetic madness 118; quotes Longinus 144, 150; as a reader 64; on Shakespeare 677; translation of Plutarch 493; *Of Dramatic Poesy* 227, 413, 425, 452, 544, 579, 677; *Apology for Heroic Poetry* 165, 174, 185, 190; *Fables* 162; *Indian Emperor* 653; *The Indian Queen* 653; *The Rival Ladies* 650; *Troilus and Cressida* 150, 164, 352, 610; *Three Poets* 286

dualism, of word and idea (content and language) 273, 305, 409, 453-4, 456, 497-8, 669, 672, 674; the basis of Dante's theory of poetry 201

Du Bartas, Guillaume, 306, 582, 587; not poet but versifier 306

d'Urfé, Honoré, as an example 584

Dutch language 457

E

Earle, George, *Microcosmography* 317

education, Greek 54; poetry in 6, 61; what it is 57

Edwards, Richard, *Damon and Pythias* 136

effect, total 129, 526; mean 196

effort. *See* labor, study

eikastike. *See* icastic

elocutionist 9, 16, 20, 114; emotion of 15; and generalship 21; judgment of 19; knowledge of 16; knowledge of the arts 18

eloquence 8, 453; what it consists in 218; of Crassus, Antonius, and Cicero 455. *See also* oratory

Elyot, Sir Thomas, 233-41, 425, 432, 560, 599; *The Governor* 233-41

embroidery, its qualities 41

emotion 153, 154, 194, 198; of characters felt by poet 94, 131, 216; declining, gives way to character 158; essential to excellence 153-4; inspired, a source of excellence 153; justifies figures 170; nourished by poetry 31, 51, 314-5; ill-timed 149

Empedocles 70, 99, 100, 111, 142, 307, 364, 366, 371, 408, 474, 567

end, defined 79; of poetry 375, 376, 418, 449, 470, 590; of tragedy 77, 317, 328, 329, 353, 513-4; of tragicomedy 513, 521, 540; of comedy 328, 329; of drama 576; architectonic 513, 521, 524; instrumental 513, 521, 524; of the *Divine Comedy* 204

energy (*energia*), poetic 165, 453, 677

English, drama 449, 628-44; defended 600; highest development of Renaissance practice 505; superior to ancient 602; regular 636; history 589; language 405, 455-7, 558, 650; fit for poetry 668; highest perfection in 638; poetry 668; surveyed 446-9; methods, better 635; plots, confused 621; stage, defended 628; stage, tumults on, 623

enigmas, in poetry 402

Ennius 130, 136, 408, 442; carelessness of 136

entanglement. *See* complication

entrance and exit, reason for 627

entremês, or comic interlude 542

CORRIGENDA

References are to page, paragraph (sometimes omitted), and line, or in the index to the head-word. The entire line to be corrected is given in revised form, except proper names which stand alone.

Page 69, line 7: For "poetry and most music . . .", read: "poetry, and most poetry accompanied with the flute and lyre all fall into the"

Page 70, line 1: For "But the art which . . .", read: "But the work which imitates by means of words only, in prose or"

Page 74, line 4 from bottom (Chapter IV): For "tone. Then there is . . .", read: "tone. Then there is the number of acts. And as to the other"

Page 76, note 26: For "Fontanelle", read: "Fontenelle"

Page 77, line 5: For "as species, as it were . . .", read: "as species, as it were.³³ Yet every tragedy has spectacle and character"

Page 82, par. 3, line 2: For "an episodic plot . . .", read: "an episodic plot I mean one in which the events do not have to"

Page 84, par. 2, line 10: For "Such a recognition . . .", read: "Such a recognition and peripety will produce either pity or fear, and"

Page 85, par. 3, line 8: For "advisable to show . . .", read: "advisable to show good men changing from good fortune to bad fortune, for this is neither fearful nor pitiable, but abominable. And bad men should not change from bad fortune to good fortune for this is"

Page 85, par. 3, line 2 from bottom: For "feeling is not . . .", read: "feeling is neither pitiable nor fearful.⁶⁷ Nor, further, should a very wicked man fall from good fortune to bad fortune; such a thing touches"

Page 86, line 1: For "our human feeling . . .", read: "our human feeling, but produces neither pity nor fear, for pity is felt for the undeserving man in his misfortune and fear for a man of the same sort; hence the situation is neither pitiable nor fearful."

Page 86, par. 2, line 1: For "There remains then . . .", read: "There remains, then, the man who occupies the middle ground. He is not unusual in virtue and"

Page 88, line 2: For "terrible and what sorts . . .", read: "terrible or what sorts are pitiable. It is necessary for such deeds"

Page 89, note 83: For "Fontanelle", read: "Fontenelle"

Page 95, line 1: For "for himself . . .", read: "for himself,¹¹⁶ and after that to fill in the speeches and give the"

Page 95, line 16: For "characters, the episodes . . .", read: "characters, the actions may be composed, with a view to making"

Page 95, line 19: For "dramas the episodes . . .", read: "dramas the actions are short, but an epic poem is lengthened out"

Page 95, par. 1, last line: For "indispensable . . .", read: "indispensable; all the rest is expansion.¹¹⁷ "

Page 96, par. 2, line 5: For "which is simple . . .", read: "which is ruled by thought, such as the *Phoricides* and the plays on Prometheus"

Page 96, par. 3, line 2: For "types, or if he cannot . . .", read: "parts, or if he cannot attain that, to employ the most important ones"

Page 96, par. 3, line 5: For "good in each part . . .", read: "good in one thing or part in one tragedy, the critics think that any one poet of the present should in one play surpass his predecessors in each and all of the four parts."

Page 118, note 4: This note is in part superseded by my article "Aristotle's Four Species of Tragedy and Their Importance for Dramatic Criticism," *American Journal of Philology*, 68 (1947), 363 ff. Especially I reject page 120, par. 3, thinking it probable that the fourth class is the tragedy of thought or idea. *Prometheus Bound* is much concerned with tyranny. (*See the following two corrections.*)

Page 118, note 4, line 2 from bottom: For "the last two, . . .", read: "the last two." (Omit: "and the species . . . dealing with suffering.")

Page 120–121, beginning par. 2: Omit three paragraphs. ("If Aristotle's meaning . . . Need it be spectacular?") Substitute the following text:

Rostagni's explanation is ingenious. I offer it partly to show that my own is subject to debate. Aristotle recognized the importance of spectacle for the effect of tragedy (14.53b; 26.62a). Yet in producing it, the stage-designer is more important than the poet; indeed tragedy can produce its effect upon a reader without stage or actors (6.50b; 14.53b). There is no indication in the *Poetics* of any intention for dealing with the art of staging; concern is with what is done by the dramatist, the poet. According to Bywater, "throughout the *Poetics*, Aristotle resolutely ignores" scenery and costume "as outside the art of poetry proper." In a treatise of the dramatic writer's art, would he have named one of his classes of tragedy from an activity only secondary for the poet? That one of the classes is the spectacular, is therefore a notion that can be abandoned.

Aristotle's simple tragedy is one lacking recognitions and discoveries (10.52a; 24.59b). Such a tragedy, if excellent in pathos, in presentation of character, even in spectacle, would be assigned to one of those classes. Simplicity—lack of complexity—is too negative to define a type, though the descriptive word is useful when speaking of the unlabored plot. For example, the plot of *Oedipus King* might have been simpler—and less effective. The truth about Oedipus might have come in routine investigation, instead of by reversal of the intention of the informant. The reversal comes from Sophocles' development of the story beyond the outline of the tradition.

In his analyses of tragedy, moreover, Aristotle mentions the element of thought, classing it with character in that character and thought are the two causes for dramatic action, for the good or bad fortune of the agents (6.50ab; 19.56ab; 24.60b; 25.61a). Since "thought is shown in everything that the characters must bring about through speech" (50b), and a tragedy is made up of speeches, thought is the tragic writer's steady concern. So necessary an element—demanding from the poet, along with character, attention second only to that given to the all-important action—has a proper place in all analyses of tragedy. For Aristotle, it does appear in all his analyses, unless it be excluded from that in Chapter 18. It is a natural filler of the hiatus there.

In Chapter 18, Aristotle gives examples of the fourth species for which we are searching: "the *Phorcides* and the plays on Prometheus and all that have their scenes in Hades." Of the first, nothing is known. Assertions that Aristotle here excludes Aeschylus' *Prometheus Bound* are not convincing. As is evident to any reader, and as many critics have said, the most important idea of that tragedy is tyranny. Prometheus' sufferings result from his meditation and conclusion on this subject. Thus the play illustrates Aristotle's statement that thought is a cause for dramatic action. Hades as a scene for tragedy suggests the lower world of Plato's *Phaedo* (113 f.). Souls are judged; they pay the penalty for evil deeds and are rewarded for good ones; they beseech those they have injured to grant them release. In his vision of the lower world (Plato, *Republic* 10.612 ff.), Er saw the wicked scourged and torn by thorns. When souls choose their future, some hastily take the tyrant's lot, which they then lament, execrating Fortune. Among the others, Ajax, for example, chose the life of a lion, because, remembering the injustice done him about the arms of Achilles, he would not be a man. Odysseus, remembering his former toils, searched for the lot of an obscure man with no responsibilities; finally he found it, lying neglected; he would have chosen it, he said, if he had been given first choice. A dramatist, putting such characters in Hades, would find much for them to say in explanation of their conduct. Or there is Odysseus' visit to Hades, in the course of which he hears Achilles speak on his unhappiness. Homer allows these characters little activity; like Prometheus fixed on his rock, they can do little more than utter their thoughts, whether in conversation with a visitor, or before Minos the judge. The place of thought, in dramas with scenes in the lower world, would be large.

Thus in tragedy, as Aristotle conceives it, thought is so important that it fitly appears as one of the qualities which, when especially developed, can give its characteristic name to one class of tragedy. Until we know—if ever we can—with what Aristotle filled what is now the hiatus in his eighteenth chapter, thought may stand as a species of tragedy harmonious with the nature of the *Poetics*.[1]

Page 120, note 1: For "In the last Rostagni's . . .", read: "In the last, Rostagni's . . ."

Page 150, note 6: For "*Dion;* I have changed them . . .", read: "*Dion;* I have changed them in order to preserve the "turn." See entry under *turn* in the index.

Page 216, line 7: For "*Hecuba*", read: "*Hecyra*"

Page 230, note 21: Omit line 2. Insert: Licamelculo is illustrated by a passage from *Tom Jones*:

Squire Western then bespattered the youth with abundance of that language which passes between country gentlemen who embrace opposite sides of the question, with frequent applications to him to salute that part which is generally introduced into all controversies that arise among the lower orders of the English gentry at horse-races, cock-matches, and other public places. Allusions to this part are likewise often made for the sake of the jest. In reality, it lies in desiring another to kiss your a— for having just before threatened to kick his; for I have observed very accurately that no one ever desires you to kick that which belongs to himself, nor offers to kiss this part in another.

It may likewise seem surprising that in the many thousand kind invitations of this sort, no one, I believe, hath ever seen a single instance where

---

[1] For details, such as opinions on tyranny in *Prometheus Unbound*, see my article on "Aristotle's Four Species of Tragedy (Poetics 18) and Their Importance for Dramatic Criticism," *American Journal of Philology*, 68 (1947), 363–381.

the desire hath been complied with—a great instance of their want of polite-
ness, for in town nothing can be more common than for the finest gentlemen
to perform this ceremony every day to their superiors, without having that
favor once requested of them. (Book 6, chap. 9.)

Page 247, line 6 from bottom: For "Ruscelli", read: "Rucellai"

Page 328, note 46: For "Fiametta", read: "Fiammetta"

Page 458, note 136: For "Landion's", read: "Landino's"

Page 489, note 80: For "For Damascus, . . .", read: "For Damascus, see Ariosto,
Orlando Furioso 17.81 ff." (Cancel the second sentence.)

Page 690: For "Fontanelle", read: "Fontenelle"

Page 690, fortune, insert: 255.

Page 695, Milton, line 3 from end, read: "follows Horace 143;"

Page 700: For "Ruscelli", read: "Rucellai"

Page 701, sentence, line 5: For "Heywood", substitute: "Webster"

Page 702, tragedy, add: "High rank 508;"